CHESTERTON CLASSICS COLLECTION

Orthodoxy, Heretics, What's Wrong With The World, What I Saw In America

G.K. CHESTERTON

This work is a product of its time and place and may include values, images, events, and language that are offensive to modern sensibilities. Reader discretion is advised

Orthodoxy: Originally published in 1908, this work is in the public domain.

Heretics: Originally published in 1905, this work is in the public domain.

What's Wrong With The World: Originally published in 1910, this work is in the public domain.

What I Saw In America: Originally published in 1922, this work is in the public domain.

No copyright claim is made with respect to public domain works.

This work reflects minor editorial revisions to the original texts.

Cover design created using Canva.com and reproduced pursuant to its free media licence agreement.

TABLE OF CONTENTS

ORTHODOXY 1
PREFACE 1
I INTRODUCTION IN DEFENCE OF EVERYTHING ELSE 1
II THE MANIAC 2
III THE SUICIDE OF THOUGHT 6
IV THE ETHICS OF ELFLAND 11
V THE FLAG OF THE WORLD 16
VI THE PARADOXES OF CHRISTIANITY 20
VII THE ETERNAL REVOLUTION 26
VIII THE ROMANCE OF ORTHODOXY 32
IX AUTHORITY AND THE ADVENTURER 37

HERETICS 44
I. INTRODUCTORY REMARKS ON THE IMPORTANCE OF ORTHODOXY 44
II. ON THE NEGATIVE SPIRIT 46
III. ON MR. RUDYARD KIPLING AND MAKING THE WORLD SMALL 47
IV. MR. BERNARD SHAW 50
V. MR. H. G. WELLS AND THE GIANTS 52
VI. CHRISTMAS AND THE AESTHETES 55
VII. OMAR AND THE SACRED VINE 57
VIII. THE MILDNESS OF THE YELLOW PRESS 58
IX. THE MOODS OF MR. GEORGE MOORE 61
X. ON SANDALS AND SIMPLICITY 61
XI SCIENCE AND THE SAVAGES 62
XII PAGANISM AND MR. LOWES DICKINSON 64
XIII. CELTS AND CELTOPHILES 67
XIV ON CERTAIN MODERN WRITERS AND THE INSTITUTION OF THE FAMILY ... 68
XV ON SMART NOVELISTS AND THE SMART SET 70
XVI ON MR. MCCABE AND A DIVINE FRIVOLITY 73
XVII ON THE WIT OF WHISTLER 76
XVIII THE FALLACY OF THE YOUNG NATION 78
XIX SLUM NOVELISTS AND THE SLUMS 81
XX. CONCLUDING REMARKS ON THE IMPORTANCE OF ORTHODOXY 83

WHAT'S WRONG WITH THE WORLD 87
PART ONE. THE HOMELESSNESS OF MAN 87
I. THE MEDICAL MISTAKE 87

II. WANTED, AN UNPRACTICAL MAN	87
III. THE NEW HYPOCRITE	88
IV. THE FEAR OF THE PAST	90
V. THE UNFINISHED TEMPLE	91
VI. THE ENEMIES OF PROPERTY	93
VII. THE FREE FAMILY	93
VIII. THE WILDNESS OF DOMESTICITY	94
IX. HISTORY OF HUDGE AND GUDGE	95
X. OPPRESSION BY OPTIMISM	96
XI. THE HOMELESSNESS OF JONES	97
PART TWO. IMPERIALISM, OR THE MISTAKE ABOUT MAN	98
I. THE CHARM OF JINGOISM	98
II. WISDOM AND THE WEATHER	98
III. THE COMMON VISION	100
IV. THE INSANE NECESSITY	101
PART THREE. FEMINISM, OR THE MISTAKE ABOUT WOMAN	102
I. THE UNMILITARY SUFFRAGETTE	102
II. THE UNIVERSAL STICK	103
III. THE EMANCIPATION OF DOMESTICITY	104
IV. THE ROMANCE OF THRIFT	105
V. THE COLDNESS OF CHLOE	106
VI. THE PEDANT AND THE SAVAGE	107
VII. THE MODERN SURRENDER OF WOMAN	108
VIII. THE BRAND OF THE FLEUR-DE-LIS	108
IX. SINCERITY AND THE GALLOWS	109
X. THE HIGHER ANARCHY	110
XI. THE QUEEN AND THE SUFFRAGETTES	111
XII. THE MODERN SLAVE	111
PART FOUR. EDUCATION: OR THE MISTAKE ABOUT THE CHILD	112
I. THE CALVINISM OF TO-DAY	112
II. THE TRIBAL TERROR	112
III. THE TRICKS OF ENVIRONMENT	113
IV. THE TRUTH ABOUT EDUCATION	113
V. AN EVIL CRY	114
VI. AUTHORITY THE UNAVOIDABLE	114
VII. THE HUMILITY OF MRS. GRUNDY	115
VIII. THE BROKEN RAINBOW	116
IX. THE NEED FOR NARROWNESS	117
X. THE CASE FOR THE PUBLIC SCHOOLS	117
XI. THE SCHOOL FOR HYPOCRITES	119
XII. THE STALENESS OF THE NEW SCHOOLS	120
XIII. THE OUTLAWED PARENT	121

XIV. FOLLY AND FEMALE EDUCATION ... 121
PART FIVE. THE HOME OF MAN ... 122
I. THE EMPIRE OF THE INSECT ... 122
II. THE FALLACY OF THE UMBRELLA STAND ... 123
III. THE DREADFUL DUTY OF GUDGE ... 124
IV. A LAST INSTANCE ... 125
V. CONCLUSION ... 125
THREE NOTES ... 126
I. ON FEMALE SUFFRAGE ... 126
II. ON CLEANLINESS IN EDUCATION ... 126
III. ON PEASANT PROPRIETORSHIP ... 127

WHAT I SAW IN AMERICA ... 128
WHAT IS AMERICA? ... 128
A MEDITATION IN A NEW YORK HOTEL ... 131
A MEDITATION IN BROADWAY ... 134
IRISH AND OTHER INTERVIEWERS ... 137
SOME AMERICAN CITIES ... 140
IN THE AMERICAN COUNTRY ... 144
THE AMERICAN BUSINESS MAN ... 147
PRESIDENTS AND PROBLEMS ... 152
PROHIBITION IN FACT AND FANCY ... 156
FADS AND PUBLIC OPINION ... 160
THE EXTRAORDINARY AMERICAN ... 164
THE REPUBLICAN IN THE RUINS ... 166
IS THE ATLANTIC NARROWING? ... 169
LINCOLN AND LOST CAUSES ... 172
WELLS AND THE WORLD STATE ... 174
A NEW MARTIN CHUZZLEWIT ... 178
THE SPIRIT OF AMERICA ... 181
THE SPIRIT OF ENGLAND ... 183
THE FUTURE OF DEMOCRACY ... 186

ORTHODOXY

PREFACE

This book is meant to be a companion to "Heretics," and to put the positive side in addition to the negative. Many critics complained of the book called "Heretics" because it merely criticised current philosophies without offering any alternative philosophy. This book is an attempt to answer the challenge. It is unavoidably affirmative and therefore unavoidably autobiographical. The writer has been driven back upon somewhat the same difficulty as that which beset Newman in writing his Apologia; he has been forced to be egotistical only in order to be sincere. While everything else may be different the motive in both cases is the same. It is the purpose of the writer to attempt an explanation, not of whether the Christian Faith can be believed, but of how he personally has come to believe it. The book is therefore arranged upon the positive principle of a riddle and its answer. It deals first with all the writer's own solitary and sincere speculations and then with all the startling style in which they were all suddenly satisfied by the Christian Theology. The writer regards it as amounting to a convincing creed. But if it is not that it is at least a repeated and surprising coincidence.

Gilbert K. Chesterton.

I INTRODUCTION IN DEFENCE OF EVERYTHING ELSE

THE only possible excuse for this book is that it is an answer to a challenge. Even a bad shot is dignified when he accepts a duel. When some time ago I published a series of hasty but sincere papers, under the name of "Heretics," several critics for whose intellect I have a warm respect (I may mention specially Mr. G.S.Street) said that it was all very well for me to tell everybody to affirm his cosmic theory, but that I had carefully avoided supporting my precepts with example. "I will begin to worry about my philosophy," said Mr. Street, "when Mr. Chesterton has given us his." It was perhaps an incautious suggestion to make to a person only too ready to write books upon the feeblest provocation. But after all, though Mr. Street has inspired and created this book, he need not read it. If he does read it, he will find that in its pages I have attempted in a vague and personal way, in a set of mental pictures rather than in a series of deductions, to state the philosophy in which I have come to believe. I will not call it my philosophy; for I did not make it. God and humanity made it; and it made me.

I have often had a fancy for writing a romance about an English yachtsman who slightly miscalculated his course and discovered England under the impression that it was a new island in the South Seas. I always find, however, that I am either too busy or too lazy to write this fine work, so I may as well give it away for the purposes of philosophical illustration. There will probably be a general impression that the man who landed (armed to the teeth and talking by signs) to plant the British flag on that barbaric temple which turned out to be the Pavilion at Brighton, felt rather a fool. I am not here concerned to deny that he looked a fool. But if you imagine that he felt a fool, or at any rate that the sense of folly was his sole or his dominant emotion, then you have not studied with sufficient delicacy the rich romantic nature of the hero of this tale. His mistake was really a most enviable mistake; and he knew it, if he was the man I take him for. What could be more delightful than to have in the same few minutes all the fascinating terrors of going abroad combined with all the humane security of coming home again? What could be better than to have all the fun of discovering South Africa without the disgusting necessity of landing there? What could be more glorious than to brace one's self up to discover New South Wales and then realize, with a gush of happy tears, that it was really old South Wales. This at least seems to me the main problem for philosophers, and is in a manner the main problem of this book. How can we contrive to be at once astonished at the world and yet at home in it? How can this queer cosmic town, with its many-legged citizens, with its monstrous and ancient lamps, how can this world give us at once the fascination of a strange town and the comfort and honour of being our own town?

To show that a faith or a philosophy is true from every standpoint would be too big an undertaking even for a much bigger book than this; it is necessary to follow one path of argument; and this is the path that I here propose to follow. I wish to set forth my faith as particularly answering this double spiritual need, the need for that mixture of the familiar and the unfamiliar which Christendom has rightly named romance. For the very word "romance" has in it the mystery and ancient meaning of Rome. Any one setting out to dispute anything ought always to begin by saying what he does not dispute. Beyond stating what he proposes to prove he should always state what he does not propose to prove. The thing I do not propose to prove, the thing I propose to take as common ground between myself and any average reader, is this desirability of an active and imaginative life, picturesque and full of a poetical curiosity, a life such as western man at any rate always seems to have desired. If a man says that extinction is better than existence or blank existence better than variety and adventure, then he is not one of the ordinary people to whom I am talking. If a man prefers nothing I can give him nothing. But nearly all people I have ever met in this western society in which I live would agree to the general proposition that we need this life of practical romance; the combination of something that is strange with something that is secure. We need so to view the world as to combine an idea of wonder and an idea of welcome. We need to be happy in this wonderland without once being merely comfortable. It is THIS achievement of my creed that I shall chiefly pursue in these pages.

But I have a peculiar reason for mentioning the man in a yacht, who discovered England. For I am that man in a yacht. I discovered England. I do not see how this book can avoid being egotistical; and I do not quite see (to tell the truth) how it can avoid being dull. Dulness will, however, free me from the charge which I most lament; the charge of being flippant. Mere light sophistry is the thing that I happen to despise most of all things, and it is perhaps a wholesome fact that this is the thing of which I am generally accused. I know nothing so contemptible as a mere paradox; a mere ingenious defence of the indefensible. If it were true (as has been said) that Mr. Bernard Shaw lived upon paradox, then he ought to be a mere common millionaire; for a man of his mental activity could invent a sophistry every six minutes. It is as easy as lying; because it is lying. The truth is, of course, that Mr. Shaw is cruelly hampered by the fact that he cannot tell any lie unless he thinks it is the truth. I find myself under the same intolerable bondage. I never in my life said anything merely because I thought it funny; though of course, I have had ordinary human vainglory, and may have thought it funny because I had said it. It is one thing to describe an interview with a gorgon or a griffin, a creature who does not exist. It is another thing to discover that the rhinoceros does exist and then take pleasure in the fact that he looks as if he didn't. One searches for truth, but it may be that one pursues instinctively the more extraordinary truths. And I offer this book with the heartiest sentiments to all the jolly people who hate what I write, and regard it (very justly, for all I know), as a piece of poor clowning or a single tiresome joke.

For if this book is a joke it is a joke against me. I am the man who with the utmost daring discovered what had been discovered before. If there is an element of farce in what follows, the farce is at my own expense; for this book explains how I fancied I was the first to set foot in Brighton and then found I was the last. It recounts my elephantine adventures in pursuit of the obvious. No one can think my case more ludicrous than I think it myself; no reader can accuse me here of trying to make a fool of him: I am the fool of this story, and no rebel shall hurl me from my throne. I freely confess all the idiotic ambitions of the end of the nineteenth century. I did, like all other solemn little boys, try to be in advance of the age. Like them I tried to be some ten minutes in advance of the truth. And I found that I was eighteen hundred years behind it. I did strain my voice with a painfully juvenile exaggeration in uttering my truths. And I was punished in the fittest and funniest way, for I have kept my truths: but I have discovered, not that they were not truths, but simply that they were not mine. When I fancied that I stood alone I was really in the ridiculous position of being backed up by all Christendom. It may be, Heaven forgive me, that I did try to be original; but I only succeeded in inventing all by myself an inferior copy of the existing traditions of civilized religion. The man from the yacht thought he was the first to find England; I thought I was the first to find Europe. I did try to found a heresy of my own; and when I had put the last touches to it, I discovered that it was orthodoxy.

It may be that somebody will be entertained by the account of this happy fiasco. It might amuse a friend or an enemy to read how I gradually learnt from the truth of some stray legend or from the falsehood of some dominant philosophy, things that I might have learnt from my catechism—if I had ever learnt it. There may or may not be some entertainment in reading how I found at last in an anarchist club or a Babylonian temple what I might have found in the nearest parish church. If any one is entertained by learning how the flowers of the field or the phrases in an omnibus, the accidents of politics or the pains of youth came together in a certain order to produce a certain conviction of Christian orthodoxy, he may possibly read this book. But there is in everything a reasonable division of labour. I have written the book, and nothing on earth would induce me to read it.

I add one purely pedantic note which comes, as a note naturally should, at the beginning of the book. These essays are concerned only to discuss the actual fact that the central Christian theology (sufficiently summarized in the Apostles' Creed) is the best root of energy and sound ethics. They are not intended to discuss the very fascinating but quite different question of what is the present seat of authority for the proclamation of that creed. When the word "orthodoxy" is used here it means the Apostles' Creed, as understood by everybody calling himself Christian until a very short time ago and the general historic conduct of those who held such a creed. I have been forced by mere space to confine myself to what I have got from this creed; I do not touch the matter much disputed among modern Christians, of where we ourselves got it. This is not an ecclesiastical treatise but a sort of slovenly autobiography. But if any one wants my opinions about the actual nature of the authority, Mr. G.S.Street has only to throw me another challenge, and I will write him another book.

II THE MANIAC

Thoroughly worldly people never understand even the world; they rely altogether on a few cynical maxims which are not true. Once I remember walking with a prosperous publisher, who made a remark which I had often heard before; it is, indeed, almost a motto of the modern world. Yet I had heard it once too often, and I saw suddenly that there was nothing in it. The publisher said of somebody, "That man will get on; he believes in himself." And I remember that as I lifted my head to listen, my eye caught an omnibus on which was written "Hanwell." I said to him, "Shall I tell you where the men are who believe most in themselves? For I can tell you. I know of men who believe in themselves more colossally than Napoleon or Caesar. I know where flames the fixed star of certainty and success. I can guide you to the thrones of the Super-men. The men who really believe in themselves are all in lunatic asylums." He said mildly that there were a good many men after all who believed in themselves and who were not in lunatic asylums. "Yes, there are," I retorted, "and you of all men ought to know them. That drunken poet from whom you would not take a dreary tragedy, he believed in himself. That elderly minister with an epic from whom you were hiding in a back room, he believed in himself. If you consulted your business experience instead of your ugly individualistic philosophy, you would know that believing in himself is one of the commonest signs of a rotter. Actors who can't act believe in themselves; and debtors who won't pay. It would be much truer to say that a man will certainly fail, because he believes in himself. Complete self-confidence is not merely a sin; complete self-confidence is a weakness. Believing utterly in one's self is a hysterical and superstitious belief like believing in Joanna Southcote: the man who has it has `Hanwell' written on his face as plain as it is written on that omnibus." And to all this my friend the publisher made this very deep and effective reply, "Well, if a man is not to believe in himself, in what is he to believe?" After a long pause I replied, "I will go home and write a book in answer to that question." This is the book that I have written in answer to it.

But I think this book may well start where our argument started— in the neighbourhood of the mad-house. Modern masters of science are much impressed with the need of beginning all inquiry with a fact. The ancient masters of religion were quite equally impressed with that necessity. They began with the fact of sin—a fact as practical as potatoes. Whether or no man could be washed in miraculous waters, there was no doubt at any rate that he wanted washing. But certain religious leaders in London, not mere materialists, have begun in our day not to deny the highly disputable water, but to deny the indisputable dirt. Certain new theologians dispute original sin, which is the only part of Christian theology which can really be proved. Some followers of the Reverend R.J.Campbell, in their almost too fastidious spirituality, admit divine sinlessness, which they cannot see even in their dreams. But they essentially deny human sin, which they can see in the street. The strongest saints and the strongest sceptics alike took positive evil as the starting-point of their argument. If it be true (as it certainly is) that a man can feel exquisite happiness in skinning a cat, then the religious philosopher can only draw one of two deductions. He must either deny the existence of God, as all atheists do; or he must deny the present union between God and man, as all Christians do. The new theologians seem to think it a highly rationalistic solution to deny the cat.

In this remarkable situation it is plainly not now possible (with any hope of a universal appeal) to start, as our fathers did, with the fact of sin. This very fact which was to them (and is to me) as plain as a pikestaff, is the very fact that has been specially diluted or denied. But though moderns deny the existence of sin, I do not think that they have yet denied the existence of a lunatic asylum. We all agree still that there is a collapse of the intellect as unmistakable as a falling house. Men deny hell, but not, as yet, Hanwell. For the purpose of our primary argument the one may very well stand where the other stood. I mean that as all thoughts and theories were once judged by whether they tended to make a man lose his soul, so for our present purpose all modern thoughts and theories may be judged by whether they tend to make a man lose his wits.

It is true that some speak lightly and loosely of insanity as in itself attractive. But a moment's thought will show that if disease is beautiful, it is generally some one else's disease. A blind man may be picturesque; but it requires two eyes to see the picture.

And similarly even the wildest poetry of insanity can only be enjoyed by the sane. To the insane man his insanity is quite prosaic, because it is quite true. A man who thinks himself a chicken is to himself as ordinary as a chicken. A man who thinks he is a bit of glass is to himself as dull as a bit of glass. It is the homogeneity of his mind which makes him dull, and which makes him mad. It is only because we see the irony of his idea that we think him even amusing; it is only because he does not see the irony of his idea that he is put in Hanwell at all. In short, oddities only strike ordinary people. Oddities do not strike odd people. This is why ordinary people have a much more exciting time; while odd people are always complaining of the dulness of life. This is also why the new novels die so quickly, and why the old fairy tales endure for ever. The old fairy tale makes the hero a normal human boy; it is his adventures that are startling; they startle him because he is normal. But in the modern psychological novel the hero is abnormal; the centre is not central. Hence the fiercest adventures fail to affect him adequately, and the book is monotonous. You can make a story out of a hero among dragons; but not out of a dragon among dragons. The fairy tale discusses what a sane man will do in a mad world. The sober realistic novel of to-day discusses what an essential lunatic will do in a dull world.

Let us begin, then, with the mad-house; from this evil and fantastic inn let us set forth on our intellectual journey. Now, if we are to glance at the philosophy of sanity, the first thing to do in the matter is to blot out one big and common mistake. There is a notion adrift everywhere that imagination, especially mystical imagination, is dangerous to man's mental balance. Poets are commonly spoken of as psychologically unreliable; and generally there is a vague association between wreathing laurels in your hair and sticking straws in it. Facts and history utterly contradict this view. Most of the very great poets have been not only sane, but extremely business-like; and if Shakespeare ever really held horses, it was because he was much the safest man to hold them. Imagination does not breed insanity. Exactly what does breed insanity is reason. Poets do not go mad; but chess-players do. Mathematicians go mad, and cashiers; but creative artists very seldom. I am not, as will be seen, in any sense attacking logic: I only say that this danger does lie in logic, not in imagination. Artistic paternity is as wholesome as physical paternity. Moreover, it is worthy of remark that when a poet really was morbid it was commonly because he had some weak spot of rationality on his brain. Poe, for instance, really was morbid; not because he was poetical, but because he was specially analytical. Even chess was too poetical for him; he disliked chess because it was full of knights and castles, like a poem. He avowedly preferred the black discs of draughts, because they were more like the mere black dots on a diagram. Perhaps the strongest case of all is this: that only one great English poet went mad, Cowper. And he was definitely driven mad by logic, by the ugly and alien logic of predestination. Poetry was not the disease, but the medicine; poetry partly kept him in health. He could sometimes forget the red and thirsty hell to which his hideous necessitarianism dragged him among the wide waters and the white flat lilies of the Ouse. He was damned by John Calvin; he was almost saved by John Gilpin. Everywhere we see that men do not go mad by dreaming. Critics are much madder than poets. Homer is complete and calm enough; it is his critics who tear him into extravagant tatters. Shakespeare is quite himself; it is only some of his critics who have discovered that he was somebody else. And though St. John the Evangelist saw many strange monsters in his vision, he saw no creature so wild as one of his own commentators. The general fact is simple. Poetry is sane because it floats easily in an infinite sea; reason seeks to cross the infinite sea, and so make it finite. The result is mental exhaustion, like the physical exhaustion of Mr. Holbein. To accept everything is an exercise, to understand everything a strain. The poet only desires exaltation and expansion, a world to stretch himself in. The poet only asks to get his head into the heavens. It is the logician who seeks to get the heavens into his head. And it is his head that splits.

It is a small matter, but not irrelevant, that this striking mistake is commonly supported by a striking misquotation. We have all heard people cite the celebrated line of Dryden as "Great genius is to madness near allied." But Dryden did not say that great genius was to madness near allied. Dryden was a great genius himself, and knew better. It would have been hard to find a man more romantic than he, or more sensible. What Dryden said was this, "Great wits are oft to madness near allied"; and that is true. It is the pure promptitude of the intellect that is in peril of a breakdown. Also people might remember of what sort of man Dryden was talking. He was not talking of any unworldly visionary like Vaughan or George Herbert. He was talking of a cynical man of the world, a sceptic, a diplomatist, a great practical politician. Such men are indeed to madness near allied. Their incessant calculation of their own brains and other people's brains is a dangerous trade. It is always perilous to the mind to reckon up the mind. A flippant person has asked why we say, "As mad as a hatter." A more flippant person might answer that a hatter is mad because he has to measure the human head.

And if great reasoners are often maniacal, it is equally true that maniacs are commonly great reasoners. When I was engaged in a controversy with the CLARION on the matter of free will, that able writer Mr. R.B.Suthers said that free will was lunacy, because it meant causeless actions, and the actions of a lunatic would be causeless. I do not dwell here upon the disastrous lapse in determinist logic. Obviously if any actions, even a lunatic's, can be causeless, determinism is done for. If the chain of causation can be broken for a madman, it can be broken for a man. But my purpose is to point out something more practical. It was natural, perhaps, that a modern Marxian Socialist should not know anything about free will. But it was certainly remarkable that a modern Marxian Socialist should not know anything about lunatics. Mr. Suthers evidently did not know anything about lunatics. The last thing that can be said of a lunatic is that his actions are causeless. If any human acts may loosely be called causeless, they are the minor acts of a healthy man; whistling as he walks; slashing the grass with a stick; kicking his heels or rubbing his hands. It is the happy man who does the useless things; the sick man is not strong enough to be idle. It is exactly such careless and causeless actions that the madman could never understand; for the madman (like the determinist) generally sees too much cause in everything. The madman would read a conspiratorial significance into those empty activities. He would think that the lopping of the grass was an attack on private property. He would think that the kicking of the heels was a signal to an accomplice. If the madman could for an instant become careless, he would become sane. Every one who has had the misfortune to talk with people in the heart or on the edge of mental disorder, knows that their most sinister quality is a horrible clarity of detail; a connecting of one thing with another in a map more elaborate than a maze. If you argue with a madman, it is extremely probable that you will get the worst of it; for in many ways his mind moves all the quicker for not being delayed by the things that go with good judgment. He is not hampered by a sense of humour or by charity, or by the dumb certainties of experience. He is the more logical for losing certain sane affections. Indeed, the common phrase for insanity is in this respect a misleading one. The madman is not the man who has lost his reason. The madman is the man who has lost everything except his reason.

The madman's explanation of a thing is always complete, and often in a purely rational sense satisfactory. Or, to speak more strictly, the insane explanation, if not conclusive, is at least unanswerable; this may be observed specially in the two or three commonest kinds of madness. If a man says (for instance) that men have a conspiracy against him, you cannot dispute it except by saying that all the men deny that they are conspirators; which is exactly what conspirators would do. His explanation covers the facts as much as yours. Or if a man says that he is the rightful King of England, it is no complete answer to say that the existing authorities call him mad; for if he were King of England that might be the wisest thing for the existing authorities to do. Or if a man says that he is Jesus Christ, it is no answer to tell him that the world denies his divinity; for the world denied Christ's.

Nevertheless he is wrong. But if we attempt to trace his error in exact terms, we shall not find it quite so easy as we had supposed. Perhaps the nearest we can get to expressing it is to say this: that his mind moves in a perfect but narrow circle. A small circle is quite as infinite as a large circle; but, though it is quite as infinite, it is not so large. In the same way the insane explanation is quite as complete as the sane one, but it is not so large. A bullet is quite as round as the world, but it is not the world. There is such a thing as a narrow universality; there is such a thing as a small and cramped eternity; you may see it in many modern religions. Now, speaking quite externally and empirically, we may say that the strongest and most unmistakable MARK of madness is this combination between a logical completeness and a spiritual contraction. The lunatic's theory explains a large number of things, but it does not explain them in a large way. I mean that if you or I were dealing with a mind that was growing morbid, we should be chiefly concerned not so much to give it arguments as to give it air, to convince it that there was something cleaner and cooler outside the suffocation of a single argument. Suppose, for instance, it were the first case that I took as typical; suppose it were the case of a man who accused everybody of conspiring against him. If we could express our deepest feelings of protest and appeal against this obsession, I suppose we should say something like this: "Oh, I admit that you have your case and have it by heart, and that many things do fit into other things as you say. I admit that your explanation explains a great deal; but what a great deal it leaves out! Are there no other stories in the world except yours; and are all men busy with your business? Suppose we grant the details; perhaps when the man in the street did not seem to see you it was only his cunning; perhaps when the policeman asked you your name it was only because he knew it already. But how much happier you would be if you only knew that these people cared nothing about you! How much larger your life would be if your self could become smaller in it; if you could really look at other men with common curiosity and pleasure; if you could see them walking as they are in their sunny selfishness and their virile indifference! You would begin to be interested in them, because they were not interested in you. You would break out of this tiny and tawdry theatre in which your own little plot is always being played, and you would find yourself under a freer sky, in a street full of splendid strangers." Or suppose it were the second case of madness, that of a man who claims the crown, your impulse would be to answer, "All right! Perhaps you know that you are the King of England; but why do you care? Make one magnificent effort and you will be a human being and look down on all the kings of the earth." Or it might be the third case, of the madman who called himself Christ. If we said what we felt, we should say, "So you are the Creator and Redeemer of the world: but what a small world it must be! What a little heaven you must inhabit, with angels no bigger than butterflies! How sad it must be to be God; and an inadequate God! Is there really no life fuller and no love more marvellous than yours; and is it really in your small and painful pity that all flesh must put its faith? How much happier you would be, how much more of you there would be, if the hammer of a higher God could smash your small cosmos, scattering the stars like spangles, and leave you in the open, free like other men to look up as well as down!"

And it must be remembered that the most purely practical science does take this view of mental evil; it does not seek to argue with it like a heresy but simply to snap it like a spell. Neither modern science nor ancient religion believes in complete free thought. Theology rebukes certain thoughts by calling them blasphemous. Science rebukes certain thoughts by calling them morbid. For example, some religious societies discouraged men more or less from thinking about sex. The new scientific society definitely discourages men from thinking about death; it is a fact, but it is considered a morbid fact. And in dealing with those whose morbidity has a touch of mania, modern science cares far less for pure logic than a dancing Dervish. In these cases it is not enough that the unhappy man should desire truth; he must desire health. Nothing can save him but a blind hunger for normality, like that of a beast. A man cannot think himself out of mental evil; for it is actually the organ of thought that has become diseased, ungovernable, and, as it were, independent. He can only be saved by will or faith. The moment his mere reason moves, it moves in the old circular rut; he will go round and round his logical circle, just as a man in a third-class carriage on the Inner Circle will go round and round the Inner Circle unless he performs the voluntary, vigorous, and mystical act of getting out at Gower Street. Decision is the whole business here; a door must be shut for ever. Every remedy is a desperate remedy. Every cure is a miraculous cure. Curing a madman is not arguing with a philosopher; it is casting out a devil. And however quietly doctors and psychologists may go to work in the matter, their attitude is profoundly intolerant— as intolerant as Bloody Mary. Their attitude is really this: that the man must stop thinking, if he is to go on living. Their counsel is one of intellectual amputation. If thy HEAD offend thee, cut it off; for it is better, not merely to enter the Kingdom of Heaven as a child, but to enter it as an imbecile, rather than with your whole intellect to be cast into hell— or into Hanwell.

Such is the madman of experience; he is commonly a reasoner, frequently a successful reasoner. Doubtless he could be vanquished in mere reason, and the case against him put logically. But it can be put much more precisely in more general and even aesthetic terms. He is in the clean and well-lit prison of one idea: he is sharpened to one painful point. He is without healthy hesitation and healthy complexity. Now, as I explain in the introduction, I have determined in these early chapters to give not so much a diagram of a doctrine as some pictures of a point of view. And I have described at length my vision of the maniac for this reason: that just as I am affected by the maniac, so I am affected by most modern thinkers. That unmistakable mood or note that I hear from Hanwell, I hear also from half the chairs of science and seats of learning to-day; and most of the mad doctors are mad doctors in more senses than one. They all have exactly that combination we have noted: the combination of an expansive and exhaustive reason with a contracted common sense. They are universal only in the sense that they take one thin explanation and carry it very far. But a pattern can stretch for ever and still be a small pattern. They see a chess-board white on black, and if the universe is paved with it, it is still white on black. Like the lunatic, they cannot alter their standpoint; they cannot make a mental effort and suddenly see it black on white.

Take first the more obvious case of materialism. As an explanation of the world, materialism has a sort of insane simplicity. It has just the quality of the madman's argument; we have at once the sense of it covering everything and the sense of it leaving everything out. Contemplate some able and sincere materialist, as, for instance, Mr. McCabe, and you will have exactly this unique sensation. He understands everything, and everything does not seem worth understanding. His cosmos may be complete in every rivet and cog-wheel, but still his cosmos is smaller than our world. Somehow his scheme, like the lucid scheme of the madman, seems unconscious of the alien energies and the large indifference of the earth; it is not thinking of the real things of the earth, of fighting peoples or proud mothers, or first love or fear upon the sea. The earth is so very large, and the cosmos is so very small. The cosmos is about the smallest hole that a man can hide his head in.

It must be understood that I am not now discussing the relation of these creeds to truth; but, for the present, solely their relation to health. Later in the argument I hope to attack the question of objective verity; here I speak only of a phenomenon of psychology. I do not for the present attempt to prove to Haeckel that materialism is untrue, any more than I attempted to prove to the man who thought he was Christ that he was labouring under an error. I merely remark here on the fact that both cases have the same kind of completeness and the same kind of incompleteness. You can explain a man's detention at Hanwell by an indifferent public by saying that it is the crucifixion of a god of whom the world is not worthy. The explanation does explain. Similarly you may explain the order in the universe by saying that all things, even the souls of men, are leaves inevitably unfolding on an utterly unconscious tree—the blind destiny of matter. The explanation does explain, though not, of course, so completely as the madman's. But the point here is that the normal human mind not only objects to both, but feels to both the same objection. Its approximate statement is that if the man in Hanwell is the real God, he is not much of a god. And, similarly, if the cosmos of the materialist is the real cosmos, it is not much of a cosmos. The thing has shrunk. The deity is less divine than many men; and (according to Haeckel) the whole of life is something much more grey, narrow, and trivial than many separate aspects of it. The parts seem greater than the whole.

For we must remember that the materialist philosophy (whether true or not) is certainly much more limiting than any religion. In one sense, of course, all intelligent ideas are narrow. They cannot be broader than themselves. A Christian is only restricted in the same sense that an atheist is restricted. He cannot think Christianity false and continue to be a Christian; and the atheist cannot think atheism false and continue to be an atheist. But as it happens, there is a very special sense in which materialism has more restrictions than spiritualism. Mr. McCabe thinks me a slave because I am not allowed to believe in determinism. I think Mr. McCabe a slave because he is not allowed to believe in fairies. But if we examine the two vetoes we shall see that his is really much more of a pure veto than mine. The Christian is quite free to believe that there is a considerable amount of settled order and inevitable development in the universe. But the materialist is not allowed to admit into his spotless machine the slightest speck of spiritualism or miracle. Poor Mr. McCabe is not allowed to retain even the tiniest imp, though it might be hiding in a pimpernel. The Christian admits that the universe is manifold and even miscellaneous, just as a sane man knows that he is complex. The sane man knows that he has a touch of the beast, a touch of the devil, a touch of the saint, a touch of the citizen. Nay, the really sane man knows that he has a touch of the madman. But the materialist's world is quite simple and solid, just as the madman is quite sure he is sane. The materialist is sure that history has been simply and solely a chain of causation, just as the interesting person before mentioned is quite sure that he is simply and solely a chicken. Materialists and madmen never have doubts.

Spiritual doctrines do not actually limit the mind as do materialistic denials. Even if I believe in immortality I need not think about it. But if I disbelieve in immortality I must not think about it. In the first case the road is open and I can go as far as I like; in the second the road is shut. But the case is even stronger, and the parallel with madness is yet more strange. For it was our case against the exhaustive and logical theory of the lunatic that, right or wrong, it gradually destroyed his humanity. Now it is the charge against the main deductions of the materialist that, right or wrong, they gradually destroy his humanity; I do not mean only kindness, I mean hope, courage, poetry, initiative, all that is human. For instance, when materialism leads men to complete fatalism (as it generally does), it is quite idle to pretend that it is in any sense a liberating force. It is absurd to say that you are especially advancing freedom when you only use free thought to destroy free will. The determinists come to bind, not to loose. They may well call their law the "chain" of causation. It is the worst chain that ever fettered a human being. You may use the language of liberty, if you like, about materialistic teaching, but it is obvious that this is just as inapplicable to it as a whole as the same language when applied to a man locked up in a mad-house. You may say, if you like, that the man is free to think himself a poached egg. But it is surely a more massive and important fact that if he is a poached egg he is not free to eat, drink, sleep, walk, or smoke a cigarette. Similarly you may say, if you like, that the bold determinist speculator is free to disbelieve in the reality of the will. But it is a much more massive and important fact that he is not free to raise, to curse, to thank, to justify, to urge, to punish, to resist temptations, to incite mobs, to make New Year resolutions, to pardon sinners, to rebuke tyrants, or even to say "thank you" for the mustard.

In passing from this subject I may note that there is a queer fallacy to the effect that materialistic fatalism is in some way favourable to mercy, to the abolition of cruel punishments or punishments of any kind. This is startlingly the reverse of the truth. It is quite tenable that the doctrine of necessity makes no difference at all; that it leaves the flogger flogging and the kind friend exhorting as before. But obviously if it stops either of them it stops the kind exhortation. That the sins are inevitable does not prevent punishment; if it prevents anything it prevents persuasion. Determinism is quite as likely to lead to cruelty as it is certain to lead to cowardice. Determinism is not inconsistent with the cruel treatment of criminals. What it is (perhaps) inconsistent with is the generous treatment of criminals; with any appeal to their better feelings or encouragement in their moral struggle. The determinist does not believe in appealing to the will, but he does believe in changing the environment. He must not say to the sinner, "Go and sin no more," because the sinner cannot help it. But he can put him in boiling oil; for boiling oil is an environment. Considered as a figure, therefore, the materialist has the fantastic outline of the figure of the madman. Both take up a position at once unanswerable and intolerable.

Of course it is not only of the materialist that all this is true. The same would apply to the other extreme of speculative logic. There is a sceptic far more terrible than he who believes that everything began in matter. It is possible to meet the sceptic who believes that everything began in himself. He doubts not the existence of angels or devils, but the existence of men and cows. For him his own friends are a mythology made up by himself. He created his own father and his own mother. This horrible fancy has in it something decidedly attractive to the somewhat mystical egoism of our day. That publisher who thought that men would get on if they believed in themselves, those seekers after the Superman who are always looking for him in the looking-glass, those writers who talk about impressing their personalities instead of creating life for the world, all these people have really only an inch between them and this awful emptiness. Then when this kindly world all round the man has been blackened out like a lie; when friends fade into ghosts, and the foundations of the world fail; then when the man, believing in nothing and in no man, is alone in his own nightmare, then the great individualistic motto shall be written over him in avenging irony. The stars will be only dots in the blackness of his own brain; his mother's face will be only a sketch from his own insane pencil on the walls of his cell. But over his cell shall be written, with dreadful truth, "He believes in himself."

All that concerns us here, however, is to note that this panegoistic extreme of thought exhibits the same paradox as the other extreme of materialism. It is equally complete in theory and equally crippling in practice. For the sake of simplicity, it is easier to state the notion by saying that a man can believe that he is always in a dream. Now, obviously there can be no positive proof given to him that he is not in a dream, for the simple reason that no proof can be offered that might not be offered in a dream. But if the man began to burn down London and say that his housekeeper would soon call him to breakfast, we should take him and put him with other logicians in a place which has often been alluded to in the course of this chapter. The man who cannot believe his senses, and the man who cannot believe anything else, are both insane, but their insanity is proved not by any error in their argument, but by the manifest mistake of their whole lives. They have both locked themselves up in two boxes, painted inside with the sun and stars; they are both unable to get out, the one into the health and happiness of heaven, the other even into the health and happiness of the earth. Their position is quite reasonable; nay, in a sense it is infinitely reasonable, just as a threepenny bit is infinitely circular. But there is such a thing as a mean infinity, a base and slavish eternity. It is amusing to notice that many of the moderns, whether sceptics or mystics, have taken as their sign a certain eastern symbol, which is the very symbol of this ultimate nullity. When they wish to represent eternity, they represent it by a serpent with his tail in his mouth. There is a startling sarcasm in the image of that very unsatisfactory meal. The eternity of the material fatalists, the eternity of the eastern pessimists, the eternity of the supercilious theosophists and higher scientists of to-day is, indeed, very well presented by a serpent eating his tail, a degraded animal who destroys even himself.

This chapter is purely practical and is concerned with what actually is the chief mark and element of insanity; we may say in summary that it is reason used without root, reason in the void. The man who begins to think without the proper first principles goes mad; he begins to think at the wrong end. And for the rest of these pages we have to try and discover what is the right end. But we may ask in conclusion, if this be what drives men mad, what is it that keeps them sane? By the end of this book I hope to give a definite, some will think a far too definite, answer. But for the moment it is possible in the same solely practical manner to give a general answer touching what in actual human history keeps men sane. Mysticism keeps men sane. As long as you have mystery you have health; when you destroy mystery you create morbidity. The ordinary man has always been sane because the ordinary man has always been a mystic. He has permitted the twilight. He has always had one foot in earth and the other in fairyland. He has always left himself free to doubt his gods; but (unlike the agnostic of to-day) free also to believe in them. He has always cared more for truth than for consistency. If he saw two truths that seemed to contradict each other, he would take the two truths and the contradiction along with them. His spiritual sight is stereoscopic, like his physical sight: he sees two different pictures at once and yet sees all the better for that. Thus he has always believed that there was such a thing as fate, but such a thing as free will also. Thus he believed that children were indeed the kingdom of heaven, but nevertheless ought to be obedient to the kingdom of earth. He admired youth because it was young and age because it was not. It is exactly this balance of apparent contradictions that has been the whole buoyancy of the healthy man. The whole secret of mysticism is this: that man can understand everything by the help of what he does not understand. The morbid logician seeks to make everything lucid, and succeeds in making everything mysterious. The mystic allows one thing to be mysterious, and everything else becomes lucid. The determinist makes the theory of causation quite clear, and then finds that he cannot say "if you please" to the housemaid. The Christian permits free will to remain a sacred mystery; but because of this his relations with the housemaid become of a sparkling and crystal clearness. He puts the seed of dogma in a central darkness; but it branches forth in all directions with abounding natural health. As we have taken the circle as the symbol of reason and madness, we may very well take the cross as the symbol at once of mystery and of health. Buddhism is centripetal, but Christianity is centrifugal: it breaks out. For the circle is perfect and infinite in its nature; but it is fixed for ever in its size; it can never be larger or smaller. But the cross, though it has at its heart a collision and a contradiction, can extend its four arms for ever without altering its shape. Because it has a paradox in its centre it can grow without changing. The circle returns upon itself and is bound. The cross opens its arms to the four winds; it is a signpost for free travellers.

Symbols alone are of even a cloudy value in speaking of this deep matter; and another symbol from physical nature will express sufficiently well the real place of mysticism before mankind. The one created thing which we cannot look at is the one thing in the light of which we look at everything. Like the sun at noonday, mysticism explains everything else by the blaze of its own victorious invisibility. Detached intellectualism is (in the exact sense of a popular phrase) all moonshine; for it is light without heat, and it is secondary light, reflected from a dead world. But the Greeks were right when they made Apollo the god both of imagination and of sanity; for he was both the patron of poetry and the patron of healing. Of necessary dogmas and a special creed I shall speak later. But that transcendentalism by which all men live has primarily much the position of the sun in the sky. We are conscious of it as of a kind of splendid confusion; it is something both shining and shapeless, at once a blaze and a blur. But the circle of the moon is as clear and unmistakable, as recurrent and inevitable, as the circle of Euclid on a blackboard. For the moon is utterly reasonable; and the moon is the mother of lunatics and has given to them all her name.

III THE SUICIDE OF THOUGHT

The phrases of the street are not only forcible but subtle: for a figure of speech can often get into a crack too small for a definition. Phrases like "put out" or "off colour" might have been coined by Mr. Henry James in an agony of verbal precision. And there is no more subtle truth than that of the everyday phrase about a man having "his heart in the right place." It involves the idea of normal proportion; not only does a certain function exist, but it is rightly related to other functions. Indeed, the negation of this phrase would describe with peculiar accuracy the somewhat morbid mercy and perverse tenderness of the most representative moderns. If, for instance, I had to describe with fairness the character of Mr. Bernard Shaw, I could not express myself more exactly than by saying that he has a heroically large and generous heart; but not a heart in the right place. And this is so of the typical society of our time.

The modern world is not evil; in some ways the modern world is far too good. It is full of wild and wasted virtues. When a religious scheme is shattered (as Christianity was shattered at the Reformation), it is not merely the vices that are let loose. The vices are, indeed, let loose, and they wander and do damage. But the virtues are let loose also; and the virtues wander more wildly, and the virtues do more terrible damage. The modern world is full of the old Christian virtues gone mad. The virtues have gone mad because they have been isolated from each other and are wandering alone. Thus some scientists care for truth; and their truth is pitiless. Thus some humanitarians only care for pity; and their pity (I am sorry to say) is often untruthful. For example, Mr. Blatchford attacks Christianity because he is mad on one

Christian virtue: the merely mystical and almost irrational virtue of charity. He has a strange idea that he will make it easier to forgive sins by saying that there are no sins to forgive. Mr. Blatchford is not only an early Christian, he is the only early Christian who ought really to have been eaten by lions. For in his case the pagan accusation is really true: his mercy would mean mere anarchy. He really is the enemy of the human race— because he is so human. As the other extreme, we may take the acrid realist, who has deliberately killed in himself all human pleasure in happy tales or in the healing of the heart. Torquemada tortured people physically for the sake of moral truth. Zola tortured people morally for the sake of physical truth. But in Torquemada's time there was at least a system that could to some extent make righteousness and peace kiss each other. Now they do not even bow. But a much stronger case than these two of truth and pity can be found in the remarkable case of the dislocation of humility.

It is only with one aspect of humility that we are here concerned. Humility was largely meant as a restraint upon the arrogance and infinity of the appetite of man. He was always outstripping his mercies with his own newly invented needs. His very power of enjoyment destroyed half his joys. By asking for pleasure, he lost the chief pleasure; for the chief pleasure is surprise. Hence it became evident that if a man would make his world large, he must be always making himself small. Even the haughty visions, the tall cities, and the toppling pinnacles are the creations of humility. Giants that tread down forests like grass are the creations of humility. Towers that vanish upwards above the loneliest star are the creations of humility. For towers are not tall unless we look up at them; and giants are not giants unless they are larger than we. All this gigantesque imagination, which is, perhaps, the mightiest of the pleasures of man, is at bottom entirely humble. It is impossible without humility to enjoy anything— even pride.

But what we suffer from to-day is humility in the wrong place. Modesty has moved from the organ of ambition. Modesty has settled upon the organ of conviction; where it was never meant to be. A man was meant to be doubtful about himself, but undoubting about the truth; this has been exactly reversed. Nowadays the part of a man that a man does assert is exactly the part he ought not to assert—himself. The part he doubts is exactly the part he ought not to doubt—the Divine Reason. Huxley preached a humility content to learn from Nature. But the new sceptic is so humble that he doubts if he can even learn. Thus we should be wrong if we had said hastily that there is no humility typical of our time. The truth is that there is a real humility typical of our time; but it so happens that it is practically a more poisonous humility than the wildest prostrations of the ascetic. The old humility was a spur that prevented a man from stopping; not a nail in his boot that prevented him from going on. For the old humility made a man doubtful about his efforts, which might make him work harder. But the new humility makes a man doubtful about his aims, which will make him stop working altogether.

At any street corner we may meet a man who utters the frantic and blasphemous statement that he may be wrong. Every day one comes across somebody who says that of course his view may not be the right one. Of course his view must be the right one, or it is not his view. We are on the road to producing a race of men too mentally modest to believe in the multiplication table. We are in danger of seeing philosophers who doubt the law of gravity as being a mere fancy of their own. Scoffers of old time were too proud to be convinced; but these are too humble to be convinced. The meek do inherit the earth; but the modern sceptics are too meek even to claim their inheritance. It is exactly this intellectual helplessness which is our second problem.

The last chapter has been concerned only with a fact of observation: that what peril of morbidity there is for man comes rather from his reason than his imagination. It was not meant to attack the authority of reason; rather it is the ultimate purpose to defend it. For it needs defence. The whole modern world is at war with reason; and the tower already reels.

The sages, it is often said, can see no answer to the riddle of religion. But the trouble with our sages is not that they cannot see the answer; it is that they cannot even see the riddle. They are like children so stupid as to notice nothing paradoxical in the playful assertion that a door is not a door. The modern latitudinarians speak, for instance, about authority in religion not only as if there were no reason in it, but as if there had never been any reason for it. Apart from seeing its philosophical basis, they cannot even see its historical cause. Religious authority has often, doubtless, been oppressive or unreasonable; just as every legal system (and especially our present one) has been callous and full of a cruel apathy. It is rational to attack the police; nay, it is glorious. But the modern critics of religious authority are like men who should attack the police without ever having heard of burglars. For there is a great and possible peril to the human mind: a peril as practical as burglary. Against it religious authority was reared, rightly or wrongly, as a barrier. And against it something certainly must be reared as a barrier, if our race is to avoid ruin.

That peril is that the human intellect is free to destroy itself. Just as one generation could prevent the very existence of the next generation, by all entering a monastery or jumping into the sea, so one set of thinkers can in some degree prevent further thinking by teaching the next generation that there is no validity in any human thought. It is idle to talk always of the alternative of reason and faith. Reason is itself a matter of faith. It is an act of faith to assert that our thoughts have any relation to reality at all. If you are merely a sceptic, you must sooner or later ask yourself the question, "Why should ANYTHING go right; even observation and deduction? Why should not good logic be as misleading as bad logic? They are both movements in the brain of a bewildered ape?" The young sceptic says, "I have a right to think for myself." But the old sceptic, the complete sceptic, says, "I have no right to think for myself. I have no right to think at all."

There is a thought that stops thought. That is the only thought that ought to be stopped. That is the ultimate evil against which all religious authority was aimed. It only appears at the end of decadent ages like our own: and already Mr. H.G.Wells has raised its ruinous banner; he has written a delicate piece of scepticism called "Doubts of the Instrument." In this he questions the brain itself, and endeavours to remove all reality from all his own assertions, past, present, and to come. But it was against this remote ruin that all the military systems in religion were originally ranked and ruled. The creeds and the crusades, the hierarchies and the horrible persecutions were not organized, as is ignorantly said, for the suppression of reason. They were organized for the difficult defence of reason. Man, by a blind instinct, knew that if once things were wildly questioned, reason could be questioned first. The authority of priests to absolve, the authority of popes to define the authority, even of inquisitors to terrify: these were all only dark defences erected round one central authority, more undemonstrable, more supernatural than all—the authority of a man to think. We know now that this is so; we have no excuse for not knowing it. For we can hear scepticism crashing through the old ring of authorities, and at the same moment we can see reason swaying upon her throne. In so far as religion is gone, reason is going. For they are both of the same primary and authoritative kind. They are both methods of proof which cannot themselves be proved. And in the act of destroying the idea of Divine authority we have largely destroyed the idea of that human authority by which we do a long-division sum. With a long and sustained tug we have attempted to pull the mitre off pontifical man; and his head has come off with it.

Lest this should be called loose assertion, it is perhaps desirable, though dull, to run rapidly through the chief modern fashions of thought which have this effect of stopping thought itself. Materialism and the view of everything as a personal illusion have some such effect; for if the mind is mechanical, thought cannot be very exciting, and if the cosmos is unreal, there is nothing to think about. But in these cases the effect is indirect and doubtful. In some cases it is direct and clear; notably in the case of what is generally called evolution.

Evolution is a good example of that modern intelligence which, if it destroys anything, destroys itself. Evolution is either an innocent scientific description of how certain earthly things came about; or, if it is anything more than this, it is an attack upon thought itself. If evolution destroys anything, it does not destroy religion but rationalism. If evolution simply means that a positive thing called an ape turned very slowly into a positive thing called a man, then it is stingless for the most orthodox; for a personal God might just as well do things slowly as quickly, especially if, like the Christian God, he were outside time. But if it means anything more, it means that there is no such thing as an ape to change, and no such thing as a man for him to change into. It means that there is no such thing as a thing. At best, there is only one thing, and that is a flux of everything and anything. This is an attack not upon the faith, but upon the mind; you cannot think if there are no things to think about. You cannot think if you are not separate from the subject of thought. Descartes said, "I think; therefore I am." The philosophic evolutionist reverses and negatives the epigram. He says, "I am not; therefore I cannot think."

Then there is the opposite attack on thought: that urged by Mr. H.G.Wells when he insists that every separate thing is "unique," and there are no categories at all. This also is merely destructive. Thinking means connecting things, and stops if they cannot be connected. It need hardly be said that this scepticism forbidding thought necessarily forbids speech; a man cannot open his mouth without contradicting it. Thus when Mr. Wells says (as he did somewhere), "All chairs are quite different," he utters not merely a misstatement, but a contradiction in terms. If all chairs were quite different, you could not call them "all chairs."

Akin to these is the false theory of progress, which maintains that we alter the test instead of trying to pass the test. We often hear it said, for instance, "What is right in one age is wrong in another." This is quite reasonable, if it means that there is a fixed aim, and that certain methods attain at certain times and not at other times. If women, say, desire to be elegant, it may be that they are improved at one time by growing fatter and at another time by growing thinner. But you cannot say that they are improved by ceasing to wish to be elegant and beginning to wish to be oblong. If the standard changes, how can there be improvement, which implies a standard? Nietzsche started a nonsensical idea that men had once sought as good what we now call evil; if it were so, we could not talk of surpassing or even falling short of them. How can you overtake Jones if you walk in the other direction? You cannot discuss whether one people has succeeded more in being miserable than another succeeded in being happy. It would be like discussing whether Milton was more puritanical than a pig is fat.

It is true that a man (a silly man) might make change itself his object or ideal. But as an ideal, change itself becomes unchangeable. If the change-worshipper wishes to estimate his own progress, he must be sternly loyal to the ideal of change; he must not begin to flirt gaily with the ideal of monotony. Progress itself cannot progress. It is worth remark, in passing, that when Tennyson, in a wild and rather weak manner, welcomed the idea of infinite alteration in society, he instinctively took a metaphor which suggests an imprisoned tedium. He wrote—

"Let the great world spin for ever down the ringing grooves of change."

He thought of change itself as an unchangeable groove; and so it is. Change is about the narrowest and hardest groove that a man can get into.

The main point here, however, is that this idea of a fundamental alteration in the standard is one of the things that make thought about the past or future simply impossible. The theory of a complete change of standards in human history does not merely deprive us of the pleasure of honouring our fathers; it deprives us even of the more modern and aristocratic pleasure of despising them.

This bald summary of the thought-destroying forces of our time would not be complete without some reference to pragmatism; for though I have here used and should everywhere defend the pragmatist method as a preliminary guide to truth, there is an extreme application of it which involves the absence of all truth whatever. My meaning can be put shortly thus. I agree with the pragmatists that apparent objective truth is not the whole matter; that there is an authoritative need to believe the things that are necessary to the human mind. But I say that one of those necessities precisely is a belief in objective truth. The pragmatist tells a man to think what he must think and never mind the Absolute. But precisely one of the things that he must think is the Absolute. This philosophy, indeed, is a kind of verbal paradox. Pragmatism is a matter of human needs; and one of the first of human needs is to be something more than a pragmatist. Extreme pragmatism is just as inhuman as the determinism it so powerfully attacks. The determinist (who, to do him justice, does not pretend to be a human being) makes nonsense of the human sense of actual choice. The pragmatist, who professes to be specially human, makes nonsense of the human sense of actual fact.

To sum up our contention so far, we may say that the most characteristic current philosophies have not only a touch of mania, but a touch of suicidal mania. The mere questioner has knocked his head against the limits of human thought; and cracked it. This is what makes so futile the warnings of the orthodox and the boasts of the advanced about the dangerous boyhood of free thought. What we are looking at is not the boyhood of free thought; it is the old age and ultimate dissolution of free thought. It is vain for bishops and pious bigwigs to discuss what dreadful things will happen if wild scepticism runs its course. It has run its course. It is vain for eloquent atheists to talk of the great truths that will be revealed if once we see free thought begin. We have seen it end. It has no more questions to ask; it has questioned itself. You cannot call up any wilder vision than a city in which men ask themselves if they have any selves. You cannot fancy a more sceptical world than that in which men doubt if there is a world. It might certainly have reached its bankruptcy more quickly and cleanly if it had not been feebly hampered by the application of indefensible laws of blasphemy or by the absurd pretence that modern England is Christian. But it would have reached the bankruptcy anyhow. Militant atheists are still unjustly persecuted; but rather because they are an old minority than because they are a new one. Free thought has exhausted its own freedom. It is weary of its own success. If any eager freethinker now hails philosophic freedom as the dawn, he is only like the man in Mark Twain who came out wrapped in blankets to see the sun rise and was just in time to see it set. If any frightened curate still says that it will be awful if the darkness of free thought should spread, we can only answer him in the high and powerful words of Mr. Belloc, "Do not, I beseech you, be troubled about the increase of forces already in dissolution. You have mistaken the hour of the night: it is already morning." We have no more questions left to ask. We have looked for questions in the darkest corners and on the wildest peaks. We have found all the questions that can be found. It is time we gave up looking for questions and began looking for answers.

But one more word must be added. At the beginning of this preliminary negative sketch I said that our mental ruin has been wrought by wild reason, not by wild imagination. A man does not go mad because he makes a statue a mile high, but he may go mad by thinking it out in square inches. Now, one school of thinkers has seen this and jumped at it as a way of renewing the pagan health of the world. They see that reason destroys; but Will, they say, creates. The ultimate authority, they say, is in will, not in reason. The supreme point is not why a man demands a thing, but the fact that he does demand it. I have no space to trace or expound this philosophy of Will. It came, I suppose, through Nietzsche, who preached something that is called egoism. That, indeed, was simpleminded enough; for Nietzsche denied egoism simply by preaching it. To preach anything is to give it away. First, the egoist calls life a war without mercy, and then he takes the greatest possible trouble to drill his enemies in war. To preach egoism is to practise altruism. But however it began, the view is common enough in current literature. The main defence of these thinkers is that they are not thinkers; they are makers. They say that choice is itself the divine thing. Thus Mr. Bernard Shaw has attacked the old idea that men's acts are to be judged by the standard of the desire of happiness. He says that a man does not act for his happiness, but from his will. He does not say, "Jam will make me happy," but "I want jam." And in all this others follow him with yet greater enthusiasm. Mr. John Davidson, a remarkable poet, is so passionately excited about it that he is obliged to write prose. He publishes a short play with several long prefaces. This is natural enough in Mr. Shaw, for all his plays are prefaces: Mr. Shaw is (I suspect) the only man on earth who has never written any poetry. But that Mr. Davidson (who can write excellent poetry) should write instead laborious metaphysics in defence of this doctrine of will, does show that the doctrine of will has taken hold of men. Even Mr. H.G.Wells has half spoken in its language; saying that one should test acts not like a thinker, but like an artist, saying, "I FEEL this curve is right," or "that line SHALL go thus." They are all excited; and well they may be. For by this doctrine of the divine authority of will, they think they can break out of the doomed fortress of rationalism. They think they can escape.

But they cannot escape. This pure praise of volition ends in the same break up and blank as the mere pursuit of logic. Exactly as complete free thought involves the doubting of thought itself, so the acceptation of mere "willing" really paralyzes the will. Mr. Bernard Shaw has not perceived the real difference between the old utilitarian test of pleasure (clumsy, of course, and easily misstated) and that which he propounds. The real difference between the test of happiness and the test of will is simply that the test of happiness is a test and the other isn't. You can discuss whether a man's act in jumping over a cliff was directed towards happiness; you cannot discuss whether it was derived from will. Of course it was. You can praise an action by saying that it is calculated to bring pleasure or pain to discover truth or to save the soul. But you cannot praise an action because it shows will; for to say that is merely to say that it is an action. By this praise of will you cannot really choose one course as better than another. And yet choosing one course as better than another is the very definition of the will you are praising.

The worship of will is the negation of will. To admire mere choice is to refuse to choose. If Mr. Bernard Shaw comes up to me and says, "Will something," that is tantamount to saying, "I do not mind what you will," and that is tantamount to saying, "I have no will in the matter." You cannot admire will in general, because the essence of will is that it is particular. A brilliant anarchist like Mr. John Davidson feels an irritation against ordinary morality, and therefore he invokes will—will to anything. He only wants humanity to want something. But humanity does want something. It wants ordinary morality. He rebels against the law and tells us to will something or anything. But we have willed something. We have willed the law against which he rebels.

All the will-worshippers, from Nietzsche to Mr. Davidson, are really quite empty of volition. They cannot will, they can hardly wish. And if any one wants a proof of this, it can be found quite easily. It can be found in this fact: that they always talk of will as something that expands and breaks out. But it is quite the opposite. Every act of will is an act of self-limitation. To desire action is to desire limitation. In that sense every act is an act of self-sacrifice. When you choose anything, you reject everything else. That objection, which men of this school used to make to the act of marriage, is really an objection to every act. Every act is an irrevocable selection and exclusion. Just as when you marry one woman you give up all the others, so when you take one course of action you give up all the other courses. If you become King of England, you give up the post of Beadle in Brompton. If you go to Rome, you sacrifice a rich suggestive life in Wimbledon. It is the existence of this negative or limiting side of will that makes most of the talk of the anarchic will-worshippers little better than nonsense. For instance, Mr. John Davidson tells us to have nothing to do with "Thou shalt not"; but it is surely obvious that "Thou shalt not" is only one of the necessary corollaries of "I will." "I will go to the Lord Mayor's Show, and thou shalt not stop me." Anarchism adjures us to be bold creative artists, and care for no laws or limits. But it is impossible to be an artist and not care for laws and limits. Art is limitation; the essence of every picture is the frame. If you draw a giraffe, you must draw him with a long neck. If, in your bold creative way, you hold yourself free to draw a giraffe with a short neck, you will really find that you are not free to draw a giraffe. The moment you step into the world of facts, you step into a world of limits. You can free things from alien or accidental laws, but not from the laws of their own nature. You may, if you like, free a tiger from his bars; but do not free him from his stripes. Do not free a camel of the burden of his hump: you may be freeing him from being a camel. Do not go about as a demagogue, encouraging triangles to break out of the prison of their three sides. If a triangle breaks out of its three sides, its life comes to a lamentable end. Somebody wrote a work called "The Loves of the Triangles"; I never read it, but I am sure that if triangles ever were loved, they were loved for being triangular. This is certainly the case with all artistic creation, which is in some ways the most decisive example of pure will. The artist loves his limitations: they constitute the THING he is doing. The painter is glad that the canvas is flat. The sculptor is glad that the clay is colourless.

In case the point is not clear, an historic example may illustrate it. The French Revolution was really an heroic and decisive thing, because the Jacobins willed something definite and limited. They desired the freedoms of democracy, but also all the vetoes of democracy. They wished to have votes and NOT to have titles. Republicanism had an ascetic side in Franklin or Robespierre as well as an expansive side in Danton or Wilkes. Therefore they have created something with a solid substance and shape, the square social equality and peasant wealth of France. But since then the revolutionary or speculative mind of Europe has been weakened by shrinking from any proposal because of the limits of that proposal. Liberalism has been degraded into liberality. Men have tried to turn "revolutionise" from a transitive to an intransitive verb. The Jacobin could tell you not only the system he would rebel against, but (what was more important) the system he would NOT rebel against, the system he would trust. But the new rebel is a Sceptic, and will not entirely trust anything. He has no loyalty; therefore he can never be really a revolutionist. And the fact that he doubts everything really gets in his way when he wants to denounce anything. For all denunciation implies a moral doctrine of some kind; and the modern revolutionist doubts not only the institution he denounces, but the doctrine by which he denounces it. Thus he writes one book complaining that imperial oppression insults the purity of women, and then he writes another book (about the sex problem) in which he insults it himself. He curses the Sultan because Christian girls lose their virginity, and then curses Mrs. Grundy because they keep it. As a politician, he will cry out that war is a waste of life, and then, as a philosopher, that all life is waste of time. A Russian pessimist will denounce a policeman for killing a peasant, and then prove by the highest philosophical principles that the peasant ought to have killed himself. A man denounces marriage as a lie, and then denounces aristocratic profligates for treating it as a lie. He calls a flag a bauble, and then blames the oppressors of Poland or Ireland because they take away that bauble. The man of this school goes first to a political meeting, where he complains that savages are treated as if they were beasts; then he takes his hat and umbrella and goes on to a scientific meeting, where he proves that they practically are beasts. In short, the modern revolutionist, being an infinite sceptic, is always engaged in undermining his own mines. In his book on politics he attacks men for trampling on morality; in his book on ethics he attacks morality for trampling on men. Therefore the modern man in revolt has become practically useless for all purposes of revolt. By rebelling against everything he has lost his right to rebel against anything.

It may be added that the same blank and bankruptcy can be observed in all fierce and terrible types of literature, especially in satire. Satire may be mad and anarchic, but it presupposes an admitted superiority in certain things over others; it presupposes a standard. When little boys in the street laugh at the fatness of some distinguished journalist, they are unconsciously assuming a standard of Greek sculpture. They are appealing to the marble Apollo. And the curious disappearance of satire from our literature is an instance of the fierce things fading for want of any principle to be fierce about. Nietzsche had some natural talent for sarcasm: he could sneer, though he could not laugh; but there is always something bodiless and without weight in his satire, simply because it has not any mass of common morality behind it. He is himself more preposterous than anything he denounces. But, indeed, Nietzsche will stand very well as the type of the whole of this failure of abstract violence. The softening of the brain which ultimately overtook him was not a physical accident. If Nietzsche had not ended in imbecility, Nietzscheism would end in imbecility. Thinking in isolation and with pride ends in being an idiot. Every man who will not have softening of the heart must at last have softening of the brain.

This last attempt to evade intellectualism ends in intellectualism, and therefore in death. The sortie has failed. The wild worship of lawlessness and the materialist worship of law end in the same void. Nietzsche scales staggering mountains, but he turns up ultimately in Tibet. He sits down beside Tolstoy in the land of nothing and Nirvana. They are both helpless—one because he must not grasp anything, and the other because he must not let go of anything. The Tolstoyan's will is frozen by a Buddhist instinct that all special actions are evil. But the Nietzscheite's will is quite equally frozen by his view that all special actions are good; for if all special actions are good, none of them are special. They stand at the crossroads, and one hates all the roads and the other likes all the roads. The result is—well, some things are not hard to calculate. They stand at the cross-roads.

Here I end (thank God) the first and dullest business of this book—the rough review of recent thought. After this I begin to sketch a view of life which may not interest my reader, but which, at any rate, interests me. In front of me, as I close this page, is a pile of modern books that I have been turning over for the purpose—a pile of ingenuity, a pile of futility. By the accident of my present detachment, I can see the inevitable smash of the philosophies of Schopenhauer and Tolstoy, Nietzsche and Shaw, as clearly as an inevitable railway smash could be seen from a balloon. They are all on the road to the emptiness of the asylum. For madness may be defined as using mental activity so as to reach mental helplessness; and they have nearly reached it. He who thinks he is made of glass, thinks to the destruction of thought; for glass cannot think. So he who wills to reject nothing, wills the destruction of will; for will is not only the choice of something, but the rejection of almost everything. And as I turn and tumble over the clever, wonderful, tiresome, and useless modern books, the title of one of them rivets my eye. It is called "Jeanne d'Arc," by Anatole France. I have only glanced at it, but a glance was enough to remind me of Renan's "Vie de Jesus." It has the same strange method of the reverent sceptic. It discredits supernatural stories that have some foundation, simply by telling natural stories that have no foundation. Because we cannot believe in what a saint did, we are to pretend that we know exactly what he felt. But I do not mention either book in order to criticise it, but because the accidental combination of the names called up two startling images of Sanity which blasted all the books before me. Joan of Arc was not stuck at the cross-roads, either by rejecting all the paths like Tolstoy, or by accepting them all like Nietzsche. She chose a path, and went down it like a thunderbolt. Yet Joan, when I came to think of her, had in her all that was true either in Tolstoy or Nietzsche, all that was even tolerable in either of them. I thought of all that is noble in Tolstoy, the pleasure in plain things, especially in plain pity, the actualities of the earth, the reverence for the poor, the dignity of the bowed back. Joan of Arc had all that and with this great addition, that she endured poverty as well as admiring it; whereas Tolstoy is only a typical aristocrat trying to find out its secret. And then I thought of all that was brave and proud and pathetic in poor Nietzsche, and his mutiny against the emptiness and timidity of our time. I thought of his cry for the ecstatic equilibrium of danger, his hunger for the rush of great horses, his cry to arms. Well, Joan of Arc had all that, and again with this difference, that she did not praise fighting, but fought. We KNOW that she was not afraid of an army, while Nietzsche, for all we know, was afraid of a cow. Tolstoy only praised the peasant; she was the peasant. Nietzsche only praised the warrior; she was the warrior. She beat them both at their own antagonistic ideals; she was more gentle than the one, more violent than the other. Yet she was a perfectly practical person who did something, while they are wild speculators who do nothing. It was impossible that the thought should not cross my mind that she and her faith had perhaps some secret of moral unity and utility that has been lost. And with that thought came a larger one, and the colossal figure of her Master had also crossed the theatre of my thoughts. The same modern difficulty which darkened the subject-matter of Anatole France also darkened that of Ernest Renan. Renan also divided his hero's pity from his hero's pugnacity. Renan even represented the righteous anger at Jerusalem as a mere nervous breakdown after the idyllic expectations of Galilee. As if there were any inconsistency between having a love for humanity and having a hatred for inhumanity! Altruists, with thin, weak voices, denounce Christ as an egoist. Egoists (with even thinner and weaker voices) denounce Him as an altruist. In our present atmosphere such cavils are comprehensible enough. The love of a hero is more terrible than the hatred of a tyrant. The hatred of a hero is more generous than the love of a philanthropist. There is a huge and heroic sanity of which moderns can only collect the fragments. There is a giant of whom we see only the lopped arms and legs walking about. They have torn the soul of Christ into silly strips, labelled egoism and altruism, and they are equally puzzled by His insane magnificence and His insane meekness. They have parted His garments among them, and for His vesture they have cast lots; though the coat was without seam woven from the top throughout.

IV THE ETHICS OF ELFLAND

When the business man rebukes the idealism of his office-boy, it is commonly in some such speech as this: "Ah, yes, when one is young, one has these ideals in the abstract and these castles in the air; but in middle age they all break up like clouds, and one comes down to a belief in practical politics, to using the machinery one has and getting on with the world as it is." Thus, at least, venerable and philanthropic old men now in their honoured graves used to talk to me when I was a boy. But since then I have grown up and have discovered that these philanthropic old men were telling lies. What has really happened is exactly the opposite of what they said would happen. They said that I should lose my ideals and begin to believe in the methods of practical politicians. Now, I have not lost my ideals in the least; my faith in fundamentals is exactly what it always was. What I have lost is my old childlike faith in practical politics. I am still as much concerned as ever about the Battle of Armageddon; but I am not so much concerned about the General Election. As a babe I leapt up on my mother's knee at the mere mention of it. No; the vision is always solid and reliable. The vision is always a fact. It is the reality that is often a fraud. As much as I ever did, more than I ever did, I believe in Liberalism. But there was a rosy time of innocence when I believed in Liberals.

I take this instance of one of the enduring faiths because, having now to trace the roots of my personal speculation, this may be counted, I think, as the only positive bias. I was brought up a Liberal, and have always believed in democracy, in the elementary liberal doctrine of a self-governing humanity. If any one finds the phrase vague or threadbare, I can only pause for a moment to explain that the principle of democracy, as I mean it, can be stated in two propositions. The first is this: that the things common to all men are more important than the things peculiar to any men. Ordinary things are more valuable than extraordinary things; nay, they are more extraordinary. Man is something more awful than men; something more strange. The sense of the miracle of humanity itself should be always more vivid to us than any marvels of power, intellect, art, or civilization. The mere man on two legs, as such, should be felt as something more heartbreaking than any music and more startling than any caricature. Death is more tragic even than death by starvation. Having a nose is more comic even than having a Norman nose.

This is the first principle of democracy: that the essential things in men are the things they hold in common, not the things they hold separately. And the second principle is merely this: that the political instinct or desire is one of these things which they hold in common. Falling in love is more poetical than dropping into poetry. The democratic contention is that government (helping to rule the tribe) is a thing like falling in love, and not a thing like dropping into poetry. It is not something analogous to playing the church organ, painting on vellum, discovering the North Pole (that insidious habit), looping the loop, being Astronomer Royal, and so on. For these things we do not wish a man to do at all unless he does them well. It is, on the contrary, a thing analogous to writing one's own love-letters or blowing one's own nose. These things we want a man to do for himself, even if he does them badly. I am not here arguing the truth of any of these conceptions; I know that some moderns are asking to have their wives chosen by scientists, and they may soon be asking, for all I know, to have their noses blown by nurses. I merely say that mankind does recognize these universal human functions, and that democracy classes government among them. In short, the democratic faith is this: that the most terribly important things must be left to ordinary men themselves—the mating of the sexes, the rearing of the young, the laws of the state. This is democracy; and in this I have always believed.

But there is one thing that I have never from my youth up been able to understand. I have never been able to understand where people got the idea that democracy was in some way opposed to tradition. It is obvious that tradition is only democracy extended through time. It is trusting to a consensus of common human voices rather than to some isolated or arbitrary record. The man who quotes some German historian against the tradition of the Catholic Church, for instance, is strictly appealing to aristocracy. He is appealing to the superiority of one expert against the awful authority of a mob. It is quite easy to see why a legend is treated, and ought to be treated, more respectfully than a book of history. The legend is generally made by the majority of people in the village, who are sane. The book is generally written by the one man in the village who is mad. Those who urge against tradition that men in the past were ignorant may go and urge it at the Carlton Club, along with the statement that voters in the slums are ignorant. It will not do for us. If we attach great importance to the opinion of ordinary men in great unanimity when we are dealing with daily matters, there is no reason why we should disregard it when we are dealing with history or fable. Tradition may be defined as an extension of the franchise. Tradition means giving votes to the most obscure of all classes, our ancestors. It is the democracy of the dead. Tradition refuses to submit to the small and arrogant oligarchy of those who merely happen to be walking about. All democrats object to men being disqualified by the accident of birth; tradition objects to their being disqualified by the accident of death. Democracy tells us not to neglect a good man's opinion, even if he is our groom; tradition asks us not to neglect a good man's opinion, even if he is our father. I, at any rate, cannot separate the two ideas of democracy and tradition; it seems evident to me that they are the same idea. We will have the dead at our councils. The ancient Greeks voted by stones; these shall vote by tombstones. It is all quite regular and official, for most tombstones, like most ballot papers, are marked with a cross.

I have first to say, therefore, that if I have had a bias, it was always a bias in favour of democracy, and therefore of tradition. Before we come to any theoretic or logical beginnings I am content to allow for that personal equation; I have always been more inclined to believe the ruck of hard-working people than to believe that special and troublesome literary class to which I belong. I prefer even the fancies and prejudices of the people who see life from the inside to the clearest demonstrations of the people who see life from the outside. I would always trust the old wives' fables against the old maids' facts. As long as wit is mother wit it can be as wild as it pleases.

Now, I have to put together a general position, and I pretend to no training in such things. I propose to do it, therefore, by writing down one after another the three or four fundamental ideas which I have found for myself, pretty much in the way that I found them. Then I shall roughly synthesise them, summing up my personal philosophy or natural religion; then I shall describe my startling discovery that the whole thing had been discovered before. It had been discovered by Christianity. But of these profound persuasions which I have to recount in order, the earliest was concerned with this element of popular tradition. And without the foregoing explanation touching tradition and democracy I could hardly make my mental experience clear. As it is, I do not know whether I can make it clear, but I now propose to try.

My first and last philosophy, that which I believe in with unbroken certainty, I learnt in the nursery. I generally learnt it from a nurse; that is, from the solemn and star-appointed priestess at once of democracy and tradition. The things I believed most then, the things I believe most now, are the things called fairy tales. They seem to me to be the entirely reasonable things. They are not fantasies: compared with them other things are fantastic. Compared with them religion and rationalism are both abnormal, though religion is abnormally right and rationalism abnormally wrong. Fairyland is nothing but the sunny country of common sense. It is not earth that judges heaven, but heaven that judges earth; so for me at least it was not earth that criticised elfland, but elfland that criticised the earth. I knew the magic beanstalk before I had tasted beans; I was sure of the Man in the Moon before I was certain of the moon. This was at one with all popular tradition. Modern minor poets are naturalists, and talk about the bush or the brook; but the singers of the old epics and fables were supernaturalists, and talked about the gods of brook and bush. That is what the moderns mean when they say that the ancients did not "appreciate Nature," because they said that Nature was divine. Old nurses do not tell children about the grass, but about the fairies that dance on the grass; and the old Greeks could not see the trees for the dryads.

But I deal here with what ethic and philosophy come from being fed on fairy tales. If I were describing them in detail I could note many noble and healthy principles that arise from them. There is the chivalrous lesson of "Jack the Giant Killer"; that giants should be killed because they are gigantic. It is a manly mutiny against pride as such. For the rebel is older than all the kingdoms, and the Jacobin has more tradition than the Jacobite. There is the lesson of "Cinderella," which is the same as that of the Magnificat— EXALTAVIT HUMILES. There is the great lesson of "Beauty and the Beast"; that a thing must be loved BEFORE it is loveable. There is the terrible allegory of the "Sleeping Beauty," which tells how the human creature was blessed with all birthday gifts, yet cursed with death; and how death also may perhaps be softened to a sleep. But I am not concerned with any of the separate statutes of elfland, but with the whole spirit of its law, which I learnt before I could speak, and shall retain when I cannot write. I am concerned with a certain way of looking at life, which was created in me by the fairy tales, but has since been meekly ratified by the mere facts.

It might be stated this way. There are certain sequences or developments (cases of one thing following another), which are, in the true sense of the word, reasonable. They are, in the true sense of the word, necessary. Such are mathematical and merely logical sequences. We in fairyland (who are the most reasonable of all creatures) admit that reason and that necessity. For instance, if the Ugly Sisters are older than Cinderella, it is (in an iron and awful sense) NECESSARY that Cinderella is younger than the Ugly Sisters. There is no getting out of it. Haeckel may talk as much fatalism about that fact as he pleases: it really must be. If Jack is the son of a miller, a miller is the father of Jack. Cold reason decrees it from her awful throne: and we in fairyland submit. If the three brothers all ride horses, there are six animals and eighteen legs involved: that is true rationalism, and fairyland is full of it. But as I put my head over the hedge of the elves and began to take notice of the natural world, I observed an extraordinary thing. I observed that learned men in spectacles were talking of the actual things that happened— dawn and death and so on—as if THEY were rational and inevitable. They talked as if the fact that trees bear fruit were just as NECESSARY as the fact that two and one trees make three. But it is not. There is an enormous difference by the test of fairyland; which is the test of the imagination. You cannot IMAGINE two and one not making three. But you can easily imagine trees not growing fruit; you can imagine them growing golden candlesticks or tigers hanging on by the tail. These men in spectacles spoke much of a man named Newton, who was hit by an apple, and who discovered a law. But they could not be got to see the distinction between a true law, a law of reason, and the mere fact of apples falling. If the apple hit Newton's nose, Newton's nose hit the apple. That is a true necessity: because we cannot conceive the one occurring without the other. But we can quite well conceive the apple not falling on his nose; we can fancy it flying ardently through the air to hit some other nose, of which it had a more definite dislike. We have always in our fairy tales kept this sharp distinction between the science of mental relations, in which there really are laws, and the science of physical facts, in which there are no laws, but only weird repetitions. We believe in bodily miracles, but not in mental impossibilities. We believe that a Bean-stalk climbed up to Heaven; but that does not at all confuse our convictions on the philosophical question of how many beans make five.

Here is the peculiar perfection of tone and truth in the nursery tales. The man of science says, "Cut the stalk, and the apple will fall"; but he says it calmly, as if the one idea really led up to the other. The witch in the fairy tale says, "Blow the horn, and the ogre's castle will fall"; but she does not say it as if it were something in which the effect obviously arose out of the cause. Doubtless she has given the advice to many champions, and has seen many castles fall, but she does not lose either her wonder or her reason. She does not muddle her head until it imagines a necessary mental connection between a horn and a falling tower. But the scientific men do muddle their heads, until they imagine a necessary mental connection between an apple leaving the tree and an apple reaching the ground. They do really talk as if they had found not only a set of marvellous facts, but a truth connecting those facts. They do talk as if the connection of two strange things physically connected them philosophically. They feel that because one incomprehensible thing constantly follows another incomprehensible thing the two together somehow make up a comprehensible thing. Two black riddles make a white answer.

In fairyland we avoid the word "law"; but in the land of science they are singularly fond of it. Thus they will call some interesting conjecture about how forgotten folks pronounced the alphabet, Grimm's Law. But Grimm's Law is far less intellectual than Grimm's Fairy Tales. The tales are, at any rate, certainly tales; while the law is not a law. A law implies that we know the nature of the generalisation and enactment; not merely that we have noticed some of the effects. If there is a law that pick-pockets shall go to prison, it implies that there is an imaginable mental connection between the idea of prison and the idea of picking pockets. And we know what the idea is. We can say why we take liberty from a man who takes liberties. But we cannot say why an egg can turn into a chicken any more than we can say why a bear could turn into a fairy prince. As IDEAS, the egg and the chicken are further off from each other than the bear and the prince; for no egg in itself suggests a chicken, whereas some princes do suggest bears. Granted, then, that certain transformations do happen, it is essential that we should regard them in the philosophic manner of fairy tales, not in the unphilosophic manner of science and the "Laws of Nature." When we are asked why eggs turn to birds or fruits fall in autumn, we must answer exactly as the fairy godmother would answer if Cinderella asked her why mice turned to horses or her clothes fell from her at twelve o'clock. We must answer that it is MAGIC. It is not a "law," for we do not understand its general formula. It is not a necessity, for though we can count on it happening practically, we have no right to say that it must always happen. It is no argument for unalterable law (as Huxley fancied) that we count on the ordinary course of things. We do not count on it; we bet on it. We risk the remote possibility of a miracle as we do that of a poisoned pancake or a world-destroying comet. We leave it out of account, not because it is a miracle, and therefore an impossibility, but because it is a miracle, and therefore an exception. All the terms used in the science books, "law," "necessity," "order," "tendency," and so on, are really unintellectual, because they assume an inner synthesis, which we do not possess. The only words that ever satisfied me as describing Nature are the terms used in the fairy books, "charm," "spell," "enchantment." They express the arbitrariness of the fact and its mystery. A tree grows fruit because it is a MAGIC tree. Water runs downhill because it is bewitched. The sun shines because it is bewitched.

I deny altogether that this is fantastic or even mystical. We may have some mysticism later on; but this fairy-tale language about things is simply rational and agnostic. It is the only way I can express in words my clear and definite perception that one thing is quite distinct from another; that there is no logical connection between flying and laying eggs. It is the man who talks about "a law" that he has never seen who is the mystic. Nay, the ordinary scientific man is strictly a sentimentalist. He is a sentimentalist in this essential sense, that he is soaked and swept away by mere associations. He has so often seen birds fly and lay eggs that he feels as if there must be some dreamy, tender connection between the two ideas, whereas there is none. A forlorn lover might be unable to dissociate the moon from lost love; so the materialist is unable to dissociate the moon from the tide. In both cases there is no connection, except that one has seen them together. A sentimentalist might shed tears at the smell of apple-blossom, because, by a dark association of his own, it reminded him of his boyhood. So the materialist professor (though he conceals his tears) is yet a sentimentalist, because, by a dark association of his own, apple-blossoms remind him of apples. But the cool rationalist from fairyland does not see why, in the abstract, the apple tree should not grow crimson tulips; it sometimes does in his country.

This elementary wonder, however, is not a mere fancy derived from the fairy tales; on the contrary, all the fire of the fairy tales is derived from this. Just as we all like love tales because there is an instinct of sex, we all like astonishing tales because they touch the nerve of the ancient instinct of astonishment. This is proved by the fact that when we are very young children we do not need fairy tales: we only need tales. Mere life is interesting enough. A child of seven is excited by being told that Tommy opened a door and saw a dragon. But a child of three is excited by being told that Tommy opened a door. Boys like romantic tales; but babies like realistic tales—because they find them romantic. In fact, a baby is about the only person, I should think, to whom a modern realistic novel could be read without boring him. This proves that even nursery tales only echo an almost pre-natal leap of interest and amazement. These tales say that apples were golden only to refresh the forgotten moment when we found that they were green. They make rivers run with wine only to make us remember, for one wild moment, that they run with water. I have said that this is wholly reasonable and even agnostic. And, indeed, on this point I am all for the higher agnosticism; its better name is Ignorance. We have all read in scientific books, and, indeed, in all romances, the story of the man who has forgotten his name. This man walks about the streets and can see and appreciate everything; only he cannot remember who he is. Well, every man is that man in the story. Every man has forgotten who he is. One may understand the cosmos, but never the ego; the self is more distant than any star. Thou shalt love the Lord thy God; but thou shalt not know thyself. We are all under the same mental calamity; we have all forgotten our names. We have all forgotten what we really are. All that we call common sense and rationality and practicality and positivism only means that for certain dead levels of our life we forget that we have forgotten. All that we call spirit and art and ecstasy only means that for one awful instant we remember that we forget.

But though (like the man without memory in the novel) we walk the streets with a sort of half-witted admiration, still it is admiration. It is admiration in English and not only admiration in Latin. The wonder has a positive element of praise. This is the next milestone to be definitely marked on our road through fairyland. I shall speak in the next chapter about optimists and pessimists in their intellectual aspect, so far as they have one. Here I am only trying to describe the enormous emotions which cannot be described. And the strongest emotion was that life was as precious as it was puzzling. It was an ecstasy because it was an adventure; it was an adventure because it was an opportunity. The goodness of the fairy tale was not affected by the fact that there might be more dragons than princesses; it was good to be in a fairy tale. The test of all happiness is gratitude; and I felt grateful, though I hardly knew to whom. Children are grateful when Santa Claus puts in their stockings gifts of toys or sweets. Could I not be grateful to Santa Claus when he put in my stockings the gift of two miraculous legs? We thank people for birthday presents of cigars and slippers. Can I thank no one for the birthday present of birth?

There were, then, these two first feelings, indefensible and indisputable. The world was a shock, but it was not merely shocking; existence was a surprise, but it was a pleasant surprise. In fact, all my first views were exactly uttered in a riddle that stuck in my brain from boyhood. The question was, "What did the first frog say?" And the answer was, "Lord, how you made me jump!" That says succinctly all that I am saying. God made the frog jump; but the frog prefers jumping. But when these things are settled there enters the second great principle of the fairy philosophy.

Any one can see it who will simply read "Grimm's Fairy Tales" or the fine collections of Mr. Andrew Lang. For the pleasure of pedantry I will call it the Doctrine of Conditional Joy. Touchstone talked of much virtue in an "if"; according to elfin ethics all virtue is in an "if." The note of the fairy utterance always is, "You may live in a palace of gold and sapphire, if you do not say the word `cow'"; or "You may live happily with the King's daughter, if you do not show her an onion." The vision always hangs upon a veto. All the dizzy and colossal things conceded depend upon one small thing withheld. All the wild and whirling things that are let loose depend upon one thing that is forbidden. Mr. W.B.Yeats, in his exquisite and piercing elfin poetry, describes the elves as lawless; they plunge in innocent anarchy on the unbridled horses of the air—

"Ride on the crest of the dishevelled tide, And dance upon the mountains like a flame."

It is a dreadful thing to say that Mr. W.B.Yeats does not understand fairyland. But I do say it. He is an ironical Irishman, full of intellectual reactions. He is not stupid enough to understand fairyland. Fairies prefer people of the yokel type like myself; people who gape and grin and do as they are told. Mr. Yeats reads into elfland all the righteous insurrection of his own race. But the lawlessness of Ireland is a Christian lawlessness, founded on reason and justice. The Fenian is rebelling against something he understands only too well; but the true citizen of fairyland is obeying something that he does not understand at all. In the fairy tale an incomprehensible happiness rests upon an incomprehensible condition. A box is opened, and all evils fly out. A word is forgotten, and cities perish. A lamp is lit, and love flies away. A flower is plucked, and human lives are forfeited. An apple is eaten, and the hope of God is gone.

This is the tone of fairy tales, and it is certainly not lawlessness or even liberty, though men under a mean modern tyranny may think it liberty by comparison. People out of Portland Gaol might think Fleet Street free; but closer study will prove that both fairies and journalists are the slaves of duty. Fairy godmothers seem at least as strict as other godmothers. Cinderella received a coach out of Wonderland and a coachman out of nowhere, but she received a command—which might have come out of Brixton—that she should be back by twelve. Also, she had a glass slipper; and it cannot be a coincidence that glass is so common a substance in folk-lore. This princess lives in a glass castle, that princess on a glass hill; this one sees all things in a mirror; they may all live in glass houses if they will not throw stones. For this thin glitter of glass everywhere is the expression of the fact that the happiness is bright but brittle, like the substance most easily smashed by a housemaid or a cat. And this fairy-tale sentiment also sank into me and became my sentiment towards the whole world. I felt and feel that life itself is as bright as the diamond, but as brittle as the window-pane; and when the heavens were compared to the terrible crystal I can remember a shudder. I was afraid that God would drop the cosmos with a crash.

Remember, however, that to be breakable is not the same as to be perishable. Strike a glass, and it will not endure an instant; simply do not strike it, and it will endure a thousand years. Such, it seemed, was the joy of man, either in elfland or on earth; the happiness depended on NOT DOING SOMETHING which you could at any moment do and which, very often, it was not obvious why you should not do. Now, the point here is that to ME this did not seem unjust. If the miller's third son said to the fairy, "Explain why I must not stand on my head in the fairy palace," the other might fairly reply, "Well, if it comes to that, explain the fairy palace." If Cinderella says, "How is it that I must leave the ball at twelve?" her godmother might answer, "How is it that you are going there till twelve?" If I leave a man in my will ten talking elephants and a hundred winged horses, he cannot complain if the conditions partake of the slight eccentricity of the gift. He must not look a winged horse in the mouth. And it seemed to me that existence was itself so very eccentric a legacy that I could not complain of not understanding the limitations of the vision when I did not understand the vision they limited. The frame was no stranger than the picture. The veto might well be as wild as the vision; it might be as startling as the sun, as elusive as the waters, as fantastic and terrible as the towering trees.

For this reason (we may call it the fairy godmother philosophy) I never could join the young men of my time in feeling what they called the general sentiment of REVOLT. I should have resisted, let us hope, any rules that were evil, and with these and their definition I shall deal in another chapter. But I did not feel disposed to resist any rule merely because it was mysterious. Estates are sometimes held by foolish forms, the breaking of a stick or the payment of a peppercorn: I was willing to hold the huge estate of earth and heaven by any such feudal fantasy. It could not well be wilder than the fact that I was allowed to hold it at all. At this stage I give only one ethical instance to show my meaning. I could never mix in the common murmur of that rising generation against monogamy, because no restriction on sex seemed so odd and unexpected as sex itself. To be allowed, like Endymion, to make love to the moon and then to complain that Jupiter kept his own moons in a harem seemed to me (bred on fairy tales like Endymion's) a vulgar anti-climax. Keeping to one woman is a small price for so much as seeing one woman. To complain that I could only be married once was like complaining that I had only been born once. It was incommensurate with the terrible excitement of which one was talking. It showed, not an exaggerated sensibility to sex, but a curious insensibility to it. A man is a fool who complains that he cannot enter Eden by five gates at once. Polygamy is a lack of the realization of sex; it is like a man plucking five pears in mere absence of mind. The aesthetes touched the last insane limits of language in their eulogy on lovely things. The thistledown made them weep; a burnished beetle brought them to their knees. Yet their emotion never impressed me for an instant, for this reason, that it never occurred to them to pay for their pleasure in any sort of symbolic sacrifice. Men (I felt) might fast forty days for the sake of hearing a blackbird sing. Men might go through fire to find a cowslip. Yet these lovers of beauty could not even keep sober for the blackbird. They would not go through common Christian marriage by way of recompense to the cowslip. Surely one might pay for extraordinary joy in ordinary morals. Oscar Wilde said that sunsets were not valued because we could not pay for sunsets. But Oscar Wilde was wrong; we can pay for sunsets. We can pay for them by not being Oscar Wilde.

Well, I left the fairy tales lying on the floor of the nursery, and I have not found any books so sensible since. I left the nurse guardian of tradition and democracy, and I have not found any modern type so sanely radical or so sanely conservative. But the matter for important comment was here: that when I first went out into the mental atmosphere of the modern world, I found that the modern world was positively opposed on two points to my nurse and to the nursery tales. It has taken me a long time to find out that the modern world is wrong and my nurse was right. The really curious thing was this: that modern thought contradicted this basic creed of my boyhood on its two most essential doctrines. I have explained that the fairy tales founded in me two convictions; first, that this world is a wild and startling place, which might have been quite different, but which is quite delightful; second, that before this wildness and delight one may well be modest and submit to the queerest limitations of so queer a kindness. But I found the whole modern world running like a high tide against both my tendernesses; and the shock of that collision created two sudden and spontaneous sentiments, which I have had ever since and which, crude as they were, have since hardened into convictions.

First, I found the whole modern world talking scientific fatalism; saying that everything is as it must always have been, being unfolded without fault from the beginning. The leaf on the tree is green because it could never have been anything else. Now, the fairy-tale philosopher is glad that the leaf is green precisely because it might have been scarlet. He feels as if it had turned green an instant before he looked at it. He is pleased that snow is white on the strictly reasonable ground that it might have been black. Every colour has in it a bold quality as of choice; the red of garden roses is not only decisive but dramatic, like suddenly spilt blood. He feels that something has been DONE. But the great determinists of the nineteenth century were strongly against this native feeling that something had happened an instant before. In fact, according to them, nothing ever really had happened since the beginning of the world. Nothing ever had happened since existence had happened; and even about the date of that they were not very sure.

The modern world as I found it was solid for modern Calvinism, for the necessity of things being as they are. But when I came to ask them I found they had really no proof of this unavoidable repetition in things except the fact that the things were repeated. Now, the mere repetition made the things to me rather more weird than more rational. It was as if, having seen a curiously shaped nose in the street and dismissed it as an accident, I had then seen six other noses of the same astonishing shape. I should have fancied for a moment that it must be some local secret society. So one elephant having a trunk was odd; but all elephants having trunks looked like a plot. I speak here only of an emotion, and of an emotion at once stubborn and subtle. But the repetition in Nature seemed sometimes to be an excited repetition, like that of an angry schoolmaster saying the same thing over and over again. The grass seemed signalling to me with all its fingers at once; the crowded stars seemed bent upon being understood. The sun would make me see him if he rose a thousand times. The recurrences of the universe rose to the maddening rhythm of an incantation, and I began to see an idea.

All the towering materialism which dominates the modern mind rests ultimately upon one assumption; a false assumption. It is supposed that if a thing goes on repeating itself it is probably dead; a piece of clockwork. People feel that if the universe was personal it would vary; if the sun were alive it would dance. This is a fallacy even in relation to known fact. For the variation in human affairs is generally brought into them, not by life, but by death; by the dying down or breaking off of their strength or desire. A man varies his movements because of some slight element of failure or fatigue. He gets into an omnibus because he is tired of walking; or he walks because he is tired of sitting still. But if his life and joy were so gigantic that he never tired of going to Islington, he might go to Islington as regularly as the Thames goes to Sheerness. The very speed and ecstasy of his life would have the stillness of death. The sun rises every morning. I do not rise every morning; but the variation is due not to my activity, but to my inaction. Now, to put the matter in a popular phrase, it might be true that the sun rises regularly because he never gets tired of rising. His routine might be due, not to a lifelessness, but to a rush of life. The thing I mean can be seen, for instance, in children, when they find some game or joke that they specially enjoy. A child kicks his legs rhythmically through excess, not absence, of life. Because children have abounding vitality, because they are in spirit fierce and free, therefore they want things repeated and unchanged. They always say, "Do it again"; and the grown-up person does it again until he is nearly dead. For grown-up people are not strong enough to exult in monotony. But perhaps God is strong enough to exult in monotony. It is possible that God says every morning, "Do it again" to the sun; and every evening, "Do it again" to the moon. It may not be automatic necessity that makes all daisies alike; it may be that God makes every daisy separately, but has never got tired of making them. It may be that He has the eternal appetite of infancy; for we have sinned and grown old, and our Father is younger than we. The repetition in Nature may not be a mere recurrence; it may be a theatrical ENCORE. Heaven may ENCORE the bird who laid an egg. If the human being conceives and brings forth a human child instead of bringing forth a fish, or a bat, or a griffin, the reason may not be that we are fixed in an animal fate without life or purpose. It may be that our little tragedy has touched the gods, that they admire it from their starry galleries, and that at the end of every human drama man is called again and again before the curtain. Repetition may go on for millions of years, by mere choice, and at any instant it may stop. Man may stand on the earth generation after generation, and yet each birth be his positively last appearance.

This was my first conviction; made by the shock of my childish emotions meeting the modern creed in mid-career. I had always vaguely felt facts to be miracles in the sense that they are wonderful: now I began to think them miracles in the stricter sense that they were WILFUL. I mean that they were, or might be, repeated exercises of some will. In short, I had always believed that the world involved magic: now I thought that perhaps it involved a magician. And this pointed a profound emotion always present and sub-conscious; that this world of ours has some purpose; and if there is a purpose, there is a person. I had always felt life first as a story: and if there is a story there is a story-teller.

But modern thought also hit my second human tradition. It went against the fairy feeling about strict limits and conditions. The one thing it loved to talk about was expansion and largeness. Herbert Spencer would have been greatly annoyed if any one had called him an imperialist, and therefore it is highly regrettable that nobody did. But he was an imperialist of the lowest type. He popularized this contemptible notion that the size of the solar system ought to over-awe the spiritual dogma of man. Why should a man surrender his dignity to the solar system any more than to a whale? If mere size proves that man is not the image of God, then a whale may be the image of God; a somewhat formless image; what one might call an impressionist portrait. It is quite futile to argue that man is small compared to the cosmos; for man was always small compared to the nearest tree. But Herbert Spencer, in his headlong imperialism, would insist that we had in some way been conquered and annexed by the astronomical universe. He spoke about men and their ideals exactly as the most insolent Unionist talks about the Irish and their ideals. He turned mankind into a small nationality. And his evil influence can be seen even in the most spirited and honourable of later scientific authors; notably in the early romances of Mr. H.G.Wells. Many moralists have in an exaggerated way represented the earth as wicked. But Mr. Wells and his school made the heavens wicked. We should lift up our eyes to the stars from whence would come our ruin.

But the expansion of which I speak was much more evil than all this. I have remarked that the materialist, like the madman, is in prison; in the prison of one thought. These people seemed to think it singularly inspiring to keep on saying that the prison was very large. The size of this scientific universe gave one no novelty, no relief. The cosmos went on for ever, but not in its wildest constellation could there be anything really interesting; anything, for instance, such as forgiveness or free will. The grandeur or infinity of the secret of its cosmos added nothing to it. It was like telling a prisoner in Reading gaol that he would be glad to hear that the gaol now covered half the county. The warder would have nothing to show the man except more and more long corridors of stone lit by ghastly lights and empty of all that is human. So these expanders of the universe had nothing to show us except more and more infinite corridors of space lit by ghastly suns and empty of all that is divine.

In fairyland there had been a real law; a law that could be broken, for the definition of a law is something that can be broken. But the machinery of this cosmic prison was something that could not be broken; for we ourselves were only a part of its machinery. We were either unable to do things or we were destined to do them. The idea of the mystical condition quite disappeared; one can neither have the firmness of keeping laws nor the fun of breaking them. The largeness of this universe had nothing of that freshness and airy outbreak which we have praised in the universe of the poet. This modern universe is literally an empire; that is, it was vast, but it is not free. One went into larger and larger windowless rooms, rooms big with Babylonian perspective; but one never found the smallest window or a whisper of outer air.

Their infernal parallels seemed to expand with distance; but for me all good things come to a point, swords for instance. So finding the boast of the big cosmos so unsatisfactory to my emotions I began to argue about it a little; and I soon found that the whole attitude was even shallower than could have been expected. According to these people the cosmos was one thing since it had one unbroken rule. Only (they would say) while it is one thing, it is also the only thing there is. Why, then, should one worry particularly to call it large? There is nothing to compare it with. It would be just as sensible to call it small. A man may say, "I like this vast cosmos, with its throng of stars and its crowd of varied creatures." But if it comes to that why should not a man say, "I like this cosy little cosmos, with its decent number of stars and as neat a provision of live stock as I wish to see"? One is as good as the other; they are both mere sentiments. It is mere sentiment to rejoice that the sun is larger than the earth; it is quite as sane a sentiment to rejoice that the sun is no larger than it is. A man chooses to have an emotion about the largeness of the world; why should he not choose to have an emotion about its smallness?

It happened that I had that emotion. When one is fond of anything one addresses it by diminutives, even if it is an elephant or a life-guardsman. The reason is, that anything, however huge, that can be conceived of as complete, can be conceived of as small. If military moustaches did not suggest a sword or tusks a tail, then the object would be vast because it would be immeasurable. But the moment you can imagine a guardsman you can imagine a small guardsman. The moment you really see an elephant you can call it "Tiny." If you can make a statue of a thing you can make a statuette of it. These people professed that the universe was one coherent thing; but they were not fond of the universe. But I was frightfully fond of the universe and wanted to address it by a diminutive. I often did so; and it never seemed to mind. Actually and in truth I did feel that these dim dogmas of vitality were better expressed by calling the world small than by calling it large. For about infinity there was a sort of carelessness which was the reverse of the fierce and pious care which I felt touching the pricelessness and the peril of life. They showed only a dreary waste; but I felt a sort of sacred thrift. For economy is far more romantic than extravagance. To them stars were an unending income of halfpence; but I felt about the golden sun and the silver moon as a schoolboy feels if he has one sovereign and one shilling.

These subconscious convictions are best hit off by the colour and tone of certain tales. Thus I have said that stories of magic alone can express my sense that life is not only a pleasure but a kind of eccentric privilege. I may express this other feeling of cosmic cosiness by allusion to another book always read in boyhood, "Robinson Crusoe," which I read about this time, and which owes its eternal vivacity to the fact that it celebrates the poetry of limits, nay, even the wild romance of prudence. Crusoe is a man on a small rock with a few comforts just snatched from the sea: the best thing in the book is simply the list of things saved from the wreck. The greatest of poems is an inventory. Every kitchen tool becomes ideal because Crusoe might have dropped it in the sea. It is a good exercise, in empty or ugly hours of the day, to look at anything, the coal-scuttle or the book-case, and think how happy one could be to have brought it out of the sinking ship on to the solitary island. But it is a better exercise still to remember how all things have had this hair-breadth escape: everything has been saved from a wreck. Every man has had one horrible adventure: as a hidden untimely birth he had not been, as infants that never see the light. Men spoke much in my boyhood of restricted or ruined men of genius: and it was common to say that many a man was a Great Might-Have-Been. To me it is a more solid and startling fact that any man in the street is a Great Might-Not-Have-Been.

But I really felt (the fancy may seem foolish) as if all the order and number of things were the romantic remnant of Crusoe's ship. That there are two sexes and one sun, was like the fact that there were two guns and one axe. It was poignantly urgent that none should be lost; but somehow, it was rather fun that none could be added. The trees and the planets seemed like things saved from the wreck: and when I saw the Matterhorn I was glad that it had not been overlooked in the confusion. I felt economical about the stars as if they were sapphires (they are called so in Milton's Eden): I hoarded the hills. For the universe is a single jewel, and while it is a natural cant to talk of a jewel as peerless and priceless, of this jewel it is literally true. This cosmos is indeed without peer and without price: for there cannot be another one.

Thus ends, in unavoidable inadequacy, the attempt to utter the unutterable things. These are my ultimate attitudes towards life; the soils for the seeds of doctrine. These in some dark way I thought before I could write, and felt before I could think: that we may proceed more easily afterwards, I will roughly recapitulate them now. I felt in my bones; first, that this world does not explain itself. It may be a miracle with a supernatural explanation; it may be a conjuring trick, with a natural explanation. But the explanation of the conjuring trick, if it is to satisfy me, will have to be better than the natural explanations I have heard. The thing is magic, true or false. Second, I came to feel as if magic must have a meaning, and meaning must have some one to mean it. There was something personal in the world, as in a work of art; whatever it meant it meant violently. Third, I thought this purpose beautiful in its old design, in spite of its defects, such as dragons. Fourth, that the proper form of thanks to it is some form of humility and restraint: we should thank God for beer and Burgundy by not drinking too much of them. We owed, also, an obedience to whatever made us. And last, and strangest, there had come into my mind a vague and vast impression that in some way all good was a remnant to be stored and held sacred out of some primordial ruin. Man had saved his good as Crusoe saved his goods: he had saved them from a wreck. All this I felt and the age gave me no encouragement to feel it. And all this time I had not even thought of Christian theology.

V THE FLAG OF THE WORLD

When I was a boy there were two curious men running about who were called the optimist and the pessimist. I constantly used the words myself, but I cheerfully confess that I never had any very special idea of what they meant. The only thing which might be considered evident was that they could not mean what they said; for the ordinary verbal explanation was that the optimist thought this world as good as it could be, while the pessimist thought it as bad as it could be. Both these statements being obviously raving nonsense, one had to cast about for other explanations. An optimist could not mean a man who thought everything right and nothing wrong. For that is meaningless; it is like calling everything right and nothing left. Upon the whole, I came to the conclusion that the optimist thought everything good except the pessimist, and that the pessimist thought everything bad, except himself. It would be unfair to omit altogether from the list the mysterious but suggestive definition said to have been given by a little girl, "An optimist is a man who looks after your eyes, and a pessimist is a man who looks after your feet." I am not sure that this is not the best definition of all. There is even a sort of allegorical truth in it. For there might, perhaps, be a profitable distinction drawn between that more dreary thinker who thinks merely of our contact with the earth from moment to moment, and that happier thinker who considers rather our primary power of vision and of choice of road.

But this is a deep mistake in this alternative of the optimist and the pessimist. The assumption of it is that a man criticises this world as if he were house-hunting, as if he were being shown over a new suite of apartments. If a man came to this world from some other world in full possession of his powers he might discuss whether the advantage of midsummer woods made up for the disadvantage of mad dogs, just as a man looking for lodgings might balance the presence of a telephone against the absence of a sea view. But no man is in that position. A man belongs to this world before he begins to ask if it is nice to belong to it. He has fought for the flag, and often won heroic victories for the flag long before he has ever enlisted. To put shortly what seems the essential matter, he has a loyalty long before he has any admiration.

In the last chapter it has been said that the primary feeling that this world is strange and yet attractive is best expressed in fairy tales. The reader may, if he likes, put down the next stage to that bellicose and even jingo literature which commonly comes next in the history of a boy. We all owe much sound morality to the penny dreadfuls. Whatever the reason, it seemed and still seems to me that our attitude towards life can be better expressed in terms of a kind of military loyalty than in terms of criticism and approval. My acceptance of the universe is not optimism, it is more like patriotism. It is a matter of primary loyalty. The world is not a lodging-house at Brighton, which we are to leave because it is miserable. It is the fortress of our family, with the flag flying on the turret, and the more miserable it is the less we should leave it. The point is not that this world is too sad to love or too glad not to love; the point is that when you do love a thing, its gladness is a reason for loving it, and its sadness a reason for loving it more. All optimistic thoughts about England and all pessimistic thoughts about her are alike reasons for the English patriot. Similarly, optimism and pessimism are alike arguments for the cosmic patriot.

Let us suppose we are confronted with a desperate thing—say Pimlico. If we think what is really best for Pimlico we shall find the thread of thought leads to the throne or the mystic and the arbitrary. It is not enough for a man to disapprove of Pimlico: in that case he will merely cut his throat or move to Chelsea. Nor, certainly, is it enough for a man to approve of Pimlico: for then it will remain Pimlico, which would be awful. The only way out of it seems to be for somebody to love Pimlico: to love it with a transcendental tie and without any earthly reason. If there arose a man who loved Pimlico, then Pimlico would rise into ivory towers and golden pinnacles; Pimlico would attire herself as a woman does when she is loved. For decoration is not given to hide horrible things: but to decorate things already adorable. A mother does not give her child a blue bow because he is so ugly without it. A lover does not give a girl a necklace to hide her neck. If men loved Pimlico as mothers love children, arbitrarily, because it is THEIRS, Pimlico in a year or two might be fairer than Florence. Some readers will say that this is a mere fantasy. I answer that this is the actual history of mankind. This, as a fact, is how cities did grow great. Go back to the darkest roots of civilization and you will find them knotted round some sacred stone or encircling some sacred well. People first paid honour to a spot and afterwards gained glory for it. Men did not love Rome because she was great. She was great because they had loved her.

The eighteenth-century theories of the social contract have been exposed to much clumsy criticism in our time; in so far as they meant that there is at the back of all historic government an idea of content and co-operation, they were demonstrably right. But they really were wrong, in so far as they suggested that men had ever aimed at order or ethics directly by a conscious exchange of interests. Morality did not begin by one man saying to another, "I will not hit you if you do not hit me"; there is no trace of such a transaction. There IS a trace of both men having said, "We must not hit each other in the holy place." They gained their morality by guarding their religion. They did not cultivate courage. They fought for the shrine, and found they had become courageous. They did not cultivate cleanliness. They purified themselves for the altar, and found that they were clean. The history of the Jews is the only early document known to most Englishmen, and the facts can be judged sufficiently from that. The Ten Commandments which have been found substantially common to mankind were merely military commands; a code of regimental orders, issued to protect a certain ark across a certain desert. Anarchy was evil because it endangered the sanctity. And only when they made a holy day for God did they find they had made a holiday for men.

If it be granted that this primary devotion to a place or thing is a source of creative energy, we can pass on to a very peculiar fact. Let us reiterate for an instant that the only right optimism is a sort of universal patriotism. What is the matter with the pessimist? I think it can be stated by saying that he is the cosmic anti-patriot. And what is the matter with the anti-patriot? I think it can be stated, without undue bitterness, by saying that he is the candid friend. And what is the matter with the candid friend? There we strike the rock of real life and immutable human nature.

I venture to say that what is bad in the candid friend is simply that he is not candid. He is keeping something back— his own gloomy pleasure in saying unpleasant things. He has a secret desire to hurt, not merely to help. This is certainly, I think, what makes a certain sort of anti-patriot irritating to healthy citizens. I do not speak (of course) of the anti-patriotism which only irritates feverish stockbrokers and gushing actresses; that is only patriotism speaking plainly. A man who says that no patriot should attack the Boer War until it is over is not worth answering intelligently; he is saying that no good son should warn his mother off a cliff until she has fallen over it. But there is an anti-patriot who honestly angers honest men, and the explanation of him is, I think, what I have suggested: he is the uncandid candid friend; the man who says, "I am sorry to say we are ruined," and is not sorry at all. And he may be said, without rhetoric, to be a traitor; for he is using that ugly knowledge which was allowed him to strengthen the army, to discourage people from joining it. Because he is allowed to be pessimistic as a military adviser he is being pessimistic as a recruiting sergeant. Just in the same way the pessimist (who is the cosmic anti-patriot) uses the freedom that life allows to her counsellors to lure away the people from her flag. Granted that he states only facts, it is still essential to know what are his emotions, what is his motive. It may be that twelve hundred men in Tottenham are down with smallpox; but we want to know whether this is stated by some great philosopher who wants to curse the gods, or only by some common clergyman who wants to help the men.

The evil of the pessimist is, then, not that he chastises gods and men, but that he does not love what he chastises—he has not this primary and supernatural loyalty to things. What is the evil of the man commonly called an optimist? Obviously, it is felt that the optimist, wishing to defend the honour of this world, will defend the indefensible. He is the jingo of the universe; he will say, "My cosmos, right or wrong." He will be less inclined to the reform of things; more inclined to a sort of front-bench official answer to all attacks, soothing every one with assurances. He will not wash the world, but whitewash the world. All this (which is true of a type of optimist) leads us to the one really interesting point of psychology, which could not be explained without it.

We say there must be a primal loyalty to life: the only question is, shall it be a natural or a supernatural loyalty? If you like to put it so, shall it be a reasonable or an unreasonable loyalty? Now, the extraordinary thing is that the bad optimism (the whitewashing, the weak defence of everything) comes in with the reasonable optimism. Rational optimism leads to stagnation: it is irrational optimism that leads to reform. Let me explain by using once more the parallel of patriotism. The man who is most likely to ruin the place he loves is exactly the man who loves it with a reason. The man who will improve the place is the man who loves it without a reason. If a man loves some feature of Pimlico (which seems unlikely), he may find himself defending that feature against Pimlico itself. But if he simply loves Pimlico itself, he may lay it waste and turn it into the New Jerusalem. I do not deny that reform may be excessive; I only say that it is the mystic patriot who reforms. Mere jingo self-contentment is commonest among those who have some pedantic reason for their patriotism. The worst jingoes do not love England, but a theory of England. If we love England for being an empire, we may overrate the success with which we rule the Hindoos. But if we love it only for being a nation, we can face all events: for it would be a nation even if the Hindoos ruled us. Thus also only those will permit their patriotism to falsify history whose patriotism depends on history. A man who loves England for being English will not mind how she arose. But a man who loves England for being Anglo-Saxon may go against all facts for his fancy. He may end (like Carlyle and Freeman) by maintaining that the Norman Conquest was a Saxon Conquest. He may end in utter unreason—because he has a reason. A man who loves France for being military will palliate the army of 1870. But a man who loves France for being France will improve the army of 1870. This is exactly what the French have done, and France is a good instance of the working paradox. Nowhere else is patriotism more purely abstract and arbitrary;

and nowhere else is reform more drastic and sweeping. The more transcendental is your patriotism, the more practical are your politics.

Perhaps the most everyday instance of this point is in the case of women; and their strange and strong loyalty. Some stupid people started the idea that because women obviously back up their own people through everything, therefore women are blind and do not see anything. They can hardly have known any women. The same women who are ready to defend their men through thick and thin are (in their personal intercourse with the man) almost morbidly lucid about the thinness of his excuses or the thickness of his head. A man's friend likes him but leaves him as he is: his wife loves him and is always trying to turn him into somebody else. Women who are utter mystics in their creed are utter cynics in their criticism. Thackeray expressed this well when he made Pendennis' mother, who worshipped her son as a god, yet assume that he would go wrong as a man. She underrated his virtue, though she overrated his value. The devotee is entirely free to criticise; the fanatic can safely be a sceptic. Love is not blind; that is the last thing that it is. Love is bound; and the more it is bound the less it is blind.

This at least had come to be my position about all that was called optimism, pessimism, and improvement. Before any cosmic act of reform we must have a cosmic oath of allegiance. A man must be interested in life, then he could be disinterested in his views of it. "My son give me thy heart"; the heart must be fixed on the right thing: the moment we have a fixed heart we have a free hand. I must pause to anticipate an obvious criticism. It will be said that a rational person accepts the world as mixed of good and evil with a decent satisfaction and a decent endurance. But this is exactly the attitude which I maintain to be defective. It is, I know, very common in this age; it was perfectly put in those quiet lines of Matthew Arnold which are more piercingly blasphemous than the shrieks of Schopenhauer—

"Enough we live:—and if a life, With large results so little rife, Though bearable, seem hardly worth This pomp of worlds, this pain of birth."

I know this feeling fills our epoch, and I think it freezes our epoch. For our Titanic purposes of faith and revolution, what we need is not the cold acceptance of the world as a compromise, but some way in which we can heartily hate and heartily love it. We do not want joy and anger to neutralize each other and produce a surly contentment; we want a fiercer delight and a fiercer discontent. We have to feel the universe at once as an ogre's castle, to be stormed, and yet as our own cottage, to which we can return at evening.

No one doubts that an ordinary man can get on with this world: but we demand not strength enough to get on with it, but strength enough to get it on. Can he hate it enough to change it, and yet love it enough to think it worth changing? Can he look up at its colossal good without once feeling acquiescence? Can he look up at its colossal evil without once feeling despair? Can he, in short, be at once not only a pessimist and an optimist, but a fanatical pessimist and a fanatical optimist? Is he enough of a pagan to die for the world, and enough of a Christian to die to it? In this combination, I maintain, it is the rational optimist who fails, the irrational optimist who succeeds. He is ready to smash the whole universe for the sake of itself.

I put these things not in their mature logical sequence, but as they came: and this view was cleared and sharpened by an accident of the time. Under the lengthening shadow of Ibsen, an argument arose whether it was not a very nice thing to murder one's self. Grave moderns told us that we must not even say "poor fellow," of a man who had blown his brains out, since he was an enviable person, and had only blown them out because of their exceptional excellence. Mr. William Archer even suggested that in the golden age there would be penny-in-the-slot machines, by which a man could kill himself for a penny. In all this I found myself utterly hostile to many who called themselves liberal and humane. Not only is suicide a sin, it is the sin. It is the ultimate and absolute evil, the refusal to take an interest in existence; the refusal to take the oath of loyalty to life. The man who kills a man, kills a man. The man who kills himself, kills all men; as far as he is concerned he wipes out the world. His act is worse (symbolically considered) than any rape or dynamite outrage. For it destroys all buildings: it insults all women. The thief is satisfied with diamonds; but the suicide is not: that is his crime. He cannot be bribed, even by the blazing stones of the Celestial City. The thief compliments the things he steals, if not the owner of them. But the suicide insults everything on earth by not stealing it. He defiles every flower by refusing to live for its sake. There is not a tiny creature in the cosmos at whom his death is not a sneer. When a man hangs himself on a tree, the leaves might fall off in anger and the birds fly away in fury: for each has received a personal affront. Of course there may be pathetic emotional excuses for the act. There often are for rape, and there almost always are for dynamite. But if it comes to clear ideas and the intelligent meaning of things, then there is much more rational and philosophic truth in the burial at the cross-roads and the stake driven through the body, than in Mr. Archer's suicidal automatic machines. There is a meaning in burying the suicide apart. The man's crime is different from other crimes—for it makes even crimes impossible.

About the same time I read a solemn flippancy by some free thinker: he said that a suicide was only the same as a martyr. The open fallacy of this helped to clear the question. Obviously a suicide is the opposite of a martyr. A martyr is a man who cares so much for something outside him, that he forgets his own personal life. A suicide is a man who cares so little for anything outside him, that he wants to see the last of everything. One wants something to begin: the other wants everything to end. In other words, the martyr is noble, exactly because (however he renounces the world or execrates all humanity) he confesses this ultimate link with life; he sets his heart outside himself: he dies that something may live. The suicide is ignoble because he has not this link with being: he is a mere destroyer; spiritually, he destroys the universe. And then I remembered the stake and the cross-roads, and the queer fact that Christianity had shown this weird harshness to the suicide. For Christianity had shown a wild encouragement of the martyr. Historic Christianity was accused, not entirely without reason, of carrying martyrdom and asceticism to a point, desolate and pessimistic. The early Christian martyrs talked of death with a horrible happiness. They blasphemed the beautiful duties of the body: they smelt the grave afar off like a field of flowers. All this has seemed to many the very poetry of pessimism. Yet there is the stake at the crossroads to show what Christianity thought of the pessimist.

This was the first of the long train of enigmas with which Christianity entered the discussion. And there went with it a peculiarity of which I shall have to speak more markedly, as a note of all Christian notions, but which distinctly began in this one. The Christian attitude to the martyr and the suicide was not what is so often affirmed in modern morals. It was not a matter of degree. It was not that a line must be drawn somewhere, and that the self-slayer in exaltation fell within the line, the self-slayer in sadness just beyond it. The Christian feeling evidently was not merely that the suicide was carrying martyrdom too far. The Christian feeling was furiously for one and furiously against the other: these two things that looked so much alike were at opposite ends of heaven and hell. One man flung away his life; he was so good that his dry bones could heal cities in pestilence. Another man flung away life; he was so bad that his bones would pollute his brethren's. I am not saying this fierceness was right; but why was it so fierce?

Here it was that I first found that my wandering feet were in some beaten track. Christianity had also felt this opposition of the martyr to the suicide: had it perhaps felt it for the same reason? Had Christianity felt what I felt, but could not (and cannot) express—this need for a first loyalty to things, and then for a ruinous reform of things? Then I remembered that it was actually the charge against Christianity that it combined these two things which I was wildly trying to combine. Christianity was accused, at one and the same time, of being too optimistic about the universe and of being too pessimistic about the world. The coincidence made me suddenly stand still.

An imbecile habit has arisen in modern controversy of saying that such and such a creed can be held in one age but cannot be held in another. Some dogma, we are told, was credible in the twelfth century, but is not credible in the twentieth. You might as well say that a certain philosophy can be believed on Mondays, but cannot be believed on Tuesdays. You might as well say of a view of the cosmos that it was suitable to half-past three, but not suitable to half-past four. What a man can believe depends upon his philosophy, not upon the clock or the century. If a man believes in unalterable natural law, he cannot believe in any miracle in any age. If a man believes in a will behind law, he can believe in any miracle in any age. Suppose, for the sake of argument, we are concerned with a case of thaumaturgic healing. A materialist of the twelfth century could not believe it any more than a materialist of the twentieth century. But a Christian Scientist of the twentieth century can believe it as much as a Christian of the twelfth century. It is simply a matter of a man's theory of things. Therefore in dealing with any historical answer, the point is not whether it was given in our time, but whether it was given in answer to our question. And the more I thought about when and how Christianity had come into the world, the more I felt that it had actually come to answer this question.

It is commonly the loose and latitudinarian Christians who pay quite indefensible compliments to Christianity. They talk as if there had never been any piety or pity until Christianity came, a point on which any mediaeval would have been eager to correct them. They represent that the remarkable thing about Christianity was that it was the first to preach simplicity or self-restraint, or inwardness and sincerity. They will think me very narrow (whatever that means) if I say that the remarkable thing about Christianity was that it was the first to preach Christianity. Its peculiarity was that it was peculiar, and simplicity and sincerity are not peculiar, but obvious ideals for all mankind. Christianity was the answer to a riddle, not the last truism uttered after a long talk. Only the other day I saw in an excellent weekly paper of Puritan tone this remark, that Christianity when stripped of its armour of dogma (as who should speak of a man stripped of his armour of bones), turned out to be nothing but the Quaker doctrine of the Inner Light. Now, if I were to say that Christianity came into the world specially to destroy the doctrine of the Inner Light, that would be an exaggeration. But it would be very much nearer to the truth. The last Stoics, like Marcus Aurelius, were exactly the people who did believe in the Inner Light. Their dignity, their weariness, their sad external care for others, their incurable internal care for themselves, were all due to the Inner Light, and existed only by that dismal illumination. Notice that Marcus Aurelius insists, as such introspective moralists always do, upon small things done or undone; it is because he has not hate or love enough to make a moral revolution. He gets up early in the morning, just as our own aristocrats living the Simple Life get up early in the morning; because such altruism is much easier than stopping the games of the amphitheatre or giving the English people back their land. Marcus Aurelius is the most intolerable of human types. He is an unselfish egoist. An unselfish egoist is a man who has pride without the excuse of passion. Of all conceivable forms of enlightenment the worst is what these people call the Inner Light. Of all horrible religions the most horrible is the worship of the god within. Any one who knows any body knows how it would work; any one who knows any one from the Higher Thought Centre knows how it does work. That Jones shall worship the god within him turns out ultimately to mean that Jones shall worship Jones. Let Jones worship the sun or moon, anything rather than the Inner Light; let Jones worship cats or crocodiles, if he can find any in his street, but not the god within. Christianity came into the world firstly in order to assert with violence that a man had not only to look inwards, but to look outwards, to behold with astonishment and enthusiasm a divine company and a divine captain. The only fun of being a Christian was that a man was not left alone with the Inner Light, but definitely recognized an outer light, fair as the sun, clear as the moon, terrible as an army with banners.

All the same, it will be as well if Jones does not worship the sun and moon. If he does, there is a tendency for him to imitate them; to say, that because the sun burns insects alive, he may burn insects alive. He thinks that because the sun gives people sun-stroke, he may give his neighbour measles. He thinks that because the moon is said to drive men mad, he may drive his wife mad. This ugly side of mere external optimism had also shown itself in the ancient world. About the time when the Stoic idealism had begun to show the weaknesses of pessimism, the old nature worship of the ancients had begun to show the enormous weaknesses of optimism. Nature worship is natural enough while the society is young, or, in other words, Pantheism is all right as long as it is the worship of Pan. But Nature has another side which experience and sin are not slow in finding out, and it is no flippancy to say of the god Pan that he soon showed the cloven hoof. The only objection to Natural Religion is that somehow it always becomes unnatural. A man loves Nature in the morning for her innocence and amiability, and at nightfall, if he is loving her still, it is for her darkness and her cruelty. He washes at dawn in clear water as did the Wise Man of the Stoics, yet, somehow at the dark end of the day, he is bathing in hot bull's blood, as did Julian the Apostate. The mere pursuit of health always leads to something unhealthy. Physical nature must not be made the direct object of obedience; it must be enjoyed, not worshipped. Stars and mountains must not be taken seriously. If they are, we end where the pagan nature worship ended. Because the earth is kind, we can imitate all her cruelties. Because sexuality is sane, we can all go mad about sexuality. Mere optimism had reached its insane and appropriate termination. The theory that everything was good had become an orgy of everything that was bad.

On the other side our idealist pessimists were represented by the old remnant of the Stoics. Marcus Aurelius and his friends had really given up the idea of any god in the universe and looked only to the god within. They had no hope of any virtue in nature, and hardly any hope of any virtue in society. They had not enough interest in the outer world really to wreck or revolutionise it. They did not love the city enough to set fire to it. Thus the ancient world was exactly in our own desolate dilemma. The only people who really enjoyed this world were busy breaking it up; and the virtuous people did not care enough about them to knock them down. In this dilemma (the same as ours) Christianity suddenly stepped in and offered a singular answer, which the world eventually accepted as THE answer. It was the answer then, and I think it is the answer now.

This answer was like the slash of a sword; it sundered; it did not in any sense sentimentally unite. Briefly, it divided God from the cosmos. That transcendence and distinctness of the deity which some Christians now want to remove from Christianity, was really the only reason why any one wanted to be a Christian. It was the whole point of the Christian answer to the unhappy pessimist and the still more unhappy optimist. As I am here only concerned with their particular problem, I shall indicate only briefly this great metaphysical suggestion. All descriptions of the creating or sustaining principle in things must be metaphorical, because they must be verbal. Thus the pantheist is forced to speak of God in all things as if he were in a box. Thus the evolutionist has, in his very name, the idea of being unrolled like a carpet. All terms, religious and irreligious, are open to this charge. The only question is whether all terms are useless, or whether one can, with such a phrase, cover a distinct IDEA about the origin of things. I think one can, and so evidently does the evolutionist, or he would not talk about evolution. And the root phrase for all Christian theism was this, that God was a creator, as an artist is a creator. A poet is so separate from his poem that he himself speaks of it as a little thing he has "thrown off." Even in giving it forth he has flung it away. This principle that all creation and procreation is a breaking off is at least as consistent through the cosmos as the evolutionary principle that all growth is a branching out. A woman loses a child even in having a child. All creation is separation. Birth is as solemn a parting as death.

It was the prime philosophic principle of Christianity that this divorce in the divine act of making (such as severs the poet from the poem or the mother from the new-born child) was the true description of the act whereby the absolute energy made the world. According to most philosophers, God in making the world enslaved it. According to Christianity, in making it, He set it free. God had written, not so much a poem, but rather a play; a play he had planned as perfect, but which had necessarily been left to human actors and stage-managers, who had since made a great mess of it. I will discuss the truth of this theorem later. Here I have only to point out with what a startling smoothness it passed the dilemma we have discussed in this chapter. In this way at least one could be both happy and indignant without degrading one's self to be either a pessimist or an optimist. On this system one could fight all the forces of existence without deserting the flag of existence. One could be at peace with the universe and yet be at war with the world. St. George could still fight the dragon, however big the monster bulked in the cosmos, though he were bigger than the mighty cities or bigger than the everlasting hills. If he were as big as the world he could yet be killed in the name of the world. St. George had not to consider any obvious odds or proportions in the scale of things, but only the original secret of their design. He can shake his sword at the dragon, even if it is everything; even if the empty heavens over his head are only the huge arch of its open jaws.

And then followed an experience impossible to describe. It was as if I had been blundering about since my birth with two huge and unmanageable machines, of different shapes and without apparent connection—the world and the Christian tradition. I had found this hole in the world: the fact that one must somehow find a way of loving the world without trusting it; somehow one must love the world without being worldly. I found this projecting feature of Christian theology, like a sort of hard spike, the dogmatic insistence that God was personal, and had made a world separate from Himself. The spike of dogma fitted exactly into the hole in the world—it had evidently been meant to go there— and then the strange thing began to happen. When once these two parts of the two machines had come together, one after another, all the other parts fitted and fell in with an eerie exactitude. I could hear bolt after bolt over all the machinery falling into its place with a kind of click of relief. Having got one part right, all the other parts were repeating that rectitude, as clock after clock strikes noon. Instinct after instinct was answered by doctrine after doctrine. Or, to vary the metaphor, I was like one who had advanced into a hostile country to take one high fortress. And when that fort had fallen the whole country surrendered and turned solid behind me. The whole land was lit up, as it were, back to the first fields of my childhood. All those blind fancies of boyhood which in the fourth chapter I have tried in vain to trace on the darkness,

became suddenly transparent and sane. I was right when I felt that roses were red by some sort of choice: it was the divine choice. I was right when I felt that I would almost rather say that grass was the wrong colour than say it must by necessity have been that colour: it might verily have been any other. My sense that happiness hung on the crazy thread of a condition did mean something when all was said: it meant the whole doctrine of the Fall. Even those dim and shapeless monsters of notions which I have not been able to describe, much less defend, stepped quietly into their places like colossal caryatides of the creed. The fancy that the cosmos was not vast and void, but small and cosy, had a fulfilled significance now, for anything that is a work of art must be small in the sight of the artist; to God the stars might be only small and dear, like diamonds. And my haunting instinct that somehow good was not merely a tool to be used, but a relic to be guarded, like the goods from Crusoe's ship— even that had been the wild whisper of something originally wise, for, according to Christianity, we were indeed the survivors of a wreck, the crew of a golden ship that had gone down before the beginning of the world.

But the important matter was this, that it entirely reversed the reason for optimism. And the instant the reversal was made it felt like the abrupt ease when a bone is put back in the socket. I had often called myself an optimist, to avoid the too evident blasphemy of pessimism. But all the optimism of the age had been false and disheartening for this reason, that it had always been trying to prove that we fit in to the world. The Christian optimism is based on the fact that we do NOT fit in to the world. I had tried to be happy by telling myself that man is an animal, like any other which sought its meat from God. But now I really was happy, for I had learnt that man is a monstrosity. I had been right in feeling all things as odd, for I myself was at once worse and better than all things. The optimist's pleasure was prosaic, for it dwelt on the naturalness of everything; the Christian pleasure was poetic, for it dwelt on the unnaturalness of everything in the light of the supernatural. The modern philosopher had told me again and again that I was in the right place, and I had still felt depressed even in acquiescence. But I had heard that I was in the WRONG place, and my soul sang for joy, like a bird in spring. The knowledge found out and illuminated forgotten chambers in the dark house of infancy. I knew now why grass had always seemed to me as queer as the green beard of a giant, and why I could feel homesick at home.

VI THE PARADOXES OF CHRISTIANITY

The real trouble with this world of ours is not that it is an unreasonable world, nor even that it is a reasonable one. The commonest kind of trouble is that it is nearly reasonable, but not quite. Life is not an illogicality; yet it is a trap for logicians. It looks just a little more mathematical and regular than it is; its exactitude is obvious, but its inexactitude is hidden; its wildness lies in wait. I give one coarse instance of what I mean. Suppose some mathematical creature from the moon were to reckon up the human body; he would at once see that the essential thing about it was that it was duplicate. A man is two men, he on the right exactly resembling him on the left. Having noted that there was an arm on the right and one on the left, a leg on the right and one on the left, he might go further and still find on each side the same number of fingers, the same number of toes, twin eyes, twin ears, twin nostrils, and even twin lobes of the brain. At last he would take it as a law; and then, where he found a heart on one side, would deduce that there was another heart on the other. And just then, where he most felt he was right, he would be wrong.

It is this silent swerving from accuracy by an inch that is the uncanny element in everything. It seems a sort of secret treason in the universe. An apple or an orange is round enough to get itself called round, and yet is not round after all. The earth itself is shaped like an orange in order to lure some simple astronomer into calling it a globe. A blade of grass is called after the blade of a sword, because it comes to a point; but it doesn't. Everywhere in things there is this element of the quiet and incalculable. It escapes the rationalists, but it never escapes till the last moment. From the grand curve of our earth it could easily be inferred that every inch of it was thus curved. It would seem rational that as a man has a brain on both sides, he should have a heart on both sides. Yet scientific men are still organizing expeditions to find the North Pole, because they are so fond of flat country. Scientific men are also still organizing expeditions to find a man's heart; and when they try to find it, they generally get on the wrong side of him.

Now, actual insight or inspiration is best tested by whether it guesses these hidden malformations or surprises. If our mathematician from the moon saw the two arms and the two ears, he might deduce the two shoulder-blades and the two halves of the brain. But if he guessed that the man's heart was in the right place, then I should call him something more than a mathematician. Now, this is exactly the claim which I have since come to propound for Christianity. Not merely that it deduces logical truths, but that when it suddenly becomes illogical, it has found, so to speak, an illogical truth. It not only goes right about things, but it goes wrong (if one may say so) exactly where the things go wrong. Its plan suits the secret irregularities, and expects the unexpected. It is simple about the simple truth; but it is stubborn about the subtle truth. It will admit that a man has two hands, it will not admit (though all the Modernists wail to it) the obvious deduction that he has two hearts. It is my only purpose in this chapter to point this out; to show that whenever we feel there is something odd in Christian theology, we shall generally find that there is something odd in the truth.

I have alluded to an unmeaning phrase to the effect that such and such a creed cannot be believed in our age. Of course, anything can be believed in any age. But, oddly enough, there really is a sense in which a creed, if it is believed at all, can be believed more fixedly in a complex society than in a simple one. If a man finds Christianity true in Birmingham, he has actually clearer reasons for faith than if he had found it true in Mercia. For the more complicated seems the coincidence, the less it can be a coincidence. If snowflakes fell in the shape, say, of the heart of Midlothian, it might be an accident. But if snowflakes fell in the exact shape of the maze at Hampton Court, I think one might call it a miracle. It is exactly as of such a miracle that I have since come to feel of the philosophy of Christianity. The complication of our modern world proves the truth of the creed more perfectly than any of the plain problems of the ages of faith. It was in Notting Hill and Battersea that I began to see that Christianity was true. This is why the faith has that elaboration of doctrines and details which so much distresses those who admire Christianity without believing in it. When once one believes in a creed, one is proud of its complexity, as scientists are proud of the complexity of science. It shows how rich it is in discoveries. If it is right at all, it is a compliment to say that it's elaborately right. A stick might fit a hole or a stone a hollow by accident. But a key and a lock are both complex. And if a key fits a lock, you know it is the right key.

But this involved accuracy of the thing makes it very difficult to do what I now have to do, to describe this accumulation of truth. It is very hard for a man to defend anything of which he is entirely convinced. It is comparatively easy when he is only partially convinced. He is partially convinced because he has found this or that proof of the thing, and he can expound it. But a man is not really convinced of a philosophic theory when he finds that something proves it. He is only really convinced when he finds that everything proves it. And the more converging reasons he finds pointing to this conviction, the more bewildered he is if asked suddenly to sum them up. Thus, if one asked an ordinary intelligent man, on the spur of the moment, "Why do you prefer civilization to savagery?" he would look wildly round at object after object, and would only be able to answer vaguely, "Why, there is that bookcase . . . and the coals in the coal-scuttle . . . and pianos . . . and policemen." The whole case for civilization is that the case for it is complex. It has done so many things. But that very multiplicity of proof which ought to make reply overwhelming makes reply impossible.

There is, therefore, about all complete conviction a kind of huge helplessness. The belief is so big that it takes a long time to get it into action. And this hesitation chiefly arises, oddly enough, from an indifference about where one should begin. All roads lead to Rome; which is one reason why many people never get there. In the case of this defence of the Christian conviction I confess that I would as soon begin the argument with one thing as another; I would begin it with a turnip or a taximeter cab. But if I am to be at all careful about making my meaning clear, it will, I think, be wiser to continue the current arguments of the last chapter, which was concerned to urge the first of these mystical coincidences, or rather ratifications. All I had hitherto heard of Christian theology had alienated me from it. I was a pagan at the age of twelve, and a complete agnostic by the age of sixteen; and I cannot understand any one passing the age of seventeen without having asked himself so simple a question. I did, indeed, retain a cloudy reverence for a cosmic deity and a great historical interest in the Founder of Christianity. But I certainly regarded Him as a man; though perhaps I thought that, even in that point, He had an advantage over some of His modern critics. I read the scientific and sceptical literature of my time—all of it, at least, that I could find written in English and lying about; and I read nothing else; I mean I read nothing else on any other note of philosophy. The penny dreadfuls which I also read were indeed in a healthy and heroic tradition of Christianity; but I did not know this at the time. I never read a line of Christian apologetics. I read as little as I can of them now. It was Huxley and Herbert Spencer and Bradlaugh who brought me back to orthodox theology. They sowed in my mind my first wild doubts of doubt. Our grandmothers were quite right when they said that Tom Paine and the free-thinkers unsettled the mind. They do. They unsettled mine horribly. The rationalist made me question whether reason was of any use whatever; and when I had finished Herbert Spencer I had got as far as doubting (for the first time) whether evolution had occurred at all. As I laid down the last of Colonel Ingersoll's atheistic lectures the dreadful thought broke across my mind, "Almost thou persuadest me to be a Christian." I was in a desperate way.

This odd effect of the great agnostics in arousing doubts deeper than their own might be illustrated in many ways. I take only one. As I read and re-read all the non-Christian or anti-Christian accounts of the faith, from Huxley to Bradlaugh, a slow and awful impression grew gradually but graphically upon my mind—the impression that Christianity must be a most extraordinary thing. For not only (as I understood) had Christianity the most flaming vices, but it had apparently a mystical talent for combining vices which seemed inconsistent with each other. It was attacked on all sides and for all contradictory reasons. No sooner had one rationalist demonstrated that it was too far to the east than another demonstrated with equal clearness that it was much too far to the west. No sooner had my indignation died down at its angular and aggressive squareness than I was called up again to notice and condemn its enervating and sensual roundness. In case any reader has not come across the thing I mean, I will give such instances as I remember at random of this self-contradiction in the sceptical attack. I give four or five of them; there are fifty more.

Thus, for instance, I was much moved by the eloquent attack on Christianity as a thing of inhuman gloom; for I thought (and still think) sincere pessimism the unpardonable sin. Insincere pessimism is a social accomplishment, rather agreeable than otherwise; and fortunately nearly all pessimism is insincere. But if Christianity was, as these people said, a thing purely pessimistic and opposed to life, then I was quite prepared to blow up St. Paul's Cathedral. But the extraordinary thing is this. They did prove to me in Chapter I. (to my complete satisfaction) that Christianity was too pessimistic; and then, in Chapter II., they began to prove to me that it was a great deal too optimistic. One accusation against Christianity was that it prevented men, by morbid tears and terrors, from seeking joy and liberty in the bosom of Nature. But another accusation was that it comforted men with a fictitious providence, and put them in a pink-and-white nursery. One great agnostic asked why Nature was not beautiful enough, and why it was hard to be free. Another great agnostic objected that Christian optimism, "the garment of make-believe woven by pious hands," hid from us the fact that Nature was ugly, and that it was impossible to be free. One rationalist had hardly done calling Christianity a nightmare before another began to call it a fool's paradise. This puzzled me; the charges seemed inconsistent. Christianity could not at once be the black mask on a white world, and also the white mask on a black world. The state of the Christian could not be at once so comfortable that he was a coward to cling to it, and so uncomfortable that he was a fool to stand it. If it falsified human vision it must falsify it one way or another; it could not wear both green and rose-coloured spectacles. I rolled on my tongue with a terrible joy, as did all young men of that time, the taunts which Swinburne hurled at the dreariness of the creed—

"Thou hast conquered, O pale Galilaean, the world has grown gray with Thy breath."

But when I read the same poet's accounts of paganism (as in "Atalanta"), I gathered that the world was, if possible, more gray before the Galilean breathed on it than afterwards. The poet maintained, indeed, in the abstract, that life itself was pitch dark. And yet, somehow, Christianity had darkened it. The very man who denounced Christianity for pessimism was himself a pessimist. I thought there must be something wrong. And it did for one wild moment cross my mind that, perhaps, those might not be the very best judges of the relation of religion to happiness who, by their own account, had neither one nor the other.

It must be understood that I did not conclude hastily that the accusations were false or the accusers fools. I simply deduced that Christianity must be something even weirder and wickeder than they made out. A thing might have these two opposite vices; but it must be a rather queer thing if it did. A man might be too fat in one place and too thin in another; but he would be an odd shape. At this point my thoughts were only of the odd shape of the Christian religion; I did not allege any odd shape in the rationalistic mind.

Here is another case of the same kind. I felt that a strong case against Christianity lay in the charge that there is something timid, monkish, and unmanly about all that is called "Christian," especially in its attitude towards resistance and fighting. The great sceptics of the nineteenth century were largely virile. Bradlaugh in an expansive way, Huxley, in a reticent way, were decidedly men. In comparison, it did seem tenable that there was something weak and over patient about Christian counsels. The Gospel paradox about the other cheek, the fact that priests never fought, a hundred things made plausible the accusation that Christianity was an attempt to make a man too like a sheep. I read it and believed it, and if I had read nothing different, I should have gone on believing it. But I read something very different. I turned the next page in my agnostic manual, and my brain turned up-side down. Now I found that I was to hate Christianity not for fighting too little, but for fighting too much. Christianity, it seemed, was the mother of wars. Christianity had deluged the world with blood. I had got thoroughly angry with the Christian, because he never was angry. And now I was told to be angry with him because his anger had been the most huge and horrible thing in human history; because his anger had soaked the earth and smoked to the sun. The very people who reproached Christianity with the meekness and non-resistance of the monasteries were the very people who reproached it also with the violence and valour of the Crusades. It was the fault of poor old Christianity (somehow or other) both that Edward the Confessor did not fight and that Richard Coeur de Leon did. The Quakers (we were told) were the only characteristic Christians; and yet the massacres of Cromwell and Alva were characteristic Christian crimes. What could it all mean? What was this Christianity which always forbade war and always produced wars? What could be the nature of the thing which one could abuse first because it would not fight, and second because it was always fighting? In what world of riddles was born this monstrous murder and this monstrous meekness? The shape of Christianity grew a queerer shape every instant.

I take a third case; the strangest of all, because it involves the one real objection to the faith. The one real objection to the Christian religion is simply that it is one religion. The world is a big place, full of very different kinds of people. Christianity (it may reasonably be said) is one thing confined to one kind of people; it began in Palestine, it has practically stopped with Europe. I was duly impressed with this argument in my youth, and I was much drawn towards the doctrine often preached in Ethical Societies— I mean the doctrine that there is one great unconscious church of all humanity founded on the omnipresence of the human conscience. Creeds, it was said, divided men; but at least morals united them. The soul might seek the strangest and most remote lands and ages and still find essential ethical common sense. It might find Confucius under Eastern trees, and he would be writing "Thou shalt not steal." It might decipher the darkest hieroglyphic on the most primeval desert, and the meaning when deciphered would be "Little boys should tell the truth." I believed this doctrine of the brotherhood of all men in the possession of a moral sense, and I believe it still—with other things. And I was thoroughly annoyed with Christianity for suggesting (as I supposed) that whole ages and empires of men had utterly escaped this light of justice and reason. But then I found an astonishing thing. I found that the very people who said that mankind was one church from Plato to Emerson were the very people who said that morality had changed altogether, and that what was right in one age was wrong in another. If I asked, say, for an altar, I was told that we needed none, for men our brothers gave us clear oracles and one creed in their universal customs and ideals. But if I mildly pointed out that one of men's universal customs was to have an altar, then my agnostic teachers turned clean round and told me that men had always been in darkness and the superstitions of savages. I found it was their daily taunt against Christianity that it was the light of one people and had left all others to die in the dark. But I also found that it was their special boast for themselves that science and progress were the discovery of one people, and that all other peoples had died in the dark. Their chief insult to Christianity was actually their chief compliment to themselves, and there seemed to be a strange unfairness about all their relative insistence on the two things. When considering some pagan or agnostic, we were to remember that all men had one religion; when considering some mystic or spiritualist, we were only to consider what absurd religions some men had. We could trust the ethics of Epictetus, because ethics had never changed. We must not trust the ethics of Bossuet, because ethics had changed. They changed in two hundred years, but not in two thousand.

This began to be alarming. It looked not so much as if Christianity was bad enough to include any vices, but rather as if any stick was good enough to beat Christianity with. What again could this astonishing thing be like which people were so anxious to contradict, that in doing so they did not mind contradicting themselves? I saw the same thing on every side. I can give no further space to this discussion of it in detail; but lest any one supposes that I have unfairly selected three accidental cases I will run briefly through a few others. Thus, certain sceptics wrote that the great crime of Christianity had been its attack on the family; it had dragged women to the loneliness and contemplation of the cloister, away from their homes and their children. But, then, other sceptics (slightly more advanced) said that the great crime of Christianity was forcing the family and marriage upon us; that it doomed women to the drudgery of their homes and children, and forbade them loneliness and contemplation. The charge was actually reversed. Or, again, certain phrases in the Epistles or the marriage service, were said by the anti-Christians to show contempt for woman's intellect. But I found that the anti-Christians themselves had a contempt for woman's intellect; for it was their great sneer at the Church on the Continent that "only women" went to it. Or again, Christianity was reproached with its naked and hungry habits; with its sackcloth and dried peas. But the next minute Christianity was being reproached with its pomp and its ritualism; its shrines of porphyry and its robes of gold. It was abused for being too plain and for being too coloured. Again Christianity had always been accused of restraining sexuality too much, when Bradlaugh the Malthusian discovered that it restrained it too little. It is often accused in the same breath of prim respectability and of religious extravagance. Between the covers of the same atheistic pamphlet I have found the faith rebuked for its disunion, "One thinks one thing, and one another," and rebuked also for its union, "It is difference of opinion that prevents the world from going to the dogs." In the same conversation a free-thinker, a friend of mine, blamed Christianity for despising Jews, and then despised it himself for being Jewish.

I wished to be quite fair then, and I wish to be quite fair now; and I did not conclude that the attack on Christianity was all wrong. I only concluded that if Christianity was wrong, it was very wrong indeed. Such hostile horrors might be combined in one thing, but that thing must be very strange and solitary. There are men who are misers, and also spendthrifts; but they are rare. There are men sensual and also ascetic; but they are rare. But if this mass of mad contradictions really existed, quakerish and bloodthirsty, too gorgeous and too thread-bare, austere, yet pandering preposterously to the lust of the eye, the enemy of women and their foolish refuge, a solemn pessimist and a silly optimist, if this evil existed, then there was in this evil something quite supreme and unique. For I found in my rationalist teachers no explanation of such exceptional corruption. Christianity (theoretically speaking) was in their eyes only one of the ordinary myths and errors of mortals. THEY gave me no key to this twisted and unnatural badness. Such a paradox of evil rose to the stature of the supernatural. It was, indeed, almost as supernatural as the infallibility of the Pope. An historic institution, which never went right, is really quite as much of a miracle as an institution that cannot go wrong. The only explanation which immediately occurred to my mind was that Christianity did not come from heaven, but from hell. Really, if Jesus of Nazareth was not Christ, He must have been Antichrist.

And then in a quiet hour a strange thought struck me like a still thunderbolt. There had suddenly come into my mind another explanation. Suppose we heard an unknown man spoken of by many men. Suppose we were puzzled to hear that some men said he was too tall and some too short; some objected to his fatness, some lamented his leanness; some thought him too dark, and some too fair. One explanation (as has been already admitted) would be that he might be an odd shape. But there is another explanation. He might be the right shape. Outrageously tall men might feel him to be short. Very short men might feel him to be tall. Old bucks who are growing stout might consider him insufficiently filled out; old beaux who were growing thin might feel that he expanded beyond the narrow lines of elegance. Perhaps Swedes (who have pale hair like tow) called him a dark man, while negroes considered him distinctly blonde. Perhaps (in short) this extraordinary thing is really the ordinary thing; at least the normal thing, the centre. Perhaps, after all, it is Christianity that is sane and all its critics that are mad—in various ways. I tested this idea by asking myself whether there was about any of the accusers anything morbid that might explain the accusation. I was startled to find that this key fitted a lock. For instance, it was certainly odd that the modern world charged Christianity at once with bodily austerity and with artistic pomp. But then it was also odd, very odd, that the modern world itself combined extreme bodily luxury with an extreme absence of artistic pomp. The modern man thought Becket's robes too rich and his meals too poor. But then the modern man was really exceptional in history; no man before ever ate such elaborate dinners in such ugly clothes. The modern man found the church too simple exactly where modern life is too complex; he found the church too gorgeous exactly where modern life is too dingy. The man who disliked the plain fasts and feasts was mad on entrees. The man who disliked vestments wore a pair of preposterous trousers. And surely if there was any insanity involved in the matter at all it was in the trousers, not in the simply falling robe. If there was any insanity at all, it was in the extravagant entrees, not in the bread and wine.

I went over all the cases, and I found the key fitted so far. The fact that Swinburne was irritated at the unhappiness of Christians and yet more irritated at their happiness was easily explained. It was no longer a complication of diseases in Christianity, but a complication of diseases in Swinburne. The restraints of Christians saddened him simply because he was more hedonist than a healthy man should be. The faith of Christians angered him because he was more pessimist than a healthy man should be. In the same way the Malthusians by instinct attacked Christianity; not because there is anything especially anti-Malthusian about Christianity, but because there is something a little anti-human about Malthusianism.

Nevertheless it could not, I felt, be quite true that Christianity was merely sensible and stood in the middle. There was really an element in it of emphasis and even frenzy which had justified the secularists in their superficial criticism. It might be wise, I began more and more to think that it was wise, but it was not merely worldly wise; it was not merely temperate and respectable. Its fierce crusaders and meek saints might balance each other; still, the crusaders were very fierce and the saints were very meek, meek beyond all decency. Now, it was just at this point of the speculation that I remembered my thoughts about the martyr and the suicide. In that matter there had been this combination between two almost insane positions which yet somehow amounted to sanity. This was just such another contradiction; and this I had already found to be true. This was exactly one of the paradoxes in which sceptics found the creed wrong; and in this I had found it right. Madly as Christians might love the martyr or hate the suicide, they never felt these passions more madly than I had felt them long before I dreamed of Christianity. Then the most difficult and interesting part of the mental process opened, and I began to trace this idea darkly through all the enormous thoughts of our theology. The idea was that which I had outlined touching the optimist and the pessimist; that we want not an amalgam or compromise, but both things at the top of their energy; love and wrath both burning. Here I shall only trace it in relation to ethics. But I need not remind the reader that the idea of this combination is indeed central in orthodox theology. For orthodox theology has specially insisted that Christ was not a being apart from God and man, like an elf, nor yet a being half human and half not, like a centaur, but both things at once and both things thoroughly, very man and very God. Now let me trace this notion as I found it.

All sane men can see that sanity is some kind of equilibrium; that one may be mad and eat too much, or mad and eat too little. Some moderns have indeed appeared with vague versions of progress and evolution which seeks to destroy the MESON or balance of Aristotle. They seem to suggest that we are meant to starve progressively, or to go on eating larger and larger breakfasts every morning for ever. But the great truism of the MESON remains for all thinking men, and these people have not upset any balance except their own. But granted that we have all to keep a balance, the real interest comes in with the question of how that balance can be kept. That was the problem which Paganism tried to solve: that was the problem which I think Christianity solved and solved in a very strange way.

Paganism declared that virtue was in a balance; Christianity declared it was in a conflict: the collision of two passions apparently opposite. Of course they were not really inconsistent; but they were such that it was hard to hold simultaneously. Let us follow for a moment the clue of the martyr and the suicide; and take the case of courage. No quality has ever so much addled the brains and tangled the definitions of merely rational sages. Courage is almost a contradiction in terms. It means a strong desire to live taking the form of a readiness to die. "He that will lose his life, the same shall save it," is not a piece of mysticism for saints and heroes. It is a piece of everyday advice for sailors or mountaineers. It might be printed in an Alpine guide or a drill book. This paradox is the whole principle of courage; even of quite earthly or quite brutal courage. A man cut off by the sea may save his life if he will risk it on the precipice.

He can only get away from death by continually stepping within an inch of it. A soldier surrounded by enemies, if he is to cut his way out, needs to combine a strong desire for living with a strange carelessness about dying. He must not merely cling to life, for then he will be a coward, and will not escape. He must not merely wait for death, for then he will be a suicide, and will not escape. He must seek his life in a spirit of furious indifference to it; he must desire life like water and yet drink death like wine. No philosopher, I fancy, has ever expressed this romantic riddle with adequate lucidity, and I certainly have not done so. But Christianity has done more: it has marked the limits of it in the awful graves of the suicide and the hero, showing the distance between him who dies for the sake of living and him who dies for the sake of dying. And it has held up ever since above the European lances the banner of the mystery of chivalry: the Christian courage, which is a disdain of death; not the Chinese courage, which is a disdain of life.

And now I began to find that this duplex passion was the Christian key to ethics everywhere. Everywhere the creed made a moderation out of the still crash of two impetuous emotions. Take, for instance, the matter of modesty, of the balance between mere pride and mere prostration. The average pagan, like the average agnostic, would merely say that he was content with himself, but not insolently self-satisfied, that there were many better and many worse, that his deserts were limited, but he would see that he got them. In short, he would walk with his head in the air; but not necessarily with his nose in the air. This is a manly and rational position, but it is open to the objection we noted against the compromise between optimism and pessimism—the "resignation" of Matthew Arnold. Being a mixture of two things, it is a dilution of two things; neither is present in its full strength or contributes its full colour. This proper pride does not lift the heart like the tongue of trumpets; you cannot go clad in crimson and gold for this. On the other hand, this mild rationalist modesty does not cleanse the soul with fire and make it clear like crystal; it does not (like a strict and searching humility) make a man as a little child, who can sit at the feet of the grass. It does not make him look up and see marvels; for Alice must grow small if she is to be Alice in Wonderland. Thus it loses both the poetry of being proud and the poetry of being humble. Christianity sought by this same strange expedient to save both of them.

It separated the two ideas and then exaggerated them both. In one way Man was to be haughtier than he had ever been before; in another way he was to be humbler than he had ever been before. In so far as I am Man I am the chief of creatures. In so far as I am a man I am the chief of sinners. All humility that had meant pessimism, that had meant man taking a vague or mean view of his whole destiny—all that was to go. We were to hear no more the wail of Ecclesiastes that humanity had no pre-eminence over the brute, or the awful cry of Homer that man was only the saddest of all the beasts of the field. Man was a statue of God walking about the garden. Man had pre-eminence over all the brutes; man was only sad because he was not a beast, but a broken god. The Greek had spoken of men creeping on the earth, as if clinging to it. Now Man was to tread on the earth as if to subdue it. Christianity thus held a thought of the dignity of man that could only be expressed in crowns rayed like the sun and fans of peacock plumage. Yet at the same time it could hold a thought about the abject smallness of man that could only be expressed in fasting and fantastic submission, in the gray ashes of St. Dominic and the white snows of St. Bernard. When one came to think of ONE'S SELF, there was vista and void enough for any amount of bleak abnegation and bitter truth. There the realistic gentleman could let himself go—as long as he let himself go at himself. There was an open playground for the happy pessimist. Let him say anything against himself short of blaspheming the original aim of his being; let him call himself a fool and even a damned fool (though that is Calvinistic); but he must not say that fools are not worth saving. He must not say that a man, QUA man, can be valueless. Here, again in short, Christianity got over the difficulty of combining furious opposites, by keeping them both, and keeping them both furious. The Church was positive on both points. One can hardly think too little of one's self. One can hardly think too much of one's soul.

Take another case: the complicated question of charity, which some highly uncharitable idealists seem to think quite easy. Charity is a paradox, like modesty and courage. Stated baldly, charity certainly means one of two things—pardoning unpardonable acts, or loving unlovable people. But if we ask ourselves (as we did in the case of pride) what a sensible pagan would feel about such a subject, we shall probably be beginning at the bottom of it. A sensible pagan would say that there were some people one could forgive, and some one couldn't: a slave who stole wine could be laughed at; a slave who betrayed his benefactor could be killed, and cursed even after he was killed. In so far as the act was pardonable, the man was pardonable. That again is rational, and even refreshing; but it is a dilution. It leaves no place for a pure horror of injustice, such as that which is a great beauty in the innocent. And it leaves no place for a mere tenderness for men as men, such as is the whole fascination of the charitable. Christianity came in here as before. It came in startlingly with a sword, and clove one thing from another. It divided the crime from the criminal. The criminal we must forgive unto seventy times seven. The crime we must not forgive at all. It was not enough that slaves who stole wine inspired partly anger and partly kindness. We must be much more angry with theft than before, and yet much kinder to thieves than before. There was room for wrath and love to run wild. And the more I considered Christianity, the more I found that while it had established a rule and order, the chief aim of that order was to give room for good things to run wild.

Mental and emotional liberty are not so simple as they look. Really they require almost as careful a balance of laws and conditions as do social and political liberty. The ordinary aesthetic anarchist who sets out to feel everything freely gets knotted at last in a paradox that prevents him feeling at all. He breaks away from home limits to follow poetry. But in ceasing to feel home limits he has ceased to feel the "Odyssey." He is free from national prejudices and outside patriotism. But being outside patriotism he is outside "Henry V." Such a literary man is simply outside all literature: he is more of a prisoner than any bigot. For if there is a wall between you and the world, it makes little difference whether you describe yourself as locked in or as locked out. What we want is not the universality that is outside all normal sentiments; we want the universality that is inside all normal sentiments. It is all the difference between being free from them, as a man is free from a prison, and being free of them as a man is free of a city. I am free from Windsor Castle (that is, I am not forcibly detained there), but I am by no means free of that building. How can man be approximately free of fine emotions, able to swing them in a clear space without breakage or wrong? THIS was the achievement of this Christian paradox of the parallel passions. Granted the primary dogma of the war between divine and diabolic, the revolt and ruin of the world, their optimism and pessimism, as pure poetry, could be loosened like cataracts.

St. Francis, in praising all good, could be a more shouting optimist than Walt Whitman. St. Jerome, in denouncing all evil, could paint the world blacker than Schopenhauer. Both passions were free because both were kept in their place. The optimist could pour out all the praise he liked on the gay music of the march, the golden trumpets, and the purple banners going into battle. But he must not call the fight needless. The pessimist might draw as darkly as he chose the sickening marches or the sanguine wounds. But he must not call the fight hopeless. So it was with all the other moral problems, with pride, with protest, and with compassion. By defining its main doctrine, the Church not only kept seemingly inconsistent things side by side, but, what was more, allowed them to break out in a sort of artistic violence otherwise possible only to anarchists. Meekness grew more dramatic than madness. Historic Christianity rose into a high and strange COUP DE THEATRE of morality—things that are to virtue what the crimes of Nero are to vice. The spirits of indignation and of charity took terrible and attractive forms, ranging from that monkish fierceness that scourged like a dog the first and greatest of the Plantagenets, to the sublime pity of St. Catherine, who, in the official shambles, kissed the bloody head of the criminal. Poetry could be acted as well as composed. This heroic and monumental manner in ethics has entirely vanished with supernatural religion. They, being humble, could parade themselves: but we are too proud to be prominent. Our ethical teachers write reasonably for prison reform; but we are not likely to see Mr. Cadbury, or any eminent philanthropist, go into Reading Gaol and embrace the strangled corpse before it is cast into the quicklime. Our ethical teachers write mildly against the power of millionaires; but we are not likely to see Mr. Rockefeller, or any modern tyrant, publicly whipped in Westminster Abbey.

Thus, the double charges of the secularists, though throwing nothing but darkness and confusion on themselves, throw a real light on the faith. It is true that the historic Church has at once emphasised celibacy and emphasised the family; has at once (if one may put it so) been fiercely for having children and fiercely for not having children. It has kept them side by side like two strong colours, red and white, like the red and white upon the shield of St. George. It has always had a healthy hatred of pink. It hates that combination of two colours which is the feeble expedient of the philosophers. It hates that evolution of black into white which is tantamount to a dirty gray. In fact, the whole theory of the Church on virginity might be symbolized in the statement that white is a colour: not merely the absence of a colour. All that I am urging here can be expressed by saying that Christianity sought in most of these cases to keep two colours coexistent but pure. It is not a mixture like russet or purple; it is rather like a shot silk, for a shot silk is always at right angles, and is in the pattern of the cross.

So it is also, of course, with the contradictory charges of the anti-Christians about submission and slaughter. It IS true that the Church told some men to fight and others not to fight; and it IS true that those who fought were like thunderbolts and those who did not fight were like statues. All this simply means that the Church preferred to use its Supermen and to use its Tolstoyans. There must be SOME good in the life of battle, for so many good men have enjoyed being soldiers. There must be SOME good in the idea of non-resistance, for so many good men seem to enjoy being Quakers. All that the Church did (so far as that goes) was to prevent either of these good things from ousting the other. They existed side by side. The Tolstoyans, having all the scruples of monks, simply became monks. The Quakers became a club instead of becoming a sect. Monks said all that Tolstoy says; they poured out lucid lamentations about the cruelty of battles and the vanity of revenge. But the Tolstoyans are not quite right enough to run the whole world; and in the ages of faith they were not allowed to run it. The world did not lose the last charge of Sir James Douglas or the banner of Joan the Maid. And sometimes this pure gentleness and this pure fierceness met and justified their juncture; the paradox of all the prophets was fulfilled, and, in the soul of St. Louis, the lion lay down with the lamb. But remember that this text is too lightly interpreted. It is constantly assured, especially in our Tolstoyan tendencies, that when the lion lies down with the lamb the lion becomes lamblike. But that is brutal annexation and imperialism on the part of the lamb. That is simply the lamb absorbing the lion instead of the lion eating the lamb. The real problem is—Can the lion lie down with the lamb and still retain his royal ferocity? THAT is the problem the Church attempted; THAT is the miracle she achieved.

This is what I have called guessing the hidden eccentricities of life. This is knowing that a man's heart is to the left and not in the middle. This is knowing not only that the earth is round, but knowing exactly where it is flat. Christian doctrine detected the oddities of life. It not only discovered the law, but it foresaw the exceptions. Those underrate Christianity who say that it discovered mercy; any one might discover mercy. In fact every one did. But to discover a plan for being merciful and also severe— THAT was to anticipate a strange need of human nature. For no one wants to be forgiven for a big sin as if it were a little one. Any one might say that we should be neither quite miserable nor quite happy. But to find out how far one MAY be quite miserable without making it impossible to be quite happy—that was a discovery in psychology. Any one might say, "Neither swagger nor grovel"; and it would have been a limit. But to say, "Here you can swagger and there you can grovel"—that was an emancipation.

This was the big fact about Christian ethics; the discovery of the new balance. Paganism had been like a pillar of marble, upright because proportioned with symmetry. Christianity was like a huge and ragged and romantic rock, which, though it sways on its pedestal at a touch, yet, because its exaggerated excrescences exactly balance each other, is enthroned there for a thousand years. In a Gothic cathedral the columns were all different, but they were all necessary. Every support seemed an accidental and fantastic support; every buttress was a flying buttress. So in Christendom apparent accidents balanced. Becket wore a hair shirt under his gold and crimson, and there is much to be said for the combination; for Becket got the benefit of the hair shirt while the people in the street got the benefit of the crimson and gold. It is at least better than the manner of the modern millionaire, who has the black and the drab outwardly for others, and the gold next his heart. But the balance was not always in one man's body as in Becket's; the balance was often distributed over the whole body of Christendom. Because a man prayed and fasted on the Northern snows, flowers could be flung at his festival in the Southern cities; and because fanatics drank water on the sands of Syria, men could still drink cider in the orchards of England. This is what makes Christendom at once so much more perplexing and so much more interesting than the Pagan empire; just as Amiens Cathedral is not better but more interesting than the Parthenon. If any one wants a modern proof of all this, let him consider the curious fact that, under Christianity, Europe (while remaining a unity) has broken up into individual nations. Patriotism is a perfect example of this deliberate balancing of one emphasis against another emphasis. The instinct of the Pagan empire would have said, "You shall all be Roman citizens, and grow alike; let the German grow less slow and reverent; the Frenchmen less experimental and swift." But the instinct of Christian Europe says, "Let the German remain slow and reverent, that the Frenchman may the more safely be swift and experimental. We will make an equipoise out of these excesses. The absurdity called Germany shall correct the insanity called France."

Last and most important, it is exactly this which explains what is so inexplicable to all the modern critics of the history of Christianity. I mean the monstrous wars about small points of theology, the earthquakes of emotion about a gesture or a word. It was only a matter of an inch; but an inch is everything when you are balancing. The Church could not afford to swerve a hair's breadth on some things if she was to continue her great and daring experiment of the irregular equilibrium. Once let one idea become less powerful and some other idea would become too powerful. It was no flock of sheep the Christian shepherd was leading, but a herd of bulls and tigers, of terrible ideals and devouring doctrines, each one of them strong enough to turn to a false religion and lay waste the world. Remember that the Church went in specifically for dangerous ideas; she was a lion tamer. The idea of birth through a Holy Spirit, of the death of a divine being, of the forgiveness of sins, or the fulfilment of prophecies, are ideas which, any one can see, need but a touch to turn them into something blasphemous or ferocious. The smallest link was let drop by the artificers of the Mediterranean, and the lion of ancestral pessimism burst his chain in the forgotten forests of the north. Of these theological equalisations I have to speak afterwards. Here it is enough to notice that if some small mistake were made in doctrine, huge blunders might be made in human happiness. A sentence phrased wrong about the nature of symbolism would have broken all the best statues in Europe. A slip in the definitions might stop all the dances; might wither all the Christmas trees or break all the Easter eggs. Doctrines had to be defined within strict limits, even in order that man might enjoy general human liberties. The Church had to be careful, if only that the world might be careless.

This is the thrilling romance of Orthodoxy. People have fallen into a foolish habit of speaking of orthodoxy as something heavy, humdrum, and safe. There never was anything so perilous or so exciting as orthodoxy. It was sanity: and to be sane is more dramatic than to be mad. It was the equilibrium of a man behind madly rushing horses, seeming to stoop this way and to sway that, yet in every attitude having the grace of statuary and the accuracy of arithmetic. The Church in its early days went fierce and fast with any warhorse; yet it is utterly unhistoric to say that she merely went mad along one idea, like a vulgar fanaticism. She swerved to left and right, so exactly as to avoid enormous obstacles. She left on one hand the huge bulk of Arianism, buttressed by all the worldly powers to make Christianity too worldly. The next instant she was swerving to avoid an orientalism, which would have made it too unworldly. The orthodox Church never took the tame course or accepted the conventions; the orthodox Church was never respectable. It would have been easier to have accepted the earthly power of the Arians. It would have been easy, in the Calvinistic seventeenth century, to fall into the bottomless pit of predestination. It is easy to be a madman: it is easy to be a heretic. It is always easy to let the age have its head; the difficult thing is to keep one's own. It is always easy to be a modernist; as it is easy to be a snob. To have fallen into any of those open traps of error and exaggeration which fashion after fashion and sect after sect set along the historic path of Christendom—that would indeed have been simple. It is always simple to fall; there are an infinity of angles at which one falls, only one at which one stands. To have fallen into any one of the fads from Gnosticism to Christian Science would indeed have been obvious and tame. But to have avoided them all has been one whirling adventure; and in my vision the heavenly chariot flies thundering through the ages, the dull heresies sprawling and prostrate, the wild truth reeling but erect.

VII THE ETERNAL REVOLUTION

The following propositions have been urged: First, that some faith in our life is required even to improve it; second, that some dissatisfaction with things as they are is necessary even in order to be satisfied; third, that to have this necessary content and necessary discontent it is not sufficient to have the obvious equilibrium of the Stoic. For mere resignation has neither the gigantic levity of pleasure nor the superb intolerance of pain. There is a vital objection to the advice merely to grin and bear it. The objection is that if you merely bear it, you do not grin. Greek heroes do not grin: but gargoyles do—because they are Christian. And when a Christian is pleased, he is (in the most exact sense) frightfully pleased; his pleasure is frightful. Christ prophesied the whole of Gothic architecture in that hour when nervous and respectable people (such people as now object to barrel organs) objected to the shouting of the gutter-snipes of Jerusalem. He said, "If these were silent, the very stones would cry out." Under the impulse of His spirit arose like a clamorous chorus the facades of the mediaeval cathedrals, thronged with shouting faces and open mouths. The prophecy has fulfilled itself: the very stones cry out.

If these things be conceded, though only for argument, we may take up where we left it the thread of the thought of the natural man, called by the Scotch (with regrettable familiarity), "The Old Man." We can ask the next question so obviously in front of us. Some satisfaction is needed even to make things better. But what do we mean by making things better? Most modern talk on this matter is a mere argument in a circle—that circle which we have already made the symbol of madness and of mere rationalism. Evolution is only good if it produces good; good is only good if it helps evolution. The elephant stands on the tortoise, and the tortoise on the elephant.

Obviously, it will not do to take our ideal from the principle in nature; for the simple reason that (except for some human or divine theory), there is no principle in nature. For instance, the cheap anti-democrat of to-day will tell you solemnly that there is no equality in nature. He is right, but he does not see the logical addendum. There is no equality in nature; also there is no inequality in nature. Inequality, as much as equality, implies a standard of value. To read aristocracy into the anarchy of animals is just as sentimental as to read democracy into it. Both aristocracy and democracy are human ideals: the one saying that all men are valuable, the other that some men are more valuable. But nature does not say that cats are more valuable than mice; nature makes no remark on the subject. She does not even say that the cat is enviable or the mouse pitiable. We think the cat superior because we have (or most of us have) a particular philosophy to the effect that life is better than death. But if the mouse were a German pessimist mouse, he might not think that the cat had beaten him at all. He might think he had beaten the cat by getting to the grave first. Or he might feel that he had actually inflicted frightful punishment on the cat by keeping him alive. Just as a microbe might feel proud of spreading a pestilence, so the pessimistic mouse might exult to think that he was renewing in the cat the torture of conscious existence. It all depends on the philosophy of the mouse. You cannot even say that there is victory or superiority in nature unless you have some doctrine about what things are superior. You cannot even say that the cat scores unless there is a system of scoring. You cannot even say that the cat gets the best of it unless there is some best to be got.

We cannot, then, get the ideal itself from nature, and as we follow here the first and natural speculation, we will leave out (for the present) the idea of getting it from God. We must have our own vision. But the attempts of most moderns to express it are highly vague.

Some fall back simply on the clock: they talk as if mere passage through time brought some superiority; so that even a man of the first mental calibre carelessly uses the phrase that human morality is never up to date. How can anything be up to date?— a date has no character. How can one say that Christmas celebrations are not suitable to the twenty-fifth of a month? What the writer meant, of course, was that the majority is behind his favourite minority—or in front of it. Other vague modern people take refuge in material metaphors; in fact, this is the chief mark of vague modern people. Not daring to define their doctrine of what is good, they use physical figures of speech without stint or shame, and, what is worst of all, seem to think these cheap analogies are exquisitely spiritual and superior to the old morality. Thus they think it intellectual to talk about things being "high." It is at least the reverse of intellectual; it is a mere phrase from a steeple or a weathercock. "Tommy was a good boy" is a pure philosophical statement, worthy of Plato or Aquinas. "Tommy lived the higher life" is a gross metaphor from a ten-foot rule.

This, incidentally, is almost the whole weakness of Nietzsche, whom some are representing as a bold and strong thinker. No one will deny that he was a poetical and suggestive thinker; but he was quite the reverse of strong. He was not at all bold. He never put his own meaning before himself in bald abstract words: as did Aristotle and Calvin, and even Karl Marx, the hard, fearless men of thought. Nietzsche always escaped a question by a physical metaphor, like a cheery minor poet. He said, "beyond good and evil," because he had not the courage to say, "more good than good and evil," or, "more evil than good and evil." Had he faced his thought without metaphors, he would have seen that it was nonsense. So, when he describes his hero, he does not dare to say, "the purer man," or "the happier man," or "the sadder man," for all these are ideas; and ideas are alarming. He says "the upper man," or "over man," a physical metaphor from acrobats or alpine climbers. Nietzsche is truly a very timid thinker. He does not really know in the least what sort of man he wants evolution to produce. And if he does not know, certainly the ordinary evolutionists, who talk about things being "higher," do not know either.

Then again, some people fall back on sheer submission and sitting still. Nature is going to do something some day; nobody knows what, and nobody knows when. We have no reason for acting, and no reason for not acting. If anything happens it is right: if anything is prevented it was wrong. Again, some people try to anticipate nature by doing something, by doing anything. Because we may possibly grow wings they cut off their legs. Yet nature may be trying to make them centipedes for all they know.

Lastly, there is a fourth class of people who take whatever it is that they happen to want, and say that that is the ultimate aim of evolution. And these are the only sensible people. This is the only really healthy way with the word evolution, to work for what you want, and to call THAT evolution. The only intelligible sense that progress or advance can have among men, is that we have a definite vision, and that we wish to make the whole world like that vision. If you like to put it so, the essence of the doctrine is that what we have around us is the mere method and preparation for something that we have to create. This is not a world, but rather the material for a world. God has given us not so much the colours of a picture as the colours of a palette. But he has also given us a subject, a model, a fixed vision. We must be clear about what we want to paint. This adds a further principle to our previous list of principles. We have said we must be fond of this world, even in order to change it. We now add that we must be fond of another world (real or imaginary) in order to have something to change it to.

We need not debate about the mere words evolution or progress: personally I prefer to call it reform. For reform implies form. It implies that we are trying to shape the world in a particular image; to make it something that we see already in our minds. Evolution is a metaphor from mere automatic unrolling. Progress is a metaphor from merely walking along a road—very likely the wrong road. But reform is a metaphor for reasonable and determined men: it means that we see a certain thing out of shape and we mean to put it into shape. And we know what shape.

Now here comes in the whole collapse and huge blunder of our age. We have mixed up two different things, two opposite things. Progress should mean that we are always changing the world to suit the vision. Progress does mean (just now) that we are always changing the vision. It should mean that we are slow but sure in bringing justice and mercy among men: it does mean that we are very swift in doubting the desirability of justice and mercy: a wild page from any Prussian sophist makes men doubt it. Progress should mean that we are always walking towards the New Jerusalem. It does mean that the New Jerusalem is always walking away from us. We are not altering the real to suit the ideal. We are altering the ideal: it is easier.

Silly examples are always simpler; let us suppose a man wanted a particular kind of world; say, a blue world. He would have no cause to complain of the slightness or swiftness of his task; he might toil for a long time at the transformation; he could work away (in every sense) until all was blue. He could have heroic adventures; the putting of the last touches to a blue tiger. He could have fairy dreams; the dawn of a blue moon. But if he worked hard, that high-minded reformer would certainly (from his own point of view) leave the world better and bluer than he found it. If he altered a blade of grass to his favourite colour every day, he would get on slowly. But if he altered his favourite colour every day, he would not get on at all. If, after reading a fresh philosopher, he started to paint everything red or yellow, his work would be thrown away: there would be nothing to show except a few blue tigers walking about, specimens of his early bad manner. This is exactly the position of the average modern thinker. It will be said that this is avowedly a preposterous example. But it is literally the fact of recent history. The great and grave changes in our political civilization all belonged to the early nineteenth century, not to the later. They belonged to the black and white epoch when men believed fixedly in Toryism, in Protestantism, in Calvinism, in Reform, and not unfrequently in Revolution. And whatever each man believed in he hammered at steadily, without scepticism: and there was a time when the Established Church might have fallen, and the House of Lords nearly fell. It was because Radicals were wise enough to be constant and consistent; it was because Radicals were wise enough to be Conservative. But in the existing atmosphere there is not enough time and tradition in Radicalism to pull anything down. There is a great deal of truth in Lord Hugh Cecil's suggestion (made in a fine speech) that the era of change is over, and that ours is an era of conservation and repose. But probably it would pain Lord Hugh Cecil if he realized (what is certainly the case) that ours is only an age of conservation because it is an age of complete unbelief. Let beliefs fade fast and frequently, if you wish institutions to remain the same. The more the life of the mind is unhinged, the more the machinery of matter will be left to itself. The net result of all our political suggestions, Collectivism, Tolstoyanism, Neo-Feudalism, Communism, Anarchy, Scientific Bureaucracy—the plain fruit of all of them is that the Monarchy and the House of Lords will remain. The net result of all the new religions will be that the Church of England will not (for heaven knows how long) be disestablished. It was Karl Marx, Nietzsche, Tolstoy, Cunninghame Grahame, Bernard Shaw and Auberon Herbert, who between them, with bowed gigantic backs, bore up the throne of the Archbishop of Canterbury.

We may say broadly that free thought is the best of all the safeguards against freedom. Managed in a modern style the emancipation of the slave's mind is the best way of preventing the emancipation of the slave. Teach him to worry about whether he wants to be free, and he will not free himself. Again, it may be said that this instance is remote or extreme. But, again, it is exactly true of the men in the streets around us. It is true that the negro slave, being a debased barbarian, will probably have either a human affection of loyalty, or a human affection for liberty. But the man we see every day—the worker in Mr. Gradgrind's factory, the little clerk in Mr. Gradgrind's office—he is too mentally worried to believe in freedom. He is kept quiet with revolutionary literature. He is calmed and kept in his place by a constant succession of wild philosophies. He is a Marxian one day, a Nietzscheite the next day, a Superman (probably) the next day; and a slave every day. The only thing that remains after all the philosophies is the factory. The only man who gains by all the philosophies is Gradgrind. It would be worth his while to keep his commercial helotry supplied with sceptical literature. And now I come to think of it, of course, Gradgrind is famous for giving libraries. He shows his sense. All modern books are on his side. As long as the vision of heaven is always changing, the vision of earth will be exactly the same. No ideal will remain long enough to be realized, or even partly realized. The modern young man will never change his environment; for he will always change his mind.

This, therefore, is our first requirement about the ideal towards which progress is directed; it must be fixed. Whistler used to make many rapid studies of a sitter; it did not matter if he tore up twenty portraits. But it would matter if he looked up twenty times, and each time saw a new person sitting placidly for his portrait. So it does not matter (comparatively speaking) how often humanity fails to imitate its ideal; for then all its old failures are fruitful. But it does frightfully matter how often humanity changes its ideal; for then all its old failures are fruitless. The question therefore becomes this: How can we keep the artist discontented with his pictures while preventing him from being vitally discontented with his art? How can we make a man always dissatisfied with his work, yet always satisfied with working? How can we make sure that the portrait painter will throw the portrait out of window instead of taking the natural and more human course of throwing the sitter out of window?

A strict rule is not only necessary for ruling; it is also necessary for rebelling. This fixed and familiar ideal is necessary to any sort of revolution. Man will sometimes act slowly upon new ideas; but he will only act swiftly upon old ideas. If I am merely to float or fade or evolve, it may be towards something anarchic; but if I am to riot, it must be for something respectable. This is the whole weakness of certain schools of progress and moral evolution. They suggest that there has been a slow movement towards morality, with an imperceptible ethical change in every year or at every instant. There is only one great disadvantage in this theory. It talks of a slow movement towards justice; but it does not permit a swift movement. A man is not allowed to leap up and declare a certain state of things to be intrinsically intolerable. To make the matter clear, it is better to take a specific example. Certain of the idealistic vegetarians, such as Mr. Salt, say that the time has now come for eating no meat; by implication they assume that at one time it was right to eat meat, and they suggest (in words that could be quoted) that some day it may be wrong to eat milk and eggs. I do not discuss here the question of what is justice to animals. I only say that whatever is justice ought, under given conditions, to be prompt justice. If an animal is wronged, we ought to be able to rush to his rescue. But how can we rush if we are, perhaps, in advance of our time? How can we rush to catch a train which may not arrive for a few centuries? How can I denounce a man for skinning cats, if he is only now what I may possibly become in drinking a glass of milk? A splendid and insane Russian sect ran about taking all the cattle out of all the carts. How can I pluck up courage to take the horse out of my hansom-cab, when I do not know whether my evolutionary watch is only a little fast or the cabman's a little slow? Suppose I say to a sweater, "Slavery suited one stage of evolution." And suppose he answers, "And sweating suits this stage of evolution." How can I answer if there is no eternal test? If sweaters can be behind the current morality, why should not philanthropists be in front of it? What on earth is the current morality, except in its literal sense—the morality that is always running away?

Thus we may say that a permanent ideal is as necessary to the innovator as to the conservative; it is necessary whether we wish the king's orders to be promptly executed or whether we only wish the king to be promptly executed. The guillotine has many sins, but to do it justice there is nothing evolutionary about it. The favourite evolutionary argument finds its best answer in the axe. The Evolutionist says, "Where do you draw the line?" the Revolutionist answers, "I draw it HERE: exactly between your head and body." There must at any given moment be an abstract right and wrong if any blow is to be struck; there must be something eternal if there is to be anything sudden. Therefore for all intelligible human purposes, for altering things or for keeping things as they are, for founding a system for ever, as in China, or for altering it every month as in the early French Revolution, it is equally necessary that the vision should be a fixed vision. This is our first requirement.

When I had written this down, I felt once again the presence of something else in the discussion: as a man hears a church bell above the sound of the street. Something seemed to be saying, "My ideal at least is fixed; for it was fixed before the foundations of the world. My vision of perfection assuredly cannot be altered; for it is called Eden. You may alter the place to which you are going; but you cannot alter the place from which you have come. To the orthodox there must always be a case for revolution; for in the hearts of men God has been put under the feet of Satan. In the upper world hell once rebelled against heaven. But in this world heaven is rebelling against hell. For the orthodox there can always be a revolution; for a revolution is a restoration. At any instant you may strike a blow for the perfection which no man has seen since Adam. No unchanging custom, no changing evolution can make the original good any thing but good. Man may have had concubines as long as cows have had horns: still they are not a part of him if they are sinful. Men may have been under oppression ever since fish were under water; still they ought not to be, if oppression is sinful. The chain may seem as natural to the slave, or the paint to the harlot, as does the plume to the bird or the burrow to the fox; still they are not, if they are sinful. I lift my prehistoric legend to defy all your history. Your vision is not merely a fixture: it is a fact." I paused to note the new coincidence of Christianity: but I passed on.

I passed on to the next necessity of any ideal of progress. Some people (as we have said) seem to believe in an automatic and impersonal progress in the nature of things. But it is clear that no political activity can be encouraged by saying that progress is natural and inevitable; that is not a reason for being active, but rather a reason for being lazy. If we are bound to improve, we need not trouble to improve. The pure doctrine of progress is the best of all reasons for not being a progressive. But it is to none of these obvious comments that I wish primarily to call attention.

The only arresting point is this: that if we suppose improvement to be natural, it must be fairly simple. The world might conceivably be working towards one consummation, but hardly towards any particular arrangement of many qualities. To take our original simile: Nature by herself may be growing more blue; that is, a process so simple that it might be impersonal. But Nature cannot be making a careful picture made of many picked colours, unless Nature is personal. If the end of the world were mere darkness or mere light it might come as slowly and inevitably as dusk or dawn. But if the end of the world is to be a piece of elaborate and artistic chiaroscuro, then there must be design in it, either human or divine. The world, through mere time, might grow black like an old picture, or white like an old coat; but if it is turned into a particular piece of black and white art— then there is an artist.

If the distinction be not evident, I give an ordinary instance. We constantly hear a particularly cosmic creed from the modern humanitarians;

I use the word humanitarian in the ordinary sense, as meaning one who upholds the claims of all creatures against those of humanity. They suggest that through the ages we have been growing more and more humane, that is to say, that one after another, groups or sections of beings, slaves, children, women, cows, or what not, have been gradually admitted to mercy or to justice. They say that we once thought it right to eat men (we didn't); but I am not here concerned with their history, which is highly unhistorical. As a fact, anthropophagy is certainly a decadent thing, not a primitive one. It is much more likely that modern men will eat human flesh out of affectation than that primitive man ever ate it out of ignorance. I am here only following the outlines of their argument, which consists in maintaining that man has been progressively more lenient, first to citizens, then to slaves, then to animals, and then (presumably) to plants. I think it wrong to sit on a man. Soon, I shall think it wrong to sit on a horse. Eventually (I suppose) I shall think it wrong to sit on a chair. That is the drive of the argument. And for this argument it can be said that it is possible to talk of it in terms of evolution or inevitable progress. A perpetual tendency to touch fewer and fewer things might—one feels, be a mere brute unconscious tendency, like that of a species to produce fewer and fewer children. This drift may be really evolutionary, because it is stupid.

Darwinism can be used to back up two mad moralities, but it cannot be used to back up a single sane one. The kinship and competition of all living creatures can be used as a reason for being insanely cruel or insanely sentimental; but not for a healthy love of animals. On the evolutionary basis you may be inhumane, or you may be absurdly humane; but you cannot be human. That you and a tiger are one may be a reason for being tender to a tiger. Or it may be a reason for being as cruel as the tiger. It is one way to train the tiger to imitate you, it is a shorter way to imitate the tiger. But in neither case does evolution tell you how to treat a tiger reasonably, that is, to admire his stripes while avoiding his claws.

If you want to treat a tiger reasonably, you must go back to the garden of Eden. For the obstinate reminder continued to recur: only the supernatural has taken a sane view of Nature. The essence of all pantheism, evolutionism, and modern cosmic religion is really in this proposition: that Nature is our mother. Unfortunately, if you regard Nature as a mother, you discover that she is a step-mother. The main point of Christianity was this: that Nature is not our mother: Nature is our sister. We can be proud of her beauty, since we have the same father; but she has no authority over us; we have to admire, but not to imitate. This gives to the typically Christian pleasure in this earth a strange touch of lightness that is almost frivolity. Nature was a solemn mother to the worshippers of Isis and Cybele. Nature was a solemn mother to Wordsworth or to Emerson. But Nature is not solemn to Francis of Assisi or to George Herbert. To St. Francis, Nature is a sister, and even a younger sister: a little, dancing sister, to be laughed at as well as loved.

This, however, is hardly our main point at present; I have admitted it only in order to show how constantly, and as it were accidentally, the key would fit the smallest doors. Our main point is here, that if there be a mere trend of impersonal improvement in Nature, it must presumably be a simple trend towards some simple triumph. One can imagine that some automatic tendency in biology might work for giving us longer and longer noses. But the question is, do we want to have longer and longer noses? I fancy not; I believe that we most of us want to say to our noses, "thus far, and no farther; and here shall thy proud point be stayed:" we require a nose of such length as may ensure an interesting face. But we cannot imagine a mere biological trend towards producing interesting faces; because an interesting face is one particular arrangement of eyes, nose, and mouth, in a most complex relation to each other. Proportion cannot be a drift: it is either an accident or a design. So with the ideal of human morality and its relation to the humanitarians and the anti-humanitarians. It is conceivable that we are going more and more to keep our hands off things: not to drive horses; not to pick flowers. We may eventually be bound not to disturb a man's mind even by argument; not to disturb the sleep of birds even by coughing. The ultimate apotheosis would appear to be that of a man sitting quite still, nor daring to stir for fear of disturbing a fly, nor to eat for fear of incommoding a microbe. To so crude a consummation as that we might perhaps unconsciously drift. But do we want so crude a consummation? Similarly, we might unconsciously evolve along the opposite or Nietzschian line of development—superman crushing superman in one tower of tyrants until the universe is smashed up for fun. But do we want the universe smashed up for fun? Is it not quite clear that what we really hope for is one particular management and proposition of these two things; a certain amount of restraint and respect, a certain amount of energy and mastery? If our life is ever really as beautiful as a fairy-tale, we shall have to remember that all the beauty of a fairy-tale lies in this: that the prince has a wonder which just stops short of being fear. If he is afraid of the giant, there is an end of him; but also if he is not astonished at the giant, there is an end of the fairy-tale. The whole point depends upon his being at once humble enough to wonder, and haughty enough to defy. So our attitude to the giant of the world must not merely be increasing delicacy or increasing contempt: it must be one particular proportion of the two—which is exactly right. We must have in us enough reverence for all things outside us to make us tread fearfully on the grass. We must also have enough disdain for all things outside us, to make us, on due occasion, spit at the stars. Yet these two things (if we are to be good or happy) must be combined, not in any combination, but in one particular combination. The perfect happiness of men on the earth (if it ever comes) will not be a flat and solid thing, like the satisfaction of animals. It will be an exact and perilous balance; like that of a desperate romance. Man must have just enough faith in himself to have adventures, and just enough doubt of himself to enjoy them.

This, then, is our second requirement for the ideal of progress. First, it must be fixed; second, it must be composite. It must not (if it is to satisfy our souls) be the mere victory of some one thing swallowing up everything else, love or pride or peace or adventure; it must be a definite picture composed of these elements in their best proportion and relation. I am not concerned at this moment to deny that some such good culmination may be, by the constitution of things, reserved for the human race. I only point out that if this composite happiness is fixed for us it must be fixed by some mind; for only a mind can place the exact proportions of a composite happiness. If the beatification of the world is a mere work of nature, then it must be as simple as the freezing of the world, or the burning up of the world. But if the beatification of the world is not a work of nature but a work of art, then it involves an artist. And here again my contemplation was cloven by the ancient voice which said, "I could have told you all this a long time ago. If there is any certain progress it can only be my kind of progress, the progress towards a complete city of virtues and dominations where righteousness and peace contrive to kiss each other. An impersonal force might be leading you to a wilderness of perfect flatness or a peak of perfect height. But only a personal God can possibly be leading you (if, indeed, you are being led) to a city with just streets and architectural proportions, a city in which each of you can contribute exactly the right amount of your own colour to the many coloured coat of Joseph."

Twice again, therefore, Christianity had come in with the exact answer that I required. I had said, "The ideal must be fixed," and the Church had answered, "Mine is literally fixed, for it existed before anything else." I said secondly, "It must be artistically combined, like a picture"; and the Church answered, "Mine is quite literally a picture, for I know who painted it." Then I went on to the third thing, which, as it seemed to me, was needed for an Utopia or goal of progress. And of all the three it is infinitely the hardest to express. Perhaps it might be put thus: that we need watchfulness even in Utopia, lest we fall from Utopia as we fell from Eden.

We have remarked that one reason offered for being a progressive is that things naturally tend to grow better. But the only real reason for being a progressive is that things naturally tend to grow worse. The corruption in things is not only the best argument for being progressive; it is also the only argument against being conservative. The conservative theory would really be quite sweeping and unanswerable if it were not for this one fact. But all conservatism is based upon the idea that if you leave things alone you leave them as they are. But you do not. If you leave a thing alone you leave it to a torrent of change. If you leave a white post alone it will soon be a black post. If you particularly want it to be white you must be always painting it again; that is, you must be always having a revolution. Briefly, if you want the old white post you must have a new white post. But this which is true even of inanimate things is in a quite special and terrible sense true of all human things. An almost unnatural vigilance is really required of the citizen because of the horrible rapidity with which human institutions grow old. It is the custom in passing romance and journalism to talk of men suffering under old tyrannies. But, as a fact, men have almost always suffered under new tyrannies; under tyrannies that had been public liberties hardly twenty years before. Thus England went mad with joy over the patriotic monarchy of Elizabeth; and then (almost immediately afterwards) went mad with rage in the trap of the tyranny of Charles the First. So, again, in France the monarchy became intolerable, not just after it had been tolerated, but just after it had been adored. The son of Louis the well-beloved was Louis the guillotined. So in the same way in England in the nineteenth century the Radical manufacturer was entirely trusted as a mere tribune of the people, until suddenly we heard the cry of the Socialist that he was a tyrant eating the people like bread. So again, we have almost up to the last instant trusted the newspapers as organs of public opinion. Just recently some of us have seen (not slowly, but with a start) that they are obviously nothing of the kind. They are, by the nature of the case, the hobbies of a few rich men. We have not any need to rebel against antiquity; we have to rebel against novelty. It is the new rulers, the capitalist or the editor, who really hold up the modern world. There is no fear that a modern king will attempt to override the constitution; it is more likely that he will ignore the constitution and work behind its back; he will take no advantage of his kingly power; it is more likely that he will take advantage of his kingly powerlessness, of the fact that he is free from criticism and publicity. For the king is the most private person of our time. It will not be necessary for any one to fight again against the proposal of a censorship of the press. We do not need a censorship of the press. We have a censorship by the press.

This startling swiftness with which popular systems turn oppressive is the third fact for which we shall ask our perfect theory of progress to allow. It must always be on the look out for every privilege being abused, for every working right becoming a wrong. In this matter I am entirely on the side of the revolutionists. They are really right to be always suspecting human institutions; they are right not to put their trust in princes nor in any child of man. The chieftain chosen to be the friend of the people becomes the enemy of the people; the newspaper started to tell the truth now exists to prevent the truth being told. Here, I say, I felt that I was really at last on the side of the revolutionary. And then I caught my breath again: for I remembered that I was once again on the side of the orthodox.

Christianity spoke again and said: "I have always maintained that men were naturally backsliders; that human virtue tended of its own nature to rust or to rot; I have always said that human beings as such go wrong, especially happy human beings, especially proud and prosperous human beings. This eternal revolution, this suspicion sustained through centuries, you (being a vague modern) call the doctrine of progress. If you were a philosopher you would call it, as I do, the doctrine of original sin. You may call it the cosmic advance as much as you like; I call it what it is—the Fall."

I have spoken of orthodoxy coming in like a sword; here I confess it came in like a battle-axe. For really (when I came to think of it) Christianity is the only thing left that has any real right to question the power of the well-nurtured or the well-bred. I have listened often enough to Socialists, or even to democrats, saying that the physical conditions of the poor must of necessity make them mentally and morally degraded. I have listened to scientific men (and there are still scientific men not opposed to democracy) saying that if we give the poor healthier conditions vice and wrong will disappear. I have listened to them with a horrible attention, with a hideous fascination. For it was like watching a man energetically sawing from the tree the branch he is sitting on. If these happy democrats could prove their case, they would strike democracy dead. If the poor are thus utterly demoralized, it may or may not be practical to raise them. But it is certainly quite practical to disfranchise them. If the man with a bad bedroom cannot give a good vote, then the first and swiftest deduction is that he shall give no vote. The governing class may not unreasonably say: "It may take us some time to reform his bedroom. But if he is the brute you say, it will take him very little time to ruin our country. Therefore we will take your hint and not give him the chance." It fills me with horrible amusement to observe the way in which the earnest Socialist industriously lays the foundation of all aristocracy, expatiating blandly upon the evident unfitness of the poor to rule. It is like listening to somebody at an evening party apologising for entering without evening dress, and explaining that he had recently been intoxicated, had a personal habit of taking off his clothes in the street, and had, moreover, only just changed from prison uniform. At any moment, one feels, the host might say that really, if it was as bad as that, he need not come in at all. So it is when the ordinary Socialist, with a beaming face, proves that the poor, after their smashing experiences, cannot be really trustworthy. At any moment the rich may say, "Very well, then, we won't trust them," and bang the door in his face. On the basis of Mr. Blatchford's view of heredity and environment, the case for the aristocracy is quite overwhelming. If clean homes and clean air make clean souls, why not give the power (for the present at any rate) to those who undoubtedly have the clean air? If better conditions will make the poor more fit to govern themselves, why should not better conditions already make the rich more fit to govern them? On the ordinary environment argument the matter is fairly manifest. The comfortable class must be merely our vanguard in Utopia.

Is there any answer to the proposition that those who have had the best opportunities will probably be our best guides? Is there any answer to the argument that those who have breathed clean air had better decide for those who have breathed foul? As far as I know, there is only one answer, and that answer is Christianity. Only the Christian Church can offer any rational objection to a complete confidence in the rich. For she has maintained from the beginning that the danger was not in man's environment, but in man. Further, she has maintained that if we come to talk of a dangerous environment, the most dangerous environment of all is the commodious environment. I know that the most modern manufacture has been really occupied in trying to produce an abnormally large needle. I know that the most recent biologists have been chiefly anxious to discover a very small camel. But if we diminish the camel to his smallest, or open the eye of the needle to its largest—if, in short, we assume the words of Christ to have meant the very least that they could mean, His words must at the very least mean this— that rich men are not very likely to be morally trustworthy. Christianity even when watered down is hot enough to boil all modern society to rags. The mere minimum of the Church would be a deadly ultimatum to the world. For the whole modern world is absolutely based on the assumption, not that the rich are necessary (which is tenable), but that the rich are trustworthy, which (for a Christian) is not tenable. You will hear everlastingly, in all discussions about newspapers, companies, aristocracies, or party politics, this argument that the rich man cannot be bribed. The fact is, of course, that the rich man is bribed; he has been bribed already. That is why he is a rich man. The whole case for Christianity is that a man who is dependent upon the luxuries of this life is a corrupt man, spiritually corrupt, politically corrupt, financially corrupt. There is one thing that Christ and all the Christian saints have said with a sort of savage monotony. They have said simply that to be rich is to be in peculiar danger of moral wreck. It is not demonstrably un-Christian to kill the rich as violators of definable justice. It is not demonstrably un-Christian to crown the rich as convenient rulers of society. It is not certainly un-Christian to rebel against the rich or to submit to the rich. But it is quite certainly un-Christian to trust the rich, to regard the rich as more morally safe than the poor. A Christian may consistently say, "I respect that man's rank, although he takes bribes." But a Christian cannot say, as all modern men are saying at lunch and breakfast, "a man of that rank would not take bribes." For it is a part of Christian dogma that any man in any rank may take bribes. It is a part of Christian dogma; it also happens by a curious coincidence that it is a part of obvious human history. When people say that a man "in that position" would be incorruptible, there is no need to bring Christianity into the discussion. Was Lord Bacon a bootblack? Was the Duke of Marlborough a crossing sweeper? In the best Utopia, I must be prepared for the moral fall of any man in any position at any moment; especially for my fall from my position at this moment.

Much vague and sentimental journalism has been poured out to the effect that Christianity is akin to democracy, and most of it is scarcely strong or clear enough to refute the fact that the two things have often quarrelled. The real ground upon which Christianity and democracy are one is very much deeper. The one specially and peculiarly un-Christian idea is the idea of Carlyle— the idea that the man should rule who feels that he can rule. Whatever else is Christian, this is heathen. If our faith comments on government at all, its comment must be this—that the man should rule who does NOT think that he can rule. Carlyle's hero may say, "I will be king"; but the Christian saint must say "Nolo episcopari." If the great paradox of Christianity means anything, it means this— that we must take the crown in our hands, and go hunting in dry places and dark corners of the earth until we find the one man who feels himself unfit to wear it. Carlyle was quite wrong; we have not got to crown the exceptional man who knows he can rule. Rather we must crown the much more exceptional man who knows he can't.

Now, this is one of the two or three vital defences of working democracy. The mere machinery of voting is not democracy, though at present it is not easy to effect any simpler democratic method. But even the machinery of voting is profoundly Christian in this practical sense—that it is an attempt to get at the opinion of those who would be too modest to offer it. It is a mystical adventure; it is specially trusting those who do not trust themselves. That enigma is strictly peculiar to Christendom. There is nothing really humble about the abnegation of the Buddhist; the mild Hindoo is mild, but he is not meek. But there is something psychologically Christian about the idea of seeking for the opinion of the obscure rather than taking the obvious course of accepting the opinion of the prominent. To say that voting is particularly Christian may seem somewhat curious. To say that canvassing is Christian may seem quite crazy. But canvassing is very Christian in its primary idea. It is encouraging the humble; it is saying to the modest man, "Friend, go up higher." Or if there is some slight defect in canvassing, that is in its perfect and rounded piety, it is only because it may possibly neglect to encourage the modesty of the canvasser.

Aristocracy is not an institution: aristocracy is a sin; generally a very venial one. It is merely the drift or slide of men into a sort of natural pomposity and praise of the powerful, which is the most easy and obvious affair in the world.

It is one of the hundred answers to the fugitive perversion of modern "force" that the promptest and boldest agencies are also the most fragile or full of sensibility. The swiftest things are the softest things. A bird is active, because a bird is soft. A stone is helpless, because a stone is hard. The stone must by its own nature go downwards, because hardness is weakness. The bird can of its nature go upwards, because fragility is force. In perfect force there is a kind of frivolity, an airiness that can maintain itself in the air. Modern investigators of miraculous history have solemnly admitted that a characteristic of the great saints is their power of "levitation." They might go further; a characteristic of the great saints is their power of levity. Angels can fly because they can take themselves lightly. This has been always the instinct of Christendom, and especially the instinct of Christian art. Remember how Fra Angelico represented all his angels, not only as birds, but almost as butterflies. Remember how the most earnest mediaeval art was full of light and fluttering draperies, of quick and capering feet. It was the one thing that the modern Pre-raphaelites could not imitate in the real Pre-raphaelites. Burne-Jones could never recover the deep levity of the Middle Ages. In the old Christian pictures the sky over every figure is like a blue or gold parachute. Every figure seems ready to fly up and float about in the heavens. The tattered cloak of the beggar will bear him up like the rayed plumes of the angels. But the kings in their heavy gold and the proud in their robes of purple will all of their nature sink downwards, for pride cannot rise to levity or levitation. Pride is the downward drag of all things into an easy solemnity. One "settles down" into a sort of selfish seriousness; but one has to rise to a gay self-forgetfulness. A man "falls" into a brown study; he reaches up at a blue sky. Seriousness is not a virtue. It would be a heresy, but a much more sensible heresy, to say that seriousness is a vice. It is really a natural trend or lapse into taking one's self gravely, because it is the easiest thing to do. It is much easier to write a good TIMES leading article than a good joke in PUNCH. For solemnity flows out of men naturally; but laughter is a leap. It is easy to be heavy: hard to be light. Satan fell by the force of gravity.

Now, it is the peculiar honour of Europe since it has been Christian that while it has had aristocracy it has always at the back of its heart treated aristocracy as a weakness—generally as a weakness that must be allowed for. If any one wishes to appreciate this point, let him go outside Christianity into some other philosophical atmosphere. Let him, for instance, compare the classes of Europe with the castes of India. There aristocracy is far more awful, because it is far more intellectual. It is seriously felt that the scale of classes is a scale of spiritual values; that the baker is better than the butcher in an invisible and sacred sense. But no Christianity, not even the most ignorant or perverse, ever suggested that a baronet was better than a butcher in that sacred sense. No Christianity, however ignorant or extravagant, ever suggested that a duke would not be damned. In pagan society there may have been (I do not know) some such serious division between the free man and the slave. But in Christian society we have always thought the gentleman a sort of joke, though I admit that in some great crusades and councils he earned the right to be called a practical joke. But we in Europe never really and at the root of our souls took aristocracy seriously. It is only an occasional non-European alien (such as Dr. Oscar Levy, the only intelligent Nietzscheite) who can even manage for a moment to take aristocracy seriously. It may be a mere patriotic bias, though I do not think so, but it seems to me that the English aristocracy is not only the type, but is the crown and flower of all actual aristocracies; it has all the oligarchical virtues as well as all the defects. It is casual, it is kind, it is courageous in obvious matters; but it has one great merit that overlaps even these. The great and very obvious merit of the English aristocracy is that nobody could possibly take it seriously.

In short, I had spelled out slowly, as usual, the need for an equal law in Utopia; and, as usual, I found that Christianity had been there before me. The whole history of my Utopia has the same amusing sadness. I was always rushing out of my architectural study with plans for a new turret only to find it sitting up there in the sunlight, shining, and a thousand years old. For me, in the ancient and partly in the modern sense, God answered the prayer, "Prevent us, O Lord, in all our doings." Without vanity, I really think there was a moment when I could have invented the marriage vow (as an institution) out of my own head; but I discovered, with a sigh, that it had been invented already. But, since it would be too long a business to show how, fact by fact and inch by inch, my own conception of Utopia was only answered in the New Jerusalem, I will take this one case of the matter of marriage as indicating the converging drift, I may say the converging crash of all the rest.

When the ordinary opponents of Socialism talk about impossibilities and alterations in human nature they always miss an important distinction. In modern ideal conceptions of society there are some desires that are possibly not attainable: but there are some desires that are not desirable. That all men should live in equally beautiful houses is a dream that may or may not be attained. But that all men should live in the same beautiful house is not a dream at all; it is a nightmare. That a man should love all old women is an ideal that may not be attainable. But that a man should regard all old women exactly as he regards his mother is not only an unattainable ideal, but an ideal which ought not to be attained. I do not know if the reader agrees with me in these examples; but I will add the example which has always affected me most. I could never conceive or tolerate any Utopia which did not leave to me the liberty for which I chiefly care, the liberty to bind myself. Complete anarchy would not merely make it impossible to have any discipline or fidelity; it would also make it impossible to have any fun. To take an obvious instance, it would not be worth while to bet if a bet were not binding. The dissolution of all contracts would not only ruin morality but spoil sport. Now betting and such sports are only the stunted and twisted shapes of the original instinct of man for adventure and romance, of which much has been said in these pages. And the perils, rewards, punishments, and fulfilments of an adventure must be real, or the adventure is only a shifting and heartless nightmare. If I bet I must be made to pay, or there is no poetry in betting. If I challenge I must be made to fight, or there is no poetry in challenging. If I vow to be faithful I must be cursed when I am unfaithful, or there is no fun in vowing. You could not even make a fairy tale from the experiences of a man who, when he was swallowed by a whale, might find himself at the top of the Eiffel Tower, or when he was turned into a frog might begin to behave like a flamingo. For the purpose even of the wildest romance results must be real; results must be irrevocable. Christian marriage is the great example of a real and irrevocable result; and that is why it is the chief subject and centre of all our romantic writing. And this is my last instance of the things that I should ask, and ask imperatively, of any social paradise; I should ask to be kept to my bargain, to have my oaths and engagements taken seriously; I should ask Utopia to avenge my honour on myself.

All my modern Utopian friends look at each other rather doubtfully, for their ultimate hope is the dissolution of all special ties. But again I seem to hear, like a kind of echo, an answer from beyond the world. "You will have real obligations, and therefore real adventures when you get to my Utopia. But the hardest obligation and the steepest adventure is to get there."

VIII THE ROMANCE OF ORTHODOXY

It is customary to complain of the bustle and strenuousness of our epoch. But in truth the chief mark of our epoch is a profound laziness and fatigue; and the fact is that the real laziness is the cause of the apparent bustle. Take one quite external case; the streets are noisy with taxicabs and motorcars; but this is not due to human activity but to human repose. There would be less bustle if there were more activity, if people were simply walking about. Our world would be more silent if it were more strenuous. And this which is true of the apparent physical bustle is true also of the apparent bustle of the intellect. Most of the machinery of modern language is labour-saving machinery; and it saves mental labour very much more than it ought. Scientific phrases are used like scientific wheels and piston-rods to make swifter and smoother yet the path of the comfortable. Long words go rattling by us like long railway trains. We know they are carrying thousands who are too tired or too indolent to walk and think for themselves. It is a good exercise to try for once in a way to express any opinion one holds in words of one syllable. If you say "The social utility of the indeterminate sentence is recognized by all criminologists as a part of our sociological evolution towards a more humane and scientific view of punishment," you can go on talking like that for hours with hardly a movement of the gray matter inside your skull. But if you begin "I wish Jones to go to gaol and Brown to say when Jones shall come out," you will discover, with a thrill of horror, that you are obliged to think. The long words are not the hard words, it is the short words that are hard. There is much more metaphysical subtlety in the word "damn" than in the word "degeneration."

But these long comfortable words that save modern people the toil of reasoning have one particular aspect in which they are especially ruinous and confusing. This difficulty occurs when the same long word is used in different connections to mean quite different things. Thus, to take a well-known instance, the word "idealist" has one meaning as a piece of philosophy and quite another as a piece of moral rhetoric. In the same way the scientific materialists have had just reason to complain of people mixing up "materialist" as a term of cosmology with "materialist" as a moral taunt. So, to take a cheaper instance, the man who hates "progressives" in London always calls himself a "progressive" in South Africa.

A confusion quite as unmeaning as this has arisen in connection with the word "liberal" as applied to religion and as applied to politics and society. It is often suggested that all Liberals ought to be freethinkers, because they ought to love everything that is free. You might just as well say that all idealists ought to be High Churchmen, because they ought to love everything that is high. You might as well say that Low Churchmen ought to like Low Mass, or that Broad Churchmen ought to like broad jokes. The thing is a mere accident of words. In actual modern Europe a freethinker does not mean a man who thinks for himself. It means a man who, having thought for himself, has come to one particular class of conclusions, the material origin of phenomena, the impossibility of miracles, the improbability of personal immortality and so on. And none of these ideas are particularly liberal. Nay, indeed almost all these ideas are definitely illiberal, as it is the purpose of this chapter to show.

In the few following pages I propose to point out as rapidly as possible that on every single one of the matters most strongly insisted on by liberalisers of theology their effect upon social practice would be definitely illiberal. Almost every contemporary proposal to bring freedom into the church is simply a proposal to bring tyranny into the world. For freeing the church now does not even mean freeing it in all directions. It means freeing that peculiar set of dogmas loosely called scientific, dogmas of monism, of pantheism, or of Arianism, or of necessity. And every one of these (and we will take them one by one) can be shown to be the natural ally of oppression. In fact, it is a remarkable circumstance (indeed not so very remarkable when one comes to think of it) that most things are the allies of oppression. There is only one thing that can never go past a certain point in its alliance with oppression—and that is orthodoxy. I may, it is true, twist orthodoxy so as partly to justify a tyrant. But I can easily make up a German philosophy to justify him entirely.

Now let us take in order the innovations that are the notes of the new theology or the modernist church. We concluded the last chapter with the discovery of one of them. The very doctrine which is called the most old-fashioned was found to be the only safeguard of the new democracies of the earth. The doctrine seemingly most unpopular was found to be the only strength of the people. In short, we found that the only logical negation of oligarchy was in the affirmation of original sin. So it is, I maintain, in all the other cases.

I take the most obvious instance first, the case of miracles. For some extraordinary reason, there is a fixed notion that it is more liberal to disbelieve in miracles than to believe in them. Why, I cannot imagine, nor can anybody tell me. For some inconceivable cause a "broad" or "liberal" clergyman always means a man who wishes at least to diminish the number of miracles; it never means a man who wishes to increase that number. It always means a man who is free to disbelieve that Christ came out of His grave; it never means a man who is free to believe that his own aunt came out of her grave. It is common to find trouble in a parish because the parish priest cannot admit that St. Peter walked on water; yet how rarely do we find trouble in a parish because the clergyman says that his father walked on the Serpentine? And this is not because (as the swift secularist debater would immediately retort) miracles cannot be believed in our experience. It is not because "miracles do not happen," as in the dogma which Matthew Arnold recited with simple faith. More supernatural things are ALLEGED to have happened in our time than would have been possible eighty years ago. Men of science believe in such marvels much more than they did: the most perplexing, and even horrible, prodigies of mind and spirit are always being unveiled in modern psychology. Things that the old science at least would frankly have rejected as miracles are hourly being asserted by the new science. The only thing which is still old-fashioned enough to reject miracles is the New Theology. But in truth this notion that it is "free" to deny miracles has nothing to do with the evidence for or against them. It is a lifeless verbal prejudice of which the original life and beginning was not in the freedom of thought, but simply in the dogma of materialism. The man of the nineteenth century did not disbelieve in the Resurrection because his liberal Christianity allowed him to doubt it. He disbelieved in it because his very strict materialism did not allow him to believe it. Tennyson, a very typical nineteenth century man, uttered one of the instinctive truisms of his contemporaries when he said that there was faith in their honest doubt. There was indeed. Those words have a profound and even a horrible truth. In their doubt of miracles there was a faith in a fixed and godless fate; a deep and sincere faith in the incurable routine of the cosmos. The doubts of the agnostic were only the dogmas of the monist.

Of the fact and evidence of the supernatural I will speak afterwards. Here we are only concerned with this clear point; that in so far as the liberal idea of freedom can be said to be on either side in the discussion about miracles, it is obviously on the side of miracles. Reform or (in the only tolerable sense) progress means simply the gradual control of matter by mind. A miracle simply means the swift control of matter by mind. If you wish to feed the people, you may think that feeding them miraculously in the wilderness is impossible—but you cannot think it illiberal. If you really want poor children to go to the seaside, you cannot think it illiberal that they should go there on flying dragons; you can only think it unlikely. A holiday, like Liberalism, only means the liberty of man. A miracle only means the liberty of God. You may conscientiously deny either of them, but you cannot call your denial a triumph of the liberal idea. The Catholic Church believed that man and God both had a sort of spiritual freedom. Calvinism took away the freedom from man, but left it to God. Scientific materialism binds the Creator Himself; it chains up God as the Apocalypse chained the devil. It leaves nothing free in the universe. And those who assist this process are called the "liberal theologians."

This, as I say, is the lightest and most evident case. The assumption that there is something in the doubt of miracles akin to liberality or reform is literally the opposite of the truth. If a man cannot believe in miracles there is an end of the matter; he is not particularly liberal, but he is perfectly honourable and logical, which are much better things. But if he can believe in miracles, he is certainly the more liberal for doing so; because they mean first, the freedom of the soul, and secondly, its control over the tyranny of circumstance. Sometimes this truth is ignored in a singularly naive way, even by the ablest men. For instance, Mr. Bernard Shaw speaks with hearty old-fashioned contempt for the idea of miracles, as if they were a sort of breach of faith on the part of nature: he seems strangely unconscious that miracles are only the final flowers of his own favourite tree, the doctrine of the omnipotence of will. Just in the same way he calls the desire for immortality a paltry selfishness, forgetting that he has just called the desire for life a healthy and heroic selfishness. How can it be noble to wish to make one's life infinite and yet mean to wish to make it immortal? No, if it is desirable that man should triumph over the cruelty of nature or custom, then miracles are certainly desirable; we will discuss afterwards whether they are possible.

But I must pass on to the larger cases of this curious error; the notion that the "liberalising" of religion in some way helps the liberation of the world. The second example of it can be found in the question of pantheism—or rather of a certain modern attitude which is often called immanentism, and which often is Buddhism. But this is so much more difficult a matter that I must approach it with rather more preparation.

The things said most confidently by advanced persons to crowded audiences are generally those quite opposite to the fact; it is actually our truisms that are untrue. Here is a case. There is a phrase of facile liberality uttered again and again at ethical societies and parliaments of religion: "the religions of the earth differ in rites and forms, but they are the same in what they teach." It is false; it is the opposite of the fact. The religions of the earth do not greatly differ in rites and forms; they do greatly differ in what they teach. It is as if a man were to say, "Do not be misled by the fact that the CHURCH TIMES and the FREETHINKER look utterly different, that one is painted on vellum and the other carved on marble, that one is triangular and the other hectagonal; read them and you will see that they say the same thing." The truth is, of course, that they are alike in everything except in the fact that they don't say the same thing. An atheist stockbroker in Surbiton looks exactly like a Swedenborgian stockbroker in Wimbledon. You may walk round and round them and subject them to the most personal and offensive study without seeing anything Swedenborgian in the hat or anything particularly godless in the umbrella. It is exactly in their souls that they are divided. So the truth is that the difficulty of all the creeds of the earth is not as alleged in this cheap maxim: that they agree in meaning, but differ in machinery. It is exactly the opposite. They agree in machinery; almost every great religion on earth works with the same external methods, with priests, scriptures, altars, sworn brotherhoods, special feasts. They agree in the mode of teaching; what they differ about is the thing to be taught. Pagan optimists and Eastern pessimists would both have temples, just as Liberals and Tories would both have newspapers. Creeds that exist to destroy each other both have scriptures, just as armies that exist to destroy each other both have guns.

The great example of this alleged identity of all human religions is the alleged spiritual identity of Buddhism and Christianity. Those who adopt this theory generally avoid the ethics of most other creeds, except, indeed, Confucianism, which they like because it is not a creed. But they are cautious in their praises of Mahommedanism, generally confining themselves to imposing its morality only upon the refreshment of the lower classes. They seldom suggest the Mahommedan view of marriage (for which there is a great deal to be said), and towards Thugs and fetish worshippers their attitude may even be called cold. But in the case of the great religion of Gautama they feel sincerely a similarity.

Students of popular science, like Mr. Blatchford, are always insisting that Christianity and Buddhism are very much alike, especially Buddhism. This is generally believed, and I believed it myself until I read a book giving the reasons for it. The reasons were of two kinds: resemblances that meant nothing because they were common to all humanity, and resemblances which were not resemblances at all. The author solemnly explained that the two creeds were alike in things in which all creeds are alike, or else he described them as alike in some point in which they are quite obviously different. Thus, as a case of the first class, he said that both Christ and Buddha were called by the divine voice coming out of the sky, as if you would expect the divine voice to come out of the coal-cellar. Or, again, it was gravely urged that these two Eastern teachers, by a singular coincidence, both had to do with the washing of feet. You might as well say that it was a remarkable coincidence that they both had feet to wash. And the other class of similarities were those which simply were not similar. Thus this reconciler of the two religions draws earnest attention to the fact that at certain religious feasts the robe of the Lama is rent in pieces out of respect, and the remnants highly valued. But this is the reverse of a resemblance, for the garments of Christ were not rent in pieces out of respect, but out of derision; and the remnants were not highly valued except for what they would fetch in the rag shops. It is rather like alluding to the obvious connection between the two ceremonies of the sword: when it taps a man's shoulder, and when it cuts off his head. It is not at all similar for the man. These scraps of puerile pedantry would indeed matter little if it were not also true that the alleged philosophical resemblances are also of these two kinds, either proving too much or not proving anything. That Buddhism approves of mercy or of self-restraint is not to say that it is specially like Christianity; it is only to say that it is not utterly unlike all human existence. Buddhists disapprove in theory of cruelty or excess because all sane human beings disapprove in theory of cruelty or excess. But to say that Buddhism and Christianity give the same philosophy of these things is simply false. All humanity does agree that we are in a net of sin. Most of humanity agrees that there is some way out. But as to what is the way out, I do not think that there are two institutions in the universe which contradict each other so flatly as Buddhism and Christianity.

Even when I thought, with most other well-informed, though unscholarly, people, that Buddhism and Christianity were alike, there was one thing about them that always perplexed me; I mean the startling difference in their type of religious art. I do not mean in its technical style of representation, but in the things that it was manifestly meant to represent. No two ideals could be more opposite than a Christian saint in a Gothic cathedral and a Buddhist saint in a Chinese temple. The opposition exists at every point; but perhaps the shortest statement of it is that the Buddhist saint always has his eyes shut, while the Christian saint always has them very wide open. The Buddhist saint has a sleek and harmonious body, but his eyes are heavy and sealed with sleep. The mediaeval saint's body is wasted to its crazy bones, but his eyes are frightfully alive. There cannot be any real community of spirit between forces that produced symbols so different as that. Granted that both images are extravagances, are perversions of the pure creed, it must be a real divergence which could produce such opposite extravagances. The Buddhist is looking with a peculiar intentness inwards. The Christian is staring with a frantic intentness outwards. If we follow that clue steadily we shall find some interesting things.

A short time ago Mrs. Besant, in an interesting essay, announced that there was only one religion in the world, that all faiths were only versions or perversions of it, and that she was quite prepared to say what it was. According to Mrs. Besant this universal Church is simply the universal self. It is the doctrine that we are really all one person; that there are no real walls of individuality between man and man. If I may put it so, she does not tell us to love our neighbours; she tells us to be our neighbours. That is Mrs. Besant's thoughtful and suggestive description of the religion in which all men must find themselves in agreement. And I never heard of any suggestion in my life with which I more violently disagree. I want to love my neighbour not because he is I, but precisely because he is not I. I want to adore the world, not as one likes a looking-glass, because it is one's self, but as one loves a woman, because she is entirely different. If souls are separate love is possible. If souls are united love is obviously impossible. A man may be said loosely to love himself, but he can hardly fall in love with himself, or, if he does, it must be a monotonous courtship. If the world is full of real selves, they can be really unselfish selves.

But upon Mrs. Besant's principle the whole cosmos is only one enormously selfish person.

It is just here that Buddhism is on the side of modern pantheism and immanence. And it is just here that Christianity is on the side of humanity and liberty and love. Love desires personality; therefore love desires division. It is the instinct of Christianity to be glad that God has broken the universe into little pieces, because they are living pieces. It is her instinct to say "little children love one another" rather than to tell one large person to love himself. This is the intellectual abyss between Buddhism and Christianity; that for the Buddhist or Theosophist personality is the fall of man, for the Christian it is the purpose of God, the whole point of his cosmic idea. The world-soul of the Theosophists asks man to love it only in order that man may throw himself into it. But the divine centre of Christianity actually threw man out of it in order that he might love it. The oriental deity is like a giant who should have lost his leg or hand and be always seeking to find it; but the Christian power is like some giant who in a strange generosity should cut off his right hand, so that it might of its own accord shake hands with him. We come back to the same tireless note touching the nature of Christianity; all modern philosophies are chains which connect and fetter; Christianity is a sword which separates and sets free. No other philosophy makes God actually rejoice in the separation of the universe into living souls. But according to orthodox Christianity this separation between God and man is sacred, because this is eternal. That a man may love God it is necessary that there should be not only a God to be loved, but a man to love him. All those vague theosophical minds for whom the universe is an immense melting-pot are exactly the minds which shrink instinctively from that earthquake saying of our Gospels, which declare that the Son of God came not with peace but with a sundering sword. The saying rings entirely true even considered as what it obviously is; the statement that any man who preaches real love is bound to beget hate. It is as true of democratic fraternity as a divine love; sham love ends in compromise and common philosophy; but real love has always ended in bloodshed. Yet there is another and yet more awful truth behind the obvious meaning of this utterance of our Lord. According to Himself the Son was a sword separating brother and brother that they should for an aeon hate each other. But the Father also was a sword, which in the black beginning separated brother and brother, so that they should love each other at last.

This is the meaning of that almost insane happiness in the eyes of the mediaeval saint in the picture. This is the meaning of the sealed eyes of the superb Buddhist image. The Christian saint is happy because he has verily been cut off from the world; he is separate from things and is staring at them in astonishment. But why should the Buddhist saint be astonished at things?— since there is really only one thing, and that being impersonal can hardly be astonished at itself. There have been many pantheist poems suggesting wonder, but no really successful ones. The pantheist cannot wonder, for he cannot praise God or praise anything as really distinct from himself. Our immediate business here, however, is with the effect of this Christian admiration (which strikes outwards, towards a deity distinct from the worshipper) upon the general need for ethical activity and social reform. And surely its effect is sufficiently obvious. There is no real possibility of getting out of pantheism, any special impulse to moral action. For pantheism implies in its nature that one thing is as good as another; whereas action implies in its nature that one thing is greatly preferable to another. Swinburne in the high summer of his scepticism tried in vain to wrestle with this difficulty. In "Songs before Sunrise," written under the inspiration of Garibaldi and the revolt of Italy he proclaimed the newer religion and the purer God which should wither up all the priests of the world:

"What doest thou now Looking Godward to cry I am I, thou art thou, I am low, thou art high, I am thou that thou seekest to find him, find thou but thyself, thou art I."

Of which the immediate and evident deduction is that tyrants are as much the sons of God as Garibaldis; and that King Bomba of Naples having, with the utmost success, "found himself" is identical with the ultimate good in all things. The truth is that the western energy that dethrones tyrants has been directly due to the western theology that says "I am I, thou art thou." The same spiritual separation which looked up and saw a good king in the universe looked up and saw a bad king in Naples. The worshippers of Bomba's god dethroned Bomba. The worshippers of Swinburne's god have covered Asia for centuries and have never dethroned a tyrant. The Indian saint may reasonably shut his eyes because he is looking at that which is I and Thou and We and They and It. It is a rational occupation: but it is not true in theory and not true in fact that it helps the Indian to keep an eye on Lord Curzon. That external vigilance which has always been the mark of Christianity (the command that we should WATCH and pray) has expressed itself both in typical western orthodoxy and in typical western politics: but both depend on the idea of a divinity transcendent, different from ourselves, a deity that disappears. Certainly the most sagacious creeds may suggest that we should pursue God into deeper and deeper rings of the labyrinth of our own ego. But only we of Christendom have said that we should hunt God like an eagle upon the mountains: and we have killed all monsters in the chase.

Here again, therefore, we find that in so far as we value democracy and the self-renewing energies of the west, we are much more likely to find them in the old theology than the new. If we want reform, we must adhere to orthodoxy: especially in this matter (so much disputed in the counsels of Mr. R.J.Campbell), the matter of insisting on the immanent or the transcendent deity. By insisting specially on the immanence of God we get introspection, self-isolation, quietism, social indifference—Tibet. By insisting specially on the transcendence of God we get wonder, curiosity, moral and political adventure, righteous indignation—Christendom. Insisting that God is inside man, man is always inside himself. By insisting that God transcends man, man has transcended himself.

If we take any other doctrine that has been called old-fashioned we shall find the case the same. It is the same, for instance, in the deep matter of the Trinity. Unitarians (a sect never to be mentioned without a special respect for their distinguished intellectual dignity and high intellectual honour) are often reformers by the accident that throws so many small sects into such an attitude. But there is nothing in the least liberal or akin to reform in the substitution of pure monotheism for the Trinity. The complex God of the Athanasian Creed may be an enigma for the intellect; but He is far less likely to gather the mystery and cruelty of a Sultan than the lonely god of Omar or Mahomet. The god who is a mere awful unity is not only a king but an Eastern king. The HEART of humanity, especially of European humanity, is certainly much more satisfied by the strange hints and symbols that gather round the Trinitarian idea, the image of a council at which mercy pleads as well as justice, the conception of a sort of liberty and variety existing even in the inmost chamber of the world. For Western religion has always felt keenly the idea "it is not well for man to be alone." The social instinct asserted itself everywhere as when the Eastern idea of hermits was practically expelled by the Western idea of monks. So even asceticism became brotherly; and the Trappists were sociable even when they were silent. If this love of a living complexity be our test, it is certainly healthier to have the Trinitarian religion than the Unitarian. For to us Trinitarians (if I may say it with reverence)—to us God Himself is a society. It is indeed a fathomless mystery of theology, and even if I were theologian enough to deal with it directly, it would not be relevant to do so here. Suffice it to say here that this triple enigma is as comforting as wine and open as an English fireside; that this thing that bewilders the intellect utterly quiets the heart: but out of the desert, from the dry places and the dreadful suns, come the cruel children of the lonely God; the real Unitarians who with scimitar in hand have laid waste the world. For it is not well for God to be alone.

Again, the same is true of that difficult matter of the danger of the soul, which has unsettled so many just minds. To hope for all souls is imperative; and it is quite tenable that their salvation is inevitable. It is tenable, but it is not specially favourable to activity or progress. Our fighting and creative society ought rather to insist on the danger of everybody, on the fact that every man is hanging by a thread or clinging to a precipice. To say that all will be well anyhow is a comprehensible remark: but it cannot be called the blast of a trumpet. Europe ought rather to emphasize possible perdition; and Europe always has emphasized it. Here its highest religion is at one with all its cheapest romances. To the Buddhist or the eastern fatalist existence is a science or a plan, which must end up in a certain way. But to a Christian existence is a STORY, which may end up in any way. In a thrilling novel (that purely Christian product) the hero is not eaten by cannibals; but it is essential to the existence of the thrill that he MIGHT be eaten by cannibals. The hero must (so to speak) be an eatable hero. So Christian morals have always said to the man, not that he would lose his soul, but that he must take care that he didn't. In Christian morals, in short, it is wicked to call a man "damned": but it is strictly religious and philosophic to call him damnable.

All Christianity concentrates on the man at the cross-roads. The vast and shallow philosophies, the huge syntheses of humbug, all talk about ages and evolution and ultimate developments. The true philosophy is concerned with the instant. Will a man take this road or that?—that is the only thing to think about, if you enjoy thinking. The aeons are easy enough to think about, any one can think about them. The instant is really awful: and it is because our religion has intensely felt the instant, that it has in literature dealt much with battle and in theology dealt much with hell. It is full of DANGER, like a boy's book: it is at an immortal crisis. There is a great deal of real similarity between popular fiction and the religion of the western people. If you say that popular fiction is vulgar and tawdry, you only say what the dreary and well-informed say also about the images in the Catholic churches. Life (according to the faith) is very like a serial story in a magazine: life ends with the promise (or menace) "to be continued in our next." Also, with a noble vulgarity, life imitates the serial and leaves off at the exciting moment. For death is distinctly an exciting moment.

But the point is that a story is exciting because it has in it so strong an element of will, of what theology calls free-will. You cannot finish a sum how you like. But you can finish a story how you like. When somebody discovered the Differential Calculus there was only one Differential Calculus he could discover. But when Shakespeare killed Romeo he might have married him to Juliet's old nurse if he had felt inclined. And Christendom has excelled in the narrative romance exactly because it has insisted on the theological free-will. It is a large matter and too much to one side of the road to be discussed adequately here; but this is the real objection to that torrent of modern talk about treating crime as disease, about making a prison merely a hygienic environment like a hospital, of healing sin by slow scientific methods. The fallacy of the whole thing is that evil is a matter of active choice whereas disease is not. If you say that you are going to cure a profligate as you cure an asthmatic, my cheap and obvious answer is, "Produce the people who want to be asthmatics as many people want to be profligates." A man may lie still and be cured of a malady. But he must not lie still if he wants to be cured of a sin; on the contrary, he must get up and jump about violently. The whole point indeed is perfectly expressed in the very word which we use for a man in hospital; "patient" is in the passive mood; "sinner" is in the active. If a man is to be saved from influenza, he may be a patient. But if he is to be saved from forging, he must be not a patient but an IMPATIENT. He must be personally impatient with forgery. All moral reform must start in the active not the passive will.

Here again we reach the same substantial conclusion. In so far as we desire the definite reconstructions and the dangerous revolutions which have distinguished European civilization, we shall not discourage the thought of possible ruin; we shall rather encourage it. If we want, like the Eastern saints, merely to contemplate how right things are, of course we shall only say that they must go right. But if we particularly want to MAKE them go right, we must insist that they may go wrong.

Lastly, this truth is yet again true in the case of the common modern attempts to diminish or to explain away the divinity of Christ. The thing may be true or not; that I shall deal with before I end. But if the divinity is true it is certainly terribly revolutionary. That a good man may have his back to the wall is no more than we knew already; but that God could have his back to the wall is a boast for all insurgents for ever. Christianity is the only religion on earth that has felt that omnipotence made God incomplete. Christianity alone has felt that God, to be wholly God, must have been a rebel as well as a king. Alone of all creeds, Christianity has added courage to the virtues of the Creator. For the only courage worth calling courage must necessarily mean that the soul passes a breaking point—and does not break. In this indeed I approach a matter more dark and awful than it is easy to discuss; and I apologise in advance if any of my phrases fall wrong or seem irreverent touching a matter which the greatest saints and thinkers have justly feared to approach. But in that terrific tale of the Passion there is a distinct emotional suggestion that the author of all things (in some unthinkable way) went not only through agony, but through doubt. It is written, "Thou shalt not tempt the Lord thy God." No; but the Lord thy God may tempt Himself; and it seems as if this was what happened in Gethsemane. In a garden Satan tempted man: and in a garden God tempted God. He passed in some superhuman manner through our human horror of pessimism. When the world shook and the sun was wiped out of heaven, it was not at the crucifixion, but at the cry from the cross: the cry which confessed that God was forsaken of God. And now let the revolutionists choose a creed from all the creeds and a god from all the gods of the world, carefully weighing all the gods of inevitable recurrence and of unalterable power. They will not find another god who has himself been in revolt. Nay, (the matter grows too difficult for human speech,) but let the atheists themselves choose a god. They will find only one divinity who ever uttered their isolation; only one religion in which God seemed for an instant to be an atheist.

These can be called the essentials of the old orthodoxy, of which the chief merit is that it is the natural fountain of revolution and reform; and of which the chief defect is that it is obviously only an abstract assertion. Its main advantage is that it is the most adventurous and manly of all theologies. Its chief disadvantage is simply that it is a theology. It can always be urged against it that it is in its nature arbitrary and in the air. But it is not so high in the air but that great archers spend their whole lives in shooting arrows at it—yes, and their last arrows; there are men who will ruin themselves and ruin their civilization if they may ruin also this old fantastic tale. This is the last and most astounding fact about this faith; that its enemies will use any weapon against it, the swords that cut their own fingers, and the firebrands that burn their own homes. Men who begin to fight the Church for the sake of freedom and humanity end by flinging away freedom and humanity if only they may fight the Church.

This is no exaggeration; I could fill a book with the instances of it. Mr. Blatchford set out, as an ordinary Bible-smasher, to prove that Adam was guiltless of sin against God; in manoeuvring so as to maintain this he admitted, as a mere side issue, that all the tyrants, from Nero to King Leopold, were guiltless of any sin against humanity. I know a man who has such a passion for proving that he will have no personal existence after death that he falls back on the position that he has no personal existence now. He invokes Buddhism and says that all souls fade into each other; in order to prove that he cannot go to heaven he proves that he cannot go to Hartlepool. I have known people who protested against religious education with arguments against any education, saying that the child's mind must grow freely or that the old must not teach the young. I have known people who showed that there could be no divine judgment by showing that there can be no human judgment, even for practical purposes. They burned their own corn to set fire to the church; they smashed their own tools to smash it; any stick was good enough to beat it with, though it were the last stick of their own dismembered furniture. We do not admire, we hardly excuse, the fanatic who wrecks this world for love of the other. But what are we to say of the fanatic who wrecks this world out of hatred of the other? He sacrifices the very existence of humanity to the non-existence of God. He offers his victims not to the altar, but merely to assert the idleness of the altar and the emptiness of the throne. He is ready to ruin even that primary ethic by which all things live, for his strange and eternal vengeance upon some one who never lived at all.

And yet the thing hangs in the heavens unhurt. Its opponents only succeed in destroying all that they themselves justly hold dear. They do not destroy orthodoxy; they only destroy political and common courage sense. They do not prove that Adam was not responsible to God; how could they prove it? They only prove (from their premises) that the Czar is not responsible to Russia. They do not prove that Adam should not have been punished by God; they only prove that the nearest sweater should not be punished by men. With their oriental doubts about personality they do not make certain that we shall have no personal life hereafter; they only make certain that we shall not have a very jolly or complete one here. With their paralysing hints of all conclusions coming out wrong they do not tear the book of the Recording Angel; they only make it a little harder to keep the books of Marshall & Snelgrove. Not only is the faith the mother of all worldly energies, but its foes are the fathers of all worldly confusion. The secularists have not wrecked divine things; but the secularists have wrecked secular things, if that is any comfort to them. The Titans did not scale heaven; but they laid waste the world.

IX AUTHORITY AND THE ADVENTURER

The last chapter has been concerned with the contention that orthodoxy is not only (as is often urged) the only safe guardian of morality or order, but is also the only logical guardian of liberty, innovation and advance. If we wish to pull down the prosperous oppressor we cannot do it with the new doctrine of human perfectibility; we can do it with the old doctrine of Original Sin. If we want to uproot inherent cruelties or lift up lost populations we cannot do it with the scientific theory that matter precedes mind; we can do it with the supernatural theory that mind precedes matter. If we wish specially to awaken people to social vigilance and tireless pursuit of practise, we cannot help it much by insisting on the Immanent God and the Inner Light: for these are at best reasons for contentment; we can help it much by insisting on the transcendent God and the flying and escaping gleam; for that means divine discontent. If we wish particularly to assert the idea of a generous balance against that of a dreadful autocracy we shall instinctively be Trinitarian rather than Unitarian. If we desire European civilization to be a raid and a rescue, we shall insist rather that souls are in real peril than that their peril is ultimately unreal. And if we wish to exalt the outcast and the crucified, we shall rather wish to think that a veritable God was crucified, rather than a mere sage or hero. Above all, if we wish to protect the poor we shall be in favour of fixed rules and clear dogmas. The RULES of a club are occasionally in favour of the poor member. The drift of a club is always in favour of the rich one.

And now we come to the crucial question which truly concludes the whole matter. A reasonable agnostic, if he has happened to agree with me so far, may justly turn round and say, "You have found a practical philosophy in the doctrine of the Fall; very well. You have found a side of democracy now dangerously neglected wisely asserted in Original Sin; all right. You have found a truth in the doctrine of hell; I congratulate you. You are convinced that worshippers of a personal God look outwards and are progressive; I congratulate them. But even supposing that those doctrines do include those truths, why cannot you take the truths and leave the doctrines? Granted that all modern society is trusting the rich too much because it does not allow for human weakness; granted that orthodox ages have had a great advantage because (believing in the Fall) they did allow for human weakness, why cannot you simply allow for human weakness without believing in the Fall? If you have discovered that the idea of damnation represents a healthy idea of danger, why can you not simply take the idea of danger and leave the idea of damnation? If you see clearly the kernel of common-sense in the nut of Christian orthodoxy, why cannot you simply take the kernel and leave the nut? Why cannot you (to use that cant phrase of the newspapers which I, as a highly scholarly agnostic, am a little ashamed of using) why cannot you simply take what is good in Christianity, what you can define as valuable, what you can comprehend, and leave all the rest, all the absolute dogmas that are in their nature incomprehensible?" This is the real question; this is the last question; and it is a pleasure to try to answer it.

The first answer is simply to say that I am a rationalist. I like to have some intellectual justification for my intuitions. If I am treating man as a fallen being it is an intellectual convenience to me to believe that he fell; and I find, for some odd psychological reason, that I can deal better with a man's exercise of freewill if I believe that he has got it. But I am in this matter yet more definitely a rationalist. I do not propose to turn this book into one of ordinary Christian apologetics; I should be glad to meet at any other time the enemies of Christianity in that more obvious arena. Here I am only giving an account of my own growth in spiritual certainty. But I may pause to remark that the more I saw of the merely abstract arguments against the Christian cosmology the less I thought of them. I mean that having found the moral atmosphere of the Incarnation to be common sense, I then looked at the established intellectual arguments against the Incarnation and found them to be common nonsense. In case the argument should be thought to suffer from the absence of the ordinary apologetic I will here very briefly summarise my own arguments and conclusions on the purely objective or scientific truth of the matter.

If I am asked, as a purely intellectual question, why I believe in Christianity, I can only answer, "For the same reason that an intelligent agnostic disbelieves in Christianity." I believe in it quite rationally upon the evidence. But the evidence in my case, as in that of the intelligent agnostic, is not really in this or that alleged demonstration; it is in an enormous accumulation of small but unanimous facts. The secularist is not to be blamed because his objections to Christianity are miscellaneous and even scrappy; it is precisely such scrappy evidence that does convince the mind. I mean that a man may well be less convinced of a philosophy from four books, than from one book, one battle, one landscape, and one old friend. The very fact that the things are of different kinds increases the importance of the fact that they all point to one conclusion. Now, the non-Christianity of the average educated man to-day is almost always, to do him justice, made up of these loose but living experiences. I can only say that my evidences for Christianity are of the same vivid but varied kind as his evidences against it. For when I look at these various anti-Christian truths, I simply discover that none of them are true. I discover that the true tide and force of all the facts flows the other way. Let us take cases. Many a sensible modern man must have abandoned Christianity under the pressure of three such converging convictions as these: first, that men, with their shape, structure, and sexuality, are, after all, very much like beasts, a mere variety of the animal kingdom; second, that primeval religion arose in ignorance and fear; third, that priests have blighted societies with bitterness and gloom. Those three anti-Christian arguments are very different; but they are all quite logical and legitimate; and they all converge. The only objection to them (I discover) is that they are all untrue. If you leave off looking at books about beasts and men, if you begin to look at beasts and men then (if you have any humour or imagination, any sense of the frantic or the farcical) you will observe that the startling thing is not how like man is to the brutes, but how unlike he is. It is the monstrous scale of his divergence that requires an explanation. That man and brute are like is, in a sense, a truism; but that being so like they should then be so insanely unlike, that is the shock and the enigma. That an ape has hands is far less interesting to the philosopher than the fact that having hands he does next to nothing with them; does not play knuckle-bones or the violin; does not carve marble or carve mutton. People talk of barbaric architecture and debased art. But elephants do not build colossal temples of ivory even in a roccoco style; camels do not paint even bad pictures, though equipped with the material of many camel's-hair brushes. Certain modern dreamers say that ants and bees have a society superior to ours. They have, indeed, a civilization; but that very truth only reminds us that it is an inferior civilization. Who ever found an ant-hill decorated with the statues of celebrated ants? Who has seen a bee-hive carved with the images of gorgeous queens of old? No; the chasm between man and other creatures may have a natural explanation, but it is a chasm. We talk of wild animals; but man is the only wild animal. It is man that has broken out. All other animals are tame animals; following the rugged respectability of the tribe or type. All other animals are domestic animals; man alone is ever undomestic, either as a profligate or a monk. So that this first superficial reason for materialism is, if anything, a reason for its opposite; it is exactly where biology leaves off that all religion begins.

It would be the same if I examined the second of the three chance rationalist arguments; the argument that all that we call divine began in some darkness and terror. When I did attempt to examine the foundations of this modern idea I simply found that there were none. Science knows nothing whatever about pre-historic man; for the excellent reason that he is pre-historic. A few professors choose to conjecture that such things as human sacrifice were once innocent and general and that they gradually dwindled; but there is no direct evidence of it, and the small amount of indirect evidence is very much the other way. In the earliest legends we have, such as the tales of Isaac and of Iphigenia, human sacrifice is not introduced as something old, but rather as something new; as a strange and frightful exception darkly demanded by the gods. History says nothing; and legends all say that the earth was kinder in its earliest time. There is no tradition of progress; but the whole human race has a tradition of the Fall. Amusingly enough, indeed, the very dissemination of this idea is used against its authenticity. Learned men literally say that this pre-historic calamity cannot be true because every race of mankind remembers it. I cannot keep pace with these paradoxes.

And if we took the third chance instance, it would be the same; the view that priests darken and embitter the world. I look at the world and simply discover that they don't. Those countries in Europe which are still influenced by priests, are exactly the countries where there is still singing and dancing and coloured dresses and art in the open-air. Catholic doctrine and discipline may be walls; but they are the walls of a playground. Christianity is the only frame which has preserved the pleasure of Paganism. We might fancy some children playing on the flat grassy top of some tall island in the sea. So long as there was a wall round the cliff's edge they could fling themselves into every frantic game and make the place the noisiest of nurseries. But the walls were knocked down, leaving the naked peril of the precipice. They did not fall over; but when their friends returned to them they were all huddled in terror in the centre of the island; and their song had ceased.

Thus these three facts of experience, such facts as go to make an agnostic, are, in this view, turned totally round. I am left saying, "Give me an explanation, first, of the towering eccentricity of man among the brutes; second, of the vast human tradition of some ancient happiness; third, of the partial perpetuation of such pagan joy in the countries of the Catholic Church." One explanation, at any rate, covers all three: the theory that twice was the natural order interrupted by some explosion or revelation such as people now call "psychic." Once Heaven came upon the earth with a power or seal called the image of God, whereby man took command of Nature; and once again (when in empire after empire men had been found wanting) Heaven came to save mankind in the awful shape of a man. This would explain why the mass of men always look backwards; and why the only corner where they in any sense look forwards is the little continent where Christ has His Church. I know it will be said that Japan has become progressive. But how can this be an answer when even in saying "Japan has become progressive," we really only mean, "Japan has become European"? But I wish here not so much to insist on my own explanation as to insist on my original remark. I agree with the ordinary unbelieving man in the street in being guided by three or four odd facts all pointing to something; only when I came to look at the facts I always found they pointed to something else.

I have given an imaginary triad of such ordinary anti-Christian arguments; if that be too narrow a basis I will give on the spur of the moment another. These are the kind of thoughts which in combination create the impression that Christianity is something weak and diseased. First, for instance, that Jesus was a gentle creature, sheepish and unworldly, a mere ineffectual appeal to the world; second, that Christianity arose and flourished in the dark ages of ignorance, and that to these the Church would drag us back; third, that the people still strongly religious or (if you will) superstitious—such people as the Irish—are weak, unpractical, and behind the times. I only mention these ideas to affirm the same thing: that when I looked into them independently I found, not that the conclusions were unphilosophical, but simply that the facts were not facts. Instead of looking at books and pictures about the New Testament I looked at the New Testament. There I found an account, not in the least of a person with his hair parted in the middle or his hands clasped in appeal, but of an extraordinary being with lips of thunder and acts of lurid decision, flinging down tables, casting out devils, passing with the wild secrecy of the wind from mountain isolation to a sort of dreadful demagogy; a being who often acted like an angry god— and always like a god. Christ had even a literary style of his own, not to be found, I think, elsewhere; it consists of an almost furious use of the A FORTIORI. His "how much more" is piled one upon another like castle upon castle in the clouds. The diction used ABOUT Christ has been, and perhaps wisely, sweet and submissive. But the diction used by Christ is quite curiously gigantesque; it is full of camels leaping through needles and mountains hurled into the sea. Morally it is equally terrific; he called himself a sword of slaughter, and told men to buy swords if they sold their coats for them. That he used other even wilder words on the side of non-resistance greatly increases the mystery; but it also, if anything, rather increases the violence. We cannot even explain it by calling such a being insane; for insanity is usually along one consistent channel. The maniac is generally a monomaniac. Here we must remember the difficult definition of Christianity already given; Christianity is a superhuman paradox whereby two opposite passions may blaze beside each other. The one explanation of the Gospel language that does explain it, is that it is the survey of one who from some supernatural height beholds some more startling synthesis.

I take in order the next instance offered: the idea that Christianity belongs to the Dark Ages. Here I did not satisfy myself with reading modern generalisations; I read a little history. And in history I found that Christianity, so far from belonging to the Dark Ages, was the one path across the Dark Ages that was not dark. It was a shining bridge connecting two shining civilizations. If any one says that the faith arose in ignorance and savagery the answer is simple: it didn't. It arose in the Mediterranean civilization in the full summer of the Roman Empire. The world was swarming with sceptics, and pantheism was as plain as the sun, when Constantine nailed the cross to the mast. It is perfectly true that afterwards the ship sank; but it is far more extraordinary that the ship came up again: repainted and glittering, with the cross still at the top. This is the amazing thing the religion did: it turned a sunken ship into a submarine. The ark lived under the load of waters; after being buried under the debris of dynasties and clans, we arose and remembered Rome. If our faith had been a mere fad of the fading empire, fad would have followed fad in the twilight, and if the civilization ever re-emerged (and many such have never re-emerged) it would have been under some new barbaric flag. But the Christian Church was the last life of the old society and was also the first life of the new. She took the people who were forgetting how to make an arch and she taught them to invent the Gothic arch. In a word, the most absurd thing that could be said of the Church is the thing we have all heard said of it. How can we say that the Church wishes to bring us back into the Dark Ages? The Church was the only thing that ever brought us out of them.

I added in this second trinity of objections an idle instance taken from those who feel such people as the Irish to be weakened or made stagnant by superstition. I only added it because this is a peculiar case of a statement of fact that turns out to be a statement of falsehood. It is constantly said of the Irish that they are impractical. But if we refrain for a moment from looking at what is said about them and look at what is DONE about them, we shall see that the Irish are not only practical, but quite painfully successful. The poverty of their country, the minority of their members are simply the conditions under which they were asked to work; but no other group in the British Empire has done so much with such conditions. The Nationalists were the only minority that ever succeeded in twisting the whole British Parliament sharply out of its path. The Irish peasants are the only poor men in these islands who have forced their masters to disgorge. These people, whom we call priest-ridden, are the only Britons who will not be squire-ridden. And when I came to look at the actual Irish character, the case was the same. Irishmen are best at the specially HARD professions—the trades of iron, the lawyer, and the soldier. In all these cases, therefore, I came back to the same conclusion: the sceptic was quite right to go by the facts, only he had not looked at the facts. The sceptic is too credulous; he believes in newspapers or even in encyclopedias. Again the three questions left me with three very antagonistic questions. The average sceptic wanted to know how I explained the namby-pamby note in the Gospel, the connection of the creed with mediaeval darkness and the political impracticability of the Celtic Christians. But I wanted to ask, and to ask with an earnestness amounting to urgency, "What is this incomparable energy which appears first in one walking the earth like a living judgment and this energy which can die with a dying civilization and yet force it to a resurrection from the dead; this energy which last of all can inflame a bankrupt peasantry with so fixed a faith in justice that they get what they ask, while others go empty away; so that the most helpless island of the Empire can actually help itself?"

There is an answer: it is an answer to say that the energy is truly from outside the world; that it is psychic, or at least one of the results of a real psychical disturbance. The highest gratitude and respect are due to the great human civilizations such as the old Egyptian or the existing Chinese. Nevertheless it is no injustice for them to say that only modern Europe has exhibited incessantly a power of self-renewal recurring often at the shortest intervals and descending to the smallest facts of building or costume. All other societies die finally and with dignity. We die daily. We are always being born again with almost indecent obstetrics. It is hardly an exaggeration to say that there is in historic Christendom a sort of unnatural life: it could be explained as a supernatural life. It could be explained as an awful galvanic life working in what would have been a corpse. For our civilization OUGHT to have died, by all parallels, by all sociological probability, in the Ragnorak of the end of Rome. That is the weird inspiration of our estate: you and I have no business to be here at all. We are all REVENANTS; all living Christians are dead pagans walking about. Just as Europe was about to be gathered in silence to Assyria and Babylon, something entered into its body. And Europe has had a strange life—it is not too much to say that it has had the JUMPS— ever since.

I have dealt at length with such typical triads of doubt in order to convey the main contention—that my own case for Christianity is rational; but it is not simple. It is an accumulation of varied facts, like the attitude of the ordinary agnostic. But the ordinary agnostic has got his facts all wrong. He is a non-believer for a multitude of reasons; but they are untrue reasons. He doubts because the Middle Ages were barbaric, but they weren't; because Darwinism is demonstrated, but it isn't; because miracles do not happen, but they do; because monks were lazy, but they were very industrious; because nuns are unhappy, but they are particularly cheerful; because Christian art was sad and pale, but it was picked out in peculiarly bright colours and gay with gold; because modern science is moving away from the supernatural, but it isn't, it is moving towards the supernatural with the rapidity of a railway train.

But among these million facts all flowing one way there is, of course, one question sufficiently solid and separate to be treated briefly, but by itself; I mean the objective occurrence of the supernatural. In another chapter I have indicated the fallacy of the ordinary supposition that the world must be impersonal because it is orderly. A person is just as likely to desire an orderly thing as a disorderly thing. But my own positive conviction that personal creation is more conceivable than material fate, is, I admit, in a sense, undiscussable. I will not call it a faith or an intuition, for those words are mixed up with mere emotion, it is strictly an intellectual conviction; but it is a PRIMARY intellectual conviction like the certainty of self of the good of living. Any one who likes, therefore, may call my belief in God merely mystical; the phrase is not worth fighting about. But my belief that miracles have happened in human history is not a mystical belief at all; I believe in them upon human evidences as I do in the discovery of America. Upon this point there is a simple logical fact that only requires to be stated and cleared up. Somehow or other an extraordinary idea has arisen that the disbelievers in miracles consider them coldly and fairly, while believers in miracles accept them only in connection with some dogma. The fact is quite the other way. The believers in miracles accept them (rightly or wrongly) because they have evidence for them. The disbelievers in miracles deny them (rightly or wrongly) because they have a doctrine against them. The open, obvious, democratic thing is to believe an old apple-woman when she bears testimony to a miracle, just as you believe an old apple-woman when she bears testimony to a murder. The plain, popular course is to trust the peasant's word about the ghost exactly as far as you trust the peasant's word about the landlord. Being a peasant he will probably have a great deal of healthy agnosticism about both. Still you could fill the British Museum with evidence uttered by the peasant, and given in favour of the ghost. If it comes to human testimony there is a choking cataract of human testimony in favour of the supernatural. If you reject it, you can only mean one of two things. You reject the peasant's story about the ghost either because the man is a peasant or because the story is a ghost story. That is, you either deny the main principle of democracy, or you affirm the main principle of materialism— the abstract impossibility of miracle. You have a perfect right to do so; but in that case you are the dogmatist. It is we Christians who accept all actual evidence—it is you rationalists who refuse actual evidence being constrained to do so by your creed. But I am not constrained by any creed in the matter, and looking impartially into certain miracles of mediaeval and modern times, I have come to the conclusion that they occurred. All argument against these plain facts is always argument in a circle. If I say, "Mediaeval documents attest certain miracles as much as they attest certain battles," they answer, "But mediaevals were superstitious"; if I want to know in what they were superstitious, the only ultimate answer is that they believed in the miracles. If I say "a peasant saw a ghost," I am told, "But peasants are so credulous." If I ask, "Why credulous?" the only answer is—that they see ghosts. Iceland is impossible because only stupid sailors have seen it; and the sailors are only stupid because they say they have seen Iceland. It is only fair to add that there is another argument that the unbeliever may rationally use against miracles, though he himself generally forgets to use it.

He may say that there has been in many miraculous stories a notion of spiritual preparation and acceptance: in short, that the miracle could only come to him who believed in it. It may be so, and if it is so how are we to test it? If we are inquiring whether certain results follow faith, it is useless to repeat wearily that (if they happen) they do follow faith. If faith is one of the conditions, those without faith have a most healthy right to laugh. But they have no right to judge. Being a believer may be, if you like, as bad as being drunk; still if we were extracting psychological facts from drunkards, it would be absurd to be always taunting them with having been drunk. Suppose we were investigating whether angry men really saw a red mist before their eyes. Suppose sixty excellent householders swore that when angry they had seen this crimson cloud: surely it would be absurd to answer "Oh, but you admit you were angry at the time." They might reasonably rejoin (in a stentorian chorus), "How the blazes could we discover, without being angry, whether angry people see red?" So the saints and ascetics might rationally reply, "Suppose that the question is whether believers can see visions—even then, if you are interested in visions it is no point to object to believers." You are still arguing in a circle—in that old mad circle with which this book began.

The question of whether miracles ever occur is a question of common sense and of ordinary historical imagination: not of any final physical experiment. One may here surely dismiss that quite brainless piece of pedantry which talks about the need for "scientific conditions" in connection with alleged spiritual phenomena. If we are asking whether a dead soul can communicate with a living it is ludicrous to insist that it shall be under conditions in which no two living souls in their senses would seriously communicate with each other. The fact that ghosts prefer darkness no more disproves the existence of ghosts than the fact that lovers prefer darkness disproves the existence of love. If you choose to say, "I will believe that Miss Brown called her fiance a periwinkle or, any other endearing term, if she will repeat the word before seventeen psychologists," then I shall reply, "Very well, if those are your conditions, you will never get the truth, for she certainly will not say it." It is just as unscientific as it is unphilosophical to be surprised that in an unsympathetic atmosphere certain extraordinary sympathies do not arise. It is as if I said that I could not tell if there was a fog because the air was not clear enough; or as if I insisted on perfect sunlight in order to see a solar eclipse.

As a common-sense conclusion, such as those to which we come about sex or about midnight (well knowing that many details must in their own nature be concealed) I conclude that miracles do happen. I am forced to it by a conspiracy of facts: the fact that the men who encounter elves or angels are not the mystics and the morbid dreamers, but fishermen, farmers, and all men at once coarse and cautious; the fact that we all know men who testify to spiritualistic incidents but are not spiritualists, the fact that science itself admits such things more and more every day. Science will even admit the Ascension if you call it Levitation, and will very likely admit the Resurrection when it has thought of another word for it. I suggest the Regalvanisation. But the strongest of all is the dilemma above mentioned, that these supernatural things are never denied except on the basis either of anti-democracy or of materialist dogmatism—I may say materialist mysticism. The sceptic always takes one of the two positions; either an ordinary man need not be believed, or an extraordinary event must not be believed. For I hope we may dismiss the argument against wonders attempted in the mere recapitulation of frauds, of swindling mediums or trick miracles. That is not an argument at all, good or bad. A false ghost disproves the reality of ghosts exactly as much as a forged banknote disproves the existence of the Bank of England— if anything, it proves its existence.

Given this conviction that the spiritual phenomena do occur (my evidence for which is complex but rational), we then collide with one of the worst mental evils of the age. The greatest disaster of the nineteenth century was this: that men began to use the word "spiritual" as the same as the word "good." They thought that to grow in refinement and uncorporeality was to grow in virtue. When scientific evolution was announced, some feared that it would encourage mere animality. It did worse: it encouraged mere spirituality. It taught men to think that so long as they were passing from the ape they were going to the angel. But you can pass from the ape and go to the devil. A man of genius, very typical of that time of bewilderment, expressed it perfectly. Benjamin Disraeli was right when he said he was on the side of the angels. He was indeed; he was on the side of the fallen angels. He was not on the side of any mere appetite or animal brutality; but he was on the side of all the imperialism of the princes of the abyss; he was on the side of arrogance and mystery, and contempt of all obvious good. Between this sunken pride and the towering humilities of heaven there are, one must suppose, spirits of shapes and sizes. Man, in encountering them, must make much the same mistakes that he makes in encountering any other varied types in any other distant continent. It must be hard at first to know who is supreme and who is subordinate. If a shade arose from the under world, and stared at Piccadilly, that shade would not quite understand the idea of an ordinary closed carriage. He would suppose that the coachman on the box was a triumphant conqueror, dragging behind him a kicking and imprisoned captive. So, if we see spiritual facts for the first time, we may mistake who is uppermost. It is not enough to find the gods; they are obvious;

we must find God, the real chief of the gods. We must have a long historic experience in supernatural phenomena— in order to discover which are really natural. In this light I find the history of Christianity, and even of its Hebrew origins, quite practical and clear. It does not trouble me to be told that the Hebrew god was one among many. I know he was, without any research to tell me so. Jehovah and Baal looked equally important, just as the sun and the moon looked the same size. It is only slowly that we learn that the sun is immeasurably our master, and the small moon only our satellite. Believing that there is a world of spirits, I shall walk in it as I do in the world of men, looking for the thing that I like and think good. Just as I should seek in a desert for clean water, or toil at the North Pole to make a comfortable fire, so I shall search the land of void and vision until I find something fresh like water, and comforting like fire; until I find some place in eternity, where I am literally at home. And there is only one such place to be found.

I have now said enough to show (to any one to whom such an explanation is essential) that I have in the ordinary arena of apologetics, a ground of belief. In pure records of experiment (if these be taken democratically without contempt or favour) there is evidence first, that miracles happen, and second that the nobler miracles belong to our tradition. But I will not pretend that this curt discussion is my real reason for accepting Christianity instead of taking the moral good of Christianity as I should take it out of Confucianism.

I have another far more solid and central ground for submitting to it as a faith, instead of merely picking up hints from it as a scheme. And that is this: that the Christian Church in its practical relation to my soul is a living teacher, not a dead one. It not only certainly taught me yesterday, but will almost certainly teach me to-morrow. Once I saw suddenly the meaning of the shape of the cross; some day I may see suddenly the meaning of the shape of the mitre. One fine morning I saw why windows were pointed; some fine morning I may see why priests were shaven. Plato has told you a truth; but Plato is dead. Shakespeare has startled you with an image; but Shakespeare will not startle you with any more. But imagine what it would be to live with such men still living, to know that Plato might break out with an original lecture to-morrow, or that at any moment Shakespeare might shatter everything with a single song. The man who lives in contact with what he believes to be a living Church is a man always expecting to meet Plato and Shakespeare to-morrow at breakfast. He is always expecting to see some truth that he has never seen before. There is one only other parallel to this position; and that is the parallel of the life in which we all began. When your father told you, walking about the garden, that bees stung or that roses smelt sweet, you did not talk of taking the best out of his philosophy. When the bees stung you, you did not call it an entertaining coincidence. When the rose smelt sweet you did not say "My father is a rude, barbaric symbol, enshrining (perhaps unconsciously) the deep delicate truths that flowers smell." No: you believed your father, because you had found him to be a living fountain of facts, a thing that really knew more than you; a thing that would tell you truth to-morrow, as well as to-day. And if this was true of your father, it was even truer of your mother; at least it was true of mine, to whom this book is dedicated. Now, when society is in a rather futile fuss about the subjection of women, will no one say how much every man owes to the tyranny and privilege of women, to the fact that they alone rule education until education becomes futile: for a boy is only sent to be taught at school when it is too late to teach him anything. The real thing has been done already, and thank God it is nearly always done by women. Every man is womanised, merely by being born. They talk of the masculine woman; but every man is a feminised man. And if ever men walk to Westminster to protest against this female privilege, I shall not join their procession.

For I remember with certainty this fixed psychological fact; that the very time when I was most under a woman's authority, I was most full of flame and adventure. Exactly because when my mother said that ants bit they did bite, and because snow did come in winter (as she said); therefore the whole world was to me a fairyland of wonderful fulfilments, and it was like living in some Hebraic age, when prophecy after prophecy came true. I went out as a child into the garden, and it was a terrible place to me, precisely because I had a clue to it: if I had held no clue it would not have been terrible, but tame. A mere unmeaning wilderness is not even impressive. But the garden of childhood was fascinating, exactly because everything had a fixed meaning which could be found out in its turn. Inch by inch I might discover what was the object of the ugly shape called a rake; or form some shadowy conjecture as to why my parents kept a cat.

So, since I have accepted Christendom as a mother and not merely as a chance example, I have found Europe and the world once more like the little garden where I stared at the symbolic shapes of cat and rake; I look at everything with the old elvish ignorance and expectancy. This or that rite or doctrine may look as ugly and extraordinary as a rake; but I have found by experience that such things end somehow in grass and flowers. A clergyman may be apparently as useless as a cat, but he is also as fascinating, for there must be some strange reason for his existence. I give one instance out of a hundred; I have not myself any instinctive kinship with that enthusiasm for physical virginity, which has certainly been a note of historic Christianity. But when I look not at myself but at the world, I perceive that this enthusiasm is not only a note of Christianity, but a note of Paganism, a note of high human nature in many spheres. The Greeks felt virginity when they carved Artemis, the Romans when they robed the vestals, the worst and wildest of the great Elizabethan playwrights clung to the literal purity of a woman as to the central pillar of the world. Above all, the modern world (even while mocking sexual innocence) has flung itself into a generous idolatry of sexual innocence— the great modern worship of children. For any man who loves children will agree that their peculiar beauty is hurt by a hint of physical sex. With all this human experience, allied with the Christian authority, I simply conclude that I am wrong, and the church right; or rather that I am defective, while the church is universal. It takes all sorts to make a church; she does not ask me to be celibate. But the fact that I have no appreciation of the celibates, I accept like the fact that I have no ear for music. The best human experience is against me, as it is on the subject of Bach. Celibacy is one flower in my father's garden, of which I have not been told the sweet or terrible name. But I may be told it any day.

This, therefore, is, in conclusion, my reason for accepting the religion and not merely the scattered and secular truths out of the religion. I do it because the thing has not merely told this truth or that truth, but has revealed itself as a truth-telling thing. All other philosophies say the things that plainly seem to be true; only this philosophy has again and again said the thing that does not seem to be true, but is true. Alone of all creeds it is convincing where it is not attractive; it turns out to be right, like my father in the garden. Theosophists for instance will preach an obviously attractive idea like re-incarnation; but if we wait for its logical results, they are spiritual superciliousness and the cruelty of caste. For if a man is a beggar by his own pre-natal sins, people will tend to despise the beggar. But Christianity preaches an obviously unattractive idea, such as original sin; but when we wait for its results, they are pathos and brotherhood, and a thunder of laughter and pity; for only with original sin we can at once pity the beggar and distrust the king. Men of science offer us health, an obvious benefit; it is only afterwards that we discover that by health, they mean bodily slavery and spiritual tedium. Orthodoxy makes us jump by the sudden brink of hell; it is only afterwards that we realise that jumping was an athletic exercise highly beneficial to our health. It is only afterwards that we realise that this danger is the root of all drama and romance. The strongest argument for the divine grace is simply its ungraciousness. The unpopular parts of Christianity turn out when examined to be the very props of the people. The outer ring of Christianity is a rigid guard of ethical abnegations and professional priests; but inside that inhuman guard you will find the old human life dancing like children, and drinking wine like men; for Christianity is the only frame for pagan freedom. But in the modern philosophy the case is opposite; it is its outer ring that is obviously artistic and emancipated; its despair is within.

And its despair is this, that it does not really believe that there is any meaning in the universe; therefore it cannot hope to find any romance; its romances will have no plots. A man cannot expect any adventures in the land of anarchy. But a man can expect any number of adventures if he goes travelling in the land of authority. One can find no meanings in a jungle of scepticism; but the man will find more and more meanings who walks through a forest of doctrine and design. Here everything has a story tied to its tail, like the tools or pictures in my father's house; for it is my father's house. I end where I began—at the right end. I have entered at last the gate of all good philosophy. I have come into my second childhood.

But this larger and more adventurous Christian universe has one final mark difficult to express; yet as a conclusion of the whole matter I will attempt to express it. All the real argument about religion turns on the question of whether a man who was born upside down can tell when he comes right way up. The primary paradox of Christianity is that the ordinary condition of man is not his sane or sensible condition; that the normal itself is an abnormality. That is the inmost philosophy of the Fall. In Sir Oliver Lodge's interesting new Catechism, the first two questions were: "What are you?" and "What, then, is the meaning of the Fall of Man?" I remember amusing myself by writing my own answers to the questions; but I soon found that they were very broken and agnostic answers. To the question, "What are you?" I could only answer, "God knows." And to the question, "What is meant by the Fall?" I could answer with complete sincerity, "That whatever I am, I am not myself." This is the prime paradox of our religion; something that we have never in any full sense known, is not only better than ourselves, but even more natural to us than ourselves. And there is really no test of this except the merely experimental one with which these pages began, the test of the padded cell and the open door. It is only since I have known orthodoxy that I have known mental emancipation. But, in conclusion, it has one special application to the ultimate idea of joy.

It is said that Paganism is a religion of joy and Christianity of sorrow; it would be just as easy to prove that Paganism is pure sorrow and Christianity pure joy. Such conflicts mean nothing and lead nowhere. Everything human must have in it both joy and sorrow; the only matter of interest is the manner in which the two things are balanced or divided. And the really interesting thing is this, that the pagan was (in the main) happier and happier as he approached the earth, but sadder and sadder as he approached the heavens. The gaiety of the best Paganism, as in the playfulness of Catullus or Theocritus, is, indeed, an eternal gaiety never to be forgotten by a grateful humanity. But it is all a gaiety about the facts of life, not about its origin. To the pagan the small things are as sweet as the small brooks breaking out of the mountain; but the broad things are as bitter as the sea. When the pagan looks at the very core of the cosmos he is struck cold. Behind the gods, who are merely despotic, sit the fates, who are deadly. Nay, the fates are worse than deadly; they are dead. And when rationalists say that the ancient world was more enlightened than the Christian, from their point of view they are right. For when they say "enlightened" they mean darkened with incurable despair. It is profoundly true that the ancient world was more modern than the Christian. The common bond is in the fact that ancients and moderns have both been miserable about existence, about everything, while mediaevals were happy about that at least. I freely grant that the pagans, like the moderns, were only miserable about everything—they were quite jolly about everything else. I concede that the Christians of the Middle Ages were only at peace about everything—they were at war about everything else. But if the question turn on the primary pivot of the cosmos, then there was more cosmic contentment in the narrow and bloody streets of Florence than in the theatre of Athens or the open garden of Epicurus. Giotto lived in a gloomier town than Euripides, but he lived in a gayer universe.

The mass of men have been forced to be gay about the little things, but sad about the big ones. Nevertheless (I offer my last dogma defiantly) it is not native to man to be so. Man is more himself, man is more manlike, when joy is the fundamental thing in him, and grief the superficial. Melancholy should be an innocent interlude, a tender and fugitive frame of mind; praise should be the permanent pulsation of the soul. Pessimism is at best an emotional half-holiday; joy is the uproarious labour by which all things live. Yet, according to the apparent estate of man as seen by the pagan or the agnostic, this primary need of human nature can never be fulfilled. Joy ought to be expansive; but for the agnostic it must be contracted, it must cling to one corner of the world. Grief ought to be a concentration; but for the agnostic its desolation is spread through an unthinkable eternity. This is what I call being born upside down. The sceptic may truly be said to be topsy-turvy; for his feet are dancing upwards in idle ecstasies, while his brain is in the abyss. To the modern man the heavens are actually below the earth. The explanation is simple; he is standing on his head; which is a very weak pedestal to stand on. But when he has found his feet again he knows it. Christianity satisfies suddenly and perfectly man's ancestral instinct for being the right way up; satisfies it supremely in this; that by its creed joy becomes something gigantic and sadness something special and small. The vault above us is not deaf because the universe is an idiot; the silence is not the heartless silence of an endless and aimless world. Rather the silence around us is a small and pitiful stillness like the prompt stillness in a sick-room. We are perhaps permitted tragedy as a sort of merciful comedy: because the frantic energy of divine things would knock us down like a drunken farce. We can take our own tears more lightly than we could take the tremendous levities of the angels. So we sit perhaps in a starry chamber of silence, while the laughter of the heavens is too loud for us to hear.

Joy, which was the small publicity of the pagan, is the gigantic secret of the Christian. And as I close this chaotic volume I open again the strange small book from which all Christianity came; and I am again haunted by a kind of confirmation. The tremendous figure which fills the Gospels towers in this respect, as in every other, above all the thinkers who ever thought themselves tall. His pathos was natural, almost casual. The Stoics, ancient and modern, were proud of concealing their tears. He never concealed His tears; He showed them plainly on His open face at any daily sight, such as the far sight of His native city. Yet He concealed something. Solemn supermen and imperial diplomatists are proud of restraining their anger. He never restrained His anger. He flung furniture down the front steps of the Temple, and asked men how they expected to escape the damnation of Hell. Yet He restrained something. I say it with reverence; there was in that shattering personality a thread that must be called shyness. There was something that He hid from all men when He went up a mountain to pray. There was something that He covered constantly by abrupt silence or impetuous isolation. There was some one thing that was too great for God to show us when He walked upon our earth; and I have sometimes fancied that it was His mirth.

HERETICS

I. INTRODUCTORY REMARKS ON THE IMPORTANCE OF ORTHODOXY

Nothing more strangely indicates an enormous and silent evil of modern society than the extraordinary use which is made nowadays of the word "orthodox." In former days the heretic was proud of not being a heretic. It was the kingdoms of the world and the police and the judges who were heretics. He was orthodox. He had no pride in having rebelled against them; they had rebelled against him. The armies with their cruel security, the kings with their cold faces, the decorous processes of State, the reasonable processes of law—all these like sheep had gone astray. The man was proud of being orthodox, was proud of being right. If he stood alone in a howling wilderness he was more than a man; he was a church. He was the centre of the universe; it was round him that the stars swung. All the tortures torn out of forgotten hells could not make him admit that he was heretical. But a few modern phrases have made him boast of it. He says, with a conscious laugh, "I suppose I am very heretical," and looks round for applause. The word "heresy" not only means no longer being wrong; it practically means being clear-headed and courageous. The word "orthodoxy" not only no longer means being right; it practically means being wrong. All this can mean one thing, and one thing only. It means that people care less for whether they are philosophically right. For obviously a man ought to confess himself crazy before he confesses himself heretical. The Bohemian, with a red tie, ought to pique himself on his orthodoxy. The dynamiter, laying a bomb, ought to feel that, whatever else he is, at least he is orthodox.

It is foolish, generally speaking, for a philosopher to set fire to another philosopher in Smithfield Market because they do not agree in their theory of the universe. That was done very frequently in the last decadence of the Middle Ages, and it failed altogether in its object. But there is one thing that is infinitely more absurd and unpractical than burning a man for his philosophy. This is the habit of saying that his philosophy does not matter, and this is done universally in the twentieth century, in the decadence of the great revolutionary period. General theories are everywhere contemned; the doctrine of the Rights of Man is dismissed with the doctrine of the Fall of Man. Atheism itself is too theological for us to-day. Revolution itself is too much of a system; liberty itself is too much of a restraint. We will have no generalizations. Mr. Bernard Shaw has put the view in a perfect epigram: "The golden rule is that there is no golden rule." We are more and more to discuss details in art, politics, literature. A man's opinion on tramcars matters; his opinion on Botticelli matters; his opinion on all things does not matter. He may turn over and explore a million objects, but he must not find that strange object, the universe; for if he does he will have a religion, and be lost. Everything matters—except everything.

Examples are scarcely needed of this total levity on the subject of cosmic philosophy. Examples are scarcely needed to show that, whatever else we think of as affecting practical affairs, we do not think it matters whether a man is a pessimist or an optimist, a Cartesian or a Hegelian, a materialist or a spiritualist. Let me, however, take a random instance. At any innocent tea-table we may easily hear a man say, "Life is not worth living." We regard it as we regard the statement that it is a fine day; nobody thinks that it can possibly have any serious effect on the man or on the world. And yet if that utterance were really believed, the world would stand on its head. Murderers would be given medals for saving men from life; firemen would be denounced for keeping men from death; poisons would be used as medicines; doctors would be called in when people were well; the Royal Humane Society would be rooted out like a horde of assassins. Yet we never speculate as to whether the conversational pessimist will strengthen or disorganize society; for we are convinced that theories do not matter.

This was certainly not the idea of those who introduced our freedom. When the old Liberals removed the gags from all the heresies, their idea was that religious and philosophical discoveries might thus be made. Their view was that cosmic truth was so important that every one ought to bear independent testimony. The modern idea is that cosmic truth is so unimportant that it cannot matter what any one says. The former freed inquiry as men loose a noble hound; the latter frees inquiry as men fling back into the sea a fish unfit for eating. Never has there been so little discussion about the nature of men as now, when, for the first time, any one can discuss it. The old restriction meant that only the orthodox were allowed to discuss religion. Modern liberty means that nobody is allowed to discuss it. Good taste, the last and vilest of human superstitions, has succeeded in silencing us where all the rest have failed. Sixty years ago it was bad taste to be an avowed atheist. Then came the Bradlaughites, the last religious men, the last men who cared about God; but they could not alter it. It is still bad taste to be an avowed atheist. But their agony has achieved just this—that now it is equally bad taste to be an avowed Christian. Emancipation has only locked the saint in the same tower of silence as the heresiarch. Then we talk about Lord Anglesey and the weather, and call it the complete liberty of all the creeds.

But there are some people, nevertheless—and I am one of them—who think that the most practical and important thing about a man is still his view of the universe. We think that for a landlady considering a lodger, it is important to know his income, but still more important to know his philosophy. We think that for a general about to fight an enemy, it is important to know the enemy's numbers, but still more important to know the enemy's philosophy. We think the question is not whether the theory of the cosmos affects matters, but whether in the long run, anything else affects them. In the fifteenth century men cross-examined and tormented a man because he preached some immoral attitude; in the nineteenth century we feted and flattered Oscar Wilde because he preached such an attitude, and then broke his heart in penal servitude because he carried it out. It may be a question which of the two methods was the more cruel; there can be no kind of question which was the more ludicrous. The age of the Inquisition has not at least the disgrace of having produced a society which made an idol of the very same man for preaching the very same things which it made him a convict for practising.

Now, in our time, philosophy or religion, our theory, that is, about ultimate things, has been driven out, more or less simultaneously, from two fields which it used to occupy. General ideals used to dominate literature. They have been driven out by the cry of "art for art's sake." General ideals used to dominate politics. They have been driven out by the cry of "efficiency," which may roughly be translated as "politics for politics' sake." Persistently for the last twenty years the ideals of order or liberty have dwindled in our books; the ambitions of wit and eloquence have dwindled in our parliaments. Literature has purposely become less political; politics have purposely become less literary. General theories of the relation of things have thus been extruded from both; and we are in a position to ask, "What have we gained or lost by this extrusion? Is literature better, is politics better, for having discarded the moralist and the philosopher?"

When everything about a people is for the time growing weak and ineffective, it begins to talk about efficiency. So it is that when a man's body is a wreck he begins, for the first time, to talk about health. Vigorous organisms talk not about their processes, but about their aims. There cannot be any better proof of the physical efficiency of a man than that he talks cheerfully of a journey to the end of the world. And there cannot be any better proof of the practical efficiency of a nation than that it talks constantly of a journey to the end of the world, a journey to the Judgment Day and the New Jerusalem. There can be no stronger sign of a coarse material health than the tendency to run after high and wild ideals; it is in the first exuberance of infancy that we cry for the moon. None of the strong men in the strong ages would have understood what you meant by working for efficiency. Hildebrand would have said that he was working not for efficiency, but for the Catholic Church. Danton would have said that he was working not for efficiency, but for liberty, equality, and fraternity. Even if the ideal of such men were simply the ideal of kicking a man downstairs, they thought of the end like men, not of the process like paralytics. They did not say, "Efficiently elevating my right leg, using, you will notice, the muscles of the thigh and calf, which are in excellent order, I—" Their feeling was quite different. They were so filled with the beautiful vision of the man lying flat at the foot of the staircase that in that ecstasy the rest followed in a flash. In practice, the habit of generalizing and idealizing did not by any means mean worldly weakness. The time of big theories was the time of big results. In the era of sentiment and fine words, at the end of the eighteenth century, men were really robust and effective. The sentimentalists conquered Napoleon. The cynics could not catch De Wet. A hundred years ago our affairs for good or evil were wielded triumphantly by rhetoricians. Now our affairs are hopelessly muddled by strong, silent men. And just as this repudiation of big words and big visions has brought forth a race of small men in politics, so it has brought forth a race of small men in the arts. Our modern politicians claim the colossal license of Caesar and the Superman, claim that they are too practical to be pure and too patriotic to be moral; but the upshot of it all is that a mediocrity is Chancellor of the Exchequer. Our new artistic philosophers call for the same moral license, for a freedom to wreck heaven and earth with their energy; but the upshot of it all is that a mediocrity is Poet Laureate. I do not say that there are no stronger men than these; but will any one say that there are any men stronger than those men of old who were dominated by their philosophy and steeped in their religion? Whether bondage be better than freedom may be discussed. But that their bondage came to more than our freedom it will be difficult for any one to deny.

The theory of the unmorality of art has established itself firmly in the strictly artistic classes. They are free to produce anything they like. They are free to write a "Paradise Lost" in which Satan shall conquer God. They are free to write a "Divine Comedy" in which heaven shall be under the floor of hell. And what have they done? Have they produced in their universality anything grander or more beautiful than the things uttered by the fierce Ghibbeline Catholic, by the rigid Puritan schoolmaster? We know that they have produced only a few roundels. Milton does not merely beat them at his piety, he beats them at their own irreverence. In all their little books of verse you will not find a finer defiance of God than Satan's. Nor will you find the grandeur of paganism felt as that fiery Christian felt it who described Faranata lifting his head as in disdain of hell. And the reason is very obvious. Blasphemy is an artistic effect, because blasphemy depends upon a philosophical conviction. Blasphemy depends upon belief and is fading with it. If any one doubts this, let him sit down seriously and try to think blasphemous thoughts about Thor. I think his family will find him at the end of the day in a state of some exhaustion.

Neither in the world of politics nor that of literature, then, has the rejection of general theories proved a success. It may be that there have been many moonstruck and misleading ideals that have from time to time perplexed mankind. But assuredly there has been no ideal in practice so moonstruck and misleading as the ideal of practicality. Nothing has lost so many opportunities as the opportunism of Lord Rosebery. He is, indeed, a standing symbol of this epoch—the man who is theoretically a practical man, and practically more unpractical than any theorist. Nothing in this universe is so unwise as that kind of worship of worldly wisdom. A man who is perpetually thinking of whether this race or that race is strong, of whether this cause or that cause is promising, is the man who will never believe in anything long enough to make it succeed. The opportunist politician is like a man who should abandon billiards because he was beaten at billiards, and abandon golf because he was beaten at golf. There is nothing which is so weak for working purposes as this enormous importance attached to immediate victory. There is nothing that fails like success.

And having discovered that opportunism does fail, I have been induced to look at it more largely, and in consequence to see that it must fail. I perceive that it is far more practical to begin at the beginning and discuss theories. I see that the men who killed each other about the orthodoxy of the Homoousion were far more sensible than the people who are quarrelling about the Education Act. For the Christian dogmatists were trying to establish a reign of holiness, and trying to get defined, first of all, what was really holy. But our modern educationists are trying to bring about a religious liberty without attempting to settle what is religion or what is liberty. If the old priests forced a statement on mankind, at least they previously took some trouble to make it lucid. It has been left for the modern mobs of Anglicans and Nonconformists to persecute for a doctrine without even stating it.

For these reasons, and for many more, I for one have come to believe in going back to fundamentals. Such is the general idea of this book. I wish to deal with my most distinguished contemporaries, not personally or in a merely literary manner, but in relation to the real body of doctrine which they teach. I am not concerned with Mr. Rudyard Kipling as a vivid artist or a vigorous personality; I am concerned with him as a Heretic—that is to say, a man whose view of things has the hardihood to differ from mine. I am not concerned with Mr. Bernard Shaw as one of the most brilliant and one of the most honest men alive; I am concerned with him as a Heretic—that is to say, a man whose philosophy is quite solid, quite coherent, and quite wrong. I revert to the doctrinal methods of the thirteenth century, inspired by the general hope of getting something done.

Suppose that a great commotion arises in the street about something, let us say a lamp-post, which many influential persons desire to pull down. A grey-clad monk, who is the spirit of the Middle Ages, is approached upon the matter, and begins to say, in the arid manner of the Schoolmen, "Let us first of all consider, my brethren, the value of Light. If Light be in itself good—" At this point he is somewhat excusably knocked down. All the people make a rush for the lamp-post, the lamp-post is down in ten minutes, and they go about congratulating each other on their unmediaeval practicality. But as things go on they do not work out so easily. Some people have pulled the lamp-post down because they wanted the electric light; some because they wanted old iron; some because they wanted darkness, because their deeds were evil. Some thought it not enough of a lamp-post, some too much; some acted because they wanted to smash municipal machinery; some because they wanted to smash something. And there is war in the night, no man knowing whom he strikes. So, gradually and inevitably, to-day, to-morrow, or the next day, there comes back the conviction that the monk was right after all, and that all depends on what is the philosophy of Light. Only what we might have discussed under the gas-lamp, we now must discuss in the dark.

II. ON THE NEGATIVE SPIRIT

Much has been said, and said truly, of the monkish morbidity, of the hysteria which as often gone with the visions of hermits or nuns. But let us never forget that this visionary religion is, in one sense, necessarily more wholesome than our modern and reasonable morality. It is more wholesome for this reason, that it can contemplate the idea of success or triumph in the hopeless fight towards the ethical ideal, in what Stevenson called, with his usual startling felicity, "the lost fight of virtue." A modern morality, on the other hand, can only point with absolute conviction to the horrors that follow breaches of law; its only certainty is a certainty of ill. It can only point to imperfection. It has no perfection to point to. But the monk meditating upon Christ or Buddha has in his mind an image of perfect health, a thing of clear colours and clean air. He may contemplate this ideal wholeness and happiness far more than he ought; he may contemplate it to the neglect of exclusion of essential THINGS; he may contemplate it until he has become a dreamer or a driveller; but still it is wholeness and happiness that he is contemplating. He may even go mad; but he is going mad for the love of sanity. But the modern student of ethics, even if he remains sane, remains sane from an insane dread of insanity.

The anchorite rolling on the stones in a frenzy of submission is a healthier person fundamentally than many a sober man in a silk hat who is walking down Cheapside. For many such are good only through a withering knowledge of evil. I am not at this moment claiming for the devotee anything more than this primary advantage, that though he may be making himself personally weak and miserable, he is still fixing his thoughts largely on gigantic strength and happiness, on a strength that has no limits, and a happiness that has no end. Doubtless there are other objections which can be urged without unreason against the influence of gods and visions in morality, whether in the cell or street. But this advantage the mystic morality must always have—it is always jollier. A young man may keep himself from vice by continually thinking of disease. He may keep himself from it also by continually thinking of the Virgin Mary. There may be question about which method is the more reasonable, or even about which is the more efficient. But surely there can be no question about which is the more wholesome.

I remember a pamphlet by that able and sincere secularist, Mr. G. W. Foote, which contained a phrase sharply symbolizing and dividing these two methods. The pamphlet was called BEER AND BIBLE, those two very noble things, all the nobler for a conjunction which Mr. Foote, in his stern old Puritan way, seemed to think sardonic, but which I confess to thinking appropriate and charming. I have not the work by me, but I remember that Mr. Foote dismissed very contemptuously any attempts to deal with the problem of strong drink by religious offices or intercessions, and said that a picture of a drunkard's liver would be more efficacious in the matter of temperance than any prayer or praise. In that picturesque expression, it seems to me, is perfectly embodied the incurable morbidity of modern ethics. In that temple the lights are low, the crowds kneel, the solemn anthems are uplifted. But that upon the altar to which all men kneel is no longer the perfect flesh, the body and substance of the perfect man; it is still flesh, but it is diseased. It is the drunkard's liver of the New Testament that is marred for us, which we take in remembrance of him.

Now, it is this great gap in modern ethics, the absence of vivid pictures of purity and spiritual triumph, which lies at the back of the real objection felt by so many sane men to the realistic literature of the nineteenth century. If any ordinary man ever said that he was horrified by the subjects discussed in Ibsen or Maupassant, or by the plain language in which they are spoken of, that ordinary man was lying. The average conversation of average men throughout the whole of modern civilization in every class or trade is such as Zola would never dream of printing. Nor is the habit of writing thus of these things a new habit. On the contrary, it is the Victorian prudery and silence which is new still, though it is already dying. The tradition of calling a spade a spade starts very early in our literature and comes down very late. But the truth is that the ordinary honest man, whatever vague account he may have given of his feelings, was not either disgusted or even annoyed at the candour of the moderns. What disgusted him, and very justly, was not the presence of a clear realism, but the absence of a clear idealism. Strong and genuine religious sentiment has never had any objection to realism; on the contrary, religion was the realistic thing, the brutal thing, the thing that called names. This is the great difference between some recent developments of Nonconformity and the great Puritanism of the seventeenth century. It was the whole point of the Puritans that they cared nothing for decency. Modern Nonconformist newspapers distinguish themselves by suppressing precisely those nouns and adjectives which the founders of Nonconformity distinguished themselves by flinging at kings and queens. But if it was a chief claim of religion that it spoke plainly about evil, it was the chief claim of all that it spoke plainly about good. The thing which is resented, and, as I think, rightly resented, in that great modern literature of which Ibsen is typical, is that while the eye that can perceive what are the wrong things increases in an uncanny and devouring clarity, the eye which sees what things are right is growing mistier and mistier every moment, till it goes almost blind with doubt. If we compare, let us say, the morality of the DIVINE COMEDY with the morality of Ibsen's GHOSTS, we shall see all that modern ethics have really done. No one, I imagine, will accuse the author of the INFERNO of an Early Victorian prudishness or a Podsnapian optimism. But Dante describes three moral instruments—Heaven, Purgatory, and Hell, the vision of perfection, the vision of improvement, and the vision of failure. Ibsen has only one—Hell. It is often said, and with perfect truth, that no one could read a play like GHOSTS and remain indifferent to the necessity of an ethical self-command. That is quite true, and the same is to be said of the most monstrous and material descriptions of the eternal fire. It is quite certain the realists like Zola do in one sense promote morality—they promote it in the sense in which the hangman promotes it, in the sense in which the devil promotes it. But they only affect that small minority which will accept any virtue of courage. Most healthy people dismiss these moral dangers as they dismiss the possibility of bombs or microbes. Modern realists are indeed Terrorists, like the dynamiters; and they fail just as much in their effort to create a thrill. Both realists and dynamiters are well-meaning people engaged in the task, so obviously ultimately hopeless, of using science to promote morality.

I do not wish the reader to confuse me for a moment with those vague persons who imagine that Ibsen is what they call a pessimist. There are plenty of wholesome people in Ibsen, plenty of good people, plenty of happy people, plenty of examples of men acting wisely and things ending well. That is not my meaning. My meaning is that Ibsen has throughout, and does not disguise, a certain vagueness and a changing attitude as well as a doubting attitude towards what is really wisdom and virtue in this life—a vagueness which contrasts very remarkably with the decisiveness with which he pounces on something which he perceives to be a root of evil, some convention, some deception, some ignorance. We know that the hero of GHOSTS is mad, and we know why he is mad. We do also know that Dr. Stockman is sane; but we do not know why he is sane. Ibsen does not profess to know how virtue and happiness are brought about, in the sense that he professes to know how our modern sexual tragedies are brought about. Falsehood works ruin in THE PILLARS OF SOCIETY, but truth works equal ruin in THE WILD DUCK. There are no cardinal virtues of Ibsenism. There is no ideal man of Ibsen. All this is not only admitted, but vaunted in the most valuable and thoughtful of all the eulogies upon Ibsen, Mr. Bernard Shaw's QUINTESSENCE OF IBSENISM. Mr. Shaw sums up Ibsen's teaching in the phrase, "The golden rule is that there is no golden rule." In his eyes this absence of an enduring and positive ideal, this absence of a permanent key to virtue, is the one great Ibsen merit. I am not discussing now with any fullness whether this is so or not. All I venture to point out, with an increased firmness, is that this omission, good or bad, does leave us face to face with the problem of a human consciousness filled with very definite images of evil, and with no definite image of good. To us light must be henceforward the dark thing—the thing of which we cannot speak. To us, as to Milton's devils in Pandemonium, it is darkness that is visible. The human race, according to religion, fell once, and in falling gained knowledge of good and of evil. Now we have fallen a second time, and only the knowledge of evil remains to us.

A great silent collapse, an enormous unspoken disappointment, has in our time fallen on our Northern civilization. All previous ages have sweated and been crucified in an attempt to realize what is really the right life, what was really the good man. A definite part of the modern world has come beyond question to the conclusion that there is no answer to these questions, that the most that we can do is to set up a few notice-boards at places of obvious danger, to warn men, for instance, against drinking themselves to death, or ignoring the mere existence of their neighbours. Ibsen is the first to return from the baffled hunt to bring us the tidings of great failure.

Every one of the popular modern phrases and ideals is a dodge in order to shirk the problem of what is good. We are fond of talking about "liberty"; that, as we talk of it, is a dodge to avoid discussing what is good. We are fond of talking about "progress"; that is a dodge to avoid discussing what is good. We are fond of talking about "education"; that is a dodge to avoid discussing what is good. The modern man says, "Let us leave all these arbitrary standards and embrace liberty." This is, logically rendered, "Let us not decide what is good, but let it be considered good not to decide it." He says, "Away with your old moral formulae; I am for progress." This, logically stated, means, "Let us not settle what is good; but let us settle whether we are getting more of it." He says, "Neither in religion nor morality, my friend, lie the hopes of the race, but in education." This, clearly expressed, means, "We cannot decide what is good, but let us give it to our children."

Mr. H.G. Wells, that exceedingly clear-sighted man, has pointed out in a recent work that this has happened in connection with economic questions. The old economists, he says, made generalizations, and they were (in Mr. Wells's view) mostly wrong. But the new economists, he says, seem to have lost the power of making any generalizations at all. And they cover this incapacity with a general claim to be, in specific cases, regarded as "experts", a claim "proper enough in a hairdresser or a fashionable physician, but indecent in a philosopher or a man of science." But in spite of the refreshing rationality with which Mr. Wells has indicated this, it must also be said that he himself has fallen into the same enormous modern error. In the opening pages of that excellent book MANKIND IN THE MAKING, he dismisses the ideals of art, religion, abstract morality, and the rest, and says that he is going to consider men in their chief function, the function of parenthood. He is going to discuss life as a "tissue of births." He is not going to ask what will produce satisfactory saints or satisfactory heroes, but what will produce satisfactory fathers and mothers. The whole is set forward so sensibly that it is a few moments at least before the reader realises that it is another example of unconscious shirking. What is the good of begetting a man until we have settled what is the good of being a man? You are merely handing on to him a problem you dare not settle yourself. It is as if a man were asked, "What is the use of a hammer?" and answered, "To make hammers"; and when asked, "And of those hammers, what is the use?" answered, "To make hammers again". Just as such a man would be perpetually putting off the question of the ultimate use of carpentry, so Mr. Wells and all the rest of us are by these phrases successfully putting off the question of the ultimate value of the human life.

The case of the general talk of "progress" is, indeed, an extreme one. As enunciated today, "progress" is simply a comparative of which we have not settled the superlative. We meet every ideal of religion, patriotism, beauty, or brute pleasure with the alternative ideal of progress—that is to say, we meet every proposal of getting something that we know about, with an alternative proposal of getting a great deal more of nobody knows what. Progress, properly understood, has, indeed, a most dignified and legitimate meaning. But as used in opposition to precise moral ideals, it is ludicrous. So far from it being the truth that the ideal of progress is to be set against that of ethical or religious finality, the reverse is the truth. Nobody has any business to use the word "progress" unless he has a definite creed and a cast-iron code of morals. Nobody can be progressive without being doctrinal; I might almost say that nobody can be progressive without being infallible—at any rate, without believing in some infallibility. For progress by its very name indicates a direction; and the moment we are in the least doubtful about the direction, we become in the same degree doubtful about the progress. Never perhaps since the beginning of the world has there been an age that had less right to use the word "progress" than we. In the Catholic twelfth century, in the philosophic eighteenth century, the direction may have been a good or a bad one, men may have differed more or less about how far they went, and in what direction, but about the direction they did in the main agree, and consequently they had the genuine sensation of progress. But it is precisely about the direction that we disagree. Whether the future excellence lies in more law or less law, in more liberty or less liberty; whether property will be finally concentrated or finally cut up; whether sexual passion will reach its sanest in an almost virgin intellectualism or in a full animal freedom; whether we should love everybody with Tolstoy, or spare nobody with Nietzsche;—these are the things about which we are actually fighting most. It is not merely true that the age which has settled least what is progress is this "progressive" age. It is, moreover, true that the people who have settled least what is progress are the most "progressive" people in it. The ordinary mass, the men who have never troubled about progress, might be trusted perhaps to progress. The particular individuals who talk about progress would certainly fly to the four winds of heaven when the pistol-shot started the race. I do not, therefore, say that the word "progress" is unmeaning; I say it is unmeaning without the previous definition of a moral doctrine, and that it can only be applied to groups of persons who hold that doctrine in common. Progress is not an illegitimate word, but it is logically evident that it is illegitimate for us. It is a sacred word, a word which could only rightly be used by rigid believers and in the ages of faith.

III. ON MR. RUDYARD KIPLING AND MAKING THE WORLD SMALL

There is no such thing on earth as an uninteresting subject; the only thing that can exist is an uninterested person. Nothing is more keenly required than a defence of bores. When Byron divided humanity into the bores and bored, he omitted to notice that the higher qualities exist entirely in the bores, the lower qualities in the bored, among whom he counted himself. The bore, by his starry enthusiasm, his solemn happiness, may, in some sense, have proved himself poetical. The bored has certainly proved himself prosaic.

We might, no doubt, find it a nuisance to count all the blades of grass or all the leaves of the trees; but this would not be because of our boldness or gaiety, but because of our lack of boldness and gaiety. The bore would go onward, bold and gay, and find the blades of grass as splendid as the swords of an army. The bore is stronger and more joyous than we are; he is a demigod—nay, he is a god. For it is the gods who do not tire of the iteration of things; to them the nightfall is always new, and the last rose as red as the first.

The sense that everything is poetical is a thing solid and absolute; it is not a mere matter of phraseology or persuasion. It is not merely true, it is ascertainable. Men may be challenged to deny it; men may be challenged to mention anything that is not a matter of poetry. I remember a long time ago a sensible sub-editor coming up to me with a book in his hand, called "Mr. Smith," or "The Smith Family," or some such thing. He said, "Well, you won't get any of your damned mysticism out of this," or words to that effect. I am happy to say that I undeceived him; but the victory was too obvious and easy. In most cases the name is unpoetical, although the fact is poetical. In the case of Smith, the name is so poetical that it must be an arduous and heroic matter for the man to live up to it. The name of Smith is the name of the one trade that even kings respected, it could claim half the glory of that arma virumque which all epics acclaimed. The spirit of the smithy is so close to the spirit of song that it has mixed in a million poems, and every blacksmith is a harmonious blacksmith.

Even the village children feel that in some dim way the smith is poetic, as the grocer and the cobbler are not poetic, when they feast on the dancing sparks and deafening blows in the cavern of that creative violence. The brute repose of Nature, the passionate cunning of man, the strongest of earthly metals, the wierdest of earthly elements, the unconquerable iron subdued by its only conqueror, the wheel and the ploughshare, the sword and the steam-hammer, the arraying of armies and the whole legend of arms, all these things are written, briefly indeed, but quite legibly, on the visiting-card of Mr. Smith. Yet our novelists call their hero "Aylmer Valence," which means nothing, or "Vernon Raymond," which means nothing, when it is in their power to give him this sacred name of Smith—this name made of iron and flame. It would be very natural if a certain hauteur, a certain carriage of the head, a certain curl of the lip, distinguished every one whose name is Smith. Perhaps it does; I trust so. Whoever else are parvenus, the Smiths are not parvenus. From the darkest dawn of history this clan has gone forth to battle; its trophies are on every hand; its name is everywhere; it is older than the nations, and its sign is the Hammer of Thor. But as I also remarked, it is not quite the usual case. It is common enough that common things should be poetical; it is not so common that common names should be poetical. In most cases it is the name that is the obstacle. A great many people talk as if this claim of ours, that all things are poetical, were a mere literary ingenuity, a play on words. Precisely the contrary is true. It is the idea that some things are not poetical which is literary, which is a mere product of words. The word "signal-box" is unpoetical. But the thing signal-box is not unpoetical; it is a place where men, in an agony of vigilance, light blood-red and sea-green fires to keep other men from death. That is the plain, genuine description of what it is; the prose only comes in with what it is called. The word "pillar-box" is unpoetical. But the thing pillar-box is not unpoetical; it is the place to which friends and lovers commit their messages, conscious that when they have done so they are sacred, and not to be touched, not only by others, but even (religious touch!) by themselves. That red turret is one of the last of the temples. Posting a letter and getting married are among the few things left that are entirely romantic; for to be entirely romantic a thing must be irrevocable. We think a pillar-box prosaic, because there is no rhyme to it. We think a pillar-box unpoetical, because we have never seen it in a poem. But the bold fact is entirely on the side of poetry. A signal-box is only called a signal-box; it is a house of life and death. A pillar-box is only called a pillar-box; it is a sanctuary of human words. If you think the name of "Smith" prosaic, it is not because you are practical and sensible; it is because you are too much affected with literary refinements. The name shouts poetry at you. If you think of it otherwise, it is because you are steeped and sodden with verbal reminiscences, because you remember everything in Punch or Comic Cuts about Mr. Smith being drunk or Mr. Smith being henpecked. All these things were given to you poetical. It is only by a long and elaborate process of literary effort that you have made them prosaic.

Now, the first and fairest thing to say about Rudyard Kipling is that he has borne a brilliant part in thus recovering the lost provinces of poetry. He has not been frightened by that brutal materialistic air which clings only to words; he has pierced through to the romantic, imaginative matter of the things themselves. He has perceived the significance and philosophy of steam and of slang. Steam may be, if you like, a dirty by-product of science. Slang may be, if you like, a dirty by-product of language. But at least he has been among the few who saw the divine parentage of these things, and knew that where there is smoke there is fire—that is, that wherever there is the foulest of things, there also is the purest. Above all, he has had something to say, a definite view of things to utter, and that always means that a man is fearless and faces everything. For the moment we have a view of the universe, we possess it.

Now, the message of Rudyard Kipling, that upon which he has really concentrated, is the only thing worth worrying about in him or in any other man. He has often written bad poetry, like Wordsworth. He has often said silly things, like Plato. He has often given way to mere political hysteria, like Gladstone. But no one can reasonably doubt that he means steadily and sincerely to say something, and the only serious question is, What is that which he has tried to say? Perhaps the best way of stating this fairly will be to begin with that element which has been most insisted by himself and by his opponents—I mean his interest in militarism. But when we are seeking for the real merits of a man it is unwise to go to his enemies, and much more foolish to go to himself.

Now, Mr. Kipling is certainly wrong in his worship of militarism, but his opponents are, generally speaking, quite as wrong as he. The evil of militarism is not that it shows certain men to be fierce and haughty and excessively warlike. The evil of militarism is that it shows most men to be tame and timid and excessively peaceable. The professional soldier gains more and more power as the general courage of a community declines. Thus the Pretorian guard became more and more important in Rome as Rome became more and more luxurious and feeble. The military man gains the civil power in proportion as the civilian loses the military virtues. And as it was in ancient Rome so it is in contemporary Europe. There never was a time when nations were more militarist. There never was a time when men were less brave. All ages and all epics have sung of arms and the man; but we have effected simultaneously the deterioration of the man and the fantastic perfection of the arms. Militarism demonstrated the decadence of Rome, and it demonstrates the decadence of Prussia.

And unconsciously Mr. Kipling has proved this, and proved it admirably. For in so far as his work is earnestly understood the military trade does not by any means emerge as the most important or attractive. He has not written so well about soldiers as he has about railway men or bridge builders, or even journalists. The fact is that what attracts Mr. Kipling to militarism is not the idea of courage, but the idea of discipline.

There was far more courage to the square mile in the Middle Ages, when no king had a standing army, but every man had a bow or sword. But the fascination of the standing army upon Mr. Kipling is not courage, which scarcely interests him, but discipline, which is, when all is said and done, his primary theme. The modern army is not a miracle of courage; it has not enough opportunities, owing to the cowardice of everybody else. But it is really a miracle of organization, and that is the truly Kiplingite ideal. Kipling's subject is not that valour which properly belongs to war, but that interdependence and efficiency which belongs quite as much to engineers, or sailors, or mules, or railway engines. And thus it is that when he writes of engineers, or sailors, or mules, or steam-engines, he writes at his best. The real poetry, the "true romance" which Mr. Kipling has taught, is the romance of the division of labour and the discipline of all the trades. He sings the arts of peace much more accurately than the arts of war. And his main contention is vital and valuable. Every thing is military in the sense that everything depends upon obedience. There is no perfectly epicurean corner; there is no perfectly irresponsible place. Everywhere men have made the way for us with sweat and submission. We may fling ourselves into a hammock in a fit of divine carelessness. But we are glad that the net-maker did not make the hammock in a fit of divine carelessness. We may jump upon a child's rocking-horse for a joke. But we are glad that the carpenter did not leave the legs of it unglued for a joke. So far from having merely preached that a soldier cleaning his side-arm is to be adored because he is military, Kipling at his best and clearest has preached that the baker baking loaves and the tailor cutting coats is as military as anybody.

Being devoted to this multitudinous vision of duty, Mr. Kipling is naturally a cosmopolitan. He happens to find his examples in the British Empire, but almost any other empire would do as well, or, indeed, any other highly civilized country. That which he admires in the British army he would find even more apparent in the German army; that which he desires in the British police he would find flourishing, in the French police. The ideal of discipline is not the whole of life, but it is spread over the whole of the world. And the worship of it tends to confirm in Mr. Kipling a certain note of worldly wisdom, of the experience of the wanderer, which is one of the genuine charms of his best work.

The great gap in his mind is what may be roughly called the lack of patriotism—that is to say, he lacks altogether the faculty of attaching himself to any cause or community finally and tragically; for all finality must be tragic. He admires England, but he does not love her; for we admire things with reasons, but love them without reasons. He admires England because she is strong, not because she is English. There is no harshness in saying this, for, to do him justice, he avows it with his usual picturesque candour. In a very interesting poem, he says that—

"If England was what England seems"

—that is, weak and inefficient; if England were not what (as he believes) she is—that is, powerful and practical—

"How quick we'd chuck 'er! But she ain't!"

He admits, that is, that his devotion is the result of a criticism, and this is quite enough to put it in another category altogether from the patriotism of the Boers, whom he hounded down in South Africa. In speaking of the really patriotic peoples, such as the Irish, he has some difficulty in keeping a shrill irritation out of his language. The frame of mind which he really describes with beauty and nobility is the frame of mind of the cosmopolitan man who has seen men and cities.

"For to admire and for to see, For to be'old this world so wide."

He is a perfect master of that light melancholy with which a man looks back on having been the citizen of many communities, of that light melancholy with which a man looks back on having been the lover of many women. He is the philanderer of the nations. But a man may have learnt much about women in flirtations, and still be ignorant of first love; a man may have known as many lands as Ulysses, and still be ignorant of patriotism.

Mr. Rudyard Kipling has asked in a celebrated epigram what they can know of England who know England only. It is a far deeper and sharper question to ask, "What can they know of England who know only the world?" for the world does not include England any more than it includes the Church. The moment we care for anything deeply, the world—that is, all the other miscellaneous interests—becomes our enemy. Christians showed it when they talked of keeping one's self "unspotted from the world;" but lovers talk of it just as much when they talk of the "world well lost." Astronomically speaking, I understand that England is situated on the world; similarly, I suppose that the Church was a part of the world, and even the lovers inhabitants of that orb. But they all felt a certain truth—the truth that the moment you love anything the world becomes your foe. Thus Mr. Kipling does certainly know the world; he is a man of the world, with all the narrowness that belongs to those imprisoned in that planet. He knows England as an intelligent English gentleman knows Venice. He has been to England a great many times; he has stopped there for long visits. But he does not belong to it, or to any place; and the proof of it is this, that he thinks of England as a place. The moment we are rooted in a place, the place vanishes. We live like a tree with the whole strength of the universe.

The globe-trotter lives in a smaller world than the peasant. He is always breathing, an air of locality. London is a place, to be compared to Chicago; Chicago is a place, to be compared to Timbuctoo. But Timbuctoo is not a place, since there, at least, live men who regard it as the universe, and breathe, not an air of locality, but the winds of the world. The man in the saloon steamer has seen all the races of men, and he is thinking of the things that divide men—diet, dress, decorum, rings in the nose as in Africa, or in the ears as in Europe, blue paint among the ancients, or red paint among the modern Britons. The man in the cabbage field has seen nothing at all; but he is thinking of the things that unite men—hunger and babies, and the beauty of women, and the promise or menace of the sky. Mr. Kipling, with all his merits, is the globe-trotter; he has not the patience to become part of anything. So great and genuine a man is not to be accused of a merely cynical cosmopolitanism; still, his cosmopolitanism is his weakness. That weakness is splendidly expressed in one of his finest poems, "The Sestina of the Tramp Royal," in which a man declares that he can endure anything in the way of hunger or horror, but not permanent presence in one place. In this there is certainly danger. The more dead and dry and dusty a thing is the more it travels about; dust is like this and the thistle-down and the High Commissioner in South Africa. Fertile things are somewhat heavier, like the heavy fruit trees on the pregnant mud of the Nile. In the heated idleness of youth we were all rather inclined to quarrel with the implication of that proverb which says that a rolling stone gathers no moss. We were inclined to ask, "Who wants to gather moss, except silly old ladies?" But for all that we begin to perceive that the proverb is right. The rolling stone rolls echoing from rock to rock; but the rolling stone is dead. The moss is silent because the moss is alive.

The truth is that exploration and enlargement make the world smaller. The telegraph and the steamboat make the world smaller. The telescope makes the world smaller; it is only the microscope that makes it larger. Before long the world will be cloven with a war between the telescopists and the microscopists. The first study large things and live in a small world; the second study small things and live in a large world. It is inspiriting without doubt to whizz in a motor-car round the earth, to feel Arabia as a whirl of sand or China as a flash of rice-fields. But Arabia is not a whirl of sand and China is not a flash of rice-fields. They are ancient civilizations with strange virtues buried like treasures. If we wish to understand them it must not be as tourists or inquirers, it must be with the loyalty of children and the great patience of poets. To conquer these places is to lose them. The man standing in his own kitchen-garden, with fairyland opening at the gate, is the man with large ideas. His mind creates distance; the motor-car stupidly destroys it. Moderns think of the earth as a globe, as something one can easily get round, the spirit of a schoolmistress. This is shown in the odd mistake perpetually made about Cecil Rhodes. His enemies say that he may have had large ideas, but he was a bad man. His friends say that he may have been a bad man, but he certainly had large ideas. The truth is that he was not a man essentially bad, he was a man of much geniality and many good intentions, but a man with singularly small views. There is nothing large about painting the map red; it is an innocent game for children. It is just as easy to think in continents as to think in cobble-stones. The difficulty comes in when we seek to know the substance of either of them. Rhodes' prophecies about the Boer resistance are an admirable comment on how the "large ideas" prosper when it is not a question of thinking in continents but of understanding a few two-legged men. And under all this vast illusion of the cosmopolitan planet, with its empires and its Reuter's agency, the real life of man goes on concerned with this tree or that temple, with this harvest or that drinking-song, totally uncomprehended, totally untouched. And it watches from its splendid parochialism, possibly with a smile of amusement, motor-car civilization going its triumphant way, outstripping time, consuming space, seeing all and seeing nothing, roaring on at last to the capture of the solar system, only to find the sun cockney and the stars suburban.

IV. MR. BERNARD SHAW

In the glad old days, before the rise of modern morbidities, when genial old Ibsen filled the world with wholesome joy, and the kindly tales of the forgotten Emile Zola kept our firesides merry and pure, it used to be thought a disadvantage to be misunderstood. It may be doubted whether it is always or even generally a disadvantage. The man who is misunderstood has always this advantage over his enemies, that they do not know his weak point or his plan of campaign. They go out against a bird with nets and against a fish with arrows. There are several modern examples of this situation. Mr. Chamberlain, for instance, is a very good one. He constantly eludes or vanquishes his opponents because his real powers and deficiencies are quite different to those with which he is credited, both by friends and foes. His friends depict him as a strenuous man of action; his opponents depict him as a coarse man of business; when, as a fact, he is neither one nor the other, but an admirable romantic orator and romantic actor. He has one power which is the soul of melodrama—the power of pretending, even when backed by a huge majority, that he has his back to the wall. For all mobs are so far chivalrous that their heroes must make some show of misfortune—that sort of hypocrisy is the homage that strength pays to weakness. He talks foolishly and yet very finely about his own city that has never deserted him. He wears a flaming and fantastic flower, like a decadent minor poet. As for his bluffness and toughness and appeals to common sense, all that is, of course, simply the first trick of rhetoric. He fronts his audiences with the venerable affectation of Mark Antony—

"I am no orator, as Brutus is; But as you know me all, a plain blunt man."

It is the whole difference between the aim of the orator and the aim of any other artist, such as the poet or the sculptor. The aim of the sculptor is to convince us that he is a sculptor; the aim of the orator, is to convince us that he is not an orator. Once let Mr. Chamberlain be mistaken for a practical man, and his game is won. He has only to compose a theme on empire, and people will say that these plain men say great things on great occasions. He has only to drift in the large loose notions common to all artists of the second rank, and people will say that business men have the biggest ideals after all. All his schemes have ended in smoke; he has touched nothing that he did not confuse. About his figure there is a Celtic pathos; like the Gaels in Matthew Arnold's quotation, "he went forth to battle, but he always fell." He is a mountain of proposals, a mountain of failures; but still a mountain. And a mountain is always romantic.

There is another man in the modern world who might be called the antithesis of Mr. Chamberlain in every point, who is also a standing monument of the advantage of being misunderstood. Mr. Bernard Shaw is always represented by those who disagree with him, and, I fear, also (if such exist) by those who agree with him, as a capering humorist, a dazzling acrobat, a quick-change artist. It is said that he cannot be taken seriously, that he will defend anything or attack anything, that he will do anything to startle and amuse. All this is not only untrue, but it is, glaringly, the opposite of the truth; it is as wild as to say that Dickens had not the boisterous masculinity of Jane Austen. The whole force and triumph of Mr. Bernard Shaw lie in the fact that he is a thoroughly consistent man. So far from his power consisting in jumping through hoops or standing on his head, his power consists in holding his own fortress night and day. He puts the Shaw test rapidly and rigorously to everything that happens in heaven or earth. His standard never varies. The thing which weak-minded revolutionists and weak-minded Conservatives really hate (and fear) in him, is exactly this, that his scales, such as they are, are held even, and that his law, such as it is, is justly enforced. You may attack his principles, as I do; but I do not know of any instance in which you can attack their application. If he dislikes lawlessness, he dislikes the lawlessness of Socialists as much as that of Individualists. If he dislikes the fever of patriotism, he dislikes it in Boers and Irishmen as well as in Englishmen. If he dislikes the vows and bonds of marriage, he dislikes still more the fiercer bonds and wilder vows that are made by lawless love. If he laughs at the authority of priests, he laughs louder at the pomposity of men of science. If he condemns the irresponsibility of faith, he condemns with a sane consistency the equal irresponsibility of art. He has pleased all the bohemians by saying that women are equal to men; but he has infuriated them by suggesting that men are equal to women. He is almost mechanically just; he has something of the terrible quality of a machine. The man who is really wild and whirling, the man who is really fantastic and incalculable, is not Mr. Shaw, but the average Cabinet Minister. It is Sir Michael Hicks-Beach who jumps through hoops. It is Sir Henry Fowler who stands on his head. The solid and respectable statesman of that type does really leap from position to position; he is really ready to defend anything or nothing; he is really not to be taken seriously. I know perfectly well what Mr. Bernard Shaw will be saying thirty years hence; he will be saying what he has always said. If thirty years hence I meet Mr. Shaw, a reverent being with a silver beard sweeping the earth, and say to him, "One can never, of course, make a verbal attack upon a lady," the patriarch will lift his aged hand and fell me to the earth. We know, I say, what Mr. Shaw will be, saying thirty years hence. But is there any one so darkly read in stars and oracles that he will dare to predict what Mr. Asquith will be saying thirty years hence?

The truth is, that it is quite an error to suppose that absence of definite convictions gives the mind freedom and agility. A man who believes something is ready and witty, because he has all his weapons about him. He can apply his test in an instant. The man engaged in conflict with a man like Mr. Bernard Shaw may fancy he has ten faces; similarly a man engaged against a brilliant duellist may fancy that the sword of his foe has turned to ten swords in his hand. But this is not really because the man is playing with ten swords, it is because he is aiming very straight with one. Moreover, a man with a definite belief always appears bizarre, because he does not change with the world; he has climbed into a fixed star, and the earth whizzes below him like a zoetrope. Millions of mild black-coated men call themselves sane and sensible merely because they always catch the fashionable insanity, because they are hurried into madness after madness by the maelstrom of the world.

People accuse Mr. Shaw and many much sillier persons of "proving that black is white." But they never ask whether the current colour-language is always correct. Ordinary sensible phraseology sometimes calls black white, it certainly calls yellow white and green white and reddish-brown white. We call wine "white wine" which is as yellow as a Blue-coat boy's legs. We call grapes "white grapes" which are manifestly pale green. We give to the European, whose complexion is a sort of pink drab, the horrible title of a "white man"—a picture more blood-curdling than any spectre in Poe.

Now, it is undoubtedly true that if a man asked a waiter in a restaurant for a bottle of yellow wine and some greenish-yellow grapes, the waiter would think him mad. It is undoubtedly true that if a Government official, reporting on the Europeans in Burmah, said, "There are only two thousand pinkish men here" he would be accused of cracking jokes, and kicked out of his post. But it is equally obvious that both men would have come to grief through telling the strict truth. That too truthful man in the restaurant; that too truthful man in Burmah, is Mr. Bernard Shaw. He appears eccentric and grotesque because he will not accept the general belief that white is yellow. He has based all his brilliancy and solidity upon the hackneyed, but yet forgotten, fact that truth is stranger than fiction. Truth, of course, must of necessity be stranger than fiction, for we have made fiction to suit ourselves.

So much then a reasonable appreciation will find in Mr. Shaw to be bracing and excellent. He claims to see things as they are; and some things, at any rate, he does see as they are, which the whole of our civilization does not see at all. But in Mr. Shaw's realism there is something lacking, and that thing which is lacking is serious.

Mr. Shaw's old and recognized philosophy was that powerfully presented in "The Quintessence of Ibsenism." It was, in brief, that conservative ideals were bad, not because they were conservative, but because they were ideals. Every ideal prevented men from judging justly the particular case; every moral generalization oppressed the individual; the golden rule was there was no golden rule. And the objection to this is simply that it pretends to free men, but really restrains them from doing the only thing that men want to do. What is the good of telling a community that it has every liberty except the liberty to make laws? The liberty to make laws is what constitutes a free people. And what is the good of telling a man (or a philosopher) that he has every liberty except the liberty to make generalizations. Making generalizations is what makes him a man. In short, when Mr. Shaw forbids men to have strict moral ideals, he is acting like one who should forbid them to have children. The saying that "the golden rule is that there is no golden rule," can, indeed, be simply answered by being turned round. That there is no golden rule is itself a golden rule, or rather it is much worse than a golden rule. It is an iron rule; a fetter on the first movement of a man.

But the sensation connected with Mr. Shaw in recent years has been his sudden development of the religion of the Superman. He who had to all appearance mocked at the faiths in the forgotten past discovered a new god in the unimaginable future. He who had laid all the blame on ideals set up the most impossible of all ideals, the ideal of a new creature. But the truth, nevertheless, is that any one who knows Mr. Shaw's mind adequately, and admires it properly, must have guessed all this long ago.

For the truth is that Mr. Shaw has never seen things as they really are. If he had he would have fallen on his knees before them. He has always had a secret ideal that has withered all the things of this world. He has all the time been silently comparing humanity with something that was not human, with a monster from Mars, with the Wise Man of the Stoics, with the Economic Man of the Fabians, with Julius Caesar, with Siegfried, with the Superman. Now, to have this inner and merciless standard may be a very good thing, or a very bad one, it may be excellent or unfortunate, but it is not seeing things as they are. It is not seeing things as they are to think first of a Briareus with a hundred hands, and then call every man a cripple for only having two. It is not seeing things as they are to start with a vision of Argus with his hundred eyes, and then jeer at every man with two eyes as if he had only one. And it is not seeing things as they are to imagine a demigod of infinite mental clarity, who may or may not appear in the latter days of the earth, and then to see all men as idiots. And this is what Mr. Shaw has always in some degree done. When we really see men as they are, we do not criticise, but worship; and very rightly. For a monster with mysterious eyes and miraculous thumbs, with strange dreams in his skull, and a queer tenderness for this place or that baby, is truly a wonderful and unnerving matter. It is only the quite arbitrary and priggish habit of comparison with something else which makes it possible to be at our ease in front of him. A sentiment of superiority keeps us cool and practical; the mere facts would make our knees knock under as with religious fear. It is the fact that every instant of conscious life is an unimaginable prodigy. It is the fact that every face in the street has the incredible unexpectedness of a fairy-tale. The thing which prevents a man from realizing this is not any clear-sightedness or experience, it is simply a habit of pedantic and fastidious comparisons between one thing and another. Mr. Shaw, on the practical side perhaps the most humane man alive, is in this sense inhumane. He has even been infected to some extent with the primary intellectual weakness of his new master, Nietzsche, the strange notion that the greater and stronger a man was the more he would despise other things. The greater and stronger a man is the more he would be inclined to prostrate himself before a periwinkle. That Mr. Shaw keeps a lifted head and a contemptuous face before the colossal panorama of empires and civilizations, this does not in itself convince one that he sees things as they are. I should be most effectively convinced that he did if I found him staring with religious astonishment at his own feet. "What are those two beautiful and industrious beings," I can imagine him murmuring to himself, "whom I see everywhere, serving me I know not why? What fairy godmother bade them come trotting out of elfland when I was born? What god of the borderland, what barbaric god of legs, must I propitiate with fire and wine, lest they run away with me?"

The truth is, that all genuine appreciation rests on a certain mystery of humility and almost of darkness. The man who said, "Blessed is he that expecteth nothing, for he shall not be disappointed," put the eulogy quite inadequately and even falsely. The truth "Blessed is he that expecteth nothing, for he shall be gloriously surprised." The man who expects nothing sees redder roses than common men can see, and greener grass, and a more startling sun. Blessed is he that expecteth nothing, for he shall possess the cities and the mountains; blessed is the meek, for he shall inherit the earth. Until we realize that things might not be we cannot realize that things are. Until we see the background of darkness we cannot admire the light as a single and created thing. As soon as we have seen that darkness, all light is lightening, sudden, blinding, and divine. Until we picture nonentity we underrate the victory of God, and can realize none of the trophies of His ancient war. It is one of the million wild jests of truth that we know nothing until we know nothing.

Now this is, I say deliberately, the only defect in the greatness of Mr. Shaw, the only answer to his claim to be a great man, that he is not easily pleased. He is an almost solitary exception to the general and essential maxim, that little things please great minds. And from this absence of that most uproarious of all things, humility, comes incidentally the peculiar insistence on the Superman. After belabouring a great many people for a great many years for being unprogressive, Mr. Shaw has discovered, with characteristic sense, that it is very doubtful whether any existing human being with two legs can be progressive at all. Having come to doubt whether humanity can be combined with progress, most people, easily pleased, would have elected to abandon progress and remain with humanity. Mr. Shaw, not being easily pleased, decides to throw over humanity with all its limitations and go in for progress for its own sake. If man, as we know him, is incapable of the philosophy of progress, Mr. Shaw asks, not for a new kind of philosophy, but for a new kind of man. It is rather as if a nurse had tried a rather bitter food for some years on a baby, and on discovering that it was not suitable, should not throw away the food and ask for a new food, but throw the baby out of window, and ask for a new baby. Mr. Shaw cannot understand that the thing which is valuable and lovable in our eyes is man—the old beer-drinking, creed-making, fighting, failing, sensual, respectable man. And the things that have been founded on this creature immortally remain; the things that have been founded on the fancy of the Superman have died with the dying civilizations which alone have given them birth. When Christ at a symbolic moment was establishing His great society, He chose for its corner-stone neither the brilliant Paul nor the mystic John, but a shuffler, a snob a coward—in a word, a man. And upon this rock He has built His Church, and the gates of Hell have not prevailed against it. All the empires and the kingdoms have failed, because of this inherent and continual weakness, that they were founded by strong men and upon strong men. But this one thing, the historic Christian Church, was founded on a weak man, and for that reason it is indestructible. For no chain is stronger than its weakest link.

V. MR. H. G. WELLS AND THE GIANTS

We ought to see far enough into a hypocrite to see even his sincerity. We ought to be interested in that darkest and most real part of a man in which dwell not the vices that he does not display, but the virtues that he cannot. And the more we approach the problems of human history with this keen and piercing charity, the smaller and smaller space we shall allow to pure hypocrisy of any kind. The hypocrites shall not deceive us into thinking them saints; but neither shall they deceive us into thinking them hypocrites. And an increasing number of cases will crowd into our field of inquiry, cases in which there is really no question of hypocrisy at all, cases in which people were so ingenuous that they seemed absurd, and so absurd that they seemed disingenuous.

There is one striking instance of an unfair charge of hypocrisy. It is always urged against the religious in the past, as a point of inconsistency and duplicity, that they combined a profession of almost crawling humility with a keen struggle for earthly success and considerable triumph in attaining it. It is felt as a piece of humbug, that a man should be very punctilious in calling himself a miserable sinner, and also very punctilious in calling himself King of France. But the truth is that there is no more conscious inconsistency between the humility of a Christian and the rapacity of a Christian than there is between the humility of a lover and the rapacity of a lover. The truth is that there are no things for which men will make such herculean efforts as the things of which they know they are unworthy. There never was a man in love who did not declare that, if he strained every nerve to breaking, he was going to have his desire. And there never was a man in love who did not declare also that he ought not to have it. The whole secret of the practical success of Christendom lies in the Christian humility, however imperfectly fulfilled. For with the removal of all question of merit or payment, the soul is suddenly released for incredible voyages. If we ask a sane man how much he merits, his mind shrinks instinctively and instantaneously. It is doubtful whether he merits six feet of earth. But if you ask him what he can conquer—he can conquer the stars. Thus comes the thing called Romance, a purely Christian product. A man cannot deserve adventures; he cannot earn dragons and hippogriffs. The mediaeval Europe which asserted humility gained Romance; the civilization which gained Romance has gained the habitable globe. How different the Pagan and Stoical feeling was from this has been admirably expressed in a famous quotation. Addison makes the great Stoic say—

"'Tis not in mortals to command success; But we'll do more, Sempronius, we'll deserve it."

But the spirit of Romance and Christendom, the spirit which is in every lover, the spirit which has bestridden the earth with European adventure, is quite opposite. 'Tis not in mortals to deserve success. But we'll do more, Sempronius; we'll obtain it.

And this gay humility, this holding of ourselves lightly and yet ready for an infinity of unmerited triumphs, this secret is so simple that every one has supposed that it must be something quite sinister and mysterious. Humility is so practical a virtue that men think it must be a vice. Humility is so successful that it is mistaken for pride. It is mistaken for it all the more easily because it generally goes with a certain simple love of splendour which amounts to vanity. Humility will always, by preference, go clad in scarlet and gold; pride is that which refuses to let gold and scarlet impress it or please it too much. In a word, the failure of this virtue actually lies in its success; it is too successful as an investment to be believed in as a virtue. Humility is not merely too good for this world; it is too practical for this world; I had almost said it is too worldly for this world.

The instance most quoted in our day is the thing called the humility of the man of science; and certainly it is a good instance as well as a modern one. Men find it extremely difficult to believe that a man who is obviously uprooting mountains and dividing seas, tearing down temples and stretching out hands to the stars, is really a quiet old gentleman who only asks to be allowed to indulge his harmless old hobby and follow his harmless old nose. When a man splits a grain of sand and the universe is turned upside down in consequence, it is difficult to realize that to the man who did it, the splitting of the grain is the great affair, and the capsizing of the cosmos quite a small one. It is hard to enter into the feelings of a man who regards a new heaven and a new earth in the light of a by-product. But undoubtedly it was to this almost eerie innocence of the intellect that the great men of the great scientific period, which now appears to be closing, owed their enormous power and triumph. If they had brought the heavens down like a house of cards their plea was not even that they had done it on principle; their quite unanswerable plea was that they had done it by accident. Whenever there was in them the least touch of pride in what they had done, there was a good ground for attacking them; but so long as they were wholly humble, they were wholly victorious. There were possible answers to Huxley; there was no answer possible to Darwin. He was convincing because of his unconsciousness; one might almost say because of his dulness. This childlike and prosaic mind is beginning to wane in the world of science. Men of science are beginning to see themselves, as the fine phrase is, in the part; they are beginning to be proud of their humility. They are beginning to be aesthetic, like the rest of the world, beginning to spell truth with a capital T, beginning to talk of the creeds they imagine themselves to have destroyed, of the discoveries that their forbears made. Like the modern English, they are beginning to be soft about their own hardness. They are becoming conscious of their own strength—that is, they are growing weaker. But one purely modern man has emerged in the strictly modern decades who does carry into our world the clear personal simplicity of the old world of science. One man of genius we have who is an artist, but who was a man of science, and who seems to be marked above all things with this great scientific humility. I mean Mr. H. G. Wells. And in his case, as in the others above spoken of, there must be a great preliminary difficulty in convincing the ordinary person that such a virtue is predicable of such a man. Mr. Wells began his literary work with violent visions—visions of the last pangs of this planet; can it be that a man who begins with violent visions is humble? He went on to wilder and wilder stories about carving beasts into men and shooting angels like birds. Is the man who shoots angels and carves beasts into men humble? Since then he has done something bolder than either of these blasphemies; he has prophesied the political future of all men; prophesied it with aggressive authority and a ringing decision of detail. Is the prophet of the future of all men humble? It will indeed be difficult, in the present condition of current thought about such things as pride and humility, to answer the query of how a man can be humble who does such big things and such bold things. For the only answer is the answer which I gave at the beginning of this essay. It is the humble man who does the big things. It is the humble man who does the bold things. It is the humble man who has the sensational sights vouchsafed to him, and this for three obvious reasons: first, that he strains his eyes more than any other men to see them; second, that he is more overwhelmed and uplifted with them when they come; third, that he records them more exactly and sincerely and with less adulteration from his more commonplace and more conceited everyday self. Adventures are to those to whom they are most unexpected—that is, most romantic. Adventures are to the shy: in this sense adventures are to the unadventurous.

Now, this arresting, mental humility in Mr. H. G. Wells may be, like a great many other things that are vital and vivid, difficult to illustrate by examples, but if I were asked for an example of it, I should have no difficulty about which example to begin with. The most interesting thing about Mr. H. G. Wells is that he is the only one of his many brilliant contemporaries who has not stopped growing. One can lie awake at night and hear him grow. Of this growth the most evident manifestation is indeed a gradual change of opinions; but it is no mere change of opinions. It is not a perpetual leaping from one position to another like that of Mr. George Moore. It is a quite continuous advance along a quite solid road in a quite definable direction. But the chief proof that it is not a piece of fickleness and vanity is the fact that it has been upon the whole an advance from more startling opinions to more humdrum opinions. It has been even in some sense an advance from unconventional opinions to conventional opinions. This fact fixes Mr. Wells's honesty and proves him to be no poseur. Mr. Wells once held that the upper classes and the lower classes would be so much differentiated in the future that one class would eat the other. Certainly no paradoxical charlatan who had once found arguments for so startling a view would ever have deserted it except for something yet more startling. Mr. Wells has deserted it in favour of the blameless belief that both classes will be ultimately subordinated or assimilated to a sort of scientific middle class, a class of engineers. He has abandoned the sensational theory with the same honourable gravity and simplicity with which he adopted it. Then he thought it was true; now he thinks it is not true. He has come to the most dreadful conclusion a literary man can come to, the conclusion that the ordinary view is the right one. It is only the last and wildest kind of courage that can stand on a tower before ten thousand people and tell them that twice two is four.

Mr. H. G. Wells exists at present in a gay and exhilarating progress of conservativism. He is finding out more and more that conventions, though silent, are alive. As good an example as any of this humility and sanity of his may be found in his change of view on the subject of science and marriage. He once held, I believe, the opinion which some singular sociologists still hold, that human creatures could successfully be paired and bred after the manner of dogs or horses. He no longer holds that view. Not only does he no longer hold that view, but he has written about it in "Mankind in the Making" with such smashing sense and humour, that I find it difficult to believe that anybody else can hold it either. It is true that his chief objection to the proposal is that it is physically impossible, which seems to me a very slight objection, and almost negligible compared with the others. The one objection to scientific marriage which is worthy of final attention is simply that such a thing could only be imposed on unthinkable slaves and cowards. I do not know whether the scientific marriage-mongers are right (as they say) or wrong (as Mr. Wells says) in saying that medical supervision would produce strong and healthy men. I am only certain that if it did, the first act of the strong and healthy men would be to smash the medical supervision.

The mistake of all that medical talk lies in the very fact that it connects the idea of health with the idea of care. What has health to do with care? Health has to do with carelessness. In special and abnormal cases it is necessary to have care. When we are peculiarly unhealthy it may be necessary to be careful in order to be healthy. But even then we are only trying to be healthy in order to be careless. If we are doctors we are speaking to exceptionally sick men, and they ought to be told to be careful. But when we are sociologists we are addressing the normal man, we are addressing humanity. And humanity ought to be told to be recklessness itself. For all the fundamental functions of a healthy man ought emphatically to be performed with pleasure and for pleasure; they emphatically ought not to be performed with precaution or for precaution. A man ought to eat because he has a good appetite to satisfy, and emphatically not because he has a body to sustain. A man ought to take exercise not because he is too fat, but because he loves foils or horses or high mountains, and loves them for their own sake. And a man ought to marry because he has fallen in love, and emphatically not because the world requires to be populated. The food will really renovate his tissues as long as he is not thinking about his tissues. The exercise will really get him into training so long as he is thinking about something else. And the marriage will really stand some chance of producing a generous-blooded generation if it had its origin in its own natural and generous excitement. It is the first law of health that our necessities should not be accepted as necessities; they should be accepted as luxuries. Let us, then, be careful about the small things, such as a scratch or a slight illness, or anything that can be managed with care. But in the name of all sanity, let us be careless about the important things, such as marriage, or the fountain of our very life will fail.

Mr. Wells, however, is not quite clear enough of the narrower scientific outlook to see that there are some things which actually ought not to be scientific. He is still slightly affected with the great scientific fallacy; I mean the habit of beginning not with the human soul, which is the first thing a man learns about, but with some such thing as protoplasm, which is about the last. The one defect in his splendid mental equipment is that he does not sufficiently allow for the stuff or material of men. In his new Utopia he says, for instance, that a chief point of the Utopia will be a disbelief in original sin. If he had begun with the human soul—that is, if he had begun on himself—he would have found original sin almost the first thing to be believed in. He would have found, to put the matter shortly, that a permanent possibility of selfishness arises from the mere fact of having a self, and not from any accidents of education or ill-treatment. And the weakness of all Utopias is this, that they take the greatest difficulty of man and assume it to be overcome, and then give an elaborate account of the overcoming of the smaller ones. They first assume that no man will want more than his share, and then are very ingenious in explaining whether his share will be delivered by motor-car or balloon. And an even stronger example of Mr. Wells's indifference to the human psychology can be found in his cosmopolitanism, the abolition in his Utopia of all patriotic boundaries. He says in his innocent way that Utopia must be a world-state, or else people might make war on it. It does not seem to occur to him that, for a good many of us, if it were a world-state we should still make war on it to the end of the world. For if we admit that there must be varieties in art or opinion what sense is there in thinking there will not be varieties in government? The fact is very simple. Unless you are going deliberately to prevent a thing being good, you cannot prevent it being worth fighting for. It is impossible to prevent a possible conflict of civilizations, because it is impossible to prevent a possible conflict between ideals. If there were no longer our modern strife between nations, there would only be a strife between Utopias. For the highest thing does not tend to union only; the highest thing, tends also to differentiation. You can often get men to fight for the union; but you can never prevent them from fighting also for the differentiation. This variety in the highest thing is the meaning of the fierce patriotism, the fierce nationalism of the great European civilization. It is also, incidentally, the meaning of the doctrine of the Trinity.

But I think the main mistake of Mr. Wells's philosophy is a somewhat deeper one, one that he expresses in a very entertaining manner in the introductory part of the new Utopia. His philosophy in some sense amounts to a denial of the possibility of philosophy itself. At least, he maintains that there are no secure and reliable ideas upon which we can rest with a final mental satisfaction. It will be both clearer, however, and more amusing to quote Mr. Wells himself.

He says, "Nothing endures, nothing is precise and certain (except the mind of a pedant).... Being indeed!—there is no being, but a universal becoming of individualities, and Plato turned his back on truth when he turned towards his museum of specific ideals." Mr. Wells says, again, "There is no abiding thing in what we know. We change from weaker to stronger lights, and each more powerful light pierces our hitherto opaque foundations and reveals fresh and different opacities below." Now, when Mr. Wells says things like this, I speak with all respect when I say that he does not observe an evident mental distinction. It cannot be true that there is nothing abiding in what we know. For if that were so we should not know it all and should not call it knowledge. Our mental state may be very different from that of somebody else some thousands of years back; but it cannot be entirely different, or else we should not be conscious of a difference. Mr. Wells must surely realize the first and simplest of the paradoxes that sit by the springs of truth. He must surely see that the fact of two things being different implies that they are similar. The hare and the tortoise may differ in the quality of swiftness, but they must agree in the quality of motion. The swiftest hare cannot be swifter than an isosceles triangle or the idea of pinkness. When we say the hare moves faster, we say that the tortoise moves. And when we say of a thing that it moves, we say, without need of other words, that there are things that do not move. And even in the act of saying that things change, we say that there is something unchangeable.

But certainly the best example of Mr. Wells's fallacy can be found in the example which he himself chooses. It is quite true that we see a dim light which, compared with a darker thing, is light, but which, compared with a stronger light, is darkness. But the quality of light remains the same thing, or else we should not call it a stronger light or recognize it as such. If the character of light were not fixed in the mind, we should be quite as likely to call a denser shadow a stronger light, or vice versa If the character of light became even for an instant unfixed, if it became even by a hair's-breadth doubtful, if, for example, there crept into our idea of light some vague idea of blueness, then in that flash we have become doubtful whether the new light has more light or less. In brief, the progress may be as varying as a cloud, but the direction must be as rigid as a French road. North and South are relative in the sense that I am North of Bournemouth and South of Spitzbergen. But if there be any doubt of the position of the North Pole, there is in equal degree a doubt of whether I am South of Spitzbergen at all. The absolute idea of light may be practically unattainable. We may not be able to procure pure light. We may not be able to get to the North Pole. But because the North Pole is unattainable, it does not follow that it is indefinable. And it is only because the North Pole is not indefinable that we can make a satisfactory map of Brighton and Worthing.

In other words, Plato turned his face to truth but his back on Mr. H. G. Wells, when he turned to his museum of specified ideals. It is precisely here that Plato shows his sense. It is not true that everything changes; the things that change are all the manifest and material things. There is something that does not change; and that is precisely the abstract quality, the invisible idea. Mr. Wells says truly enough, that a thing which we have seen in one connection as dark we may see in another connection as light. But the thing common to both incidents is the mere idea of light—which we have not seen at all. Mr. Wells might grow taller and taller for unending aeons till his head was higher than the loneliest star. I can imagine his writing a good novel about it. In that case he would see the trees first as tall things and then as short things; he would see the clouds first as high and then as low. But there would remain with him through the ages in that starry loneliness the idea of tallness; he would have in the awful spaces for companion and comfort the definite conception that he was growing taller and not (for instance) growing fatter.

And now it comes to my mind that Mr. H. G. Wells actually has written a very delightful romance about men growing as tall as trees; and that here, again, he seems to me to have been a victim of this vague relativism. "The Food of the Gods" is, like Mr. Bernard Shaw's play, in essence a study of the Superman idea. And it lies, I think, even through the veil of a half-pantomimic allegory, open to the same intellectual attack. We cannot be expected to have any regard for a great creature if he does not in any manner conform to our standards. For unless he passes our standard of greatness we cannot even call him great. Nietszche summed up all that is interesting in the Superman idea when he said, "Man is a thing which has to be surpassed." But the very word "surpass" implies the existence of a standard common to us and the thing surpassing us. If the Superman is more manly than men are, of course they will ultimately deify him, even if they happen to kill him first. But if he is simply more supermanly, they may be quite indifferent to him as they would be to another seemingly aimless monstrosity. He must submit to our test even in order to overawe us. Mere force or size even is a standard; but that alone will never make men think a man their superior. Giants, as in the wise old fairy-tales, are vermin. Supermen, if not good men, are vermin.

"The Food of the Gods" is the tale of "Jack the Giant-Killer" told from the point of view of the giant. This has not, I think, been done before in literature; but I have little doubt that the psychological substance of it existed in fact. I have little doubt that the giant whom Jack killed did regard himself as the Superman. It is likely enough that he considered Jack a narrow and parochial person who wished to frustrate a great forward movement of the life-force. If (as not unfrequently was the case) he happened to have two heads, he would point out the elementary maxim which declares them to be better than one. He would enlarge on the subtle modernity of such an equipment, enabling a giant to look at a subject from two points of view, or to correct himself with promptitude. But Jack was the champion of the enduring human standards, of the principle of one man one head and one man one conscience, of the single head and the single heart and the single eye. Jack was quite unimpressed by the question of whether the giant was a particularly gigantic giant. All he wished to know was whether he was a good giant— that is, a giant who was any good to us. What were the giant's religious views; what his views on politics and the duties of the citizen? Was he fond of children—or fond of them only in a dark and sinister sense? To use a fine phrase for emotional sanity, was his heart in the right place? Jack had sometimes to cut him up with a sword in order to find out. The old and correct story of Jack the Giant-Killer is simply the whole story of man; if it were understood we should need no Bibles or histories. But the modern world in particular does not seem to understand it at all. The modern world, like Mr. Wells is on the side of the giants; the safest place, and therefore the meanest and the most prosaic. The modern world, when it praises its little Caesars, talks of being strong and brave: but it does not seem to see the eternal paradox involved in the conjunction of these ideas. The strong cannot be brave. Only the weak can be brave; and yet again, in practice, only those who can be brave can be trusted, in time of doubt, to be strong. The only way in which a giant could really keep himself in training against the inevitable Jack would be by continually fighting other giants ten times as big as himself. That is by ceasing to be a giant and becoming a Jack. Thus that sympathy with the small or the defeated as such, with which we Liberals and Nationalists have been often reproached, is not a useless sentimentalism at all, as Mr. Wells and his friends fancy. It is the first law of practical courage. To be in the weakest camp is to be in the strongest school. Nor can I imagine anything that would do humanity more good than the advent of a race of Supermen, for them to fight like dragons. If the Superman is better than we, of course we need not fight him; but in that case, why not call him the Saint? But if he is merely stronger (whether physically, mentally, or morally stronger, I do not care a farthing), then he ought to have to reckon with us at least for all the strength we have. It we are weaker than he, that is no reason why we should be weaker than ourselves. If we are not tall enough to touch the giant's knees, that is no reason why we should become shorter by falling on our own. But that is at bottom the meaning of all modern hero-worship and celebration of the Strong Man, the Caesar the Superman. That he may be something more than man, we must be something less.

Doubtless there is an older and better hero-worship than this. But the old hero was a being who, like Achilles, was more human than humanity itself. Nietzsche's Superman is cold and friendless. Achilles is so foolishly fond of his friend that he slaughters armies in the agony of his bereavement. Mr. Shaw's sad Caesar says in his desolate pride, "He who has never hoped can never despair." The Man-God of old answers from his awful hill, "Was ever sorrow like unto my sorrow?" A great man is not a man so strong that he feels less than other men; he is a man so strong that he feels more. And when Nietszche says, "A new commandment I give to you, 'be hard,'" he is really saying, "A new commandment I give to you, 'be dead.'" Sensibility is the definition of life.

I recur for a last word to Jack the Giant-Killer. I have dwelt on this matter of Mr. Wells and the giants, not because it is specially prominent in his mind; I know that the Superman does not bulk so large in his cosmos as in that of Mr. Bernard Shaw. I have dwelt on it for the opposite reason; because this heresy of immoral hero-worship has taken, I think, a slighter hold of him, and may perhaps still be prevented from perverting one of the best thinkers of the day. In the course of "The New Utopia" Mr. Wells makes more than one admiring allusion to Mr. W. E. Henley. That clever and unhappy man lived in admiration of a vague violence, and was always going back to rude old tales and rude old ballads, to strong and primitive literatures, to find the praise of strength and the justification of tyranny. But he could not find it. It is not there. The primitive literature is shown in the tale of Jack the Giant-Killer. The strong old literature is all in praise of the weak. The rude old tales are as tender to minorities as any modern political idealist. The rude old ballads are as sentimentally concerned for the under-dog as the Aborigines Protection Society. When men were tough and raw, when they lived amid hard knocks and hard laws, when they knew what fighting really was, they had only two kinds of songs. The first was a rejoicing that the weak had conquered the strong, the second a lamentation that the strong had, for once in a way, conquered the weak. For this defiance of the statu quo, this constant effort to alter the existing balance, this premature challenge to the powerful, is the whole nature and inmost secret of the psychological adventure which is called man. It is his strength to disdain strength. The forlorn hope is not only a real hope, it is the only real hope of mankind. In the coarsest ballads of the greenwood men are admired most when they defy, not only the king, but what is more to the point, the hero. The moment Robin Hood becomes a sort of Superman, that moment the chivalrous chronicler shows us Robin thrashed by a poor tinker whom he thought to thrust aside. And the chivalrous chronicler makes Robin Hood receive the thrashing in a glow of admiration. This magnanimity is not a product of modern humanitarianism; it is not a product of anything to do with peace. This magnanimity is merely one of the lost arts of war. The Henleyites call for a sturdy and fighting England, and they go back to the fierce old stories of the sturdy and fighting English. And the thing that they find written across that fierce old literature everywhere, is "the policy of Majuba."

VI. CHRISTMAS AND THE AESTHETES

The world is round, so round that the schools of optimism and pessimism have been arguing from the beginning whether it is the right way up. The difficulty does not arise so much from the mere fact that good and evil are mingled in roughly equal proportions; it arises chiefly from the fact that men always differ about what parts are good and what evil. Hence the difficulty which besets "undenominational religions." They profess to include what is beautiful in all creeds, but they appear to many to have collected all that is dull in them. All the colours mixed together in purity ought to make a perfect white. Mixed together on any human paint-box, they make a thing like mud, and a thing very like many new religions. Such a blend is often something much worse than any one creed taken separately, even the creed of the Thugs. The error arises from the difficulty of detecting what is really the good part and what is really the bad part of any given religion. And this pathos falls rather heavily on those persons who have the misfortune to think of some religion or other, that the parts commonly counted good are bad, and the parts commonly counted bad are good.

It is tragic to admire and honestly admire a human group, but to admire it in a photographic negative. It is difficult to congratulate all their whites on being black and all their blacks on their whiteness. This will often happen to us in connection with human religions. Take two institutions which bear witness to the religious energy of the nineteenth century. Take the Salvation Army and the philosophy of Auguste Comte.

The usual verdict of educated people on the Salvation Army is expressed in some such words as these: "I have no doubt they do a great deal of good, but they do it in a vulgar and profane style; their aims are excellent, but their methods are wrong." To me, unfortunately, the precise reverse of this appears to be the truth. I do not know whether the aims of the Salvation Army are excellent, but I am quite sure their methods are admirable. Their methods are the methods of all intense and hearty religions; they are popular like all religion, military like all religion, public and sensational like all religion. They are not reverent any more than Roman Catholics are reverent, for reverence in the sad and delicate meaning of the term reverence is a thing only possible to infidels. That beautiful twilight you will find in Euripides, in Renan, in Matthew Arnold; but in men who believe you will not find it—you will find only laughter and war. A man cannot pay that kind of reverence to truth solid as marble; they can only be reverent towards a beautiful lie. And the Salvation Army, though their voice has broken out in a mean environment and an ugly shape, are really the old voice of glad and angry faith, hot as the riots of Dionysus, wild as the gargoyles of Catholicism, not to be mistaken for a philosophy. Professor Huxley, in one of his clever phrases, called the Salvation Army "corybantic Christianity." Huxley was the last and noblest of those Stoics who have never understood the Cross. If he had understood Christianity he would have known that there never has been, and never can be, any Christianity that is not corybantic.

And there is this difference between the matter of aims and the matter of methods, that to judge of the aims of a thing like the Salvation Army is very difficult, to judge of their ritual and atmosphere very easy. No one, perhaps, but a sociologist can see whether General Booth's housing scheme is right. But any healthy person can see that banging brass cymbals together must be right. A page of statistics, a plan of model dwellings, anything which is rational, is always difficult for the lay mind. But the thing which is irrational any one can understand. That is why religion came so early into the world and spread so far, while science came so late into the world and has not spread at all. History unanimously attests the fact that it is only mysticism which stands the smallest chance of being understanded of the people. Common sense has to be kept as an esoteric secret in the dark temple of culture. And so while the philanthropy of the Salvationists and its genuineness may be a reasonable matter for the discussion of the doctors, there can be no doubt about the genuineness of their brass bands, for a brass band is purely spiritual, and seeks only to quicken the internal life. The object of philanthropy is to do good; the object of religion is to be good, if only for a moment, amid a crash of brass.

And the same antithesis exists about another modern religion—I mean the religion of Comte, generally known as Positivism, or the worship of humanity. Such men as Mr. Frederic Harrison, that brilliant and chivalrous philosopher, who still, by his mere personality, speaks for the creed, would tell us that he offers us the philosophy of Comte, but not all Comte's fantastic proposals for pontiffs and ceremonials, the new calendar, the new holidays and saints' days. He does not mean that we should dress ourselves up as priests of humanity or let off fireworks because it is Milton's birthday. To the solid English Comtist all this appears, he confesses, to be a little absurd. To me it appears the only sensible part of Comtism. As a philosophy it is unsatisfactory. It is evidently impossible to worship humanity, just as it is impossible to worship the Savile Club; both are excellent institutions to which we may happen to belong. But we perceive clearly that the Savile Club did not make the stars and does not fill the universe. And it is surely unreasonable to attack the doctrine of the Trinity as a piece of bewildering mysticism, and then to ask men to worship a being who is ninety million persons in one God, neither confounding the persons nor dividing the substance.

But if the wisdom of Comte was insufficient, the folly of Comte was wisdom. In an age of dusty modernity, when beauty was thought of as something barbaric and ugliness as something sensible, he alone saw that men must always have the sacredness of mummery. He saw that while the brutes have all the useful things, the things that are truly human are the useless ones. He saw the falsehood of that almost universal notion of to-day, the notion that rites and forms are something artificial, additional, and corrupt. Ritual is really much older than thought; it is much simpler and much wilder than thought. A feeling touching the nature of things does not only make men feel that there are certain proper things to say; it makes them feel that there are certain proper things to do. The more agreeable of these consist of dancing, building temples, and shouting very loud; the less agreeable, of wearing green carnations and burning other philosophers alive. But everywhere the religious dance came before the religious hymn, and man was a ritualist before he could speak. If Comtism had spread the world would have been converted, not by the Comtist philosophy, but by the Comtist calendar. By discouraging what they conceive to be the weakness of their master, the English Positivists have broken the strength of their religion. A man who has faith must be prepared not only to be a martyr, but to be a fool. It is absurd to say that a man is ready to toil and die for his convictions when he is not even ready to wear a wreath round his head for them. I myself, to take a corpus vile, am very certain that I would not read the works of Comte through for any consideration whatever. But I can easily imagine myself with the greatest enthusiasm lighting a bonfire on Darwin Day.

That splendid effort failed, and nothing in the style of it has succeeded. There has been no rationalist festival, no rationalist ecstasy. Men are still in black for the death of God. When Christianity was heavily bombarded in the last century upon no point was it more persistently and brilliantly attacked than upon that of its alleged enmity to human joy. Shelley and Swinburne and all their armies have passed again and again over the ground, but they have not altered it. They have not set up a single new trophy or ensign for the world's merriment to rally to. They have not given a name or a new occasion of gaiety. Mr. Swinburne does not hang up his stocking on the eve of the birthday of Victor Hugo. Mr. William Archer does not sing carols descriptive of the infancy of Ibsen outside people's doors in the snow. In the round of our rational and mournful year one festival remains out of all those ancient gaieties that once covered the whole earth. Christmas remains to remind us of those ages, whether Pagan or Christian, when the many acted poetry instead of the few writing it. In all the winter in our woods there is no tree in glow but the holly.

The strange truth about the matter is told in the very word "holiday." A bank holiday means presumably a day which bankers regard as holy. A half-holiday means, I suppose, a day on which a schoolboy is only partially holy. It is hard to see at first sight why so human a thing as leisure and larkiness should always have a religious origin. Rationally there appears no reason why we should not sing and give each other presents in honour of anything—the birth of Michael Angelo or the opening of Euston Station. But it does not work. As a fact, men only become greedily and gloriously material about something spiritualistic. Take away the Nicene Creed and similar things, and you do some strange wrong to the sellers of sausages. Take away the strange beauty of the saints, and what has remained to us is the far stranger ugliness of Wandsworth. Take away the supernatural, and what remains is the unnatural.

And now I have to touch upon a very sad matter. There are in the modern world an admirable class of persons who really make protest on behalf of that antiqua pulchritudo of which Augustine spoke, who do long for the old feasts and formalities of the childhood of the world. William Morris and his followers showed how much brighter were the dark ages than the age of Manchester. Mr. W. B. Yeats frames his steps in prehistoric dances, but no man knows and joins his voice to forgotten choruses that no one but he can hear. Mr. George Moore collects every fragment of Irish paganism that the forgetfulness of the Catholic Church has left or possibly her wisdom preserved. There are innumerable persons with eye-glasses and green garments who pray for the return of the maypole or the Olympian games. But there is about these people a haunting and alarming something which suggests that it is just possible that they do not keep Christmas. It is painful to regard human nature in such a light, but it seems somehow possible that Mr. George Moore does not wave his spoon and shout when the pudding is set alight. It is even possible that Mr. W. B. Yeats never pulls crackers. If so, where is the sense of all their dreams of festive traditions? Here is a solid and ancient festive tradition still plying a roaring trade in the streets, and they think it vulgar. if this is so, let them be very certain of this, that they are the kind of people who in the time of the maypole would have thought the maypole vulgar; who in the time of the Canterbury pilgrimage would have thought the Canterbury pilgrimage vulgar; who in the time of the Olympian games would have thought the Olympian games vulgar. Nor can there be any reasonable doubt that they were vulgar. Let no man deceive himself; if by vulgarity we mean coarseness of speech, rowdiness of behaviour, gossip, horseplay, and some heavy drinking, vulgarity there always was wherever there was joy, wherever there was faith in the gods. Wherever you have belief you will have hilarity, wherever you have hilarity you will have some dangers. And as creed and mythology produce this gross and vigorous life, so in its turn this gross and vigorous life will always produce creed and mythology. If we ever get the English back on to the English land they will become again a religious people, if all goes well, a superstitious people. The absence from modern life of both the higher and lower forms of faith is largely due to a divorce from nature and the trees and clouds. If we have no more turnip ghosts it is chiefly from the lack of turnips.

VII. OMAR AND THE SACRED VINE

A new morality has burst upon us with some violence in connection with the problem of strong drink; and enthusiasts in the matter range from the man who is violently thrown out at 12.30, to the lady who smashes American bars with an axe. In these discussions it is almost always felt that one very wise and moderate position is to say that wine or such stuff should only be drunk as a medicine. With this I should venture to disagree with a peculiar ferocity. The one genuinely dangerous and immoral way of drinking wine is to drink it as a medicine. And for this reason, If a man drinks wine in order to obtain pleasure, he is trying to obtain something exceptional, something he does not expect every hour of the day, something which, unless he is a little insane, he will not try to get every hour of the day. But if a man drinks wine in order to obtain health, he is trying to get something natural; something, that is, that he ought not to be without; something that he may find it difficult to reconcile himself to being without. The man may not be seduced who has seen the ecstasy of being ecstatic; it is more dazzling to catch a glimpse of the ecstasy of being ordinary. If there were a magic ointment, and we took it to a strong man, and said, "This will enable you to jump off the Monument," doubtless he would jump off the Monument, but he would not jump off the Monument all day long to the delight of the City. But if we took it to a blind man, saying, "This will enable you to see," he would be under a heavier temptation. It would be hard for him not to rub it on his eyes whenever he heard the hoof of a noble horse or the birds singing at daybreak. It is easy to deny one's self festivity; it is difficult to deny one's self normality. Hence comes the fact which every doctor knows, that it is often perilous to give alcohol to the sick even when they need it. I need hardly say that I do not mean that I think the giving of alcohol to the sick for stimulus is necessarily unjustifiable. But I do mean that giving it to the healthy for fun is the proper use of it, and a great deal more consistent with health.

The sound rule in the matter would appear to be like many other sound rules—a paradox. Drink because you are happy, but never because you are miserable. Never drink when you are wretched without it, or you will be like the grey-faced gin-drinker in the slum; but drink when you would be happy without it, and you will be like the laughing peasant of Italy. Never drink because you need it, for this is rational drinking, and the way to death and hell. But drink because you do not need it, for this is irrational drinking, and the ancient health of the world.

For more than thirty years the shadow and glory of a great Eastern figure has lain upon our English literature. Fitzgerald's translation of Omar Khayyam concentrated into an immortal poignancy all the dark and drifting hedonism of our time. Of the literary splendour of that work it would be merely banal to speak; in few other of the books of men has there been anything so combining the gay pugnacity of an epigram with the vague sadness of a song. But of its philosophical, ethical, and religious influence which has been almost as great as its brilliancy, I should like to say a word, and that word, I confess, one of uncompromising hostility. There are a great many things which might be said against the spirit of the Rubaiyat, and against its prodigious influence. But one matter of indictment towers ominously above the rest—a genuine disgrace to it, a genuine calamity to us. This is the terrible blow that this great poem has struck against sociability and the joy of life. Some one called Omar "the sad, glad old Persian." Sad he is; glad he is not, in any sense of the word whatever. He has been a worse foe to gladness than the Puritans.

A pensive and graceful Oriental lies under the rose-tree with his wine-pot and his scroll of poems. It may seem strange that any one's thoughts should, at the moment of regarding him, fly back to the dark bedside where the doctor doles out brandy. It may seem stranger still that they should go back to the grey wastrel shaking with gin in Houndsditch. But a great philosophical unity links the three in an evil bond. Omar Khayyam's wine-bibbing is bad, not because it is wine-bibbing. It is bad, and very bad, because it is medical wine-bibbing. It is the drinking of a man who drinks because he is not happy. His is the wine that shuts out the universe, not the wine that reveals it. It is not poetical drinking, which is joyous and instinctive; it is rational drinking, which is as prosaic as an investment, as unsavoury as a dose of camomile. Whole heavens above it, from the point of view of sentiment, though not of style, rises the splendour of some old English drinking-song—

"Then pass the bowl, my comrades all, And let the zider vlow."

For this song was caught up by happy men to express the worth of truly worthy things, of brotherhood and garrulity, and the brief and kindly leisure of the poor. Of course, the great part of the more stolid reproaches directed against the Omarite morality are as false and babyish as such reproaches usually are. One critic, whose work I have read, had the incredible foolishness to call Omar an atheist and a materialist. It is almost impossible for an Oriental to be either; the East understands metaphysics too well for that. Of course, the real objection which a philosophical Christian would bring against the religion of Omar, is not that he gives no place to God, it is that he gives too much place to God. His is that terrible theism which can imagine nothing else but deity, and which denies altogether the outlines of human personality and human will.

"The ball no question makes of Ayes or Noes, But Here or There as strikes the Player goes; And He that tossed you down into the field, He knows about it all—he knows—he knows."

A Christian thinker such as Augustine or Dante would object to this because it ignores free-will, which is the valour and dignity of the soul. The quarrel of the highest Christianity with this scepticism is not in the least that the scepticism denies the existence of God; it is that it denies the existence of man.

In this cult of the pessimistic pleasure-seeker the Rubaiyat stands first in our time; but it does not stand alone. Many of the most brilliant intellects of our time have urged us to the same self-conscious snatching at a rare delight. Walter Pater said that we were all under sentence of death, and the only course was to enjoy exquisite moments simply for those moments' sake. The same lesson was taught by the very powerful and very desolate philosophy of Oscar Wilde. It is the carpe diem religion; but the carpe diem religion is not the religion of happy people, but of very unhappy people. Great joy does, not gather the rosebuds while it may; its eyes are fixed on the immortal rose which Dante saw. Great joy has in it the sense of immortality; the very splendour of youth is the sense that it has all space to stretch its legs in. In all great comic literature, in "Tristram Shandy" or "Pickwick", there is this sense of space and incorruptibility; we feel the characters are deathless people in an endless tale.

It is true enough, of course, that a pungent happiness comes chiefly in certain passing moments; but it is not true that we should think of them as passing, or enjoy them simply "for those moments' sake." To do this is to rationalize the happiness, and therefore to destroy it. Happiness is a mystery like religion, and should never be rationalized. Suppose a man experiences a really splendid moment of pleasure. I do not mean something connected with a bit of enamel, I mean something with a violent happiness in it—an almost painful happiness. A man may have, for instance, a moment of ecstasy in first love, or a moment of victory in battle. The lover enjoys the moment, but precisely not for the moment's sake. He enjoys it for the woman's sake, or his own sake. The warrior enjoys the moment, but not for the sake of the moment; he enjoys it for the sake of the flag. The cause which the flag stands for may be foolish and fleeting; the love may be calf-love, and last a week. But the patriot thinks of the flag as eternal; the lover thinks of his love as something that cannot end. These moments are filled with eternity; these moments are joyful because they do not seem momentary. Once look at them as moments after Pater's manner, and they become as cold as Pater and his style. Man cannot love mortal things. He can only love immortal things for an instant.

Pater's mistake is revealed in his most famous phrase. He asks us to burn with a hard, gem-like flame. Flames are never hard and never gem-like—they cannot be handled or arranged. So human emotions are never hard and never gem-like; they are always dangerous, like flames, to touch or even to examine. There is only one way in which our passions can become hard and gem-like, and that is by becoming as cold as gems. No blow then has ever been struck at the natural loves and laughter of men so sterilizing as this carpe diem of the aesthetes. For any kind of pleasure a totally different spirit is required; a certain shyness, a certain indeterminate hope, a certain boyish expectation. Purity and simplicity are essential to passions—yes even to evil passions. Even vice demands a sort of virginity.

Omar's (or Fitzgerald's) effect upon the other world we may let go, his hand upon this world has been heavy and paralyzing. The Puritans, as I have said, are far jollier than he. The new ascetics who follow Thoreau or Tolstoy are much livelier company; for, though the surrender of strong drink and such luxuries may strike us as an idle negation, it may leave a man with innumerable natural pleasures, and, above all, with man's natural power of happiness. Thoreau could enjoy the sunrise without a cup of coffee. If Tolstoy cannot admire marriage, at least he is healthy enough to admire mud. Nature can be enjoyed without even the most natural luxuries. A good bush needs no wine. But neither nature nor wine nor anything else can be enjoyed if we have the wrong attitude towards happiness, and Omar (or Fitzgerald) did have the wrong attitude towards happiness. He and those he has influenced do not see that if we are to be truly gay, we must believe that there is some eternal gaiety in the nature of things. We cannot enjoy thoroughly even a pas-de-quatre at a subscription dance unless we believe that the stars are dancing to the same tune. No one can be really hilarious but the serious man. "Wine," says the Scripture, "maketh glad the heart of man," but only of the man who has a heart. The thing called high spirits is possible only to the spiritual. Ultimately a man cannot rejoice in anything except the nature of things. Ultimately a man can enjoy nothing except religion. Once in the world's history men did believe that the stars were dancing to the tune of their temples, and they danced as men have never danced since. With this old pagan eudaemonism the sage of the Rubaiyat has quite as little to do as he has with any Christian variety. He is no more a Bacchanal than he is a saint. Dionysus and his church was grounded on a serious joie-de-vivre like that of Walt Whitman. Dionysus made wine, not a medicine, but a sacrament. Jesus Christ also made wine, not a medicine, but a sacrament. But Omar makes it, not a sacrament, but a medicine. He feasts because life is not joyful; he revels because he is not glad. "Drink," he says, "for you know not whence you come nor why. Drink, for you know not when you go nor where. Drink, because the stars are cruel and the world as idle as a humming-top. Drink, because there is nothing worth trusting, nothing worth fighting for. Drink, because all things are lapsed in a base equality and an evil peace." So he stands offering us the cup in his hand. And at the high altar of Christianity stands another figure, in whose hand also is the cup of the vine. "Drink" he says "for the whole world is as red as this wine, with the crimson of the love and wrath of God. Drink, for the trumpets are blowing for battle and this is the stirrup-cup. Drink, for this my blood of the new testament that is shed for you. Drink, for I know of whence you come and why. Drink, for I know of when you go and where."

VIII. THE MILDNESS OF THE YELLOW PRESS

There is a great deal of protest made from one quarter or another nowadays against the influence of that new journalism which is associated with the names of Sir Alfred Harmsworth and Mr. Pearson. But almost everybody who attacks it attacks on the ground that it is very sensational, very violent and vulgar and startling. I am speaking in no affected contrariety, but in the simplicity of a genuine personal impression, when I say that this journalism offends as being not sensational or violent enough. The real vice is not that it is startling, but that it is quite insupportably tame. The whole object is to keep carefully along a certain level of the expected and the commonplace; it may be low, but it must take care also to be flat. Never by any chance in it is there any of that real plebeian pungency which can be heard from the ordinary cabman in the ordinary street. We have heard of a certain standard of decorum which demands that things should be funny without being vulgar, but the standard of this decorum demands that if things are vulgar they shall be vulgar without being funny. This journalism does not merely fail to exaggerate life—it positively underrates it; and it has to do so because it is intended for the faint and languid recreation of men whom the fierceness of modern life has fatigued. This press is not the yellow press at all; it is the drab press. Sir Alfred Harmsworth must not address to the tired clerk any observation more witty than the tired clerk might be able to address to Sir Alfred Harmsworth. It must not expose anybody (anybody who is powerful, that is), it must not offend anybody, it must not even please anybody, too much. A general vague idea that in spite of all this, our yellow press is sensational, arises from such external accidents as large type or lurid headlines. It is quite true that these editors print everything they possibly can in large capital letters. But they do this, not because it is startling, but because it is soothing. To people wholly weary or partly drunk in a dimly lighted train, it is a simplification and a comfort to have things presented in this vast and obvious manner. The editors use this gigantic alphabet in dealing with their readers, for exactly the same reason that parents and governesses use a similar gigantic alphabet in teaching children to spell. The nursery authorities do not use an A as big as a horseshoe in order to make the child jump; on the contrary, they use it to put the child at his ease, to make things smoother and more evident. Of the same character is the dim and quiet dame school which Sir Alfred Harmsworth and Mr. Pearson keep. All their sentiments are spelling-book sentiments—that is to say, they are sentiments with which the pupil is already respectfully familiar. All their wildest posters are leaves torn from a copy-book.

Of real sensational journalism, as it exists in France, in Ireland, and in America, we have no trace in this country. When a journalist in Ireland wishes to create a thrill, he creates a thrill worth talking about. He denounces a leading Irish member for corruption, or he charges the whole police system with a wicked and definite conspiracy. When a French journalist desires a frisson there is a frisson; he discovers, let us say, that the President of the Republic has murdered three wives. Our yellow journalists invent quite as unscrupulously as this; their moral condition is, as regards careful veracity, about the same. But it is their mental calibre which happens to be such that they can only invent calm and even reassuring things. The fictitious version of the massacre of the envoys of Pekin was mendacious, but it was not interesting, except to those who had private reasons for terror or sorrow. It was not connected with any bold and suggestive view of the Chinese situation. It revealed only a vague idea that nothing could be impressive except a great deal of blood. Real sensationalism, of which I happen to be very fond, may be either moral or immoral. But even when it is most immoral, it requires moral courage. For it is one of the most dangerous things on earth genuinely to surprise anybody. If you make any sentient creature jump, you render it by no means improbable that it will jump on you. But the leaders of this movement have no moral courage or immoral courage; their whole method consists in saying, with large and elaborate emphasis, the things which everybody else says casually, and without remembering what they have said. When they brace themselves up to attack anything, they never reach the point of attacking anything which is large and real, and would resound with the shock. They do not attack the army as men do in France, or the judges as men do in Ireland, or the democracy itself as men did in England a hundred years ago. They attack something like the War Office—something, that is, which everybody attacks and nobody bothers to defend, something which is an old joke in fourth-rate comic papers. just as a man shows he has a weak voice by straining it to shout, so they show the hopelessly unsensational nature of their minds when they really try to be sensational. With the whole world full of big and dubious institutions, with the whole wickedness of civilization staring them in the face, their idea of being bold and bright is to attack the War Office. They might as well start a campaign against the weather, or form a secret society in order to make jokes about mothers-in-law. Nor is it only from the point of view of particular amateurs of the sensational such as myself, that it is permissible to say, in the words of Cowper's Alexander Selkirk, that "their tameness is shocking to me." The whole modern world is pining for a genuinely sensational journalism. This has been discovered by that very able and honest journalist, Mr. Blatchford, who started his campaign against Christianity, warned on all sides, I believe, that it would ruin his paper, but who continued from an honourable sense of intellectual responsibility. He discovered, however, that while he had undoubtedly shocked his readers, he had also greatly advanced his newspaper. It was bought—first, by all the people who agreed with him and wanted to read it; and secondly, by all the people who disagreed with him, and wanted to write him letters. Those letters were voluminous (I helped, I am glad to say, to swell their volume), and they were generally inserted with a generous fulness. Thus was accidentally discovered (like the steam-engine) the great journalistic maxim—that if an editor can only make people angry enough, they will write half his newspaper for him for nothing.

Some hold that such papers as these are scarcely the proper objects of so serious a consideration; but that can scarcely be maintained from a political or ethical point of view. In this problem of the mildness and tameness of the Harmsworth mind there is mirrored the outlines of a much larger problem which is akin to it.

The Harmsworthian journalist begins with a worship of success and violence, and ends in sheer timidity and mediocrity. But he is not alone in this, nor does he come by this fate merely because he happens personally to be stupid. Every man, however brave, who begins by worshipping violence, must end in mere timidity. Every man, however wise, who begins by worshipping success, must end in mere mediocrity. This strange and paradoxical fate is involved, not in the individual, but in the philosophy, in the point of view. It is not the folly of the man which brings about this necessary fall; it is his wisdom. The worship of success is the only one out of all possible worships of which this is true, that its followers are foredoomed to become slaves and cowards. A man may be a hero for the sake of Mrs. Gallup's ciphers or for the sake of human sacrifice, but not for the sake of success. For obviously a man may choose to fail because he loves Mrs. Gallup or human sacrifice; but he cannot choose to fail because he loves success. When the test of triumph is men's test of everything, they never endure long enough to triumph at all. As long as matters are really hopeful, hope is a mere flattery or platitude; it is only when everything is hopeless that hope begins to be a strength at all. Like all the Christian virtues, it is as unreasonable as it is indispensable.

It was through this fatal paradox in the nature of things that all these modern adventurers come at last to a sort of tedium and acquiescence. They desired strength; and to them to desire strength was to admire strength; to admire strength was simply to admire the statu quo. They thought that he who wished to be strong ought to respect the strong. They did not realize the obvious verity that he who wishes to be strong must despise the strong. They sought to be everything, to have the whole force of the cosmos behind them, to have an energy that would drive the stars. But they did not realize the two great facts—first, that in the attempt to be everything the first and most difficult step is to be something; second, that the moment a man is something, he is essentially defying everything. The lower animals, say the men of science, fought their way up with a blind selfishness. If this be so, the only real moral of it is that our unselfishness, if it is to triumph, must be equally blind. The mammoth did not put his head on one side and wonder whether mammoths were a little out of date. Mammoths were at least as much up to date as that individual mammoth could make them. The great elk did not say, "Cloven hoofs are very much worn now." He polished his own weapons for his own use. But in the reasoning animal there has arisen a more horrible danger, that he may fail through perceiving his own failure. When modern sociologists talk of the necessity of accommodating one's self to the trend of the time, they forget that the trend of the time at its best consists entirely of people who will not accommodate themselves to anything. At its worst it consists of many millions of frightened creatures all accommodating themselves to a trend that is not there. And that is becoming more and more the situation of modern England. Every man speaks of public opinion, and means by public opinion, public opinion minus his opinion. Every man makes his contribution negative under the erroneous impression that the next man's contribution is positive. Every man surrenders his fancy to a general tone which is itself a surrender. And over all the heartless and fatuous unity spreads this new and wearisome and platitudinous press, incapable of invention, incapable of audacity, capable only of a servility all the more contemptible because it is not even a servility to the strong. But all who begin with force and conquest will end in this.

The chief characteristic of the "New journalism" is simply that it is bad journalism. It is beyond all comparison the most shapeless, careless, and colourless work done in our day.

I read yesterday a sentence which should be written in letters of gold and adamant; it is the very motto of the new philosophy of Empire. I found it (as the reader has already eagerly guessed) in Pearson's Magazine, while I was communing (soul to soul) with Mr. C. Arthur Pearson, whose first and suppressed name I am afraid is Chilperic. It occurred in an article on the American Presidential Election. This is the sentence, and every one should read it carefully, and roll it on the tongue, till all the honey be tasted.

"A little sound common sense often goes further with an audience of American working-men than much high-flown argument. A speaker who, as he brought forward his points, hammered nails into a board, won hundreds of votes for his side at the last Presidential Election."

I do not wish to soil this perfect thing with comment; the words of Mercury are harsh after the songs of Apollo. But just think for a moment of the mind, the strange inscrutable mind, of the man who wrote that, of the editor who approved it, of the people who are probably impressed by it, of the incredible American working-man, of whom, for all I know, it may be true. Think what their notion of "common sense" must be! It is delightful to realize that you and I are now able to win thousands of votes should we ever be engaged in a Presidential Election, by doing something of this kind. For I suppose the nails and the board are not essential to the exhibition of "common sense;" there may be variations. We may read—

"A little common sense impresses American working-men more than high-flown argument. A speaker who, as he made his points, pulled buttons off his waistcoat, won thousands of votes for his side." Or, "Sound common sense tells better in America than high-flown argument. Thus Senator Budge, who threw his false teeth in the air every time he made an epigram, won the solid approval of American working-men." Or again, "The sound common sense of a gentleman from Earlswood, who stuck straws in his hair during the progress of his speech, assured the victory of Mr. Roosevelt."

There are many other elements in this article on which I should love to linger. But the matter which I wish to point out is that in that sentence is perfectly revealed the whole truth of what our Chamberlainites, hustlers, bustlers, Empire-builders, and strong, silent men, really mean by "commonsense." They mean knocking, with deafening noise and dramatic effect, meaningless bits of iron into a useless bit of wood. A man goes on to an American platform and behaves like a mountebank fool with a board and a hammer; well, I do not blame him; I might even admire him. He may be a dashing and quite decent strategist. He may be a fine romantic actor, like Burke flinging the dagger on the floor. He may even (for all I know) be a sublime mystic, profoundly impressed with the ancient meaning of the divine trade of the Carpenter, and offering to the people a parable in the form of a ceremony. All I wish to indicate is the abyss of mental confusion in which such wild ritualism can be called "sound common sense." And it is in that abyss of mental confusion, and in that alone, that the new Imperialism lives and moves and has its being. The whole glory and greatness of Mr. Chamberlain consists in this: that if a man hits the right nail on the head nobody cares where he hits it to or what it does. They care about the noise of the hammer, not about the silent drip of the nail.

Before and throughout the African war, Mr. Chamberlain was always knocking in nails, with ringing decisiveness. But when we ask, "But what have these nails held together? Where is your carpentry? Where are your contented Outlanders? Where is your free South Africa? Where is your British prestige? What have your nails done?" then what answer is there? We must go back (with an affectionate sigh) to our Pearson for the answer to the question of what the nails have done: "The speaker who hammered nails into a board won thousands of votes."

Now the whole of this passage is admirably characteristic of the new journalism which Mr. Pearson represents, the new journalism which has just purchased the Standard. To take one instance out of hundreds, the incomparable man with the board and nails is described in the Pearson's article as calling out (as he smote the symbolic nail), "Lie number one. Nailed to the Mast! Nailed to the Mast!" In the whole office there was apparently no compositor or office-boy to point out that we speak of lies being nailed to the counter, and not to the mast. Nobody in the office knew that Pearson's Magazine was falling into a stale Irish bull, which must be as old as St. Patrick. This is the real and essential tragedy of the sale of the Standard. It is not merely that journalism is victorious over literature. It is that bad journalism is victorious over good journalism.

It is not that one article which we consider costly and beautiful is being ousted by another kind of article which we consider common or unclean. It is that of the same article a worse quality is preferred to a better. If you like popular journalism (as I do), you will know that Pearson's Magazine is poor and weak popular journalism. You will know it as certainly as you know bad butter. You will know as certainly that it is poor popular journalism as you know that the Strand, in the great days of Sherlock Holmes, was good popular journalism. Mr. Pearson has been a monument of this enormous banality. About everything he says and does there is something infinitely weak-minded. He clamours for home trades and employs foreign ones to print his paper. When this glaring fact is pointed out, he does not say that the thing was an oversight, like a sane man. He cuts it off with scissors, like a child of three. His very cunning is infantile. And like a child of three, he does not cut it quite off. In all human records I doubt if there is such an example of a profound simplicity in deception. This is the sort of intelligence which now sits in the seat of the sane and honourable old Tory journalism. If it were really the triumph of the tropical exuberance of the Yankee press, it would be vulgar, but still tropical. But it is not. We are delivered over to the bramble, and from the meanest of the shrubs comes the fire upon the cedars of Lebanon.

The only question now is how much longer the fiction will endure that journalists of this order represent public opinion. It may be doubted whether any honest and serious Tariff Reformer would for a moment maintain that there was any majority for Tariff Reform in the country comparable to the ludicrous preponderance which money has given it among the great dailies. The only inference is that for purposes of real public opinion the press is now a mere plutocratic oligarchy. Doubtless the public buys the wares of these men, for one reason or another. But there is no more reason to suppose that the public admires their politics than that the public admires the delicate philosophy of Mr. Crosse or the darker and sterner creed of Mr. Blackwell. If these men are merely tradesmen, there is nothing to say except that there are plenty like them in the Battersea Park Road, and many much better. But if they make any sort of attempt to be politicians, we can only point out to them that they are not as yet even good journalists.

IX. THE MOODS OF MR. GEORGE MOORE

Mr. George Moore began his literary career by writing his personal confessions; nor is there any harm in this if he had not continued them for the remainder of his life. He is a man of genuinely forcible mind and of great command over a kind of rhetorical and fugitive conviction which excites and pleases. He is in a perpetual state of temporary honesty. He has admired all the most admirable modern eccentrics until they could stand it no longer. Everything he writes, it is to be fully admitted, has a genuine mental power. His account of his reason for leaving the Roman Catholic Church is possibly the most admirable tribute to that communion which has been written of late years. For the fact of the matter is, that the weakness which has rendered barren the many brilliancies of Mr. Moore is actually that weakness which the Roman Catholic Church is at its best in combating. Mr. Moore hates Catholicism because it breaks up the house of looking-glasses in which he lives. Mr. Moore does not dislike so much being asked to believe in the spiritual existence of miracles or sacraments, but he does fundamentally dislike being asked to believe in the actual existence of other people. Like his master Pater and all the aesthetes, his real quarrel with life is that it is not a dream that can be moulded by the dreamer. It is not the dogma of the reality of the other world that troubles him, but the dogma of the reality of this world.

The truth is that the tradition of Christianity (which is still the only coherent ethic of Europe) rests on two or three paradoxes or mysteries which can easily be impugned in argument and as easily justified in life. One of them, for instance, is the paradox of hope or faith—that the more hopeless is the situation the more hopeful must be the man. Stevenson understood this, and consequently Mr. Moore cannot understand Stevenson. Another is the paradox of charity or chivalry that the weaker a thing is the more it should be respected, that the more indefensible a thing is the more it should appeal to us for a certain kind of defence. Thackeray understood this, and therefore Mr. Moore does not understand Thackeray. Now, one of these very practical and working mysteries in the Christian tradition, and one which the Roman Catholic Church, as I say, has done her best work in singling out, is the conception of the sinfulness of pride. Pride is a weakness in the character; it dries up laughter, it dries up wonder, it dries up chivalry and energy. The Christian tradition understands this; therefore Mr. Moore does not understand the Christian tradition.

For the truth is much stranger even than it appears in the formal doctrine of the sin of pride. It is not only true that humility is a much wiser and more vigorous thing than pride. It is also true that vanity is a much wiser and more vigorous thing than pride. Vanity is social—it is almost a kind of comradeship; pride is solitary and uncivilized. Vanity is active; it desires the applause of infinite multitudes; pride is passive, desiring only the applause of one person, which it already has. Vanity is humorous, and can enjoy the joke even of itself; pride is dull, and cannot even smile. And the whole of this difference is the difference between Stevenson and Mr. George Moore, who, as he informs us, has "brushed Stevenson aside." I do not know where he has been brushed to, but wherever it is I fancy he is having a good time, because he had the wisdom to be vain, and not proud. Stevenson had a windy vanity; Mr. Moore has a dusty egoism. Hence Stevenson could amuse himself as well as us with his vanity; while the richest effects of Mr. Moore's absurdity are hidden from his eyes.

If we compare this solemn folly with the happy folly with which Stevenson belauds his own books and berates his own critics, we shall not find it difficult to guess why it is that Stevenson at least found a final philosophy of some sort to live by, while Mr. Moore is always walking the world looking for a new one. Stevenson had found that the secret of life lies in laughter and humility. Self is the gorgon. Vanity sees it in the mirror of other men and lives. Pride studies it for itself and is turned to stone.

It is necessary to dwell on this defect in Mr. Moore, because it is really the weakness of work which is not without its strength. Mr. Moore's egoism is not merely a moral weakness, it is a very constant and influential aesthetic weakness as well. We should really be much more interested in Mr. Moore if he were not quite so interested in himself. We feel as if we were being shown through a gallery of really fine pictures, into each of which, by some useless and discordant convention, the artist had represented the same figure in the same attitude. "The Grand Canal with a distant view of Mr. Moore," "Effect of Mr. Moore through a Scotch Mist," "Mr. Moore by Firelight," "Ruins of Mr. Moore by Moonlight," and so on, seems to be the endless series. He would no doubt reply that in such a book as this he intended to reveal himself. But the answer is that in such a book as this he does not succeed. One of the thousand objections to the sin of pride lies precisely in this, that self-consciousness of necessity destroys self-revelation. A man who thinks a great deal about himself will try to be many-sided, attempt a theatrical excellence at all points, will try to be an encyclopaedia of culture, and his own real personality will be lost in that false universalism. Thinking about himself will lead to trying to be the universe; trying to be the universe will lead to ceasing to be anything. If, on the other hand, a man is sensible enough to think only about the universe; he will think about it in his own individual way. He will keep virgin the secret of God; he will see the grass as no other man can see it, and look at a sun that no man has ever known. This fact is very practically brought out in Mr. Moore's "Confessions." In reading them we do not feel the presence of a clean-cut personality like that of Thackeray and Matthew Arnold. We only read a number of quite clever and largely conflicting opinions which might be uttered by any clever person, but which we are called upon to admire specifically, because they are uttered by Mr. Moore. He is the only thread that connects Catholicism and Protestantism, realism and mysticism—he or rather his name. He is profoundly absorbed even in views he no longer holds, and he expects us to be. And he intrudes the capital "I" even where it need not be intruded—even where it weakens the force of a plain statement. Where another man would say, "It is a fine day," Mr. Moore says, "Seen through my temperament, the day appeared fine." Where another man would say "Milton has obviously a fine style," Mr. Moore would say, "As a stylist Milton had always impressed me." The Nemesis of this self-centred spirit is that of being totally ineffectual. Mr. Moore has started many interesting crusades, but he has abandoned them before his disciples could begin. Even when he is on the side of the truth he is as fickle as the children of falsehood. Even when he has found reality he cannot find rest. One Irish quality he has which no Irishman was ever without—pugnacity; and that is certainly a great virtue, especially in the present age. But he has not the tenacity of conviction which goes with the fighting spirit in a man like Bernard Shaw. His weakness of introspection and selfishness in all their glory cannot prevent him fighting; but they will always prevent him winning.

X. ON SANDALS AND SIMPLICITY

The great misfortune of the modern English is not at all that they are more boastful than other people (they are not); it is that they are boastful about those particular things which nobody can boast of without losing them. A Frenchman can be proud of being bold and logical, and still remain bold and logical. A German can be proud of being reflective and orderly, and still remain reflective and orderly. But an Englishman cannot be proud of being simple and direct, and still remain simple and direct. In the matter of these strange virtues, to know them is to kill them. A man may be conscious of being heroic or conscious of being divine, but he cannot (in spite of all the Anglo-Saxon poets) be conscious of being unconscious.

Now, I do not think that it can be honestly denied that some portion of this impossibility attaches to a class very different in their own opinion, at least, to the school of Anglo-Saxonism. I mean that school of the simple life, commonly associated with Tolstoy. If a perpetual talk about one's own robustness leads to being less robust, it is even more true that a perpetual talking about one's own simplicity leads to being less simple. One great complaint, I think, must stand against the modern upholders of the simple life—the simple life in all its varied forms, from vegetarianism to the honourable consistency of the Doukhobors. This complaint against them stands, that they would make us simple in the unimportant things, but complex in the important things. They would make us simple in the things that do not matter—that is, in diet, in costume, in etiquette, in economic system. But they would make us complex in the things that do matter—in philosophy, in loyalty, in spiritual acceptance, and spiritual rejection. It does not so very much matter whether a man eats a grilled tomato or a plain tomato; it does very much matter whether he eats a plain tomato with a grilled mind. The only kind of simplicity worth preserving is the simplicity of the heart, the simplicity which accepts and enjoys. There may be a reasonable doubt as to what system preserves this; there can surely be no doubt that a system of simplicity destroys it. There is more simplicity in the man who eats caviar on impulse than in the man who eats grape-nuts on principle. The chief error of these people is to be found in the very phrase to which they are most attached—"plain living and high thinking." These people do not stand in need of, will not be improved by, plain living and high thinking. They stand in need of the contrary. They would be improved by high living and plain thinking. A little high living (I say, having a full sense of responsibility, a little high living) would teach them the force and meaning of the human festivities, of the banquet that has gone on from the beginning of the world. It would teach them the historic fact that the artificial is, if anything, older than the natural. It would teach them that the loving-cup is as old as any hunger. It would teach them that ritualism is older than any religion. And a little plain thinking would teach them how harsh and fanciful are the mass of their own ethics, how very civilized and very complicated must be the brain of the Tolstoyan who really believes it to be evil to love one's country and wicked to strike a blow.

A man approaches, wearing sandals and simple raiment, a raw tomato held firmly in his right hand, and says, "The affections of family and country alike are hindrances to the fuller development of human love;" but the plain thinker will only answer him, with a wonder not untinged with admiration, "What a great deal of trouble you must have taken in order to feel like that." High living will reject the tomato. Plain thinking will equally decisively reject the idea of the invariable sinfulness of war. High living will convince us that nothing is more materialistic than to despise a pleasure as purely material. And plain thinking will convince us that nothing is more materialistic than to reserve our horror chiefly for material wounds.

The only simplicity that matters is the simplicity of the heart. If that be gone, it can be brought back by no turnips or cellular clothing; but only by tears and terror and the fires that are not quenched. If that remain, it matters very little if a few Early Victorian armchairs remain along with it. Let us put a complex entree into a simple old gentleman; let us not put a simple entree into a complex old gentleman. So long as human society will leave my spiritual inside alone, I will allow it, with a comparative submission, to work its wild will with my physical interior. I will submit to cigars. I will meekly embrace a bottle of Burgundy. I will humble myself to a hansom cab. If only by this means I may preserve to myself the virginity of the spirit, which enjoys with astonishment and fear. I do not say that these are the only methods of preserving it. I incline to the belief that there are others. But I will have nothing to do with simplicity which lacks the fear, the astonishment, and the joy alike. I will have nothing to do with the devilish vision of a child who is too simple to like toys.

The child is, indeed, in these, and many other matters, the best guide. And in nothing is the child so righteously childlike, in nothing does he exhibit more accurately the sounder order of simplicity, than in the fact that he sees everything with a simple pleasure, even the complex things. The false type of naturalness harps always on the distinction between the natural and the artificial. The higher kind of naturalness ignores that distinction. To the child the tree and the lamp-post are as natural and as artificial as each other; or rather, neither of them are natural but both supernatural. For both are splendid and unexplained. The flower with which God crowns the one, and the flame with which Sam the lamplighter crowns the other, are equally of the gold of fairy-tales. In the middle of the wildest fields the most rustic child is, ten to one, playing at steam-engines. And the only spiritual or philosophical objection to steam-engines is not that men pay for them or work at them, or make them very ugly, or even that men are killed by them; but merely that men do not play at them. The evil is that the childish poetry of clockwork does not remain. The wrong is not that engines are too much admired, but that they are not admired enough. The sin is not that engines are mechanical, but that men are mechanical.

In this matter, then, as in all the other matters treated in this book, our main conclusion is that it is a fundamental point of view, a philosophy or religion which is needed, and not any change in habit or social routine. The things we need most for immediate practical purposes are all abstractions. We need a right view of the human lot, a right view of the human society; and if we were living eagerly and angrily in the enthusiasm of those things, we should, ipso facto, be living simply in the genuine and spiritual sense. Desire and danger make every one simple. And to those who talk to us with interfering eloquence about Jaeger and the pores of the skin, and about Plasmon and the coats of the stomach, at them shall only be hurled the words that are hurled at fops and gluttons, "Take no thought what ye shall eat or what ye shall drink, or wherewithal ye shall be clothed. For after all these things do the Gentiles seek. But seek first the kingdom of God and His righteousness, and all these things shall be added unto you." Those amazing words are not only extraordinarily good, practical politics; they are also superlatively good hygiene. The one supreme way of making all those processes go right, the processes of health, and strength, and grace, and beauty, the one and only way of making certain of their accuracy, is to think about something else. If a man is bent on climbing into the seventh heaven, he may be quite easy about the pores of his skin. If he harnesses his waggon to a star, the process will have a most satisfactory effect upon the coats of his stomach. For the thing called "taking thought," the thing for which the best modern word is "rationalizing," is in its nature, inapplicable to all plain and urgent things. Men take thought and ponder rationalistically, touching remote things—things that only theoretically matter, such as the transit of Venus. But only at their peril can men rationalize about so practical a matter as health.

XI SCIENCE AND THE SAVAGES

A permanent disadvantage of the study of folk-lore and kindred subjects is that the man of science can hardly be in the nature of things very frequently a man of the world. He is a student of nature; he is scarcely ever a student of human nature. And even where this difficulty is overcome, and he is in some sense a student of human nature, this is only a very faint beginning of the painful progress towards being human. For the study of primitive race and religion stands apart in one important respect from all, or nearly all, the ordinary scientific studies. A man can understand astronomy only by being an astronomer; he can understand entomology only by being an entomologist (or, perhaps, an insect); but he can understand a great deal of anthropology merely by being a man. He is himself the animal which he studies. Hence arises the fact which strikes the eye everywhere in the records of ethnology and folk-lore—the fact that the same frigid and detached spirit which leads to success in the study of astronomy or botany leads to disaster in the study of mythology or human origins. It is necessary to cease to be a man in order to do justice to a microbe; it is not necessary to cease to be a man in order to do justice to men. That same suppression of sympathies, that same waving away of intuitions or guess-work which make a man preternaturally clever in dealing with the stomach of a spider, will make him preternaturally stupid in dealing with the heart of man. He is making himself inhuman in order to understand humanity. An ignorance of the other world is boasted by many men of science; but in this matter their defect arises, not from ignorance of the other world, but from ignorance of this world. For the secrets about which anthropologists concern themselves can be best learnt, not from books or voyages, but from the ordinary commerce of man with man. The secret of why some savage tribe worships monkeys or the moon is not to be found even by travelling among those savages and taking down their answers in a note-book, although the cleverest man may pursue this course. The answer to the riddle is in England; it is in London; nay, it is in his own heart. When a man has discovered why men in Bond Street wear black hats he will at the same moment have discovered why men in Timbuctoo wear red feathers. The mystery in the heart of some savage war-dance should not be studied in books of scientific travel; it should be studied at a subscription ball. If a man desires to find out the origins of religions, let him not go to the Sandwich Islands; let him go to church. If a man wishes to know the origin of human society, to know what society, philosophically speaking, really is, let him not go into the British Museum; let him go into society.

This total misunderstanding of the real nature of ceremonial gives rise to the most awkward and dehumanized versions of the conduct of men in rude lands or ages. The man of science, not realizing that ceremonial is essentially a thing which is done without a reason, has to find a reason for every sort of ceremonial, and, as might be supposed, the reason is generally a very absurd one—absurd because it originates not in the simple mind of the barbarian, but in the sophisticated mind of the professor. The teamed man will say, for instance, "The natives of Mumbojumbo Land believe that the dead man can eat and will require food upon his journey to the other world. This is attested by the fact that they place food in the grave, and that any family not complying with this rite is the object of the anger of the priests and the tribe." To any one acquainted with humanity this way of talking is topsy-turvy. It is like saying, "The English in the twentieth century believed that a dead man could smell. This is attested by the fact that they always covered his grave with lilies, violets, or other flowers. Some priestly and tribal terrors were evidently attached to the neglect of this action, as we have records of several old ladies who were very much disturbed in mind because their wreaths had not arrived in time for the funeral." It may be of course that savages put food with a dead man because they think that a dead man can eat, or weapons with a dead man because they think that a dead man can fight. But personally I do not believe that they think anything of the kind. I believe they put food or weapons on the dead for the same reason that we put flowers, because it is an exceedingly natural and obvious thing to do. We do not understand, it is true, the emotion which makes us think it obvious and natural; but that is because, like all the important emotions of human existence it is essentially irrational. We do not understand the savage for the same reason that the savage does not understand himself. And the savage does not understand himself for the same reason that we do not understand ourselves either.

The obvious truth is that the moment any matter has passed through the human mind it is finally and for ever spoilt for all purposes of science. It has become a thing incurably mysterious and infinite; this mortal has put on immortality. Even what we call our material desires are spiritual, because they are human. Science can analyse a pork-chop, and say how much of it is phosphorus and how much is protein; but science cannot analyse any man's wish for a pork-chop, and say how much of it is hunger, how much custom, how much nervous fancy, how much a haunting love of the beautiful. The man's desire for the pork-chop remains literally as mystical and ethereal as his desire for heaven. All attempts, therefore, at a science of any human things, at a science of history, a science of folk-lore, a science of sociology, are by their nature not merely hopeless, but crazy. You can no more be certain in economic history that a man's desire for money was merely a desire for money than you can be certain in hagiology that a saint's desire for God was merely a desire for God. And this kind of vagueness in the primary phenomena of the study is an absolutely final blow to anything in the nature of a science. Men can construct a science with very few instruments, or with very plain instruments; but no one on earth could construct a science with unreliable instruments. A man might work out the whole of mathematics with a handful of pebbles, but not with a handful of clay which was always falling apart into new fragments, and falling together into new combinations. A man might measure heaven and earth with a reed, but not with a growing reed.

As one of the enormous follies of folk-lore, let us take the case of the transmigration of stories, and the alleged unity of their source. Story after story the scientific mythologists have cut out of its place in history, and pinned side by side with similar stories in their museum of fables. The process is industrious, it is fascinating, and the whole of it rests on one of the plainest fallacies in the world. That a story has been told all over the place at some time or other, not only does not prove that it never really happened; it does not even faintly indicate or make slightly more probable that it never happened. That a large number of fishermen have falsely asserted that they have caught a pike two feet long, does not in the least affect the question of whether any one ever really did so. That numberless journalists announce a Franco-German war merely for money is no evidence one way or the other upon the dark question of whether such a war ever occurred. Doubtless in a few hundred years the innumerable Franco-German wars that did not happen will have cleared the scientific mind of any belief in the legendary war of '70 which did. But that will be because if folk-lore students remain at all, their nature will be unchanged; and their services to folk-lore will be still as they are at present, greater than they know. For in truth these men do something far more godlike than studying legends; they create them.

There are two kinds of stories which the scientists say cannot be true, because everybody tells them. The first class consists of the stories which are told everywhere, because they are somewhat odd or clever; there is nothing in the world to prevent their having happened to somebody as an adventure any more than there is anything to prevent their having occurred, as they certainly did occur, to somebody as an idea. But they are not likely to have happened to many people. The second class of their "myths" consist of the stories that are told everywhere for the simple reason that they happen everywhere. Of the first class, for instance, we might take such an example as the story of William Tell, now generally ranked among legends upon the sole ground that it is found in the tales of other peoples. Now, it is obvious that this was told everywhere because whether true or fictitious it is what is called "a good story;" it is odd, exciting, and it has a climax. But to suggest that some such eccentric incident can never have happened in the whole history of archery, or that it did not happen to any particular person of whom it is told, is stark impudence. The idea of shooting at a mark attached to some valuable or beloved person is an idea doubtless that might easily have occurred to any inventive poet. But it is also an idea that might easily occur to any boastful archer. It might be one of the fantastic caprices of some story-teller. It might equally well be one of the fantastic caprices of some tyrant. It might occur first in real life and afterwards occur in legends. Or it might just as well occur first in legends and afterwards occur in real life. If no apple has ever been shot off a boy's head from the beginning of the world, it may be done tomorrow morning, and by somebody who has never heard of William Tell.

This type of tale, indeed, may be pretty fairly paralleled with the ordinary anecdote terminating in a repartee or an Irish bull. Such a retort as the famous "je ne vois pas la necessite" we have all seen attributed to Talleyrand, to Voltaire, to Henri Quatre, to an anonymous judge, and so on. But this variety does not in any way make it more likely that the thing was never said at all. It is highly likely that it was really said by somebody unknown. It is highly likely that it was really said by Talleyrand. In any case, it is not any more difficult to believe that the mot might have occurred to a man in conversation than to a man writing memoirs. It might have occurred to any of the men I have mentioned. But there is this point of distinction about it, that it is not likely to have occurred to all of them. And this is where the first class of so-called myth differs from the second to which I have previously referred. For there is a second class of incident found to be common to the stories of five or six heroes, say to Sigurd, to Hercules, to Rustem, to the Cid, and so on. And the peculiarity of this myth is that not only is it highly reasonable to imagine that it really happened to one hero, but it is highly reasonable to imagine that it really happened to all of them. Such a story, for instance, is that of a great man having his strength swayed or thwarted by the mysterious weakness of a woman. The anecdotal story, the story of William Tell, is as I have said, popular, because it is peculiar. But this kind of story, the story of Samson and Delilah of Arthur and Guinevere, is obviously popular because it is not peculiar. It is popular as good, quiet fiction is popular, because it tells the truth about people. If the ruin of Samson by a woman, and the ruin of Hercules by a woman, have a common legendary origin, it is gratifying to know that we can also explain, as a fable, the ruin of Nelson by a woman and the ruin of Parnell by a woman. And, indeed, I have no doubt whatever that, some centuries hence, the students of folk-lore will refuse altogether to believe that Elizabeth Barrett eloped with Robert Browning, and will prove their point up to the hilt by the unquestionable fact that the whole fiction of the period was full of such elopements from end to end.

Possibly the most pathetic of all the delusions of the modern students of primitive belief is the notion they have about the thing they call anthropomorphism. They believe that primitive men attributed phenomena to a god in human form in order to explain them, because his mind in its sullen limitation could not reach any further than his own clownish existence. The thunder was called the voice of a man, the lightning the eyes of a man, because by this explanation they were made more reasonable and comfortable. The final cure for all this kind of philosophy is to walk down a lane at night. Any one who does so will discover very quickly that men pictured something semi-human at the back of all things, not because such a thought was natural, but because it was supernatural; not because it made things more comprehensible, but because it made them a hundred times more incomprehensible and mysterious. For a man walking down a lane at night can see the conspicuous fact that as long as nature keeps to her own course, she has no power with us at all. As long as a tree is a tree, it is a top-heavy monster with a hundred arms, a thousand tongues, and only one leg. But so long as a tree is a tree, it does not frighten us at all. It begins to be something alien, to be something strange, only when it looks like ourselves. When a tree really looks like a man our knees knock under us. And when the whole universe looks like a man we fall on our faces.

XII PAGANISM AND MR. LOWES DICKINSON

Of the New Paganism (or neo-Paganism), as it was preached flamboyantly by Mr. Swinburne or delicately by Walter Pater, there is no necessity to take any very grave account, except as a thing which left behind it incomparable exercises in the English language. The New Paganism is no longer new, and it never at any time bore the smallest resemblance to Paganism. The ideas about the ancient civilization which it has left loose in the public mind are certainly extraordinary enough. The term "pagan" is continually used in fiction and light literature as meaning a man without any religion, whereas a pagan was generally a man with about half a dozen. The pagans, according to this notion, were continually crowning themselves with flowers and dancing about in an irresponsible state, whereas, if there were two things that the best pagan civilization did honestly believe in, they were a rather too rigid dignity and a much too rigid responsibility. Pagans are depicted as above all things inebriate and lawless, whereas they were above all things reasonable and respectable. They are praised as disobedient when they had only one great virtue—civic obedience. They are envied and admired as shamelessly happy when they had only one great sin—despair.

Mr. Lowes Dickinson, the most pregnant and provocative of recent writers on this and similar subjects, is far too solid a man to have fallen into this old error of the mere anarchy of Paganism. In order to make hay of that Hellenic enthusiasm which has as its ideal mere appetite and egotism, it is not necessary to know much philosophy, but merely to know a little Greek. Mr. Lowes Dickinson knows a great deal of philosophy, and also a great deal of Greek, and his error, if error he has, is not that of the crude hedonist. But the contrast which he offers between Christianity and Paganism in the matter of moral ideals—a contrast which he states very ably in a paper called "How long halt ye?" which appeared in the Independent Review—does, I think, contain an error of a deeper kind. According to him, the ideal of Paganism was not, indeed, a mere frenzy of lust and liberty and caprice, but was an ideal of full and satisfied humanity. According to him, the ideal of Christianity was the ideal of asceticism. When I say that I think this idea wholly wrong as a matter of philosophy and history, I am not talking for the moment about any ideal Christianity of my own, or even of any primitive Christianity undefiled by after events. I am not, like so many modern Christian idealists, basing my case upon certain things which Christ said. Neither am I, like so many other Christian idealists, basing my case upon certain things that Christ forgot to say. I take historic Christianity with all its sins upon its head; I take it, as I would take Jacobinism, or Mormonism, or any other mixed or unpleasing human product, and I say that the meaning of its action was not to be found in asceticism. I say that its point of departure from Paganism was not asceticism. I say that its point of difference with the modern world was not asceticism. I say that St. Simeon Stylites had not his main inspiration in asceticism. I say that the main Christian impulse cannot be described as asceticism, even in the ascetics.

Let me set about making the matter clear. There is one broad fact about the relations of Christianity and Paganism which is so simple that many will smile at it, but which is so important that all moderns forget it. The primary fact about Christianity and Paganism is that one came after the other. Mr. Lowes Dickinson speaks of them as if they were parallel ideals—even speaks as if Paganism were the newer of the two, and the more fitted for a new age. He suggests that the Pagan ideal will be the ultimate good of man; but if that is so, we must at least ask with more curiosity than he allows for, why it was that man actually found his ultimate good on earth under the stars, and threw it away again. It is this extraordinary enigma to which I propose to attempt an answer.

There is only one thing in the modern world that has been face to face with Paganism; there is only one thing in the modern world which in that sense knows anything about Paganism: and that is Christianity. That fact is really the weak point in the whole of that hedonistic neo-Paganism of which I have spoken. All that genuinely remains of the ancient hymns or the ancient dances of Europe, all that has honestly come to us from the festivals of Phoebus or Pan, is to be found in the festivals of the Christian Church. If any one wants to hold the end of a chain which really goes back to the heathen mysteries, he had better take hold of a festoon of flowers at Easter or a string of sausages at Christmas. Everything else in the modern world is of Christian origin, even everything that seems most anti-Christian. The French Revolution is of Christian origin. The newspaper is of Christian origin. The anarchists are of Christian origin. Physical science is of Christian origin. The attack on Christianity is of Christian origin. There is one thing, and one thing only, in existence at the present day which can in any sense accurately be said to be of pagan origin, and that is Christianity.

The real difference between Paganism and Christianity is perfectly summed up in the difference between the pagan, or natural, virtues, and those three virtues of Christianity which the Church of Rome calls virtues of grace. The pagan, or rational, virtues are such things as justice and temperance, and Christianity has adopted them. The three mystical virtues which Christianity has not adopted, but invented, are faith, hope, and charity. Now much easy and foolish Christian rhetoric could easily be poured out upon those three words, but I desire to confine myself to the two facts which are evident about them. The first evident fact (in marked contrast to the delusion of the dancing pagan)—the first evident fact, I say, is that the pagan virtues, such as justice and temperance, are the sad virtues, and that the mystical virtues of faith, hope, and charity are the gay and exuberant virtues. And the second evident fact, which is even more evident, is the fact that the pagan virtues are the reasonable virtues, and that the Christian virtues of faith, hope, and charity are in their essence as unreasonable as they can be.

As the word "unreasonable" is open to misunderstanding, the matter may be more accurately put by saying that each one of these Christian or mystical virtues involves a paradox in its own nature, and that this is not true of any of the typically pagan or rationalist virtues. Justice consists in finding out a certain thing due to a certain man and giving it to him. Temperance consists in finding out the proper limit of a particular indulgence and adhering to that. But charity means pardoning what is unpardonable, or it is no virtue at all. Hope means hoping when things are hopeless, or it is no virtue at all. And faith means believing the incredible, or it is no virtue at all.

It is somewhat amusing, indeed, to notice the difference between the fate of these three paradoxes in the fashion of the modern mind. Charity is a fashionable virtue in our time; it is lit up by the gigantic firelight of Dickens. Hope is a fashionable virtue to-day; our attention has been arrested for it by the sudden and silver trumpet of Stevenson. But faith is unfashionable, and it is customary on every side to cast against it the fact that it is a paradox. Everybody mockingly repeats the famous childish definition that faith is "the power of believing that which we know to be untrue." Yet it is not one atom more paradoxical than hope or charity. Charity is the power of defending that which we know to be indefensible. Hope is the power of being cheerful in circumstances which we know to be desperate. It is true that there is a state of hope which belongs to bright prospects and the morning; but that is not the virtue of hope. The virtue of hope exists only in earthquake and, eclipse. It is true that there is a thing crudely called charity, which means charity to the deserving poor; but charity to the deserving is not charity at all, but justice. It is the undeserving who require it, and the ideal either does not exist at all, or exists wholly for them. For practical purposes it is at the hopeless moment that we require the hopeful man, and the virtue either does not exist at all, or begins to exist at that moment. Exactly at the instant when hope ceases to be reasonable it begins to be useful. Now the old pagan world went perfectly straightforward until it discovered that going straightforward is an enormous mistake. It was nobly and beautifully reasonable, and discovered in its death-pang this lasting and valuable truth, a heritage for the ages, that reasonableness will not do. The pagan age was truly an Eden or golden age, in this essential sense, that it is not to be recovered. And it is not to be recovered in this sense again that, while we are certainly jollier than the pagans, and much more right than the pagans, there is not one of us who can, by the utmost stretch of energy, be so sensible as the pagans. That naked innocence of the intellect cannot be recovered by any man after Christianity; and for this excellent reason, that every man after Christianity knows it to be misleading. Let me take an example, the first that occurs to the mind, of this impossible plainness in the pagan point of view. The greatest tribute to Christianity in the modern world is Tennyson's "Ulysses." The poet reads into the story of Ulysses the conception of an incurable desire to wander. But the real Ulysses does not desire to wander at all. He desires to get home. He displays his heroic and unconquerable qualities in resisting the misfortunes which baulk him; but that is all. There is no love of adventure for its own sake; that is a Christian product. There is no love of Penelope for her own sake; that is a Christian product. Everything in that old world would appear to have been clean and obvious. A good man was a good man; a bad man was a bad man. For this reason they had no charity; for charity is a reverent agnosticism towards the complexity of the soul. For this reason they had no such thing as the art of fiction, the novel; for the novel is a creation of the mystical idea of charity. For them a pleasant landscape was pleasant, and an unpleasant landscape unpleasant. Hence they had no idea of romance; for romance consists in thinking a thing more delightful because it is dangerous; it is a Christian idea. In a word, we cannot reconstruct or even imagine the beautiful and astonishing pagan world. It was a world in which common sense was really common.

My general meaning touching the three virtues of which I have spoken will now, I hope, be sufficiently clear. They are all three paradoxical, they are all three practical, and they are all three paradoxical because they are practical. it is the stress of ultimate need, and a terrible knowledge of things as they are, which led men to set up these riddles, and to die for them. Whatever may be the meaning of the contradiction, it is the fact that the only kind of hope that is of any use in a battle is a hope that denies arithmetic. Whatever may be the meaning of the contradiction, it is the fact that the only kind of charity which any weak spirit wants, or which any generous spirit feels, is the charity which forgives the sins that are like scarlet. Whatever may be the meaning of faith, it must always mean a certainty about something we cannot prove. Thus, for instance, we believe by faith in the existence of other people.

But there is another Christian virtue, a virtue far more obviously and historically connected with Christianity, which will illustrate even better the connection between paradox and practical necessity. This virtue cannot be questioned in its capacity as a historical symbol; certainly Mr. Lowes Dickinson will not question it. It has been the boast of hundreds of the champions of Christianity. It has been the taunt of hundreds of the opponents of Christianity. It is, in essence, the basis of Mr. Lowes Dickinson's whole distinction between Christianity and Paganism. I mean, of course, the virtue of humility. I admit, of course, most readily, that a great deal of false Eastern humility (that is, of strictly ascetic humility) mixed itself with the main stream of European Christianity. We must not forget that when we speak of Christianity we are speaking of a whole continent for about a thousand years. But of this virtue even more than of the other three, I would maintain the general proposition adopted above. Civilization discovered Christian humility for the same urgent reason that it discovered faith and charity—that is, because Christian civilization had to discover it or die.

The great psychological discovery of Paganism, which turned it into Christianity, can be expressed with some accuracy in one phrase. The pagan set out, with admirable sense, to enjoy himself. By the end of his civilization he had discovered that a man cannot enjoy himself and continue to enjoy anything else. Mr. Lowes Dickinson has pointed out in words too excellent to need any further elucidation, the absurd shallowness of those who imagine that the pagan enjoyed himself only in a materialistic sense. Of course, he enjoyed himself, not only intellectually even, he enjoyed himself morally, he enjoyed himself spiritually. But it was himself that he was enjoying; on the face of it, a very natural thing to do. Now, the psychological discovery is merely this, that whereas it had been supposed that the fullest possible enjoyment is to be found by extending our ego to infinity, the truth is that the fullest possible enjoyment is to be found by reducing our ego to zero.

Humility is the thing which is for ever renewing the earth and the stars. It is humility, and not duty, which preserves the stars from wrong, from the unpardonable wrong of casual resignation; it is through humility that the most ancient heavens for us are fresh and strong. The curse that came before history has laid on us all a tendency to be weary of wonders. If we saw the sun for the first time it would be the most fearful and beautiful of meteors. Now that we see it for the hundredth time we call it, in the hideous and blasphemous phrase of Wordsworth, "the light of common day." We are inclined to increase our claims. We are inclined to demand six suns, to demand a blue sun, to demand a green sun. Humility is perpetually putting us back in the primal darkness. There all light is lightning, startling and instantaneous. Until we understand that original dark, in which we have neither sight nor expectation, we can give no hearty and childlike praise to the splendid sensationalism of things. The terms "pessimism" and "optimism," like most modern terms, are unmeaning. But if they can be used in any vague sense as meaning something, we may say that in this great fact pessimism is the very basis of optimism. The man who destroys himself creates the universe. To the humble man, and to the humble man alone, the sun is really a sun; to the humble man, and to the humble man alone, the sea is really a sea. When he looks at all the faces in the street, he does not only realize that men are alive, he realizes with a dramatic pleasure that they are not dead.

I have not spoken of another aspect of the discovery of humility as a psychological necessity, because it is more commonly insisted on, and is in itself more obvious. But it is equally clear that humility is a permanent necessity as a condition of effort and self-examination. It is one of the deadly fallacies of Jingo politics that a nation is stronger for despising other nations. As a matter of fact, the strongest nations are those, like Prussia or Japan, which began from very mean beginnings, but have not been too proud to sit at the feet of the foreigner and learn everything from him. Almost every obvious and direct victory has been the victory of the plagiarist. This is, indeed, only a very paltry by-product of humility, but it is a product of humility, and, therefore, it is successful. Prussia had no Christian humility in its internal arrangements; hence its internal arrangements were miserable. But it had enough Christian humility slavishly to copy France (even down to Frederick the Great's poetry), and that which it had the humility to copy it had ultimately the honour to conquer. The case of the Japanese is even more obvious; their only Christian and their only beautiful quality is that they have humbled themselves to be exalted. All this aspect of humility, however, as connected with the matter of effort and striving for a standard set above us, I dismiss as having been sufficiently pointed out by almost all idealistic writers.

It may be worth while, however, to point out the interesting disparity in the matter of humility between the modern notion of the strong man and the actual records of strong men. Carlyle objected to the statement that no man could be a hero to his valet. Every sympathy can be extended towards him in the matter if he merely or mainly meant that the phrase was a disparagement of hero-worship. Hero-worship is certainly a generous and human impulse; the hero may be faulty, but the worship can hardly be. It may be that no man would be a hero to his valet. But any man would be a valet to his hero. But in truth both the proverb itself and Carlyle's stricture upon it ignore the most essential matter at issue. The ultimate psychological truth is not that no man is a hero to his valet. The ultimate psychological truth, the foundation of Christianity, is that no man is a hero to himself. Cromwell, according to Carlyle, was a strong man. According to Cromwell, he was a weak one.

The weak point in the whole of Carlyle's case for aristocracy lies, indeed, in his most celebrated phrase. Carlyle said that men were mostly fools. Christianity, with a surer and more reverent realism, says that they are all fools. This doctrine is sometimes called the doctrine of original sin. It may also be described as the doctrine of the equality of men. But the essential point of it is merely this, that whatever primary and far-reaching moral dangers affect any man, affect all men. All men can be criminals, if tempted; all men can be heroes, if inspired. And this doctrine does away altogether with Carlyle's pathetic belief (or any one else's pathetic belief) in "the wise few." There are no wise few. Every aristocracy that has ever existed has behaved, in all essential points, exactly like a small mob. Every oligarchy is merely a knot of men in the street—that is to say, it is very jolly, but not infallible. And no oligarchies in the world's history have ever come off so badly in practical affairs as the very proud oligarchies—the oligarchy of Poland, the oligarchy of Venice. And the armies that have most swiftly and suddenly broken their enemies in pieces have been the religious armies—the Moslem Armies, for instance, or the Puritan Armies. And a religious army may, by its nature, be defined as an army in which every man is taught not to exalt but to abase himself. Many modern Englishmen talk of themselves as the sturdy descendants of their sturdy Puritan fathers. As a fact, they would run away from a cow. If you asked one of their Puritan fathers, if you asked Bunyan, for instance, whether he was sturdy, he would have answered, with tears, that he was as weak as water. And because of this he would have borne tortures. And this virtue of humility, while being practical enough to win battles, will always be paradoxical enough to puzzle pedants. It is at one with the virtue of charity in this respect. Every generous person will admit that the one kind of sin which charity should cover is the sin which is inexcusable. And every generous person will equally agree that the one kind of pride which is wholly damnable is the pride of the man who has something to be proud of. The pride which, proportionally speaking, does not hurt the character, is the pride in things which reflect no credit on the person at all. Thus it does a man no harm to be proud of his country, and comparatively little harm to be proud of his remote ancestors. It does him more harm to be proud of having made money, because in that he has a little more reason for pride. It does him more harm still to be proud of what is nobler than money—intellect. And it does him most harm of all to value himself for the most valuable thing on earth—goodness. The man who is proud of what is really creditable to him is the Pharisee, the man whom Christ Himself could not forbear to strike.

My objection to Mr. Lowes Dickinson and the reassertors of the pagan ideal is, then, this. I accuse them of ignoring definite human discoveries in the moral world, discoveries as definite, though not as material, as the discovery of the circulation of the blood. We cannot go back to an ideal of reason and sanity. For mankind has discovered that reason does not lead to sanity. We cannot go back to an ideal of pride and enjoyment. For mankind has discovered that pride does not lead to enjoyment. I do not know by what extraordinary mental accident modern writers so constantly connect the idea of progress with the idea of independent thinking. Progress is obviously the antithesis of independent thinking. For under independent or individualistic thinking, every man starts at the beginning, and goes, in all probability, just as far as his father before him. But if there really be anything of the nature of progress, it must mean, above all things, the careful study and assumption of the whole of the past. I accuse Mr. Lowes Dickinson and his school of reaction in the only real sense. If he likes, let him ignore these great historic mysteries—the mystery of charity, the mystery of chivalry, the mystery of faith. If he likes, let him ignore the plough or the printing-press. But if we do revive and pursue the pagan ideal of a simple and rational self-completion we shall end—where Paganism ended. I do not mean that we shall end in destruction. I mean that we shall end in Christianity.

XIII. CELTS AND CELTOPHILES

Science in the modern world has many uses; its chief use, however, is to provide long words to cover the errors of the rich. The word "kleptomania" is a vulgar example of what I mean. It is on a par with that strange theory, always advanced when a wealthy or prominent person is in the dock, that exposure is more of a punishment for the rich than for the poor. Of course, the very reverse is the truth. Exposure is more of a punishment for the poor than for the rich. The richer a man is the easier it is for him to be a tramp. The richer a man is the easier it is for him to be popular and generally respected in the Cannibal Islands. But the poorer a man is the more likely it is that he will have to use his past life whenever he wants to get a bed for the night. Honour is a luxury for aristocrats, but it is a necessity for hall-porters. This is a secondary matter, but it is an example of the general proposition I offer—the proposition that an enormous amount of modern ingenuity is expended on finding defences for the indefensible conduct of the powerful. As I have said above, these defences generally exhibit themselves most emphatically in the form of appeals to physical science. And of all the forms in which science, or pseudo-science, has come to the rescue of the rich and stupid, there is none so singular as the singular invention of the theory of races.

When a wealthy nation like the English discovers the perfectly patent fact that it is making a ludicrous mess of the government of a poorer nation like the Irish, it pauses for a moment in consternation, and then begins to talk about Celts and Teutons. As far as I can understand the theory, the Irish are Celts and the English are Teutons. Of course, the Irish are not Celts any more than the English are Teutons. I have not followed the ethnological discussion with much energy, but the last scientific conclusion which I read inclined on the whole to the summary that the English were mainly Celtic and the Irish mainly Teutonic. But no man alive, with even the glimmering of a real scientific sense, would ever dream of applying the terms "Celtic" or "Teutonic" to either of them in any positive or useful sense.

That sort of thing must be left to people who talk about the Anglo-Saxon race, and extend the expression to America. How much of the blood of the Angles and Saxons (whoever they were) there remains in our mixed British, Roman, German, Dane, Norman, and Picard stock is a matter only interesting to wild antiquaries. And how much of that diluted blood can possibly remain in that roaring whirlpool of America into which a cataract of Swedes, Jews, Germans, Irishmen, and Italians is perpetually pouring, is a matter only interesting to lunatics. It would have been wiser for the English governing class to have called upon some other god. All other gods, however weak and warring, at least boast of being constant. But science boasts of being in a flux for ever; boasts of being unstable as water.

And England and the English governing class never did call on this absurd deity of race until it seemed, for an instant, that they had no other god to call on. All the most genuine Englishmen in history would have yawned or laughed in your face if you had begun to talk about Anglo-Saxons. If you had attempted to substitute the ideal of race for the ideal of nationality, I really do not like to think what they would have said. I certainly should not like to have been the officer of Nelson who suddenly discovered his French blood on the eve of Trafalgar. I should not like to have been the Norfolk or Suffolk gentleman who had to expound to Admiral Blake by what demonstrable ties of genealogy he was irrevocably bound to the Dutch. The truth of the whole matter is very simple. Nationality exists, and has nothing in the world to do with race. Nationality is a thing like a church or a secret society; it is a product of the human soul and will; it is a spiritual product. And there are men in the modern world who would think anything and do anything rather than admit that anything could be a spiritual product.

A nation, however, as it confronts the modern world, is a purely spiritual product. Sometimes it has been born in independence, like Scotland. Sometimes it has been born in dependence, in subjugation, like Ireland. Sometimes it is a large thing cohering out of many smaller things, like Italy. Sometimes it is a small thing breaking away from larger things, like Poland. But in each and every case its quality is purely spiritual, or, if you will, purely psychological. It is a moment when five men become a sixth man. Every one knows it who has ever founded a club. It is a moment when five places become one place. Every one must know it who has ever had to repel an invasion. Mr. Timothy Healy, the most serious intellect in the present House of Commons, summed up nationality to perfection when he simply called it something for which people will die, As he excellently said in reply to Lord Hugh Cecil, "No one, not even the noble lord, would die for the meridian of Greenwich." And that is the great tribute to its purely psychological character. It is idle to ask why Greenwich should not cohere in this spiritual manner while Athens or Sparta did. It is like asking why a man falls in love with one woman and not with another.

Now, of this great spiritual coherence, independent of external circumstances, or of race, or of any obvious physical thing, Ireland is the most remarkable example. Rome conquered nations, but Ireland has conquered races. The Norman has gone there and become Irish, the Scotchman has gone there and become Irish, the Spaniard has gone there and become Irish, even the bitter soldier of Cromwell has gone there and become Irish. Ireland, which did not exist even politically, has been stronger than all the races that existed scientifically. The purest Germanic blood, the purest Norman blood, the purest blood of the passionate Scotch patriot, has not been so attractive as a nation without a flag. Ireland, unrecognized and oppressed, has easily absorbed races, as such trifles are easily absorbed. She has easily disposed of physical science, as such superstitions are easily disposed of. Nationality in its weakness has been stronger than ethnology in its strength. Five triumphant races have been absorbed, have been defeated by a defeated nationality.

This being the true and strange glory of Ireland, it is impossible to hear without impatience of the attempt so constantly made among her modern sympathizers to talk about

Celts and Celticism. Who were the Celts? I defy anybody to say. Who are the Irish? I defy any one to be indifferent, or to pretend not to know. Mr. W. B. Yeats, the great Irish genius who has appeared in our time, shows his own admirable penetration in discarding altogether the argument from a Celtic race. But he does not wholly escape, and his followers hardly ever escape, the general objection to the Celtic argument. The tendency of that argument is to represent the Irish or the Celts as a strange and separate race, as a tribe of eccentrics in the modern world immersed in dim legends and fruitless dreams. Its tendency is to exhibit the Irish as odd, because they see the fairies. Its trend is to make the Irish seem weird and wild because they sing old songs and join in strange dances. But this is quite an error; indeed, it is the opposite of the truth. It is the English who are odd because they do not see the fairies. It is the inhabitants of Kensington who are weird and wild because they do not sing old songs and join in strange dances. In all this the Irish are not in the least strange and separate, are not in the least Celtic, as the word is commonly and popularly used. In all this the Irish are simply an ordinary sensible nation, living the life of any other ordinary and sensible nation which has not been either sodden with smoke or oppressed by money-lenders, or otherwise corrupted with wealth and science. There is nothing Celtic about having legends. It is merely human. The Germans, who are (I suppose) Teutonic, have hundreds of legends, wherever it happens that the Germans are human. There is nothing Celtic about loving poetry; the English loved poetry more, perhaps, than any other people before they came under the shadow of the chimney-pot and the shadow of the chimney-pot hat. It is not Ireland which is mad and mystic; it is Manchester which is mad and mystic, which is incredible, which is a wild exception among human things. Ireland has no need to play the silly game of the science of races; Ireland has no need to pretend to be a tribe of visionaries apart. In the matter of visions, Ireland is more than a nation, it is a model nation.

XIV ON CERTAIN MODERN WRITERS AND THE INSTITUTION OF THE FAMILY

The family may fairly be considered, one would think, an ultimate human institution. Every one would admit that it has been the main cell and central unit of almost all societies hitherto, except, indeed, such societies as that of Lacedaemon, which went in for "efficiency," and has, therefore, perished, and left not a trace behind. Christianity, even enormous as was its revolution, did not alter this ancient and savage sanctity; it merely reversed it. It did not deny the trinity of father, mother, and child. It merely read it backwards, making it run child, mother, father. This it called, not the family, but the Holy Family, for many things are made holy by being turned upside down. But some sages of our own decadence have made a serious attack on the family. They have impugned it, as I think wrongly; and its defenders have defended it, and defended it wrongly. The common defence of the family is that, amid the stress and fickleness of life, it is peaceful, pleasant, and at one. But there is another defence of the family which is possible, and to me evident; this defence is that the family is not peaceful and not pleasant and not at one.

It is not fashionable to say much nowadays of the advantages of the small community. We are told that we must go in for large empires and large ideas. There is one advantage, however, in the small state, the city, or the village, which only the wilfully blind can overlook. The man who lives in a small community lives in a much larger world. He knows much more of the fierce varieties and uncompromising divergences of men. The reason is obvious. In a large community we can choose our companions. In a small community our companions are chosen for us. Thus in all extensive and highly civilized societies groups come into existence founded upon what is called sympathy, and shut out the real world more sharply than the gates of a monastery. There is nothing really narrow about the clan; the thing which is really narrow is the clique. The men of the clan live together because they all wear the same tartan or are all descended from the same sacred cow; but in their souls, by the divine luck of things, there will always be more colours than in any tartan. But the men of the clique live together because they have the same kind of soul, and their narrowness is a narrowness of spiritual coherence and contentment, like that which exists in hell. A big society exists in order to form cliques. A big society is a society for the promotion of narrowness. It is a machinery for the purpose of guarding the solitary and sensitive individual from all experience of the bitter and bracing human compromises. It is, in the most literal sense of the words, a society for the prevention of Christian knowledge.

We can see this change, for instance, in the modern transformation of the thing called a club. When London was smaller, and the parts of London more self-contained and parochial, the club was what it still is in villages, the opposite of what it is now in great cities. Then the club was valued as a place where a man could be sociable. Now the club is valued as a place where a man can be unsociable. The more the enlargement and elaboration of our civilization goes on the more the club ceases to be a place where a man can have a noisy argument, and becomes more and more a place where a man can have what is somewhat fantastically called a quiet chop. Its aim is to make a man comfortable, and to make a man comfortable is to make him the opposite of sociable. Sociability, like all good things, is full of discomforts, dangers, and renunciations. The club tends to produce the most degraded of all combinations—the luxurious anchorite, the man who combines the self-indulgence of Lucullus with the insane loneliness of St. Simeon Stylites.

If we were to-morrow morning snowed up in the street in which we live, we should step suddenly into a much larger and much wilder world than we have ever known. And it is the whole effort of the typically modern person to escape from the street in which he lives. First he invents modern hygiene and goes to Margate. Then he invents modern culture and goes to Florence. Then he invents modern imperialism and goes to Timbuctoo. He goes to the fantastic borders of the earth. He pretends to shoot tigers. He almost rides on a camel. And in all this he is still essentially fleeing from the street in which he was born; and of this flight he is always ready with his own explanation. He says he is fleeing from his street because it is dull; he is lying. He is really fleeing from his street because it is a great deal too exciting. It is exciting because it is exacting; it is exacting because it is alive. He can visit Venice because to him the Venetians are only Venetians; the people in his own street are men. He can stare at the Chinese because for him the Chinese are a passive thing to be stared at; if he stares at the old lady in the next garden, she becomes active. He is forced to flee, in short, from the too stimulating society of his equals—of free men, perverse, personal, deliberately different from himself. The street in Brixton is too glowing and overpowering. He has to soothe and quiet himself among tigers and vultures, camels and crocodiles. These creatures are indeed very different from himself. But they do not put their shape or colour or custom into a decisive intellectual competition with his own. They do not seek to destroy his principles and assert their own; the stranger monsters of the suburban street do seek to do this. The camel does not contort his features into a fine sneer because Mr. Robinson has not got a hump; the cultured gentleman at No. 5 does exhibit a sneer because Robinson has not got a dado. The vulture will not roar with laughter because a man does not fly; but the major at No. 9 will roar with laughter because a man does not smoke. The complaint we commonly have to make of our neighbours is that they will not, as we express it, mind their own business. We do not really mean that they will not mind their own business. If our neighbours did not mind their own business they would be asked abruptly for their rent, and would rapidly cease to be our neighbours. What we really mean when we say that they cannot mind their own business is something much deeper. We do not dislike them because they have so little force and fire that they cannot be interested in themselves. We dislike them because they have so much force and fire that they can be interested in us as well. What we dread about our neighbours, in short, is not the narrowness of their horizon, but their superb tendency to broaden it. And all aversions to ordinary humanity have this general character. They are not aversions to its feebleness (as is pretended), but to its energy. The misanthropes pretend that they despise humanity for its weakness. As a matter of fact, they hate it for its strength.

Of course, this shrinking from the brutal vivacity and brutal variety of common men is a perfectly reasonable and excusable thing as long as it does not pretend to any point of superiority. It is when it calls itself aristocracy or aestheticism or a superiority to the bourgeoisie that its inherent weakness has in justice to be pointed out. Fastidiousness is the most pardonable of vices; but it is the most unpardonable of virtues. Nietzsche, who represents most prominently this pretentious claim of the fastidious, has a description somewhere—a very powerful description in the purely literary sense—of the disgust and disdain which consume him at the sight of the common people with their common faces, their common voices, and their common minds. As I have said, this attitude is almost beautiful if we may regard it as pathetic. Nietzsche's aristocracy has about it all the sacredness that belongs to the weak. When he makes us feel that he cannot endure the innumerable faces, the incessant voices, the overpowering omnipresence which belongs to the mob, he will have the sympathy of anybody who has ever been sick on a steamer or tired in a crowded omnibus. Every man has hated mankind when he was less than a man. Every man has had humanity in his eyes like a blinding fog, humanity in his nostrils like a suffocating smell. But when Nietzsche has the incredible lack of humour and lack of imagination to ask us to believe that his aristocracy is an aristocracy of strong muscles or an aristocracy of strong wills, it is necessary to point out the truth. It is an aristocracy of weak nerves.

We make our friends; we make our enemies; but God makes our next-door neighbour. Hence he comes to us clad in all the careless terrors of nature; he is as strange as the stars, as reckless and indifferent as the rain. He is Man, the most terrible of the beasts. That is why the old religions and the old scriptural language showed so sharp a wisdom when they spoke, not of one's duty towards humanity, but one's duty towards one's neighbour. The duty towards humanity may often take the form of some choice which is personal or even pleasurable. That duty may be a hobby; it may even be a dissipation. We may work in the East End because we are peculiarly fitted to work in the East End, or because we think we are; we may fight for the cause of international peace because we are very fond of fighting. The most monstrous martyrdom, the most repulsive experience, may be the result of choice or a kind of taste. We may be so made as to be particularly fond of lunatics or specially interested in leprosy. We may love negroes because they are black or German Socialists because they are pedantic. But we have to love our neighbour because he is there—a much more alarming reason for a much more serious operation. He is the sample of humanity which is actually given us. Precisely because he may be anybody he is everybody. He is a symbol because he is an accident.

Doubtless men flee from small environments into lands that are very deadly. But this is natural enough; for they are not fleeing from death. They are fleeing from life. And this principle applies to ring within ring of the social system of humanity. It is perfectly reasonable that men should seek for some particular variety of the human type, so long as they are seeking for that variety of the human type, and not for mere human variety. It is quite proper that a British diplomatist should seek the society of Japanese generals, if what he wants is Japanese generals. But if what he wants is people different from himself, he had much better stop at home and discuss religion with the housemaid. It is quite reasonable that the village genius should come up to conquer London if what he wants is to conquer London. But if he wants to conquer something fundamentally and symbolically hostile and also very strong, he had much better remain where he is and have a row with the rector. The man in the suburban street is quite right if he goes to Ramsgate for the sake of Ramsgate—a difficult thing to imagine. But if, as he expresses it, he goes to Ramsgate "for a change," then he would have a much more romantic and even melodramatic change if he jumped over the wall into his neighbours garden. The consequences would be bracing in a sense far beyond the possibilities of Ramsgate hygiene.

Now, exactly as this principle applies to the empire, to the nation within the empire, to the city within the nation, to the street within the city, so it applies to the home within the street. The institution of the family is to be commended for precisely the same reasons that the institution of the nation, or the institution of the city, are in this matter to be commended. It is a good thing for a man to live in a family for the same reason that it is a good thing for a man to be besieged in a city. It is a good thing for a man to live in a family in the same sense that it is a beautiful and delightful thing for a man to be snowed up in a street. They all force him to realize that life is not a thing from outside, but a thing from inside. Above all, they all insist upon the fact that life, if it be a truly stimulating and fascinating life, is a thing which, of its nature, exists in spite of ourselves. The modern writers who have suggested, in a more or less open manner, that the family is a bad institution, have generally confined themselves to suggesting, with much sharpness, bitterness, or pathos, that perhaps the family is not always very congenial. Of course the family is a good institution because it is uncongenial. It is wholesome precisely because it contains so many divergencies and varieties. It is, as the sentimentalists say, like a little kingdom, and, like most other little kingdoms, is generally in a state of something resembling anarchy. It is exactly because our brother George is not interested in our religious difficulties, but is interested in the Trocadero Restaurant, that the family has some of the bracing qualities of the commonwealth. It is precisely because our uncle Henry does not approve of the theatrical ambitions of our sister Sarah that the family is like humanity. The men and women who, for good reasons and bad, revolt against the family, are, for good reasons and bad, simply revolting against mankind. Aunt Elizabeth is unreasonable, like mankind. Papa is excitable, like mankind Our youngest brother is mischievous, like mankind. Grandpapa is stupid, like the world; he is old, like the world.

Those who wish, rightly or wrongly, to step out of all this, do definitely wish to step into a narrower world. They are dismayed and terrified by the largeness and variety of the family. Sarah wishes to find a world wholly consisting of private theatricals; George wishes to think the Trocadero a cosmos. I do not say, for a moment, that the flight to this narrower life may not be the right thing for the individual, any more than I say the same thing about flight into a monastery. But I do say that anything is bad and artificial which tends to make these people succumb to the strange delusion that they are stepping into a world which is actually larger and more varied than their own. The best way that a man could test his readiness to encounter the common variety of mankind would be to climb down a chimney into any house at random, and get on as well as possible with the people inside. And that is essentially what each one of us did on the day that he was born.

This is, indeed, the sublime and special romance of the family. It is romantic because it is a toss-up. It is romantic because it is everything that its enemies call it. It is romantic because it is arbitrary. It is romantic because it is there. So long as you have groups of men chosen rationally, you have some special or sectarian atmosphere. It is when you have groups of men chosen irrationally that you have men. The element of adventure begins to exist; for an adventure is, by its nature, a thing that comes to us. It is a thing that chooses us, not a thing that we choose. Falling in love has been often regarded as the supreme adventure, the supreme romantic accident. In so much as there is in it something outside ourselves, something of a sort of merry fatalism, this is very true. Love does take us and transfigure and torture us. It does break our hearts with an unbearable beauty, like the unbearable beauty of music. But in so far as we have certainly something to do with the matter; in so far as we are in some sense prepared to fall in love and in some sense jump into it; in so far as we do to some extent choose and to some extent even judge—in all this falling in love is not truly romantic, is not truly adventurous at all. In this degree the supreme adventure is not falling in love. The supreme adventure is being born. There we do walk suddenly into a splendid and startling trap. There we do see something of which we have not dreamed before. Our father and mother do lie in wait for us and leap out on us, like brigands from a bush. Our uncle is a surprise. Our aunt is, in the beautiful common expression, a bolt from the blue. When we step into the family, by the act of being born, we do step into a world which is incalculable, into a world which has its own strange laws, into a world which could do without us, into a world that we have not made. In other words, when we step into the family we step into a fairy-tale.

This colour as of a fantastic narrative ought to cling to the family and to our relations with it throughout life. Romance is the deepest thing in life; romance is deeper even than reality. For even if reality could be proved to be misleading, it still could not be proved to be unimportant or unimpressive. Even if the facts are false, they are still very strange. And this strangeness of life, this unexpected and even perverse element of things as they fall out, remains incurably interesting. The circumstances we can regulate may become tame or pessimistic; but the "circumstances over which we have no control" remain god-like to those who, like Mr. Micawber, can call on them and renew their strength. People wonder why the novel is the most popular form of literature; people wonder why it is read more than books of science or books of metaphysics. The reason is very simple; it is merely that the novel is more true than they are. Life may sometimes legitimately appear as a book of science. Life may sometimes appear, and with a much greater legitimacy, as a book of metaphysics. But life is always a novel. Our existence may cease to be a song; it may cease even to be a beautiful lament. Our existence may not be an intelligible justice, or even a recognizable wrong. But our existence is still a story. In the fiery alphabet of every sunset is written, "to be continued in our next." If we have sufficient intellect, we can finish a philosophical and exact deduction, and be certain that we are finishing it right. With the adequate brain-power we could finish any scientific discovery, and be certain that we were finishing it right. But not with the most gigantic intellect could we finish the simplest or silliest story, and be certain that we were finishing it right. That is because a story has behind it, not merely intellect which is partly mechanical, but will, which is in its essence divine. The narrative writer can send his hero to the gallows if he likes in the last chapter but one. He can do it by the same divine caprice whereby he, the author, can go to the gallows himself, and to hell afterwards if he chooses. And the same civilization, the chivalric European civilization which asserted freewill in the thirteenth century, produced the thing called "fiction" in the eighteenth. When Thomas Aquinas asserted the spiritual liberty of man, he created all the bad novels in the circulating libraries.

But in order that life should be a story or romance to us, it is necessary that a great part of it, at any rate, should be settled for us without our permission. If we wish life to be a system, this may be a nuisance; but if we wish it to be a drama, it is an essential. It may often happen, no doubt, that a drama may be written by somebody else which we like very little. But we should like it still less if the author came before the curtain every hour or so, and forced on us the whole trouble of inventing the next act. A man has control over many things in his life; he has control over enough things to be the hero of a novel. But if he had control over everything, there would be so much hero that there would be no novel. And the reason why the lives of the rich are at bottom so tame and uneventful is simply that they can choose the events. They are dull because they are omnipotent. They fail to feel adventures because they can make the adventures. The thing which keeps life romantic and full of fiery possibilities is the existence of these great plain limitations which force all of us to meet the things we do not like or do not expect. It is vain for the supercilious moderns to talk of being in uncongenial surroundings. To be in a romance is to be in uncongenial surroundings. To be born into this earth is to be born into uncongenial surroundings, hence to be born into a romance. Of all these great limitations and frameworks which fashion and create the poetry and variety of life, the family is the most definite and important. Hence it is misunderstood by the moderns, who imagine that romance would exist most perfectly in a complete state of what they call liberty. They think that if a man makes a gesture it would be a startling and romantic matter that the sun should fall from the sky. But the startling and romantic thing about the sun is that it does not fall from the sky. They are seeking under every shape and form a world where there are no limitations—that is, a world where there are no outlines; that is, a world where there are no shapes. There is nothing baser than that infinity. They say they wish to be, as strong as the universe, but they really wish the whole universe as weak as themselves.

XV ON SMART NOVELISTS AND THE SMART SET

In one sense, at any rate, it is more valuable to read bad literature than good literature. Good literature may tell us the mind of one man; but bad literature may tell us the mind of many men. A good novel tells us the truth about its hero; but a bad novel tells us the truth about its author. It does much more than that, it tells us the truth about its readers; and, oddly enough, it tells us this all the more the more cynical and immoral be the motive of its manufacture. The more dishonest a book is as a book the more honest it is as a public document. A sincere novel exhibits the simplicity of one particular man; an insincere novel exhibits the simplicity of mankind. The pedantic decisions and definable readjustments of man may be found in scrolls and statute books and scriptures; but men's basic assumptions and everlasting energies are to be found in penny dreadfuls and halfpenny novelettes. Thus a man, like many men of real culture in our day, might learn from good literature nothing except the power to appreciate good literature. But from bad literature he might learn to govern empires and look over the map of mankind.

There is one rather interesting example of this state of things in which the weaker literature is really the stronger and the stronger the weaker. It is the case of what may be called, for the sake of an approximate description, the literature of aristocracy; or, if you prefer the description, the literature of snobbishness. Now if any one wishes to find a really effective and comprehensible and permanent case for aristocracy well and sincerely stated, let him read, not the modern philosophical conservatives, not even Nietzsche, let him read the Bow Bells Novelettes. Of the case of Nietzsche I am confessedly more doubtful. Nietzsche and the Bow Bells Novelettes have both obviously the same fundamental character; they both worship the tall man with curling moustaches and herculean bodily power, and they both worship him in a manner which is somewhat feminine and hysterical. Even here, however, the Novelette easily maintains its philosophical superiority, because it does attribute to the strong man those virtues which do commonly belong to him, such virtues as laziness and kindliness and a rather reckless benevolence, and a great dislike of hurting the weak. Nietzsche, on the other hand, attributes to the strong man that scorn against weakness which only exists among invalids. It is not, however, of the secondary merits of the great German philosopher, but of the primary merits of the Bow Bells Novelettes, that it is my present affair to speak. The picture of aristocracy in the popular sentimental novelette seems to me very satisfactory as a permanent political and philosophical guide. It may be inaccurate about details such as the title by which a baronet is addressed or the width of a mountain chasm which a baronet can conveniently leap, but it is not a bad description of the general idea and intention of aristocracy as they exist in human affairs. The essential dream of aristocracy is magnificence and valour; and if the Family Herald Supplement sometimes distorts or exaggerates these things, at least, it does not fall short in them. It never errs by making the mountain chasm too narrow or the title of the baronet insufficiently impressive. But above this sane reliable old literature of snobbishness there has arisen in our time another kind of literature of snobbishness which, with its much higher pretensions, seems to me worthy of very much less respect. Incidentally (if that matters), it is much better literature. But it is immeasurably worse philosophy, immeasurably worse ethics and politics, immeasurably worse vital rendering of aristocracy and humanity as they really are. From such books as those of which I wish now to speak we can discover what a clever man can do with the idea of aristocracy. But from the Family Herald Supplement literature we can learn what the idea of aristocracy can do with a man who is not clever. And when we know that we know English history.

This new aristocratic fiction must have caught the attention of everybody who has read the best fiction for the last fifteen years. It is that genuine or alleged literature of the Smart Set which represents that set as distinguished, not only by smart dresses, but by smart sayings. To the bad baronet, to the good baronet, to the romantic and misunderstood baronet who is supposed to be a bad baronet, but is a good baronet, this school has added a conception undreamed of in the former years—the conception of an amusing baronet. The aristocrat is not merely to be taller than mortal men and stronger and handsomer, he is also to be more witty. He is the long man with the short epigram. Many eminent, and deservedly eminent, modern novelists must accept some responsibility for having supported this worst form of snobbishness—an intellectual snobbishness. The talented author of "Dodo" is responsible for having in some sense created the fashion as a fashion. Mr. Hichens, in the "Green Carnation," reaffirmed the strange idea that young noblemen talk well; though his case had some vague biographical foundation, and in consequence an excuse. Mrs. Craigie is considerably guilty in the matter, although, or rather because, she has combined the aristocratic note with a note of some moral and even religious sincerity. When you are saving a man's soul, even in a novel, it is indecent to mention that he is a gentleman. Nor can blame in this matter be altogether removed from a man of much greater ability, and a man who has proved his possession of the highest of human instinct, the romantic instinct—I mean Mr. Anthony Hope. In a galloping, impossible melodrama like "The Prisoner of Zenda," the blood of kings fanned an excellent fantastic thread or theme. But the blood of kings is not a thing that can be taken seriously. And when, for example, Mr. Hope devotes so much serious and sympathetic study to the man called Tristram of Blent, a man who throughout burning boyhood thought of nothing but a silly old estate, we feel even in Mr. Hope the hint of this excessive concern about the oligarchic idea. It is hard for any ordinary person to feel so much interest in a young man whose whole aim is to own the house of Blent at the time when every other young man is owning the stars.

Mr. Hope, however, is a very mild case, and in him there is not only an element of romance, but also a fine element of irony which warns us against taking all this elegance too seriously. Above all, he shows his sense in not making his noblemen so incredibly equipped with impromptu repartee. This habit of insisting on the wit of the wealthier classes is the last and most servile of all the servilities. It is, as I have said, immeasurably more contemptible than the snobbishness of the novelette which describes the nobleman as smiling like an Apollo or riding a mad elephant. These may be exaggerations of beauty and courage, but beauty and courage are the unconscious ideals of aristocrats, even of stupid aristocrats.

The nobleman of the novelette may not be sketched with any very close or conscientious attention to the daily habits of noblemen. But he is something more important than a reality; he is a practical ideal. The gentleman of fiction may not copy the gentleman of real life; but the gentleman of real life is copying the gentleman of fiction. He may not be particularly good-looking, but he would rather be good-looking than anything else; he may not have ridden on a mad elephant, but he rides a pony as far as possible with an air as if he had. And, upon the whole, the upper class not only especially desire these qualities of beauty and courage, but in some degree, at any rate, especially possess them. Thus there is nothing really mean or sycophantic about the popular literature which makes all its marquises seven feet high. It is snobbish, but it is not servile. Its exaggeration is based on an exuberant and honest admiration; its honest admiration is based upon something which is in some degree, at any rate, really there. The English lower classes do not fear the English upper classes in the least; nobody could. They simply and freely and sentimentally worship them. The strength of the aristocracy is not in the aristocracy at all; it is in the slums. It is not in the House of Lords; it is not in the Civil Service; it is not in the Government offices; it is not even in the huge and disproportionate monopoly of the English land. It is in a certain spirit. It is in the fact that when a navvy wishes to praise a man, it comes readily to his tongue to say that he has behaved like a gentleman. From a democratic point of view he might as well say that he had behaved like a viscount. The oligarchic character of the modern English commonwealth does not rest, like many oligarchies, on the cruelty of the rich to the poor. It does not even rest on the kindness of the rich to the poor. It rests on the perennial and unfailing kindness of the poor to the rich.

The snobbishness of bad literature, then, is not servile; but the snobbishness of good literature is servile. The old-fashioned halfpenny romance where the duchesses sparkled with diamonds was not servile; but the new romance where they sparkle with epigrams is servile. For in thus attributing a special and startling degree of intellect and conversational or controversial power to the upper classes, we are attributing something which is not especially their virtue or even especially their aim. We are, in the words of Disraeli (who, being a genius and not a gentleman, has perhaps primarily to answer for the introduction of this method of flattering the gentry), we are performing the essential function of flattery which is flattering the people for the qualities they have not got. Praise may be gigantic and insane without having any quality of flattery so long as it is praise of something that is noticeably in existence. A man may say that a giraffe's head strikes the stars, or that a whale fills the German Ocean, and still be only in a rather excited state about a favourite animal. But when he begins to congratulate the giraffe on his feathers, and the whale on the elegance of his legs, we find ourselves confronted with that social element which we call flattery. The middle and lower orders of London can sincerely, though not perhaps safely, admire the health and grace of the English aristocracy. And this for the very simple reason that the aristocrats are, upon the whole, more healthy and graceful than the poor. But they cannot honestly admire the wit of the aristocrats. And this for the simple reason that the aristocrats are not more witty than the poor, but a very great deal less so. A man does not hear, as in the smart novels, these gems of verbal felicity dropped between diplomatists at dinner. Where he really does hear them is between two omnibus conductors in a block in Holborn. The witty peer whose impromptus fill the books of Mrs. Craigie or Miss Fowler, would, as a matter of fact, be torn to shreds in the art of conversation by the first boot-black he had the misfortune to fall foul of. The poor are merely sentimental, and very excusably sentimental, if they praise the gentleman for having a ready hand and ready money. But they are strictly slaves and sycophants if they praise him for having a ready tongue. For that they have far more themselves.

The element of oligarchical sentiment in these novels, however, has, I think, another and subtler aspect, an aspect more difficult to understand and more worth understanding. The modern gentleman, particularly the modern English gentleman, has become so central and important in these books, and through them in the whole of our current literature and our current mode of thought, that certain qualities of his, whether original or recent, essential or accidental, have altered the quality of our English comedy. In particular, that stoical ideal, absurdly supposed to be the English ideal, has stiffened and chilled us. It is not the English ideal; but it is to some extent the aristocratic ideal; or it may be only the ideal of aristocracy in its autumn or decay. The gentleman is a Stoic because he is a sort of savage, because he is filled with a great elemental fear that some stranger will speak to him. That is why a third-class carriage is a community, while a first-class carriage is a place of wild hermits. But this matter, which is difficult, I may be permitted to approach in a more circuitous way.

The haunting element of ineffectualness which runs through so much of the witty and epigrammatic fiction fashionable during the last eight or ten years, which runs through such works of a real though varying ingenuity as "Dodo," or "Concerning Isabel Carnaby," or even "Some Emotions and a Moral," may be expressed in various ways, but to most of us I think it will ultimately amount to the same thing. This new frivolity is inadequate because there is in it no strong sense of an unuttered joy. The men and women who exchange the repartees may not only be hating each other, but hating even themselves. Any one of them might be bankrupt that day, or sentenced to be shot the next. They are joking, not because they are merry, but because they are not; out of the emptiness of the heart the mouth speaketh. Even when they talk pure nonsense it is a careful nonsense—a nonsense of which they are economical, or, to use the perfect expression of Mr. W. S. Gilbert in "Patience," it is such "precious nonsense." Even when they become light-headed they do not become light-hearted. All those who have read anything of the rationalism of the moderns know that their Reason is a sad thing. But even their unreason is sad.

The causes of this incapacity are also not very difficult to indicate. The chief of all, of course, is that miserable fear of being sentimental, which is the meanest of all the modern terrors—meaner even than the terror which produces hygiene. Everywhere the robust and uproarious humour has come from the men who were capable not merely of sentimentalism, but a very silly sentimentalism. There has been no humour so robust or uproarious as that of the sentimentalist Steele or the sentimentalist Sterne or the sentimentalist Dickens. These creatures who wept like women were the creatures who laughed like men. It is true that the humour of Micawber is good literature and that the pathos of little Nell is bad. But the kind of man who had the courage to write so badly in the one case is the kind of man who would have the courage to write so well in the other. The same unconsciousness, the same violent innocence, the same gigantesque scale of action which brought the Napoleon of Comedy his Jena brought him also his Moscow. And herein is especially shown the frigid and feeble limitations of our modern wits. They make violent efforts, they make heroic and almost pathetic efforts, but they cannot really write badly. There are moments when we almost think that they are achieving the effect, but our hope shrivels to nothing the moment we compare their little failures with the enormous imbecilities of Byron or Shakespeare.

For a hearty laugh it is necessary to have touched the heart. I do not know why touching the heart should always be connected only with the idea of touching it to compassion or a sense of distress. The heart can be touched to joy and triumph; the heart can be touched to amusement. But all our comedians are tragic comedians. These later fashionable writers are so pessimistic in bone and marrow that they never seem able to imagine the heart having any concern with mirth. When they speak of the heart, they always mean the pangs and disappointments of the emotional life. When they say that a man's heart is in the right place, they mean, apparently, that it is in his boots. Our ethical societies understand fellowship, but they do not understand good fellowship. Similarly, our wits understand talk, but not what Dr. Johnson called a good talk. In order to have, like Dr. Johnson, a good talk, it is emphatically necessary to be, like Dr. Johnson, a good man—to have friendship and honour and an abysmal tenderness. Above all, it is necessary to be openly and indecently humane, to confess with fulness all the primary pities and fears of Adam. Johnson was a clear-headed humorous man, and therefore he did not mind talking seriously about religion. Johnson was a brave man, one of the bravest that ever walked, and therefore he did not mind avowing to any one his consuming fear of death.

The idea that there is something English in the repression of one's feelings is one of those ideas which no Englishman ever heard of until England began to be governed exclusively by Scotchmen, Americans, and Jews. At the best, the idea is a generalization from the Duke of Wellington—who was an Irishman. At the worst, it is a part of that silly Teutonism which knows as little about England as it does about anthropology, but which is always talking about Vikings. As a matter of fact, the Vikings did not repress their feelings in the least. They cried like babies and kissed each other like girls; in short, they acted in that respect like Achilles and all strong heroes the children of the gods. And though the English nationality has probably not much more to do with the Vikings than the French nationality or the Irish nationality, the English have certainly been the children of the Vikings in the matter of tears and kisses. It is not merely true that all the most typically English men of letters, like Shakespeare and Dickens, Richardson and Thackeray, were sentimentalists. It is also true that all the most typically English men of action were sentimentalists, if possible, more sentimental. In the great Elizabethan age, when the English nation was finally hammered out, in the great eighteenth century when the British Empire was being built up everywhere, where in all these times, where was this symbolic stoical Englishman who dresses in drab and black and represses his feelings? Were all the Elizabethan palladins and pirates like that? Were any of them like that? Was Grenville concealing his emotions when he broke wine-glasses to pieces with his teeth and bit them till the blood poured down? Was Essex restraining his excitement when he threw his hat into the sea? Did Raleigh think it sensible to answer the Spanish guns only, as Stevenson says, with a flourish of insulting trumpets? Did Sydney ever miss an opportunity of making a theatrical remark in the whole course of his life and death? Were even the Puritans Stoics? The English Puritans repressed a good deal, but even they were too English to repress their feelings. It was by a great miracle of genius assuredly that Carlyle contrived to admire simultaneously two things so irreconcilably opposed as silence and Oliver Cromwell. Cromwell was the very reverse of a strong, silent man. Cromwell was always talking, when he was not crying. Nobody, I suppose, will accuse the author of "Grace Abounding" of being ashamed of his feelings. Milton, indeed, it might be possible to represent as a Stoic; in some sense he was a Stoic, just as he was a prig and a polygamist and several other unpleasant and heathen things. But when we have passed that great and desolate name, which may really be counted an exception, we find the tradition of English emotionalism immediately resumed and unbrokenly continuous. Whatever may have been the moral beauty of the passions of Etheridge and Dorset, Sedley and Buckingham, they cannot be accused of the fault of fastidiously concealing them. Charles the Second was very popular with the English because, like all the jolly English kings, he displayed his passions. William the Dutchman was very unpopular with the English because, not being an Englishman, he did hide his emotions. He was, in fact, precisely the ideal Englishman of our modern theory; and precisely for that reason all the real Englishmen loathed him like leprosy. With the rise of the great England of the eighteenth century, we find this open and emotional tone still maintained in letters and politics, in arts and in arms. Perhaps the only quality which was possessed in common by the great Fielding, and the great Richardson was that neither of them hid their feelings. Swift, indeed, was hard and logical, because Swift was Irish. And when we pass to the soldiers and the rulers, the patriots and the empire-builders of the eighteenth century, we find, as I have said, that they were, If possible, more romantic than the romancers, more poetical than the poets. Chatham, who showed the world all his strength, showed the House of Commons all his weakness. Wolfe walked about the room with a drawn sword calling himself Caesar and Hannibal, and went to death with poetry in his mouth. Clive was a man of the same type as Cromwell or Bunyan, or, for the matter of that, Johnson—that is, he was a strong, sensible man with a kind of running spring of hysteria and melancholy in him. Like Johnson, he was all the more healthy because he was morbid. The tales of all the admirals and adventurers of that England are full of braggadocio, of sentimentality, of splendid affectation. But it is scarcely necessary to multiply examples of the essentially romantic Englishman when one example towers above them all. Mr. Rudyard Kipling has said complacently of the English, "We do not fall on the neck and kiss when we come together." It is true that this ancient and universal custom has vanished with the modern weakening of England. Sydney would have thought nothing of kissing Spenser. But I willingly concede that Mr. Broderick would not be likely to kiss Mr. Arnold-Foster, if that be any proof of the increased manliness and military greatness of England. But the Englishman who does not show his feelings has not altogether given up the power of seeing something English in the great sea-hero of the Napoleonic war. You cannot break the legend of Nelson. And across the sunset of that glory is written in flaming letters for ever the great English sentiment, "Kiss me, Hardy."

This ideal of self-repression, then, is, whatever else it is, not English. It is, perhaps, somewhat Oriental, it is slightly Prussian, but in the main it does not come, I think, from any racial or national source. It is, as I have said, in some sense aristocratic; it comes not from a people, but from a class. Even aristocracy, I think, was not quite so stoical in the days when it was really strong. But whether this unemotional ideal be the genuine tradition of the gentleman, or only one of the inventions of the modern gentleman (who may be called the decayed gentleman), it certainly has something to do with the unemotional quality in these society novels. From representing aristocrats as people who suppressed their feelings, it has been an easy step to representing aristocrats as people who had no feelings to suppress. Thus the modern oligarchist has made a virtue for the oligarchy of the hardness as well as the brightness of the diamond. Like a sonneteer addressing his lady in the seventeenth century, he seems to use the word "cold" almost as a eulogium, and the word "heartless" as a kind of compliment. Of course, in people so incurably kind-hearted and babyish as are the English gentry, it would be impossible to create anything that can be called positive cruelty; so in these books they exhibit a sort of negative cruelty. They cannot be cruel in acts, but they can be so in words. All this means one thing, and one thing only. It means that the living and invigorating ideal of England must be looked for in the masses; it must be looked for where Dickens found it—Dickens among whose glories it was to be a humorist, to be a sentimentalist, to be an optimist, to be a poor man, to be an Englishman, but the greatest of whose glories was that he saw all mankind in its amazing and tropical luxuriance, and did not even notice the aristocracy; Dickens, the greatest of whose glories was that he could not describe a gentleman.

XVI ON MR. MCCABE AND A DIVINE FRIVOLITY

A critic once remonstrated with me saying, with an air of indignant reasonableness, "If you must make jokes, at least you need not make them on such serious subjects." I replied with a natural simplicity and wonder, "About what other subjects can one make jokes except serious subjects?" It is quite useless to talk about profane jesting. All jesting is in its nature profane, in the sense that it must be the sudden realization that something which thinks itself solemn is not so very solemn after all. If a joke is not a joke about religion or morals, it is a joke about police-magistrates or scientific professors or undergraduates dressed up as Queen Victoria. And people joke about the police-magistrate more than they joke about the Pope, not because the police-magistrate is a more frivolous subject, but, on the contrary, because the police-magistrate is a more serious subject than the Pope. The Bishop of Rome has no jurisdiction in this realm of England; whereas the police-magistrate may bring his solemnity to bear quite suddenly upon us. Men make jokes about old scientific professors, even more than they make them about bishops—not because science is lighter than religion, but because science is always by its nature more solemn and austere than religion. It is not I; it is not even a particular class of journalists or jesters who make jokes about the matters which are of most awful import; it is the whole human race. If there is one thing more than another which any one will admit who has the smallest knowledge of the world, it is that men are always speaking gravely and earnestly and with the utmost possible care about the things that are not important, but always talking frivolously about the things that are. Men talk for hours with the faces of a college of cardinals about things like golf, or tobacco, or waistcoats, or party politics. But all the most grave and dreadful things in the world are the oldest jokes in the world—being married; being hanged.

One gentleman, however, Mr. McCabe, has in this matter made to me something that almost amounts to a personal appeal; and as he happens to be a man for whose sincerity and intellectual virtue I have a high respect, I do not feel inclined to let it pass without some attempt to satisfy my critic in the matter. Mr. McCabe devotes a considerable part of the last essay in the collection called "Christianity and Rationalism on Trial" to an objection, not to my thesis, but to my method, and a very friendly and dignified appeal to me to alter it. I am much inclined to defend myself in this matter out of mere respect for Mr. McCabe, and still more so out of mere respect for the truth which is, I think, in danger by his error, not only in this question, but in others. In order that there may be no injustice done in the matter, I will quote Mr. McCabe himself. "But before I follow Mr. Chesterton in some detail I would make a general observation on his method. He is as serious as I am in his ultimate purpose, and I respect him for that. He knows, as I do, that humanity stands at a solemn parting of the ways. Towards some unknown goal it presses through the ages, impelled by an overmastering desire of happiness. To-day it hesitates, lightheartedly enough, but every serious thinker knows how momentous the decision may be. It is, apparently, deserting the path of religion and entering upon the path of secularism. Will it lose itself in quagmires of sensuality down this new path, and pant and toil through years of civic and industrial anarchy, only to learn it had lost the road, and must return to religion? Or will it find that at last it is leaving the mists and the quagmires behind it; that it is ascending the slope of the hill so long dimly discerned ahead, and making straight for the long-sought Utopia? This is the drama of our time, and every man and every woman should understand it.

"Mr. Chesterton understands it. Further, he gives us credit for understanding it. He has nothing of that paltry meanness or strange density of so many of his colleagues, who put us down as aimless iconoclasts or moral anarchists. He admits that we are waging a thankless war for what we take to be Truth and Progress. He is doing the same. But why, in the name of all that is reasonable, should we, when we are agreed on the momentousness of the issue either way, forthwith desert serious methods of conducting the controversy? Why, when the vital need of our time is to induce men and women to collect their thoughts occasionally, and be men and women—nay, to remember that they are really gods that hold the destinies of humanity on their knees—why should we think that this kaleidoscopic play of phrases is inopportune? The ballets of the Alhambra, and the fireworks of the Crystal Palace, and Mr. Chesterton's Daily News articles, have their place in life. But how a serious social student can think of curing the thoughtlessness of our generation by strained paradoxes; of giving people a sane grasp of social problems by literary sleight-of-hand; of settling important questions by a reckless shower of rocket-metaphors and inaccurate 'facts,' and the substitution of imagination for judgment, I cannot see."

I quote this passage with a particular pleasure, because Mr. McCabe certainly cannot put too strongly the degree to which I give him and his school credit for their complete sincerity and responsibility of philosophical attitude. I am quite certain that they mean every word they say. I also mean every word I say. But why is it that Mr. McCabe has some sort of mysterious hesitation about admitting that I mean every word I say; why is it that he is not quite as certain of my mental responsibility as I am of his mental responsibility? If we attempt to answer the question directly and well, we shall, I think, have come to the root of the matter by the shortest cut.

Mr. McCabe thinks that I am not serious but only funny, because Mr. McCabe thinks that funny is the opposite of serious. Funny is the opposite of not funny, and of nothing else. The question of whether a man expresses himself in a grotesque or laughable phraseology, or in a stately and restrained phraseology, is not a question of motive or of moral state, it is a question of instinctive language and self-expression. Whether a man chooses to tell the truth in long sentences or short jokes is a problem analogous to whether he chooses to tell the truth in French or German. Whether a man preaches his gospel grotesquely or gravely is merely like the question of whether he preaches it in prose or verse. The question of whether Swift was funny in his irony is quite another sort of question to the question of whether Swift was serious in his pessimism. Surely even Mr. McCabe would not maintain that the more funny "Gulliver" is in its method the less it can be sincere in its object. The truth is, as I have said, that in this sense the two qualities of fun and seriousness have nothing whatever to do with each other, they are no more comparable than black and triangular. Mr. Bernard Shaw is funny and sincere. Mr. George Robey is funny and not sincere. Mr. McCabe is sincere and not funny. The average Cabinet Minister is not sincere and not funny.

In short, Mr. McCabe is under the influence of a primary fallacy which I have found very common in men of the clerical type. Numbers of clergymen have from time to time reproached me for making jokes about religion; and they have almost always invoked the authority of that very sensible commandment which says, "Thou shalt not take the name of the Lord thy God in vain." Of course, I pointed out that I was not in any conceivable sense taking the name in vain. To take a thing and make a joke out of it is not to take it in vain. It is, on the contrary, to take it and use it for an uncommonly good object. To use a thing in vain means to use it without use. But a joke may be exceedingly useful; it may contain the whole earthly sense, not to mention the whole heavenly sense, of a situation. And those who find in the Bible the commandment can find in the Bible any number of the jokes. In the same book in which God's name is fenced from being taken in vain, God himself overwhelms Job with a torrent of terrible levities. The same book which says that God's name must not be taken vainly, talks easily and carelessly about God laughing and God winking. Evidently it is not here that we have to look for genuine examples of what is meant by a vain use of the name. And it is not very difficult to see where we have really to look for it. The people (as I tactfully pointed out to them) who really take the name of the Lord in vain are the clergymen themselves. The thing which is fundamentally and really frivolous is not a careless joke. The thing which is fundamentally and really frivolous is a careless solemnity. If Mr. McCabe really wishes to know what sort of guarantee of reality and solidity is afforded by the mere act of what is called talking seriously, let him spend a happy Sunday in going the round of the pulpits. Or, better still, let him drop in at the House of Commons or the House of Lords. Even Mr. McCabe would admit that these men are solemn—more solemn than I am. And even Mr. McCabe, I think, would admit that these men are frivolous—more frivolous than I am. Why should Mr. McCabe be so eloquent about the danger arising from fantastic and paradoxical writers? Why should he be so ardent in desiring grave and verbose writers? There are not so very many fantastic and paradoxical writers. But there are a gigantic number of grave and verbose writers; and it is by the efforts of the grave and verbose writers that everything that Mr. McCabe detests (and everything that I detest, for that matter) is kept in existence and energy. How can it have come about that a man as intelligent as Mr. McCabe can think that paradox and jesting stop the way? It is solemnity that is stopping the way in every department of modern effort. It is his own favourite "serious methods;" it is his own favourite "momentousness;" it is his own favourite "judgment" which stops the way everywhere. Every man who has ever headed a deputation to a minister knows this. Every man who has ever written a letter to the Times knows it. Every rich man who wishes to stop the mouths of the poor talks about "momentousness." Every Cabinet minister who has not got an answer suddenly develops a "judgment." Every sweater who uses vile methods recommends "serious methods." I said a moment ago that sincerity had nothing to do with solemnity, but I confess that I am not so certain that I was right. In the modern world, at any rate, I am not so sure that I was right. In the modern world solemnity is the direct enemy of sincerity. In the modern world sincerity is almost always on one side, and solemnity almost always on the other. The only answer possible to the fierce and glad attack of sincerity is the miserable answer of solemnity. Let Mr. McCabe, or any one else who is much concerned that we should be grave in order to be sincere, simply imagine the scene in some government office in which Mr. Bernard Shaw should head a Socialist deputation to Mr. Austen Chamberlain. On which side would be the solemnity? And on which the sincerity?

I am, indeed, delighted to discover that Mr. McCabe reckons Mr. Shaw along with me in his system of condemnation of frivolity. He said once, I believe, that he always wanted Mr. Shaw to label his paragraphs serious or comic. I do not know which paragraphs of Mr. Shaw are paragraphs to be labelled serious; but surely there can be no doubt that this paragraph of Mr. McCabe's is one to be labelled comic. He also says, in the article I am now discussing, that Mr. Shaw has the reputation of deliberately saying everything which his hearers do not expect him to say. I need not labour the inconclusiveness and weakness of this, because it has already been dealt with in my remarks on Mr. Bernard Shaw. Suffice it to say here that the only serious reason which I can imagine inducing any one person to listen to any other is, that the first person looks to the second person with an ardent faith and a fixed attention, expecting him to say what he does not expect him to say. It may be a paradox, but that is because paradoxes are true. It may not be rational, but that is because rationalism is wrong. But clearly it is quite true that whenever we go to hear a prophet or teacher we may or may not expect wit, we may or may not expect eloquence, but we do expect what we do not expect. We may not expect the true, we may not even expect the wise, but we do expect the unexpected. If we do not expect the unexpected, why do we go there at all? If we expect the expected, why do we not sit at home and expect it by ourselves? If Mr. McCabe means merely this about Mr. Shaw, that he always has some unexpected application of his doctrine to give to those who listen to him, what he says is quite true, and to say it is only to say that Mr. Shaw is an original man. But if he means that Mr. Shaw has ever professed or preached any doctrine but one, and that his own, then what he says is not true. It is not my business to defend Mr. Shaw; as has been seen already, I disagree with him altogether. But I do not mind, on his behalf offering in this matter a flat defiance to all his ordinary opponents, such as Mr. McCabe. I defy Mr. McCabe, or anybody else, to mention one single instance in which Mr. Shaw has, for the sake of wit or novelty, taken up any position which was not directly deducible from the body of his doctrine as elsewhere expressed. I have been, I am happy to say, a tolerably close student of Mr. Shaw's utterances, and I request Mr. McCabe, if he will not believe that I mean anything else, to believe that I mean this challenge.

All this, however, is a parenthesis. The thing with which I am here immediately concerned is Mr. McCabe's appeal to me not to be so frivolous. Let me return to the actual text of that appeal. There are, of course, a great many things that I might say about it in detail. But I may start with saying that Mr. McCabe is in error in supposing that the danger which I anticipate from the disappearance of religion is the increase of sensuality. On the contrary, I should be inclined to anticipate a decrease in sensuality, because I anticipate a decrease in life. I do not think that under modern Western materialism we should have anarchy. I doubt whether we should have enough individual valour and spirit even to have liberty. It is quite an old-fashioned fallacy to suppose that our objection to scepticism is that it removes the discipline from life. Our objection to scepticism is that it removes the motive power. Materialism is not a thing which destroys mere restraint. Materialism itself is the great restraint. The McCabe school advocates a political liberty, but it denies spiritual liberty. That is, it abolishes the laws which could be broken, and substitutes laws that cannot. And that is the real slavery.

The truth is that the scientific civilization in which Mr. McCabe believes has one rather particular defect; it is perpetually tending to destroy that democracy or power of the ordinary man in which Mr. McCabe also believes. Science means specialism, and specialism means oligarchy. If you once establish the habit of trusting particular men to produce particular results in physics or astronomy, you leave the door open for the equally natural demand that you should trust particular men to do particular things in government and the coercing of men. If, you feel it to be reasonable that one beetle should be the only study of one man, and that one man the only student of that one beetle, it is surely a very harmless consequence to go on to say that politics should be the only study of one man, and that one man the only student of politics. As I have pointed out elsewhere in this book, the expert is more aristocratic than the aristocrat, because the aristocrat is only the man who lives well, while the expert is the man who knows better. But if we look at the progress of our scientific civilization we see a gradual increase everywhere of the specialist over the popular function. Once men sang together round a table in chorus; now one man sings alone, for the absurd reason that he can sing better. If scientific civilization goes on (which is most improbable) only one man will laugh, because he can laugh better than the rest.

I do not know that I can express this more shortly than by taking as a text the single sentence of Mr. McCabe, which runs as follows: "The ballets of the Alhambra and the fireworks of the Crystal Palace and Mr. Chesterton's Daily News articles have their places in life." I wish that my articles had as noble a place as either of the other two things mentioned. But let us ask ourselves (in a spirit of love, as Mr. Chadband would say), what are the ballets of the Alhambra? The ballets of the Alhambra are institutions in which a particular selected row of persons in pink go through an operation known as dancing. Now, in all commonwealths dominated by a religion—in the Christian commonwealths of the Middle Ages and in many rude societies—this habit of dancing was a common habit with everybody, and was not necessarily confined to a professional class. A person could dance without being a dancer; a person could dance without being a specialist; a person could dance without being pink. And, in proportion as Mr. McCabe's scientific civilization advances—that is, in proportion as religious civilization (or real civilization) decays—the more and more "well trained," the more and more pink, become the people who do dance, and the more and more numerous become the people who don't. Mr. McCabe may recognize an example of what I mean in the gradual discrediting in society of the ancient European waltz or dance with partners, and the substitution of that horrible and degrading oriental interlude which is known as skirt-dancing. That is the whole essence of decadence, the effacement of five people who do a thing for fun by one person who does it for money. Now it follows, therefore, that when Mr. McCabe says that the ballets of the Alhambra and my articles "have their place in life," it ought to be pointed out to him that he is doing his best to create a world in which dancing, properly speaking, will have no place in life at all. He is, indeed, trying to create a world in which there will be no life for dancing to have a place in. The very fact that Mr. McCabe thinks of dancing as a thing belonging to some hired women at the Alhambra is an illustration of the same principle by which he is able to think of religion as a thing belonging to some hired men in white neckties. Both these things are things which should not be done for us, but by us. If Mr. McCabe were really religious he would be happy. If he were really happy he would dance.

Briefly, we may put the matter in this way. The main point of modern life is not that the Alhambra ballet has its place in life. The main point, the main enormous tragedy of modern life, is that Mr. McCabe has not his place in the Alhambra ballet. The joy of changing and graceful posture, the joy of suiting the swing of music to the swing of limbs, the joy of whirling drapery, the joy of standing on one leg,—all these should belong by rights to Mr. McCabe and to me; in short, to the ordinary healthy citizen. Probably we should not consent to go through these evolutions. But that is because we are miserable moderns and rationalists. We do not merely love ourselves more than we love duty; we actually love ourselves more than we love joy.

When, therefore, Mr. McCabe says that he gives the Alhambra dances (and my articles) their place in life, I think we are justified in pointing out that by the very nature of the case of his philosophy and of his favourite civilization he gives them a very inadequate place. For (if I may pursue the too flattering parallel) Mr. McCabe thinks of the Alhambra and of my articles as two very odd and absurd things, which some special people do (probably for money) in order to amuse him. But if he had ever felt himself the ancient, sublime, elemental, human instinct to dance, he would have discovered that dancing is not a frivolous thing at all, but a very serious thing. He would have discovered that it is the one grave and chaste and decent method of expressing a certain class of emotions. And similarly, if he had ever had, as Mr. Shaw and I have had, the impulse to what he calls paradox, he would have discovered that paradox again is not a frivolous thing, but a very serious thing. He would have found that paradox simply means a certain defiant joy which belongs to belief. I should regard any civilization which was without a universal habit of uproarious dancing as being, from the full human point of view, a defective civilization. And I should regard any mind which had not got the habit in one form or another of uproarious thinking as being, from the full human point of view, a defective mind. It is vain for Mr. McCabe to say that a ballet is a part of him. He should be part of a ballet, or else he is only part of a man. It is in vain for him to say that he is "not quarrelling with the importation of humour into the controversy." He ought himself to be importing humour into every controversy; for unless a man is in part a humorist, he is only in part a man. To sum up the whole matter very simply, if Mr. McCabe asks me why I import frivolity into a discussion of the nature of man, I answer, because frivolity is a part of the nature of man. If he asks me why I introduce what he calls paradoxes into a philosophical problem, I answer, because all philosophical problems tend to become paradoxical. If he objects to my treating of life riotously, I reply that life is a riot. And I say that the Universe as I see it, at any rate, is very much more like the fireworks at the Crystal Palace than it is like his own philosophy. About the whole cosmos there is a tense and secret festivity—like preparations for Guy Fawkes' day. Eternity is the eve of something. I never look up at the stars without feeling that they are the fires of a schoolboy's rocket, fixed in their everlasting fall.

XVII ON THE WIT OF WHISTLER

That capable and ingenious writer, Mr. Arthur Symons, has included in a book of essays recently published, I believe, an apologia for "London Nights," in which he says that morality should be wholly subordinated to art in criticism, and he uses the somewhat singular argument that art or the worship of beauty is the same in all ages, while morality differs in every period and in every respect. He appears to defy his critics or his readers to mention any permanent feature or quality in ethics. This is surely a very curious example of that extravagant bias against morality which makes so many ultra-modern aesthetes as morbid and fanatical as any Eastern hermit. Unquestionably it is a very common phrase of modern intellectualism to say that the morality of one age can be entirely different to the morality of another. And like a great many other phrases of modern intellectualism, it means literally nothing at all. If the two moralities are entirely different, why do you call them both moralities? It is as if a man said, "Camels in various places are totally diverse; some have six legs, some have none, some have scales, some have feathers, some have horns, some have wings, some are green, some are triangular. There is no point which they have in common." The ordinary man of sense would reply, "Then what makes you call them all camels? What do you mean by a camel? How do you know a camel when you see one?" Of course, there is a permanent substance of morality, as much as there is a permanent substance of art; to say that is only to say that morality is morality, and that art is art. An ideal art critic would, no doubt, see the enduring beauty under every school; equally an ideal moralist would see the enduring ethic under every code. But practically some of the best Englishmen that ever lived could see nothing but filth and idolatry in the starry piety of the Brahmin. And it is equally true that practically the greatest group of artists that the world has ever seen, the giants of the Renaissance, could see nothing but barbarism in the ethereal energy of Gothic.

This bias against morality among the modern aesthetes is nothing very much paraded. And yet it is not really a bias against morality; it is a bias against other people's morality. It is generally founded on a very definite moral preference for a certain sort of life, pagan, plausible, humane. The modern aesthete, wishing us to believe that he values beauty more than conduct, reads Mallarme, and drinks absinthe in a tavern. But this is not only his favourite kind of beauty; it is also his favourite kind of conduct. If he really wished us to believe that he cared for beauty only, he ought to go to nothing but Wesleyan school treats, and paint the sunlight in the hair of the Wesleyan babies. He ought to read nothing but very eloquent theological sermons by old-fashioned Presbyterian divines. Here the lack of all possible moral sympathy would prove that his interest was purely verbal or pictorial, as it is; in all the books he reads and writes he clings to the skirts of his own morality and his own immorality. The champion of l'art pour l'art is always denouncing Ruskin for his moralizing. If he were really a champion of l'art pour l'art, he would be always insisting on Ruskin for his style.

The doctrine of the distinction between art and morality owes a great part of its success to art and morality being hopelessly mixed up in the persons and performances of its greatest exponents. Of this lucky contradiction the very incarnation was Whistler. No man ever preached the impersonality of art so well; no man ever preached the impersonality of art so personally. For him pictures had nothing to do with the problems of character; but for all his fiercest admirers his character was, as a matter of fact far more interesting than his pictures. He gloried in standing as an artist apart from right and wrong. But he succeeded by talking from morning till night about his rights and about his wrongs. His talents were many, his virtues, it must be confessed, not many, beyond that kindness to tried friends, on which many of his biographers insist, but which surely is a quality of all sane men, of pirates and pickpockets; beyond this, his outstanding virtues limit themselves chiefly to two admirable ones—courage and an abstract love of good work. Yet I fancy he won at last more by those two virtues than by all his talents. A man must be something of a moralist if he is to preach, even if he is to preach unmorality. Professor Walter Raleigh, in his "In Memoriam: James McNeill Whistler," insists, truly enough, on the strong streak of an eccentric honesty in matters strictly pictorial, which ran through his complex and slightly confused character. "He would destroy any of his works rather than leave a careless or inexpressive touch within the limits of the frame. He would begin again a hundred times over rather than attempt by patching to make his work seem better than it was."

No one will blame Professor Raleigh, who had to read a sort of funeral oration over Whistler at the opening of the Memorial

Exhibition, if, finding himself in that position, he confined himself mostly to the merits and the stronger qualities of his subject. We should naturally go to some other type of composition for a proper consideration of the weaknesses of Whistler. But these must never be omitted from our view of him. Indeed, the truth is that it was not so much a question of the weaknesses of Whistler as of the intrinsic and primary weakness of Whistler. He was one of those people who live up to their emotional incomes, who are always taut and tingling with vanity. Hence he had no strength to spare; hence he had no kindness, no geniality; for geniality is almost definable as strength to spare. He had no god-like carelessness; he never forgot himself; his whole life was, to use his own expression, an arrangement. He went in for "the art of living"—a miserable trick. In a word, he was a great artist; but emphatically not a great man. In this connection I must differ strongly with Professor Raleigh upon what is, from a superficial literary point of view, one of his most effective points. He compares Whistler's laughter to the laughter of another man who was a great man as well as a great artist. "His attitude to the public was exactly the attitude taken up by Robert Browning, who suffered as long a period of neglect and mistake, in those lines of 'The Ring and the Book'—

"'Well, British Public, ye who like me not, (God love you!) and will have your proper laugh At the dark question; laugh it! I'd laugh first.'

"Mr. Whistler," adds Professor Raleigh, "always laughed first." The truth is, I believe, that Whistler never laughed at all. There was no laughter in his nature; because there was no thoughtlessness and self-abandonment, no humility. I cannot understand anybody reading "The Gentle Art of Making Enemies" and thinking that there is any laughter in the wit. His wit is a torture to him. He twists himself into arabesques of verbal felicity; he is full of a fierce carefulness; he is inspired with the complete seriousness of sincere malice. He hurts himself to hurt his opponent. Browning did laugh, because Browning did not care; Browning did not care, because Browning was a great man. And when Browning said in brackets to the simple, sensible people who did not like his books, "God love you!" he was not sneering in the least. He was laughing—that is to say, he meant exactly what he said.

There are three distinct classes of great satirists who are also great men—that is to say, three classes of men who can laugh at something without losing their souls. The satirist of the first type is the man who, first of all enjoys himself, and then enjoys his enemies. In this sense he loves his enemy, and by a kind of exaggeration of Christianity he loves his enemy the more the more he becomes an enemy. He has a sort of overwhelming and aggressive happiness in his assertion of anger; his curse is as human as a benediction. Of this type of satire the great example is Rabelais. This is the first typical example of satire, the satire which is voluble, which is violent, which is indecent, but which is not malicious. The satire of Whistler was not this. He was never in any of his controversies simply happy; the proof of it is that he never talked absolute nonsense. There is a second type of mind which produces satire with the quality of greatness. That is embodied in the satirist whose passions are released and let go by some intolerable sense of wrong. He is maddened by the sense of men being maddened; his tongue becomes an unruly member, and testifies against all mankind. Such a man was Swift, in whom the saeva indignatio was a bitterness to others, because it was a bitterness to himself. Such a satirist Whistler was not. He did not laugh because he was happy, like Rabelais. But neither did he laugh because he was unhappy, like Swift.

The third type of great satire is that in which he satirist is enabled to rise superior to his victim in the only serious sense which superiority can bear, in that of pitying the sinner and respecting the man even while he satirises both. Such an achievement can be found in a thing like Pope's "Atticus" a poem in which the satirist feels that he is satirising the weaknesses which belong specially to literary genius. Consequently he takes a pleasure in pointing out his enemy's strength before he points out his weakness. That is, perhaps, the highest and most honourable form of satire. That is not the satire of Whistler. He is not full of a great sorrow for the wrong done to human nature; for him the wrong is altogether done to himself.

He was not a great personality, because he thought so much about himself. And the case is stronger even than that. He was sometimes not even a great artist, because he thought so much about art. Any man with a vital knowledge of the human psychology ought to have the most profound suspicion of anybody who claims to be an artist, and talks a great deal about art. Art is a right and human thing, like walking or saying one's prayers; but the moment it begins to be talked about very solemnly, a man may be fairly certain that the thing has come into a congestion and a kind of difficulty.

The artistic temperament is a disease that afflicts amateurs. It is a disease which arises from men not having sufficient power of expression to utter and get rid of the element of art in their being. It is healthful to every sane man to utter the art within him; it is essential to every sane man to get rid of the art within him at all costs. Artists of a large and wholesome vitality get rid of their art easily, as they breathe easily, or perspire easily. But in artists of less force, the thing becomes a pressure, and produces a definite pain, which is called the artistic temperament. Thus, very great artists are able to be ordinary men—men like Shakespeare or Browning. There are many real tragedies of the artistic temperament, tragedies of vanity or violence or fear. But the great tragedy of the artistic temperament is that it cannot produce any art.

Whistler could produce art; and in so far he was a great man. But he could not forget art; and in so far he was only a man with the artistic temperament. There can be no stronger manifestation of the man who is a really great artist than the fact that he can dismiss the subject of art; that he can, upon due occasion, wish art at the bottom of the sea. Similarly, we should always be much more inclined to trust a solicitor who did not talk about conveyancing over the nuts and wine. What we really desire of any man conducting any business is that the full force of an ordinary man should be put into that particular study. We do not desire that the full force of that study should be put into an ordinary man. We do not in the least wish that our particular law-suit should pour its energy into our barrister's games with his children, or rides on his bicycle, or meditations on the morning star. But we do, as a matter of fact, desire that his games with his children, and his rides on his bicycle, and his meditations on the morning star should pour something of their energy into our law-suit. We do desire that if he has gained any especial lung development from the bicycle, or any bright and pleasing metaphors from the morning star, that the should be placed at our disposal in that particular forensic controversy. In a word, we are very glad that he is an ordinary man, since that may help him to be an exceptional lawyer.

Whistler never ceased to be an artist. As Mr. Max Beerbohm pointed out in one of his extraordinarily sensible and sincere critiques, Whistler really regarded Whistler as his greatest work of art. The white lock, the single eyeglass, the remarkable hat—these were much dearer to him than any nocturnes or arrangements that he ever threw off. He could throw off the nocturnes; for some mysterious reason he could not throw off the hat. He never threw off from himself that disproportionate accumulation of aestheticism which is the burden of the amateur.

It need hardly be said that this is the real explanation of the thing which has puzzled so many dilettante critics, the problem of the extreme ordinariness of the behaviour of so many great geniuses in history. Their behaviour was so ordinary that it was not recorded; hence it was so ordinary that it seemed mysterious.

Hence people say that Bacon wrote Shakespeare. The modern artistic temperament cannot understand how a man who could write such lyrics as Shakespeare wrote, could be as keen as Shakespeare was on business transactions in a little town in Warwickshire. The explanation is simple enough; it is that Shakespeare had a real lyrical impulse, wrote a real lyric, and so got rid of the impulse and went about his business. Being an artist did not prevent him from being an ordinary man, any more than being a sleeper at night or being a diner at dinner prevented him from being an ordinary man.

All very great teachers and leaders have had this habit of assuming their point of view to be one which was human and casual, one which would readily appeal to every passing man. If a man is genuinely superior to his fellows the first thing that he believes in is the equality of man. We can see this, for instance, in that strange and innocent rationality with which Christ addressed any motley crowd that happened to stand about Him. "What man of you having a hundred sheep, and losing one, would not leave the ninety and nine in the wilderness, and go after that which was lost?" Or, again, "What man of you if his son ask for bread will he give him a stone, or if he ask for a fish will he give him a serpent?" This plainness, this almost prosaic camaraderie, is the note of all very great minds.

To very great minds the things on which men agree are so immeasurably more important than the things on which they differ, that the latter, for all practical purposes, disappear. They have too much in them of an ancient laughter even to endure to discuss the difference between the hats of two men who were both born of a woman, or between the subtly varied cultures of two men who have both to die. The first-rate great man is equal with other men, like Shakespeare. The second-rate great man is on his knees to other men, like Whitman. The third-rate great man is superior to other men, like Whistler.

XVIII THE FALLACY OF THE YOUNG NATION

To say that a man is an idealist is merely to say that he is a man; but, nevertheless, it might be possible to effect some valid distinction between one kind of idealist and another. One possible distinction, for instance, could be effected by saying that humanity is divided into conscious idealists and unconscious idealists. In a similar way, humanity is divided into conscious ritualists and unconscious ritualists. The curious thing is, in that example as in others, that it is the conscious ritualism which is comparatively simple, the unconscious ritual which is really heavy and complicated. The ritual which is comparatively rude and straightforward is the ritual which people call "ritualistic." It consists of plain things like bread and wine and fire, and men falling on their faces. But the ritual which is really complex, and many coloured, and elaborate, and needlessly formal, is the ritual which people enact without knowing it. It consists not of plain things like wine and fire, but of really peculiar, and local, and exceptional, and ingenious things—things like door-mats, and door-knockers, and electric bells, and silk hats, and white ties, and shiny cards, and confetti. The truth is that the modern man scarcely ever gets back to very old and simple things except when he is performing some religious mummery. The modern man can hardly get away from ritual except by entering a ritualistic church. In the case of these old and mystical formalities we can at least say that the ritual is not mere ritual; that the symbols employed are in most cases symbols which belong to a primary human poetry. The most ferocious opponent of the Christian ceremonials must admit that if Catholicism had not instituted the bread and wine, somebody else would most probably have done so. Any one with a poetical instinct will admit that to the ordinary human instinct bread symbolizes something which cannot very easily be symbolized otherwise; that wine, to the ordinary human instinct, symbolizes something which cannot very easily be symbolized otherwise. But white ties in the evening are ritual, and nothing else but ritual. No one would pretend that white ties in the evening are primary and poetical. Nobody would maintain that the ordinary human instinct would in any age or country tend to symbolize the idea of evening by a white necktie. Rather, the ordinary human instinct would, I imagine, tend to symbolize evening by cravats with some of the colours of the sunset, not white neckties, but tawny or crimson neckties—neckties of purple or olive, or some darkened gold. Mr. J. A. Kensit, for example, is under the impression that he is not a ritualist. But the daily life of Mr. J. A. Kensit, like that of any ordinary modern man, is, as a matter of fact, one continual and compressed catalogue of mystical mummery and flummery. To take one instance out of an inevitable hundred: I imagine that Mr. Kensit takes off his hat to a lady; and what can be more solemn and absurd, considered in the abstract, than, symbolizing the existence of the other sex by taking off a portion of your clothing and waving it in the air? This, I repeat, is not a natural and primitive symbol, like fire or food. A man might just as well have to take off his waistcoat to a lady; and if a man, by the social ritual of his civilization, had to take off his waistcoat to a lady, every chivalrous and sensible man would take off his waistcoat to a lady. In short, Mr. Kensit, and those who agree with him, may think, and quite sincerely think, that men give too much incense and ceremonial to their adoration of the other world. But nobody thinks that he can give too much incense and ceremonial to the adoration of this world. All men, then, are ritualists, but are either conscious or unconscious ritualists. The conscious ritualists are generally satisfied with a few very simple and elementary signs; the unconscious ritualists are not satisfied with anything short of the whole of human life, being almost insanely ritualistic. The first is called a ritualist because he invents and remembers one rite; the other is called an anti-ritualist because he obeys and forgets a thousand. And a somewhat similar distinction to this which I have drawn with some unavoidable length, between the conscious ritualist and the unconscious ritualist, exists between the conscious idealist and the unconscious idealist. It is idle to inveigh against cynics and materialists—there are no cynics, there are no materialists. Every man is idealistic; only it so often happens that he has the wrong ideal. Every man is incurably sentimental; but, unfortunately, it is so often a false sentiment. When we talk, for instance, of some unscrupulous commercial figure, and say that he would do anything for money, we use quite an inaccurate expression, and we slander him very much. He would not do anything for money. He would do some things for money; he would sell his soul for money, for instance; and, as Mirabeau humorously said, he would be quite wise "to take money for muck." He would oppress humanity for money; but then it happens that humanity and the soul are not things that he believes in; they are not his ideals. But he has his own dim and delicate ideals; and he would not violate these for money. He would not drink out of the soup-tureen, for money. He would not wear his coat-tails in front, for money. He would not spread a report that he had softening of the brain, for money. In the actual practice of life we find, in the matter of ideals, exactly what we have already found in the matter of ritual. We find that while there is a perfectly genuine danger of fanaticism from the men who have unworldly ideals, the permanent and urgent danger of fanaticism is from the men who have worldly ideals.

People who say that an ideal is a dangerous thing, that it deludes and intoxicates, are perfectly right. But the ideal which intoxicates most is the least idealistic kind of ideal. The ideal which intoxicates least is the very ideal ideal; that sobers us suddenly, as all heights and precipices and great distances do. Granted that it is a great evil to mistake a cloud for a cape; still, the cloud, which can be most easily mistaken for a cape, is the cloud that is nearest the earth. Similarly, we may grant that it may be dangerous to mistake an ideal for something practical. But we shall still point out that, in this respect, the most dangerous ideal of all is the ideal which looks a little practical. It is difficult to attain a high ideal; consequently, it is almost impossible to persuade ourselves that we have attained it. But it is easy to attain a low ideal; consequently, it is easier still to persuade ourselves that we have attained it when we have done nothing of the kind. To take a random example. It might be called a high ambition to wish to be an archangel; the man who entertained such an ideal would very possibly exhibit asceticism, or even frenzy, but not, I think, delusion. He would not think he was an archangel, and go about flapping his hands under the impression that they were wings. But suppose that a sane man had a low ideal; suppose he wished to be a gentleman. Any one who knows the world knows that in nine weeks he would have persuaded himself that he was a gentleman; and this being manifestly not the case, the result will be very real and practical dislocations and calamities in social life. It is not the wild ideals which wreck the practical world; it is the tame ideals.

The matter may, perhaps, be illustrated by a parallel from our modern politics. When men tell us that the old Liberal politicians of the type of Gladstone cared only for ideals, of course, they are talking nonsense—they cared for a great many other things, including votes. And when men tell us that modern politicians of the type of Mr. Chamberlain or, in another way, Lord Rosebery, care only for votes or for material interest, then again they are talking nonsense—these men care for ideals like all other men. But the real distinction which may be drawn is this, that to the older politician the ideal was an ideal, and nothing else. To the new politician his dream is not only a good dream, it is a reality. The old politician would have said, "It would be a good thing if there were a Republican Federation dominating the world." But the modern politician does not say, "It would be a good thing if there were a British Imperialism dominating the world." He says, "It is a good thing that there is a British Imperialism dominating the world;" whereas clearly there is nothing of the kind. The old Liberal would say "There ought to be a good Irish government in Ireland." But the ordinary modern Unionist does not say, "There ought to be a good English government in Ireland." He says, "There is a good English government in Ireland;" which is absurd. In short, the modern politicians seem to think that a man becomes practical merely by making assertions entirely about practical things. Apparently, a delusion does not matter as long as it is a materialistic delusion. Instinctively most of us feel that, as a practical matter, even the contrary is true. I certainly would much rather share my apartments with a gentleman who thought he was God than with a gentleman who thought he was a grasshopper. To be continually haunted by practical images and practical problems, to be constantly thinking of things as actual, as urgent, as in process of completion—these things do not prove a man to be practical; these things, indeed, are among the most ordinary signs of a lunatic. That our modern statesmen are materialistic is nothing against their being also morbid. Seeing angels in a vision may make a man a supernaturalist to excess. But merely seeing snakes in delirium tremens does not make him a naturalist.

And when we come actually to examine the main stock notions of our modern practical politicians, we find that those main stock notions are mainly delusions. A great many instances might be given of the fact. We might take, for example, the case of that strange class of notions which underlie the word "union," and all the eulogies heaped upon it. Of course, union is no more a good thing in itself than separation is a good thing in itself. To have a party in favour of union and a party in favour of separation is as absurd as to have a party in favour of going upstairs and a party in favour of going downstairs. The question is not whether we go up or down stairs, but where we are going to, and what we are going, for? Union is strength; union is also weakness. It is a good thing to harness two horses to a cart; but it is not a good thing to try and turn two hansom cabs into one four-wheeler. Turning ten nations into one empire may happen to be as feasible as turning ten shillings into one half-sovereign. Also it may happen to be as preposterous as turning ten terriers into one mastiff. The question in all cases is not a question of union or absence of union, but of identity or absence of identity. Owing to certain historical and moral causes, two nations may be so united as upon the whole to help each other. Thus England and Scotland pass their time in paying each other compliments; but their energies and atmospheres run distinct and parallel, and consequently do not clash. Scotland continues to be educated and Calvinistic; England continues to be uneducated and happy. But owing to certain other Moral and certain other political causes, two nations may be so united as only to hamper each other; their lines do clash and do not run parallel. Thus, for instance, England and Ireland are so united that the Irish can sometimes rule England, but can never rule Ireland. The educational systems, including the last Education Act, are here, as in the case of Scotland, a very good test of the matter. The overwhelming majority of Irishmen believe in a strict Catholicism; the overwhelming majority of Englishmen believe in a vague Protestantism. The Irish party in the Parliament of Union is just large enough to prevent the English education being indefinitely Protestant, and just small enough to prevent the Irish education being definitely Catholic. Here we have a state of things which no man in his senses would ever dream of wishing to continue if he had not been bewitched by the sentimentalism of the mere word "union."

This example of union, however, is not the example which I propose to take of the ingrained futility and deception underlying all the assumptions of the modern practical politician. I wish to speak especially of another and much more general delusion. It pervades the minds and speeches of all the practical men of all parties; and it is a childish blunder built upon a single false metaphor. I refer to the universal modern talk about young nations and new nations; about America being young, about New Zealand being new. The whole thing is a trick of words. America is not young, New Zealand is not new. It is a very discussable question whether they are not both much older than England or Ireland.

Of course we may use the metaphor of youth about America or the colonies, if we use it strictly as implying only a recent origin. But if we use it (as we do use it) as implying vigour, or vivacity, or crudity, or inexperience, or hope, or a long life before them or any of the romantic attributes of youth, then it is surely as clear as daylight that we are duped by a stale figure of speech. We can easily see the matter clearly by applying it to any other institution parallel to the institution of an independent nationality. If a club called "The Milk and Soda League" (let us say) was set up yesterday, as I have no doubt it was, then, of course, "The Milk and Soda League" is a young club in the sense that it was set up yesterday, but in no other sense. It may consist entirely of moribund old gentlemen. It may be moribund itself. We may call it a young club, in the light of the fact that it was founded yesterday. We may also call it a very old club in the light of the fact that it will most probably go bankrupt to-morrow. All this appears very obvious when we put it in this form. Any one who adopted the young-community delusion with regard to a bank or a butcher's shop would be sent to an asylum. But the whole modern political notion that America and the colonies must be very vigorous because they are very new, rests upon no better foundation. That America was founded long after England does not make it even in the faintest degree more probable that America will not perish a long time before England. That England existed before her colonies does not make it any the less likely that she will exist after her colonies. And when we look at the actual history of the world, we find that great European nations almost invariably have survived the vitality of their colonies. When we look at the actual history of the world, we find, that if there is a thing that is born old and dies young, it is a colony. The Greek colonies went to pieces long before the Greek civilization. The Spanish colonies have gone to pieces long before the nation of Spain—nor does there seem to be any reason to doubt the possibility or even the probability of the conclusion that the colonial civilization, which owes its origin to England, will be much briefer and much less vigorous than the civilization of England itself. The English nation will still be going the way of all European nations when the Anglo-Saxon race has gone the way of all fads. Now, of course, the interesting question is, have we, in the case of America and the colonies, any real evidence of a moral and intellectual youth as opposed to the indisputable triviality of a merely chronological youth? Consciously or unconsciously, we know that we have no such evidence, and consciously or unconsciously, therefore, we proceed to make it up. Of this pure and placid invention, a good example, for instance, can be found in a recent poem of Mr. Rudyard Kipling's. Speaking of the English people and the South African War Mr. Kipling says that "we fawned on the younger nations for the men that could shoot and ride." Some people considered this sentence insulting. All that I am concerned with at present is the evident fact that it is not true. The colonies provided very useful volunteer troops, but they did not provide the best troops, nor achieve the most successful exploits. The best work in the war on the English side was done, as might have been expected, by the best English regiments. The men who could shoot and ride were not the enthusiastic corn merchants from Melbourne, any more than they were the enthusiastic clerks from Cheapside. The men who could shoot and ride were the men who had been taught to shoot and ride in the discipline of the standing army of a great European power. Of course, the colonials are as brave and athletic as any other average white men. Of course, they acquitted themselves with reasonable credit. All I have here to indicate is that, for the purposes of this theory of the new nation, it is necessary to maintain that the colonial forces were more useful or more heroic than the gunners at Colenso or the Fighting Fifth. And of this contention there is not, and never has been, one stick or straw of evidence.

A similar attempt is made, and with even less success, to represent the literature of the colonies as something fresh and vigorous and important. The imperialist magazines are constantly springing upon us some genius from Queensland or Canada, through whom we are expected to smell the odours of the bush or the prairie. As a matter of fact, any one who is even slightly interested in literature as such (and I, for one, confess that I am only slightly interested in literature as such), will freely admit that the stories of these geniuses smell of nothing but printer's ink, and that not of first-rate quality. By a great effort of Imperial imagination the generous English people reads into these works a force and a novelty. But the force and the novelty are not in the new writers; the force and the novelty are in the ancient heart of the English. Anybody who studies them impartially will know that the first-rate writers of the colonies are not even particularly novel in their note and atmosphere, are not only not producing a new kind of good literature, but are not even in any particular sense producing a new kind of bad literature. The first-rate writers of the new countries are really almost exactly like the second-rate writers of the old countries. Of course they do feel the mystery of the wilderness, the mystery of the bush, for all simple and honest men feel this in Melbourne, or Margate, or South St. Pancras. But when they write most sincerely and most successfully, it is not with a background of the mystery of the bush, but with a background, expressed or assumed, of our own romantic cockney civilization. What really moves their souls with a kindly terror is not the mystery of the wilderness, but the Mystery of a Hansom Cab.

Of course there are some exceptions to this generalization. The one really arresting exception is Olive Schreiner, and she is quite as certainly an exception that proves the rule. Olive Schreiner is a fierce, brilliant, and realistic novelist; but she is all this precisely because she is not English at all. Her tribal kinship is with the country of Teniers and Maarten Maartens—that is, with a country of realists. Her literary kinship is with the pessimistic fiction of the continent; with the novelists whose very pity is cruel. Olive Schreiner is the one English colonial who is not conventional, for the simple reason that South Africa is the one English colony which is not English, and probably never will be. And, of course, there are individual exceptions in a minor way. I remember in particular some Australian tales by Mr. McIlwain which were really able and effective, and which, for that reason, I suppose, are not presented to the public with blasts of a trumpet. But my general contention if put before any one with a love of letters, will not be disputed if it is understood. It is not the truth that the colonial civilization as a whole is giving us, or shows any signs of giving us, a literature which will startle and renovate our own. It may be a very good thing for us to have an affectionate illusion in the matter; that is quite another affair. The colonies may have given England a new emotion; I only say that they have not given the world a new book.

Touching these English colonies, I do not wish to be misunderstood. I do not say of them or of America that they have not a future, or that they will not be great nations. I merely deny the whole established modern expression about them. I deny that they are "destined" to a future. I deny that they are "destined" to be great nations. I deny (of course) that any human thing is destined to be anything. All the absurd physical metaphors, such as youth and age, living and dying, are, when applied to nations, but pseudo-scientific attempts to conceal from men the awful liberty of their lonely souls.

In the case of America, indeed, a warning to this effect is instant and essential. America, of course, like every other human thing, can in spiritual sense live or die as much as it chooses. But at the present moment the matter which America has very seriously to consider is not how near it is to its birth and beginning, but how near it may be to its end. It is only a verbal question whether the American civilization is young; it may become a very practical and urgent question whether it is dying. When once we have cast aside, as we inevitably have after a moment's thought, the fanciful physical metaphor involved in the word "youth," what serious evidence have we that America is a fresh force and not a stale one? It has a great many people, like China; it has a great deal of money, like defeated Carthage or dying Venice. It is full of bustle and excitability, like Athens after its ruin, and all the Greek cities in their decline. It is fond of new things; but the old are always fond of new things. Young men read chronicles, but old men read newspapers. It admires strength and good looks; it admires a big and barbaric beauty in its women, for instance; but so did Rome when the Goth was at the gates. All these are things quite compatible with fundamental tedium and decay. There are three main shapes or symbols in which a nation can show itself essentially glad and great—by the heroic in government, by the heroic in arms, and by the heroic in art. Beyond government, which is, as it were, the very shape and body of a nation, the most significant thing about any citizen is his artistic attitude towards a holiday and his moral attitude towards a fight—that is, his way of accepting life and his way of accepting death.

Subjected to these eternal tests, America does not appear by any means as particularly fresh or untouched. She appears with all the weakness and weariness of modern England or of any other Western power. In her politics she has broken up exactly as England has broken up, into a bewildering opportunism and insincerity. In the matter of war and the national attitude towards war, her resemblance to England is even more manifest and melancholy. It may be said with rough accuracy that there are three stages in the life of a strong people. First, it is a small power, and fights small powers. Then it is a great power, and fights great powers. Then it is a great power, and fights small powers, but pretends that they are great powers, in order to rekindle the ashes of its ancient emotion and vanity. After that, the next step is to become a small power itself. England exhibited this symptom of decadence very badly in the war with the Transvaal; but America exhibited it worse in the war with Spain. There was exhibited more sharply and absurdly than anywhere else the ironic contrast between the very careless choice of a strong line and the very careful choice of a weak enemy. America added to all her other late Roman or Byzantine elements the element of the Caracallan triumph, the triumph over nobody.

But when we come to the last test of nationality, the test of art and letters, the case is almost terrible. The English colonies have produced no great artists; and that fact may prove that they are still full of silent possibilities and reserve force. But America has produced great artists. And that fact most certainly proves that she is full of a fine futility and the end of all things. Whatever the American men of genius are, they are not young gods making a young world. Is the art of Whistler a brave, barbaric art, happy and headlong? Does Mr. Henry James infect us with the spirit of a schoolboy? No; the colonies have not spoken, and they are safe. Their silence may be the silence of the unborn. But out of America has come a sweet and startling cry, as unmistakable as the cry of a dying man.

XIX SLUM NOVELISTS AND THE SLUMS

Odd ideas are entertained in our time about the real nature of the doctrine of human fraternity. The real doctrine is something which we do not, with all our modern humanitarianism, very clearly understand, much less very closely practise. There is nothing, for instance, particularly undemocratic about kicking your butler downstairs. It may be wrong, but it is not unfraternal. In a certain sense, the blow or kick may be considered as a confession of equality: you are meeting your butler body to body; you are almost according him the privilege of the duel. There is nothing, undemocratic, though there may be something unreasonable, in expecting a great deal from the butler, and being filled with a kind of frenzy of surprise when he falls short of the divine stature. The thing which is really undemocratic and unfraternal is not to expect the butler to be more or less divine. The thing which is really undemocratic and unfraternal is to say, as so many modern humanitarians say, "Of course one must make allowances for those on a lower plane." All things considered indeed, it may be said, without undue exaggeration, that the really undemocratic and unfraternal thing is the common practice of not kicking the butler downstairs.

It is only because such a vast section of the modern world is out of sympathy with the serious democratic sentiment that this statement will seem to many to be lacking in seriousness. Democracy is not philanthropy; it is not even altruism or social reform. Democracy is not founded on pity for the common man; democracy is founded on reverence for the common man, or, if you will, even on fear of him. It does not champion man because man is so miserable, but because man is so sublime. It does not object so much to the ordinary man being a slave as to his not being a king, for its dream is always the dream of the first Roman republic, a nation of kings.

Next to a genuine republic, the most democratic thing in the world is a hereditary despotism. I mean a despotism in which there is absolutely no trace whatever of any nonsense about intellect or special fitness for the post. Rational despotism—that is, selective despotism—is always a curse to mankind, because with that you have the ordinary man misunderstood and misgoverned by some prig who has no brotherly respect for him at all. But irrational despotism is always democratic, because it is the ordinary man enthroned. The worst form of slavery is that which is called Caesarism, or the choice of some bold or brilliant man as despot because he is suitable. For that means that men choose a representative, not because he represents them, but because he does not. Men trust an ordinary man like George III or William IV. because they are themselves ordinary men and understand him. Men trust an ordinary man because they trust themselves. But men trust a great man because they do not trust themselves. And hence the worship of great men always appears in times of weakness and cowardice; we never hear of great men until the time when all other men are small.

Hereditary despotism is, then, in essence and sentiment democratic because it chooses from mankind at random. If it does not declare that every man may rule, it declares the next most democratic thing; it declares that any man may rule. Hereditary aristocracy is a far worse and more dangerous thing, because the numbers and multiplicity of an aristocracy make it sometimes possible for it to figure as an aristocracy of intellect. Some of its members will presumably have brains, and thus they, at any rate, will be an intellectual aristocracy within the social one. They will rule the aristocracy by virtue of their intellect, and they will rule the country by virtue of their aristocracy. Thus a double falsity will be set up, and millions of the images of God, who, fortunately for their wives and families, are neither gentlemen nor clever men, will be represented by a man like Mr. Balfour or Mr. Wyndham, because he is too gentlemanly to be called merely clever, and just too clever to be called merely a gentleman. But even an hereditary aristocracy may exhibit, by a sort of accident, from time to time some of the basically democratic quality which belongs to a hereditary despotism. It is amusing to think how much conservative ingenuity has been wasted in the defence of the House of Lords by men who were desperately endeavouring to prove that the House of Lords consisted of clever men. There is one really good defence of the House of Lords, though admirers of the peerage are strangely coy about using it; and that is, that the House of Lords, in its full and proper strength, consists of stupid men. It really would be a plausible defence of that otherwise indefensible body to point out that the clever men in the Commons, who owed their power to cleverness, ought in the last resort to be checked by the average man in the Lords, who owed their power to accident. Of course, there would be many answers to such a contention, as, for instance, that the House of Lords is largely no longer a House of Lords, but a House of tradesmen and financiers, or that the bulk of the commonplace nobility do not vote, and so leave the chamber to the prigs and the specialists and the mad old gentlemen with hobbies. But on some occasions the House of Lords, even under all these disadvantages, is in some sense representative. When all the peers flocked together to vote against Mr. Gladstone's second Home Rule Bill, for instance, those who said that the peers represented the English people, were perfectly right. All those dear old men who happened to be born peers were at that moment, and upon that question, the precise counterpart of all the dear old men who happened to be born paupers or middle-class gentlemen. That mob of peers did really represent the English people—that is to say, it was honest, ignorant, vaguely excited, almost unanimous, and obviously wrong. Of course, rational democracy is better as an expression of the public will than the haphazard hereditary method. While we are about having any kind of democracy, let it be rational democracy. But if we are to have any kind of oligarchy, let it be irrational oligarchy. Then at least we shall be ruled by men.

But the thing which is really required for the proper working of democracy is not merely the democratic system, or even the democratic philosophy, but the democratic emotion. The democratic emotion, like most elementary and indispensable things, is a thing difficult to describe at any time. But it is peculiarly difficult to describe it in our enlightened age, for the simple reason that it is peculiarly difficult to find it. It is a certain instinctive attitude which feels the things in which all men agree to be unspeakably important, and all the things in which they differ (such as mere brains) to be almost unspeakably unimportant. The nearest approach to it in our ordinary life would be the promptitude with which we should consider mere humanity in any circumstance of shock or death. We should say, after a somewhat disturbing discovery, "There is a dead man under the sofa." We should not be likely to say, "There is a dead man of considerable personal refinement under the sofa." We should say, "A woman has fallen into the water." We should not say, "A highly educated woman has fallen into the water." Nobody would say, "There are the remains of a clear thinker in your back garden." Nobody would say, "Unless you hurry up and stop him, a man with a very fine ear for music will have jumped off that cliff." But this emotion, which all of us have in connection with such things as birth and death, is to some people native and constant at all ordinary times and in all ordinary places. It was native to St. Francis of Assisi. It was native to Walt Whitman. In this strange and splendid degree it cannot be expected, perhaps, to pervade a whole commonwealth or a whole civilization; but one commonwealth may have it much more than another commonwealth, one civilization much more than another civilization. No community, perhaps, ever had it so much as the early Franciscans. No community, perhaps, ever had it so little as ours.

Everything in our age has, when carefully examined, this fundamentally undemocratic quality. In religion and morals we should admit, in the abstract, that the sins of the educated classes were as great as, or perhaps greater than, the sins of the poor and ignorant. But in practice the great difference between the mediaeval ethics and ours is that ours concentrate attention on the sins which are the sins of the ignorant, and practically deny that the sins which are the sins of the educated are sins at all. We are always talking about the sin of intemperate drinking, because it is quite obvious that the poor have it more than the rich. But we are always denying that there is any such thing as the sin of pride, because it would be quite obvious that the rich have it more than the poor. We are always ready to make a saint or prophet of the educated man who goes into cottages to give a little kindly advice to the uneducated. But the medieval idea of a saint or prophet was something quite different. The mediaeval saint or prophet was an uneducated man who walked into grand houses to give a little kindly advice to the educated. The old tyrants had enough insolence to despoil the poor, but they had not enough insolence to preach to them. It was the gentleman who oppressed the slums; but it was the slums that admonished the gentleman. And just as we are undemocratic in faith and morals, so we are, by the very nature of our attitude in such matters, undemocratic in the tone of our practical politics. It is a sufficient proof that we are not an essentially democratic state that we are always wondering what we shall do with the poor. If we were democrats, we should be wondering what the poor will do with us. With us the governing class is always saying to itself, "What laws shall we make?" In a purely democratic state it would be always saying, "What laws can we obey?" A purely democratic state perhaps there has never been. But even the feudal ages were in practice thus far democratic, that every feudal potentate knew that any laws which he made would in all probability return upon himself. His feathers might be cut off for breaking a sumptuary law. His head might be cut off for high treason. But the modern laws are almost always laws made to affect the governed class, but not the governing. We have public-house licensing laws, but not sumptuary laws. That is to say, we have laws against the festivity and hospitality of the poor, but no laws against the festivity and hospitality of the rich. We have laws against blasphemy—that is, against a kind of coarse and offensive speaking in which nobody but a rough and obscure man would be likely to indulge. But we have no laws against heresy—that is, against the intellectual poisoning of the whole people, in which only a prosperous and prominent man would be likely to be successful. The evil of aristocracy is not that it necessarily leads to the infliction of bad things or the suffering of sad ones; the evil of aristocracy is that it places everything in the hands of a class of people who can always inflict what they can never suffer. Whether what they inflict is, in their intention, good or bad, they become equally frivolous. The case against the governing class of modern England is not in the least that it is selfish; if you like, you may call the English oligarchs too fantastically unselfish. The case against them simply is that when they legislate for all men, they always omit themselves.

We are undemocratic, then, in our religion, as is proved by our efforts to "raise" the poor. We are undemocratic in our government, as is proved by our innocent attempt to govern them well. But above all we are undemocratic in our literature, as is proved by the torrent of novels about the poor and serious studies of the poor which pour from our publishers every month. And the more "modern" the book is the more certain it is to be devoid of democratic sentiment.

A poor man is a man who has not got much money. This may seem a simple and unnecessary description, but in the face of a great mass of modern fact and fiction, it seems very necessary indeed; most of our realists and sociologists talk about a poor man as if he were an octopus or an alligator. There is no more need to study the psychology of poverty than to study the psychology of bad temper, or the psychology of vanity, or the psychology of animal spirits. A man ought to know something of the emotions of an insulted man, not by being insulted, but simply by being a man. And he ought to know something of the emotions of a poor man, not by being poor, but simply by being a man. Therefore, in any writer who is describing poverty, my first objection to him will be that he has studied his subject. A democrat would have imagined it.

A great many hard things have been said about religious slumming and political or social slumming, but surely the most despicable of all is artistic slumming. The religious teacher is at least supposed to be interested in the costermonger because he is a man; the politician is in some dim and perverted sense interested in the costermonger because he is a citizen; it is only the wretched writer who is interested in the costermonger merely because he is a costermonger. Nevertheless, so long as he is merely seeking impressions, or in other words copy, his trade, though dull, is honest. But when he endeavours to represent that he is describing the spiritual core of a costermonger, his dim vices and his delicate virtues, then we must object that his claim is preposterous; we must remind him that he is a journalist and nothing else. He has far less psychological authority even than the foolish missionary. For he is in the literal and derivative sense a journalist, while the missionary is an eternalist. The missionary at least pretends to have a version of the man's lot for all time; the journalist only pretends to have a version of it from day to day. The missionary comes to tell the poor man that he is in the same condition with all men. The journalist comes to tell other people how different the poor man is from everybody else.

If the modern novels about the slums, such as novels of Mr. Arthur Morrison, or the exceedingly able novels of Mr. Somerset Maugham, are intended to be sensational, I can only say that that is a noble and reasonable object, and that they attain it. A sensation, a shock to the imagination, like the contact with cold water, is always a good and exhilarating thing; and, undoubtedly, men will always seek this sensation (among other forms) in the form of the study of the strange antics of remote or alien peoples. In the twelfth century men obtained this sensation by reading about dog-headed men in Africa. In the twentieth century they obtained it by reading about pig-headed Boers in Africa. The men of the twentieth century were certainly, it must be admitted, somewhat the more credulous of the two. For it is not recorded of the men in the twelfth century that they organized a sanguinary crusade solely for the purpose of altering the singular formation of the heads of the Africans. But it may be, and it may even legitimately be, that since all these monsters have faded from the popular mythology, it is necessary to have in our fiction the image of the horrible and hairy East-ender, merely to keep alive in us a fearful and childlike wonder at external peculiarities. But the Middle Ages (with a great deal more common sense than it would now be fashionable to admit) regarded natural history at bottom rather as a kind of joke; they regarded the soul as very important. Hence, while they had a natural history of dog-headed men, they did not profess to have a psychology of dog-headed men. They did not profess to mirror the mind of a dog-headed man, to share his tenderest secrets, or mount with his most celestial musings. They did not write novels about the semi-canine creature, attributing to him all the oldest morbidities and all the newest fads. It is permissible to present men as monsters if we wish to make the reader jump; and to make anybody jump is always a Christian act. But it is not permissible to present men as regarding themselves as monsters, or as making themselves jump. To summarize, our slum fiction is quite defensible as aesthetic fiction; it is not defensible as spiritual fact.

One enormous obstacle stands in the way of its actuality. The men who write it, and the men who read it, are men of the middle classes or the upper classes; at least, of those who are loosely termed the educated classes. Hence, the fact that it is the life as the refined man sees it proves that it cannot be the life as the unrefined man lives it. Rich men write stories about poor men, and describe them as speaking with a coarse, or heavy, or husky enunciation. But if poor men wrote novels about you or me they would describe us as speaking with some absurd shrill and affected voice, such as we only hear from a duchess in a three-act farce. The slum novelist gains his whole effect by the fact that some detail is strange to the reader; but that detail by the nature of the case cannot be strange in itself. It cannot be strange to the soul which he is professing to study. The slum novelist gains his effects by describing the same grey mist as draping the dingy factory and the dingy tavern. But to the man he is supposed to be studying there must be exactly the same difference between the factory and the tavern that there is to a middle-class man between a late night at the office and a supper at Pagani's. The slum novelist is content with pointing out that to the eye of his particular class a pickaxe looks dirty and a pewter pot looks dirty. But the man he is supposed to be studying sees the difference between them exactly as a clerk sees the difference between a ledger and an edition de luxe. The chiaroscuro of the life is inevitably lost; for to us the high lights and the shadows are a light grey. But the high lights and the shadows are not a light grey in that life any more than in any other. The kind of man who could really express the pleasures of the poor would be also the kind of man who could share them. In short, these books are not a record of the psychology of poverty. They are a record of the psychology of wealth and culture when brought in contact with poverty. They are not a description of the state of the slums. They are only a very dark and dreadful description of the state of the slummers. One might give innumerable examples of the essentially unsympathetic and unpopular quality of these realistic writers. But perhaps the simplest and most obvious example with which we could conclude is the mere fact that these writers are realistic. The poor have many other vices, but, at least, they are never realistic. The poor are melodramatic and romantic in grain; the poor all believe in high moral platitudes and copy-book maxims; probably this is the ultimate meaning of the great saying, "Blessed are the poor." Blessed are the poor, for they are always making life, or trying to make life like an Adelphi play. Some innocent educationalists and philanthropists (for even philanthropists can be innocent) have expressed a grave astonishment that the masses prefer shilling shockers to scientific treatises and melodramas to problem plays. The reason is very simple. The realistic story is certainly more artistic than the melodramatic story. If what you desire is deft handling, delicate proportions, a unit of artistic atmosphere, the realistic story has a full advantage over the melodrama. In everything that is light and bright and ornamental the realistic story has a full advantage over the melodrama. But, at least, the melodrama has one indisputable advantage over the realistic story. The melodrama is much more like life. It is much more like man, and especially the poor man. It is very banal and very inartistic when a poor woman at the Adelphi says, "Do you think I will sell my own child?" But poor women in the Battersea High Road do say, "Do you think I will sell my own child?" They say it on every available occasion; you can hear a sort of murmur or babble of it all the way down the street. It is very stale and weak dramatic art (if that is all) when the workman confronts his master and says, "I'm a man." But a workman does say "I'm a man" two or three times every day. In fact, it is tedious, possibly, to hear poor men being melodramatic behind the footlights; but that is because one can always hear them being melodramatic in the street outside. In short, melodrama, if it is dull, is dull because it is too accurate. Somewhat the same problem exists in the case of stories about schoolboys. Mr. Kipling's "Stalky and Co." is much more amusing (if you are talking about amusement) than the late Dean Farrar's "Eric; or, Little by Little." But "Eric" is immeasurably more like real school-life. For real school-life, real boyhood, is full of the things of which Eric is full— priggishness, a crude piety, a silly sin, a weak but continual attempt at the heroic, in a word, melodrama. And if we wish to lay a firm basis for any efforts to help the poor, we must not become realistic and see them from the outside. We must become melodramatic, and see them from the inside. The novelist must not take out his notebook and say, "I am an expert." No; he must imitate the workman in the Adelphi play. He must slap himself on the chest and say, "I am a man."

XX. CONCLUDING REMARKS ON THE IMPORTANCE OF ORTHODOXY

Whether the human mind can advance or not, is a question too little discussed, for nothing can be more dangerous than to found our social philosophy on any theory which is debatable but has not been debated. But if we assume, for the sake of argument, that there has been in the past, or will be in the future, such a thing as a growth or improvement of the human mind itself, there still remains a very sharp objection to be raised against the modern version of that improvement. The vice of the modern notion of mental progress is that it is always something concerned with the breaking of bonds, the effacing of boundaries, the casting away of dogmas. But if there be such a thing as mental growth, it must mean the growth into more and more definite convictions, into more and more dogmas. The human brain is a machine for coming to conclusions; if it cannot come to conclusions it is rusty. When we hear of a man too clever to believe, we are hearing of something having almost the character of a contradiction in terms. It is like hearing of a nail that was too good to hold down a carpet; or a bolt that was too strong to keep a door shut. Man can hardly be defined, after the fashion of Carlyle, as an animal who makes tools; ants and beavers and many other animals make tools, in the sense that they make an apparatus. Man can be defined as an animal that makes dogmas. As he piles doctrine on doctrine and conclusion on conclusion in the formation of some tremendous scheme of philosophy and religion, he is, in the only legitimate sense of which the expression is capable, becoming more and more human. When he drops one doctrine after another in a refined scepticism, when he declines to tie himself to a system, when he says that he has outgrown definitions, when he says that he disbelieves in finality, when, in his own imagination, he sits as God, holding no form of creed but contemplating all, then he is by that very process sinking slowly backwards into the vagueness of the vagrant animals and the unconsciousness of the grass. Trees have no dogmas. Turnips are singularly broad-minded.

If then, I repeat, there is to be mental advance, it must be mental advance in the construction of a definite philosophy of life. And that philosophy of life must be right and the other philosophies wrong. Now of all, or nearly all, the able modern writers whom I have briefly studied in this book, this is especially and pleasingly true, that they do each of them have a constructive and affirmative view, and that they do take it seriously and ask us to take it seriously. There is nothing merely sceptically progressive about Mr. Rudyard Kipling. There is nothing in the least broad minded about Mr. Bernard Shaw. The paganism of Mr. Lowes Dickinson is more grave than any Christianity. Even the opportunism of Mr. H. G. Wells is more dogmatic than the idealism of anybody else. Somebody complained, I think, to Matthew Arnold that he was getting as dogmatic as Carlyle. He replied, "That may be true; but you overlook an obvious difference. I am dogmatic and right, and Carlyle is dogmatic and wrong." The strong humour of the remark ought not to disguise from us its everlasting seriousness and common sense; no man ought to write at all, or even to speak at all, unless he thinks that he is in truth and the other man in error. In similar style, I hold that I am dogmatic and right, while Mr. Shaw is dogmatic and wrong. But my main point, at present, is to notice that the chief among these writers I have discussed do most sanely and courageously offer themselves as dogmatists, as founders of a system. It may be true that the thing in Mr. Shaw most interesting to me, is the fact that Mr. Shaw is wrong. But it is equally true that the thing in Mr. Shaw most interesting to himself, is the fact that Mr. Shaw is right. Mr. Shaw may have none with him but himself; but it is not for himself he cares. It is for the vast and universal church, of which he is the only member.

The two typical men of genius whom I have mentioned here, and with whose names I have begun this book, are very symbolic, if only because they have shown that the fiercest dogmatists can make the best artists. In the fin de siecle atmosphere every one was crying out that literature should be free from all causes and all ethical creeds. Art was to produce only exquisite workmanship, and it was especially the note of those days to demand brilliant plays and brilliant short stories. And when they got them, they got them from a couple of moralists. The best short stories were written by a man trying to preach Imperialism. The best plays were written by a man trying to preach Socialism. All the art of all the artists looked tiny and tedious beside the art which was a byproduct of propaganda.

The reason, indeed, is very simple. A man cannot be wise enough to be a great artist without being wise enough to wish to be a philosopher. A man cannot have the energy to produce good art without having the energy to wish to pass beyond it. A small artist is content with art; a great artist is content with nothing except everything. So we find that when real forces, good or bad, like Kipling and G. B. S., enter our arena, they bring with them not only startling and arresting art, but very startling and arresting dogmas. And they care even more, and desire us to care even more, about their startling and arresting dogmas than about their startling and arresting art. Mr. Shaw is a good dramatist, but what he desires more than anything else to be is a good politician. Mr. Rudyard Kipling is by divine caprice and natural genius an unconventional poet; but what he desires more than anything else to be is a conventional poet. He desires to be the poet of his people, bone of their bone, and flesh of their flesh, understanding their origins, celebrating their destiny. He desires to be Poet Laureate, a most sensible and honourable and public-spirited desire. Having been given by the gods originality—that is, disagreement with others—he desires divinely to agree with them. But the most striking instance of all, more striking, I think, even than either of these, is the instance of Mr. H. G. Wells. He began in a sort of insane infancy of pure art. He began by making a new heaven and a new earth, with the same irresponsible instinct by which men buy a new necktie or button-hole. He began by trifling with the stars and systems in order to make ephemeral anecdotes; he killed the universe for a joke. He has since become more and more serious, and has become, as men inevitably do when they become more and more serious, more and more parochial. He was frivolous about the twilight of the gods; but he is serious about the London omnibus. He was careless in "The Time Machine," for that dealt only with the destiny of all things; but he is careful, and even cautious, in "Mankind in the Making," for that deals with the day after to-morrow. He began with the end of the world, and that was easy. Now he has gone on to the beginning of the world, and that is difficult. But the main result of all this is the same as in the other cases. The men who have really been the bold artists, the realistic artists, the uncompromising artists, are the men who have turned out, after all, to be writing "with a purpose." Suppose that any cool and cynical art-critic, any art-critic fully impressed with the conviction that artists were greatest when they were most purely artistic, suppose that a man who professed ably a humane aestheticism, as did Mr. Max Beerbohm, or a cruel aestheticism, as did Mr. W. E. Henley, had cast his eye over the whole fictional literature which was recent in the year 1895, and had been asked to select the three most vigorous and promising and original artists and artistic works, he would, I think, most certainly have said that for a fine artistic audacity, for a real artistic delicacy, or for a whiff of true novelty in art, the things that stood first were "Soldiers Three," by a Mr. Rudyard Kipling; "Arms and the Man," by a Mr. Bernard Shaw; and "The Time Machine," by a man called Wells. And all these men have shown themselves ingrainedly didactic. You may express the matter if you will by saying that if we want doctrines we go to the great artists. But it is clear from the psychology of the matter that this is not the true statement; the true statement is that when we want any art tolerably brisk and bold we have to go to the doctrinaires.

In concluding this book, therefore, I would ask, first and foremost, that men such as these of whom I have spoken should not be insulted by being taken for artists. No man has any right whatever merely to enjoy the work of Mr. Bernard Shaw; he might as well enjoy the invasion of his country by the French. Mr. Shaw writes either to convince or to enrage us. No man has any business to be a Kiplingite without being a politician, and an Imperialist politician. If a man is first with us, it should be because of what is first with him. If a man convinces us at all, it should be by his convictions. If we hate a poem of Kipling's from political passion, we are hating it for the same reason that the poet loved it; if we dislike him because of his opinions, we are disliking him for the best of all possible reasons. If a man comes into Hyde Park to preach it is permissible to hoot him; but it is discourteous to applaud him as a performing bear. And an artist is only a performing bear compared with the meanest man who fancies he has anything to say.

There is, indeed, one class of modern writers and thinkers who cannot altogether be overlooked in this question, though there is no space here for a lengthy account of them, which, indeed, to confess the truth, would consist chiefly of abuse. I mean those who get over all these abysses and reconcile all these wars by talking about "aspects of truth," by saying that the art of Kipling represents one aspect of the truth, and the art of William

Watson another; the art of Mr. Bernard Shaw one aspect of the truth, and the art of Mr. Cunningham Grahame another; the art of Mr. H. G. Wells one aspect, and the art of Mr. Coventry Patmore (say) another. I will only say here that this seems to me an evasion which has not even had the sense to disguise itself ingeniously in words. If we talk of a certain thing being an aspect of truth, it is evident that we claim to know what is truth; just as, if we talk of the hind leg of a dog, we claim to know what is a dog. Unfortunately, the philosopher who talks about aspects of truth generally also asks, "What is truth?" Frequently even he denies the existence of truth, or says it is inconceivable by the human intelligence. How, then, can he recognize its aspects? I should not like to be an artist who brought an architectural sketch to a builder, saying, "This is the south aspect of Sea-View Cottage. Sea-View Cottage, of course, does not exist." I should not even like very much to have to explain, under such circumstances, that Sea-View Cottage might exist, but was unthinkable by the human mind. Nor should I like any better to be the bungling and absurd metaphysician who professed to be able to see everywhere the aspects of a truth that is not there. Of course, it is perfectly obvious that there are truths in Kipling, that there are truths in Shaw or Wells. But the degree to which we can perceive them depends strictly upon how far we have a definite conception inside us of what is truth. It is ludicrous to suppose that the more sceptical we are the more we see good in everything. It is clear that the more we are certain what good is, the more we shall see good in everything.

I plead, then, that we should agree or disagree with these men. I plead that we should agree with them at least in having an abstract belief. But I know that there are current in the modern world many vague objections to having an abstract belief, and I feel that we shall not get any further until we have dealt with some of them. The first objection is easily stated.

A common hesitation in our day touching the use of extreme convictions is a sort of notion that extreme convictions specially upon cosmic matters, have been responsible in the past for the thing which is called bigotry. But a very small amount of direct experience will dissipate this view. In real life the people who are most bigoted are the people who have no convictions at all. The economists of the Manchester school who disagree with Socialism take Socialism seriously. It is the young man in Bond Street, who does not know what socialism means much less whether he agrees with it, who is quite certain that these socialist fellows are making a fuss about nothing. The man who understands the Calvinist philosophy enough to agree with it must understand the Catholic philosophy in order to disagree with it. It is the vague modern who is not at all certain what is right who is most certain that Dante was wrong. The serious opponent of the Latin Church in history, even in the act of showing that it produced great infamies, must know that it produced great saints. It is the hard-headed stockbroker, who knows no history and believes no religion, who is, nevertheless, perfectly convinced that all these priests are knaves. The Salvationist at the Marble Arch may be bigoted, but he is not too bigoted to yearn from a common human kinship after the dandy on church parade. But the dandy on church parade is so bigoted that he does not in the least yearn after the Salvationist at the Marble Arch. Bigotry may be roughly defined as the anger of men who have no opinions. It is the resistance offered to definite ideas by that vague bulk of people whose ideas are indefinite to excess. Bigotry may be called the appalling frenzy of the indifferent. This frenzy of the indifferent is in truth a terrible thing; it has made all monstrous and widely pervading persecutions. In this degree it was not the people who cared who ever persecuted; the people who cared were not sufficiently numerous. It was the people who did not care who filled the world with fire and oppression. It was the hands of the indifferent that lit the faggots; it was the hands of the indifferent that turned the rack. There have come some persecutions out of the pain of a passionate certainty; but these produced, not bigotry, but fanaticism—a very different and a somewhat admirable thing. Bigotry in the main has always been the pervading omnipotence of those who do not care crushing out those who care in darkness and blood.

There are people, however, who dig somewhat deeper than this into the possible evils of dogma. It is felt by many that strong philosophical conviction, while it does not (as they perceive) produce that sluggish and fundamentally frivolous condition which we call bigotry, does produce a certain concentration, exaggeration, and moral impatience, which we may agree to call fanaticism. They say, in brief, that ideas are dangerous things. In politics, for example, it is commonly urged against a man like Mr. Balfour, or against a man like Mr. John Morley, that a wealth of ideas is dangerous. The true doctrine on this point, again, is surely not very difficult to state. Ideas are dangerous, but the man to whom they are least dangerous is the man of ideas. He is acquainted with ideas, and moves among them like a lion-tamer. Ideas are dangerous, but the man to whom they are most dangerous is the man of no ideas. The man of no ideas will find the first idea fly to his head like wine to the head of a teetotaller. It is a common error, I think, among the Radical idealists of my own party and period to suggest that financiers and business men are a danger to the empire because they are so sordid or so materialistic. The truth is that financiers and business men are a danger to the empire because they can be sentimental about any sentiment, and idealistic about any ideal, any ideal that they find lying about. just as a boy who has not known much of women is apt too easily to take a woman for the woman, so these practical men, unaccustomed to causes, are always inclined to think that if a thing is proved to be an ideal it is proved to be the ideal. Many, for example, avowedly followed Cecil Rhodes because he had a vision. They might as well have followed him because he had a nose; a man without some kind of dream of perfection is quite as much of a monstrosity as a noseless man. People say of such a figure, in almost feverish whispers, "He knows his own mind," which is exactly like saying in equally feverish whispers, "He blows his own nose." Human nature simply cannot subsist without a hope and aim of some kind; as the sanity of the Old Testament truly said, where there is no vision the people perisheth. But it is precisely because an ideal is necessary to man that the man without ideals is in permanent danger of fanaticism. There is nothing which is so likely to leave a man open to the sudden and irresistible inroad of an unbalanced vision as the cultivation of business habits. All of us know angular business men who think that the earth is flat, or that Mr. Kruger was at the head of a great military despotism, or that men are graminivorous, or that Bacon wrote Shakespeare. Religious and philosophical beliefs are, indeed, as dangerous as fire, and nothing can take from them that beauty of danger. But there is only one way of really guarding ourselves against the excessive danger of them, and that is to be steeped in philosophy and soaked in religion.

Briefly, then, we dismiss the two opposite dangers of bigotry and fanaticism, bigotry which is a too great vagueness and fanaticism which is a too great concentration. We say that the cure for the bigot is belief; we say that the cure for the idealist is ideas. To know the best theories of existence and to choose the best from them (that is, to the best of our own strong conviction) appears to us the proper way to be neither bigot nor fanatic, but something more firm than a bigot and more terrible than a fanatic, a man with a definite opinion. But that definite opinion must in this view begin with the basic matters of human thought, and these must not be dismissed as irrelevant, as religion, for instance, is too often in our days dismissed as irrelevant. Even if we think religion insoluble, we cannot think it irrelevant. Even if we ourselves have no view of the ultimate verities, we must feel that wherever such a view exists in a man it must be more important than anything else in him. The instant that the thing ceases to be the unknowable, it becomes the indispensable. There can be no doubt, I think, that the idea does exist in our time that there is something narrow or irrelevant or even mean about attacking a man's religion, or arguing from it in matters of politics or ethics. There can be quite as little doubt that such an accusation of narrowness is itself almost grotesquely narrow. To take an example from comparatively current events: we all know that it was not uncommon for a man to be considered a scarecrow of bigotry and obscurantism because he distrusted the Japanese, or lamented the rise of the Japanese, on the ground that the Japanese were Pagans. Nobody would think that there was anything antiquated or fanatical about distrusting a people because of some difference between them and us in practice or political machinery. Nobody would think it bigoted to say of a people, "I distrust their influence because they are Protectionists." No one would think it narrow to say, "I lament their rise because they are Socialists, or Manchester Individualists, or strong believers in militarism and conscription." A difference of opinion about the nature of Parliaments matters very much; but a difference of opinion about the nature of sin does not matter at all. A difference of opinion about the object of taxation matters very much; but a difference of opinion about the object of human existence does not matter at all. We have a right to distrust a man who is in a different kind of municipality; but we have no right to mistrust a man who is in a different kind of cosmos. This sort of enlightenment is surely about the most unenlightened that it is possible to imagine. To recur to the phrase which I employed earlier, this is tantamount to saying that everything is important with the exception of everything. Religion is exactly the thing which cannot be left out—because it includes everything. The most absent-minded person cannot well pack his Gladstone-bag and leave out the bag. We have a general view of existence, whether we like it or not; it alters or, to speak more accurately, it creates and involves everything we say or do, whether we like it or not. If we regard the Cosmos as a dream, we regard the Fiscal Question as a dream. If we regard the Cosmos as a joke, we regard St. Paul's Cathedral as a joke. If everything is bad, then we must believe (if it be possible) that beer is bad; if everything be good, we are forced to the rather fantastic conclusion that scientific philanthropy is good. Every man in the street must hold a metaphysical system, and hold it firmly. The possibility is that he may have held it so firmly and so long as to have forgotten all about its existence.

This latter situation is certainly possible; in fact, it is the situation of the whole modern world. The modern world is filled with men who hold dogmas so strongly that they do not even know that they are dogmas. It may be said even that the modern world, as a corporate body, holds certain dogmas so strongly that it does not know that they are dogmas. It may be thought "dogmatic," for instance, in some circles accounted progressive, to assume the perfection or improvement of man in another world. But it is not thought "dogmatic" to assume the perfection or improvement of man in this world; though that idea of progress is quite as unproved as the idea of immortality, and from a rationalistic point of view quite as improbable. Progress happens to be one of our dogmas, and a dogma means a thing which is not thought dogmatic. Or, again, we see nothing "dogmatic" in the inspiring, but certainly most startling, theory of physical science, that we should collect facts for the sake of facts, even though they seem as useless as sticks and straws. This is a great and suggestive idea, and its utility may, if you will, be proving itself, but its utility is, in the abstract, quite as disputable as the utility of that calling on oracles or consulting shrines which is also said to prove itself. Thus, because we are not in a civilization which believes strongly in oracles or sacred places, we see the full frenzy of those who killed themselves to find the sepulchre of Christ. But being in a civilization which does believe in this dogma of fact for facts' sake, we do not see the full frenzy of those who kill themselves to find the North Pole. I am not speaking of a tenable ultimate utility which is true both of the Crusades and the polar explorations. I mean merely that we do see the superficial and aesthetic singularity, the startling quality, about the idea of men crossing a continent with armies to conquer the place where a man died. But we do not see the aesthetic singularity and startling quality of men dying in agonies to find a place where no man can live—a place only interesting because it is supposed to be the meeting-place of some lines that do not exist.

Let us, then, go upon a long journey and enter on a dreadful search. Let us, at least, dig and seek till we have discovered our own opinions. The dogmas we really hold are far more fantastic, and, perhaps, far more beautiful than we think. In the course of these essays I fear that I have spoken from time to time of rationalists and rationalism, and that in a disparaging sense. Being full of that kindliness which should come at the end of everything, even of a book, I apologize to the rationalists even for calling them rationalists. There are no rationalists. We all believe fairy-tales, and live in them. Some, with a sumptuous literary turn, believe in the existence of the lady clothed with the sun. Some, with a more rustic, elvish instinct, like Mr. McCabe, believe merely in the impossible sun itself. Some hold the undemonstrable dogma of the existence of God; some the equally undemonstrable dogma of the existence of the man next door.

Truths turn into dogmas the instant that they are disputed. Thus every man who utters a doubt defines a religion. And the scepticism of our time does not really destroy the beliefs, rather it creates them; gives them their limits and their plain and defiant shape. We who are Liberals once held Liberalism lightly as a truism. Now it has been disputed, and we hold it fiercely as a faith. We who believe in patriotism once thought patriotism to be reasonable, and thought little more about it. Now we know it to be unreasonable, and know it to be right. We who are Christians never knew the great philosophic common sense which inheres in that mystery until the anti-Christian writers pointed it out to us. The great march of mental destruction will go on. Everything will be denied. Everything will become a creed. It is a reasonable position to deny the stones in the street; it will be a religious dogma to assert them. It is a rational thesis that we are all in a dream; it will be a mystical sanity to say that we are all awake. Fires will be kindled to testify that two and two make four. Swords will be drawn to prove that leaves are green in summer. We shall be left defending, not only the incredible virtues and sanities of human life, but something more incredible still, this huge impossible universe which stares us in the face. We shall fight for visible prodigies as if they were invisible. We shall look on the impossible grass and the skies with a strange courage. We shall be of those who have seen and yet have believed.

THE END

WHAT'S WRONG WITH THE WORLD

PART ONE. THE HOMELESSNESS OF MAN

I. THE MEDICAL MISTAKE

A book of modern social inquiry has a shape that is somewhat sharply defined. It begins as a rule with an analysis, with statistics, tables of population, decrease of crime among Congregationalists, growth of hysteria among policemen, and similar ascertained facts; it ends with a chapter that is generally called "The Remedy." It is almost wholly due to this careful, solid, and scientific method that "The Remedy" is never found. For this scheme of medical question and answer is a blunder; the first great blunder of sociology. It is always called stating the disease before we find the cure. But it is the whole definition and dignity of man that in social matters we must actually find the cure before we find the disease.

The fallacy is one of the fifty fallacies that come from the modern madness for biological or bodily metaphors. It is convenient to speak of the Social Organism, just as it is convenient to speak of the British Lion. But Britain is no more an organism than Britain is a lion. The moment we begin to give a nation the unity and simplicity of an animal, we begin to think wildly. Because every man is a biped, fifty men are not a centipede. This has produced, for instance, the gaping absurdity of perpetually talking about "young nations" and "dying nations," as if a nation had a fixed and physical span of life. Thus people will say that Spain has entered a final senility; they might as well say that Spain is losing all her teeth. Or people will say that Canada should soon produce a literature; which is like saying that Canada must soon grow a new moustache. Nations consist of people; the first generation may be decrepit, or the ten thousandth may be vigorous. Similar applications of the fallacy are made by those who see in the increasing size of national possessions, a simple increase in wisdom and stature, and in favor with God and man. These people, indeed, even fall short in subtlety of the parallel of a human body. They do not even ask whether an empire is growing taller in its youth, or only growing fatter in its old age. But of all the instances of error arising from this physical fancy, the worst is that we have before us: the habit of exhaustively describing a social sickness, and then propounding a social drug.

Now we do talk first about the disease in cases of bodily breakdown; and that for an excellent reason. Because, though there may be doubt about the way in which the body broke down, there is no doubt at all about the shape in which it should be built up again. No doctor proposes to produce a new kind of man, with a new arrangement of eyes or limbs. The hospital, by necessity, may send a man home with one leg less: but it will not (in a creative rapture) send him home with one leg extra. Medical science is content with the normal human body, and only seeks to restore it.

But social science is by no means always content with the normal human soul; it has all sorts of fancy souls for sale. Man as a social idealist will say "I am tired of being a Puritan; I want to be a Pagan," or "Beyond this dark probation of Individualism I see the shining paradise of Collectivism." Now in bodily ills there is none of this difference about the ultimate ideal. The patient may or may not want quinine; but he certainly wants health. No one says "I am tired of this headache; I want some toothache," or "The only thing for this Russian influenza is a few German measles," or "Through this dark probation of catarrh I see the shining paradise of rheumatism." But exactly the whole difficulty in our public problems is that some men are aiming at cures which other men would regard as worse maladies; are offering ultimate conditions as states of health which others would uncompromisingly call states of disease. Mr. Belloc once said that he would no more part with the idea of property than with his teeth; yet to Mr. Bernard Shaw property is not a tooth, but a toothache. Lord Milner has sincerely attempted to introduce German efficiency; and many of us would as soon welcome German measles. Dr. Saleeby would honestly like to have Eugenics; but I would rather have rheumatics.

This is the arresting and dominant fact about modern social discussion; that the quarrel is not merely about the difficulties, but about the aim. We agree about the evil; it is about the good that we should tear each other's eyes out. We all admit that a lazy aristocracy is a bad thing. We should not by any means all admit that an active aristocracy would be a good thing. We all feel angry with an irreligious priesthood; but some of us would go mad with disgust at a really religious one. Everyone is indignant if our army is weak, including the people who would be even more indignant if it were strong. The social case is exactly the opposite of the medical case. We do not disagree, like doctors, about the precise nature of the illness, while agreeing about the nature of health. On the contrary, we all agree that England is unhealthy, but half of us would not look at her in what the other half would call blooming health. Public abuses are so prominent and pestilent that they sweep all generous people into a sort of fictitious unanimity. We forget that, while we agree about the abuses of things, we should differ very much about the uses of them. Mr. Cadbury and I would agree about the bad public house. It would be precisely in front of the good public-house that our painful personal fracas would occur.

I maintain, therefore, that the common sociological method is quite useless: that of first dissecting abject poverty or cataloguing prostitution. We all dislike abject poverty; but it might be another business if we began to discuss independent and dignified poverty. We all disapprove of prostitution; but we do not all approve of purity. The only way to discuss the social evil is to get at once to the social ideal. We can all see the national madness; but what is national sanity? I have called this book "What Is Wrong with the World?" and the upshot of the title can be easily and clearly stated. What is wrong is that we do not ask what is right.

II. WANTED, AN UNPRACTICAL MAN

There is a popular philosophical joke intended to typify the endless and useless arguments of philosophers; I mean the joke about which came first, the chicken or the egg? I am not sure that properly understood, it is so futile an inquiry after all. I am not concerned here to enter on those deep metaphysical and theological differences of which the chicken and egg debate is a frivolous, but a very felicitous, type. The evolutionary materialists are appropriately enough represented in the vision of all things coming from an egg, a dim and monstrous oval germ that had laid itself by accident. That other supernatural school of thought (to which I personally adhere) would be not unworthily typified in the fancy that this round world of ours is but an egg brooded upon by a sacred unbegotten bird; the mystic dove of the prophets. But it is to much humbler functions that I here call the awful power of such a distinction. Whether or no the living bird is at the beginning of our mental chain, it is absolutely necessary that it should be at the end of our mental chain. The bird is the thing to be aimed at—not with a gun, but a life-bestowing wand. What is essential to our right thinking is this: that the egg and the bird must not be thought of as equal cosmic occurrences recurring alternatively forever. They must not become a mere egg and bird pattern, like the egg and dart pattern. One is a means and the other an end; they are in different mental worlds. Leaving the complications of the human breakfast-table out of account, in an elemental sense, the egg only exists to produce the chicken. But the chicken does not exist only in order to produce another egg. He may also exist to amuse himself, to praise God, and even to suggest ideas to a French dramatist. Being a conscious life, he is, or may be, valuable in himself. Now our modern politics are full of a noisy forgetfulness; forgetfulness that the production of this happy and conscious life is after all the aim of all complexities and compromises. We talk of nothing but useful men and working institutions; that is, we only think of the chickens as things that will lay more eggs. Instead of seeking to breed our ideal bird, the eagle of Zeus or the Swan of Avon, or whatever we happen to want, we talk entirely in terms of the process and the embryo. The process itself, divorced from its divine object, becomes doubtful and even morbid; poison enters the embryo of everything; and our politics are rotten eggs.

Idealism is only considering everything in its practical essence. Idealism only means that we should consider a poker in reference to poking before we discuss its suitability for wife-beating; that we should ask if an egg is good enough for practical poultry-rearing before we decide that the egg is bad enough for practical politics. But I know that this primary pursuit of the theory (which is but pursuit of the aim) exposes one to the cheap charge of fiddling while Rome is burning. A school, of which Lord Rosebery is representative, has endeavored to substitute for the moral or social ideals which have hitherto been the motive of politics a general coherency or completeness in the social system which has gained the nick-name of "efficiency." I am not very certain of the secret doctrine of this sect in the matter. But, as far as I can make out, "efficiency" means that we ought to discover everything about a machine except what it is for. There has arisen in our time a most singular fancy: the fancy that when things go very wrong we need a practical man. It would be far truer to say, that when things go very wrong we need an unpractical man. Certainly, at least, we need a theorist. A practical man means a man accustomed to mere daily practice, to the way things commonly work. When things will not work, you must have the thinker, the man who has some doctrine about why they work at all. It is wrong to fiddle while Rome is burning; but it is quite right to study the theory of hydraulics while Rome is burning.

It is then necessary to drop one's daily agnosticism and attempt rerum cognoscere causas. If your aeroplane has a slight indisposition, a handy man may mend it. But, if it is seriously ill, it is all the more likely that some absent-minded old professor with wild white hair will have to be dragged out of a college or laboratory to analyze the evil. The more complicated the smash, the whiter-haired and more absent-minded will be the theorist who is needed to deal with it; and in some extreme cases, no one but the man (probably insane) who invented your flying-ship could possibly say what was the matter with it.

"Efficiency," of course, is futile for the same reason that strong men, will-power and the superman are futile. That is, it is futile because it only deals with actions after they have been performed. It has no philosophy for incidents before they happen; therefore it has no power of choice. An act can only be successful or unsuccessful when it is over; if it is to begin, it must be, in the abstract, right or wrong. There is no such thing as backing a winner; for he cannot be a winner when he is backed. There is no such thing as fighting on the winning side; one fights to find out which is the winning side. If any operation has occurred, that operation was efficient. If a man is murdered, the murder was efficient. A tropical sun is as efficient in making people lazy as a Lancashire foreman bully in making them energetic. Maeterlinck is as efficient in filling a man with strange spiritual tremors as Messrs. Crosse and Blackwell are in filling a man with jam. But it all depends on what you want to be filled with. Lord Rosebery, being a modern skeptic, probably prefers the spiritual tremors. I, being an orthodox Christian, prefer the jam. But both are efficient when they have been effected; and inefficient until they are effected. A man who thinks much about success must be the drowsiest sentimentalist; for he must be always looking back. If he only likes victory he must always come late for the battle. For the man of action there is nothing but idealism.

This definite ideal is a far more urgent and practical matter in our existing English trouble than any immediate plans or proposals. For the present chaos is due to a sort of general oblivion of all that men were originally aiming at. No man demands what he desires; each man demands what he fancies he can get. Soon people forget what the man really wanted first; and after a successful and vigorous political life, he forgets it himself. The whole is an extravagant riot of second bests, a pandemonium of pis-aller. Now this sort of pliability does not merely prevent any heroic consistency, it also prevents any really practical compromise. One can only find the middle distance between two points if the two points will stand still. We may make an arrangement between two litigants who cannot both get what they want; but not if they will not even tell us what they want. The keeper of a restaurant would much prefer that each customer should give his order smartly, though it were for stewed ibis or boiled elephant, rather than that each customer should sit holding his head in his hands, plunged in arithmetical calculations about how much food there can be on the premises. Most of us have suffered from a certain sort of ladies who, by their perverse unselfishness, give more trouble than the selfish; who almost clamor for the unpopular dish and scramble for the worst seat. Most of us have known parties or expeditions full of this seething fuss of self-effacement. From much meaner motives than those of such admirable women, our practical politicians keep things in the same confusion through the same doubt about their real demands. There is nothing that so much prevents a settlement as a tangle of small surrenders. We are bewildered on every side by politicians who are in favor of secular education, but think it hopeless to work for it; who desire total prohibition, but are certain they should not demand it; who regret compulsory education, but resignedly continue it; or who want peasant proprietorship and therefore vote for something else. It is this dazed and floundering opportunism that gets in the way of everything. If our statesmen were visionaries something practical might be done. If we ask for something in the abstract we might get something in the concrete. As it is, it is not only impossible to get what one wants, but it is impossible to get any part of it, because nobody can mark it out plainly like a map. That clear and even hard quality that there was in the old bargaining has wholly vanished. We forget that the word "compromise" contains, among other things, the rigid and ringing word "promise." Moderation is not vague; it is as definite as perfection. The middle point is as fixed as the extreme point.

If I am made to walk the plank by a pirate, it is vain for me to offer, as a common-sense compromise, to walk along the plank for a reasonable distance. It is exactly about the reasonable distance that the pirate and I differ. There is an exquisite mathematical split second at which the plank tips up. My common-sense ends just before that instant; the pirate's common-sense begins just beyond it. But the point itself is as hard as any geometrical diagram; as abstract as any theological dogma.

III. THE NEW HYPOCRITE

But this new cloudy political cowardice has rendered useless the old English compromise. People have begun to be terrified of an improvement merely because it is complete. They call it utopian and revolutionary that anyone should really have his own way, or anything be really done, and done with. Compromise used to mean that half a loaf was better than no bread. Among modern statesmen it really seems to mean that half a loaf is better than a whole loaf.

As an instance to sharpen the argument, I take the one case of our everlasting education bills. We have actually contrived to invent a new kind of hypocrite. The old hypocrite, Tartuffe or Pecksniff, was a man whose aims were really worldly and practical, while he pretended that they were religious. The new hypocrite is one whose aims are really religious, while he pretends that they are worldly and practical. The Rev. Brown, the Wesleyan minister, sturdily declares that he cares nothing for creeds, but only for education; meanwhile, in truth, the wildest Wesleyanism is tearing his soul. The Rev. Smith, of the Church of England, explains gracefully, with the Oxford manner, that the only question for him is the prosperity and efficiency of the schools; while in truth all the evil passions of a curate are roaring within him. It is a fight of creeds masquerading as policies. I think these reverend gentlemen do themselves wrong; I think they are more pious than they will admit. Theology is not (as some suppose) expunged as an error. It is merely concealed, like a sin. Dr. Clifford really wants a theological atmosphere as much as Lord Halifax; only it is a different one. If Dr. Clifford would ask plainly for Puritanism and Lord Halifax ask plainly for Catholicism, something might be done for them. We are all, one hopes, imaginative enough to recognize the dignity and distinctness of another religion, like Islam or the cult of Apollo. I am quite ready to respect another man's faith; but it is too much to ask that I should respect his doubt, his worldly hesitations and fictions, his political bargain and make-believe. Most Nonconformists with an instinct for English history could see something poetic and national about the Archbishop of Canterbury as an Archbishop of Canterbury. It is when he does the rational British statesman that they very justifiably get annoyed. Most Anglicans with an eye for pluck and simplicity could admire Dr. Clifford as a Baptist minister. It is when he says that he is simply a citizen that nobody can possibly believe him.

But indeed the case is yet more curious than this. The one argument that used to be urged for our creedless vagueness was that at least it saved us from fanaticism. But it does not even do that. On the contrary, it creates and renews fanaticism with a force quite peculiar to itself. This is at once so strange and so true that I will ask the reader's attention to it with a little more precision.

Some people do not like the word "dogma." Fortunately they are free, and there is an alternative for them. There are two things, and two things only, for the human mind, a dogma and a prejudice. The Middle Ages were a rational epoch, an age of doctrine. Our age is, at its best, a poetical epoch, an age of prejudice. A doctrine is a definite point; a prejudice is a direction. That an ox may be eaten, while a man should not be eaten, is a doctrine. That as little as possible of anything should be eaten is a prejudice; which is also sometimes called an ideal. Now a direction is always far more fantastic than a plan. I would rather have the most archaic map of the road to Brighton than a general recommendation to turn to the left. Straight lines that are not parallel must meet at last; but curves may recoil forever. A pair of lovers might walk along the frontier of France and Germany, one on the one side and one on the other, so long as they were not vaguely told to keep away from each other. And this is a strictly true parable of the effect of our modern vagueness in losing and separating men as in a mist.

It is not merely true that a creed unites men. Nay, a difference of creed unites men—so long as it is a clear difference. A boundary unites. Many a magnanimous Moslem and chivalrous Crusader must have been nearer to each other, because they were both dogmatists, than any two homeless agnostics in a pew of Mr. Campbell's chapel. "I say God is One," and "I say God is One but also Three," that is the beginning of a good quarrelsome, manly friendship. But our age would turn these creeds into tendencies. It would tell the Trinitarian to follow multiplicity as such (because it was his "temperament"), and he would turn up later with three hundred and thirty-three persons in the Trinity. Meanwhile, it would turn the Moslem into a Monist: a frightful intellectual fall. It would force that previously healthy person not only to admit that there was one God, but to admit that there was nobody else. When each had, for a long enough period, followed the gleam of his own nose (like the Dong) they would appear again; the Christian a Polytheist, and the Moslem a Panegoist, both quite mad, and far more unfit to understand each other than before.

It is exactly the same with politics. Our political vagueness divides men, it does not fuse them. Men will walk along the edge of a chasm in clear weather, but they will edge miles away from it in a fog. So a Tory can walk up to the very edge of Socialism, if he knows what is Socialism. But if he is told that Socialism is a spirit, a sublime atmosphere, a noble, indefinable tendency, why, then he keeps out of its way; and quite right too. One can meet an assertion with argument; but healthy bigotry is the only way in which one can meet a tendency. I am told that the Japanese method of wrestling consists not of suddenly pressing, but of suddenly giving way. This is one of my many reasons for disliking the Japanese civilization. To use surrender as a weapon is the very worst spirit of the East. But certainly there is no force so hard to fight as the force which it is easy to conquer; the force that always yields and then returns. Such is the force of a great impersonal prejudice, such as possesses the modern world on so many points. Against this there is no weapon at all except a rigid and steely sanity, a resolution not to listen to fads, and not to be infected by diseases.

In short, the rational human faith must armor itself with prejudice in an age of prejudices, just as it armoured itself with logic in an age of logic. But the difference between the two mental methods is marked and unmistakable. The essential of the difference is this: that prejudices are divergent, whereas creeds are always in collision. Believers bump into each other; whereas bigots keep out of each other's way. A creed is a collective thing, and even its sins are sociable. A prejudice is a private thing, and even its tolerance is misanthropic. So it is with our existing divisions. They keep out of each other's way; the Tory paper and the Radical paper do not answer each other; they ignore each other. Genuine controversy, fair cut and thrust before a common audience, has become in our special epoch very rare. For the sincere controversialist is above all things a good listener. The really burning enthusiast never interrupts; he listens to the enemy's arguments as eagerly as a spy would listen to the enemy's arrangements. But if you attempt an actual argument with a modern paper of opposite politics, you will find that no medium is admitted between violence and evasion. You will have no answer except slanging or silence. A modern editor must not have that eager ear that goes with the honest tongue. He may be deaf and silent; and that is called dignity. Or he may be deaf and noisy; and that is called slashing journalism. In neither case is there any controversy; for the whole object of modern party combatants is to charge out of earshot.

The only logical cure for all this is the assertion of a human ideal. In dealing with this, I will try to be as little transcendental as is consistent with reason; it is enough to say that unless we have some doctrine of a divine man, all abuses may be excused, since evolution may turn them into uses. It will be easy for the scientific plutocrat to maintain that humanity will adapt itself to any conditions which we now consider evil. The old tyrants invoked the past; the new tyrants will invoke the future evolution has produced the snail and the owl; evolution can produce a workman who wants no more space than a snail, and no more light than an owl. The employer need not mind sending a Kaffir to work underground; he will soon become an underground animal, like a mole. He need not mind sending a diver to hold his breath in the deep seas; he will soon be a deep-sea animal. Men need not trouble to alter conditions, conditions will so soon alter men. The head can be beaten small enough to fit the hat. Do not knock the fetters off the slave; knock the slave until he forgets the fetters. To all this plausible modern argument for oppression, the only adequate answer is, that there is a permanent human ideal that must not be either confused or destroyed. The most important man on earth is the perfect man who is not there. The Christian religion has specially uttered the ultimate sanity of Man, says Scripture, who shall judge the incarnate and human truth. Our lives and laws are not judged by divine superiority, but simply by human perfection. It is man, says Aristotle, who is the measure. It is the Son of Man, says Scripture, who shall judge the quick and the dead.

Doctrine, therefore, does not cause dissensions; rather a doctrine alone can cure our dissensions. It is necessary to ask, however, roughly, what abstract and ideal shape in state or family would fulfil the human hunger; and this apart from whether we can completely obtain it or not. But when we come to ask what is the need of normal men, what is the desire of all nations, what is the ideal house, or road, or rule, or republic, or king, or priesthood, then we are confronted with a strange and irritating difficulty peculiar to the present time; and we must call a temporary halt and examine that obstacle.

IV. THE FEAR OF THE PAST

The last few decades have been marked by a special cultivation of the romance of the future. We seem to have made up our minds to misunderstand what has happened; and we turn, with a sort of relief, to stating what will happen—which is (apparently) much easier. The modern man no longer presents the memoirs of his great grandfather; but is engaged in writing a detailed and authoritative biography of his great-grandson. Instead of trembling before the specters of the dead, we shudder abjectly under the shadow of the babe unborn. This spirit is apparent everywhere, even to the creation of a form of futurist romance. Sir Walter Scott stands at the dawn of the nineteenth century for the novel of the past; Mr. H. G. Wells stands at the dawn of the twentieth century for the novel of the future. The old story, we know, was supposed to begin: "Late on a winter's evening two horsemen might have been seen—." The new story has to begin: "Late on a winter's evening two aviators will be seen—." The movement is not without its elements of charm; there is something spirited, if eccentric, in the sight of so many people fighting over again the fights that have not yet happened; of people still glowing with the memory of tomorrow morning. A man in advance of the age is a familiar phrase enough. An age in advance of the age is really rather odd.

But when full allowance has been made for this harmless element of poetry and pretty human perversity in the thing, I shall not hesitate to maintain here that this cult of the future is not only a weakness but a cowardice of the age. It is the peculiar evil of this epoch that even its pugnacity is fundamentally frightened; and the Jingo is contemptible not because he is impudent, but because he is timid. The reason why modern armaments do not inflame the imagination like the arms and emblazonments of the Crusades is a reason quite apart from optical ugliness or beauty. Some battleships are as beautiful as the sea; and many Norman nosepieces were as ugly as Norman noses. The atmospheric ugliness that surrounds our scientific war is an emanation from that evil panic which is at the heart of it. The charge of the Crusades was a charge; it was charging towards God, the wild consolation of the braver. The charge of the modern armaments is not a charge at all. It is a rout, a retreat, a flight from the devil, who will catch the hindmost. It is impossible to imagine a mediaeval knight talking of longer and longer French lances, with precisely the quivering employed about larger and larger German ships The man who called the Blue Water School the "Blue Funk School" uttered a psychological truth which that school itself would scarcely essentially deny. Even the two-power standard, if it be a necessity, is in a sense a degrading necessity. Nothing has more alienated many magnanimous minds from Imperial enterprises than the fact that they are always exhibited as stealthy or sudden defenses against a world of cold rapacity and fear. The Boer War, for instance, was colored not so much by the creed that we were doing something right, as by the creed that Boers and Germans were probably doing something wrong; driving us (as it was said) to the sea. Mr. Chamberlain, I think, said that the war was a feather in his cap and so it was: a white feather.

Now this same primary panic that I feel in our rush towards patriotic armaments I feel also in our rush towards future visions of society. The modern mind is forced towards the future by a certain sense of fatigue, not unmixed with terror, with which it regards the past. It is propelled towards the coming time; it is, in the exact words of the popular phrase, knocked into the middle of next week. And the goad which drives it on thus eagerly is not an affectation for futurity Futurity does not exist, because it is still future. Rather it is a fear of the past; a fear not merely of the evil in the past, but of the good in the past also. The brain breaks down under the unbearable virtue of mankind. There have been so many flaming faiths that we cannot hold; so many harsh heroisms that we cannot imitate; so many great efforts of monumental building or of military glory which seem to us at once sublime and pathetic. The future is a refuge from the fierce competition of our forefathers. The older generation, not the younger, is knocking at our door. It is agreeable to escape, as Henley said, into the Street of By-and-Bye, where stands the Hostelry of Never. It is pleasant to play with children, especially unborn children. The future is a blank wall on which every man can write his own name as large as he likes; the past I find already covered with illegible scribbles, such as Plato, Isaiah, Shakespeare, Michael Angelo, Napoleon. I can make the future as narrow as myself; the past is obliged to be as broad and turbulent as humanity. And the upshot of this modern attitude is really this: that men invent new ideals because they dare not attempt old ideals. They look forward with enthusiasm, because they are afraid to look back.

Now in history there is no Revolution that is not a Restoration. Among the many things that leave me doubtful about the modern habit of fixing eyes on the future, none is stronger than this: that all the men in history who have really done anything with the future have had their eyes fixed upon the past. I need not mention the Renaissance, the very word proves my case. The originality of Michael Angelo and Shakespeare began with the digging up of old vases and manuscripts. The mildness of poets absolutely arose out of the mildness of antiquaries. So the great mediaeval revival was a memory of the Roman Empire. So the Reformation looked back to the Bible and Bible times. So the modern Catholic movement has looked back to patristic times. But that modern movement which many would count the most anarchic of all is in this sense the most conservative of all. Never was the past more venerated by men than it was by the French Revolutionists. They invoked the little republics of antiquity with the complete confidence of one who invokes the gods. The Sans-culottes believed (as their name might imply) in a return to simplicity. They believed most piously in a remote past; some might call it a mythical past. For some strange reason man must always thus plant his fruit trees in a graveyard. Man can only find life among the dead. Man is a misshapen monster, with his feet set forward and his face turned back. He can make the future luxuriant and gigantic, so long as he is thinking about the past. When he tries to think about the future itself, his mind diminishes to a pin point with imbecility, which some call Nirvana. To-morrow is the Gorgon; a man must only see it mirrored in the shining shield of yesterday. If he sees it directly he is turned to stone. This has been the fate of all those who have really seen fate and futurity as clear and inevitable. The Calvinists, with their perfect creed of predestination, were turned to stone. The modern sociological scientists (with their excruciating Eugenics) are turned to stone. The only difference is that the Puritans make dignified, and the Eugenists somewhat amusing, statues.

But there is one feature in the past which more than all the rest defies and depresses the moderns and drives them towards this featureless future. I mean the presence in the past of huge ideals, unfulfilled and sometimes abandoned. The sight of these splendid failures is melancholy to a restless and rather morbid generation; and they maintain a strange silence about them—sometimes amounting to an unscrupulous silence. They keep them entirely out of their newspapers and almost entirely out of their history books. For example, they will often tell you (in their praises of the coming age) that we are moving on towards a United States of Europe. But they carefully omit to tell you that we are moving away from a United States of Europe, that such a thing existed literally in Roman and essentially in mediaeval times. They never admit that the international hatreds (which they call barbaric) are really very recent, the mere breakdown of the ideal of the Holy Roman Empire. Or again, they will tell you that there is going to be a social revolution, a great rising of the poor against the rich; but they never rub it in that France made that magnificent attempt, unaided, and that we and all the world allowed it to be trampled out and forgotten. I say decisively that nothing is so marked in modern writing as the prediction of such ideals in the future combined with the ignoring of them in the past. Anyone can test this for himself. Read any thirty or forty pages of pamphlets advocating peace in Europe and see how many of them praise the old Popes or Emperors for keeping the peace in Europe. Read any armful of essays and poems in praise of social democracy, and see how many of them praise the old Jacobins who created democracy and died for it. These colossal ruins are to the modern only enormous eyesores. He looks back along the valley of the past and sees a perspective of splendid but unfinished cities. They are unfinished, not always through enmity or accident, but often through fickleness, mental fatigue, and the lust for alien philosophies. We have not only left undone those things that we ought to have done, but we have even left undone those things that we wanted to do

It is very currently suggested that the modern man is the heir of all the ages, that he has got the good out of these successive human experiments. I know not what to say in answer to this, except to ask the reader to look at the modern man, as I have just looked at the modern man—in the looking-glass. Is it really true that you and I are two starry towers built up of all the most towering visions of the past? Have we really fulfilled all the great historic ideals one after the other, from our naked ancestor who was brave enough to kill a mammoth with a stone knife, through the Greek citizen and the Christian saint to our own grandfather or great-grandfather, who may have been sabred by the Manchester Yeomanry or shot in the '48? Are we still strong enough to spear mammoths, but now tender enough to spare them? Does the cosmos contain any mammoth that we have either speared or spared? When we decline (in a marked manner) to fly the red flag and fire across a barricade like our grandfathers, are we really declining in deference to sociologists—or to soldiers? Have we indeed outstripped the warrior and passed the ascetical saint? I fear we only outstrip the warrior in the sense that we should probably run away from him. And if we have passed the saint, I fear we have passed him without bowing.

This is, first and foremost, what I mean by the narrowness of the new ideas, the limiting effect of the future. Our modern prophetic idealism is narrow because it has undergone a persistent process of elimination. We must ask for new things because we are not allowed to ask for old things. The whole position is based on this idea that we have got all the good that can be got out of the ideas of the past. But we have not got all the good out of them, perhaps at this moment not any of the good out of them. And the need here is a need of complete freedom for restoration as well as revolution.

We often read nowadays of the valor or audacity with which some rebel attacks a hoary tyranny or an antiquated superstition. There is not really any courage at all in attacking hoary or antiquated things, any more than in offering to fight one's grandmother. The really courageous man is he who defies tyrannies young as the morning and superstitions fresh as the first flowers. The only true free-thinker is he whose intellect is as much free from the future as from the past. He cares as little for what will be as for what has been; he cares only for what ought to be. And for my present purpose I specially insist on this abstract independence. If I am to discuss what is wrong, one of the first things that are wrong is this: the deep and silent modern assumption that past things have become impossible. There is one metaphor of which the moderns are very fond; they are always saying, "You can't put the clock back." The simple and obvious answer is "You can." A clock, being a piece of human construction, can be restored by the human finger to any figure or hour. In the same way society, being a piece of human construction, can be reconstructed upon any plan that has ever existed.

There is another proverb, "As you have made your bed, so you must lie on it"; which again is simply a lie. If I have made my bed uncomfortable, please God I will make it again. We could restore the Heptarchy or the stage coaches if we chose. It might take some time to do, and it might be very inadvisable to do it; but certainly it is not impossible as bringing back last Friday is impossible. This is, as I say, the first freedom that I claim: the freedom to restore. I claim a right to propose as a solution the old patriarchal system of a Highland clan, if that should seem to eliminate the largest number of evils. It certainly would eliminate some evils; for instance, the unnatural sense of obeying cold and harsh strangers, mere bureaucrats and policemen. I claim the right to propose the complete independence of the small Greek or Italian towns, a sovereign city of Brixton or Brompton, if that seems the best way out of our troubles. It would be a way out of some of our troubles; we could not have in a small state, for instance, those enormous illusions about men or measures which are nourished by the great national or international newspapers. You could not persuade a city state that Mr. Beit was an Englishman, or Mr. Dillon a desperado, any more than you could persuade a Hampshire Village that the village drunkard was a teetotaller or the village idiot a statesman. Nevertheless, I do not as a fact propose that the Browns and the Smiths should be collected under separate tartans. Nor do I even propose that Clapham should declare its independence. I merely declare my independence. I merely claim my choice of all the tools in the universe; and I shall not admit that any of them are blunted merely because they have been used.

V. THE UNFINISHED TEMPLE

The task of modern idealists indeed is made much too easy for them by the fact that they are always taught that if a thing has been defeated it has been disproved. Logically, the case is quite clearly the other way. The lost causes are exactly those which might have saved the world. If a man says that the Young Pretender would have made England happy, it is hard to answer him. If anyone says that the Georges made England happy, I hope we all know what to answer. That which was prevented is always impregnable; and the only perfect King of England was he who was smothered. Exactly be cause Jacobitism failed we cannot call it a failure. Precisely because the Commune collapsed as a rebellion we cannot say that it collapsed as a system. But such outbursts were brief or incidental. Few people realize how many of the largest efforts, the facts that will fill history, were frustrated in their full design and come down to us as gigantic cripples. I have only space to allude to the two largest facts of modern history: the Catholic Church and that modern growth rooted in the French Revolution.

When four knights scattered the blood and brains of St. Thomas of Canterbury, it was not only a sign of anger but of a sort of black admiration. They wished for his blood, but they wished even more for his brains. Such a blow will remain forever unintelligible unless we realise what the brains of St. Thomas were thinking about just before they were distributed over the floor. They were thinking about the great mediaeval conception that the church is the judge of the world. Becket objected to a priest being tried even by the Lord Chief Justice. And his reason was simple: because the Lord Chief Justice was being tried by the priest. The judiciary was itself sub judice. The kings were themselves in the dock. The idea was to create an invisible kingdom, without armies or prisons, but with complete freedom to condemn publicly all the kingdoms of the earth. Whether such a supreme church would have cured society we cannot affirm definitely; because the church never was a supreme church. We only know that in England at any rate the princes conquered the saints. What the world wanted we see before us; and some of us call it a failure. But we cannot call what the church wanted a failure, simply because the church failed. Tracy struck a little too soon. England had not yet made the great Protestant discovery that the king can do no wrong. The king was whipped in the cathedral; a performance which I recommend to those who regret the unpopularity of church-going. But the discovery was made; and Henry VIII scattered Becket's bones as easily as Tracy had scattered his brains.

Of course, I mean that Catholicism was not tried; plenty of Catholics were tried, and found guilty. My point is that the world did not tire of the church's ideal, but of its reality. Monasteries were impugned not for the chastity of monks, but for the unchastity of monks. Christianity was unpopular not because of the humility, but of the arrogance of Christians. Certainly, if the church failed it was largely through the churchmen. But at the same time hostile elements had certainly begun to end it long before it could have done its work. In the nature of things it needed a common scheme of life and thought in Europe. Yet the mediaeval system began to be broken to pieces intellectually, long before it showed the slightest hint of falling to pieces morally. The huge early heresies, like the Albigenses, had not the faintest excuse in moral superiority. And it is actually true that the Reformation began to tear Europe apart before the Catholic Church had had time to pull it together. The Prussians, for instance, were not converted to Christianity at all until quite close to the Reformation. The poor creatures hardly had time to become Catholics before they were told to become Protestants. This explains a great deal of their subsequent conduct. But I have only taken this as the first and most evident case of the general truth: that the great ideals of the past failed not by being outlived (which must mean over-lived), but by not being lived enough. Mankind has not passed through the Middle Ages. Rather mankind has retreated from the Middle Ages in reaction and rout. The Christian ideal has not been tried and found wanting. It has been found difficult; and left untried.

It is, of course, the same in the case of the French Revolution. A great part of our present perplexity arises from the fact that the French Revolution has half succeeded and half failed. In one sense, Valmy was the decisive battle of the West, and in another Trafalgar. We have, indeed, destroyed the largest territorial tyrannies, and created a free peasantry in almost all Christian countries except England; of which we shall say more anon. But representative government, the one universal relic, is a very poor fragment of the full republican idea. The theory of the French Revolution presupposed two things in government, things which it achieved at the time, but which it has certainly not bequeathed to its imitators in England, Germany, and America. The first of these was the idea of honorable poverty; that a statesman must be something of a stoic; the second was the idea of extreme publicity. Many imaginative English writers, including Carlyle, seem quite unable to imagine how it was that men like Robespierre and Marat were ardently admired. The best answer is that they were admired for being poor—poor when they might have been rich.

No one will pretend that this ideal exists at all in the haute politique of this country. Our national claim to political incorruptibility is actually based on exactly the opposite argument; it is based on the theory that wealthy men in assured positions will have no temptation to financial trickery. Whether the history of the English aristocracy, from the spoliation of the monasteries to the annexation of the mines, entirely supports this theory I am not now inquiring; but certainly it is our theory, that wealth will be a protection against political corruption. The English statesman is bribed not to be bribed. He is born with a silver spoon in his mouth, so that he may never afterwards be found with the silver spoons in his pocket. So strong is our faith in this protection by plutocracy, that we are more and more trusting our empire in the hands of families which inherit wealth without either blood or manners. Some of our political houses are parvenue by pedigree; they hand on vulgarity like a coat of-arms. In the case of many a modern statesman to say that he is born with a silver spoon in his mouth, is at once inadequate and excessive. He is born with a silver knife in his mouth. But all this only illustrates the English theory that poverty is perilous for a politician.

It will be the same if we compare the conditions that have come about with the Revolution legend touching publicity. The old democratic doctrine was that the more light that was let in to all departments of State, the easier it was for a righteous indignation to move promptly against wrong. In other words, monarchs were to live in glass houses, that mobs might throw stones. Again, no admirer of existing English politics (if there is any admirer of existing English politics) will really pretend that this ideal of publicity is exhausted, or even attempted. Obviously public life grows more private every day. The French have, indeed, continued the tradition of revealing secrets and making scandals; hence they are more flagrant and palpable than we, not in sin but in the confession of sin. The first trial of Dreyfus might have happened in England; it is exactly the second trial that would have been legally impossible. But, indeed, if we wish to realise how far we fall short of the original republican outline, the sharpest way to test it is to note how far we fall short even of the republican element in the older regime. Not only are we less democratic than Danton and Condorcet, but we are in many ways less democratic than Choiseul and Marie Antoinette. The richest nobles before the revolt were needy middle-class people compared with our Rothschilds and Roseberys. And in the matter of publicity the old French monarchy was infinitely more democratic than any of the monarchies of today. Practically anybody who chose could walk into the palace and see the king playing with his children, or paring his nails. The people possessed the monarch, as the people possess Primrose Hill; that is, they cannot move it, but they can sprawl all over it. The old French monarchy was founded on the excellent principle that a cat may look at a king. But nowadays a cat may not look at a king; unless it is a very tame cat. Even where the press is free for criticism it is only used for adulation. The substantial difference comes to something uncommonly like this: Eighteenth century tyranny meant that you could say "The K__ of Br__rd is a profligate." Twentieth century liberty really means that you are allowed to say "The King of Brentford is a model family man."

But we have delayed the main argument too long for the parenthetical purpose of showing that the great democratic dream, like the great mediaeval dream, has in a strict and practical sense been a dream unfulfilled. Whatever is the matter with modern England it is not that we have carried out too literally, or achieved with disappointing completeness, either the Catholicism of Becket or the equality of Marat. Now I have taken these two cases merely because they are typical of ten thousand other cases; the world is full of these unfulfilled ideas, these uncompleted temples. History does not consist of completed and crumbling ruins; rather it consists of half-built villas abandoned by a bankrupt-builder. This world is more like an unfinished suburb than a deserted cemetery.

VI. THE ENEMIES OF PROPERTY

But it is for this especial reason that such an explanation is necessary on the very threshold of the definition of ideals. For owing to that historic fallacy with which I have just dealt, numbers of readers will expect me, when I propound an ideal, to propound a new ideal. Now I have no notion at all of propounding a new ideal. There is no new ideal imaginable by the madness of modern sophists, which will be anything like so startling as fulfilling any one of the old ones. On the day that any copybook maxim is carried out there will be something like an earthquake on the earth. There is only one thing new that can be done under the sun; and that is to look at the sun. If you attempt it on a blue day in June, you will know why men do not look straight at their ideals. There is only one really startling thing to be done with the ideal, and that is to do it. It is to face the flaming logical fact, and its frightful consequences. Christ knew that it would be a more stunning thunderbolt to fulfil the law than to destroy it. It is true of both the cases I have quoted, and of every case. The pagans had always adored purity: Athena, Artemis, Vesta. It was when the virgin martyrs began defiantly to practice purity that they rent them with wild beasts, and rolled them on red-hot coals. The world had always loved the notion of the poor man uppermost; it can be proved by every legend from Cinderella to Whittington, by every poem from the Magnificat to the Marseillaise. The kings went mad against France not because she idealized this ideal, but because she realized it. Joseph of Austria and Catherine of Russia quite agreed that the people should rule; what horrified them was that the people did. The French Revolution, therefore, is the type of all true revolutions, because its ideal is as old as the Old Adam, but its fulfilment almost as fresh, as miraculous, and as new as the New Jerusalem.

But in the modern world we are primarily confronted with the extraordinary spectacle of people turning to new ideals because they have not tried the old. Men have not got tired of Christianity; they have never found enough Christianity to get tired of. Men have never wearied of political justice; they have wearied of waiting for it.

Now, for the purpose of this book, I propose to take only one of these old ideals; but one that is perhaps the oldest. I take the principle of domesticity: the ideal house; the happy family, the holy family of history. For the moment it is only necessary to remark that it is like the church and like the republic, now chiefly assailed by those who have never known it, or by those who have failed to fulfil it. Numberless modern women have rebelled against domesticity in theory because they have never known it in practice. Hosts of the poor are driven to the workhouse without ever having known the house. Generally speaking, the cultured class is shrieking to be let out of the decent home, just as the working class is shouting to be let into it.

Now if we take this house or home as a test, we may very generally lay the simple spiritual foundations of the idea. God is that which can make something out of nothing. Man (it may truly be said) is that which can make something out of anything. In other words, while the joy of God be unlimited creation, the special joy of man is limited creation, the combination of creation with limits. Man's pleasure, therefore, is to possess conditions, but also to be partly possessed by them; to be half-controlled by the flute he plays or by the field he digs. The excitement is to get the utmost out of given conditions; the conditions will stretch, but not indefinitely. A man can write an immortal sonnet on an old envelope, or hack a hero out of a lump of rock. But hacking a sonnet out of a rock would be a laborious business, and making a hero out of an envelope is almost out of the sphere of practical politics. This fruitful strife with limitations, when it concerns some airy entertainment of an educated class, goes by the name of Art. But the mass of men have neither time nor aptitude for the invention of invisible or abstract beauty. For the mass of men the idea of artistic creation can only be expressed by an idea unpopular in present discussions—the idea of property. The average man cannot cut clay into the shape of a man; but he can cut earth into the shape of a garden; and though he arranges it with red geraniums and blue potatoes in alternate straight lines, he is still an artist; because he has chosen. The average man cannot paint the sunset whose colors be admires; but he can paint his own house with what color he chooses, and though he paints it pea green with pink spots, he is still an artist; because that is his choice. Property is merely the art of the democracy. It means that every man should have something that he can shape in his own image, as he is shaped in the image of heaven. But because he is not God, but only a graven image of God, his self-expression must deal with limits; properly with limits that are strict and even small.

I am well aware that the word "property" has been defied in our time by the corruption of the great capitalists. One would think, to hear people talk, that the Rothchilds and the Rockefellers were on the side of property. But obviously they are the enemies of property; because they are enemies of their own limitations. They do not want their own land; but other people's. When they remove their neighbor's landmark, they also remove their own. A man who loves a little triangular field ought to love it because it is triangular; anyone who destroys the shape, by giving him more land, is a thief who has stolen a triangle. A man with the true poetry of possession wishes to see the wall where his garden meets Smith's garden; the hedge where his farm touches Brown's. He cannot see the shape of his own land unless he sees the edges of his neighbor's. It is the negation of property that the Duke of Sutherland should have all the farms in one estate; just as it would be the negation of marriage if he had all our wives in one harem.

VII. THE FREE FAMILY

As I have said, I propose to take only one central instance; I will take the institution called the private house or home; the shell and organ of the family. We will consider cosmic and political tendencies simply as they strike that ancient and unique roof. Very few words will suffice for all I have to say about the family itself. I leave alone the speculations about its animal origin and the details of its social reconstruction; I am concerned only with its palpable omnipresence. It is a necessity far mankind; it is (if you like to put it so) a trap for mankind. Only by the hypocritical ignoring of a huge fact can any one contrive to talk of "free love"; as if love were an episode like lighting a cigarette, or whistling a tune. Suppose whenever a man lit a cigarette, a towering genie arose from the rings of smoke and followed him everywhere as a huge slave. Suppose whenever a man whistled a tune he "drew an angel down" and had to walk about forever with a seraph on a string. These catastrophic images are but faint parallels to the earthquake consequences that Nature has attached to sex; and it is perfectly plain at the beginning that a man cannot be a free lover; he is either a traitor or a tied man. The second element that creates the family is that its consequences, though colossal, are gradual; the cigarette produces a baby giant, the song only an infant seraph. Thence arises the necessity for some prolonged system of co-operation; and thence arises the family in its full educational sense.

It may be said that this institution of the home is the one anarchist institution. That is to say, it is older than law, and stands outside the State. By its nature it is refreshed or corrupted by indefinable forces of custom or kinship. This is not to be understood as meaning that the State has no authority over families; that State authority is invoked and ought to be invoked in many abnormal cases. But in most normal cases of family joys and sorrows, the State has no mode of entry. It is not so much that the law should not interfere, as that the law cannot. Just as there are fields too far off for law, so there are fields too near; as a man may see the North Pole before he sees his own backbone. Small and near matters escape control at least as much as vast and remote ones; and the real pains and pleasures of the family form a strong instance of this. If a baby cries for the moon, the policeman cannot procure the moon—but neither can he stop the baby. Creatures so close to each other as husband and wife, or a mother and children, have powers of making each other happy or miserable with which no public coercion can deal. If a marriage could be dissolved every morning it would not give back his night's rest to a man kept awake by a curtain lecture; and what is the good of giving a man a lot of power where he only wants a little peace? The child must depend on the most imperfect mother; the mother may be devoted to the most unworthy children; in such relations legal revenges are vain. Even in the abnormal cases where the law may operate, this difficulty is constantly found; as many a bewildered magistrate knows. He has to save children from starvation by taking away their breadwinner. And he often has to break a wife's heart because her husband has already broken her head. The State has no tool delicate enough to deracinate the rooted habits and tangled affections of the family; the two sexes, whether happy or unhappy, are glued together too tightly for us to get the blade of a legal penknife in between them. The man and the woman are one flesh—yes, even when they are not one spirit. Man is a quadruped. Upon this ancient and anarchic intimacy, types of government have little or no effect; it is happy or unhappy, by its own sexual wholesomeness and genial habit, under the republic of Switzerland or the despotism of Siam. Even a republic in Siam would not have done much towards freeing the Siamese Twins.

The problem is not in marriage, but in sex; and would be felt under the freest concubinage. Nevertheless, the overwhelming mass of mankind has not believed in freedom in this matter, but rather in a more or less lasting tie. Tribes and civilizations differ about the occasions on which we may loosen the bond, but they all agree that there is a bond to be loosened, not a mere universal detachment. For the purposes of this book I am not concerned to discuss that mystical view of marriage in which I myself believe: the great European tradition which has made marriage a sacrament. It is enough to say here that heathen and Christian alike have regarded marriage as a tie; a thing not normally to be sundered. Briefly, this human belief in a sexual bond rests on a principle of which the modern mind has made a very inadequate study. It is, perhaps, most nearly paralleled by the principle of the second wind in walking.

The principle is this: that in everything worth having, even in every pleasure, there is a point of pain or tedium that must be survived, so that the pleasure may revive and endure. The joy of battle comes after the first fear of death; the joy of reading Virgil comes after the bore of learning him; the glow of the sea-bather comes after the icy shock of the sea bath; and the success of the marriage comes after the failure of the honeymoon. All human vows, laws, and contracts are so many ways of surviving with success this breaking point, this instant of potential surrender.

In everything on this earth that is worth doing, there is a stage when no one would do it, except for necessity or honor. It is then that the Institution upholds a man and helps him on to the firmer ground ahead. Whether this solid fact of human nature is sufficient to justify the sublime dedication of Christian marriage is quite an other matter, it is amply sufficient to justify the general human feeling of marriage as a fixed thing, dissolution of which is a fault or, at least, an ignominy. The essential element is not so much duration as security. Two people must be tied together in order to do themselves justice; for twenty minutes at a dance, or for twenty years in a marriage In both cases the point is, that if a man is bored in the first five minutes he must go on and force himself to be happy. Coercion is a kind of encouragement; and anarchy (or what some call liberty) is essentially oppressive, because it is essentially discouraging. If we all floated in the air like bubbles, free to drift anywhere at any instant, the practical result would be that no one would have the courage to begin a conversation. It would be so embarrassing to start a sentence in a friendly whisper, and then have to shout the last half of it because the other party was floating away into the free and formless ether. The two must hold each other to do justice to each other. If Americans can be divorced for "incompatibility of temper" I cannot conceive why they are not all divorced. I have known many happy marriages, but never a compatible one. The whole aim of marriage is to fight through and survive the instant when incompatibility becomes unquestionable. For a man and a woman, as such, are incompatible.

VIII. THE WILDNESS OF DOMESTICITY

In the course of this crude study we shall have to touch on what is called the problem of poverty, especially the dehumanized poverty of modern industrialism. But in this primary matter of the ideal the difficulty is not the problem of poverty, but the problem of wealth. It is the special psychology of leisure and luxury that falsifies life. Some experience of modern movements of the sort called "advanced" has led me to the conviction that they generally repose upon some experience peculiar to the rich. It is so with that fallacy of free love of which I have already spoken; the idea of sexuality as a string of episodes. That implies a long holiday in which to get tired of one woman, and a motor car in which to wander looking for others; it also implies money for maintenances. An omnibus conductor has hardly time to love his own wife, let alone other people's. And the success with which nuptial estrangements are depicted in modern "problem plays" is due to the fact that there is only one thing that a drama cannot depict—that is a hard day's work. I could give many other instances of this plutocratic assumption behind progressive fads. For instance, there is a plutocratic assumption behind the phrase "Why should woman be economically dependent upon man?" The answer is that among poor and practical people she isn't; except in the sense in which he is dependent upon her. A hunter has to tear his clothes; there must be somebody to mend them. A fisher has to catch fish; there must be somebody to cook them. It is surely quite clear that this modern notion that woman is a mere "pretty clinging parasite," "a plaything," etc., arose through the somber contemplation of some rich banking family, in which the banker, at least, went to the city and pretended to do something, while the banker's wife went to the Park and did not pretend to do anything at all. A poor man and his wife are a business partnership. If one partner in a firm of publishers interviews the authors while the other interviews the clerks, is one of them economically dependent? Was Hodder a pretty parasite clinging to Stoughton? Was Marshall a mere plaything for Snelgrove?

But of all the modern notions generated by mere wealth the worst is this: the notion that domesticity is dull and tame. Inside the home (they say) is dead decorum and routine; outside is adventure and variety. This is indeed a rich man's opinion. The rich man knows that his own house moves on vast and soundless wheels of wealth, is run by regiments of servants, by a swift and silent ritual. On the other hand, every sort of vagabondage of romance is open to him in the streets outside. He has plenty of money and can afford to be a tramp. His wildest adventure will end in a restaurant, while the yokel's tamest adventure may end in a police-court. If he smashes a window he can pay for it; if he smashes a man he can pension him. He can (like the millionaire in the story) buy an hotel to get a glass of gin. And because he, the luxurious man, dictates the tone of nearly all "advanced" and "progressive" thought, we have almost forgotten what a home really means to the overwhelming millions of mankind.

For the truth is, that to the moderately poor the home is the only place of liberty. Nay, it is the only place of anarchy. It is the only spot on the earth where a man can alter arrangements suddenly, make an experiment or indulge in a whim. Everywhere else he goes he must accept the strict rules of the shop, inn, club, or museum that he happens to enter. He can eat his meals on the floor in his own house if he likes. I often do it myself; it gives a curious, childish, poetic, picnic feeling. There would be considerable trouble if I tried to do it in an A.B.C. tea-shop. A man can wear a dressing gown and slippers in his house; while I am sure that this would not be permitted at the Savoy, though I never actually tested the point. If you go to a restaurant you must drink some of the wines on the wine list, all of them if you insist, but certainly some of them. But if you have a house and garden you can try to make hollyhock tea or convolvulus wine if you like. For a plain, hard-working man the home is not the one tame place in the world of adventure. It is the one wild place in the world of rules and set tasks. The home is the one place where he can put the carpet on the ceiling or the slates on the floor if he wants to. When a man spends every night staggering from bar to bar or from music-hall to music-hall, we say that he is living an irregular life. But he is not; he is living a highly regular life, under the dull, and often oppressive, laws of such places. Some times he is not allowed even to sit down in the bars; and frequently he is not allowed to sing in the music-halls. Hotels may be defined as places where you are forced to dress; and theaters may be defined as places where you are forbidden to smoke. A man can only picnic at home.

Now I take, as I have said, this small human omnipotence, this possession of a definite cell or chamber of liberty, as the working model for the present inquiry. Whether we can give every English man a free home of his own or not, at least we should desire it; and he desires it. For the moment we speak of what he wants, not of what he expects to get. He wants, for instance, a separate house; he does not want a semi-detached house. He may be forced in the commercial race to share one wall with another man. Similarly he might be forced in a three-legged race to share one leg with another man; but it is not so that he pictures himself in his dreams of elegance and liberty. Again, he does not desire a flat. He can eat and sleep and praise God in a flat; he can eat and sleep and praise God in a railway train. But a railway train is not a house, because it is a house on wheels. And a flat is not a house, because it is a house on stilts. An idea of earthy contact and foundation, as well as an idea of separation and independence, is a part of this instructive human picture.

I take, then, this one institution as a test. As every normal man desires a woman, and children born of a woman, every normal man desires a house of his own to put them into. He does not merely want a roof above him and a chair below him; he wants an objective and visible kingdom; a fire at which he can cook what food he likes, a door he can open to what friends he chooses. This is the normal appetite of men; I do not say there are not exceptions. There may be saints above the need and philanthropists below it. Opalstein, now he is a duke, may have got used to more than this; and when he was a convict may have got used to less. But the normality of the thing is enormous. To give nearly everybody ordinary houses would please nearly everybody; that is what I assert without apology. Now in modern England (as you eagerly point out) it is very difficult to give nearly everybody houses. Quite so; I merely set up the desideratum; and ask the reader to leave it standing there while he turns with me to a consideration of what really happens in the social wars of our time.

IX. HISTORY OF HUDGE AND GUDGE

There is, let us say, a certain filthy rookery in Hoxton, dripping with disease and honeycombed with crime and promiscuity. There are, let us say, two noble and courageous young men, of pure intentions and (if you prefer it) noble birth; let us call them Hudge and Gudge. Hudge, let us say, is of a bustling sort; he points out that the people must at all costs be got out of this den; he subscribes and collects money, but he finds (despite the large financial interests of the Hudges) that the thing will have to be done on the cheap if it is to be done on the spot. He therefore, runs up a row of tall bare tenements like beehives; and soon has all the poor people bundled into their little brick cells, which are certainly better than their old quarters, in so far as they are weather proof, well ventilated and supplied with clean water. But Gudge has a more delicate nature. He feels a nameless something lacking in the little brick boxes; he raises numberless objections; he even assails the celebrated Hudge Report, with the Gudge Minority Report; and by the end of a year or so has come to telling Hudge heatedly that the people were much happier where they were before. As the people preserve in both places precisely the same air of dazed amiability, it is very difficult to find out which is right. But at least one might safely say that no people ever liked stench or starvation as such, but only some peculiar pleasures en tangled with them. Not so feels the sensitive Gudge. Long before the final quarrel (Hudge v. Gudge and Another), Gudge has succeeded in persuading himself that slums and stinks are really very nice things; that the habit of sleeping fourteen in a room is what has made our England great; and that the smell of open drains is absolutely essential to the rearing of a viking breed.

But, meanwhile, has there been no degeneration in Hudge? Alas, I fear there has. Those maniacally ugly buildings which he originally put up as unpretentious sheds barely to shelter human life, grow every day more and more lovely to his deluded eye. Things he would never have dreamed of defending, except as crude necessities, things like common kitchens or infamous asbestos stoves, begin to shine quite sacredly before him, merely because they reflect the wrath of Gudge. He maintains, with the aid of eager little books by Socialists, that man is really happier in a hive than in a house. The practical difficulty of keeping total strangers out of your bedroom he describes as Brotherhood; and the necessity for climbing twenty-three flights of cold stone stairs, I dare say he calls Effort. The net result of their philanthropic adventure is this: that one has come to defending indefensible slums and still more indefensible slum-landlords, while the other has come to treating as divine the sheds and pipes which he only meant as desperate. Gudge is now a corrupt and apoplectic old Tory in the Carlton Club; if you mention poverty to him he roars at you in a thick, hoarse voice something that is conjectured to be "Do 'em good!" Nor is Hudge more happy; for he is a lean vegetarian with a gray, pointed beard and an unnaturally easy smile, who goes about telling everybody that at last we shall all sleep in one universal bedroom; and he lives in a Garden City, like one forgotten of God.

Such is the lamentable history of Hudge and Gudge; which I merely introduce as a type of an endless and exasperating misunderstanding which is always occurring in modern England. To get men out of a rookery men are put into a tenement; and at the beginning the healthy human soul loathes them both. A man's first desire is to get away as far as possible from the rookery, even should his mad course lead him to a model dwelling. The second desire is, naturally, to get away from the model dwelling, even if it should lead a man back to the rookery. But I am neither a Hudgian nor a Gudgian; and I think the mistakes of these two famous and fascinating persons arose from one simple fact. They arose from the fact that neither Hudge nor Gudge had ever thought for an instant what sort of house a man might probably like for himself. In short, they did not begin with the ideal; and, therefore, were not practical politicians.

We may now return to the purpose of our awkward parenthesis about the praise of the future and the failures of the past. A house of his own being the obvious ideal for every man, we may now ask (taking this need as typical of all such needs) why he hasn't got it; and whether it is in any philosophical sense his own fault. Now, I think that in some philosophical sense it is his own fault, I think in a yet more philosophical sense it is the fault of his philosophy. And this is what I have now to attempt to explain.

Burke, a fine rhetorician, who rarely faced realities, said, I think, that an Englishman's house is his castle. This is honestly entertaining; for as it happens the Englishman is almost the only man in Europe whose house is not his castle. Nearly everywhere else exists the assumption of peasant proprietorship; that a poor man may be a landlord, though he is only lord of his own land. Making the landlord and the tenant the same person has certain trivial advantages, as that the tenant pays no rent, while the landlord does a little work. But I am not concerned with the defense of small proprietorship, but merely with the fact that it exists almost everywhere except in England. It is also true, however, that this estate of small possession is attacked everywhere today; it has never existed among ourselves, and it may be destroyed among our neighbors. We have, therefore, to ask ourselves what it is in human affairs generally, and in this domestic ideal in particular, that has really ruined the natural human creation, especially in this country.

Man has always lost his way. He has been a tramp ever since Eden; but he always knew, or thought he knew, what he was looking for. Every man has a house somewhere in the elaborate cosmos; his house waits for him waist deep in slow Norfolk rivers or sunning itself upon Sussex downs. Man has always been looking for that home which is the subject matter of this book. But in the bleak and blinding hail of skepticism to which he has been now so long subjected, he has begun for the first time to be chilled, not merely in his hopes, but in his desires. For the first time in history he begins really to doubt the object of his wanderings on the earth. He has always lost his way; but now he has lost his address.

Under the pressure of certain upper-class philosophies (or in other words, under the pressure of Hudge and Gudge) the average man has really become bewildered about the goal of his efforts; and his efforts, therefore, grow feebler and feebler. His simple notion of having a home of his own is derided as bourgeois, as sentimental, or as despicably Christian. Under various verbal forms he is recommended to go on to the streets—which is called Individualism; or to the work-house—which is called Collectivism. We shall consider this process somewhat more carefully in a moment. But it may be said here that Hudge and Gudge, or the governing class generally, will never fail for lack of some modern phrase to cover their ancient predominance. The great lords will refuse the English peasant his three acres and a cow on advanced grounds, if they cannot refuse it longer on reactionary grounds. They will deny him the three acres on grounds of State Ownership. They will forbid him the cow on grounds of humanitarianism.

And this brings us to the ultimate analysis of this singular influence that has prevented doctrinal demands by the English people. There are, I believe, some who still deny that England is governed by an oligarchy. It is quite enough for me to know that a man might have gone to sleep some thirty years ago over the day's newspaper and woke up last week over the later newspaper, and fancied he was reading about the same people. In one paper he would have found a Lord Robert Cecil, a Mr. Gladstone, a Mr. Lyttleton, a Churchill, a Chamberlain, a Trevelyan, an Acland. In the other paper he would find a Lord Robert Cecil, a Mr. Gladstone, a Mr. Lyttleton, a Churchill, a Chamberlain, a Trevelyan, an Acland. If this is not being governed by families I cannot imagine what it is. I suppose it is being governed by extraordinary democratic coincidences.

X. OPPRESSION BY OPTIMISM

But we are not here concerned with the nature and existence of the aristocracy, but with the origin of its peculiar power, why is it the last of the true oligarchies of Europe; and why does there seem no very immediate prospect of our seeing the end of it? The explanation is simple though it remains strangely unnoticed. The friends of aristocracy often praise it for preserving ancient and gracious traditions. The enemies of aristocracy often blame it for clinging to cruel or antiquated customs. Both its enemies and its friends are wrong. Generally speaking the aristocracy does not preserve either good or bad traditions; it does not preserve anything except game. Who would dream of looking among aristocrats anywhere for an old custom? One might as well look for an old costume! The god of the aristocrats is not tradition, but fashion, which is the opposite of tradition. If you wanted to find an old-world Norwegian head-dress, would you look for it in the Scandinavian Smart Set? No; the aristocrats never have customs; at the best they have habits, like the animals. Only the mob has customs.

The real power of the English aristocrats has lain in exactly the opposite of tradition. The simple key to the power of our upper classes is this: that they have always kept carefully on the side of what is called Progress. They have always been up to date, and this comes quite easy to an aristocracy. For the aristocracy are the supreme instances of that frame of mind of which we spoke just now. Novelty is to them a luxury verging on a necessity. They, above all, are so bored with the past and with the present, that they gape, with a horrible hunger, for the future.

But whatever else the great lords forgot they never forgot that it was their business to stand for the new things, for whatever was being most talked about among university dons or fussy financiers. Thus they were on the side of the Reformation against the Church, of the Whigs against the Stuarts, of the Baconian science against the old philosophy, of the manufacturing system against the operatives, and (to-day) of the increased power of the State against the old-fashioned individualists. In short, the rich are always modern; it is their business. But the immediate effect of this fact upon the question we are studying is somewhat singular.

In each of the separate holes or quandaries in which the ordinary Englishman has been placed, he has been told that his situation is, for some particular reason, all for the best. He woke up one fine morning and discovered that the public things, which for eight hundred years he had used at once as inns and sanctuaries, had all been suddenly and savagely abolished, to increase the private wealth of about six or seven men. One would think he might have been annoyed at that; in many places he was, and was put down by the soldiery. But it was not merely the army that kept him quiet. He was kept quiet by the sages as well as the soldiers; the six or seven men who took away the inns of the poor told him that they were not doing it for themselves, but for the religion of the future, the great dawn of Protestantism and truth. So whenever a seventeenth century noble was caught pulling down a peasant's fence and stealing his field, the noble pointed excitedly at the face of Charles I or James II (which at that moment, perhaps, wore a cross expression) and thus diverted the simple peasant's attention. The great Puritan lords created the Commonwealth, and destroyed the common land. They saved their poorer countrymen from the disgrace of paying Ship Money, by taking from them the plow money and spade money which they were doubtless too weak to guard. A fine old English rhyme has immortalized this easy aristocratic habit—

You prosecute the man or woman Who steals the goose from off the common, But leave the larger felon loose Who steals the common from the goose.

But here, as in the case of the monasteries, we confront the strange problem of submission. If they stole the common from the goose, one can only say that he was a great goose to stand it. The truth is that they reasoned with the goose; they explained to him that all this was needed to get the Stuart fox over seas. So in the nineteenth century the great nobles who became mine-owners and railway directors earnestly assured everybody that they did not do this from preference, but owing to a newly discovered Economic Law. So the prosperous politicians of our own generation introduce bills to prevent poor mothers from going about with their own babies; or they calmly forbid their tenants to drink beer in public inns. But this insolence is not (as you would suppose) howled at by everybody as outrageous feudalism. It is gently rebuked as Socialism. For an aristocracy is always progressive; it is a form of going the pace. Their parties grow later and later at night; for they are trying to live to-morrow.

XI. THE HOMELESSNESS OF JONES

Thus the Future of which we spoke at the beginning has (in England at least) always been the ally of tyranny. The ordinary Englishman has been duped out of his old possessions, such as they were, and always in the name of progress. The destroyers of the abbeys took away his bread and gave him a stone, assuring him that it was a precious stone, the white pebble of the Lord's elect. They took away his maypole and his original rural life and promised him instead the Golden Age of Peace and Commerce inaugurated at the Crystal Palace. And now they are taking away the little that remains of his dignity as a householder and the head of a family, promising him instead Utopias which are called (appropriately enough) "Anticipations" or "News from Nowhere." We come back, in fact, to the main feature which has already been mentioned. The past is communal: the future must be individualist. In the past are all the evils of democracy, variety and violence and doubt, but the future is pure despotism, for the future is pure caprice. Yesterday, I know I was a human fool, but to-morrow I can easily be the Superman.

The modern Englishman, however, is like a man who should be perpetually kept out, for one reason after another, from the house in which he had meant his married life to begin. This man (Jones let us call him) has always desired the divinely ordinary things; he has married for love, he has chosen or built a small house that fits like a coat; he is ready to be a great grandfather and a local god. And just as he is moving in, something goes wrong. Some tyranny, personal or political, suddenly debars him from the home; and he has to take his meals in the front garden. A passing philosopher (who is also, by a mere coincidence, the man who turned him out) pauses, and leaning elegantly on the railings, explains to him that he is now living that bold life upon the bounty of nature which will be the life of the sublime future. He finds life in the front garden more bold than bountiful, and has to move into mean lodgings in the next spring. The philosopher (who turned him out), happening to call at these lodgings, with the probable intention of raising the rent, stops to explain to him that he is now in the real life of mercantile endeavor; the economic struggle between him and the landlady is the only thing out of which, in the sublime future, the wealth of nations can come. He is defeated in the economic struggle, and goes to the workhouse. The philosopher who turned him out (happening at that very moment to be inspecting the workhouse) assures him that he is now at last in that golden republic which is the goal of mankind; he is in an equal, scientific, Socialistic commonwealth, owned by the State and ruled by public officers; in fact, the commonwealth of the sublime future.

Nevertheless, there are signs that the irrational Jones still dreams at night of this old idea of having an ordinary home. He asked for so little, and he has been offered so much. He has been offered bribes of worlds and systems; he has been offered Eden and Utopia and the New Jerusalem, and he only wanted a house; and that has been refused him.

Such an apologue is literally no exaggeration of the facts of English history. The rich did literally turn the poor out of the old guest house on to the road, briefly telling them that it was the road of progress. They did literally force them into factories and the modern wage-slavery, assuring them all the time that this was the only way to wealth and civilization. Just as they had dragged the rustic from the convent food and ale by saying that the streets of heaven were paved with gold, so now they dragged him from the village food and ale by telling him that the streets of London were paved with gold. As he entered the gloomy porch of Puritanism, so he entered the gloomy porch of Industrialism, being told that each of them was the gate of the future. Hitherto he has only gone from prison to prison, nay, into darkening prisons, for Calvinism opened one small window upon heaven. And now he is asked, in the same educated and authoritative tones, to enter another dark porch, at which he has to surrender, into unseen hands, his children, his small possessions and all the habits of his fathers.

Whether this last opening be in truth any more inviting than the old openings of Puritanism and Industrialism can be discussed later. But there can be little doubt, I think, that if some form of Collectivism is imposed upon England it will be imposed, as everything else has been, by an instructed political class upon a people partly apathetic and partly hypnotized. The aristocracy will be as ready to "administer" Collectivism as they were to administer Puritanism or Manchesterism; in some ways such a centralized political power is necessarily attractive to them. It will not be so hard as some innocent Socialists seem to suppose to induce the Honorable Tomnoddy to take over the milk supply as well as the stamp supply—at an increased salary. Mr. Bernard Shaw has remarked that rich men are better than poor men on parish councils because they are free from "financial timidity." Now, the English ruling class is quite free from financial timidity. The Duke of Sussex will be quite ready to be Administrator of Sussex at the same screw. Sir William Harcourt, that typical aristocrat, put it quite correctly. "We" (that is, the aristocracy) "are all Socialists now."

But this is not the essential note on which I desire to end. My main contention is that, whether necessary or not, both Industrialism and Collectivism have been accepted as necessities—not as naked ideals or desires. Nobody liked the Manchester School; it was endured as the only way of producing wealth. Nobody likes the Marxian school; it is endured as the only way of preventing poverty. Nobody's real heart is in the idea of preventing a free man from owning his own farm, or an old woman from cultivating her own garden, any more than anybody's real heart was in the heartless battle of the machines. The purpose of this chapter is sufficiently served in indicating that this proposal also is a pis aller, a desperate second best—like teetotalism. I do not propose to prove here that Socialism is a poison; it is enough if I maintain that it is a medicine and not a wine.

The idea of private property universal but private, the idea of families free but still families, of domesticity democratic but still domestic, of one man one house—this remains the real vision and magnet of mankind. The world may accept something more official and general, less human and intimate. But the world will be like a broken-hearted woman who makes a humdrum marriage because she may not make a happy one; Socialism may be the world's deliverance, but it is not the world's desire.

PART TWO. IMPERIALISM, OR THE MISTAKE ABOUT MAN

I. THE CHARM OF JINGOISM

I have cast about widely to find a title for this section; and I confess that the word "Imperialism" is a clumsy version of my meaning. But no other word came nearer; "Militarism" would have been even more misleading, and "The Superman" makes nonsense of any discussion that he enters. Perhaps, upon the whole, the word "Caesarism" would have been better; but I desire a popular word; and Imperialism (as the reader will perceive) does cover for the most part the men and theories that I mean to discuss.

This small confusion is increased, however, by the fact that I do also disbelieve in Imperialism in its popular sense, as a mode or theory of the patriotic sentiment of this country. But popular Imperialism in England has very little to do with the sort of Caesarean Imperialism I wish to sketch. I differ from the Colonial idealism of Rhodes' and Kipling; but I do not think, as some of its opponents do, that it is an insolent creation of English harshness and rapacity. Imperialism, I think, is a fiction created, not by English hardness, but by English softness; nay, in a sense, even by English kindness.

The reasons for believing in Australia are mostly as sentimental as the most sentimental reasons for believing in heaven. New South Wales is quite literally regarded as a place where the wicked cease from troubling and the weary are at rest; that is, a paradise for uncles who have turned dishonest and for nephews who are born tired. British Columbia is in strict sense a fairyland, it is a world where a magic and irrational luck is supposed to attend the youngest sons. This strange optimism about the ends of the earth is an English weakness; but to show that it is not a coldness or a harshness it is quite sufficient to say that no one shared it more than that gigantic English sentimentalist—the great Charles Dickens. The end of "David Copperfield" is unreal not merely because it is an optimistic ending, but because it is an Imperialistic ending. The decorous British happiness planned out for David Copperfield and Agnes would be embarrassed by the perpetual presence of the hopeless tragedy of Emily, or the more hopeless farce of Micawber. Therefore, both Emily and Micawber are shipped off to a vague colony where changes come over them with no conceivable cause, except the climate. The tragic woman becomes contented and the comic man becomes responsible, solely as the result of a sea voyage and the first sight of a kangaroo.

To Imperialism in the light political sense, therefore, my only objection is that it is an illusion of comfort; that an Empire whose heart is failing should be specially proud of the extremities, is to me no more sublime a fact than that an old dandy whose brain is gone should still be proud of his legs. It consoles men for the evident ugliness and apathy of England with legends of fair youth and heroic strenuousness in distant continents and islands. A man can sit amid the squalor of Seven Dials and feel that life is innocent and godlike in the bush or on the veldt. Just so a man might sit in the squalor of Seven Dials and feel that life was innocent and godlike in Brixton and Surbiton. Brixton and Surbiton are "new"; they are expanding; they are "nearer to nature," in the sense that they have eaten up nature mile by mile. The only objection is the objection of fact. The young men of Brixton are not young giants. The lovers of Surbiton are not all pagan poets, singing with the sweet energy of the spring. Nor are the people of the Colonies when you meet them young giants or pagan poets. They are mostly Cockneys who have lost their last music of real things by getting out of the sound of Bow Bells. Mr. Rudyard Kipling, a man of real though decadent genius, threw a theoretic glamour over them which is already fading. Mr. Kipling is, in a precise and rather startling sense, the exception that proves the rule. For he has imagination, of an oriental and cruel kind, but he has it, not because he grew up in a new country, but precisely because he grew up in the oldest country upon earth. He is rooted in a past—an Asiatic past. He might never have written "Kabul River" if he had been born in Melbourne.

I say frankly, therefore (lest there should be any air of evasion), that Imperialism in its common patriotic pretensions appears to me both weak and perilous. It is the attempt of a European country to create a kind of sham Europe which it can dominate, instead of the real Europe, which it can only share. It is a love of living with one's inferiors. The notion of restoring the Roman Empire by oneself and for oneself is a dream that has haunted every Christian nation in a different shape and in almost every shape as a snare. The Spanish are a consistent and conservative people; therefore they embodied that attempt at Empire in long and lingering dynasties. The French are a violent people, and therefore they twice conquered that Empire by violence of arms. The English are above all a poetical and optimistic people; and therefore their Empire is something vague and yet sympathetic, something distant and yet dear. But this dream of theirs of being powerful in the uttermost places, though a native weakness, is still a weakness in them; much more of a weakness than gold was to Spain or glory to Napoleon. If ever we were in collision with our real brothers and rivals we should leave all this fancy out of account. We should no more dream of pitting Australian armies against German than of pitting Tasmanian sculpture against French. I have thus explained, lest anyone should accuse me of concealing an unpopular attitude, why I do not believe in Imperialism as commonly understood. I think it not merely an occasional wrong to other peoples, but a continuous feebleness, a running sore, in my own. But it is also true that I have dwelt on this Imperialism that is an amiable delusion partly in order to show how different it is from the deeper, more sinister and yet more persuasive thing that I have been forced to call Imperialism for the convenience of this chapter. In order to get to the root of this evil and quite un-English Imperialism we must cast back and begin anew with a more general discussion of the first needs of human intercourse.

II. WISDOM AND THE WEATHER

It is admitted, one may hope, that common things are never commonplace. Birth is covered with curtains precisely because it is a staggering and monstrous prodigy. Death and first love, though they happen to everybody, can stop one's heart with the very thought of them. But while this is granted, something further may be claimed. It is not merely true that these universal things are strange; it is moreover true that they are subtle. In the last analysis most common things will be found to be highly complicated. Some men of science do indeed get over the difficulty by dealing only with the easy part of it: thus, they will call first love the instinct of sex, and the awe of death the instinct of self-preservation. But this is only getting over the difficulty of describing peacock green by calling it blue. There is blue in it. That there is a strong physical element in both romance and the Memento Mori makes them if possible more baffling than if they had been wholly intellectual. No man could say exactly how much his sexuality was colored by a clean love of beauty, or by the mere boyish itch for irrevocable adventures, like running away to sea. No man could say how far his animal dread of the end was mixed up with mystical traditions touching morals and religion. It is exactly because these things are animal, but not quite animal, that the dance of all the difficulties begins. The materialists analyze the easy part, deny the hard part and go home to their tea.

It is complete error to suppose that because a thing is vulgar therefore it is not refined; that is, subtle and hard to define. A drawing-room song of my youth which began "In the gloaming, O, my darling," was vulgar enough as a song; but the connection between human passion and the twilight is none the less an exquisite and even inscrutable thing. Or to take another obvious instance: the jokes about a mother-in-law are scarcely delicate, but the problem of a mother-in-law is extremely delicate. A mother-in-law is subtle because she is a thing like the twilight. She is a mystical blend of two inconsistent things—law and a mother. The caricatures misrepresent her; but they arise out of a real human enigma. "Comic Cuts" deals with the difficulty wrongly, but it would need George Meredith at his best to deal with the difficulty rightly. The nearest statement of the problem perhaps is this: it is not that a mother-in-law must be nasty, but that she must be very nice.

But it is best perhaps to take in illustration some daily custom we have all heard despised as vulgar or trite. Take, for the sake of argument, the custom of talking about the weather. Stevenson calls it "the very nadir and scoff of good conversationalists." Now there are very deep reasons for talking about the weather, reasons that are delicate as well as deep; they lie in layer upon layer of stratified sagacity. First of all it is a gesture of primeval worship. The sky must be invoked; and to begin everything with the weather is a sort of pagan way of beginning everything with prayer. Jones and Brown talk about the weather: but so do Milton and Shelley. Then it is an expression of that elementary idea in politeness—equality. For the very word politeness is only the Greek for citizenship. The word politeness is akin to the word policeman: a charming thought. Properly understood, the citizen should be more polite than the gentleman; perhaps the policeman should be the most courtly and elegant of the three. But all good manners must obviously begin with the sharing of something in a simple style. Two men should share an umbrella; if they have not got an umbrella, they should at least share the rain, with all its rich potentialities of wit and philosophy. "For He maketh His sun to shine...." This is the second element in the weather; its recognition of human equality in that we all have our hats under the dark blue spangled umbrella of the universe. Arising out of this is the third wholesome strain in the custom; I mean that it begins with the body and with our inevitable bodily brotherhood. All true friendliness begins with fire and food and drink and the recognition of rain or frost. Those who will not begin at the bodily end of things are already prigs and may soon be Christian Scientists. Each human soul has in a sense to enact for itself the gigantic humility of the Incarnation. Every man must descend into the flesh to meet mankind.

Briefly, in the mere observation "a fine day" there is the whole great human idea of comradeship. Now, pure comradeship is another of those broad and yet bewildering things. We all enjoy it; yet when we come to talk about it we almost always talk nonsense, chiefly because we suppose it to be a simpler affair than it is. It is simple to conduct; but it is by no means simple to analyze. Comradeship is at the most only one half of human life; the other half is Love, a thing so different that one might fancy it had been made for another universe. And I do not mean mere sex love; any kind of concentrated passion, maternal love, or even the fiercer kinds of friendship are in their nature alien to pure comradeship. Both sides are essential to life; and both are known in differing degrees to everybody of every age or sex. But very broadly speaking it may still be said that women stand for the dignity of love and men for the dignity of comradeship. I mean that the institution would hardly be expected if the males of the tribe did not mount guard over it. The affections in which women excel have so much more authority and intensity that pure comradeship would be washed away if it were not rallied and guarded in clubs, corps, colleges, banquets and regiments. Most of us have heard the voice in which the hostess tells her husband not to sit too long over the cigars. It is the dreadful voice of Love, seeking to destroy Comradeship.

All true comradeship has in it those three elements which I have remarked in the ordinary exclamation about the weather. First, it has a sort of broad philosophy like the common sky, emphasizing that we are all under the same cosmic conditions. We are all in the same boat, the "winged rock" of Mr. Herbert Trench. Secondly, it recognizes this bond as the essential one; for comradeship is simply humanity seen in that one aspect in which men are really equal. The old writers were entirely wise when they talked of the equality of men; but they were also very wise in not mentioning women. Women are always authoritarian; they are always above or below; that is why marriage is a sort of poetical see-saw. There are only three things in the world that women do not understand; and they are Liberty, Equality, and Fraternity. But men (a class little understood in the modern world) find these things the breath of their nostrils; and our most learned ladies will not even begin to understand them until they make allowance for this kind of cool camaraderie. Lastly, it contains the third quality of the weather, the insistence upon the body and its indispensable satisfaction. No one has even begun to understand comradeship who does not accept with it a certain hearty eagerness in eating, drinking, or smoking, an uproarious materialism which to many women appears only hoggish. You may call the thing an orgy or a sacrament; it is certainly an essential. It is at root a resistance to the superciliousness of the individual. Nay, its very swaggering and howling are humble. In the heart of its rowdiness there is a sort of mad modesty; a desire to melt the separate soul into the mass of unpretentious masculinity. It is a clamorous confession of the weakness of all flesh. No man must be superior to the things that are common to men. This sort of equality must be bodily and gross and comic. Not only are we all in the same boat, but we are all seasick.

The word comradeship just now promises to become as fatuous as the word "affinity." There are clubs of a Socialist sort where all the members, men and women, call each other "Comrade." I have no serious emotions, hostile or otherwise, about this particular habit: at the worst it is conventionality, and at the best flirtation. I am convinced here only to point out a rational principle. If you choose to lump all flowers together, lilies and dahlias and tulips and chrysanthemums and call them all daisies, you will find that you have spoiled the very fine word daisy. If you choose to call every human attachment comradeship, if you include under that name the respect of a youth for a venerable prophetess, the interest of a man in a beautiful woman who baffles him, the pleasure of a philosophical old fogy in a girl who is impudent and innocent, the end of the meanest quarrel or the beginning of the most mountainous love; if you are going to call all these comradeship, you will gain nothing, you will only lose a word. Daisies are obvious and universal and open; but they are only one kind of flower. Comradeship is obvious and universal and open; but it is only one kind of affection; it has characteristics that would destroy any other kind. Anyone who has known true comradeship in a club or in a regiment, knows that it is impersonal. There is a pedantic phrase used in debating clubs which is strictly true to the masculine emotion; they call it "speaking to the question." Women speak to each other; men speak to the subject they are speaking about. Many an honest man has sat in a ring of his five best friends under heaven and forgotten who was in the room while he explained some system. This is not peculiar to intellectual men; men are all theoretical, whether they are talking about God or about golf. Men are all impersonal; that is to say, republican. No one remembers after a really good talk who has said the good things. Every man speaks to a visionary multitude; a mystical cloud, that is called the club.

It is obvious that this cool and careless quality which is essential to the collective affection of males involves disadvantages and dangers. It leads to spitting; it leads to coarse speech; it must lead to these things so long as it is honorable; comradeship must be in some degree ugly. The moment beauty is mentioned in male friendship, the nostrils are stopped with the smell of abominable things. Friendship must be physically dirty if it is to be morally clean. It must be in its shirt sleeves. The chaos of habits that always goes with males when left entirely to themselves has only one honorable cure; and that is the strict discipline of a monastery. Anyone who has seen our unhappy young idealists in East End Settlements losing their collars in the wash and living on tinned salmon will fully understand why it was decided by the wisdom of St. Bernard or St. Benedict, that if men were to live without women, they must not live without rules. Something of the same sort of artificial exactitude, of course, is obtained in an army; and an army also has to be in many ways monastic; only that it has celibacy without chastity. But these things do not apply to normal married men. These have a quite sufficient restraint on their instinctive anarchy in the savage common-sense of the other sex. There is only one very timid sort of man that is not afraid of women.

III. THE COMMON VISION

Now this masculine love of an open and level camaraderie is the life within all democracies and attempts to govern by debate; without it the republic would be a dead formula. Even as it is, of course, the spirit of democracy frequently differs widely from the letter, and a pothouse is often a better test than a Parliament. Democracy in its human sense is not arbitrament by the majority; it is not even arbitrament by everybody. It can be more nearly defined as arbitrament by anybody. I mean that it rests on that club habit of taking a total stranger for granted, of assuming certain things to be inevitably common to yourself and him. Only the things that anybody may be presumed to hold have the full authority of democracy. Look out of the window and notice the first man who walks by. The Liberals may have swept England with an over-whelming majority; but you would not stake a button that the man is a Liberal. The Bible may be read in all schools and respected in all law courts; but you would not bet a straw that he believes in the Bible. But you would bet your week's wages, let us say, that he believes in wearing clothes. You would bet that he believes that physical courage is a fine thing, or that parents have authority over children. Of course, he might be the millionth man who does not believe these things; if it comes to that, he might be the Bearded Lady dressed up as a man. But these prodigies are quite a different thing from any mere calculation of numbers. People who hold these views are not a minority, but a monstrosity. But of these universal dogmas that have full democratic authority the only test is this test of anybody. What you would observe before any newcomer in a tavern—that is the real English law. The first man you see from the window, he is the King of England.

The decay of taverns, which is but a part of the general decay of democracy, has undoubtedly weakened this masculine spirit of equality. I remember that a roomful of Socialists literally laughed when I told them that there were no two nobler words in all poetry than Public House. They thought it was a joke. Why they should think it a joke, since they want to make all houses public houses, I cannot imagine. But if anyone wishes to see the real rowdy egalitarianism which is necessary (to males, at least) he can find it as well as anywhere in the great old tavern disputes which come down to us in such books as Boswell's Johnson. It is worth while to mention that one name especially because the modern world in its morbidity has done it a strange injustice. The demeanor of Johnson, it is said, was "harsh and despotic." It was occasionally harsh, but it was never despotic. Johnson was not in the least a despot; Johnson was a demagogue, he shouted against a shouting crowd. The very fact that he wrangled with other people is proof that other people were allowed to wrangle with him. His very brutality was based on the idea of an equal scrimmage, like that of football. It is strictly true that he bawled and banged the table because he was a modest man. He was honestly afraid of being overwhelmed or even overlooked. Addison had exquisite manners and was the king of his company; he was polite to everybody; but superior to everybody; therefore he has been handed down forever in the immortal insult of Pope—

"Like Cato, give his little Senate laws And sit attentive to his own applause."

Johnson, so far from being king of his company, was a sort of Irish Member in his own Parliament. Addison was a courteous superior and was hated. Johnson was an insolent equal and therefore was loved by all who knew him, and handed down in a marvellous book, which is one of the mere miracles of love.

This doctrine of equality is essential to conversation; so much may be admitted by anyone who knows what conversation is. Once arguing at a table in a tavern the most famous man on earth would wish to be obscure, so that his brilliant remarks might blaze like the stars on the background of his obscurity. To anything worth calling a man nothing can be conceived more cold or cheerless than to be king of your company. But it may be said that in masculine sports and games, other than the great game of debate, there is definite emulation and eclipse. There is indeed emulation, but this is only an ardent sort of equality. Games are competitive, because that is the only way of making them exciting. But if anyone doubts that men must forever return to the ideal of equality, it is only necessary to answer that there is such a thing as a handicap. If men exulted in mere superiority, they would seek to see how far such superiority could go; they would be glad when one strong runner came in miles ahead of all the rest. But what men like is not the triumph of superiors, but the struggle of equals; and, therefore, they introduce even into their competitive sports an artificial equality. It is sad to think how few of those who arrange our sporting handicaps can be supposed with any probability to realize that they are abstract and even severe republicans.

No; the real objection to equality and self-rule has nothing to do with any of these free and festive aspects of mankind; all men are democrats when they are happy. The philosophic opponent of democracy would substantially sum up his position by saying that it "will not work." Before going further, I will register in passing a protest against the assumption that working is the one test of humanity. Heaven does not work; it plays. Men are most themselves when they are free; and if I find that men are snobs in their work but democrats on their holidays, I shall take the liberty to believe their holidays. But it is this question of work which really perplexes the question of equality; and it is with that that we must now deal. Perhaps the truth can be put most pointedly thus: that democracy has one real enemy, and that is civilization. Those utilitarian miracles which science has made are anti-democratic, not so much in their perversion, or even in their practical result, as in their primary shape and purpose. The Frame-Breaking Rioters were right; not perhaps in thinking that machines would make fewer men workmen; but certainly in thinking that machines would make fewer men masters. More wheels do mean fewer handles; fewer handles do mean fewer hands. The machinery of science must be individualistic and isolated. A mob can shout round a palace; but a mob cannot shout down a telephone. The specialist appears and democracy is half spoiled at a stroke.

IV. THE INSANE NECESSITY

The common conception among the dregs of Darwinian culture is that men have slowly worked their way out of inequality into a state of comparative equality. The truth is, I fancy, almost exactly the opposite. All men have normally and naturally begun with the idea of equality; they have only abandoned it late and reluctantly, and always for some material reason of detail. They have never naturally felt that one class of men was superior to another; they have always been driven to assume it through certain practical limitations of space and time.

For example, there is one element which must always tend to oligarchy—or rather to despotism; I mean the element of hurry. If the house has caught fire a man must ring up the fire engines; a committee cannot ring them up. If a camp is surprised by night somebody must give the order to fire; there is no time to vote it. It is solely a question of the physical limitations of time and space; not at all of any mental limitations in the mass of men commanded. If all the people in the house were men of destiny it would still be better that they should not all talk into the telephone at once; nay, it would be better that the silliest man of all should speak uninterrupted. If an army actually consisted of nothing but Hanibals and Napoleons, it would still be better in the case of a surprise that they should not all give orders together. Nay, it would be better if the stupidest of them all gave the orders. Thus, we see that merely military subordination, so far from resting on the inequality of men, actually rests on the equality of men. Discipline does not involve the Carlylean notion that somebody is always right when everybody is wrong, and that we must discover and crown that somebody. On the contrary, discipline means that in certain frightfully rapid circumstances, one can trust anybody so long as he is not everybody. The military spirit does not mean (as Carlyle fancied) obeying the strongest and wisest man. On the contrary, the military spirit means, if anything, obeying the weakest and stupidest man, obeying him merely because he is a man, and not a thousand men. Submission to a weak man is discipline. Submission to a strong man is only servility.

Now it can be easily shown that the thing we call aristocracy in Europe is not in its origin and spirit an aristocracy at all. It is not a system of spiritual degrees and distinctions like, for example, the caste system of India, or even like the old Greek distinction between free men and slaves. It is simply the remains of a military organization, framed partly to sustain the sinking Roman Empire, partly to break and avenge the awful onslaught of Islam. The word Duke simply means Colonel, just as the word Emperor simply means Commander-in-Chief. The whole story is told in the single title of Counts of the Holy Roman Empire, which merely means officers in the European army against the contemporary Yellow Peril. Now in an army nobody ever dreams of supposing that difference of rank represents a difference of moral reality. Nobody ever says about a regiment, "Your Major is very humorous and energetic; your Colonel, of course, must be even more humorous and yet more energetic." No one ever says, in reporting a mess-room conversation, "Lieutenant Jones was very witty, but was naturally inferior to Captain Smith." The essence of an army is the idea of official inequality, founded on unofficial equality. The Colonel is not obeyed because he is the best man, but because he is the Colonel. Such was probably the spirit of the system of dukes and counts when it first arose out of the military spirit and military necessities of Rome. With the decline of those necessities it has gradually ceased to have meaning as a military organization, and become honeycombed with unclean plutocracy. Even now it is not a spiritual aristocracy—it is not so bad as all that. It is simply an army without an enemy—billeted upon the people.

Man, therefore, has a specialist as well as comrade-like aspect; and the case of militarism is not the only case of such specialist submission. The tinker and tailor, as well as the soldier and sailor, require a certain rigidity of rapidity of action: at least, if the tinker is not organized that is largely why he does not tink on any large scale. The tinker and tailor often represent the two nomadic races in Europe: the Gipsy and the Jew; but the Jew alone has influence because he alone accepts some sort of discipline. Man, we say, has two sides, the specialist side where he must have subordination, and the social side where he must have equality. There is a truth in the saying that ten tailors go to make a man; but we must remember also that ten Poets Laureate or ten Astronomers Royal go to make a man, too. Ten million tradesmen go to make Man himself; but humanity consists of tradesmen when they are not talking shop. Now the peculiar peril of our time, which I call for argument's sake Imperialism or Caesarism, is the complete eclipse of comradeship and equality by specialism and domination.

There are only two kinds of social structure conceivable—personal government and impersonal government. If my anarchic friends will not have rules—they will have rulers. Preferring personal government, with its tact and flexibility, is called Royalism. Preferring impersonal government, with its dogmas and definitions, is called Republicanism. Objecting broadmindedly both to kings and creeds is called Bosh; at least, I know no more philosophic word for it. You can be guided by the shrewdness or presence of mind of one ruler, or by the equality and ascertained justice of one rule; but you must have one or the other, or you are not a nation, but a nasty mess. Now men in their aspect of equality and debate adore the idea of rules; they develop and complicate them greatly to excess. A man finds far more regulations and definitions in his club, where there are rules, than in his home, where there is a ruler. A deliberate assembly, the House of Commons, for instance, carries this mummery to the point of a methodical madness. The whole system is stiff with rigid unreason; like the Royal Court in Lewis Carroll. You would think the Speaker would speak; therefore he is mostly silent. You would think a man would take off his hat to stop and put it on to go away; therefore he takes off his hat to walk out and puts it on to stop in. Names are forbidden, and a man must call his own father "my right honorable friend the member for West Birmingham." These are, perhaps, fantasies of decay: but fundamentally they answer a masculine appetite. Men feel that rules, even if irrational, are universal; men feel that law is equal, even when it is not equitable. There is a wild fairness in the thing—as there is in tossing up.

Again, it is gravely unfortunate that when critics do attack such cases as the Commons it is always on the points (perhaps the few points) where the Commons are right. They denounce the House as the Talking-Shop, and complain that it wastes time in wordy mazes. Now this is just one respect in which the Commons are actually like the Common People. If they love leisure and long debate, it is because all men love it; that they really represent England. There the Parliament does approach to the virile virtues of the pothouse.

The real truth is that adumbrated in the introductory section when we spoke of the sense of home and property, as now we speak of the sense of counsel and community. All men do naturally love the idea of leisure, laughter, loud and equal argument; but there stands a specter in our hall. We are conscious of the towering modern challenge that is called specialism or cut-throat competition—Business. Business will have nothing to do with leisure; business will have no truck with comradeship; business will pretend to no patience with all the legal fictions and fantastic handicaps by which comradeship protects its egalitarian ideal. The modern millionaire, when engaged in the agreeable and typical task of sacking his own father, will certainly not refer to him as the right honorable clerk from the Laburnum Road, Brixton. Therefore there has arisen in modern life a literary fashion devoting itself to the romance of business, to great demigods of greed and to fairyland of finance. This popular philosophy is utterly despotic and anti-democratic; this fashion is the flower of that Caesarism against which I am concerned to protest. The ideal millionaire is strong in the possession of a brain of steel. The fact that the real millionaire is rather more often strong in the possession of a head of wood, does not alter the spirit and trend of the idolatry. The essential argument is "Specialists must be despots; men must be specialists. You cannot have equality in a soap factory; so you cannot have it anywhere. You cannot have comradeship in a wheat corner; so you cannot have it at all. We must have commercial civilization; therefore we must destroy democracy." I know that plutocrats have seldom sufficient fancy to soar to such examples as soap or wheat. They generally confine themselves, with fine freshness of mind, to a comparison between the state and a ship. One anti-democratic writer remarked that he would not like to sail in a vessel in which the cabin-boy had an equal vote with the captain. It might easily be urged in answer that many a ship (the Victoria, for instance) was sunk because an admiral gave an order which a cabin-boy could see was wrong. But this is a debating reply; the essential fallacy is both deeper and simpler. The elementary fact is that we were all born in a state; we were not all born on a ship; like some of our great British bankers. A ship still remains a specialist experiment, like a diving-bell or a flying ship: in such peculiar perils the need for promptitude constitutes the need for autocracy. But we live and die in the vessel of the state; and if we cannot find freedom camaraderie and the popular element in the state, we cannot find it at all. And the modern doctrine of commercial despotism means that we shall not find it at all. Our specialist trades in their highly civilized state cannot (it says) be run without the whole brutal business of bossing and sacking, "too old at forty" and all the rest of the filth. And they must be run, and therefore we call on Caesar. Nobody but the Superman could descend to do such dirty work.

Now (to reiterate my title) this is what is wrong. This is the huge modern heresy of altering the human soul to fit its conditions, instead of altering human conditions to fit the human soul. If soap boiling is really inconsistent with brotherhood, so much the worst for soap-boiling, not for brotherhood. If civilization really cannot get on with democracy, so much the worse for civilization, not for democracy. Certainly, it would be far better to go back to village communes, if they really are communes. Certainly, it would be better to do without soap rather than to do without society. Certainly, we would sacrifice all our wires, wheels, systems, specialties, physical science and frenzied finance for one half-hour of happiness such as has often come to us with comrades in a common tavern. I do not say the sacrifice will be necessary; I only say it will be easy.

PART THREE. FEMINISM, OR THE MISTAKE ABOUT WOMAN

I. THE UNMILITARY SUFFRAGETTE

It will be better to adopt in this chapter the same process that appeared a piece of mental justice in the last. My general opinions on the feminine question are such as many suffragists would warmly approve; and it would be easy to state them without any open reference to the current controversy. But just as it seemed more decent to say first that I was not in favor of Imperialism even in its practical and popular sense, so it seems more decent to say the same of Female Suffrage, in its practical and popular sense. In other words, it is only fair to state, however hurriedly, the superficial objection to the Suffragettes before we go on to the really subtle questions behind the Suffrage.

Well, to get this honest but unpleasant business over, the objection to the Suffragettes is not that they are Militant Suffragettes. On the contrary, it is that they are not militant enough. A revolution is a military thing; it has all the military virtues; one of which is that it comes to an end. Two parties fight with deadly weapons, but under certain rules of arbitrary honor; the party that wins becomes the government and proceeds to govern. The aim of civil war, like the aim of all war, is peace. Now the Suffragettes cannot raise civil war in this soldierly and decisive sense; first, because they are women; and, secondly, because they are very few women. But they can raise something else; which is altogether another pair of shoes. They do not create revolution; what they do create is anarchy; and the difference between these is not a question of violence, but a question of fruitfulness and finality. Revolution of its nature produces government; anarchy only produces more anarchy. Men may have what opinions they please about the beheading of King Charles or King Louis, but they cannot deny that Bradshaw and Cromwell ruled, that Carnot and Napoleon governed. Someone conquered; something occurred. You can only knock off the King's head once. But you can knock off the King's hat any number of times. Destruction is finite, obstruction is infinite: so long as rebellion takes the form of mere disorder (instead of an attempt to enforce a new order) there is no logical end to it; it can feed on itself and renew itself forever. If Napoleon had not wanted to be a Consul, but only wanted to be a nuisance, he could, possibly, have prevented any government arising successfully out of the Revolution. But such a proceeding would not have deserved the dignified name of rebellion.

It is exactly this unmilitant quality in the Suffragettes that makes their superficial problem. The problem is that their action has none of the advantages of ultimate violence; it does not afford a test. War is a dreadful thing; but it does prove two points sharply and unanswerably—numbers, and an unnatural valor. One does discover the two urgent matters; how many rebels there are alive, and how many are ready to be dead. But a tiny minority, even an interested minority, may maintain mere disorder forever. There is also, of course, in the case of these women, the further falsity that is introduced by their sex. It is false to state the matter as a mere brutal question of strength. If his muscles give a man a vote, then his horse ought to have two votes and his elephant five votes. The truth is more subtle than that; it is that bodily outbreak is a man's instinctive weapon, like the hoofs to the horse or the tusks to the elephant. All riot is a threat of war; but the woman is brandishing a weapon she can never use. There are many weapons that she could and does use. If (for example) all the women nagged for a vote they would get it in a month. But there again, one must remember, it would be necessary to get all the women to nag. And that brings us to the end of the political surface of the matter. The working objection to the Suffragette philosophy is simply that overmastering millions of women do not agree with it. I am aware that some maintain that women ought to have votes whether the majority wants them or not; but this is surely a strange and childish case of setting up formal democracy to the destruction of actual democracy. What should the mass of women decide if they do not decide their general place in the State? These people practically say that females may vote about everything except about Female Suffrage.

But having again cleared my conscience of my merely political and possibly unpopular opinion, I will again cast back and try to treat the matter in a slower and more sympathetic style; attempt to trace the real roots of woman's position in the western state, and the causes of our existing traditions or perhaps prejudices upon the point. And for this purpose it is again necessary to travel far from the modern topic, the mere Suffragette of today, and to go back to subjects which, though much more old, are, I think, considerably more fresh.

II. THE UNIVERSAL STICK

Cast your eye round the room in which you sit, and select some three or four things that have been with man almost since his beginning; which at least we hear of early in the centuries and often among the tribes. Let me suppose that you see a knife on the table, a stick in the corner, or a fire on the hearth. About each of these you will notice one speciality; that not one of them is special. Each of these ancestral things is a universal thing; made to supply many different needs; and while tottering pedants nose about to find the cause and origin of some old custom, the truth is that it had fifty causes or a hundred origins. The knife is meant to cut wood, to cut cheese, to cut pencils, to cut throats; for a myriad ingenious or innocent human objects. The stick is meant partly to hold a man up, partly to knock a man down; partly to point with like a finger-post, partly to balance with like a balancing pole, partly to trifle with like a cigarette, partly to kill with like a club of a giant; it is a crutch and a cudgel; an elongated finger and an extra leg. The case is the same, of course, with the fire; about which the strangest modern views have arisen. A queer fancy seems to be current that a fire exists to warm people. It exists to warm people, to light their darkness, to raise their spirits, to toast their muffins, to air their rooms, to cook their chestnuts, to tell stories to their children, to make checkered shadows on their walls, to boil their hurried kettles, and to be the red heart of a man's house and that hearth for which, as the great heathens said, a man should die.

Now it is the great mark of our modernity that people are always proposing substitutes for these old things; and these substitutes always answer one purpose where the old thing answered ten. The modern man will wave a cigarette instead of a stick; he will cut his pencil with a little screwing pencil-sharpener instead of a knife; and he will even boldly offer to be warmed by hot water pipes instead of a fire. I have my doubts about pencil-sharpeners even for sharpening pencils; and about hot water pipes even for heat. But when we think of all those other requirements that these institutions answered, there opens before us the whole horrible harlequinade of our civilization. We see as in a vision a world where a man tries to cut his throat with a pencil-sharpener; where a man must learn single-stick with a cigarette; where a man must try to toast muffins at electric lamps, and see red and golden castles in the surface of hot water pipes.

The principle of which I speak can be seen everywhere in a comparison between the ancient and universal things and the modern and specialist things. The object of a theodolite is to lie level; the object of a stick is to swing loose at any angle; to whirl like the very wheel of liberty. The object of a lancet is to lance; when used for slashing, gashing, ripping, lopping off heads and limbs, it is a disappointing instrument. The object of an electric light is merely to light (a despicable modesty); and the object of an asbestos stove... I wonder what is the object of an asbestos stove? If a man found a coil of rope in a desert he could at least think of all the things that can be done with a coil of rope; and some of them might even be practical. He could tow a boat or lasso a horse. He could play cat's-cradle, or pick oakum. He could construct a rope-ladder for an eloping heiress, or cord her boxes for a travelling maiden aunt. He could learn to tie a bow, or he could hang himself. Far otherwise with the unfortunate traveller who should find a telephone in the desert. You can telephone with a telephone; you cannot do anything else with it. And though this is one of the wildest joys of life, it falls by one degree from its full delirium when there is nobody to answer you. The contention is, in brief, that you must pull up a hundred roots, and not one, before you uproot any of these hoary and simple expedients. It is only with great difficulty that a modern scientific sociologist can be got to see that any old method has a leg to stand on. But almost every old method has four or five legs to stand on. Almost all the old institutions are quadrupeds; and some of them are centipedes.

Consider these cases, old and new, and you will observe the operation of a general tendency. Everywhere there was one big thing that served six purposes; everywhere now there are six small things; or, rather (and there is the trouble), there are just five and a half. Nevertheless, we will not say that this separation and specialism is entirely useless or inexcusable. I have often thanked God for the telephone; I may any day thank God for the lancet; and there is none of these brilliant and narrow inventions (except, of course, the asbestos stove) which might not be at some moment necessary and lovely. But I do not think the most austere upholder of specialism will deny that there is in these old, many-sided institutions an element of unity and universality which may well be preserved in its due proportion and place. Spiritually, at least, it will be admitted that some all-round balance is needed to equalize the extravagance of experts. It would not be difficult to carry the parable of the knife and stick into higher regions. Religion, the immortal maiden, has been a maid-of-all-work as well as a servant of mankind. She provided men at once with the theoretic laws of an unalterable cosmos and also with the practical rules of the rapid and thrilling game of morality. She taught logic to the student and told fairy tales to the children; it was her business to confront the nameless gods whose fears are on all flesh, and also to see the streets were spotted with silver and scarlet, that there was a day for wearing ribbons or an hour for ringing bells. The large uses of religion have been broken up into lesser specialities, just as the uses of the hearth have been broken up into hot water pipes and electric bulbs. The romance of ritual and colored emblem has been taken over by that narrowest of all trades, modern art (the sort called art for art's sake), and men are in modern practice informed that they may use all symbols so long as they mean nothing by them. The romance of conscience has been dried up into the science of ethics; which may well be called decency for decency's sake, decency unborn of cosmic energies and barren of artistic flower. The cry to the dim gods, cut off from ethics and cosmology, has become mere Psychical Research. Everything has been sundered from everything else, and everything has grown cold. Soon we shall hear of specialists dividing the tune from the words of a song, on the ground that they spoil each other; and I did once meet a man who openly advocated the separation of almonds and raisins. This world is all one wild divorce court; nevertheless, there are many who still hear in their souls the thunder of authority of human habit; those whom Man hath joined let no man sunder.

This book must avoid religion, but there must (I say) be many, religious and irreligious, who will concede that this power of answering many purposes was a sort of strength which should not wholly die out of our lives. As a part of personal character, even the moderns will agree that many-sidedness is a merit and a merit that may easily be overlooked. This balance and universality has been the vision of many groups of men in many ages. It was the Liberal Education of Aristotle; the jack-of-all-trades artistry of Leonardo da Vinci and his friends; the august amateurishness of the Cavalier Person of Quality like Sir William Temple or the great Earl of Dorset. It has appeared in literature in our time in the most erratic and opposite shapes, set to almost inaudible music by Walter Pater and enunciated through a foghorn by Walt Whitman. But the great mass of men have always been unable to achieve this literal universality, because of the nature of their work in the world. Not, let it be noted, because of the existence of their work. Leonardo da Vinci must have worked pretty hard; on the other hand, many a government office clerk, village constable or elusive plumber may do (to all human appearance) no work at all, and yet show no signs of the Aristotelian universalism. What makes it difficult for the average man to be a universalist is that the average man has to be a specialist; he has not only to learn one trade, but to learn it so well as to uphold him in a more or less ruthless society.

This is generally true of males from the first hunter to the last electrical engineer; each has not merely to act, but to excel. Nimrod has not only to be a mighty hunter before the Lord, but also a mighty hunter before the other hunters. The electrical engineer has to be a very electrical engineer, or he is outstripped by engineers yet more electrical. Those very miracles of the human mind on which the modern world prides itself, and rightly in the main, would be impossible without a certain concentration which disturbs the pure balance of reason more than does religious bigotry. No creed can be so limiting as that awful adjuration that the cobbler must not go beyond his last. So the largest and wildest shots of our world are but in one direction and with a defined trajectory: the gunner cannot go beyond his shot, and his shot so often falls short; the astronomer cannot go beyond his telescope and his telescope goes such a little way. All these are like men who have stood on the high peak of a mountain and seen the horizon like a single ring and who then descend down different paths towards different towns, traveling slow or fast. It is right; there must be people traveling to different towns; there must be specialists; but shall no one behold the horizon? Shall all mankind be specialist surgeons or peculiar plumbers; shall all humanity be monomaniac? Tradition has decided that only half of humanity shall be monomaniac. It has decided that in every home there shall be a tradesman and a Jack-of-all-trades. But it has also decided, among other things, that the Jack-of-all-trades shall be a Jill-of-all-trades. It has decided, rightly or wrongly, that this specialism and this universalism shall be divided between the sexes. Cleverness shall be left for men and wisdom for women. For cleverness kills wisdom; that is one of the few sad and certain things.

But for women this ideal of comprehensive capacity (or common-sense) must long ago have been washed away. It must have melted in the frightful furnaces of ambition and eager technicality. A man must be partly a one-idead man, because he is a one-weaponed man—and he is flung naked into the fight. The world's demand comes to him direct; to his wife indirectly. In short, he must (as the books on Success say) give "his best"; and what a small part of a man "his best" is! His second and third best are often much better. If he is the first violin he must fiddle for life; he must not remember that he is a fine fourth bagpipe, a fair fifteenth billiard-cue, a foil, a fountain pen, a hand at whist, a gun, and an image of God.

III. THE EMANCIPATION OF DOMESTICITY

And it should be remarked in passing that this force upon a man to develop one feature has nothing to do with what is commonly called our competitive system, but would equally exist under any rationally conceivable kind of Collectivism. Unless the Socialists are frankly ready for a fall in the standard of violins, telescopes and electric lights, they must somehow create a moral demand on the individual that he shall keep up his present concentration on these things. It was only by men being in some degree specialist that there ever were any telescopes; they must certainly be in some degree specialist in order to keep them going. It is not by making a man a State wage-earner that you can prevent him thinking principally about the very difficult way he earns his wages. There is only one way to preserve in the world that high levity and that more leisurely outlook which fulfils the old vision of universalism. That is, to permit the existence of a partly protected half of humanity; a half which the harassing industrial demand troubles indeed, but only troubles indirectly. In other words, there must be in every center of humanity one human being upon a larger plan; one who does not "give her best," but gives her all.

Our old analogy of the fire remains the most workable one. The fire need not blaze like electricity nor boil like boiling water; its point is that it blazes more than water and warms more than light. The wife is like the fire, or to put things in their proper proportion, the fire is like the wife. Like the fire, the woman is expected to cook: not to excel in cooking, but to cook; to cook better than her husband who is earning the coke by lecturing on botany or breaking stones. Like the fire, the woman is expected to tell tales to the children, not original and artistic tales, but tales—better tales than would probably be told by a first-class cook. Like the fire, the woman is expected to illuminate and ventilate, not by the most startling revelations or the wildest winds of thought, but better than a man can do it after breaking stones or lecturing. But she cannot be expected to endure anything like this universal duty if she is also to endure the direct cruelty of competitive or bureaucratic toil. Woman must be a cook, but not a competitive cook; a school mistress, but not a competitive schoolmistress; a house-decorator but not a competitive house-decorator; a dressmaker, but not a competitive dressmaker. She should have not one trade but twenty hobbies; she, unlike the man, may develop all her second bests. This is what has been really aimed at from the first in what is called the seclusion, or even the oppression, of women. Women were not kept at home in order to keep them narrow; on the contrary, they were kept at home in order to keep them broad. The world outside the home was one mass of narrowness, a maze of cramped paths, a madhouse of monomaniacs. It was only by partly limiting and protecting the woman that she was enabled to play at five or six professions and so come almost as near to God as the child when he plays at a hundred trades. But the woman's professions, unlike the child's, were all truly and almost terribly fruitful; so tragically real that nothing but her universality and balance prevented them being merely morbid. This is the substance of the contention I offer about the historic female position. I do not deny that women have been wronged and even tortured; but I doubt if they were ever tortured so much as they are tortured now by the absurd modern attempt to make them domestic empresses and competitive clerks at the same time. I do not deny that even under the old tradition women had a harder time than men; that is why we take off our hats. I do not deny that all these various female functions were exasperating; but I say that there was some aim and meaning in keeping them various. I do not pause even to deny that woman was a servant; but at least she was a general servant.

The shortest way of summarizing the position is to say that woman stands for the idea of Sanity; that intellectual home to which the mind must return after every excursion on extravagance. The mind that finds its way to wild places is the poet's; but the mind that never finds its way back is the lunatic's. There must in every machine be a part that moves and a part that stands still; there must be in everything that changes a part that is unchangeable. And many of the phenomena which moderns hastily condemn are really parts of this position of the woman as the center and pillar of health. Much of what is called her subservience, and even her pliability, is merely the subservience and pliability of a universal remedy; she varies as medicines vary, with the disease. She has to be an optimist to the morbid husband, a salutary pessimist to the happy-go-lucky husband. She has to prevent the Quixote from being put upon, and the bully from putting upon others. The French King wrote—

"*Toujours femme varie Bien fol qui s'y fie,*"

but the truth is that woman always varies, and that is exactly why we always trust her. To correct every adventure and extravagance with its antidote in common-sense is not (as the moderns seem to think) to be in the position of a spy or a slave. It is to be in the position of Aristotle or (at the lowest) Herbert Spencer, to be a universal morality, a complete system of thought. The slave flatters; the complete moralist rebukes. It is, in short, to be a Trimmer in the true sense of that honorable term; which for some reason or other is always used in a sense exactly opposite to its own. It seems really to be supposed that a Trimmer means a cowardly person who always goes over to the stronger side. It really means a highly chivalrous person who always goes over to the weaker side; like one who trims a boat by sitting where there are few people seated. Woman is a trimmer; and it is a generous, dangerous and romantic trade.

The final fact which fixes this is a sufficiently plain one. Supposing it to be conceded that humanity has acted at least not unnaturally in dividing itself into two halves, respectively typifying the ideals of special talent and of general sanity (since they are genuinely difficult to combine completely in one mind), it is not difficult to see why the line of cleavage has followed the line of sex, or why the female became the emblem of the universal and the male of the special and superior. Two gigantic facts of nature fixed it thus: first, that the woman who frequently fulfilled her functions literally could not be specially prominent in experiment and adventure; and second, that the same natural operation surrounded her with very young children, who require to be taught not so much anything as everything. Babies need not to be taught a trade, but to be introduced to a world. To put the matter shortly, woman is generally shut up in a house with a human being at the time when he asks all the questions that there are, and some that there aren't. It would be odd if she retained any of the narrowness of a specialist. Now if anyone says that this duty of general enlightenment (even when freed from modern rules and hours, and exercised more spontaneously by a more protected person) is in itself too exacting and oppressive, I can understand the view. I can only answer that our race has thought it worth while to cast this burden on women in order to keep common-sense in the world. But when people begin to talk about this domestic duty as not merely difficult but trivial and dreary, I simply give up the question. For I cannot with the utmost energy of imagination conceive what they mean. When domesticity, for instance, is called drudgery, all the difficulty arises from a double meaning in the word. If drudgery only means dreadfully hard work, I admit the woman drudges in the home, as a man might drudge at the Cathedral of Amiens or drudge behind a gun at Trafalgar. But if it means that the hard work is more heavy because it is trifling, colorless and of small import to the soul, then as I say, I give it up; I do not know what the words mean. To be Queen Elizabeth within a definite area, deciding sales, banquets, labors and holidays; to be Whiteley within a certain area, providing toys, boots, sheets, cakes and books, to be Aristotle within a certain area, teaching morals, manners, theology, and hygiene; I can understand how this might exhaust the mind, but I cannot imagine how it could narrow it. How can it be a large career to tell other people's children about the Rule of Three, and a small career to tell one's own children about the universe? How can it be broad to be the same thing to everyone, and narrow to be everything to someone? No; a woman's function is laborious, but because it is gigantic, not because it is minute. I will pity Mrs. Jones for the hugeness of her task; I will never pity her for its smallness.

But though the essential of the woman's task is universality, this does not, of course, prevent her from having one or two severe though largely wholesome prejudices. She has, on the whole, been more conscious than man that she is only one half of humanity; but she has expressed it (if one may say so of a lady) by getting her teeth into the two or three things which she thinks she stands for. I would observe here in parenthesis that much of the recent official trouble about women has arisen from the fact that they transfer to things of doubt and reason that sacred stubbornness only proper to the primary things which a woman was set to guard. One's own children, one's own altar, ought to be a matter of principle—or if you like, a matter of prejudice. On the other hand, who wrote Junius's Letters ought not to be a principle or a prejudice, it ought to be a matter of free and almost indifferent inquiry. But take an energetic modern girl secretary to a league to show that George III wrote Junius, and in three months she will believe it, too, out of mere loyalty to her employers. Modern women defend their office with all the fierceness of domesticity. They fight for desk and typewriter as for hearth and home, and develop a sort of wolfish wifehood on behalf of the invisible head of the firm. That is why they do office work so well; and that is why they ought not to do it.

IV. THE ROMANCE OF THRIFT

The larger part of womankind, however, have had to fight for things slightly more intoxicating to the eye than the desk or the typewriter; and it cannot be denied that in defending these, women have developed the quality called prejudice to a powerful and even menacing degree. But these prejudices will always be found to fortify the main position of the woman, that she is to remain a general overseer, an autocrat within small compass but on all sides. On the one or two points on which she really misunderstands the man's position, it is almost entirely in order to preserve her own. The two points on which woman, actually and of herself, is most tenacious may be roughly summarized as the ideal of thrift and the ideal of dignity.

Unfortunately for this book it is written by a male, and these two qualities, if not hateful to a man, are at least hateful in a man. But if we are to settle the sex question at all fairly, all males must make an imaginative attempt to enter into the attitude of all good women toward these two things. The difficulty exists especially, perhaps, in the thing called thrift; we men have so much encouraged each other in throwing money right and left, that there has come at last to be a sort of chivalrous and poetical air about losing sixpence. But on a broader and more candid consideration the case scarcely stands so.

Thrift is the really romantic thing; economy is more romantic than extravagance. Heaven knows I for one speak disinterestedly in the matter; for I cannot clearly remember saving a half-penny ever since I was born. But the thing is true; economy, properly understood, is the more poetic. Thrift is poetic because it is creative; waste is unpoetic because it is waste. It is prosaic to throw money away, because it is prosaic to throw anything away; it is negative; it is a confession of indifference, that is, it is a confession of failure. The most prosaic thing about the house is the dustbin, and the one great objection to the new fastidious and aesthetic homestead is simply that in such a moral menage the dustbin must be bigger than the house. If a man could undertake to make use of all things in his dustbin he would be a broader genius than Shakespeare. When science began to use by-products; when science found that colors could be made out of coaltar, she made her greatest and perhaps her only claim on the real respect of the human soul. Now the aim of the good woman is to use the by-products, or, in other words, to rummage in the dustbin.

A man can only fully comprehend it if he thinks of some sudden joke or expedient got up with such materials as may be found in a private house on a rainy day. A man's definite daily work is generally run with such rigid convenience of modern science that thrift, the picking up of potential helps here and there, has almost become unmeaning to him. He comes across it most (as I say) when he is playing some game within four walls; when in charades, a hearthrug will just do for a fur coat, or a tea-cozy just do for a cocked hat; when a toy theater needs timber and cardboard, and the house has just enough firewood and just enough bandboxes. This is the man's occasional glimpse and pleasing parody of thrift. But many a good housekeeper plays the same game every day with ends of cheese and scraps of silk, not because she is mean, but on the contrary, because she is magnanimous; because she wishes her creative mercy to be over all her works, that not one sardine should be destroyed, or cast as rubbish to the void, when she has made the pile complete.

The modern world must somehow be made to understand (in theology and other things) that a view may be vast, broad, universal, liberal and yet come into conflict with another view that is vast, broad, universal and liberal also. There is never a war between two sects, but only between two universal Catholic Churches. The only possible collision is the collision of one cosmos with another. So in a smaller way it must be first made clear that this female economic ideal is a part of that female variety of outlook and all-round art of life which we have already attributed to the sex: thrift is not a small or timid or provincial thing; it is part of that great idea of the woman watching on all sides out of all the windows of the soul and being answerable for everything. For in the average human house there is one hole by which money comes in and a hundred by which it goes out; man has to do with the one hole, woman with the hundred. But though the very stinginess of a woman is a part of her spiritual breadth, it is none the less true that it brings her into conflict with the special kind of spiritual breadth that belongs to the males of the tribe. It brings her into conflict with that shapeless cataract of Comradeship, of chaotic feasting and deafening debate, which we noted in the last section. The very touch of the eternal in the two sexual tastes brings them the more into antagonism; for one stands for a universal vigilance and the other for an almost infinite output. Partly through the nature of his moral weakness, and partly through the nature of his physical strength, the male is normally prone to expand things into a sort of eternity; he always thinks of a dinner party as lasting all night; and he always thinks of a night as lasting forever. When the working women in the poor districts come to the doors of the public houses and try to get their husbands home, simple minded "social workers" always imagine that every husband is a tragic drunkard and every wife a broken-hearted saint. It never occurs to them that the poor woman is only doing under coarser conventions exactly what every fashionable hostess does when she tries to get the men from arguing over the cigars to come and gossip over the teacups. These women are not exasperated merely at the amount of money that is wasted in beer; they are exasperated also at the amount of time that is wasted in talk. It is not merely what goeth into the mouth but what cometh out the mouth that, in their opinion, defileth a man. They will raise against an argument (like their sisters of all ranks) the ridiculous objection that nobody is convinced by it; as if a man wanted to make a body-slave of anybody with whom he had played single-stick. But the real female prejudice on this point is not without a basis; the real feeling is this, that the most masculine pleasures have a quality of the ephemeral. A duchess may ruin a duke for a diamond necklace; but there is the necklace. A coster may ruin his wife for a pot of beer; and where is the beer? The duchess quarrels with another duchess in order to crush her, to produce a result; the coster does not argue with another coster in order to convince him, but in order to enjoy at once the sound of his own voice, the clearness of his own opinions and the sense of masculine society. There is this element of a fine fruitlessness about the male enjoyments; wine is poured into a bottomless bucket; thought plunges into a bottomless abyss. All this has set woman against the Public House—that is, against the Parliament House. She is there to prevent waste; and the "pub" and the parliament are the very palaces of waste. In the upper classes the "pub" is called the club, but that makes no more difference to the reason than it does to the rhyme. High and low, the woman's objection to the Public House is perfectly definite and rational, it is that the Public House wastes the energies that could be used on the private house.

As it is about feminine thrift against masculine waste, so it is about feminine dignity against masculine rowdiness. The woman has a fixed and very well-founded idea that if she does not insist on good manners nobody else will. Babies are not always strong on the point of dignity, and grown-up men are quite unpresentable. It is true that there are many very polite men, but none that I ever heard of who were not either fascinating women or obeying them. But indeed the female ideal of dignity, like the female ideal of thrift, lies deeper and may easily be misunderstood. It rests ultimately on a strong idea of spiritual isolation; the same that makes women religious. They do not like being melted down; they dislike and avoid the mob. That anonymous quality we have remarked in the club conversation would be common impertinence in a case of ladies. I remember an artistic and eager lady asking me in her grand green drawing-room whether I believed in comradeship between the sexes, and why not. I was driven back on offering the obvious and sincere answer "Because if I were to treat you for two minutes like a comrade you would turn me out of the house." The only certain rule on this subject is always to deal with woman and never with women. "Women" is a profligate word; I have used it repeatedly in this chapter; but it always has a blackguard sound. It smells of oriental cynicism and hedonism. Every woman is a captive queen. But every crowd of women is only a harem broken loose.

I am not expressing my own views here, but those of nearly all the women I have known. It is quite unfair to say that a woman hates other women individually; but I think it would be quite true to say that she detests them in a confused heap. And this is not because she despises her own sex, but because she respects it; and respects especially that sanctity and separation of each item which is represented in manners by the idea of dignity and in morals by the idea of chastity.

V. THE COLDNESS OF CHLOE

We hear much of the human error which accepts what is sham and what is real. But it is worth while to remember that with unfamiliar things we often mistake what is real for what is sham. It is true that a very young man may think the wig of an actress is her hair. But it is equally true that a child yet younger may call the hair of a negro his wig. Just because the woolly savage is remote and barbaric he seems to be unnaturally neat and tidy. Everyone must have noticed the same thing in the fixed and almost offensive color of all unfamiliar things, tropic birds and tropic blossoms. Tropic birds look like staring toys out of a toy-shop. Tropic flowers simply look like artificial flowers, like things cut out of wax. This is a deep matter, and, I think, not unconnected with divinity; but anyhow it is the truth that when we see things for the first time we feel instantly that they are fictive creations; we feel the finger of God. It is only when we are thoroughly used to them and our five wits are wearied, that we see them as wild and objectless; like the shapeless tree-tops or the shifting cloud. It is the design in Nature that strikes us first; the sense of the crosses and confusions in that design only comes afterwards through experience and an almost eerie monotony. If a man saw the stars abruptly by accident he would think them as festive and as artificial as a firework. We talk of the folly of painting the lily; but if we saw the lily without warning we should think that it was painted. We talk of the devil not being so black as he is painted; but that very phrase is a testimony to the kinship between what is called vivid and what is called artificial. If the modern sage had only one glimpse of grass and sky, he would say that grass was not as green as it was painted; that sky was not as blue as it was painted. If one could see the whole universe suddenly, it would look like a bright-colored toy, just as the South American hornbill looks like a bright-colored toy. And so they are—both of them, I mean.

But it was not with this aspect of the startling air of artifice about all strange objects that I meant to deal. I mean merely, as a guide to history, that we should not be surprised if things wrought in fashions remote from ours seem artificial; we should convince ourselves that nine times out of ten these things are nakedly and almost indecently honest. You will hear men talk of the frosted classicism of Corneille or of the powdered pomposities of the eighteenth century, but all these phrases are very superficial. There never was an artificial epoch. There never was an age of reason. Men were always men and women women: and their two generous appetites always were the expression of passion and the telling of truth. We can see something stiff and quaint in their mode of expression, just as our descendants will see something stiff and quaint in our coarsest slum sketch or our most naked pathological play. But men have never talked about anything but important things; and the next force in femininity which we have to consider can be considered best perhaps in some dusty old volume of verses by a person of quality.

The eighteenth century is spoken of as the period of artificiality, in externals at least; but, indeed, there may be two words about that. In modern speech one uses artificiality as meaning indefinitely a sort of deceit; and the eighteenth century was far too artificial to deceive. It cultivated that completest art that does not conceal the art. Its fashions and costumes positively revealed nature by allowing artifice; as in that obvious instance of a barbering that frosted every head with the same silver. It would be fantastic to call this a quaint humility that concealed youth; but, at least, it was not one with the evil pride that conceals old age. Under the eighteenth century fashion people did not so much all pretend to be young, as all agree to be old. The same applies to the most odd and unnatural of their fashions; they were freakish, but they were not false. A lady may or may not be as red as she is painted, but plainly she was not so black as she was patched.

But I only introduce the reader into this atmosphere of the older and franker fictions that he may be induced to have patience for a moment with a certain element which is very common in the decoration and literature of that age and of the two centuries preceding it. It is necessary to mention it in such a connection because it is exactly one of those things that look as superficial as powder, and are really as rooted as hair.

In all the old flowery and pastoral love-songs, those of the seventeenth and eighteenth centuries especially, you will find a perpetual reproach against woman in the matter of her coldness; ceaseless and stale similes that compare her eyes to northern stars, her heart to ice, or her bosom to snow. Now most of us have always supposed these old and iterant phrases to be a mere pattern of dead words, a thing like a cold wall-paper. Yet I think those old cavalier poets who wrote about the coldness of Chloe had hold of a psychological truth missed in nearly all the realistic novels of today. Our psychological romancers perpetually represent wives as striking terror into their husbands by rolling on the floor, gnashing their teeth, throwing about the furniture or poisoning the coffee; all this upon some strange fixed theory that women are what they call emotional. But in truth the old and frigid form is much nearer to the vital fact. Most men if they spoke with any sincerity would agree that the most terrible quality in women, whether in friendship, courtship or marriage, was not so much being emotional as being unemotional.

There is an awful armor of ice which may be the legitimate protection of a more delicate organism; but whatever be the psychological explanation there can surely be no question of the fact. The instinctive cry of the female in anger is noli me tangere. I take this as the most obvious and at the same time the least hackneyed instance of a fundamental quality in the female tradition, which has tended in our time to be almost immeasurably misunderstood, both by the cant of moralists and the cant of immoralists. The proper name for the thing is modesty; but as we live in an age of prejudice and must not call things by their right names, we will yield to a more modern nomenclature and call it dignity. Whatever else it is, it is the thing which a thousand poets and a million lovers have called the coldness of Chloe. It is akin to the classical, and is at least the opposite of the grotesque. And since we are talking here chiefly in types and symbols, perhaps as good an embodiment as any of the idea may be found in the mere fact of a woman wearing a skirt. It is highly typical of the rabid plagiarism which now passes everywhere for emancipation, that a little while ago it was common for an "advanced" woman to claim the right to wear trousers; a right about as grotesque as the right to wear a false nose. Whether female liberty is much advanced by the act of wearing a skirt on each leg I do not know; perhaps Turkish women might offer some information on the point. But if the western woman walks about (as it were) trailing the curtains of the harem with her, it is quite certain that the woven mansion is meant for a perambulating palace, not for a perambulating prison. It is quite certain that the skirt means female dignity, not female submission; it can be proved by the simplest of all tests. No ruler would deliberately dress up in the recognized fetters of a slave; no judge would appear covered with broad arrows. But when men wish to be safely impressive, as judges, priests or kings, they do wear skirts, the long, trailing robes of female dignity The whole world is under petticoat government; for even men wear petticoats when they wish to govern.

VI. THE PEDANT AND THE SAVAGE

We say then that the female holds up with two strong arms these two pillars of civilization; we say also that she could do neither, but for her position; her curious position of private omnipotence, universality on a small scale. The first element is thrift; not the destructive thrift of the miser, but the creative thrift of the peasant; the second element is dignity, which is but the expression of sacred personality and privacy. Now I know the question that will be abruptly and automatically asked by all that know the dull tricks and turns of the modern sexual quarrel. The advanced person will at once begin to argue about whether these instincts are inherent and inevitable in woman or whether they are merely prejudices produced by her history and education. Now I do not propose to discuss whether woman could now be educated out of her habits touching thrift and dignity; and that for two excellent reasons. First it is a question which cannot conceivably ever find any answer: that is why modern people are so fond of it. From the nature of the case it is obviously impossible to decide whether any of the peculiarities of civilized man have been strictly necessary to his civilization. It is not self-evident (for instance), that even the habit of standing upright was the only path of human progress. There might have been a quadrupedal civilization, in which a city gentleman put on four boots to go to the city every morning. Or there might have been a reptilian civilization, in which he rolled up to the office on his stomach; it is impossible to say that intelligence might not have developed in such creatures. All we can say is that man as he is walks upright; and that woman is something almost more upright than uprightness.

And the second point is this: that upon the whole we rather prefer women (nay, even men) to walk upright; so we do not waste much of our noble lives in inventing any other way for them to walk. In short, my second reason for not speculating upon whether woman might get rid of these peculiarities, is that I do not want her to get rid of them; nor does she. I will not exhaust my intelligence by inventing ways in which mankind might unlearn the violin or forget how to ride horses; and the art of domesticity seems to me as special and as valuable as all the ancient arts of our race. Nor do I propose to enter at all into those formless and floundering speculations about how woman was or is regarded in the primitive times that we cannot remember, or in the savage countries which we cannot understand. Even if these people segregated their women for low or barbaric reasons it would not make our reasons barbaric; and I am haunted with a tenacious suspicion that these people's feelings were really, under other forms, very much the same as ours. Some impatient trader, some superficial missionary, walks across an island and sees the squaw digging in the fields while the man is playing a flute; and immediately says that the man is a mere lord of creation and the woman a mere serf. He does not remember that he might see the same thing in half the back gardens in Brixton, merely because women are at once more conscientious and more impatient, while men are at once more quiescent and more greedy for pleasure. It may often be in Hawaii simply as it is in Hoxton. That is, the woman does not work because the man tells her to work and she obeys. On the contrary, the woman works because she has told the man to work and he hasn't obeyed. I do not affirm that this is the whole truth, but I do affirm that we have too little comprehension of the souls of savages to know how far it is untrue. It is the same with the relations of our hasty and surface science, with the problem of sexual dignity and modesty. Professors find all over the world fragmentary ceremonies in which the bride affects some sort of reluctance, hides from her husband, or runs away from him. The professor then pompously proclaims that this is a survival of Marriage by Capture. I wonder he never says that the veil thrown over the bride is really a net. I gravely doubt whether women ever were married by capture I think they pretended to be; as they do still.

It is equally obvious that these two necessary sanctities of thrift and dignity are bound to come into collision with the wordiness, the wastefulness, and the perpetual pleasure-seeking of masculine companionship. Wise women allow for the thing; foolish women try to crush it; but all women try to counteract it, and they do well. In many a home all round us at this moment, we know that the nursery rhyme is reversed. The queen is in the counting-house, counting out the money. The king is in the parlor, eating bread and honey. But it must be strictly understood that the king has captured the honey in some heroic wars. The quarrel can be found in moldering Gothic carvings and in crabbed Greek manuscripts. In every age, in every land, in every tribe and village, has been waged the great sexual war between the Private House and the Public House. I have seen a collection of mediaeval English poems, divided into sections such as "Religious Carols," "Drinking Songs," and so on; and the section headed, "Poems of Domestic Life" consisted entirely (literally, entirely) of the complaints of husbands who were bullied by their wives. Though the English was archaic, the words were in many cases precisely the same as those which I have heard in the streets and public houses of Battersea, protests on behalf of an extension of time and talk, protests against the nervous impatience and the devouring utilitarianism of the female. Such, I say, is the quarrel; it can never be anything but a quarrel; but the aim of all morals and all society is to keep it a lovers' quarrel.

VII. THE MODERN SURRENDER OF WOMAN

But in this corner called England, at this end of the century, there has happened a strange and startling thing. Openly and to all appearance, this ancestral conflict has silently and abruptly ended; one of the two sexes has suddenly surrendered to the other. By the beginning of the twentieth century, within the last few years, the woman has in public surrendered to the man. She has seriously and officially owned that the man has been right all along; that the public house (or Parliament) is really more important than the private house; that politics are not (as woman had always maintained) an excuse for pots of beer, but are a sacred solemnity to which new female worshipers may kneel; that the talkative patriots in the tavern are not only admirable but enviable; that talk is not a waste of time, and therefore (as a consequence, surely) that taverns are not a waste of money. All we men had grown used to our wives and mothers, and grandmothers, and great aunts all pouring a chorus of contempt upon our hobbies of sport, drink and party politics. And now comes Miss Pankhurst with tears in her eyes, owning that all the women were wrong and all the men were right; humbly imploring to be admitted into so much as an outer court, from which she may catch a glimpse of those masculine merits which her erring sisters had so thoughtlessly scorned.

Now this development naturally perturbs and even paralyzes us. Males, like females, in the course of that old fight between the public and private house, had indulged in overstatement and extravagance, feeling that they must keep up their end of the see-saw. We told our wives that Parliament had sat late on most essential business; but it never crossed our minds that our wives would believe it. We said that everyone must have a vote in the country; similarly our wives said that no one must have a pipe in the drawing room. In both cases the idea was the same. "It does not matter much, but if you let those things slide there is chaos." We said that Lord Huggins or Mr. Buggins was absolutely necessary to the country. We knew quite well that nothing is necessary to the country except that the men should be men and the women women. We knew this; we thought the women knew it even more clearly; and we thought the women would say it. Suddenly, without warning, the women have begun to say all the nonsense that we ourselves hardly believed when we said it. The solemnity of politics; the necessity of votes; the necessity of Huggins; the necessity of Buggins; all these flow in a pellucid stream from the lips of all the suffragette speakers. I suppose in every fight, however old, one has a vague aspiration to conquer; but we never wanted to conquer women so completely as this. We only expected that they might leave us a little more margin for our nonsense; we never expected that they would accept it seriously as sense. Therefore I am all at sea about the existing situation; I scarcely know whether to be relieved or enraged by this substitution of the feeble platform lecture for the forcible curtain-lecture. I am lost without the trenchant and candid Mrs. Caudle. I really do not know what to do with the prostrate and penitent Miss Pankhurst. This surrender of the modern woman has taken us all so much by surprise that it is desirable to pause a moment, and collect our wits about what she is really saying.

As I have already remarked, there is one very simple answer to all this; these are not the modern women, but about one in two thousand of the modern women. This fact is important to a democrat; but it is of very little importance to the typically modern mind. Both the characteristic modern parties believed in a government by the few; the only difference is whether it is the Conservative few or Progressive few. It might be put, somewhat coarsely perhaps, by saying that one believes in any minority that is rich and the other in any minority that is mad. But in this state of things the democratic argument obviously falls out for the moment; and we are bound to take the prominent minority, merely because it is prominent. Let us eliminate altogether from our minds the thousands of women who detest this cause, and the millions of women who have hardly heard of it. Let us concede that the English people itself is not and will not be for a very long time within the sphere of practical politics. Let us confine ourselves to saying that these particular women want a vote and to asking themselves what a vote is. If we ask these ladies ourselves what a vote is, we shall get a very vague reply. It is the only question, as a rule, for which they are not prepared. For the truth is that they go mainly by precedent; by the mere fact that men have votes already. So far from being a mutinous movement, it is really a very Conservative one; it is in the narrowest rut of the British Constitution. Let us take a little wider and freer sweep of thought and ask ourselves what is the ultimate point and meaning of this odd business called voting.

VIII. THE BRAND OF THE FLEUR-DE-LIS

Seemingly from the dawn of man all nations have had governments; and all nations have been ashamed of them. Nothing is more openly fallacious than to fancy that in ruder or simpler ages ruling, judging and punishing appeared perfectly innocent and dignified. These things were always regarded as the penalties of the Fall; as part of the humiliation of mankind, as bad in themselves. That the king can do no wrong was never anything but a legal fiction; and it is a legal fiction still. The doctrine of Divine Right was not a piece of idealism, but rather a piece of realism, a practical way of ruling amid the ruin of humanity; a very pragmatist piece of faith. The religious basis of government was not so much that people put their trust in princes, as that they did not put their trust in any child of man. It was so with all the ugly institutions which disfigure human history. Torture and slavery were never talked of as good things; they were always talked of as necessary evils. A pagan spoke of one man owning ten slaves just as a modern business man speaks of one merchant sacking ten clerks: "It's very horrible; but how else can society be conducted?" A mediaeval scholastic regarded the possibility of a man being burned to death just as a modern business man regards the possibility of a man being starved to death: "It is a shocking torture; but can you organize a painless world?" It is possible that a future society may find a way of doing without the question by hunger as we have done without the question by fire. It is equally possible, for the matter of that, that a future society may reestablish legal torture with the whole apparatus of rack and fagot. The most modern of countries, America, has introduced with a vague savor of science, a method which it calls "the third degree." This is simply the extortion of secrets by nervous fatigue; which is surely uncommonly close to their extortion by bodily pain. And this is legal and scientific in America. Amateur ordinary America, of course, simply burns people alive in broad daylight, as they did in the Reformation Wars. But though some punishments are more inhuman than others there is no such thing as humane punishment. As long as nineteen men claim the right in any sense or shape to take hold of the twentieth man and make him even mildly uncomfortable, so long the whole proceeding must be a humiliating one for all concerned. And the proof of how poignantly men have always felt this lies in the fact that the headsman and the hangman, the jailors and the torturers, were always regarded not merely with fear but with contempt; while all kinds of careless smiters, bankrupt knights and swashbucklers and outlaws, were regarded with indulgence or even admiration. To kill a man lawlessly was pardoned. To kill a man lawfully was unpardonable. The most bare-faced duelist might almost brandish his weapon. But the executioner was always masked.

This is the first essential element in government, coercion; a necessary but not a noble element. I may remark in passing that when people say that government rests on force they give an admirable instance of the foggy and muddled cynicism of modernity. Government does not rest on force. Government is force; it rests on consent or a conception of justice. A king or a community holding a certain thing to be abnormal, evil, uses the general strength to crush it out; the strength is his tool, but the belief is his only sanction. You might as well say that glass is the real reason for telescopes. But arising from whatever reason the act of government is coercive and is burdened with all the coarse and painful qualities of coercion. And if anyone asks what is the use of insisting on the ugliness of this task of state violence since all mankind is condemned to employ it, I have a simple answer to that. It would be useless to insist on it if all humanity were condemned to it. But it is not irrelevant to insist on its ugliness so long as half of humanity is kept out of it.

All government then is coercive; we happen to have created a government which is not only coercive; but collective. There are only two kinds of government, as I have already said, the despotic and the democratic. Aristocracy is not a government, it is a riot; that most effective kind of riot, a riot of the rich. The most intelligent apologists of aristocracy, sophists like Burke and Nietzsche, have never claimed for aristocracy any virtues but the virtues of a riot, the accidental virtues, courage, variety and adventure. There is no case anywhere of aristocracy having established a universal and applicable order, as despots and democracies have often done; as the last Caesars created the Roman law, as the last Jacobins created the Code Napoleon. With the first of these elementary forms of government, that of the king or chieftain, we are not in this matter of the sexes immediately concerned. We shall return to it later when we remark how differently mankind has dealt with female claims in the despotic as against the democratic field. But for the moment the essential point is that in self-governing countries this coercion of criminals is a collective coercion. The abnormal person is theoretically thumped by a million fists and kicked by a million feet. If a man is flogged we all flogged him; if a man is hanged, we all hanged him. That is the only possible meaning of democracy, which can give any meaning to the first two syllables and also to the last two. In this sense each citizen has the high responsibility of a rioter. Every statute is a declaration of war, to be backed by arms. Every tribunal is a revolutionary tribunal. In a republic all punishment is as sacred and solemn as lynching.

IX. SINCERITY AND THE GALLOWS

When, therefore, it is said that the tradition against Female Suffrage keeps women out of activity, social influence and citizenship, let us a little more soberly and strictly ask ourselves what it actually does keep her out of. It does definitely keep her out of the collective act of coercion; the act of punishment by a mob. The human tradition does say that, if twenty men hang a man from a tree or lamp-post, they shall be twenty men and not women. Now I do not think any reasonable Suffragist will deny that exclusion from this function, to say the least of it, might be maintained to be a protection as well as a veto. No candid person will wholly dismiss the proposition that the idea of having a Lord Chancellor but not a Lady Chancellor may at least be connected with the idea of having a headsman but not a headswoman, a hangman but not a hangwoman. Nor will it be adequate to answer (as is so often answered to this contention) that in modern civilization women would not really be required to capture, to sentence, or to slay; that all this is done indirectly, that specialists kill our criminals as they kill our cattle. To urge this is not to urge the reality of the vote, but to urge its unreality. Democracy was meant to be a more direct way of ruling, not a more indirect way; and if we do not feel that we are all jailers, so much the worse for us, and for the prisoners. If it is really an unwomanly thing to lock up a robber or a tyrant, it ought to be no softening of the situation that the woman does not feel as if she were doing the thing that she certainly is doing. It is bad enough that men can only associate on paper who could once associate in the street; it is bad enough that men have made a vote very much of a fiction. It is much worse that a great class should claim the vote be cause it is a fiction, who would be sickened by it if it were a fact. If votes for women do not mean mobs for women they do not mean what they were meant to mean. A woman can make a cross on a paper as well as a man; a child could do it as well as a woman; and a chimpanzee after a few lessons could do it as well as a child. But nobody ought to regard it merely as making a cross on paper; everyone ought to regard it as what it ultimately is, branding the fleur-de-lis, marking the broad arrow, signing the death warrant. Both men and women ought to face more fully the things they do or cause to be done; face them or leave off doing them.

On that disastrous day when public executions were abolished, private executions were renewed and ratified, perhaps forever. Things grossly unsuited to the moral sentiment of a society cannot be safely done in broad daylight; but I see no reason why we should not still be roasting heretics alive, in a private room. It is very likely (to speak in the manner foolishly called Irish) that if there were public executions there would be no executions. The old open-air punishments, the pillory and the gibbet, at least fixed responsibility upon the law; and in actual practice they gave the mob an opportunity of throwing roses as well as rotten eggs; of crying "Hosannah" as well as "Crucify." But I do not like the public executioner being turned into the private executioner. I think it is a crooked oriental, sinister sort of business, and smells of the harem and the divan rather than of the forum and the market place. In modern times the official has lost all the social honor and dignity of the common hangman. He is only the bearer of the bowstring.

Here, however, I suggest a plea for a brutal publicity only in order to emphasize the fact that it is this brutal publicity and nothing else from which women have been excluded. I also say it to emphasize the fact that the mere modern veiling of the brutality does not make the situation different, unless we openly say that we are giving the suffrage, not only because it is power but because it is not, or in other words, that women are not so much to vote as to play voting. No suffragist, I suppose, will take up that position; and a few suffragists will wholly deny that this human necessity of pains and penalties is an ugly, humiliating business, and that good motives as well as bad may have helped to keep women out of it. More than once I have remarked in these pages that female limitations may be the limits of a temple as well as of a prison, the disabilities of a priest and not of a pariah. I noted it, I think, in the case of the pontifical feminine dress. In the same way it is not evidently irrational, if men decided that a woman, like a priest, must not be a shedder of blood.

X. THE HIGHER ANARCHY

But there is a further fact; forgotten also because we moderns forget that there is a female point of view. The woman's wisdom stands partly, not only for a wholesome hesitation about punishment, but even for a wholesome hesitation about absolute rules. There was something feminine and perversely true in that phrase of Wilde's, that people should not be treated as the rule, but all of them as exceptions. Made by a man the remark was a little effeminate; for Wilde did lack the masculine power of dogma and of democratic cooperation. But if a woman had said it it would have been simply true; a woman does treat each person as a peculiar person. In other words, she stands for Anarchy; a very ancient and arguable philosophy; not anarchy in the sense of having no customs in one's life (which is inconceivable), but anarchy in the sense of having no rules for one's mind. To her, almost certainly, are due all those working traditions that cannot be found in books, especially those of education; it was she who first gave a child a stuffed stocking for being good or stood him in the corner for being naughty. This unclassified knowledge is sometimes called rule of thumb and sometimes motherwit. The last phrase suggests the whole truth, for none ever called it fatherwit.

Now anarchy is only tact when it works badly. Tact is only anarchy when it works well. And we ought to realize that in one half of the world—the private house—it does work well. We modern men are perpetually forgetting that the case for clear rules and crude penalties is not self-evident, that there is a great deal to be said for the benevolent lawlessness of the autocrat, especially on a small scale; in short, that government is only one side of life. The other half is called Society, in which women are admittedly dominant. And they have always been ready to maintain that their kingdom is better governed than ours, because (in the logical and legal sense) it is not governed at all. "Whenever you have a real difficulty," they say, "when a boy is bumptious or an aunt is stingy, when a silly girl will marry somebody, or a wicked man won't marry somebody, all your lumbering Roman Law and British Constitution come to a standstill. A snub from a duchess or a slanging from a fish-wife are much more likely to put things straight." So, at least, rang the ancient female challenge down the ages until the recent female capitulation. So streamed the red standard of the higher anarchy until Miss Pankhurst hoisted the white flag.

It must be remembered that the modern world has done deep treason to the eternal intellect by believing in the swing of the pendulum. A man must be dead before he swings. It has substituted an idea of fatalistic alternation for the mediaeval freedom of the soul seeking truth. All modern thinkers are reactionaries; for their thought is always a reaction from what went before. When you meet a modern man he is always coming from a place, not going to it. Thus, mankind has in nearly all places and periods seen that there is a soul and a body as plainly as that there is a sun and moon. But because a narrow Protestant sect called Materialists declared for a short time that there was no soul, another narrow Protestant sect called Christian Science is now maintaining that there is no body. Now just in the same way the unreasonable neglect of government by the Manchester School has produced, not a reasonable regard for government, but an unreasonable neglect of everything else. So that to hear people talk to-day one would fancy that every important human function must be organized and avenged by law; that all education must be state education, and all employment state employment; that everybody and everything must be brought to the foot of the august and prehistoric gibbet. But a somewhat more liberal and sympathetic examination of mankind will convince us that the cross is even older than the gibbet, that voluntary suffering was before and independent of compulsory; and in short that in most important matters a man has always been free to ruin himself if he chose. The huge fundamental function upon which all anthropology turns, that of sex and childbirth, has never been inside the political state, but always outside of it. The state concerned itself with the trivial question of killing people, but wisely left alone the whole business of getting them born. A Eugenist might indeed plausibly say that the government is an absent-minded and inconsistent person who occupies himself with providing for the old age of people who have never been infants. I will not deal here in any detail with the fact that some Eugenists have in our time made the maniacal answer that the police ought to control marriage and birth as they control labor and death. Except for this inhuman handful (with whom I regret to say I shall have to deal with later) all the Eugenists I know divide themselves into two sections: ingenious people who once meant this, and rather bewildered people who swear they never meant it—nor anything else. But if it be conceded (by a breezier estimate of men) that they do mostly desire marriage to remain free from government, it does not follow that they desire it to remain free from everything. If man does not control the marriage market by law, is it controlled at all? Surely the answer is broadly that man does not control the marriage market by law, but the woman does control it by sympathy and prejudice. There was until lately a law forbidding a man to marry his deceased wife's sister; yet the thing happened constantly. There was no law forbidding a man to marry his deceased wife's scullery-maid; yet it did not happen nearly so often. It did not happen because the marriage market is managed in the spirit and by the authority of women; and women are generally conservative where classes are concerned. It is the same with that system of exclusiveness by which ladies have so often contrived (as by a process of elimination) to prevent marriages that they did not want and even sometimes procure those they did. There is no need of the broad arrow and the fleur-de lis, the turnkey's chains or the hangman's halter. You need not strangle a man if you can silence him. The branded shoulder is less effective and final than the cold shoulder; and you need not trouble to lock a man in when you can lock him out.

The same, of course, is true of the colossal architecture which we call infant education: an architecture reared wholly by women. Nothing can ever overcome that one enormous sex superiority, that even the male child is born closer to his mother than to his father. No one, staring at that frightful female privilege, can quite believe in the equality of the sexes. Here and there we read of a girl brought up like a tom-boy; but every boy is brought up like a tame girl. The flesh and spirit of femininity surround him from the first like the four walls of a house; and even the vaguest or most brutal man has been womanized by being born. Man that is born of a woman has short days and full of misery; but nobody can picture the obscenity and bestial tragedy that would belong to such a monster as man that was born of a man.

XI. THE QUEEN AND THE SUFFRAGETTES

But, indeed, with this educational matter I must of necessity embroil myself later. The fourth section of discussion is supposed to be about the child, but I think it will be mostly about the mother. In this place I have systematically insisted on the large part of life that is governed, not by man with his vote, but by woman with her voice, or more often, with her horrible silence. Only one thing remains to be added. In a sprawling and explanatory style has been traced out the idea that government is ultimately coercion, that coercion must mean cold definitions as well as cruel consequences, and that therefore there is something to be said for the old human habit of keeping one-half of humanity out of so harsh and dirty a business. But the case is stronger still.

Voting is not only coercion, but collective coercion. I think Queen Victoria would have been yet more popular and satisfying if she had never signed a death warrant. I think Queen Elizabeth would have stood out as more solid and splendid in history if she had not earned (among those who happen to know her history) the nickname of Bloody Bess. I think, in short, that the great historic woman is more herself when she is persuasive rather than coercive. But I feel all mankind behind me when I say that if a woman has this power it should be despotic power—not democratic power. There is a much stronger historic argument for giving Miss Pankhurst a throne than for giving her a vote. She might have a crown, or at least a coronet, like so many of her supporters; for these old powers are purely personal and therefore female. Miss Pankhurst as a despot might be as virtuous as Queen Victoria, and she certainly would find it difficult to be as wicked as Queen Bess, but the point is that, good or bad, she would be irresponsible—she would not be governed by a rule and by a ruler. There are only two ways of governing: by a rule and by a ruler. And it is seriously true to say of a woman, in education and domesticity, that the freedom of the autocrat appears to be necessary to her. She is never responsible until she is irresponsible. In case this sounds like an idle contradiction, I confidently appeal to the cold facts of history. Almost every despotic or oligarchic state has admitted women to its privileges. Scarcely one democratic state has ever admitted them to its rights The reason is very simple: that something female is endangered much more by the violence of the crowd. In short, one Pankhurst is an exception, but a thousand Pankhursts are a nightmare, a Bacchic orgie, a Witches Sabbath. For in all legends men have thought of women as sublime separately but horrible in a herd.

XII. THE MODERN SLAVE

Now I have only taken the test case of Female Suffrage because it is topical and concrete; it is not of great moment for me as a political proposal. I can quite imagine anyone substantially agreeing with my view of woman as universalist and autocrat in a limited area; and still thinking that she would be none the worse for a ballot paper. The real question is whether this old ideal of woman as the great amateur is admitted or not. There are many modern things which threaten it much more than suffragism; notably the increase of self-supporting women, even in the most severe or the most squalid employments. If there be something against nature in the idea of a horde of wild women governing, there is something truly intolerable in the idea of a herd of tame women being governed. And there are elements in human psychology that make this situation particularly poignant or ignominious. The ugly exactitudes of business, the bells and clocks the fixed hours and rigid departments, were all meant for the male: who, as a rule, can only do one thing and can only with the greatest difficulty be induced to do that. If clerks do not try to shirk their work, our whole great commercial system breaks down. It is breaking down, under the inroad of women who are adopting the unprecedented and impossible course of taking the system seriously and doing it well. Their very efficiency is the definition of their slavery. It is generally a very bad sign when one is trusted very much by one's employers. And if the evasive clerks have a look of being blackguards, the earnest ladies are often something very like blacklegs. But the more immediate point is that the modern working woman bears a double burden, for she endures both the grinding officialism of the new office and the distracting scrupulosity of the old home. Few men understand what conscientiousness is. They understand duty, which generally means one duty; but conscientiousness is the duty of the universalist. It is limited by no work days or holidays; it is a lawless, limitless, devouring decorum. If women are to be subjected to the dull rule of commerce, we must find some way of emancipating them from the wild rule of conscience. But I rather fancy you will find it easier to leave the conscience and knock off the commerce. As it is, the modern clerk or secretary exhausts herself to put one thing straight in the ledger and then goes home to put everything straight in the house.

This condition (described by some as emancipated) is at least the reverse of my ideal. I would give woman, not more rights, but more privileges. Instead of sending her to seek such freedom as notoriously prevails in banks and factories, I would design specially a house in which she can be free. And with that we come to the last point of all; the point at which we can perceive the needs of women, like the rights of men, stopped and falsified by something which it is the object of this book to expose.

The Feminist (which means, I think, one who dislikes the chief feminine characteristics) has heard my loose monologue, bursting all the time with one pent-up protest. At this point he will break out and say, "But what are we to do? There is modern commerce and its clerks; there is the modern family with its unmarried daughters; specialism is expected everywhere; female thrift and conscientiousness are demanded and supplied. What does it matter whether we should in the abstract prefer the old human and housekeeping woman; we might prefer the Garden of Eden. But since women have trades they ought to have trades unions. Since women work in factories, they ought to vote on factory-acts. If they are unmarried they must be commercial; if they are commercial they must be political. We must have new rules for a new world—even if it be not a better one." I said to a Feminist once: "The question is not whether women are good enough for votes: it is whether votes are good enough for women." He only answered: "Ah, you go and say that to the women chain-makers on Cradley Heath."

Now this is the attitude which I attack. It is the huge heresy of Precedent. It is the view that because we have got into a mess we must grow messier to suit it; that because we have taken a wrong turn some time ago we must go forward and not backwards; that because we have lost our way we must lose our map also; and because we have missed our ideal, we must forget it. "There are numbers of excellent people who do not think votes unfeminine; and there may be enthusiasts for our beautiful modern industry who do not think factories unfeminine." But if these things are unfeminine it is no answer to say that they fit into each other. I am not satisfied with the statement that my daughter must have unwomanly powers because she has unwomanly wrongs. Industrial soot and political printer's ink are two blacks which do not make a white. Most of the Feminists would probably agree with me that womanhood is under shameful tyranny in the shops and mills. But I want to destroy the tyranny. They want to destroy womanhood. That is the only difference.

Whether we can recover the clear vision of woman as a tower with many windows, the fixed eternal feminine from which her sons, the specialists, go forth; whether we can preserve the tradition of a central thing which is even more human than democracy and even more practical than politics; whether, in word, it is possible to re-establish the family, freed from the filthy cynicism and cruelty of the commercial epoch, I shall discuss in the last section of this book. But meanwhile do not talk to me about the poor chain-makers on Cradley Heath. I know all about them and what they are doing. They are engaged in a very wide-spread and flourishing industry of the present age. They are making chains.

PART FOUR. EDUCATION: OR THE MISTAKE ABOUT THE CHILD

I. THE CALVINISM OF TO-DAY

When I wrote a little volume on my friend Mr. Bernard Shaw, it is needless to say that he reviewed it. I naturally felt tempted to answer and to criticise the book from the same disinterested and impartial standpoint from which Mr. Shaw had criticised the subject of it. I was not withheld by any feeling that the joke was getting a little obvious; for an obvious joke is only a successful joke; it is only the unsuccessful clowns who comfort themselves with being subtle. The real reason why I did not answer Mr. Shaw's amusing attack was this: that one simple phrase in it surrendered to me all that I have ever wanted, or could want from him to all eternity. I told Mr. Shaw (in substance) that he was a charming and clever fellow, but a common Calvinist. He admitted that this was true, and there (so far as I am concerned) is an end of the matter. He said that, of course, Calvin was quite right in holding that "if once a man is born it is too late to damn or save him." That is the fundamental and subterranean secret; that is the last lie in hell.

The difference between Puritanism and Catholicism is not about whether some priestly word or gesture is significant and sacred. It is about whether any word or gesture is significant and sacred. To the Catholic every other daily act is dramatic dedication to the service of good or of evil. To the Calvinist no act can have that sort of solemnity, because the person doing it has been dedicated from eternity, and is merely filling up his time until the crack of doom. The difference is something subtler than plum-puddings or private theatricals; the difference is that to a Christian of my kind this short earthly life is intensely thrilling and precious; to a Calvinist like Mr. Shaw it is confessedly automatic and uninteresting. To me these threescore years and ten are the battle. To the Fabian Calvinist (by his own confession) they are only a long procession of the victors in laurels and the vanquished in chains. To me earthly life is the drama; to him it is the epilogue. Shavians think about the embryo; Spiritualists about the ghost; Christians about the man. It is as well to have these things clear.

Now all our sociology and eugenics and the rest of it are not so much materialist as confusedly Calvinist, they are chiefly occupied in educating the child before he exists. The whole movement is full of a singular depression about what one can do with the populace, combined with a strange disembodied gayety about what may be done with posterity. These essential Calvinists have, indeed, abolished some of the more liberal and universal parts of Calvinism, such as the belief in an intellectual design or an everlasting happiness. But though Mr. Shaw and his friends admit it is a superstition that a man is judged after death, they stick to their central doctrine, that he is judged before he is born.

In consequence of this atmosphere of Calvinism in the cultured world of to-day, it is apparently necessary to begin all arguments on education with some mention of obstetrics and the unknown world of the prenatal. All I shall have to say, however, on heredity will be very brief, because I shall confine myself to what is known about it, and that is very nearly nothing. It is by no means self-evident, but it is a current modern dogma, that nothing actually enters the body at birth except a life derived and compounded from the parents. There is at least quite as much to be said for the Christian theory that an element comes from God, or the Buddhist theory that such an element comes from previous existences. But this is not a religious work, and I must submit to those very narrow intellectual limits which the absence of theology always imposes. Leaving the soul on one side, let us suppose for the sake of argument that the human character in the first case comes wholly from parents; and then let us curtly state our knowledge rather than our ignorance.

II. THE TRIBAL TERROR

Popular science, like that of Mr. Blatchford, is in this matter as mild as old wives' tales. Mr. Blatchford, with colossal simplicity, explained to millions of clerks and workingmen that the mother is like a bottle of blue beads and the father is like a bottle of yellow beads; and so the child is like a bottle of mixed blue beads and yellow. He might just as well have said that if the father has two legs and the mother has two legs, the child will have four legs. Obviously it is not a question of simple addition or simple division of a number of hard detached "qualities," like beads. It is an organic crisis and transformation of the most mysterious sort; so that even if the result is unavoidable, it will still be unexpected. It is not like blue beads mixed with yellow beads; it is like blue mixed with yellow; the result of which is green, a totally novel and unique experience, a new emotion. A man might live in a complete cosmos of blue and yellow, like the "Edinburgh Review"; a man might never have seen anything but a golden cornfield and a sapphire sky; and still he might never have had so wild a fancy as green. If you paid a sovereign for a bluebell; if you spilled the mustard on the blue-books; if you married a canary to a blue baboon; there is nothing in any of these wild weddings that contains even a hint of green. Green is not a mental combination, like addition; it is a physical result like birth. So, apart from the fact that nobody ever really understands parents or children either, yet even if we could understand the parents, we could not make any conjecture about the children. Each time the force works in a different way; each time the constituent colors combine into a different spectacle. A girl may actually inherit her ugliness from her mother's good looks. A boy may actually get his weakness from his father's strength. Even if we admit it is really a fate, for us it must remain a fairy tale. Considered in regard to its causes, the Calvinists and materialists may be right or wrong; we leave them their dreary debate. But considered in regard to its results there is no doubt about it. The thing is always a new color; a strange star. Every birth is as lonely as a miracle. Every child is as uninvited as a monstrosity.

On all such subjects there is no science, but only a sort of ardent ignorance; and nobody has ever been able to offer any theories of moral heredity which justified themselves in the only scientific sense; that is that one could calculate on them beforehand. There are six cases, say, of a grandson having the same twitch of mouth or vice of character as his grandfather; or perhaps there are sixteen cases, or perhaps sixty. But there are not two cases, there is not one case, there are no cases at all, of anybody betting half a crown that the grandfather will have a grandson with the twitch or the vice. In short, we deal with heredity as we deal with omens, affinities and the fulfillment of dreams. The things do happen, and when they happen we record them; but not even a lunatic ever reckons on them. Indeed, heredity, like dreams and omens, is a barbaric notion; that is, not necessarily an untrue, but a dim, groping and unsystematized notion. A civilized man feels himself a little more free from his family. Before Christianity these tales of tribal doom occupied the savage north; and since the Reformation and the revolt against Christianity (which is the religion of a civilized freedom) savagery is slowly creeping back in the form of realistic novels and problem plays. The curse of Rougon-Macquart is as heathen and superstitious as the curse of Ravenswood; only not so well written. But in this twilight barbaric sense the feeling of a racial fate is not irrational, and may be allowed like a hundred other half emotions that make life whole. The only essential of tragedy is that one should take it lightly. But even when the barbarian deluge rose to its highest in the madder novels of Zola (such as that called "The Human Beast", a gross libel on beasts as well as humanity), even then the application of the hereditary idea to practice is avowedly timid and fumbling. The students of heredity are savages in this vital sense; that they stare back at marvels, but they dare not stare forward to schemes. In practice no one is mad enough to legislate or educate upon dogmas of physical inheritance; and even the language of the thing is rarely used except for special modern purposes, such as the endowment of research or the oppression of the poor.

III. THE TRICKS OF ENVIRONMENT

After all the modern clatter of Calvinism, therefore, it is only with the born child that anybody dares to deal; and the question is not eugenics but education. Or again, to adopt that rather tiresome terminology of popular science, it is not a question of heredity but of environment. I will not needlessly complicate this question by urging at length that environment also is open to some of the objections and hesitations which paralyze the employment of heredity. I will merely suggest in passing that even about the effect of environment modern people talk much too cheerfully and cheaply. The idea that surroundings will mold a man is always mixed up with the totally different idea that they will mold him in one particular way. To take the broadest case, landscape no doubt affects the soul; but how it affects it is quite another matter. To be born among pine-trees might mean loving pine-trees. It might mean loathing pine-trees. It might quite seriously mean never having seen a pine-tree. Or it might mean any mixture of these or any degree of any of them. So that the scientific method here lacks a little in precision. I am not speaking without the book; on the contrary, I am speaking with the blue book, with the guide-book and the atlas. It may be that the Highlanders are poetical because they inhabit mountains; but are the Swiss prosaic because they inhabit mountains? It may be the Swiss have fought for freedom because they had hills; did the Dutch fight for freedom because they hadn't? Personally I should think it quite likely. Environment might work negatively as well as positively. The Swiss may be sensible, not in spite of their wild skyline, but be cause of their wild skyline. The Flemings may be fantastic artists, not in spite of their dull skyline, but because of it.

I only pause on this parenthesis to show that, even in matters admittedly within its range, popular science goes a great deal too fast, and drops enormous links of logic. Nevertheless, it remains the working reality that what we have to deal with in the case of children is, for all practical purposes, environment; or, to use the older word, education. When all such deductions are made, education is at least a form of will-worship; not of cowardly fact-worship; it deals with a department that we can control; it does not merely darken us with the barbarian pessimism of Zola and the heredity-hunt. We shall certainly make fools of ourselves; that is what is meant by philosophy. But we shall not merely make beasts of ourselves; which is the nearest popular definition for merely following the laws of Nature and cowering under the vengeance of the flesh. Education contains much moonshine; but not of the sort that makes mere mooncalves and idiots the slaves of a silver magnet, the one eye of the world. In this decent arena there are fads, but not frenzies. Doubtless we shall often find a mare's nest; but it will not always be the nightmare's.

IV. THE TRUTH ABOUT EDUCATION

When a man is asked to write down what he really thinks on education, a certain gravity grips and stiffens his soul, which might be mistaken by the superficial for disgust. If it be really true that men sickened of sacred words and wearied of theology, if this largely unreasoning irritation against "dogma" did arise out of some ridiculous excess of such things among priests in the past, then I fancy we must be laying up a fine crop of cant for our descendants to grow tired of. Probably the word "education" will some day seem honestly as old and objectless as the word "justification" now seems in a Puritan folio. Gibbon thought it frightfully funny that people should have fought about the difference between the "Homoousion" and the "Homoiousion." The time will come when somebody will laugh louder to think that men thundered against Sectarian Education and also against Secular Education; that men of prominence and position actually denounced the schools for teaching a creed and also for not teaching a faith. The two Greek words in Gibbon look rather alike; but they really mean quite different things. Faith and creed do not look alike, but they mean exactly the same thing. Creed happens to be the Latin for faith.

Now having read numberless newspaper articles on education, and even written a good many of them, and having heard deafening and indeterminate discussion going on all around me almost ever since I was born, about whether religion was part of education, about whether hygiene was an essential of education, about whether militarism was inconsistent with true education, I naturally pondered much on this recurring substantive, and I am ashamed to say that it was comparatively late in life that I saw the main fact about it.

Of course, the main fact about education is that there is no such thing. It does not exist, as theology or soldiering exist. Theology is a word like geology, soldiering is a word like soldering; these sciences may be healthy or no as hobbies; but they deal with stone and kettles, with definite things. But education is not a word like geology or kettles. Education is a word like "transmission" or "inheritance"; it is not an object, but a method. It must mean the conveying of certain facts, views or qualities, to the last baby born. They might be the most trivial facts or the most preposterous views or the most offensive qualities; but if they are handed on from one generation to another they are education. Education is not a thing like theology, it is not an inferior or superior thing; it is not a thing in the same category of terms. Theology and education are to each other like a love-letter to the General Post Office. Mr. Fagin was quite as educational as Dr. Strong; in practice probably more educational. It is giving something—perhaps poison. Education is tradition, and tradition (as its name implies) can be treason.

This first truth is frankly banal; but it is so perpetually ignored in our political prosing that it must be made plain. A little boy in a little house, son of a little tradesman, is taught to eat his breakfast, to take his medicine, to love his country, to say his prayers, and to wear his Sunday clothes. Obviously Fagin, if he found such a boy, would teach him to drink gin, to lie, to betray his country, to blaspheme and to wear false whiskers. But so also Mr. Salt the vegetarian would abolish the boy's breakfast; Mrs. Eddy would throw away his medicine; Count Tolstoi would rebuke him for loving his country; Mr. Blatchford would stop his prayers, and Mr. Edward Carpenter would theoretically denounce Sunday clothes, and perhaps all clothes. I do not defend any of these advanced views, not even Fagin's.

But I do ask what, between the lot of them, has become of the abstract entity called education. It is not (as commonly supposed) that the tradesman teaches education plus Christianity; Mr. Salt, education plus vegetarianism; Fagin, education plus crime. The truth is, that there is nothing in common at all between these teachers, except that they teach. In short, the only thing they share is the one thing they profess to dislike: the general idea of authority. It is quaint that people talk of separating dogma from education. Dogma is actually the only thing that cannot be separated from education. It is education. A teacher who is not dogmatic is simply a teacher who is not teaching.

V. AN EVIL CRY

The fashionable fallacy is that by education we can give people something that we have not got. To hear people talk one would think it was some sort of magic chemistry, by which, out of a laborious hotchpotch of hygienic meals, baths, breathing exercises, fresh air and freehand drawing, we can produce something splendid by accident; we can create what we cannot conceive. These pages have, of course, no other general purpose than to point out that we cannot create anything good until we have conceived it. It is odd that these people, who in the matter of heredity are so sullenly attached to law, in the matter of environment seem almost to believe in miracle. They insist that nothing but what was in the bodies of the parents can go to make the bodies of the children. But they seem somehow to think that things can get into the heads of the children which were not in the heads of the parents, or, indeed, anywhere else.

There has arisen in this connection a foolish and wicked cry typical of the confusion. I mean the cry, "Save the children." It is, of course, part of that modern morbidity that insists on treating the State (which is the home of man) as a sort of desperate expedient in time of panic. This terrified opportunism is also the origin of the Socialist and other schemes. Just as they would collect and share all the food as men do in a famine, so they would divide the children from their fathers, as men do in a shipwreck. That a human community might conceivably not be in a condition of famine or shipwreck never seems to cross their minds. This cry of "Save the children" has in it the hateful implication that it is impossible to save the fathers; in other words, that many millions of grown-up, sane, responsible and self-supporting Europeans are to be treated as dirt or debris and swept away out of the discussion; called dipsomaniacs because they drink in public houses instead of private houses; called unemployables because nobody knows how to get them work; called dullards if they still adhere to conventions, and called loafers if they still love liberty. Now I am concerned, first and last, to maintain that unless you can save the fathers, you cannot save the children; that at present we cannot save others, for we cannot save ourselves. We cannot teach citizenship if we are not citizens; we cannot free others if we have forgotten the appetite of freedom. Education is only truth in a state of transmission; and how can we pass on truth if it has never come into our hand? Thus we find that education is of all the cases the clearest for our general purpose. It is vain to save children; for they cannot remain children. By hypothesis we are teaching them to be men; and how can it be so simple to teach an ideal manhood to others if it is so vain and hopeless to find one for ourselves?

I know that certain crazy pedants have attempted to counter this difficulty by maintaining that education is not instruction at all, does not teach by authority at all. They present the process as coming, not from the outside, from the teacher, but entirely from inside the boy. Education, they say, is the Latin for leading out or drawing out the dormant faculties of each person. Somewhere far down in the dim boyish soul is a primordial yearning to learn Greek accents or to wear clean collars; and the schoolmaster only gently and tenderly liberates this imprisoned purpose. Sealed up in the newborn babe are the intrinsic secrets of how to eat asparagus and what was the date of Bannockburn. The educator only draws out the child's own unapparent love of long division; only leads out the child's slightly veiled preference for milk pudding to tarts. I am not sure that I believe in the derivation; I have heard the disgraceful suggestion that "educator," if applied to a Roman schoolmaster, did not mean leading our young functions into freedom; but only meant taking out little boys for a walk. But I am much more certain that I do not agree with the doctrine; I think it would be about as sane to say that the baby's milk comes from the baby as to say that the baby's educational merits do. There is, indeed, in each living creature a collection of forces and functions; but education means producing these in particular shapes and training them to particular purposes, or it means nothing at all. Speaking is the most practical instance of the whole situation. You may indeed "draw out" squeals and grunts from the child by simply poking him and pulling him about, a pleasant but cruel pastime to which many psychologists are addicted. But you will wait and watch very patiently indeed before you draw the English language out of him. That you have got to put into him; and there is an end of the matter.

VI. AUTHORITY THE UNAVOIDABLE

But the important point here is only that you cannot anyhow get rid of authority in education; it is not so much (as poor Conservatives say) that parental authority ought to be preserved, as that it cannot be destroyed. Mr. Bernard Shaw once said that he hated the idea of forming a child's mind. In that case Mr. Bernard Shaw had better hang himself; for he hates something inseparable from human life. I only mentioned educere and the drawing out of the faculties in order to point out that even this mental trick does not avoid the inevitable idea of parental or scholastic authority. The educator drawing out is just as arbitrary and coercive as the instructor pouring in; for he draws out what he chooses. He decides what in the child shall be developed and what shall not be developed. He does not (I suppose) draw out the neglected faculty of forgery. He does not (so far at least) lead out, with timid steps, a shy talent for torture. The only result of all this pompous and precise distinction between the educator and the instructor is that the instructor pokes where he likes and the educator pulls where he likes. Exactly the same intellectual violence is done to the creature who is poked and pulled. Now we must all accept the responsibility of this intellectual violence. Education is violent; because it is creative. It is creative because it is human. It is as reckless as playing on the fiddle; as dogmatic as drawing a picture; as brutal as building a house. In short, it is what all human action is; it is an interference with life and growth. After that it is a trifling and even a jocular question whether we say of this tremendous tormentor, the artist Man, that he puts things into us like an apothecary, or draws things out of us, like a dentist.

The point is that Man does what he likes. He claims the right to take his mother Nature under his control; he claims the right to make his child the Superman, in his image. Once flinch from this creative authority of man, and the whole courageous raid which we call civilization wavers and falls to pieces. Now most modern freedom is at root fear. It is not so much that we are too bold to endure rules; it is rather that we are too timid to endure responsibilities. And Mr. Shaw and such people are especially shrinking from that awful and ancestral responsibility to which our fathers committed us when they took the wild step of becoming men. I mean the responsibility of affirming the truth of our human tradition and handing it on with a voice of authority, an unshaken voice. That is the one eternal education; to be sure enough that something is true that you dare to tell it to a child. From this high audacious duty the moderns are fleeing on every side; and the only excuse for them is, (of course,) that their modern philosophies are so half-baked and hypothetical that they cannot convince themselves enough to convince even a newborn babe. This, of course, is connected with the decay of democracy; and is somewhat of a separate subject. Suffice it to say here that when I say that we should instruct our children, I mean that we should do it, not that Mr. Sully or Professor Earl Barnes should do it. The trouble in too many of our modern schools is that the State, being controlled so specially by the few, allows cranks and experiments to go straight to the schoolroom when they have never passed through the Parliament, the public house, the private house, the church, or the marketplace. Obviously, it ought to be the oldest things that are taught to the youngest people; the assured and experienced truths that are put first to the baby. But in a school to-day the baby has to submit to a system that is younger than himself. The flopping infant of four actually has more experience, and has weathered the world longer, than the dogma to which he is made to submit. Many a school boasts of having the last ideas in education, when it has not even the first idea; for the first idea is that even innocence, divine as it is, may learn something from experience. But this, as I say, is all due to the mere fact that we are managed by a little oligarchy; my system presupposes that men who govern themselves will govern their children. To-day we all use Popular Education as meaning education of the people. I wish I could use it as meaning education by the people.

The urgent point at present is that these expansive educators do not avoid the violence of authority an inch more than the old school masters. Nay, it might be maintained that they avoid it less. The old village schoolmaster beat a boy for not learning grammar and sent him out into the playground to play anything he liked; or at nothing, if he liked that better. The modern scientific schoolmaster pursues him into the playground and makes him play at cricket, because exercise is so good for the health. The modern Dr. Busby is a doctor of medicine as well as a doctor of divinity. He may say that the good of exercise is self-evident; but he must say it, and say it with authority. It cannot really be self-evident or it never could have been compulsory. But this is in modern practice a very mild case. In modern practice the free educationists forbid far more things than the old-fashioned educationists. A person with a taste for paradox (if any such shameless creature could exist) might with some plausibility maintain concerning all our expansion since the failure of Luther's frank paganism and its replacement by Calvin's Puritanism, that all this expansion has not been an expansion, but the closing in of a prison, so that less and less beautiful and humane things have been permitted. The Puritans destroyed images; the Rationalists forbade fairy tales. Count Tostoi practically issued one of his papal encyclicals against music; and I have heard of modern educationists who forbid children to play with tin soldiers. I remember a meek little madman who came up to me at some Socialist soiree or other, and asked me to use my influence (have I any influence?) against adventure stories for boys. It seems they breed an appetite for blood. But never mind that; one must keep one's temper in this madhouse. I need only insist here that these things, even if a just deprivation, are a deprivation. I do not deny that the old vetoes and punishments were often idiotic and cruel; though they are much more so in a country like England (where in practice only a rich man decrees the punishment and only a poor man receives it) than in countries with a clearer popular tradition—such as Russia. In Russia flogging is often inflicted by peasants on a peasant. In modern England flogging can only in practice be inflicted by a gentleman on a very poor man. Thus only a few days ago as I write a small boy (a son of the poor, of course) was sentenced to flogging and imprisonment for five years for having picked up a small piece of coal which the experts value at 5d. I am entirely on the side of such liberals and humanitarians as have protested against this almost bestial ignorance about boys.

But I do think it a little unfair that these humanitarians, who excuse boys for being robbers, should denounce them for playing at robbers. I do think that those who understand a guttersnipe playing with a piece of coal might, by a sudden spurt of imagination, understand him playing with a tin soldier. To sum it up in one sentence: I think my meek little madman might have understood that there is many a boy who would rather be flogged, and unjustly flogged, than have his adventure story taken away.

VII. THE HUMILITY OF MRS. GRUNDY

In short, the new education is as harsh as the old, whether or no it is as high. The freest fad, as much as the strictest formula, is stiff with authority. It is because the humane father thinks soldiers wrong that they are forbidden; there is no pretense, there can be no pretense, that the boy would think so. The average boy's impression certainly would be simply this: "If your father is a Methodist you must not play with soldiers on Sunday. If your father is a Socialist you must not play with them even on week days." All educationists are utterly dogmatic and authoritarian. You cannot have free education; for if you left a child free you would not educate him at all. Is there, then, no distinction or difference between the most hide-bound conventionalists and the most brilliant and bizarre innovators? Is there no difference between the heaviest heavy father and the most reckless and speculative maiden aunt? Yes; there is. The difference is that the heavy father, in his heavy way, is a democrat. He does not urge a thing merely because to his fancy it should be done; but, because (in his own admirable republican formula) "Everybody does it." The conventional authority does claim some popular mandate; the unconventional authority does not. The Puritan who forbids soldiers on Sunday is at least expressing Puritan opinion; not merely his own opinion. He is not a despot; he is a democracy, a tyrannical democracy, a dingy and local democracy perhaps; but one that could do and has done the two ultimate virile things—fight and appeal to God. But the veto of the new educationist is like the veto of the House of Lords; it does not pretend to be representative. These innovators are always talking about the blushing modesty of Mrs. Grundy. I do not know whether Mrs. Grundy is more modest than they are; but I am sure she is more humble.

But there is a further complication. The more anarchic modern may again attempt to escape the dilemma by saying that education should only be an enlargement of the mind, an opening of all the organs of receptivity. Light (he says) should be brought into darkness; blinded and thwarted existences in all our ugly corners should merely be permitted to perceive and expand; in short, enlightenment should be shed over darkest London. Now here is just the trouble; that, in so far as this is involved, there is no darkest London. London is not dark at all; not even at night. We have said that if education is a solid substance, then there is none of it. We may now say that if education is an abstract expansion there is no lack of it. There is far too much of it. In fact, there is nothing else.

There are no uneducated people. Everybody in England is educated; only most people are educated wrong. The state schools were not the first schools, but among the last schools to be established; and London had been educating Londoners long before the London School Board. The error is a highly practical one. It is persistently assumed that unless a child is civilized by the established schools, he must remain a barbarian. I wish he did. Every child in London becomes a highly civilized person. But here are so many different civilizations, most of them born tired. Anyone will tell you that the trouble with the poor is not so much that the old are still foolish, but rather that the young are already wise. Without going to school at all, the gutter-boy would be educated. Without going to school at all, he would be over-educated. The real object of our schools should be not so much to suggest complexity as solely to restore simplicity. You will hear venerable idealists declare we must make war on the ignorance of the poor; but, indeed, we have rather to make war on their knowledge. Real educationists have to resist a kind of roaring cataract of culture. The truant is being taught all day. If the children do not look at the large letters in the spelling-book, they need only walk outside and look at the large letters on the poster. If they do not care for the colored maps provided by the school, they can gape at the colored maps provided by the Daily Mail. If they tire of electricity, they can take to electric trams. If they are unmoved by music, they can take to drink. If they will not work so as to get a prize from their school, they may work to get a prize from Prizy Bits. If they cannot learn enough about law and citizenship to please the teacher, they learn enough about them to avoid the policeman. If they will not learn history forwards from the right end in the history books, they will learn it backwards from the wrong end in the party newspapers. And this is the tragedy of the whole affair: that the London poor, a particularly quick-witted and civilized class, learn everything tail foremost, learn even what is right in the way of what is wrong. They do not see the first principles of law in a law book; they only see its last results in the police news. They do not see the truths of politics in a general survey. They only see the lies of politics, at a General Election.

But whatever be the pathos of the London poor, it has nothing to do with being uneducated. So far from being without guidance, they are guided constantly, earnestly, excitedly; only guided wrong. The poor are not at all neglected, they are merely oppressed; nay, rather they are persecuted. There are no people in London who are not appealed to by the rich; the appeals of the rich shriek from every hoarding and shout from every hustings. For it should always be remembered that the queer, abrupt ugliness of our streets and costumes are not the creation of democracy, but of aristocracy. The House of Lords objected to the Embankment being disfigured by trams. But most of the rich men who disfigure the street-walls with their wares are actually in the House of Lords. The peers make the country seats beautiful by making the town streets hideous. This, however, is parenthetical. The point is, that the poor in London are not left alone, but rather deafened and bewildered with raucous and despotic advice. They are not like sheep without a shepherd. They are more like one sheep whom twenty-seven shepherds are shouting at. All the newspapers, all the new advertisements, all the new medicines and new theologies, all the glare and blare of the gas and brass of modern times—it is against these that the national school must bear up if it can. I will not question that our elementary education is better than barbaric ignorance. But there is no barbaric ignorance. I do not doubt that our schools would be good for uninstructed boys. But there are no uninstructed boys. A modern London school ought not merely to be clearer, kindlier, more clever and more rapid than ignorance and darkness. It must also be clearer than a picture postcard, cleverer than a Limerick competition, quicker than the tram, and kindlier than the tavern. The school, in fact, has the responsibility of universal rivalry. We need not deny that everywhere there is a light that must conquer darkness. But here we demand a light that can conquer light.

VIII. THE BROKEN RAINBOW

I will take one case that will serve both as symbol and example: the case of color. We hear the realists (those sentimental fellows) talking about the gray streets and the gray lives of the poor. But whatever the poor streets are they are not gray; but motley, striped, spotted, piebald and patched like a quilt. Hoxton is not aesthetic enough to be monochrome; and there is nothing of the Celtic twilight about it. As a matter of fact, a London gutter-boy walks unscathed among furnaces of color. Watch him walk along a line of hoardings, and you will see him now against glowing green, like a traveler in a tropic forest; now black like a bird against the burning blue of the Midi; now passant across a field gules, like the golden leopards of England. He ought to understand the irrational rapture of that cry of Mr. Stephen Phillips about "that bluer blue, that greener green." There is no blue much bluer than Reckitt's Blue and no blacking blacker than Day and Martin's; no more emphatic yellow than that of Colman's Mustard. If, despite this chaos of color, like a shattered rainbow, the spirit of the small boy is not exactly intoxicated with art and culture, the cause certainly does not lie in universal grayness or the mere starving of his senses. It lies in the fact that the colors are presented in the wrong connection, on the wrong scale, and, above all, from the wrong motive. It is not colors he lacks, but a philosophy of colors. In short, there is nothing wrong with Reckitt's Blue except that it is not Reckitt's. Blue does not belong to Reckitt, but to the sky; black does not belong to Day and Martin, but to the abyss. Even the finest posters are only very little things on a very large scale. There is something specially irritant in this way about the iteration of advertisements of mustard: a condiment, a small luxury; a thing in its nature not to be taken in quantity. There is a special irony in these starving streets to see such a great deal of mustard to such very little meat. Yellow is a bright pigment; mustard is a pungent pleasure. But to look at these seas of yellow is to be like a man who should swallow gallons of mustard. He would either die, or lose the taste of mustard altogether.

Now suppose we compare these gigantic trivialities on the hoardings with those tiny and tremendous pictures in which the mediaevals recorded their dreams; little pictures where the blue sky is hardly longer than a single sapphire, and the fires of judgment only a pigmy patch of gold. The difference here is not merely that poster art is in its nature more hasty than illumination art; it is not even merely that the ancient artist was serving the Lord while the modern artist is serving the lords. It is that the old artist contrived to convey an impression that colors really were significant and precious things, like jewels and talismanic stones. The color was often arbitrary; but it was always authoritative. If a bird was blue, if a tree was golden, if a fish was silver, if a cloud was scarlet, the artist managed to convey that these colors were important and almost painfully intense; all the red red-hot and all the gold tried in the fire. Now that is the spirit touching color which the schools must recover and protect if they are really to give the children any imaginative appetite or pleasure in the thing. It is not so much an indulgence in color; it is rather, if anything, a sort of fiery thrift. It fenced in a green field in heraldry as straitly as a green field in peasant proprietorship. It would not fling away gold leaf any more than gold coin; it would not heedlessly pour out purple or crimson, any more than it would spill good wine or shed blameless blood. That is the hard task before educationists in this special matter; they have to teach people to relish colors like liquors. They have the heavy business of turning drunkards into wine tasters. If even the twentieth century succeeds in doing these things, it will almost catch up with the twelfth.

The principle covers, however, the whole of modern life. Morris and the merely aesthetic mediaevalists always indicated that a crowd in the time of Chaucer would have been brightly clad and glittering, compared with a crowd in the time of Queen Victoria. I am not so sure that the real distinction is here. There would be brown frocks of friars in the first scene as well as brown bowlers of clerks in the second. There would be purple plumes of factory girls in the second scene as well as purple lenten vestments in the first. There would be white waistcoats against white ermine; gold watch chains against gold lions. The real difference is this: that the brown earth-color of the monk's coat was instinctively chosen to express labor and humility, whereas the brown color of the clerk's hat was not chosen to express anything. The monk did mean to say that he robed himself in dust. I am sure the clerk does not mean to say that he crowns himself with clay. He is not putting dust on his head, as the only diadem of man. Purple, at once rich and somber, does suggest a triumph temporarily eclipsed by a tragedy. But the factory girl does not intend her hat to express a triumph temporarily eclipsed by a tragedy; far from it. White ermine was meant to express moral purity; white waistcoats were not. Gold lions do suggest a flaming magnanimity; gold watch chains do not. The point is not that we have lost the material hues, but that we have lost the trick of turning them to the best advantage. We are not like children who have lost their paint box and are left alone with a gray lead-pencil. We are like children who have mixed all the colors in the paint-box together and lost the paper of instructions. Even then (I do not deny) one has some fun.

Now this abundance of colors and loss of a color scheme is a pretty perfect parable of all that is wrong with our modern ideals and especially with our modern education. It is the same with ethical education, economic education, every sort of education. The growing London child will find no lack of highly controversial teachers who will teach him that geography means painting the map red; that economics means taxing the foreigner, that patriotism means the peculiarly un-English habit of flying a flag on Empire Day. In mentioning these examples specially I do not mean to imply that there are no similar crudities and popular fallacies upon the other political side. I mention them because they constitute a very special and arresting feature of the situation. I mean this, that there were always Radical revolutionists; but now there are Tory revolutionists also. The modern Conservative no longer conserves. He is avowedly an innovator. Thus all the current defenses of the House of Lords which describe it as a bulwark against the mob, are intellectually done for; the bottom has fallen out of them; because on five or six of the most turbulent topics of the day, the House of Lords is a mob itself; and exceedingly likely to behave like one.

IX. THE NEED FOR NARROWNESS

Through all this chaos, then we come back once more to our main conclusion. The true task of culture to-day is not a task of expansion, but very decidedly of selection—and rejection. The educationist must find a creed and teach it. Even if it be not a theological creed, it must still be as fastidious and as firm as theology. In short, it must be orthodox. The teacher may think it antiquated to have to decide precisely between the faith of Calvin and of Laud, the faith of Aquinas and of Swedenborg; but he still has to choose between the faith of Kipling and of Shaw, between the world of Blatchford and of General Booth. Call it, if you will, a narrow question whether your child shall be brought up by the vicar or the minister or the popish priest. You have still to face that larger, more liberal, more highly civilized question, of whether he shall be brought up by Harmsworth or by Pearson, by Mr. Eustace Miles with his Simple Life or Mr. Peter Keary with his Strenuous Life; whether he shall most eagerly read Miss Annie S. Swan or Mr. Bart Kennedy; in short, whether he shall end up in the mere violence of the S. D. F., or in the mere vulgarity of the Primrose League. They say that nowadays the creeds are crumbling; I doubt it, but at least the sects are increasing; and education must now be sectarian education, merely for practical purposes. Out of all this throng of theories it must somehow select a theory; out of all these thundering voices it must manage to hear a voice; out of all this awful and aching battle of blinding lights, without one shadow to give shape to them, it must manage somehow to trace and to track a star.

I have spoken so far of popular education, which began too vague and vast and which therefore has accomplished little. But as it happens there is in England something to compare it with. There is an institution, or class of institutions, which began with the same popular object, which has since followed a much narrower object, but which had the great advantage that it did follow some object, unlike our modern elementary schools.

In all these problems I should urge the solution which is positive, or, as silly people say, "optimistic." I should set my face, that is, against most of the solutions that are solely negative and abolitionist. Most educators of the poor seem to think that they have to teach the poor man not to drink. I should be quite content if they teach him to drink; for it is mere ignorance about how to drink and when to drink that is accountable for most of his tragedies. I do not propose (like some of my revolutionary friends) that we should abolish the public schools. I propose the much more lurid and desperate experiment that we should make them public. I do not wish to make Parliament stop working, but rather to make it work; not to shut up churches, but rather to open them; not to put out the lamp of learning or destroy the hedge of property, but only to make some rude effort to make universities fairly universal and property decently proper.

In many cases, let it be remembered, such action is not merely going back to the old ideal, but is even going back to the old reality. It would be a great step forward for the gin shop to go back to the inn. It is incontrovertibly true that to mediaevalize the public schools would be to democratize the public schools. Parliament did once really mean (as its name seems to imply) a place where people were allowed to talk. It is only lately that the general increase of efficiency, that is, of the Speaker, has made it mostly a place where people are prevented from talking. The poor do not go to the modern church, but they went to the ancient church all right; and if the common man in the past had a grave respect for property, it may conceivably have been because he sometimes had some of his own. I therefore can claim that I have no vulgar itch of innovation in anything I say about any of these institutions. Certainly I have none in that particular one which I am now obliged to pick out of the list; a type of institution to which I have genuine and personal reasons for being friendly and grateful: I mean the great Tudor foundations, the public schools of England. They have been praised for a great many things, mostly, I am sorry to say, praised by themselves and their children. And yet for some reason no one has ever praised them the one really convincing reason.

X. THE CASE FOR THE PUBLIC SCHOOLS

The word success can of course be used in two senses. It may be used with reference to a thing serving its immediate and peculiar purpose, as of a wheel going around; or it can be used with reference to a thing adding to the general welfare, as of a wheel being a useful discovery. It is one thing to say that Smith's flying machine is a failure, and quite another to say that Smith has failed to make a flying machine. Now this is very broadly the difference between the old English public schools and the new democratic schools. Perhaps the old public schools are (as I personally think they are) ultimately weakening the country rather than strengthening it, and are therefore, in that ultimate sense, inefficient. But there is such a thing as being efficiently inefficient. You can make your flying ship so that it flies, even if you also make it so that it kills you. Now the public school system may not work satisfactorily, but it works; the public schools may not achieve what we want, but they achieve what they want. The popular elementary schools do not in that sense achieve anything at all. It is very difficult to point to any guttersnipe in the street and say that he embodies the ideal for which popular education has been working, in the sense that the fresh-faced, foolish boy in "Etons" does embody the ideal for which the headmasters of Harrow and Winchester have been working. The aristocratic educationists have the positive purpose of turning out gentlemen, and they do turn out gentlemen, even when they expel them. The popular educationists would say that they had the far nobler idea of turning out citizens. I concede that it is a much nobler idea, but where are the citizens? I know that the boy in "Etons" is stiff with a rather silly and sentimental stoicism, called being a man of the world. I do not fancy that the errand-boy is rigid with that republican stoicism that is called being a citizen. The schoolboy will really say with fresh and innocent hauteur, "I am an English gentleman." I cannot so easily picture the errand-boy drawing up his head to the stars and answering, "Romanus civis sum." Let it be granted that our elementary teachers are teaching the very broadest code of morals, while our great headmasters are teaching only the narrowest code of manners. Let it be granted that both these things are being taught. But only one of them is being learned.

It is always said that great reformers or masters of events can manage to bring about some specific and practical reforms, but that they never fulfill their visions or satisfy their souls. I believe there is a real sense in which this apparent platitude is quite untrue. By a strange inversion the political idealist often does not get what he asks for, but does get what he wants. The silent pressure of his ideal lasts much longer and reshapes the world much more than the actualities by which he attempted to suggest it. What perishes is the letter, which he thought so practical. What endures is the spirit, which he felt to be unattainable and even unutterable. It is exactly his schemes that are not fulfilled; it is exactly his vision that is fulfilled. Thus the ten or twelve paper constitutions of the French Revolution, which seemed so business-like to the framers of them, seem to us to have flown away on the wind as the wildest fancies. What has not flown away, what is a fixed fact in Europe, is the ideal and vision. The Republic, the idea of a land full of mere citizens all with some minimum of manners and minimum of wealth, the vision of the eighteenth century, the reality of the twentieth. So I think it will generally be with the creator of social things, desirable or undesirable. All his schemes will fail, all his tools break in his hands. His compromises will collapse, his concessions will be useless. He must brace himself to bear his fate; he shall have nothing but his heart's desire.

Now if one may compare very small things with very great, one may say that the English aristocratic schools can claim something of the same sort of success and solid splendor as the French democratic politics. At least they can claim the same sort of superiority over the distracted and fumbling attempts of modern England to establish democratic education. Such success as has attended the public schoolboy throughout the Empire, a success exaggerated indeed by himself, but still positive and a fact of a certain indisputable shape and size, has been due to the central and supreme circumstance that the managers of our public schools did know what sort of boy they liked. They wanted something and they got something; instead of going to work in the broad-minded manner and wanting everything and getting nothing.

The only thing in question is the quality of the thing they got. There is something highly maddening in the circumstance that when modern people attack an institution that really does demand reform, they always attack it for the wrong reasons. Thus many opponents of our public schools, imagining themselves to be very democratic, have exhausted themselves in an unmeaning attack upon the study of Greek. I can understand how Greek may be regarded as useless, especially by those thirsting to throw themselves into the cut throat commerce which is the negation of citizenship; but I do not understand how it can be considered undemocratic. I quite understand why Mr. Carnegie has a hatred of Greek. It is obscurely founded on the firm and sound impression that in any self-governing Greek city he would have been killed. But I cannot comprehend why any chance democrat, say Mr. Quelch, or Mr. Will Crooks, I or Mr. John M. Robertson, should be opposed to people learning the Greek alphabet, which was the alphabet of liberty. Why should Radicals dislike Greek? In that language is written all the earliest and, Heaven knows, the most heroic history of the Radical party. Why should Greek disgust a democrat, when the very word democrat is Greek?

A similar mistake, though a less serious one, is merely attacking the athletics of public schools as something promoting animalism and brutality. Now brutality, in the only immoral sense, is not a vice of the English public schools. There is much moral bullying, owing to the general lack of moral courage in the public-school atmosphere. These schools do, upon the whole, encourage physical courage; but they do not merely discourage moral courage, they forbid it. The ultimate result of the thing is seen in the egregious English officer who cannot even endure to wear a bright uniform except when it is blurred and hidden in the smoke of battle. This, like all the affectations of our present plutocracy, is an entirely modern thing. It was unknown to the old aristocrats. The Black Prince would certainly have asked that any knight who had the courage to lift his crest among his enemies, should also have the courage to lift it among his friends. As regards moral courage, then it is not so much that the public schools support it feebly, as that they suppress it firmly. But physical courage they do, on the whole, support; and physical courage is a magnificent fundamental. The one great, wise Englishman of the eighteenth century said truly that if a man lost that virtue he could never be sure of keeping any other. Now it is one of the mean and morbid modern lies that physical courage is connected with cruelty. The Tolstoian and Kiplingite are nowhere more at one than in maintaining this. They have, I believe, some small sectarian quarrel with each other, the one saying that courage must be abandoned because it is connected with cruelty, and the other maintaining that cruelty is charming because it is a part of courage. But it is all, thank God, a lie. An energy and boldness of body may make a man stupid or reckless or dull or drunk or hungry, but it does not make him spiteful. And we may admit heartily (without joining in that perpetual praise which public-school men are always pouring upon themselves) that this does operate to the removal of mere evil cruelty in the public schools. English public school life is extremely like English public life, for which it is the preparatory school. It is like it specially in this, that things are either very open, common and conventional, or else are very secret indeed. Now there is cruelty in public schools, just as there is kleptomania and secret drinking and vices without a name. But these things do not flourish in the full daylight and common consciousness of the school, and no more does cruelty. A tiny trio of sullen-looking boys gather in corners and seem to have some ugly business always; it may be indecent literature, it may be the beginning of drink, it may occasionally be cruelty to little boys. But on this stage the bully is not a braggart. The proverb says that bullies are always cowardly, but these bullies are more than cowardly; they are shy.

As a third instance of the wrong form of revolt against the public schools, I may mention the habit of using the word aristocracy with a double implication. To put the plain truth as briefly as possible, if aristocracy means rule by a rich ring, England has aristocracy and the English public schools support it. If it means rule by ancient families or flawless blood, England has not got aristocracy, and the public schools systematically destroy it. In these circles real aristocracy, like real democracy, has become bad form. A modern fashionable host dare not praise his ancestry; it would so often be an insult to half the other oligarchs at table, who have no ancestry. We have said he has not the moral courage to wear his uniform; still less has he the moral courage to wear his coat-of-arms. The whole thing now is only a vague hotch-potch of nice and nasty gentlemen. The nice gentleman never refers to anyone else's father, the nasty gentleman never refers to his own. That is the only difference, the rest is the public-school manner. But Eton and Harrow have to be aristocratic because they consist so largely of parvenues. The public school is not a sort of refuge for aristocrats, like an asylum, a place where they go in and never come out. It is a factory for aristocrats; they come out without ever having perceptibly gone in. The poor little private schools, in their old-world, sentimental, feudal style, used to stick up a notice, "For the Sons of Gentlemen only." If the public schools stuck up a notice it ought to be inscribed, "For the Fathers of Gentlemen only." In two generations they can do the trick.

XI. THE SCHOOL FOR HYPOCRITES

These are the false accusations; the accusation of classicism, the accusation of cruelty, and the accusation of an exclusiveness based on perfection of pedigree. English public-school boys are not pedants, they are not torturers; and they are not, in the vast majority of cases, people fiercely proud of their ancestry, or even people with any ancestry to be proud of. They are taught to be courteous, to be good tempered, to be brave in a bodily sense, to be clean in a bodily sense; they are generally kind to animals, generally civil to servants, and to anyone in any sense their equal, the jolliest companions on earth. Is there then anything wrong in the public-school ideal? I think we all feel there is something very wrong in it, but a blinding network of newspaper phraseology obscures and entangles us; so that it is hard to trace to its beginning, beyond all words and phrases, the faults in this great English achievement.

Surely, when all is said, the ultimate objection to the English public school is its utterly blatant and indecent disregard of the duty of telling the truth. I know there does still linger among maiden ladies in remote country houses a notion that English schoolboys are taught to tell the truth, but it cannot be maintained seriously for a moment. Very occasionally, very vaguely, English schoolboys are told not to tell lies, which is a totally different thing. I may silently support all the obscene fictions and forgeries in the universe, without once telling a lie. I may wear another man's coat, steal another man's wit, apostatize to another man's creed, or poison another man's coffee, all without ever telling a lie. But no English school-boy is ever taught to tell the truth, for the very simple reason that he is never taught to desire the truth. From the very first he is taught to be totally careless about whether a fact is a fact; he is taught to care only whether the fact can be used on his "side" when he is engaged in "playing the game." He takes sides in his Union debating society to settle whether Charles I ought to have been killed, with the same solemn and pompous frivolity with which he takes sides in the cricket field to decide whether Rugby or Westminster shall win. He is never allowed to admit the abstract notion of the truth, that the match is a matter of what may happen, but that Charles I is a matter of what did happen—or did not. He is Liberal or Tory at the general election exactly as he is Oxford or Cambridge at the boat race. He knows that sport deals with the unknown; he has not even a notion that politics should deal with the known. If anyone really doubts this self-evident proposition, that the public schools definitely discourage the love of truth, there is one fact which I should think would settle him. England is the country of the Party System, and it has always been chiefly run by public-school men. Is there anyone out of Hanwell who will maintain that the Party System, whatever its conveniences or inconveniences, could have been created by people particularly fond of truth?

The very English happiness on this point is itself a hypocrisy. When a man really tells the truth, the first truth he tells is that he himself is a liar. David said in his haste, that is, in his honesty, that all men are liars. It was afterwards, in some leisurely official explanation, that he said the Kings of Israel at least told the truth. When Lord Curzon was Viceroy he delivered a moral lecture to the Indians on their reputed indifference to veracity, to actuality and intellectual honor. A great many people indignantly discussed whether orientals deserved to receive this rebuke; whether Indians were indeed in a position to receive such severe admonition. No one seemed to ask, as I should venture to ask, whether Lord Curzon was in a position to give it. He is an ordinary party politician; a party politician means a politician who might have belonged to either party. Being such a person, he must again and again, at every twist and turn of party strategy, either have deceived others or grossly deceived himself. I do not know the East; nor do I like what I know. I am quite ready to believe that when Lord Curzon went out he found a very false atmosphere. I only say it must have been something startlingly and chokingly false if it was falser than that English atmosphere from which he came. The English Parliament actually cares for everything except veracity. The public-school man is kind, courageous, polite, clean, companionable; but, in the most awful sense of the words, the truth is not in him.

This weakness of untruthfulness in the English public schools, in the English political system, and to some extent in the English character, is a weakness which necessarily produces a curious crop of superstitions, of lying legends, of evident delusions clung to through low spiritual self-indulgence. There are so many of these public-school superstitions that I have here only space for one of them, which may be called the superstition of soap. It appears to have been shared by the ablutionary Pharisees, who resembled the English public-school aristocrats in so many respects: in their care about club rules and traditions, in their offensive optimism at the expense of other people, and above all in their unimaginative plodding patriotism in the worst interests of their country. Now the old human common sense about washing is that it is a great pleasure. Water (applied externally) is a splendid thing, like wine. Sybarites bathe in wine, and Nonconformists drink water; but we are not concerned with these frantic exceptions. Washing being a pleasure, it stands to reason that rich people can afford it more than poor people, and as long as this was recognized all was well; and it was very right that rich people should offer baths to poor people, as they might offer any other agreeable thing—a drink or a donkey ride. But one dreadful day, somewhere about the middle of the nineteenth century, somebody discovered (somebody pretty well off) the two great modern truths, that washing is a virtue in the rich and therefore a duty in the poor. For a duty is a virtue that one can't do. And a virtue is generally a duty that one can do quite easily; like the bodily cleanliness of the upper classes. But in the public-school tradition of public life, soap has become creditable simply because it is pleasant. Baths are represented as a part of the decay of the Roman Empire; but the same baths are represented as part of the energy and rejuvenation of the British Empire. There are distinguished public school men, bishops, dons, headmasters, and high politicians, who, in the course of the eulogies which from time to time they pass upon themselves, have actually identified physical cleanliness with moral purity. They say (if I remember rightly) that a public-school man is clean inside and out. As if everyone did not know that while saints can afford to be dirty, seducers have to be clean. As if everyone did not know that the harlot must be clean, because it is her business to captivate, while the good wife may be dirty, because it is her business to clean. As if we did not all know that whenever God's thunder cracks above us, it is very likely indeed to find the simplest man in a muck cart and the most complex blackguard in a bath.

There are other instances, of course, of this oily trick of turning the pleasures of a gentleman into the virtues of an Anglo-Saxon. Sport, like soap, is an admirable thing, but, like soap, it is an agreeable thing. And it does not sum up all mortal merits to be a sportsman playing the game in a world where it is so often necessary to be a workman doing the work. By all means let a gentleman congratulate himself that he has not lost his natural love of pleasure, as against the blase, and unchildlike. But when one has the childlike joy it is best to have also the childlike unconsciousness; and I do not think we should have special affection for the little boy who ever lastingly explained that it was his duty to play Hide and Seek and one of his family virtues to be prominent in Puss in the Corner.

Another such irritating hypocrisy is the oligarchic attitude towards mendicity as against organized charity. Here again, as in the case of cleanliness and of athletics, the attitude would be perfectly human and intelligible if it were not maintained as a merit. Just as the obvious thing about soap is that it is a convenience, so the obvious thing about beggars is that they are an inconvenience. The rich would deserve very little blame if they simply said that they never dealt directly with beggars, because in modern urban civilization it is impossible to deal directly with beggars; or if not impossible, at least very difficult. But these people do not refuse money to beggars on the ground that such charity is difficult. They refuse it on the grossly hypocritical ground that such charity is easy. They say, with the most grotesque gravity, "Anyone can put his hand in his pocket and give a poor man a penny; but we, philanthropists, go home and brood and travail over the poor man's troubles until we have discovered exactly what jail, reformatory, workhouse, or lunatic asylum it will really be best for him to go to." This is all sheer lying. They do not brood about the man when they get home, and if they did it would not alter the original fact that their motive for discouraging beggars is the perfectly rational one that beggars are a bother. A man may easily be forgiven for not doing this or that incidental act of charity, especially when the question is as genuinely difficult as is the case of mendicity. But there is something quite pestilently Pecksniffian about shrinking from a hard task on the plea that it is not hard enough. If any man will really try talking to the ten beggars who come to his door he will soon find out whether it is really so much easier than the labor of writing a check for a hospital.

XII. THE STALENESS OF THE NEW SCHOOLS

For this deep and disabling reason therefore, its cynical and abandoned indifference to the truth, the English public school does not provide us with the ideal that we require. We can only ask its modern critics to remember that right or wrong the thing can be done; the factory is working, the wheels are going around, the gentlemen are being produced, with their soap, cricket and organized charity all complete. And in this, as we have said before, the public school really has an advantage over all the other educational schemes of our time. You can pick out a public-school man in any of the many companies into which they stray, from a Chinese opium den to a German Jewish dinner-party. But I doubt if you could tell which little match girl had been brought up by undenominational religion and which by secular education. The great English aristocracy which has ruled us since the Reformation is really, in this sense, a model to the moderns. It did have an ideal, and therefore it has produced a reality.

We may repeat here that these pages propose mainly to show one thing: that progress ought to be based on principle, while our modern progress is mostly based on precedent. We go, not by what may be affirmed in theory, but by what has been already admitted in practice. That is why the Jacobites are the last Tories in history with whom a high-spirited person can have much sympathy. They wanted a specific thing; they were ready to go forward for it, and so they were also ready to go back for it. But modern Tories have only the dullness of defending situations that they had not the excitement of creating. Revolutionists make a reform, Conservatives only conserve the reform. They never reform the reform, which is often very much wanted. Just as the rivalry of armaments is only a sort of sulky plagiarism, so the rivalry of parties is only a sort of sulky inheritance. Men have votes, so women must soon have votes; poor children are taught by force, so they must soon be fed by force; the police shut public houses by twelve o'clock, so soon they must shut them by eleven o'clock; children stop at school till they are fourteen, so soon they will stop till they are forty. No gleam of reason, no momentary return to first principles, no abstract asking of any obvious question, can interrupt this mad and monotonous gallop of mere progress by precedent. It is a good way to prevent real revolution. By this logic of events, the Radical gets as much into a rut as the Conservative. We meet one hoary old lunatic who says his grandfather told him to stand by one stile. We meet another hoary old lunatic who says his grandfather told him only to walk along one lane.

I say we may repeat here this primary part of the argument, because we have just now come to the place where it is most startlingly and strongly shown. The final proof that our elementary schools have no definite ideal of their own is the fact that they so openly imitate the ideals of the public schools. In the elementary schools we have all the ethical prejudices and exaggerations of Eton and Harrow carefully copied for people to whom they do not even roughly apply. We have the same wildly disproportionate doctrine of the effect of physical cleanliness on moral character. Educators and educational politicians declare, amid warm cheers, that cleanliness is far more important than all the squabbles about moral and religious training. It would really seem that so long as a little boy washes his hands it does not matter whether he is washing off his mother's jam or his brother's gore. We have the same grossly insincere pretense that sport always encourages a sense of honor, when we know that it often ruins it. Above all, we have the same great upperclass assumption that things are done best by large institutions handling large sums of money and ordering everybody about; and that trivial and impulsive charity is in some way contemptible. As Mr. Blatchford says, "The world does not want piety, but soap—and Socialism." Piety is one of the popular virtues, whereas soap and Socialism are two hobbies of the upper middle class.

These "healthy" ideals, as they are called, which our politicians and schoolmasters have borrowed from the aristocratic schools and applied to the democratic, are by no means particularly appropriate to an impoverished democracy. A vague admiration for organized government and a vague distrust of individual aid cannot be made to fit in at all into the lives of people among whom kindness means lending a saucepan and honor means keeping out of the workhouse. It resolves itself either into discouraging that system of prompt and patchwork generosity which is a daily glory of the poor, or else into hazy advice to people who have no money not to give it recklessly away. Nor is the exaggerated glory of athletics, defensible enough in dealing with the rich who, if they did not romp and race, would eat and drink unwholesomely, by any means so much to the point when applied to people, most of whom will take a great deal of exercise anyhow, with spade or hammer, pickax or saw. And for the third case, of washing, it is obvious that the same sort of rhetoric about corporeal daintiness which is proper to an ornamental class cannot, merely as it stands, be applicable to a dustman. A gentleman is expected to be substantially spotless all the time. But it is no more discreditable for a scavenger to be dirty than for a deep-sea diver to be wet. A sweep is no more disgraced when he is covered with soot than Michael Angelo when he is covered with clay, or Bayard when he is covered with blood. Nor have these extenders of the public-school tradition done or suggested anything by way of a substitute for the present snobbish system which makes cleanliness almost impossible to the poor; I mean the general ritual of linen and the wearing of the cast-off clothes of the rich. One man moves into another man's clothes as he moves into another man's house. No wonder that our educationists are not horrified at a man picking up the aristocrat's second-hand trousers, when they themselves have only taken up the aristocrat's second-hand ideas.

XIII. THE OUTLAWED PARENT

There is one thing at least of which there is never so much as a whisper inside the popular schools; and that is the opinion of the people. The only persons who seem to have nothing to do with the education of the children are the parents. Yet the English poor have very definite traditions in many ways. They are hidden under embarrassment and irony; and those psychologists who have disentangled them talk of them as very strange, barbaric and secretive things. But, as a matter of fact, the traditions of the poor are mostly simply the traditions of humanity, a thing which many of us have not seen for some time. For instance, workingmen have a tradition that if one is talking about a vile thing it is better to talk of it in coarse language; one is the less likely to be seduced into excusing it. But mankind had this tradition also, until the Puritans and their children, the Ibsenites, started the opposite idea, that it does not matter what you say so long as you say it with long words and a long face. Or again, the educated classes have tabooed most jesting about personal appearance; but in doing this they taboo not only the humor of the slums, but more than half the healthy literature of the world; they put polite nose-bags on the noses of Punch and Bardolph, Stiggins and Cyrano de Bergerac. Again, the educated classes have adopted a hideous and heathen custom of considering death as too dreadful to talk about, and letting it remain a secret for each person, like some private malformation. The poor, on the contrary, make a great gossip and display about bereavement; and they are right. They have hold of a truth of psychology which is at the back of all the funeral customs of the children of men. The way to lessen sorrow is to make a lot of it. The way to endure a painful crisis is to insist very much that it is a crisis; to permit people who must feel sad at least to feel important. In this the poor are simply the priests of the universal civilization; and in their stuffy feasts and solemn chattering there is the smell of the baked meats of Hamlet and the dust and echo of the funeral games of Patroclus.

The things philanthropists barely excuse (or do not excuse) in the life of the laboring classes are simply the things we have to excuse in all the greatest monuments of man. It may be that the laborer is as gross as Shakespeare or as garrulous as Homer; that if he is religious he talks nearly as much about hell as Dante; that if he is worldly he talks nearly as much about drink as Dickens. Nor is the poor man without historic support if he thinks less of that ceremonial washing which Christ dismissed, and rather more of that ceremonial drinking which Christ specially sanctified. The only difference between the poor man of to-day and the saints and heroes of history is that which in all classes separates the common man who can feel things from the great man who can express them. What he feels is merely the heritage of man. Now nobody expects of course that the cabmen and coal-heavers can be complete instructors of their children any more than the squires and colonels and tea merchants are complete instructors of their children. There must be an educational specialist in loco parentis. But the master at Harrow is in loco parentis; the master in Hoxton is rather contra parentem. The vague politics of the squire, the vaguer virtues of the colonel, the soul and spiritual yearnings of a tea merchant, are, in veritable practice, conveyed to the children of these people at the English public schools. But I wish here to ask a very plain and emphatic question. Can anyone alive even pretend to point out any way in which these special virtues and traditions of the poor are reproduced in the education of the poor? I do not wish the coster's irony to appeal as coarsely in the school as it does in the tap room; but does it appear at all? Is the child taught to sympathize at all with his father's admirable cheerfulness and slang? I do not expect the pathetic, eager pietas of the mother, with her funeral clothes and funeral baked meats, to be exactly imitated in the educational system; but has it any influence at all on the educational system? Does any elementary schoolmaster accord it even an instant's consideration or respect? I do not expect the schoolmaster to hate hospitals and C.O.S. centers so much as the schoolboy's father; but does he hate them at all? Does he sympathize in the least with the poor man's point of honor against official institutions? Is it not quite certain that the ordinary elementary schoolmaster will think it not merely natural but simply conscientious to eradicate all these rugged legends of a laborious people, and on principle to preach soap and Socialism against beer and liberty? In the lower classes the school master does not work for the parent, but against the parent. Modern education means handing down the customs of the minority, and rooting out the customs of the majority. Instead of their Christlike charity, their Shakespearean laughter and their high Homeric reverence for the dead, the poor have imposed on them mere pedantic copies of the prejudices of the remote rich. They must think a bathroom a necessity because to the lucky it is a luxury; they must swing Swedish clubs because their masters are afraid of English cudgels; and they must get over their prejudice against being fed by the parish, because aristocrats feel no shame about being fed by the nation.

XIV. FOLLY AND FEMALE EDUCATION

It is the same in the case of girls. I am often solemnly asked what I think of the new ideas about female education. But there are no new ideas about female education. There is not, there never has been, even the vestige of a new idea. All the educational reformers did was to ask what was being done to boys and then go and do it to girls; just as they asked what was being taught to young squires and then taught it to young chimney sweeps. What they call new ideas are very old ideas in the wrong place. Boys play football, why shouldn't girls play football; boys have school colors, why shouldn't girls have school-colors; boys go in hundreds to day-schools, why shouldn't girls go in hundreds to day-schools; boys go to Oxford, why shouldn't girls go to Oxford—in short, boys grow mustaches, why shouldn't girls grow mustaches—that is about their notion of a new idea. There is no brain-work in the thing at all; no root query of what sex is, of whether it alters this or that, and why, anymore than there is any imaginative grip of the humor and heart of the populace in the popular education. There is nothing but plodding, elaborate, elephantine imitation. And just as in the case of elementary teaching, the cases are of a cold and reckless inappropriateness. Even a savage could see that bodily things, at least, which are good for a man are very likely to be bad for a woman. Yet there is no boy's game, however brutal, which these mild lunatics have not promoted among girls. To take a stronger case, they give girls very heavy home-work; never reflecting that all girls have home-work already in their homes. It is all a part of the same silly subjugation; there must be a hard stick-up collar round the neck of a woman, because it is already a nuisance round the neck of a man. Though a Saxon serf, if he wore that collar of cardboard, would ask for his collar of brass.

It will then be answered, not without a sneer, "And what would you prefer? Would you go back to the elegant early Victorian female, with ringlets and smelling-bottle, doing a little in water colors, dabbling a little in Italian, playing a little on the harp, writing in vulgar albums and painting on senseless screens? Do you prefer that?" To which I answer, "Emphatically, yes." I solidly prefer it to the new female education, for this reason, that I can see in it an intellectual design, while there is none in the other. I am by no means sure that even in point of practical fact that elegant female would not have been more than a match for most of the inelegant females. I fancy Jane Austen was stronger, sharper and shrewder than Charlotte Bronte; I am quite certain she was stronger, sharper and shrewder than George Eliot. She could do one thing neither of them could do: she could coolly and sensibly describe a man.

I am not sure that the old great lady who could only smatter Italian was not more vigorous than the new great lady who can only stammer American; nor am I certain that the bygone duchesses who were scarcely successful when they painted Melrose Abbey, were so much more weak-minded than the modern duchesses who paint only their own faces, and are bad at that. But that is not the point. What was the theory, what was the idea, in their old, weak water-colors and their shaky Italian? The idea was the same which in a ruder rank expressed itself in home-made wines and hereditary recipes; and which still, in a thousand unexpected ways, can be found clinging to the women of the poor. It was the idea I urged in the second part of this book: that the world must keep one great amateur, lest we all become artists and perish. Somebody must renounce all specialist conquests, that she may conquer all the conquerors. That she may be a queen of life, she must not be a private soldier in it. I do not think the elegant female with her bad Italian was a perfect product, any more than I think the slum woman talking gin and funerals is a perfect product; alas! there are few perfect products. But they come from a comprehensible idea; and the new woman comes from nothing and nowhere. It is right to have an ideal, it is right to have the right ideal, and these two have the right ideal. The slum mother with her funerals is the degenerate daughter of Antigone, the obstinate priestess of the household gods. The lady talking bad Italian was the decayed tenth cousin of Portia, the great and golden Italian lady, the Renascence amateur of life, who could be a barrister because she could be anything. Sunken and neglected in the sea of modern monotony and imitation, the types hold tightly to their original truths. Antigone, ugly, dirty and often drunken, will still bury her father. The elegant female, vapid and fading away to nothing, still feels faintly the fundamental difference between herself and her husband: that he must be Something in the City, that she may be everything in the country.

There was a time when you and I and all of us were all very close to God; so that even now the color of a pebble (or a paint), the smell of a flower (or a firework), comes to our hearts with a kind of authority and certainty; as if they were fragments of a muddled message, or features of a forgotten face. To pour that fiery simplicity upon the whole of life is the only real aim of education; and closest to the child comes the woman—she understands. To say what she understands is beyond me; save only this, that it is not a solemnity. Rather it is a towering levity, an uproarious amateurishness of the universe, such as we felt when we were little, and would as soon sing as garden, as soon paint as run. To smatter the tongues of men and angels, to dabble in the dreadful sciences, to juggle with pillars and pyramids and toss up the planets like balls, this is that inner audacity and indifference which the human soul, like a conjurer catching oranges, must keep up forever. This is that insanely frivolous thing we call sanity. And the elegant female, drooping her ringlets over her water-colors, knew it and acted on it. She was juggling with frantic and flaming suns. She was maintaining the bold equilibrium of inferiorities which is the most mysterious of superiorities and perhaps the most unattainable. She was maintaining the prime truth of woman, the universal mother: that if a thing is worth doing, it is worth doing badly.

PART FIVE. THE HOME OF MAN

I. THE EMPIRE OF THE INSECT

A cultivated Conservative friend of mine once exhibited great distress because in a gay moment I once called Edmund Burke an atheist. I need scarcely say that the remark lacked something of biographical precision; it was meant to. Burke was certainly not an atheist in his conscious cosmic theory, though he had not a special and flaming faith in God, like Robespierre. Nevertheless, the remark had reference to a truth which it is here relevant to repeat. I mean that in the quarrel over the French Revolution, Burke did stand for the atheistic attitude and mode of argument, as Robespierre stood for the theistic. The Revolution appealed to the idea of an abstract and eternal justice, beyond all local custom or convenience. If there are commands of God, then there must be rights of man. Here Burke made his brilliant diversion; he did not attack the Robespierre doctrine with the old mediaeval doctrine of jus divinum (which, like the Robespierre doctrine, was theistic), he attacked it with the modern argument of scientific relativity; in short, the argument of evolution. He suggested that humanity was everywhere molded by or fitted to its environment and institutions; in fact, that each people practically got, not only the tyrant it deserved, but the tyrant it ought to have. "I know nothing of the rights of men," he said, "but I know something of the rights of Englishmen." There you have the essential atheist. His argument is that we have got some protection by natural accident and growth; and why should we profess to think beyond it, for all the world as if we were the images of God! We are born under a House of Lords, as birds under a house of leaves; we live under a monarchy as niggers live under a tropic sun; it is not their fault if they are slaves, and it is not ours if we are snobs. Thus, long before Darwin struck his great blow at democracy, the essential of the Darwinian argument had been already urged against the French Revolution. Man, said Burke in effect, must adapt himself to everything, like an animal; he must not try to alter everything, like an angel. The last weak cry of the pious, pretty, half-artificial optimism and deism of the eighteenth century came in the voice of Sterne, saying, "God tempers the wind to the shorn lamb." And Burke, the iron evolutionist, essentially answered, "No; God tempers the shorn lamb to the wind." It is the lamb that has to adapt himself. That is, he either dies or becomes a particular kind of lamb who likes standing in a draught.

The subconscious popular instinct against Darwinism was not a mere offense at the grotesque notion of visiting one's grandfather in a cage in the Regent's Park. Men go in for drink, practical jokes and many other grotesque things; they do not much mind making beasts of themselves, and would not much mind having beasts made of their forefathers. The real instinct was much deeper and much more valuable. It was this: that when once one begins to think of man as a shifting and alterable thing, it is always easy for the strong and crafty to twist him into new shapes for all kinds of unnatural purposes. The popular instinct sees in such developments the possibility of backs bowed and hunch-backed for their burden, or limbs twisted for their task. It has a very well-grounded guess that whatever is done swiftly and systematically will mostly be done by a successful class and almost solely in their interests. It has therefore a vision of inhuman hybrids and half-human experiments much in the style of Mr. Wells's "Island of Dr. Moreau." The rich man may come to breeding a tribe of dwarfs to be his jockeys, and a tribe of giants to be his hall-porters. Grooms might be born bow-legged and tailors born cross-legged; perfumers might have long, large noses and a crouching attitude, like hounds of scent; and professional wine-tasters might have the horrible expression of one tasting wine stamped upon their faces as infants. Whatever wild image one employs it cannot keep pace with the panic of the human fancy, when once it supposes that the fixed type called man could be changed. If some millionaire wanted arms, some porter must grow ten arms like an octopus; if he wants legs, some messenger-boy must go with a hundred trotting legs like a centipede. In the distorted mirror of hypothesis, that is, of the unknown, men can dimly see such monstrous and evil shapes; men run all to eye, or all to fingers, with nothing left but one nostril or one ear. That is the nightmare with which the mere notion of adaptation threatens us. That is the nightmare that is not so very far from the reality.

It will be said that not the wildest evolutionist really asks that we should become in any way unhuman or copy any other animal. Pardon me, that is exactly what not merely the wildest evolutionists urge, but some of the tamest evolutionists too. There has risen high in recent history an important cultus which bids fair to be the religion of the future—which means the religion of those few weak-minded people who live in the future. It is typical of our time that it has to look for its god through a microscope; and our time has marked a definite adoration of the insect. Like most things we call new, of course, it is not at all new as an idea; it is only new as an idolatry. Virgil takes bees seriously but I doubt if he would have kept bees as carefully as he wrote about them. The wise king told the sluggard to watch the ant, a charming occupation—for a sluggard. But in our own time has appeared a very different tone, and more than one great man, as well as numberless intelligent men, have in our time seriously suggested that we should study the insect because we are his inferiors. The old moralists merely took the virtues of man and distributed them quite decoratively and arbitrarily among the animals. The ant was an almost heraldic symbol of industry, as the lion was of courage, or, for the matter of that, the pelican of charity. But if the mediaevals had been convinced that a lion was not courageous, they would have dropped the lion and kept the courage; if the pelican is not charitable, they would say, so much the worse for the pelican. The old moralists, I say, permitted the ant to enforce and typify man's morality; they never allowed the ant to upset it. They used the ant for industry as the lark for punctuality; they looked up at the flapping birds and down at the crawling insects for a homely lesson. But we have lived to see a sect that does not look down at the insects, but looks up at the insects, that asks us essentially to bow down and worship beetles, like ancient Egyptians.

Maurice Maeterlinck is a man of unmistakable genius, and genius always carries a magnifying glass. In the terrible crystal of his lens we have seen the bees not as a little yellow swarm, but rather in golden armies and hierarchies of warriors and queens. Imagination perpetually peers and creeps further down the avenues and vistas in the tubes of science, and one fancies every frantic reversal of proportions; the earwig striding across the echoing plain like an elephant, or the grasshopper coming roaring above our roofs like a vast aeroplane, as he leaps from Hertfordshire to Surrey. One seems to enter in a dream a temple of enormous entomology, whose architecture is based on something wilder than arms or backbones; in which the ribbed columns have the half-crawling look of dim and monstrous caterpillars; or the dome is a starry spider hung horribly in the void. There is one of the modern works of engineering that gives one something of this nameless fear of the exaggerations of an underworld; and that is the curious curved architecture of the under ground railway, commonly called the Twopenny Tube. Those squat archways, without any upright line or pillar, look as if they had been tunneled by huge worms who have never learned to lift their heads. It is the very underground palace of the Serpent, the spirit of changing shape and color, that is the enemy of man.

But it is not merely by such strange aesthetic suggestions that writers like Maeterlinck have influenced us in the matter; there is also an ethical side to the business. The upshot of M. Maeterlinck's book on bees is an admiration, one might also say an envy, of their collective spirituality; of the fact that they live only for something which he calls the Soul of the Hive. And this admiration for the communal morality of insects is expressed in many other modern writers in various quarters and shapes; in Mr. Benjamin Kidd's theory of living only for the evolutionary future of our race, and in the great interest of some Socialists in ants, which they generally prefer to bees, I suppose, because they are not so brightly colored. Not least among the hundred evidences of this vague insectolatry are the floods of flattery poured by modern people on that energetic nation of the Far East of which it has been said that "Patriotism is its only religion"; or, in other words, that it lives only for the Soul of the Hive. When at long intervals of the centuries Christendom grows weak, morbid or skeptical, and mysterious Asia begins to move against us her dim populations and to pour them westward like a dark movement of matter, in such cases it has been very common to compare the invasion to a plague of lice or incessant armies of locusts. The Eastern armies were indeed like insects; in their blind, busy destructiveness, in their black nihilism of personal outlook, in their hateful indifference to individual life and love, in their base belief in mere numbers, in their pessimistic courage and their atheistic patriotism, the riders and raiders of the East are indeed like all the creeping things of the earth. But never before, I think, have Christians called a Turk a locust and meant it as a compliment. Now for the first time we worship as well as fear; and trace with adoration that enormous form advancing vast and vague out of Asia, faintly discernible amid the mystic clouds of winged creatures hung over the wasted lands, thronging the skies like thunder and discoloring the skies like rain; Beelzebub, the Lord of Flies.

In resisting this horrible theory of the Soul of the Hive, we of Christendom stand not for ourselves, but for all humanity; for the essential and distinctive human idea that one good and happy man is an end in himself, that a soul is worth saving. Nay, for those who like such biological fancies it might well be said that we stand as chiefs and champions of a whole section of nature, princes of the house whose cognizance is the backbone, standing for the milk of the individual mother and the courage of the wandering cub, representing the pathetic chivalry of the dog, the humor and perversity of cats, the affection of the tranquil horse, the loneliness of the lion. It is more to the point, however, to urge that this mere glorification of society as it is in the social insects is a transformation and a dissolution in one of the outlines which have been specially the symbols of man. In the cloud and confusion of the flies and bees is growing fainter and fainter, as is finally disappearing, the idea of the human family. The hive has become larger than the house, the bees are destroying their captors; what the locust hath left, the caterpillar hath eaten; and the little house and garden of our friend Jones is in a bad way.

II. THE FALLACY OF THE UMBRELLA STAND

When Lord Morley said that the House of Lords must be either mended or ended, he used a phrase which has caused some confusion; because it might seem to suggest that mending and ending are somewhat similar things. I wish specially to insist on the fact that mending and ending are opposite things. You mend a thing because you like it; you end a thing because you don't. To mend is to strengthen. I, for instance, disbelieve in oligarchy; so I would no more mend the House of Lords than I would mend a thumbscrew. On the other hand, I do believe in the family; therefore I would mend the family as I would mend a chair; and I will never deny for a moment that the modern family is a chair that wants mending. But here comes in the essential point about the mass of modern advanced sociologists. Here are two institutions that have always been fundamental with mankind, the family and the state. Anarchists, I believe, disbelieve in both. It is quite unfair to say that Socialists believe in the state, but do not believe in the family; thousands of Socialists believe more in the family than any Tory. But it is true to say that while anarchists would end both, Socialists are specially engaged in mending (that is, strengthening and renewing) the state; and they are not specially engaged in strengthening and renewing the family. They are not doing anything to define the functions of father, mother, and child, as such; they are not tightening the machine up again; they are not blackening in again the fading lines of the old drawing. With the state they are doing this; they are sharpening its machinery, they are blackening in its black dogmatic lines, they are making mere government in every way stronger and in some ways harsher than before. While they leave the home in ruins, they restore the hive, especially the stings. Indeed, some schemes of labor and Poor Law reform recently advanced by distinguished Socialists, amount to little more than putting the largest number of people in the despotic power of Mr. Bumble. Apparently, progress means being moved on—by the police.

The point it is my purpose to urge might perhaps be suggested thus: that Socialists and most social reformers of their color are vividly conscious of the line between the kind of things that belong to the state and the kind of things that belong to mere chaos or uncoercible nature; they may force children to go to school before the sun rises, but they will not try to force the sun to rise; they will not, like Canute, banish the sea, but only the sea-bathers. But inside the outline of the state their lines are confused, and entities melt into each other. They have no firm instinctive sense of one thing being in its nature private and another public, of one thing being necessarily bond and another free. That is why piece by piece, and quite silently, personal liberty is being stolen from Englishmen, as personal land has been silently stolen ever since the sixteenth century.

I can only put it sufficiently curtly in a careless simile. A Socialist means a man who thinks a walking-stick like an umbrella because they both go into the umbrella-stand. Yet they are as different as a battle-ax and a bootjack. The essential idea of an umbrella is breadth and protection. The essential idea of a stick is slenderness and, partly, attack. The stick is the sword, the umbrella is the shield, but it is a shield against another and more nameless enemy—the hostile but anonymous universe. More properly, therefore, the umbrella is the roof; it is a kind of collapsible house. But the vital difference goes far deeper than this; it branches off into two kingdoms of man's mind, with a chasm between. For the point is this: that the umbrella is a shield against an enemy so actual as to be a mere nuisance; whereas the stick is a sword against enemies so entirely imaginary as to be a pure pleasure. The stick is not merely a sword, but a court sword; it is a thing of purely ceremonial swagger. One cannot express the emotion in any way except by saying that a man feels more like a man with a stick in his hand, just as he feels more like a man with a sword at his side. But nobody ever had any swelling sentiments about an umbrella; it is a convenience, like a door scraper. An umbrella is a necessary evil. A walking-stick is a quite unnecessary good. This, I fancy, is the real explanation of the perpetual losing of umbrellas; one does not hear of people losing walking sticks. For a walking-stick is a pleasure, a piece of real personal property; it is missed even when it is not needed. When my right hand forgets its stick may it forget its cunning. But anybody may forget an umbrella, as anybody might forget a shed that he has stood up in out of the rain. Anybody can forget a necessary thing.

If I might pursue the figure of speech, I might briefly say that the whole Collectivist error consists in saying that because two men can share an umbrella, therefore two men can share a walking-stick. Umbrellas might possibly be replaced by some kind of common awnings covering certain streets from particular showers. But there is nothing but nonsense in the notion of swinging a communal stick; it is as if one spoke of twirling a communal mustache. It will be said that this is a frank fantasia and that no sociologists suggest such follies. Pardon me if they do. I will give a precise parallel to the case of confusion of sticks and umbrellas, a parallel from a perpetually reiterated suggestion of reform. At least sixty Socialists out of a hundred, when they have spoken of common laundries, will go on at once to speak of common kitchens. This is just as mechanical and unintelligent as the fanciful case I have quoted. Sticks and umbrellas are both stiff rods that go into holes in a stand in the hall. Kitchens and washhouses are both large rooms full of heat and damp and steam. But the soul and function of the two things are utterly opposite. There is only one way of washing a shirt; that is, there is only one right way. There is no taste and fancy in tattered shirts. Nobody says, "Tompkins likes five holes in his shirt, but I must say, give me the good old four holes." Nobody says, "This washerwoman rips up the left leg of my pyjamas; now if there is one thing I insist on it is the right leg ripped up." The ideal washing is simply to send a thing back washed. But it is by no means true that the ideal cooking is simply to send a thing back cooked. Cooking is an art; it has in it personality, and even perversity, for the definition of an art is that which must be personal and may be perverse. I know a man, not otherwise dainty, who cannot touch common sausages unless they are almost burned to a coal. He wants his sausages fried to rags, yet he does not insist on his shirts being boiled to rags. I do not say that such points of culinary delicacy are of high importance. I do not say that the communal ideal must give way to them. What I say is that the communal ideal is not conscious of their existence, and therefore goes wrong from the very start, mixing a wholly public thing with a highly individual one. Perhaps we ought to accept communal kitchens in the social crisis, just as we should accept communal cat's-meat in a siege. But the cultured Socialist, quite at his ease, by no means in a siege, talks about communal kitchens as if they were the same kind of thing as communal laundries. This shows at the start that he misunderstands human nature. It is as different as three men singing the same chorus from three men playing three tunes on the same piano.

III. THE DREADFUL DUTY OF GUDGE

In the quarrel earlier alluded to between the energetic Progressive and the obstinate Conservative (or, to talk a tenderer language, between Hudge and Gudge), the state of cross-purposes is at the present moment acute. The Tory says he wants to preserve family life in Cindertown; the Socialist very reasonably points out to him that in Cindertown at present there isn't any family life to preserve. But Hudge, the Socialist, in his turn, is highly vague and mysterious about whether he would preserve the family life if there were any; or whether he will try to restore it where it has disappeared. It is all very confusing. The Tory sometimes talks as if he wanted to tighten the domestic bonds that do not exist; the Socialist as if he wanted to loosen the bonds that do not bind anybody. The question we all want to ask of both of them is the original ideal question, "Do you want to keep the family at all?" If Hudge, the Socialist, does want the family he must be prepared for the natural restraints, distinctions and divisions of labor in the family. He must brace himself up to bear the idea of the woman having a preference for the private house and a man for the public house. He must manage to endure somehow the idea of a woman being womanly, which does not mean soft and yielding, but handy, thrifty, rather hard, and very humorous. He must confront without a quiver the notion of a child who shall be childish, that is, full of energy, but without an idea of independence; fundamentally as eager for authority as for information and butter-scotch. If a man, a woman and a child live together any more in free and sovereign households, these ancient relations will recur; and Hudge must put up with it. He can only avoid it by destroying the family, driving both sexes into sexless hives and hordes, and bringing up all children as the children of the state—like Oliver Twist. But if these stern words must be addressed to Hudge, neither shall Gudge escape a somewhat severe admonition. For the plain truth to be told pretty sharply to the Tory is this, that if he wants the family to remain, if he wants to be strong enough to resist the rending forces of our essentially savage commerce, he must make some very big sacrifices and try to equalize property. The overwhelming mass of the English people at this particular instant are simply too poor to be domestic. They are as domestic as they can manage; they are much more domestic than the governing class; but they cannot get what good there was originally meant to be in this institution, simply because they have not got enough money. The man ought to stand for a certain magnanimity, quite lawfully expressed in throwing money away: but if under given circumstances he can only do it by throwing the week's food away, then he is not magnanimous, but mean. The woman ought to stand for a certain wisdom which is well expressed in valuing things rightly and guarding money sensibly; but how is she to guard money if there is no money to guard? The child ought to look on his mother as a fountain of natural fun and poetry; but how can he unless the fountain, like other fountains, is allowed to play? What chance have any of these ancient arts and functions in a house so hideously topsy-turvy; a house where the woman is out working and the man isn't; and the child is forced by law to think his schoolmaster's requirements more important than his mother's? No, Gudge and his friends in the House of Lords and the Carlton Club must make up their minds on this matter, and that very quickly. If they are content to have England turned into a beehive and an ant-hill, decorated here and there with a few faded butterflies playing at an old game called domesticity in the intervals of the divorce court, then let them have their empire of insects; they will find plenty of Socialists who will give it to them. But if they want a domestic England, they must "shell out," as the phrase goes, to a vastly greater extent than any Radical politician has yet dared to suggest; they must endure burdens much heavier than the Budget and strokes much deadlier than the death duties; for the thing to be done is nothing more nor less than the distribution of the great fortunes and the great estates. We can now only avoid Socialism by a change as vast as Socialism. If we are to save property, we must distribute property, almost as sternly and sweepingly as did the French Revolution. If we are to preserve the family we must revolutionize the nation.

IV. A LAST INSTANCE

And now, as this book is drawing to a close, I will whisper in the reader's ear a horrible suspicion that has sometimes haunted me: the suspicion that Hudge and Gudge are secretly in partnership. That the quarrel they keep up in public is very much of a put-up job, and that the way in which they perpetually play into each other's hands is not an everlasting coincidence. Gudge, the plutocrat, wants an anarchic industrialism; Hudge, the idealist, provides him with lyric praises of anarchy. Gudge wants women-workers because they are cheaper; Hudge calls the woman's work "freedom to live her own life." Gudge wants steady and obedient workmen, Hudge preaches teetotalism—to workmen, not to Gudge—Gudge wants a tame and timid population who will never take arms against tyranny; Hudge proves from Tolstoi that nobody must take arms against anything. Gudge is naturally a healthy and well-washed gentleman; Hudge earnestly preaches the perfection of Gudge's washing to people who can't practice it. Above all, Gudge rules by a coarse and cruel system of sacking and sweating and bi-sexual toil which is totally inconsistent with the free family and which is bound to destroy it; therefore Hudge, stretching out his arms to the universe with a prophetic smile, tells us that the family is something that we shall soon gloriously outgrow.

I do not know whether the partnership of Hudge and Gudge is conscious or unconscious. I only know that between them they still keep the common man homeless. I only know I still meet Jones walking the streets in the gray twilight, looking sadly at the poles and barriers and low red goblin lanterns which still guard the house which is none the less his because he has never been in it.

V. CONCLUSION

Here, it may be said, my book ends just where it ought to begin. I have said that the strong centers of modern English property must swiftly or slowly be broken up, if even the idea of property is to remain among Englishmen. There are two ways in which it could be done, a cold administration by quite detached officials, which is called Collectivism, or a personal distribution, so as to produce what is called Peasant Proprietorship. I think the latter solution the finer and more fully human, because it makes each man as somebody blamed somebody for saying of the Pope, a sort of small god. A man on his own turf tastes eternity or, in other words, will give ten minutes more work than is required. But I believe I am justified in shutting the door on this vista of argument, instead of opening it. For this book is not designed to prove the case for Peasant Proprietorship, but to prove the case against modern sages who turn reform to a routine. The whole of this book has been a rambling and elaborate urging of one purely ethical fact. And if by any chance it should happen that there are still some who do not quite see what that point is, I will end with one plain parable, which is none the worse for being also a fact.

A little while ago certain doctors and other persons permitted by modern law to dictate to their shabbier fellow-citizens, sent out an order that all little girls should have their hair cut short. I mean, of course, all little girls whose parents were poor. Many very unhealthy habits are common among rich little girls, but it will be long before any doctors interfere forcibly with them. Now, the case for this particular interference was this, that the poor are pressed down from above into such stinking and suffocating underworlds of squalor, that poor people must not be allowed to have hair, because in their case it must mean lice in the hair. Therefore, the doctors propose to abolish the hair. It never seems to have occurred to them to abolish the lice. Yet it could be done. As is common in most modern discussions the unmentionable thing is the pivot of the whole discussion. It is obvious to any Christian man (that is, to any man with a free soul) that any coercion applied to a cabman's daughter ought, if possible, to be applied to a Cabinet Minister's daughter. I will not ask why the doctors do not, as a matter of fact apply their rule to a Cabinet Minister's daughter. I will not ask, because I know. They do not because they dare not. But what is the excuse they would urge, what is the plausible argument they would use, for thus cutting and clipping poor children and not rich? Their argument would be that the disease is more likely to be in the hair of poor people than of rich. And why? Because the poor children are forced (against all the instincts of the highly domestic working classes) to crowd together in close rooms under a wildly inefficient system of public instruction; and because in one out of the forty children there may be offense. And why? Because the poor man is so ground down by the great rents of the great ground landlords that his wife often has to work as well as he. Therefore she has no time to look after the children, therefore one in forty of them is dirty. Because the workingman has these two persons on top of him, the landlord sitting (literally) on his stomach, and the schoolmaster sitting (literally) on his head, the workingman must allow his little girl's hair, first to be neglected from poverty, next to be poisoned by promiscuity, and, lastly, to be abolished by hygiene. He, perhaps, was proud of his little girl's hair. But he does not count.

Upon this simple principle (or rather precedent) the sociological doctor drives gayly ahead. When a crapulous tyranny crushes men down into the dirt, so that their very hair is dirty, the scientific course is clear. It would be long and laborious to cut off the heads of the tyrants; it is easier to cut off the hair of the slaves. In the same way, if it should ever happen that poor children, screaming with toothache, disturbed any schoolmaster or artistic gentleman, it would be easy to pull out all the teeth of the poor; if their nails were disgustingly dirty, their nails could be plucked out; if their noses were indecently blown, their noses could be cut off. The appearance of our humbler fellow-citizen could be quite strikingly simplified before we had done with him. But all this is not a bit wilder than the brute fact that a doctor can walk into the house of a free man, whose daughter's hair may be as clean as spring flowers, and order him to cut it off. It never seems to strike these people that the lesson of lice in the slums is the wrongness of slums, not the wrongness of hair. Hair is, to say the least of it, a rooted thing. Its enemy (like the other insects and oriental armies of whom we have spoken) sweep upon us but seldom. In truth, it is only by eternal institutions like hair that we can test passing institutions like empires. If a house is so built as to knock a man's head off when he enters it, it is built wrong.

The mob can never rebel unless it is conservative, at least enough to have conserved some reasons for rebelling. It is the most awful thought in all our anarchy, that most of the ancient blows struck for freedom would not be struck at all to-day, because of the obscuration of the clean, popular customs from which they came. The insult that brought down the hammer of Wat Tyler might now be called a medical examination. That which Virginius loathed and avenged as foul slavery might now be praised as free love. The cruel taunt of Foulon, "Let them eat grass," might now be represented as the dying cry of an idealistic vegetarian. Those great scissors of science that would snip off the curls of the poor little school children are ceaselessly snapping closer and closer to cut off all the corners and fringes of the arts and honors of the poor. Soon they will be twisting necks to suit clean collars, and hacking feet to fit new boots. It never seems to strike them that the body is more than raiment; that the Sabbath was made for man; that all institutions shall be judged and damned by whether they have fitted the normal flesh and spirit. It is the test of political sanity to keep your head. It is the test of artistic sanity to keep your hair on.

Now the whole parable and purpose of these last pages, and indeed of all these pages, is this: to assert that we must instantly begin all over again, and begin at the other end. I begin with a little girl's hair. That I know is a good thing at any rate. Whatever else is evil, the pride of a good mother in the beauty of her daughter is good. It is one of those adamantine tendernesses which are the touchstones of every age and race. If other things are against it, other things must go down. If landlords and laws and sciences are against it, landlords and laws and sciences must go down. With the red hair of one she-urchin in the gutter I will set fire to all modern civilization. Because a girl should have long hair, she should have clean hair; because she should have clean hair, she should not have an unclean home: because she should not have an unclean home, she should have a free and leisured mother; because she should have a free mother, she should not have an usurious landlord; because there should not be an usurious landlord, there should be a redistribution of property; because there should be a redistribution of property, there shall be a revolution. That little urchin with the gold-red hair, whom I have just watched toddling past my house, she shall not be lopped and lamed and altered; her hair shall not be cut short like a convict's; no, all the kingdoms of the earth shall be hacked about and mutilated to suit her. She is the human and sacred image; all around her the social fabric shall sway and split and fall; the pillars of society shall be shaken, and the roofs of ages come rushing down, and not one hair of her head shall be harmed.

THREE NOTES

I. ON FEMALE SUFFRAGE

Not wishing to overload this long essay with too many parentheses, apart from its thesis of progress and precedent, I append here three notes on points of detail that may possibly be misunderstood.

The first refers to the female controversy. It may seem to many that I dismiss too curtly the contention that all women should have votes, even if most women do not desire them. It is constantly said in this connection that males have received the vote (the agricultural laborers for instance) when only a minority of them were in favor of it. Mr. Galsworthy, one of the few fine fighting intellects of our time, has talked this language in the "Nation." Now, broadly, I have only to answer here, as everywhere in this book, that history is not a toboggan slide, but a road to be reconsidered and even retraced. If we really forced General Elections upon free laborers who definitely disliked General Elections, then it was a thoroughly undemocratic thing to do; if we are democrats we ought to undo it. We want the will of the people, not the votes of the people; and to give a man a vote against his will is to make voting more valuable than the democracy it declares.

But this analogy is false, for a plain and particular reason. Many voteless women regard a vote as unwomanly. Nobody says that most voteless men regarded a vote as unmanly. Nobody says that any voteless men regarded it as unmanly. Not in the stillest hamlet or the most stagnant fen could you find a yokel or a tramp who thought he lost his sexual dignity by being part of a political mob. If he did not care about a vote it was solely because he did not know about a vote; he did not understand the word any better than Bimetallism. His opposition, if it existed, was merely negative. His indifference to a vote was really indifference.

But the female sentiment against the franchise, whatever its size, is positive. It is not negative; it is by no means indifferent. Such women as are opposed to the change regard it (rightly or wrongly) as unfeminine. That is, as insulting certain affirmative traditions to which they are attached. You may think such a view prejudiced; but I violently deny that any democrat has a right to override such prejudices, if they are popular and positive. Thus he would not have a right to make millions of Moslems vote with a cross if they had a prejudice in favor of voting with a crescent. Unless this is admitted, democracy is a farce we need scarcely keep up. If it is admitted, the Suffragists have not merely to awaken an indifferent, but to convert a hostile majority.

II. ON CLEANLINESS IN EDUCATION

On re-reading my protest, which I honestly think much needed, against our heathen idolatry of mere ablution, I see that it may possibly be misread. I hasten to say that I think washing a most important thing to be taught both to rich and poor. I do not attack the positive but the relative position of soap. Let it be insisted on even as much as now; but let other things be insisted on much more. I am even ready to admit that cleanliness is next to godliness; but the moderns will not even admit godliness to be next to cleanliness. In their talk about Thomas Becket and such saints and heroes they make soap more important than soul; they reject godliness whenever it is not cleanliness. If we resent this about remote saints and heroes, we should resent it more about the many saints and heroes of the slums, whose unclean hands cleanse the world. Dirt is evil chiefly as evidence of sloth; but the fact remains that the classes that wash most are those that work least. Concerning these, the practical course is simple; soap should be urged on them and advertised as what it is—a luxury. With regard to the poor also the practical course is not hard to harmonize with our thesis. If we want to give poor people soap we must set out deliberately to give them luxuries. If we will not make them rich enough to be clean, then emphatically we must do what we did with the saints. We must reverence them for being dirty.

III. ON PEASANT PROPRIETORSHIP

I have not dealt with any details touching distributed ownership, or its possibility in England, for the reason stated in the text. This book deals with what is wrong, wrong in our root of argument and effort. This wrong is, I say, that we will go forward because we dare not go back. Thus the Socialist says that property is already concentrated into Trusts and Stores: the only hope is to concentrate it further in the State. I say the only hope is to unconcentrate it; that is, to repent and return; the only step forward is the step backward.

But in connection with this distribution I have laid myself open to another potential mistake. In speaking of a sweeping redistribution, I speak of decision in the aim, not necessarily of abruptness in the means. It is not at all too late to restore an approximately rational state of English possessions without any mere confiscation. A policy of buying out landlordism, steadily adopted in England as it has already been adopted in Ireland (notably in Mr. Wyndham's wise and fruitful Act), would in a very short time release the lower end of the see-saw and make the whole plank swing more level. The objection to this course is not at all that it would not do, only that it will not be done. If we leave things as they are, there will almost certainly be a crash of confiscation. If we hesitate, we shall soon have to hurry. But if we start doing it quickly we have still time to do it slowly.

This point, however, is not essential to my book. All I have to urge between these two boards is that I dislike the big Whiteley shop, and that I dislike Socialism because it will (according to Socialists) be so like that shop. It is its fulfilment, not its reversal. I do not object to Socialism because it will revolutionize our commerce, but because it will leave it so horribly the same.

WHAT I SAW IN AMERICA

WHAT IS AMERICA?

I have never managed to lose my old conviction that travel narrows the mind. At least a man must make a double effort of moral humility and imaginative energy to prevent it from narrowing his mind. Indeed there is something touching and even tragic about the thought of the thoughtless tourist, who might have stayed at home loving Laplanders, embracing Chinamen, and clasping Patagonians to his heart in Hampstead or Surbiton, but for his blind and suicidal impulse to go and see what they looked like. This is not meant for nonsense; still less is it meant for the silliest sort of nonsense, which is cynicism. The human bond that he feels at home is not an illusion. On the contrary, it is rather an inner reality. Man is inside all men. In a real sense any man may be inside any men. But to travel is to leave the inside and draw dangerously near the outside. So long as he thought of men in the abstract, like naked toiling figures in some classic frieze, merely as those who labour and love their children and die, he was thinking the fundamental truth about them. By going to look at their unfamiliar manners and customs he is inviting them to disguise themselves in fantastic masks and costumes. Many modern internationalists talk as if men of different nationalities had only to meet and mix and understand each other. In reality that is the moment of supreme danger—the moment when they meet. We might shiver, as at the old euphemism by which a meeting meant a duel.

Travel ought to combine amusement with instruction; but most travellers are so much amused that they refuse to be instructed. I do not blame them for being amused; it is perfectly natural to be amused at a Dutchman for being Dutch or a Chinaman for being Chinese. Where they are wrong is that they take their own amusement seriously. They base on it their serious ideas of international instruction. It was said that the Englishman takes his pleasures sadly; and the pleasure of despising foreigners is one which he takes most sadly of all. He comes to scoff and does not remain to pray, but rather to excommunicate. Hence in international relations there is far too little laughing, and far too much sneering. But I believe that there is a better way which largely consists of laughter; a form of friendship between nations which is actually founded on differences. To hint at some such better way is the only excuse of this book.

Let me begin my American impressions with two impressions I had before I went to America. One was an incident and the other an idea; and when taken together they illustrate the attitude I mean. The first principle is that nobody should be ashamed of thinking a thing funny because it is foreign; the second is that he should be ashamed of thinking it wrong because it is funny. The reaction of his senses and superficial habits of mind against something new, and to him abnormal, is a perfectly healthy reaction. But the mind which imagines that mere unfamiliarity can possibly prove anything about inferiority is a very inadequate mind. It is inadequate even in criticising things that may really be inferior to the things involved here. It is far better to laugh at a negro for having a black face than to sneer at him for having a sloping skull. It is proportionally even more preferable to laugh rather than judge in dealing with highly civilised peoples. Therefore I put at the beginning two working examples of what I felt about America before I saw it; the sort of thing that a man has a right to enjoy as a joke, and the sort of thing he has a duty to understand and respect, because it is the explanation of the joke.

When I went to the American consulate to regularise my passports, I was capable of expecting the American consulate to be American. Embassies and consulates are by tradition like islands of the soil for which they stand; and I have often found the tradition corresponding to a truth. I have seen the unmistakable French official living on omelettes and a little wine and serving his sacred abstractions under the last palm-trees fringing a desert. In the heat and noise of quarrelling Turks and Egyptians, I have come suddenly, as with the cool shock of his own shower-bath, on the listless amiability of the English gentleman. The officials I interviewed were very American, especially in being very polite; for whatever may have been the mood or meaning of Martin Chuzzlewit, I have always found Americans by far the politest people in the world. They put in my hands a form to be filled up, to all appearance like other forms I had filled up in other passport offices. But in reality it was very different from any form I had ever filled up in my life. At least it was a little like a freer form of the game called 'Confessions' which my friends and I invented in our youth; an examination paper containing questions like, 'If you saw a rhinoceros in the front garden, what would you do?' One of my friends, I remember, wrote, 'Take the pledge.' But that is another story, and might bring Mr. Pussyfoot Johnson on the scene before his time.

One of the questions on the paper was, 'Are you an anarchist?' To which a detached philosopher would naturally feel inclined to answer, 'What the devil has that to do with you? Are you an atheist?' along with some playful efforts to cross-examine the official about what constitutes an ἀρχη . Then there was the question, 'Are you in favour of subverting the government of the United States by force?' Against this I should write, 'I prefer to answer that question at the end of my tour and not the beginning.' The inquisitor, in his more than morbid curiosity, had then written down, 'Are you a polygamist?' The answer to this is, 'No such luck' or 'Not such a fool,' according to our experience of the other sex. But perhaps a better answer would be that given to W. T. Stead when he circulated the rhetorical question, 'Shall I slay my brother Boer?'—the answer that ran, 'Never interfere in family matters.' But among many things that amused me almost to the point of treating the form thus disrespectfully, the most amusing was the thought of the ruthless outlaw who should feel compelled to treat it respectfully. I like to think of the foreign desperado, seeking to slip into America with official papers under official protection, and sitting down to write with a beautiful gravity, 'I am an anarchist. I hate you all and wish to destroy you.' Or, 'I intend to subvert by force the government of the United States as soon as possible, sticking the long sheath-knife in my left trouser-pocket into Mr. Harding at the earliest opportunity.' Or again, 'Yes, I am a polygamist all right, and my forty-seven wives are accompanying me on the voyage disguised as secretaries.' There seems to be a certain simplicity of mind about these answers; and it is reassuring to know that anarchists and polygamists are so pure and good that the police have only to ask them questions and they are certain to tell no lies.

Now that is a model of the sort of foreign practice, founded on foreign problems, at which a man's first impulse is naturally to laugh. Nor have I any intention of apologising for my laughter. A man is perfectly entitled to laugh at a thing because he happens to find it incomprehensible. What he has no right to do is to laugh at it as incomprehensible, and then criticise it as if he comprehended it. The very fact of its unfamiliarity and mystery ought to set him thinking about the deeper causes that make people so different from himself, and that without merely assuming that they must be inferior to himself.

Superficially this is rather a queer business. It would be easy enough to suggest that in this America has introduced a quite abnormal spirit of inquisition; an interference with liberty unknown among all the ancient despotisms and aristocracies. About that there will be something to be said later; but superficially it is true that this degree of officialism is comparatively unique. In a journey which I took only the year before I had occasion to have my papers passed by governments which many worthy people in the West would vaguely identify with corsairs and assassins; I have stood on the other side of Jordan, in the land ruled by a rude Arab chief, where the police looked so like brigands that one wondered what the brigands looked like. But they did not ask me whether I had come to subvert the power of the Shereef; and they did not exhibit the faintest curiosity about my personal views on the ethical basis of civil authority. These ministers of ancient Moslem despotism did not care about whether I was an anarchist; and naturally would not have minded if I had been a polygamist. The Arab chief was probably a polygamist himself. These slaves of Asiatic autocracy were content, in the old liberal fashion, to judge me by my actions; they did not inquire into my thoughts. They held their power as limited to the limitation of practice; they did not forbid me to hold a theory. It would be easy to argue here that Western democracy persecutes where even Eastern despotism tolerates or emancipates. It would be easy to develop the fancy that, as compared with the sultans of Turkey or Egypt, the American Constitution is a thing like the Spanish Inquisition.

Only the traveller who stops at that point is totally wrong; and the traveller only too often does stop at that point. He has found something to make him laugh, and he will not suffer it to make him think. And the remedy is not to unsay what he has said, not even, so to speak, to unlaugh what he has laughed, not to deny that there is something unique and curious about this American inquisition into our abstract opinions, but rather to continue the train of thought, and follow the admirable advice of Mr. H. G. Wells, who said, 'It is not much good thinking of a thing unless you think it out.' It is not to deny that American officialism is rather peculiar on this point, but to inquire what it really is which makes America peculiar, or which is peculiar to America. In short, it is to get some ultimate idea of what America *is*; and the answer to that question will reveal something much deeper and grander and more worthy of our intelligent interest.

It may have seemed something less than a compliment to compare the American Constitution to the Spanish Inquisition. But oddly enough, it does involve a truth; and still more oddly perhaps, it does involve a compliment. The American Constitution does resemble the Spanish Inquisition in this: that it is founded on a creed. America is the only nation in the world that is founded on a creed. That creed is set forth with dogmatic and even theological lucidity in the Declaration of Independence; perhaps the only piece of practical politics that is also theoretical politics and also great literature. It enunciates that all men are equal in their claim to justice, that governments exist to give them that justice, and that their authority is for that reason just. It certainly does condemn anarchism, and it does also by inference condemn atheism, since it clearly names the Creator as the ultimate authority from whom these equal rights are derived. Nobody expects a modern political system to proceed logically in the application of such dogmas, and in the matter of God and Government it is naturally God whose claim is taken more lightly. The point is that there is a creed, if not about divine, at least about human things.

Now a creed is at once the broadest and the narrowest thing in the world. In its nature it is as broad as its scheme for a brotherhood of all men. In its nature it is limited by its definition of the nature of all men. This was true of the Christian Church, which was truly said to exclude neither Jew nor Greek, but which did definitely substitute something else for Jewish religion or Greek philosophy. It was truly said to be a net drawing in of all kinds; but a net of a certain pattern, the pattern of Peter the Fisherman. And this is true even of the most disastrous distortions or degradations of that creed; and true among others of the Spanish Inquisition. It may have been narrow touching theology, it could not confess to being narrow about nationality or ethnology. The Spanish Inquisition might be admittedly Inquisitorial; but the Spanish Inquisition could not be merely Spanish. Such a Spaniard, even when he was narrower than his own creed, had to be broader than his own empire. He might burn a philosopher because he was heterodox; but he must accept a barbarian because he was orthodox. And we see, even in modern times, that the same Church which is blamed for making sages heretics is also blamed for making savages priests. Now in a much vaguer and more evolutionary fashion, there is something of the same idea at the back of the great American experiment; the experiment of a democracy of diverse races which has been compared to a melting-pot. But even that metaphor implies that the pot itself is of a certain shape and a certain substance; a pretty solid substance. The melting-pot must not melt. The original shape was traced on the lines of Jeffersonian democracy; and it will remain in that shape until it becomes shapeless. America invites all men to become citizens; but it implies the dogma that there is such a thing as citizenship. Only, so far as its primary ideal is concerned, its exclusiveness is religious because it is not racial. The missionary can condemn a cannibal, precisely because he cannot condemn a Sandwich Islander. And in something of the same spirit the American may exclude a polygamist, precisely because he cannot exclude a Turk.

Now for America this is no idle theory. It may have been theoretical, though it was thoroughly sincere, when that great Virginian gentleman declared it in surroundings that still had something of the character of an English countryside. It is not merely theoretical now. There is nothing to prevent America being literally invaded by Turks, as she is invaded by Jews or Bulgars. In the most exquisitely inconsequent of the *Bab Ballads*, we are told concerning Pasha Bailey Ben:—

One morning knocked at half-past eight
A tall Red Indian at his gate.
In Turkey, as you 'r' p'raps aware,
Red Indians are extremely rare.

But the converse need by no means be true. There is nothing in the nature of things to prevent an emigration of Turks increasing and multiplying on the plains where the Red Indians wandered; there is nothing to necessitate the Turks being extremely rare. The Red Indians, alas, are likely to be rarer. And as I much prefer Red Indians to Turks, not to mention Jews, I speak without prejudice; but the point here is that America, partly by original theory and partly by historical accident, does lie open to racial admixtures which most countries would think incongruous or comic. That is why it is only fair to read any American definitions or rules in a certain light, and relatively to a rather unique position. It is not fair to compare the position of those who may meet Turks in the back street with that of those who have never met Turks except in the *Bab Ballads*. It is not fair simply to compare America with England in its regulations about the Turk. In short, it is not fair to do what almost every Englishman probably does; to look at the American international examination paper, and laugh and be satisfied with saying, 'We don't have any of that nonsense in England.'

We do not have any of that nonsense in England because we have never attempted to have any of that philosophy in England. And, above all, because we have the enormous advantage of feeling it natural to be national, because there is nothing else to be. England in these days is not well governed; England is not well educated; England suffers from wealth and poverty that are not well distributed. But England is English; *esto perpetua*. England is English as France is French or Ireland Irish; the great mass of men taking certain national traditions for granted. Now this gives us a totally different and a very much easier task. We have not got an inquisition, because we have not got a creed; but it is arguable that we do not need a creed, because we have got a character. In any of the old nations the national unity is preserved by the national type. Because we have a type we do not need to have a test.

Take that innocent question, 'Are you an anarchist?' which is intrinsically quite as impudent as 'Are you an optimist?' or 'Are you a philanthropist?' I am not discussing here whether these things are right, but whether most of us are in a position to know them rightly. Now it is quite true that most Englishmen do not find it necessary to go about all day asking each other whether they are anarchists. It is quite true that the phrase occurs on no British forms that I have seen. But this is not only because most of the Englishmen are not anarchists. It is even more because even the anarchists are Englishmen. For instance, it would be easy to make fun of the American formula by noting that the cap would fit all sorts of bald academic heads. It might well be maintained that Herbert Spencer was an anarchist. It is practically certain that Auberon Herbert was an anarchist. But Herbert Spencer was an extraordinarily typical Englishman of the Nonconformist middle class. And Auberon Herbert was an extraordinarily typical English aristocrat of the old and genuine aristocracy. Every one knew in his heart that the squire would not throw a bomb at the Queen, and the Nonconformist would not throw a bomb at anybody. Every one knew that there was something subconscious in a man like Auberon Herbert, which would have come out only in throwing bombs at the enemies of England; as it did come out in his son and namesake, the generous and unforgotten, who fell flinging bombs from the sky far beyond the German line. Every one knows that normally, in the last resort, the English gentleman is patriotic. Every one knows that the English Nonconformist is national even when he denies that he is patriotic. Nothing is more notable indeed than the fact that nobody is more stamped with the mark of his own nation than the man who says that there ought to be no nations. Somebody called Cobden the International Man; but no man could be more English than Cobden. Everybody recognises Tolstoy as the iconoclast of all patriotism; but nobody could be more Russian than Tolstoy. In the old countries where there are these national types, the types may be allowed to hold any theories. Even if they hold certain theories, they are unlikely to do certain things. So the conscientious objector, in the English sense, may be and is one of the peculiar by-products of England. But the conscientious objector will probably have a conscientious objection to throwing bombs.

Now I am very far from intending to imply that these American tests are good tests, or that there is no danger of tyranny becoming the temptation of America. I shall have something to say later on about that temptation or tendency. Nor do I say that they apply consistently this conception of a nation with the soul of a church, protected by religious and not racial selection. If they did apply that principle consistently, they would have to exclude pessimists and rich cynics who deny the democratic ideal; an excellent thing but a rather improbable one. What I say is that when we realise that this principle exists at all, we see the whole position in a totally different perspective. We say that the Americans are doing something heroic, or doing something insane, or doing it in an unworkable or unworthy fashion, instead of simply wondering what the devil they are doing.

When we realise the democratic design of such a cosmopolitan commonwealth, and compare it with our insular reliance or instincts, we see at once why such a thing has to be not only democratic but dogmatic. We see why in some points it tends to be inquisitive or intolerant. Any one can see the practical point by merely transferring into private life a problem like that of the two academic anarchists, who might by a coincidence be called the two Herberts. Suppose a man said, 'Buffle, my old Oxford tutor, wants to meet you; I wish you'd ask him down for a day or two. He has the oddest opinions, but he's very stimulating.' It would not occur to us that the oddity of the Oxford don's opinions would lead him to blow up the house; because the Oxford don is an English type. Suppose somebody said, 'Do let me bring old Colonel Robinson down for the week-end; he's a bit of a crank but quite interesting.' We should not anticipate the colonel running amuck with a carving-knife and offering up human sacrifice in the garden; for these are not among the daily habits of an old English colonel; and because we know his habits, we do not care about his opinions. But suppose somebody offered to bring a person from the interior of Kamskatka to stay with us for a week or two, and added that his religion was a very extraordinary religion, we should feel a little more inquisitive about what kind of religion it was. If somebody wished to add a Hairy Ainu to the family party at Christmas, explaining that his point of view was so individual and interesting, we should want to know a little more about it and him. We should be tempted to draw up as fantastic an examination paper as that presented to the emigrant going to America. We should ask what a Hairy Ainu was, and how hairy he was, and above all what sort of Ainu he was. Would etiquette require us to ask him to bring his wife? And if we did ask him to bring his wife, how many wives would he bring? In short, as in the American formula, is he a polygamist? Merely as a point of housekeeping and accommodation the question is not irrelevant. Is the Hairy Ainu content with hair, or does he wear any clothes? If the police insist on his wearing clothes, will he recognise the authority of the police? In short, as in the American formula, is he an anarchist?

Of course this generalisation about America, like other historical things, is subject to all sorts of cross divisions and exceptions, to be considered in their place. The negroes are a special problem, because of what white men in the past did to them. The Japanese are a special problem, because of what men fear that they in the future may do to white men. The Jews are a special problem, because of what they and the Gentiles, in the past, present, and future, seem to have the habit of doing to each other. But the point is not that nothing exists in America except this idea; it is that nothing like this idea exists anywhere except in America. This idea is not internationalism; on the contrary it is decidedly nationalism. The Americans are very patriotic, and wish to make their new citizens patriotic Americans. But it is the idea of making a new nation literally out of any old nation that comes along. In a word, what is unique is not America but what is called Americanisation. We understand nothing till we understand the amazing ambition to Americanise the Kamskatkan and the Hairy Ainu. We are not trying to Anglicise thousands of French cooks or Italian organ-grinders. France is not trying to Gallicise thousands of English trippers or German prisoners of war. America is the one place in the world where this process, healthy or unhealthy, possible or impossible, is going on. And the process, as I have pointed out, is *not* internationalisation. It would be truer to say it is the nationalisation of the internationalised. It is making a home out of vagabonds and a nation out of exiles. This is what at once illuminates and softens the moral regulations which we may really think faddist or fanatical. They are abnormal; but in one sense this experiment of a home for the homeless is abnormal. In short, it has long been recognised that America was an asylum. It is only since Prohibition that it has looked a little like a lunatic asylum.

It was before sailing for America, as I have said, that I stood with the official paper in my hand and these thoughts in my head. It was while I stood on English soil that I passed through the two stages of smiling and then sympathising; of realising that my momentary amusement, at being asked if I were not an Anarchist, was partly due to the fact that I was not an American. And in truth I think there are some things a man ought to know about America before he sees it. What we know of a country beforehand may not affect what we see that it is; but it will vitally affect what we appreciate it for being, because it will vitally affect what we expect it to be. I can honestly say that I had never expected America to be what nine-tenths of the newspaper critics invariably assume it to be. I never thought it was a sort of Anglo-Saxon colony, knowing that it was more and more thronged with crowds of very different colonists. During the war I felt that the very worst propaganda for the Allies was the propaganda for the Anglo-Saxons. I tried to point out that in one way America is nearer to Europe than England is. If she is not nearer to Bulgaria, she is nearer to Bulgars; if she is not nearer to Bohemia, she is nearer to Bohemians. In my New York hotel the head waiter in the dining-room was a Bohemian; the head waiter in the grill-room was a Bulgar. Americans have nationalities at the end of the street which for us are at the ends of the earth. I did my best to persuade my countrymen not to appeal to the American as if he were a rather dowdy Englishman, who had been rusticating in the provinces and had not heard the latest news about the town. I shall record later some of those arresting realities which the traveller does not expect; and which, in some cases I fear, he actually does not see because he does not expect. I shall try to do justice to the psychology of what Mr. Belloc has called 'Eye-Openers in Travel.' But there are some things about America that a man ought to see even with his eyes shut. One is that a state that came into existence solely through its repudiation and abhorrence of the British Crown is not likely to be a respectful copy of the British Constitution. Another is that the chief mark of the Declaration of Independence is something that is not only absent from the British Constitution, but something which all our constitutionalists have invariably thanked God, with the jolliest boasting and bragging, that they had kept out of the British Constitution. It is the thing called abstraction or academic logic. It is the thing which such jolly people call theory; and which those who can practise it call thought. And the theory or thought is the very last to which English people are accustomed, either by their social structure or their traditional teaching. It is the theory of equality. It is the pure classic conception that no man must aspire to be anything more than a citizen, and that no man should endure to be anything less. It is by no means especially intelligible to an Englishman, who tends at his best to the virtues of the gentleman and at his worst to the vices of the snob. The idealism of England, or if you will the romance of England, has not been primarily the romance of the citizen. But the idealism of America, we may safely say, still revolves entirely round the citizen and his romance. The realities are quite another matter, and we shall consider in its place the question of whether the ideal will be able to shape the realities or will merely be beaten shapeless by them. The ideal is besieged by inequalities of the most towering and insane description in the industrial and economic field. It may be devoured by modern capitalism, perhaps the worst inequality that ever existed among men. Of all that we shall speak later. But citizenship is still the American ideal; there is an army of actualities opposed to that ideal; but there is no ideal opposed to that ideal. American plutocracy has never got itself respected like English aristocracy. Citizenship is the American ideal; and it has never been the English ideal. But it is surely an ideal that may stir some imaginative generosity and respect in an Englishman, if he will condescend to be also a man. In this vision of moulding many peoples into the visible image of the citizen, he may see a spiritual adventure which he can admire from the outside, at least as much as he admires the valour of the Moslems and much more than he admires the virtues of the Middle Ages. He need not set himself to develop equality, but he need not set himself to misunderstand it. He may at least understand what Jefferson and Lincoln meant, and he may possibly find some assistance in this task by reading what they said. He may realise that equality is not some crude fairy tale about all men being equally tall or equally tricky; which we not only cannot believe but cannot believe in anybody believing. It is an absolute of morals by which all men have a value invariable and indestructible and a dignity as intangible as death. He may at least be a philosopher and see that equality is an idea; and not merely one of these soft-headed sceptics who, having risen by low tricks to high places, drink bad champagne in tawdry hotel lounges, and tell each other twenty times over, with unwearied iteration, that equality is an illusion.

In truth it is inequality that is the illusion. The extreme disproportion between men, that we seem to see in life, is a thing of changing lights and lengthening shadows, a twilight full of fancies and distortions. We find a man famous and cannot live long enough to find him forgotten; we see a race dominant and cannot linger to see it decay. It is the experience of men that always returns to the equality of men; it is the average that ultimately justifies the average man. It is when men have seen and suffered much and come at the end of more elaborate experiments, that they see men as men under an equal light of death and daily laughter; and none the less mysterious for being many. Nor is it in vain that these Western democrats have sought the blazonry of their flag in that great multitude of immortal lights that endure behind the fires we see, and gathered them into the corner of Old Glory whose ground is like the glittering night. For veritably, in the spirit as well as in the symbol, suns and moons and meteors pass and fill our skies with a fleeting and almost theatrical conflagration; and wherever the old shadow stoops upon the earth, the stars return.

A MEDITATION IN A NEW YORK HOTEL

All this must begin with an apology and not an apologia. When I went wandering about the States disguised as a lecturer, I was well aware that I was not sufficiently well disguised to be a spy. I was even in the worst possible position to be a sight-seer. A lecturer to American audiences can hardly be in the holiday mood of a sight-seer. It is rather the audience that is sight-seeing; even if it is seeing a rather melancholy sight. Some say that people come to see the lecturer and not to hear him; in which case it seems rather a pity that he should disturb and distress their minds with a lecture. He might merely display himself on a stand or platform for a stipulated sum; or be exhibited like a monster in a menagerie. The circus elephant is not expected to make a speech. But it is equally true that the circus elephant is not allowed to write a book. His impressions of travel would be somewhat sketchy and perhaps a little over-specialised. In merely travelling from circus to circus he would, so to speak, move in rather narrow circles. Jumbo the great elephant (with whom I am hardly so ambitious as to compare myself), before he eventually went to the Barnum show, passed a considerable and I trust happy part of his life in Regent's Park. But if he had written a book on England, founded on his impressions of the Zoo, it might have been a little disproportionate and even misleading in its version of the flora and fauna of that country. He might imagine that lions and leopards were commoner than they are in our hedgerows and country lanes, or that the head and neck of a giraffe was as native to our landscapes as a village spire. And that is why I apologise in anticipation for a probable lack of proportion in this work. Like the elephant, I may have seen too much of a special enclosure where a special sort of lions are gathered together. I may exaggerate the territorial, as distinct from the vertical space occupied by the spiritual giraffe; for the giraffe may surely be regarded as an example of Uplift, and is even, in a manner of speaking, a high-brow. Above all, I shall probably make generalisations that are much too general; and are insufficient through being exaggerative. To this sort of doubt all my impressions are subject; and among them the negative generalisation with which I shall begin this rambling meditation on American hotels.

In all my American wanderings I never saw such a thing as an inn. They may exist; but they do not arrest the traveller upon every road as they do in England and in Europe. The saloons no longer existed when I was there, owing to the recent reform which restricted intoxicants to the wealthier classes. But we feel that the saloons have been there; if one may so express it, their absence is still present. They remain in the structure of the street and the idiom of the language. But the saloons were not inns. If they had been inns, it would have been far harder even for the power of modern plutocracy to root them out. There will be a very different chase when the White Hart is hunted to the forests or when the Red Lion turns to bay. But people could not feel about the American saloon as they will feel about the English inns. They could not feel that the Prohibitionist, that vulgar chucker-out, was chucking Chaucer out of the Tabard and Shakespeare out of the Mermaid. In justice to the American Prohibitionists it must be realised that they were not doing quite such desecration; and that many of them felt the saloon a specially poisonous sort of place. They did feel that drinking-places were used only as drug-shops. So they have effected the great reconstruction, by which it will be necessary to use only drug-shops as drinking-places. But I am not dealing here with the problem of Prohibition except in so far as it is involved in the statement that the saloons were in no sense inns. Secondly, of course, there are the hotels. There are indeed. There are hotels toppling to the stars, hotels covering the acreage of villages, hotels in multitudinous number like a mob of Babylonian or Assyrian monuments; but the hotels also are not inns.

Broadly speaking, there is only one hotel in America. The pattern of it, which is a very rational pattern, is repeated in cities as remote from each other as the capitals of European empires. You may find that hotel rising among the red blooms of the warm spring woods of Nebraska, or whitened with Canadian snows near the eternal noise of Niagara. And before touching on this solid and simple pattern itself, I may remark that the same system of symmetry runs through all the details of the interior. As one hotel is like another hotel, so one hotel floor is like another hotel floor. If the passage outside your bedroom door, or hallway as it is called, contains, let us say, a small table with a green vase and a stuffed flamingo, or some trifle of the sort, you may be perfectly certain that there is exactly the same table, vase, and flamingo on every one of the thirty-two landings of that towering habitation. This is where it differs most perhaps from the crooked landings and unexpected levels of the old English inns, even when they call themselves hotels. To me there was something weird, like a magic multiplication, in the exquisite sameness of these suites. It seemed to suggest the still atmosphere of some eerie psychological story. I once myself entertained the notion of a story, in which a man was to be prevented from entering his house (the scene of some crime or calamity) by people who painted and furnished the next house to look exactly like it; the assimilation going to the most fantastic lengths, such as altering the numbering of houses in the street. I came to America and found an hotel fitted and upholstered throughout for the enactment of my phantasmal fraud. I offer the skeleton of my story with all humility to some of the admirable lady writers of detective stories in America, to Miss Carolyn Wells, or Miss Mary Roberts Rhinehart, or Mrs. A. K. Green of the unforgotten Leavenworth Case. Surely it might be possible for the unsophisticated Nimrod K. Moose, of Yellow Dog Flat, to come to New York and be entangled somehow in this net of repetitions or recurrences. Surely something tells me that his beautiful daughter, the Rose of Red Murder Gulch, might seek for him in vain amid the apparently unmistakable surroundings of the thirty-second floor, while he was being quietly butchered by the floor-clerk on the thirty-third floor, an agent of the Green Claw (that formidable organisation); and all because the two floors looked exactly alike to the virginal Western eye. The original point of my own story was that the man to be entrapped walked into his own house after all, in spite of it being differently painted and numbered, simply because he was absent-minded and used to taking a certain number of mechanical steps. This would not work in the hotel; because a lift has no habits. It is typical of the real tameness of machinery, that even when we talk of a man turning mechanically we only talk metaphorically; for it is something that a mechanism cannot do. But I think there is only one real objection to my story of Mr. Moose in the New York hotel. And that is unfortunately a rather fatal one. It is that far away in the remote desolation of Yellow Dog, among those outlying and outlandish rocks that almost seem to rise beyond the sunset, there is undoubtedly an hotel of exactly the same sort, with all its floors exactly the same.

Anyhow the general plan of the American hotel is commonly the same, and, as I have said, it is a very sound one so far as it goes. When I first went into one of the big New York hotels, the first impression was certainly its bigness. It was called the Biltmore; and I wondered how many national humorists had made the obvious comment of wishing they had built less. But it was not merely the Babylonian size and scale of such things, it was the way in which they are used. They are used almost as public streets, or rather as public squares. My first impression was that I was in some sort of high street or market-place during a carnival or a revolution. True, the people looked rather rich for a revolution and rather grave for a carnival; but they were congested in great crowds that moved slowly like people passing through an overcrowded railway station. Even in the dizzy heights of such a sky-scraper there could not possibly be room for all those people to sleep in the hotel, or even to dine in it. And, as a matter of fact, they did nothing whatever except drift into it and drift out again. Most of them had no more to do with the hotel than I have with Buckingham Palace. I have never been in Buckingham Palace, and I have very seldom, thank God, been in the big hotels of this type that exist in London or Paris. But I cannot believe that mobs are perpetually pouring through the Hotel Cecil or the Savoy in this fashion, calmly coming in at one door and going out of the other. But this fact is part of the fundamental structure of the American hotel; it is built upon a compromise that makes it possible. The whole of the lower floor is thrown open to the public streets and treated as a public square. But above it and all round it runs another floor in the form of a sort of deep gallery, furnished more luxuriously and looking down on the moving mobs beneath. No one is allowed on this floor except the guests or clients of the hotel. As I have been one of them myself, I trust it is not unsympathetic to compare them to active anthropoids who can climb trees, and so look down in safety on the herds or packs of wilder animals wandering and prowling below. Of course there are modifications of this architectural plan, but they are generally approximations to it; it is the plan that seems to suit the social life of the American cities. There is generally something like a ground floor that is more public, a half-floor or gallery above that is more private, and above that the bulk of the block of bedrooms, the huge hive with its innumerable and identical cells.

The ladder of ascent in this tower is of course the lift, or, as it is called, the elevator. With all that we hear of American hustle and hurry it is rather strange that Americans seem to like more than we do to linger upon long words. And indeed there is an element of delay in their diction and spirit, very little understood, which I may discuss elsewhere. Anyhow they say elevator when we say lift, just as they say automobile when we say motor and stenographer when we say typist, or sometimes (by a slight confusion) typewriter. Which reminds me of another story that never existed, about a man who was accused of having murdered and dismembered his secretary when he had only taken his typing machine to pieces; but we must not dwell on these digressions. The Americans may have another reason for giving long and ceremonious titles to the lift. When first I came among them I had a suspicion that they possessed and practised a new and secret religion, which was the cult of the elevator. I fancied they worshipped the lift, or at any rate worshipped in the lift. The details or data of this suspicion it were now vain to collect, as I have regretfully abandoned it, except in so far as they illustrate the social principles underlying the structural plan of the building. Now an American gentleman invariably takes off his hat in the lift. He does not take off his hat in the hotel, even if it is crowded with ladies. But he always so salutes a lady in the elevator; and this marks the difference of atmosphere. The lift is a room, but the hotel is a street. But during my first delusion, of course, I assumed that he uncovered in this tiny temple merely because he was in church. There is something about the very word elevator that expresses a great deal of his vague but idealistic religion. Perhaps that flying chapel will eventually be ritualistically decorated like a chapel; possibly with a symbolic scheme of wings. Perhaps a brief religious service will be held in the elevator as it ascends; in a few well-chosen words touching the Utmost for the Highest. Possibly he would consent even to call the elevator a lift, if he could call it an uplift. There would be no difficulty, except what I cannot but regard as the chief moral problem of all optimistic modernism. I mean the difficulty of imagining a lift which is free to go up, if it is not also free to go down.

I think I know my American friends and acquaintances too well to apologise for any levity in these illustrations. Americans make fun of their own institutions; and their own journalism is full of such fanciful conjectures. The tall building is itself artistically akin to the tall story. The very word sky-scraper is an admirable example of an American lie. But I can testify quite as eagerly to the solid and sensible advantages of the symmetrical hotel. It is not only a pattern of vases and stuffed flamingoes; it is also an equally accurate pattern of cupboards and baths. It is a dignified and humane custom to have a bathroom attached to every bedroom; and my impulse to sing the praises of it brought me once at least into a rather quaint complication. I think it was in the city of Dayton; anyhow I remember there was a Laundry Convention going on in the same hotel, in a room very patriotically and properly festooned with the stars and stripes, and doubtless full of promise for the future of laundering. I was interviewed on the roof, within earshot of this debate, and may have been the victim of some association or confusion; anyhow, after answering the usual questions about Labour, the League of Nations, the length of ladies' dresses, and other great matters, I took refuge in a rhapsody of warm and well-deserved praise of American bathrooms. The editor, I understand, running a gloomy eye down the column of his contributor's 'story,' and seeing nothing but metaphysical terms such as justice, freedom, the abstract disapproval of sweating, swindling, and the like, paused at last upon the ablutionary allusion, and his eye brightened. 'That's the only copy in the whole thing,' he said, 'A Bath-Tub in Every Home.' So these words appeared in enormous letters above my portrait in the paper. It will be noted that, like many things that practical men make a great point of, they miss the point. What I had commended as new and national was a bathroom in every bedroom. Even feudal and moss-grown England is not entirely ignorant of an occasional bath-tub in the home. But what gave me great joy was what followed. I discovered with delight that many people, glancing rapidly at my portrait with its prodigious legend, imagined that it was a commercial advertisement, and that I was a very self-advertising commercial traveller. When I walked about the streets, I was supposed to be travelling in bath-tubs. Consider the caption of the portrait, and you will see how similar it is to the true commercial slogan: 'We offer a Bath-Tub in Every Home.' And this charming error was doubtless clinched by the fact that I had been found haunting the outer courts of the temple of the ancient Guild of Lavenders. I never knew how many shared the impression; I regret to say that I only traced it with certainty in two individuals. But I understand that it included the idea that I had come to the town to attend the Laundry Convention, and had made an eloquent speech to that senate, no doubt exhibiting my tubs.

Such was the penalty of too passionate and unrestrained an admiration for American bathrooms; yet the connection of ideas, however inconsequent, does cover the part of social practice for which these American institutions can really be praised. About everything like laundry or hot and cold water there is not only organisation, but what does not always or perhaps often go with it, efficiency. Americans are particular about these things of dress and decorum; and it is a virtue which I very seriously recognise, though I find it very hard to emulate. But with them it is a virtue; it is not a mere convention, still less a mere fashion. It is really related to human dignity rather than to social superiority. The really glorious thing about the American is that he does not dress like a gentleman; he dresses like a citizen or a civilised man. His Puritanic particularity on certain points is really detachable from any definite social ambitions; these things are not a part of getting into society but merely of keeping out of savagery. Those millions and millions of middling people, that huge middle class especially of the Middle West, are not near enough to any aristocracy even to be sham aristocrats, or to be real snobs. But their standards are secure; and though I do not really travel in a bath-tub, or believe in the bath-tub philosophy and religion, I will not on this matter recoil misanthropically from them: I prefer the tub of Dayton to the tub of Diogenes. On these points there is really something a million times better than efficiency, and that is something like equality.

In short, the American hotel is not America; but it is American. In some respects it is as American as the English inn is English. And it is symbolic of that society in this among other things: that it does tend too much to uniformity; but that that very uniformity disguises not a little natural dignity. The old Romans boasted that their republic was a nation of kings. If we really walked abroad in such a kingdom, we might very well grow tired of the sight of a crowd of kings, of every man with a gold crown on his head or an ivory sceptre in his hand. But it is arguable that we ought not to grow tired of the repetition of crowns and sceptres, any more than of the repetition of flowers and stars. The whole imaginative effort of Walt Whitman was really an effort to absorb and animate these multitudinous modern repetitions; and Walt Whitman would be quite capable of including in his lyric litany of optimism a list of the nine hundred and ninety-nine identical bathrooms. I do not sneer at the generous effort of the giant; though I think, when all is said, that it is a criticism of modern machinery that the effort should be gigantic as well as generous.

While there is so much repetition there is little repose. It is the pattern of a kaleidoscope rather than a wall-paper; a pattern of figures running and even leaping like the figures in a zoetrope. But even in the groups where there was no hustle there was often something of homelessness. I do not mean merely that they were not dining at home; but rather that they were not at home even when dining, and dining at their favourite hotel. They would frequently start up and dart from the room at a summons from the telephone. It may have been fanciful, but I could not help feeling a breath of home, as from a flap or flutter of St. George's Cross, when I first sat down in a Canadian hostelry, and read the announcement that no such telephonic or other summonses were allowed in the dining-room. It may have been a coincidence, and there may be American hotels with this merciful proviso and Canadian hotels without it; but the thing was symbolic even if it was not evidential. I felt as if I stood indeed upon English soil, in a place where people liked to have their meals in peace.

The process of the summons is called 'paging,' and consists of sending a little boy with a large voice through all the halls and corridors of the building, making them resound with a name. The custom is common, of course, in clubs and hotels even in England; but in England it is a mere whisper compared with the wail with which the American page repeats the formula of 'Calling Mr. So and So.' I remember a particularly crowded *parterre* in the somewhat smoky and oppressive atmosphere of Pittsburg, through which wandered a youth with a voice the like of which I have never heard in the land of the living, a voice like the cry of a lost spirit, saying again and again for ever, 'Carling Mr. Anderson.' One felt that he never would find Mr. Anderson. Perhaps there never had been any Mr. Anderson to be found. Perhaps he and every one else wandered in an abyss of bottomless scepticism; and he was but the victim of one out of numberless nightmares of eternity, as he wandered a shadow with shadows and wailed by impassable streams. This is not exactly my philosophy, but I feel sure it was his. And it is a mood that may frequently visit the mind in the centres of highly active and successful industrial civilisation.

Such are the first idle impressions of the great American hotel, gained by sitting for the first time in its gallery and gazing on its drifting crowds with thoughts equally drifting. The first impression is of something enormous and rather unnatural, an impression that is gradually tempered by experience of the kindliness and even the tameness of so much of that social order. But I should not be recording the sensations with sincerity, if I did not touch in passing the note of something unearthly about that vast system to an insular traveller who sees it for the first time. It is as if he were wandering in another world among the fixed stars; or worse still, in an ideal Utopia of the future.

Yet I am not certain; and perhaps the best of all news is that nothing is really new. I sometimes have a fancy that many of these new things in new countries are but the resurrections of old things which have been wickedly killed or stupidly stunted in old countries. I have looked over the sea of little tables in some light and airy open-air café; and my thoughts have gone back to the plain wooden bench and wooden table that stands solitary and weather-stained outside so many neglected English inns. We talk of experimenting in the French café, as of some fresh and almost impudent innovation. But our fathers had the French café, in the sense of the free-and-easy table in the sun and air. The only difference was that French democracy was allowed to develop its café, or multiply its tables, while English plutocracy prevented any such popular growth. Perhaps there are other examples of old types and patterns, lost in the old oligarchy and saved in the new democracies. I am haunted with a hint that the new structures are not so very new; and that they remind me of something very old. As I look from the balcony floor the crowds seem to float away and the colours to soften and grow pale, and I know I am in one of the simplest and most ancestral of human habitations. I am looking down from the old wooden gallery upon the courtyard of an inn. This new architectural model, which I have described, is after all one of the oldest European models, now neglected in Europe and especially in England. It was the theatre in which were enacted innumerable picaresque comedies and romantic plays, with figures ranging from Sancho Panza to Sam Weller. It served as the apparatus, like some gigantic toy set up in bricks and timber, for the ancient and perhaps eternal game of tennis. The very terms of the original game were taken from the inn courtyard, and the players scored accordingly as they hit the buttery-hatch or the roof. Singular speculations hover in my mind as the scene darkens and the quadrangle below begins to empty in the last hours of night. Some day perhaps this huge structure will be found standing in a solitude like a skeleton; and it will be the skeleton of the Spotted Dog or the Blue Boar. It will wither and decay until it is worthy at last to be a tavern. I do not know whether men will play tennis on its ground floor, with various scores and prizes for hitting the electric fan, or the lift, or the head waiter. Perhaps the very words will only remain as part of some such rustic game. Perhaps the electric fan will no longer be electric and the elevator will no longer elevate, and the waiter will only wait to be hit. But at least it is only by the decay of modern plutocracy, which seems already to have begun, that the secret of the structure even of this plutocratic palace can stand revealed. And after long years, when its lights are extinguished and only the long shadows inhabit its halls and vestibules, there may come a new noise like thunder; of D'Artagnan knocking at the door.

A MEDITATION IN BROADWAY

When I had looked at the lights of Broadway by night, I made to my American friends an innocent remark that seemed for some reason to amuse them. I had looked, not without joy, at that long kaleidoscope of coloured lights arranged in large letters and sprawling trade-marks, advertising everything, from pork to pianos, through the agency of the two most vivid and most mystical of the gifts of God; colour and fire. I said to them, in my simplicity, 'What a glorious garden of wonders this would be, to any one who was lucky enough to be unable to read.'

Here it is but a text for a further suggestion. But let us suppose that there does walk down this flaming avenue a peasant, of the sort called scornfully an illiterate peasant; by those who think that insisting on people reading and writing is the best way to keep out the spies who read in all languages and the forgers who write in all hands. On this principle indeed, a peasant merely acquainted with things of little practical use to mankind, such as ploughing, cutting wood, or growing vegetables, would very probably be excluded; and it is not for us to criticise from the outside the philosophy of those who would keep out the farmer and let in the forger. But let us suppose, if only for the sake of argument, that the peasant is walking under the artificial suns and stars of this tremendous thoroughfare; that he has escaped to the land of liberty upon some general rumour and romance of the story of its liberation, but without being yet able to understand the arbitrary signs of its alphabet. The soul of such a man would surely soar higher than the sky-scrapers, and embrace a brotherhood broader than Broadway. Realising that he had arrived on an evening of exceptional festivity, worthy to be blazoned with all this burning heraldry, he would please himself by guessing what great proclamation or principle of the Republic hung in the sky like a constellation or rippled across the street like a comet. He would be shrewd enough to guess that the three festoons fringed with fiery words of somewhat similar pattern stood for 'Government of the People, For the People, By the People'; for it must obviously be that, unless it were 'Liberty, Equality, Fraternity.' His shrewdness would perhaps be a little shaken if he knew that the triad stood for 'Tang Tonic To-day; Tang Tonic To-morrow; Tang Tonic All the Time.' He will soon identify a restless ribbon of red lettering, red hot and rebellious, as the saying, 'Give me liberty or give me death.' He will fail to identify it as the equally famous saying, 'Skyoline Has Gout Beaten to a Frazzle.' Therefore it was that I desired the peasant to walk down that grove of fiery trees, under all that golden foliage, and fruits like monstrous jewels, as innocent as Adam before the Fall. He would see sights almost as fine as the flaming sword or the purple and peacock plumage of the seraphim; so long as he did not go near the Tree of Knowledge.

In other words, if once he went to school it would be all up; and indeed I fear in any case he would soon discover his error. If he stood wildly waving his hat for liberty in the middle of the road as Chunk Chutney picked itself out in ruby stars upon the sky, he would impede the excellent but extremely rigid traffic system of New York. If he fell on his knees before a sapphire splendour, and began saying an Ave Maria under a mistaken association, he would be conducted kindly but firmly by an Irish policeman to a more authentic shrine. But though the foreign simplicity might not long survive in New York, it is quite a mistake to suppose that such foreign simplicity cannot enter New York. He may be excluded for being illiterate, but he cannot be excluded for being ignorant, nor for being innocent. Least of all can he be excluded for being wiser in his innocence than the world in its knowledge. There is here indeed more than one distinction to be made. New York is a cosmopolitan city; but it is not a city of cosmopolitans. Most of the masses in New York have a nation, whether or no it be the nation to which New York belongs. Those who are Americanised are American, and very patriotically American. Those who are not thus nationalised are not in the least internationalised. They simply continue to be themselves; the Irish are Irish; the Jews are Jewish; and all sorts of other tribes carry on the traditions of remote European valleys almost untouched. In short, there is a sort of slender bridge between their old country and their new, which they either cross or do not cross, but which they seldom simply occupy. They are exiles or they are citizens; there is no moment when they are cosmopolitans. But very often the exiles bring with them not only rooted traditions, but rooted truths.

Indeed it is to a great extent the thought of these strange souls in crude American garb that gives a meaning to the masquerade of New York. In the hotel where I stayed the head waiter in one room was a Bohemian; and I am glad to say that he called himself a Bohemian. I have already protested sufficiently, before American audiences, against the pedantry of perpetually talking about Czecho-Slovakia. I suggested to my American friends that the abandonment of the word Bohemian in its historical sense might well extend to its literary and figurative sense. We might be expected to say, 'I'm afraid Henry has got into very Czecho-Slovakian habits lately,' or 'Don't bother to dress; it's quite a Czecho-Slovakian affair.' Anyhow my Bohemian would have nothing to do with such nonsense; he called himself a son of Bohemia, and spoke as such in his criticisms of America, which were both favourable and unfavourable. He was a squat man, with a sturdy figure and a steady smile; and his eyes were like dark pools in the depth of a darker forest, but I do not think he had ever been deceived by the lights of Broadway.

But I found something like my real innocent abroad, my real peasant among the sky-signs, in another part of the same establishment. He was a much leaner man, equally dark, with a hook nose, hungry face, and fierce black moustaches. He also was a waiter, and was in the costume of a waiter, which is a smarter edition of the costume of a lecturer. As he was serving me with clam chowder or some such thing, I fell into speech with him and he told me he was a Bulgar. I said something like, 'I'm afraid I don't know as much as I ought to about Bulgaria. I suppose most of your people are agricultural, aren't they?' He did not stir an inch from his regular attitude, but he slightly lowered his low voice and said, 'Yes. From the earth we come and to the earth we return; when people get away from that they are lost.'

To hear such a thing said by the waiter was alone an epoch in the life of an unfortunate writer of fantastic novels. To see him clear away the clam chowder like an automaton, and bring me more iced water like an automaton or like nothing on earth except an American waiter (for piling up ice is the cold passion of their lives), and all this after having uttered something so dark and deep, so starkly incongruous and so startlingly true, was an indescribable thing, but very like the picture of the peasant admiring Broadway. So he passed, with his artificial clothes and manners, lit up with all the ghastly artificial light of the hotel, and all the ghastly artificial life of the city; and his heart was like his own remote and rocky valley, where those unchanging words were carved as on a rock.

I do not profess to discuss here at all adequately the question this raises about the Americanisation of the Bulgar. It has many aspects, of some of which most Englishmen and even some Americans are rather unconscious. For one thing, a man with so rugged a loyalty to land could not be Americanised in New York; but it is not so certain that he could not be Americanised in America. We might almost say that a peasantry is hidden in the heart of America. So far as our impressions go, it is a secret. It is rather an open secret; covering only some thousand square miles of open prairie. But for most of our countrymen it is something invisible, unimagined, and unvisited; the simple truth that where all those acres are there is agriculture, and where all that agriculture is there is considerable tendency towards distributive or decently equalised property, as in a peasantry. On the other hand, there are those who say that the Bulgar will never be Americanised, that he only comes to be a waiter in America that he may afford to return to be a peasant in Bulgaria. I cannot decide this issue, and indeed I did not introduce it to this end. I was led to it by a certain line of reflection that runs along the Great White Way, and I will continue to follow it. The criticism, if we could put it rightly, not only covers more than New York but more than the whole New World. Any argument against it is quite as valid against the largest and richest cities of the Old World, against London or Liverpool or Frankfort or Belfast. But it is in New York that we see the argument most clearly, because we see the thing thus towering into its own turrets and breaking into its own fireworks.

I disagree with the aesthetic condemnation of the modern city with its sky-scrapers and sky-signs. I mean that which laments the loss of beauty and its sacrifice to utility. It seems to me the very reverse of the truth. Years ago, when people used to say the Salvation Army doubtless had good intentions, but we must all deplore its methods, I pointed out that the very contrary is the case. Its method, the method of drums and democratic appeal, is that of the Franciscans or any other march of the Church Militant. It was precisely its aims that were dubious, with their dissenting morality and despotic finance. It is somewhat the same with things like the sky-signs in Broadway. The aesthete must not ask me to mingle my tears with his, because these things are merely useful and ugly. For I am not specially inclined to think them ugly; but I am strongly inclined to think them useless. As a matter of art for art's sake, they seem to me rather artistic. As a form of practical social work they seem to me stark stupid waste. If Mr. Bilge is rich enough to build a tower four hundred feet high and give it a crown of golden crescents and crimson stars, in order to draw attention to his manufacture of the Paradise Tooth Paste or The Seventh Heaven Cigar, I do not feel the least disposition to thank him for any serious form of social service. I have never tried the Seventh Heaven Cigar; indeed a premonition moves me towards the belief that I shall go down to the dust without trying it. I have every reason to doubt whether it does any particular good to those who smoke it, or any good to anybody except those who sell it. In short Mr. Bilge's usefulness consists in being useful to Mr. Bilge, and all the rest is illusion and sentimentalism. But because I know that Bilge is only Bilge, shall I stoop to the profanity of saying that fire is only fire? Shall I blaspheme crimson stars any more than crimson sunsets, or deny that those moons are golden any more than that this grass is green? If a child saw these coloured lights, he would dance with as much delight as at any other coloured toys; and it is the duty of every poet, and even of every critic, to dance in respectful imitation of the child. Indeed I am in a mood of so much sympathy with the fairy lights of this pantomime city, that I should be almost sorry to see social sanity and a sense of proportion return to extinguish them. I fear the day is breaking, and the broad daylight of tradition and ancient truth is coming to end all this delightful nightmare of New York at night. Peasants and priests and all sorts of practical and sensible people are coming back into power, and their stern realism may wither all these beautiful, unsubstantial, useless things. They will not believe in the Seventh Heaven Cigar, even when they see it shining as with stars in the seventh heaven. They will not be affected by advertisements, any more than the priests and peasants of the Middle Ages would have been affected by advertisements. Only a very soft-headed, sentimental, and rather servile generation of men could possibly be affected by advertisements at all. People who are a little more hard-headed, humorous, and intellectually independent, see the rather simple joke; and are not impressed by this or any other form of self-praise. Almost any other men in almost any other age would have seen the joke. If you had said to a man in the Stone Age, 'Ugg says Ugg makes the best stone hatchets,' he would have perceived a lack of detachment and disinterestedness about the testimonial. If you had said to a medieval peasant, 'Robert the Bowyer proclaims, with three blasts of a horn, that he makes good bows,' the peasant would have said, 'Well, of course he does,' and thought about something more important. It is only among people whose minds have been weakened by a sort of mesmerism that so transparent a trick as that of advertisement could ever have been tried at all. And if ever we have again, as for other reasons I cannot but hope we shall, a more democratic distribution of property and a more agricultural basis of national life, it would seem at first sight only too likely that all this beautiful superstition will perish, and the fairyland of Broadway with all its varied rainbows fade away. For such people the Seventh Heaven Cigar, like the nineteenth-century city, will have ended in smoke. And even the smoke of it will have vanished.

But the next stage of reflection brings us back to the peasant looking at the lights of Broadway. It is not true to say in the strict sense that the peasant has never seen such things before. The truth is that he has seen them on a much smaller scale, but for a much larger purpose. Peasants also have their ritual and ornament, but it is to adorn more real things. Apart from our first fancy about the peasant who could not read, there is no doubt about what would be apparent to a peasant who could read, and who could understand. For him also fire is sacred, for him also colour is symbolic. But where he sets up a candle to light the little shrine of St. Joseph, he finds it takes twelve hundred candles to light the Seventh Heaven Cigar. He is used to the colours in church windows showing red for martyrs or blue for madonnas; but here he can only conclude that all the colours of the rainbow belong to Mr. Bilge. Now upon the aesthetic side he might well be impressed; but it is exactly on the social and even scientific side that he has a right to criticise. If he were a Chinese peasant, for instance, and came from a land of fireworks, he would naturally suppose that he had happened to arrive at a great firework display in celebration of something; perhaps the Sacred Emperor's birthday, or rather birthnight. It would gradually dawn on the Chinese philosopher that the Emperor could hardly be born every night. And when he learnt the truth the philosopher, if he was a philosopher, would be a little disappointed ... possibly a little disdainful.

Compare, for instance, these everlasting fireworks with the damp squibs and dying bonfires of Guy Fawkes Day. That quaint and even queer national festival has been fading for some time out of English life. Still, it was a national festival, in the double sense that it represented some sort of public spirit pursued by some sort of popular impulse. People spent money on the display of fireworks; they did not get money by it. And the people who spent money were often those who had very little money to spend. It had something of the glorious and fanatical character of making the poor poorer. It did not, like the advertisements, have only the mean and materialistic character of making the rich richer. In short, it came from the people and it appealed to the nation. The historical and religious cause in which it originated is not mine; and I think it has perished partly through being tied to a historical theory for which there is no future. I think this is illustrated in the very fact that the ceremonial is merely negative and destructive. Negation and destruction are very noble things as far as they go, and when they go in the right direction; and the popular expression of them has always something hearty and human about it. I shall not therefore bring any fine or fastidious criticism, whether literary or musical, to bear upon the little boys who drag about a bolster and a paper mask, calling out

Guy Fawkes Guy

Hit him in the eye.

But I admit it is a disadvantage that they have not a saint or hero to crown in effigy as well as a traitor to burn in effigy. I admit that popular Protestantism has become too purely negative for people to wreathe in flowers the statue of Mr. Kensit or even of Dr. Clifford. I do not disguise my preference for popular Catholicism; which still has statues that can be wreathed in flowers. I wish our national feast of fireworks revolved round something positive and popular. I wish the beauty of a Catherine Wheel were displayed to the glory of St. Catherine. I should not especially complain if Roman candles were really Roman candles. But this negative character does not destroy the national character; which began at least in disinterested faith and has ended at least in disinterested fun. There is nothing disinterested at all about the new commercial fireworks. There is nothing so dignified as a dingy guy among the lights of Broadway. In that thoroughfare, indeed, the very word guy has another and milder significance. An American friend congratulated me on the impression I produced on a lady interviewer, observing, 'She says you're a regular guy.' This puzzled me a little at the time. 'Her description is no doubt correct,' I said, 'but I confess that it would never have struck me as specially complimentary.' But it appears that it is one of the most graceful of compliments, in the original American. A guy in America is a colourless term for a human being. All men are guys, being endowed by their Creator with certain ... but I am misled by another association. And a regular guy means, I presume, a reliable or respectable guy. The point here, however, is that the guy in the grotesque English sense does represent the dilapidated remnant of a real human tradition of symbolising real historic ideals by the sacramental mystery of fire. It is a great fall from the lowest of these lowly bonfires to the highest of the modern sky-signs. The new illumination does not stand for any national ideal at all; and what is yet more to the point, it does not come from any popular enthusiasm at all. That is where it differs from the narrowest national Protestantism of the English institution. Mobs have risen in support of No Popery; no mobs are likely to rise in defence of the New Puffery. Many a poor crazy Orangeman has died saying, 'To Hell with the Pope'; it is doubtful whether any man will ever, with his last breath, frame the ecstatic words, 'Try Hugby's Chewing Gum.' These modern and mercantile legends are imposed upon us by a mercantile minority, and we are merely passive to the suggestion. The hypnotist of high finance or big business merely writes his commands in heaven with a finger of fire. All men really are guys, in the sense of dummies. We are only the victims of his pyrotechnic violence; and it is he who hits us in the eye.

This is the real case against that modern society that is symbolised by such art and architecture. It is not that it is toppling, but that it is top-heavy. It is not that it is vulgar, but rather that it is not popular. In other words, the democratic ideal of countries like America, while it is still generally sincere and sometimes intense, is at issue with another tendency, an industrial progress which is of all things on earth the most undemocratic. America is not alone in possessing the industrialism, but she is alone in emphasising the ideal that strives with industrialism. Industrial capitalism and ideal democracy are everywhere in controversy; but perhaps only here are they in conflict. France has a democratic ideal; but France is not industrial. England and Germany are industrial; but England and Germany are not really democratic. Of course when I speak here of industrialism I speak of great industrial areas; there is, as will be noted later, another side to all these countries; there is in America itself not only a great deal of agricultural society, but a great deal of agricultural equality; just as there are still peasants in Germany and may some day again be peasants in England. But the point is that the ideal and its enemy the reality are here crushed very close to each other in the high, narrow city; and that the sky-scraper is truly named because its top, towering in such insolence, is scraping the stars off the American sky, the very heaven of the American spirit.

That seems to me the main outline of the whole problem. In the first chapter of this book, I have emphasised the fact that equality is still the ideal though no longer the reality of America. I should like to conclude this one by emphasising the fact that the reality of modern capitalism is menacing that ideal with terrors and even splendours that might well stagger the wavering and impressionable modern spirit. Upon the issue of that struggle depends the question of whether this new great civilisation continues to exist, and even whether any one cares if it exists or not. I have already used the parable of the American flag, and the stars that stand for a multitudinous equality; I might here take the opposite symbol of these artificial and terrestrial stars flaming on the forehead of the commercial city; and note the peril of the last illusion, which is that the artificial stars may seem to fill the heavens, and the real stars to have faded from sight. But I am content for the moment to reaffirm the merely imaginative pleasure of those dizzy turrets and dancing fires. If those nightmare buildings were really all built for nothing, how noble they would be! The fact that they were really built for something need not unduly depress us for a moment, or drag down our soaring fancies. There is something about these vertical lines that suggests a sort of rush upwards, as of great cataracts topsy-turvy. I have spoken of fireworks, but here I should rather speak of rockets. There is only something underneath the mind murmuring that nothing remains at last of a flaming rocket except a falling stick. I have spoken of Babylonian perspectives, and of words written with a fiery finger, like that huge unhuman finger that wrote on Belshazzar's wall.... But what did it write on Belshazzar's wall?... I am content once more to end on a note of doubt and a rather dark sympathy with those many-coloured solar systems turning so dizzily, far up in the divine vacuum of the night.

'From the earth we come and to the earth we return; when people get away from that they are lost.'

IRISH AND OTHER INTERVIEWERS

It is often asked what should be the first thing that a man sees when he lands in a foreign country; but I think it should be the vision of his own country. At least when I came into New York Harbour, a sort of grey and green cloud came between me and the towers with multitudinous windows, white in the winter sunlight; and I saw an old brown house standing back among the beech-trees at home, the house of only one among many friends and neighbours, but one somehow so sunken in the very heart of England as to be unconscious of her imperial or international position, and out of the sound of her perilous seas. But what made most clear the vision that revisited me was something else. Before we touched land the men of my own guild, the journalists and reporters, had already boarded the ship like pirates. And one of them spoke to me in an accent that I knew; and thanked me for all I had done for Ireland. And it was at that moment that I knew most vividly that what I wanted was to do something for England.

Then, as it chanced, I looked across at the statue of Liberty, and saw that the great bronze was gleaming green in the morning light. I had made all the obvious jokes about the statue of Liberty. I found it had a soothing effect on earnest Prohibitionists on the boat to urge, as a point of dignity and delicacy, that it ought to be given back to the French, a vicious race abandoned to the culture of the vine. I proposed that the last liquors on board should be poured out in a pagan libation before it. And then I suddenly remembered that this Liberty was still in some sense enlightening the world, or one part of the world; was a lamp for one sort of wanderer, a star of one sort of seafarer. To one persecuted people at least this land had really been an asylum; even if recent legislation (as I have said) had made them think it a lunatic asylum. They had made it so much their home that the very colour of the country seemed to change with the infusion; as the bronze of the great statue took on a semblance of the wearing of the green.

It is a commonplace that the Englishman has been stupid in his relations with the Irish; but he has been far more stupid in his relations with the Americans on the subject of the Irish. His propaganda has been worse than his practice; and his defence more ill-considered than the most indefensible things that it was intended to defend. There is in this matter a curious tangle of cross-purposes, which only a parallel example can make at all clear. And I will note the point here, because it is some testimony to its vivid importance that it was really the first I had to discuss on American soil with an American citizen. In a double sense I touched Ireland before I came to America. I will take an imaginary instance from another controversy; in order to show how the apology can be worse than the action. The best we can say for ourselves is worse than the worst that we can do.

There was a time when English poets and other publicists could always be inspired with instantaneous indignation about the persecuted Jews in Russia. We have heard less about them since we heard more about the persecuting Jews in Russia. I fear there are a great many middle-class Englishmen already who wish that Trotsky had been persecuted a little more. But even in those days Englishmen divided their minds in a curious fashion; and unconsciously distinguished between the Jews whom they had never seen, in Warsaw, and the Jews whom they had often seen in Whitechapel. It seemed to be assumed that, by a curious coincidence, Russia possessed not only the very worst Anti-Semites but the very best Semites. A moneylender in London might be like Judas Iscariot; but a moneylender in Moscow must be like Judas Maccabaeus.

Nevertheless there remained in our common sense an unconscious but fundamental comprehension of the unity of Israel; a sense that some things could be said, and some could not be said, about the Jews as a whole. Suppose that even in those days, to say nothing of these, an English protest against Russian Anti-Semitism had been answered by the Russian Anti-Semites, and suppose the answer had been somewhat as follows:—

'It is all very well for foreigners to complain of our denying civic rights to our Jewish subjects; but we know the Jews better than they do. They are a barbarous people, entirely primitive, and very like the simple savages who cannot count beyond five on their fingers. It is quite impossible to make them understand ordinary numbers, to say nothing of simple economics. They do not realise the meaning or the value of money. No Jew anywhere in the world can get into his stupid head the notion of a bargain, or of exchanging one thing for another. Their hopeless incapacity for commerce or finance would retard the progress of our people, would prevent the spread of any sort of economic education, would keep the whole country on a level lower than that of the most prehistoric methods of barter. What Russia needs most is a mercantile middle class; and it is unjust to ask us to swamp its small beginnings in thousands of these rude tribesmen, who cannot do a sum of simple addition, or understand the symbolic character of a threepenny bit. We might as well be asked to give civic rights to cows and pigs as to this unhappy, half-witted race who can no more count than the beasts of the field. In every intellectual exercise they are hopelessly incompetent; no Jew can play chess; no Jew can learn languages; no Jew has ever appeared in the smallest part in any theatrical performance; no Jew can give or take any pleasure connected with any musical instrument. These people are our subjects; and we understand them. We accept full responsibility for treating such troglodytes on our own terms.'

It would not be entirely convincing. It would sound a little far-fetched and unreal. But it would sound exactly like our utterances about the Irish, as they sound to all Americans, and rather especially to Anti-Irish Americans. That is exactly the impression we produce on the people of the United States when we say, as we do say in substance, something like this: 'We mean no harm to the poor dear Irish, so dreamy, so irresponsible, so incapable of order or organisation. If we were to withdraw from their country they would only fight among themselves; they have no notion of how to rule themselves. There is something charming about their unpracticability, about their very incapacity for the coarse business of politics. But for their own sakes it is impossible to leave these emotional visionaries to ruin themselves in the attempt to rule themselves. They are like children; but they are our own children, and we understand them. We accept full responsibility for acting as their parents and guardians.'

Now the point is not only that this view of the Irish is false, but that it is the particular view that the Americans know to be false. While we are saying that the Irish could not organise, the Americans are complaining, often very bitterly, of the power of Irish organisation. While we say that the Irishman could not rule himself, the Americans are saying, more or less humorously, that the Irishman rules them. A highly intelligent professor said to me in Boston, 'We have solved the Irish problem here; we have an entirely independent Irish Government.' While we are complaining, in an almost passionate manner, of the impotence of mere cliques of idealists and dreamers, they are complaining, often in a very indignant manner, of the power of great gangs of bosses and bullies. There are a great many Americans who pity the Irish, very naturally and very rightly, for the historic martyrdom which their patriotism has endured. But there are a great many Americans who do not pity the Irish in the least. They would be much more likely to pity the English; only this particular way of talking tends rather to make them despise the English. Thus both the friends of Ireland and the foes of Ireland tend to be the foes of England. We make one set of enemies by our action, and another by our apology.

It is a thing that can from time to time be found in history; a misunderstanding that really has a moral. The English excuse would carry much more weight if it had more sincerity and more humility. There are a considerable number of people in the United States who could sympathise with us, if we would say frankly that we fear the Irish. Those who thus despise our pity might possibly even respect our fear. The argument I have often used in other places comes back with prodigious and redoubled force, after hearing anything of American opinion; the argument that the only reasonable or reputable excuse for the English is the excuse of a patriotic sense of peril; and that the Unionist, if he must be a Unionist, should use that and no other. When the Unionist has said that he dare not let loose against himself a captive he has so cruelly wronged, he has said all that he has to say; all that he has ever had to say; all that he will ever have to say. He is like a man who has sent a virile and rather vindictive rival unjustly to penal servitude; and who connives at the continuance of the sentence, not because he himself is particularly vindictive, but because he is afraid of what the convict will do when he comes out of prison. This is not exactly a moral strength, but it is a very human weakness; and that is the most that can be said for it. All other talk, about Celtic frenzy or Catholic superstition, is cant invented to deceive himself or to deceive the world. But the vital point to realise is that it is cant that cannot possibly deceive the American world. In the matter of the Irishman the American is not to be deceived. It is not merely true to say that he knows better. It is equally true to say that he knows worse. He knows vices and evils in the Irishman that are entirely hidden in the hazy vision of the Englishman. He knows that our unreal slanders are inconsistent even with the real sins. To us Ireland is a shadowy Isle of Sunset, like Atlantis, about which we can make up legends. To him it is a positive ward or parish in the heart of his huge cities, like Whitechapel; about which even we cannot make legends but only lies. And, as I have said, there are some lies we do not tell even about Whitechapel. We do not say it is inhabited by Jews too stupid to count or know the value of a coin.

The first thing for any honest Englishman to send across the sea is this; that the English have not the shadow of a notion of what they are up against in America. They have never even heard of the batteries of almost brutal energy, of which I had thus touched a live wire even before I landed. People talk about the hypocrisy of England in dealing with a small nationality. What strikes me is the stupidity of England in supposing that she is dealing with a small nationality; when she is really dealing with a very large nationality. She is dealing with a nationality that often threatens, even numerically, to dominate all the other nationalities of the United States. The Irish are not decaying; they are not unpractical; they are scarcely even scattered; they are not even poor. They are the most powerful and practical world-combination with whom we can decide to be friends or foes; and that is why I thought first of that still and solid brown house in Buckinghamshire, standing back in the shadow of the trees.

Among my impressions of America I have deliberately put first the figure of the Irish-American interviewer, standing on the shore more symbolic than the statue of Liberty. The Irish interviewer's importance for the English lay in the fact of his being an Irishman, but there was also considerable interest in the circumstance of his being an interviewer. And as certain wild birds sometimes wing their way far out to sea and are the first signal of the shore, so the first Americans the traveller meets are often American interviewers; and they are generally birds of a feather, and they certainly flock together. In this respect, there is a slight difference in the etiquette of the craft in the two countries, which I was delighted to discuss with my fellow craftsmen. If I could at that moment have flown back to Fleet Street I am happy to reflect that nobody in the world would in the least wish to interview me. I should attract no more attention than the stone griffin opposite the Law Courts; both monsters being grotesque but also familiar. But supposing for the sake of argument that anybody did want to interview me, it is fairly certain that the fact of one paper publishing such an interview would rather prevent the other papers from doing so. The repetition of the same views of the same individual in two places would be considered rather bad journalism; it would have an air of stolen thunder, not to say stage thunder.

But in America the fact of my landing and lecturing was evidently regarded in the same light as a murder or a great fire, or any other terrible but incurable catastrophe, a matter of interest to all pressmen concerned with practical events. One of the first questions I was asked was how I should be disposed to explain the wave of crime in New York. Naturally I replied that it might possibly be due to the number of English lecturers who had recently landed. In the mood of the moment it seemed possible that, if they had all been interviewed, regrettable incidents might possibly have taken place. But this was only the mood of the moment, and even as a mood did not last more than a moment. And since it has reference to a rather common and a rather unjust conception of American journalism, I think it well to take it first as a fallacy to be refuted, though the refutation may require a rather longer approach.

I have generally found that the traveller fails to understand a foreign country, through treating it as a tendency and not as a balance. But if a thing were always tending in one direction it would soon tend to destruction. Everything that merely progresses finally perishes. Every nation, like every family, exists upon a compromise, and commonly a rather eccentric compromise; using the word 'eccentric' in the sense of something that is somehow at once crazy and healthy. Now the foreigner commonly sees some feature that he thinks fantastic without seeing the feature that balances it. The ordinary examples are obvious enough. An Englishman dining inside a hotel on the boulevards thinks the French eccentric in refusing to open a window. But he does not think the English eccentric in refusing to carry their chairs and tables out on to the pavement in Ludgate Circus. An Englishman will go poking about in little Swiss or Italian villages, in wild mountains or in remote islands, demanding tea; and never reflects that he is like a Chinaman who should enter all the wayside public-houses in Kent and Sussex and demand opium. But the point is not merely that he demands what he cannot expect to enjoy; it is that he ignores even what he does enjoy. He does not realise the sublime and starry paradox of the phrase, *vin ordinaire*, which to him should be a glorious jest like the phrase 'common gold' or 'daily diamonds.' These are the simple and self-evident cases; but there are many more subtle cases of the same thing; of the tendency to see that the nation fills up its own gap with its own substitute; or corrects its own extravagance with its own precaution. The national antidote generally grows wild in the woods side by side with the national poison. If it did not, all the natives would be dead. For it is so, as I have said, that nations necessarily die of the undiluted poison called progress.

It is so in this much-abused and over-abused example of the American journalist. The American interviewers really have exceedingly good manners for the purposes of their trade, granted that it is necessary to pursue their trade. And even what is called their hustling method can truly be said to cut both ways, or hustle both ways; for if they hustle in, they also hustle out. It may not at first sight seem the very warmest compliment to a gentleman to congratulate him on the fact that he soon goes away. But it really is a tribute to his perfection in a very delicate social art; and I am quite serious when I say that in this respect the interviewers are artists. It might be more difficult for an Englishman to come to the point, particularly the sort of point which American journalists are supposed, with some exaggeration, to aim at. It might be more difficult for an Englishman to ask a total stranger on the spur of the moment for the exact inscription on his mother's grave; but I really think that if an Englishman once got so far as that he would go very much farther, and certainly go on very much longer. The Englishman would approach the churchyard by a rather more wandering woodland path; but if once he had got to the grave I think he would have much more disposition, so to speak, to sit down on it. Our own national temperament would find it decidedly more difficult to disconnect when connections had really been established. Possibly that is the reason why our national temperament does not establish them. I suspect that the real reason that an Englishman does not talk is that he cannot leave off talking. I suspect that my solitary countrymen, hiding in separate railway compartments, are not so much retiring as a race of Trappists as escaping from a race of talkers.

However this may be, there is obviously something of practical advantage in the ease with which the American butterfly flits from flower to flower. He may in a sense force his acquaintance on us, but he does not force himself on us. Even when, to our prejudices, he seems to insist on knowing us, at least he does not insist on our knowing him. It may be, to some sensibilities, a bad thing that a total stranger should talk as if he were a friend, but it might possibly be worse if he insisted on being a friend before he would talk like one. To a great deal of the interviewing, indeed much the greater part of it, even this criticism does not apply; there is nothing which even an Englishman of extreme sensibility could regard as particularly private; the questions involved are generally entirely public, and treated with not a little public spirit. But my only reason for saying here what can be said even for the worst exceptions is to point out this general and neglected principle; that the very thing that we complain of in a foreigner generally carries with it its own foreign cure. American interviewing is generally very reasonable, and it is always very rapid. And even those to whom talking to an intelligent fellow creature is as horrible as having a tooth out may still admit that American interviewing has many of the qualities of American dentistry.

Another effect that has given rise to this fallacy, this exaggeration of the vulgarity and curiosity of the press, is the distinction between the articles and the headlines; or rather the tendency to ignore that distinction. The few really untrue and unscrupulous things I have seen in American 'stories' have always been in the headlines. And the headlines are written by somebody else; some solitary and savage cynic locked up in the office, hating all mankind, and raging and revenging himself at random, while the neat, polite, and rational pressman can safely be let loose to wander about the town.

For instance, I talked to two decidedly thoughtful fellow journalists immediately on my arrival at a town in which there had been some labour troubles. I told them my general view of Labour in the very largest and perhaps the vaguest historical outline; pointing out that the one great truth to be taught to the middle classes was that Capitalism was itself a crisis, and a passing crisis; that it was not so much that it was breaking down as that it had never really stood up. Slaveries could last, and peasantries could last; but wage-earning communities could hardly even live, and were already dying.

All this moral and even metaphysical generalisation was most fairly and most faithfully reproduced by the interviewer, who had actually heard it casually and idly spoken. But on the top of this column of political philosophy was the extraordinary announcement in enormous letters, 'Chesterton Takes Sides in Trolley Strike.' This was inaccurate. When I spoke I not only did not know that there was any trolley strike, but I did not know what a trolley strike was. I should have had an indistinct idea that a large number of citizens earned their living by carrying things about in wheel-barrows, and that they had desisted from the beneficent activities. Any one who did not happen to be a journalist, or know a little about journalism, American and English, would have supposed that the same man who wrote the article had suddenly gone mad and written the title. But I know that we have here to deal with two different types of journalists; and the man who writes the headlines I will not dare to describe; for I have not seen him except in dreams.

Another innocent complication is that the interviewer does sometimes translate things into his native language. It would not seem odd that a French interviewer should translate them into French; and it is certain that the American interviewer sometimes translates them into American. Those who imagine the two languages to be the same are more innocent than any interviewer. To take one out of the twenty examples, some of which I have mentioned elsewhere, suppose an interviewer had said that I had the reputation of being a nut. I should be flattered but faintly surprised at such a tribute to my dress and dashing exterior. I should afterwards be sobered and enlightened by discovering that in America a nut does not mean a dandy but a defective or imbecile person. And as I have here to translate their American phrase into English, it may be very defensible that they should translate my English phrases into American. Anyhow they often do translate them into American. In answer to the usual question about Prohibition I had made the usual answer, obvious to the point of dullness to those who are in daily contact with it, that it is a law that the rich make knowing they can always break it. From the printed interview it appeared that I had said, 'Prohibition! All matter of dollar sign.' This is almost avowed translation, like a French translation. Nobody can suppose that it would come natural to an Englishman to talk about a dollar, still less about a dollar sign—whatever that may be. It is exactly as if he had made me talk about the Skelt and Stevenson Toy Theatre as 'a cent plain, and two cents coloured' or condemned a parsimonious policy as dime-wise and dollar-foolish. Another interviewer once asked me who was the greatest American writer. I have forgotten exactly what I said, but after mentioning several names, I said that the greatest natural genius and artistic force was probably Walt Whitman. The printed interview is more precise; and students of my literary and conversational style will be interested to know that I said, 'See here, Walt Whitman was your one real red-blooded man.' Here again I hardly think the translation can have been quite unconscious; most of my intimates are indeed aware that I do not talk like that, but I fancy that the same fact would have dawned on the journalist to whom I had been talking. And even this trivial point carries with it the two truths which must be, I fear, the rather monotonous moral of these pages. The first is that America and England can be far better friends when sharply divided than when shapelessly amalgamated. These two journalists were false reporters, but they were true translators. They were not so much interviewers as interpreters. And the second is that in any such difference it is often wholesome to look beneath the surface for a superiority. For ability to translate does imply ability to understand; and many of these journalists really did understand. I think there are many English journalists who would be more puzzled by so simple an idea as the plutocratic foundation of Prohibition. But the American knew at once that I meant it was a matter of dollar sign; probably because he knew very well that it is.

Then again there is a curious convention by which American interviewing makes itself out much worse than it is. The reports are far more rowdy and insolent than the conversations. This is probably a part of the fact that a certain vivacity, which to some seems vitality and to some vulgarity, is not only an ambition but an ideal. It must always be grasped that this vulgarity is an ideal even more than it is a reality. It is an ideal when it is not a reality. A very quiet and intelligent young man, in a soft black hat and tortoise-shell spectacles, will ask for an interview with unimpeachable politeness, wait for his living subject with unimpeachable patience, talk to him quite sensibly for twenty minutes, and go noiselessly away. Then in the newspaper next morning you will read how he beat the bedroom door in, and pursued his victim on to the roof or dragged him from under the bed, and tore from him replies to all sorts of bald and ruthless questions printed in large black letters. I was often interviewed in the evening, and had no notion of how atrociously I had been insulted till I saw it in the paper next morning. I had no notion I had been on the rack of an inquisitor until I saw it in plain print; and then of course I believed it, with a faith and docility unknown in any previous epoch of history. An interesting essay might be written upon points upon which nations affect more vices than they possess; and it might deal more fully with the American pressman, who is a harmless clubman in private, and becomes a sort of highway-robber in print.

I have turned this chapter into something like a defence of interviewers, because I really think they are made to bear too much of the burden of the bad developments of modern journalism. But I am very far from meaning to suggest that those bad developments are not very bad. So far from wishing to minimise the evil, I would in a real sense rather magnify it. I would suggest that the evil itself is a much larger and more fundamental thing; and that to deal with it by abusing poor journalists, doing their particular and perhaps peculiar duty, is like dealing with a pestilence by rubbing at one of the spots. What is wrong with the modern world will not be righted by attributing the whole disease to each of its symptoms in turn; first to the tavern and then to the cinema and then to the reporter's room. The evil of journalism is not in the journalists. It is not in the poor men on the lower level of the profession, but in the rich men at the top of the profession; or rather in the rich men who are too much on top of the profession even to belong to it. The trouble with newspapers is the Newspaper Trust, as the trouble might be with a Wheat Trust, without involving a vilification of all the people who grow wheat. It is the American plutocracy and not the American press. What is the matter with the modern world is not modern headlines or modern films or modern machinery. What is the matter with the modern world is the modern world; and the cure will come from another.

SOME AMERICAN CITIES

There is one point, almost to be called a paradox, to be noted about New York; and that is that in one sense it is really new. The term very seldom has any relevance to the reality. The New Forest is nearly as old as the Conquest, and the New Theology is nearly as old as the Creed. Things have been offered to me as the new thought that might more properly be called the old thoughtlessness; and the thing we call the New Poor Law is already old enough to know better. But there is a sense in which New York is always new; in the sense that it is always being renewed. A stranger might well say that the chief industry of the citizens consists of destroying their city; but he soon realises that they always start it all over again with undiminished energy and hope. At first I had a fancy that they never quite finished putting up a big building without feeling that it was time to pull it down again; and that somebody began to dig up the first foundations while somebody else was putting on the last tiles. This fills the whole of this brilliant and bewildering place with a quite unique and unparalleled air of rapid ruin. Ruins spring up so suddenly like mushrooms, which with us are the growth of age like mosses, that one half expects to see ivy climbing quickly up the broken walls as in the nightmare of the Time Machine, or in some incredibly accelerated cinema.

There is no sight in any country that raises my own spirits so much as a scaffolding. It is a tragedy that they always take the scaffolding away, and leave us nothing but a mere building. If they would only take the building away and leave us a beautiful scaffolding, it would in most cases be a gain to the loveliness of earth. If I could analyse what it is that lifts the heart about the lightness and clarity of such a white and wooden skeleton, I could explain what it is that is really charming about New York; in spite of its suffering from the curse of cosmopolitanism and even the provincial superstition of progress. It is partly that all this destruction and reconstruction is an unexhausted artistic energy; but it is partly also that it is an artistic energy that does not take itself too seriously. It is first because man is here a carpenter; and secondly because he is a stage carpenter. Indeed there is about the whole scene the spirit of scene-shifting. It therefore touches whatever nerve in us has since childhood thrilled at all theatrical things. But the picture will be imperfect unless we realise something which gives it unity and marks its chief difference from the climate and colours of Western Europe. We may say that the back-scene remains the same. The sky remained, and in the depths of winter it seemed to be blue with summer; and so clear that I almost flattered myself that clouds were English products like primroses. An American would probably retort on my charge of scene-shifting by saying that at least he only shifted the towers and domes of the earth; and that in England it is the heavens that are shifty. And indeed we have changes from day to day that would seem to him as distinct as different magic-lantern slides; one view showing the Bay of Naples and the next the North Pole. I do not mean, of course, that there are no changes in American weather; but as a matter of proportion it is true that the most unstable part of our scenery is the most stable part of theirs. Indeed we might almost be pardoned the boast that Britain alone really possesses the noble thing called weather; most other countries having to be content with climate. It must be confessed, however, that they often are content with it. And the beauty of New York, which is considerable, is very largely due to the clarity that brings out the colours of varied buildings against the equal colour of the sky. Strangely enough I found myself repeating about this vista of the West two vivid lines in which Mr. W. B. Yeats has called up a vision of the East:—

And coloured like the eastern birds
At evening in their rainless skies.

To invoke a somewhat less poetic parallel, even the untravelled Englishman has probably seen American posters and trade advertisements of a patchy and gaudy kind, in which a white house or a yellow motor-car are cut out as in cardboard against a sky like blue marble. I used to think it was only New Art, but I found that it is really New York.

It is not for nothing that the very nature of local character has gained the nickname of local colour. Colour runs through all our experience; and we all know that our childhood found talismanic gems in the very paints in the paint-box, or even in their very names. And just as the very name of 'crimson lake' really suggested to me some sanguine and mysterious mere, dark yet red as blood, so the very name of 'burnt sienna' became afterwards tangled up in my mind with the notion of something traditional and tragic; as if some such golden Italian city had really been darkened by many conflagrations in the wars of mediaeval democracy. Now if one had the caprice of conceiving some city exactly contrary to one thus seared and seasoned by fire, its colour might be called up to a childish fancy by the mere name of 'raw umber'; and such a city is New York. I used to be puzzled by the name of 'raw umber,' being unable to imagine the effect of fried umber or stewed umber. But the colours of New York are exactly in that key; and might be adumbrated by phrases like raw pink or raw yellow. It is really in a sense like something uncooked; or something which the satiric would call half-baked. And yet the effect is not only beautiful, it is even delicate. I had no name for this nuance; until I saw that somebody had written of 'the pastel-tinted towers of New York'; and I knew that the name had been found. There are no paints dry enough to describe all that dry light; and it is not a box of colours but of crayons. If the Englishman returning to England is moved at the sight of a block of white chalk, the American sees rather a bundle of chalks. Nor can I imagine anything more moving. Fairy tales are told to children about a country where the trees are like sugar-sticks and the lakes like treacle, but most children would feel almost as greedy for a fairyland where the trees were like brushes of green paint and the hills were of coloured chalks.

But here what accentuates this arid freshness is the fragmentary look of the continual reconstruction and change. The strong daylight finds everywhere the broken edges of things, and the sort of hues we see in newly-turned earth or the white sections of trees. And it is in this respect that the local colour can literally be taken as local character. For New York considered in itself is primarily a place of unrest, and those who sincerely love it, as many do, love it for the romance of its restlessness. A man almost looks at a building as he passes to wonder whether it will be there when he comes back from his walk; and the doubt is part of an indescribable notion, as of a white nightmare of daylight, which is increased by the very numbering of the streets, with its tangle of numerals which at first makes an English head reel. The detail is merely a symbol; and when he is used to it he can see that it is, like the most humdrum human customs, both worse and better than his own. '271 West 52nd Street' is the easiest of all addresses to find, but the hardest of all addresses to remember. He who is, like myself, so constituted as necessarily to lose any piece of paper he has particular reason to preserve, will find himself wishing the place were called 'Pine Crest' or 'Heather Crag' like any unobtrusive villa in Streatham. But his sense of some sort of incalculable calculations, as of the vision of a mad mathematician, is rooted in a more real impression. His first feeling that his head is turning round is due to something really dizzy in the movement of a life that turns dizzily like a wheel. If there be in the modern mind something paradoxical that can find peace in change, it is here that it has indeed built its habitation or rather is still building and unbuilding it. One might fancy that it changes in everything and that nothing endures but its invisible name; and even its name, as I have said, seems to make a boast of novelty.

That is something like a sincere first impression of the atmosphere of New York. Those who think that is the atmosphere of America have never got any farther than New York. We might almost say that they have never entered America, any more than if they had been detained like undesirable aliens at Ellis Island. And indeed there are a good many undesirable aliens detained in Manhattan Island too. But of that I will not speak, being myself an alien with no particular pretensions to be desirable. Anyhow, such is New York; but such is not the New World. The great American Republic contains very considerable varieties, and of these varieties I necessarily saw far too little to allow me to generalise. But from the little I did see, I should venture on the generalisation that the great part of America is singularly and even strikingly unlike New York. It goes without saying that New York is very unlike the vast agricultural plains and small agricultural towns of the Middle West, which I did see. It may be conjectured with some confidence that it is very unlike what is called the Wild and sometimes the Woolly West, which I did not see. But I am here comparing New York, not with the newer states of the prairie or the mountains, but with the other older cities of the Atlantic coast. And New York, as it seems to me, is quite vitally different from the other historic cities of America. It is so different that it shows them all for the moment in a false light, as a long white searchlight will throw a light that is fantastic and theatrical upon ancient and quiet villages folded in the everlasting hills. Philadelphia and Boston and Baltimore are more like those quiet villages than they are like New York.

If I were to call this book 'The Antiquities of America,' I should give rise to misunderstanding and possibly to annoyance. And yet the double sense in such words is an undeserved misfortune for them. We talk of Plato or the Parthenon or the Greek passion for beauty as parts of the antique, but hardly of the antiquated. When we call them ancient it is not because they have perished, but rather because they have survived. In the same way I heard some New Yorkers refer to Philadelphia or Baltimore as 'dead towns.' They mean by a dead town a town that has had the impudence not to die. Such people are astonished to find an ancient thing alive, just as they are now astonished, and will be increasingly astonished, to find Poland or the Papacy or the French nation still alive. And what I mean by Philadelphia and Baltimore being alive is precisely what these people mean by their being dead; it is continuity; it is the presence of the life first breathed into them and of the purpose of their being; it is the benediction of the founders of the colonies and the fathers of the republic. This tradition is truly to be called life; for life alone can link the past and the future. It merely means that as what was done yesterday makes some difference to-day, so what is done to-day will make some difference to-morrow. In New York it is difficult to feel that any day will make any difference. These moderns only die daily without power to rise from the dead. But I can truly claim that in coming into some of these more stable cities of the States I felt something quite sincerely of that historic emotion which is satisfied in the eternal cities of the Mediterranean. I felt in America what many Americans suppose can only be felt in Europe. I have seldom had that sentiment stirred more simply and directly than when I saw from afar off, above the vast grey labyrinth of Philadelphia, great Penn upon his pinnacle like the graven figure of a god who had fashioned a new world; and remembered that his body lay buried in a field at the turning of a lane, a league from my own door.

For this aspect of America is rather neglected in the talk about electricity and headlines. Needless to say, the modern vulgarity of avarice and advertisement sprawls all over Philadelphia or Boston; but so it does over Winchester or Canterbury. But most people know that there is something else to be found in Canterbury or Winchester; many people know that it is rather more interesting; and some people know that Alfred can still walk in Winchester and that St. Thomas at Canterbury was killed but did not die. It is at least as possible for a Philadelphian to feel the presence of Penn and Franklin as for an Englishman to see the ghosts of Alfred and of Becket. Tradition does not mean a dead town; it does not mean that the living are dead but that the dead are alive. It means that it still matters what Penn did two hundred years ago or what Franklin did a hundred years ago; I never could feel in New York that it mattered what anybody did an hour ago. And these things did and do matter. Quakerism is not my favourite creed; but on that day when William Penn stood unarmed upon that spot and made his treaty with the Red Indians, his creed of humanity did have a triumph and a triumph that has not turned back. The praise given to him is not a priggish fiction of our conventional history, though such fictions have illogically curtailed it. The Nonconformists have been rather unfair to Penn even in picking their praises; and they generally forget that toleration cuts both ways and that an open mind is open on all sides. Those who deify him for consenting to bargain with the savages cannot forgive him for consenting to bargain with the Stuarts. And the same is true of the other city, yet more closely connected with the tolerant experiment of the Stuarts. The state of Maryland was the first experiment in religious freedom in human history. Lord Baltimore and his Catholics were a long march ahead of William Penn and his Quakers on what is now called the path of progress. That the first religious toleration ever granted in the world was granted by Roman Catholics is one of those little informing details with which our Victorian histories did not exactly teem. But when I went into my hotel at Baltimore and found two priests waiting to see me, I was moved in a new fashion, for I felt that I touched the end of a living chain. Nor was the impression accidental; it will always remain with me with a mixture of gratitude and grief, for they brought a message of welcome from a great American whose name I had known from childhood and whose career was drawing to its close; for it was but a few days after I left the city that I learned that Cardinal Gibbons was dead.

On the top of a hill on one side of the town stood the first monument raised after the Revolution to Washington. Beyond it was a new monument saluting in the name of Lafayette the American soldiers who fell fighting in France in the Great War. Between them were steps and stone seats, and I sat down on one of them and talked to two children who were clambering about the bases of the monument. I felt a profound and radiant peace in the thought that they at any rate were not going to my lecture. It made me happy that in that talk neither they nor I had any names. I was full of that indescribable waking vision of the strangeness of life, and especially of the strangeness of locality; of how we find places and lose them; and see faces for a moment in a far-off land, and it is equally mysterious if we remember and mysterious if we forget. I had even stirring in my head the suggestion of some verses that I shall never finish—

If I ever go back to Baltimore
The city of Maryland.

But the poem would have to contain far too much; for I was thinking of a thousand things at once; and wondering what the children would be like twenty years after and whether they would travel in white goods or be interested in oil, and I was not untouched (it may be said) by the fact that a neighbouring shop had provided the only sample of the substance called 'tea' ever found on the American continent; and in front of me soared up into the sky on wings of stone the column of all those high hopes of humanity a hundred years ago; and beyond there were lighted candles in the chapels and prayers in the ante-chambers, where perhaps already a Prince of the Church was dying. Only on a later page can I even attempt to comb out such a tangle of contrasts, which is indeed the tangle of America and this mortal life; but sitting there on that stone seat under that quiet sky, I had some experience of the thronging thousands of living thoughts and things, noisy and numberless as birds, that give its everlasting vivacity and vitality to a dead town.

Two other cities I visited which have this particular type of traditional character, the one being typical of the North and the other of the South. At least I may take as convenient anti-types the towns of Boston and St. Louis; and we might add Nashville as being a shade more truly southern than St. Louis. To the extreme South, in the sense of what is called the Black Belt, I never went at all. Now English travellers expect the South to be somewhat traditional; but they are not prepared for the aspects of Boston in the North which are even more so. If we wished only for an antic of antithesis, we might say that on one side the places are more prosaic than the names and on the other the names are more prosaic than the places. St. Louis is a fine town, and we recognise a fine instinct of the imagination that set on the hill overlooking the river the statue of that holy horseman who has christened the city. But the city is not as beautiful as its name; it could not be. Indeed these titles set up a standard to which the most splendid spires and turrets could not rise, and below which the commercial chimneys and sky-signs conspicuously sink. We should think it odd if Belfast had borne the name of Joan of Arc. We should be slightly shocked if the town of Johannesburg happened to be called Jesus Christ. But few have noted a blasphemy, or even a somewhat challenging benediction, to be found in the very name of San Francisco.

But on the other hand a place like Boston is much more beautiful than its name. And, as I have suggested, an Englishman's general information, or lack of information, leaves him in some ignorance of the type of beauty that turns up in that type of place. He has heard so much about the purely commercial North as against the agricultural and aristocratic South, and the traditions of Boston and Philadelphia are rather too tenuous and delicate to be seen from across the Atlantic. But here also there are traditions and a great deal of traditionalism. The circle of old families, which still meets with a certain exclusiveness in Philadelphia, is the sort of thing that we in England should expect to find rather in New Orleans. The academic aristocracy of Boston, which Oliver Wendell Holmes called the Brahmins, is still a reality though it was always a minority and is now a very small minority. An epigram, invented by Yale at the expense of Harvard, describes it as very small indeed:—

Here is to jolly old Boston, the home of the bean and the cod,
Where Cabots speak only to Lowells, and Lowells speak only to God.

But an aristocracy must be a minority, and it is arguable that the smaller it is the better. I am bound to say, however, that the distinguished Dr. Cabot, the present representative of the family, broke through any taboo that may tie his affections to his Creator and to Miss Amy Lowell, and broadened his sympathies so indiscriminately as to show kindness and hospitality to so lost a being as an English lecturer. But if the thing is hardly a limit it is very living as a memory; and Boston on this side is very much a place of memories. It would be paying it a very poor compliment merely to say that parts of it reminded me of England; for indeed they reminded me of English things that have largely vanished from England. There are old brown houses in the corners of squares and streets that are like glimpses of a man's forgotten childhood; and when I saw the long path with posts where the Autocrat may be supposed to have walked with the schoolmistress, I felt I had come to the land where old tales come true.

I pause in this place upon this particular aspect of America because it is very much missed in a mere contrast with England. I need not say that if I felt it even about slight figures of fiction, I felt it even more about solid figures of history. Such ghosts seemed particularly solid in the Southern States, precisely because of the comparative quietude and leisure of the atmosphere of the South. It was never more vivid to me than when coming in, at a quiet hour of the night, into the comparatively quiet hotel at Nashville in Tennessee, and mounting to a dim and deserted upper floor where I found myself before a faded picture; and from the dark canvas looked forth the face of Andrew Jackson, watchful like a white eagle.

At that moment, perhaps, I was in more than one sense alone. Most Englishmen know a good deal of American fiction, and nothing whatever of American history. They know more about the autocrat of the breakfast-table than about the autocrat of the army and the people, the one great democratic despot of modern times; the Napoleon of the New World. The only notion the English public ever got about American politics they got from a novel, *Uncle Tom's Cabin*; and to say the least of it, it was no exception to the prevalence of fiction over fact. Hundreds of us have heard of Tom Sawyer for one who has heard of Charles Sumner; and it is probable that most of us could pass a more detailed examination about Toddy and Budge than about Lincoln and Lee. But in the case of Andrew Jackson it may be that I felt a special sense of individual isolation; for I believe that there are even fewer among Englishmen than among Americans who realise that the energy of that great man was largely directed towards saving us from the chief evil which destroys the nations to-day. He sought to cut down, as with a sword of simplicity, the new and nameless enormity of finance; and he must have known, as by a lightning flash, that the people were behind him, because all the politicians were against him. The end of that struggle is not yet; but if the bank is stronger than the sword or the sceptre of popular sovereignty, the end will be the end of democracy. It will have to choose between accepting an acknowledged dictator and accepting dictation which it dare not acknowledge. The process will have begun by giving power to people and refusing to give them their titles; and it will have ended by giving the power to people who refuse to give us their names.

But I have a special reason for ending this chapter on the name of the great popular dictator who made war on the politicians and the financiers. This chapter does not profess to touch on one in twenty of the interesting cities of America, even in this particular aspect of their relation to the history of America, which is so much neglected in England. If that were so, there would be a great deal to say even about the newest of them; Chicago, for instance, is certainly something more than the mere pork-packing yard that English tradition suggests; and it has been building a boulevard not unworthy of its splendid position on its splendid lake. But all these cities are defiled and even diseased with industrialism. It is due to the Americans to remember that they have deliberately preserved one of their cities from such defilement and such disease. And that is the presidential city, which stands in the American mind for the same ideal as the President; the idea of the Republic that rises above modern money-getting and endures. There has really been an effort to keep the White House white. No factories are allowed in that town; no more than the necessary shops are tolerated. It is a beautiful city; and really retains something of that classical serenity of the eighteenth century in which the Fathers of the Republic moved. With all respect to the colonial place of that name, I do not suppose that Wellington is particularly like Wellington. But Washington really is like Washington.

In this, as in so many things, there is no harm in our criticising foreigners, if only we would also criticise ourselves. In other words, the world might need even less of its new charity, if it had a little more of the old humility. When we complain of American individualism, we forget that we have fostered it by ourselves having far less of this impersonal ideal of the Republic or commonwealth as a whole. When we complain, very justly, for instance, of great pictures passing into the possession of American magnates, we ought to remember that we paved the way for it by allowing them all to accumulate in the possession of English magnates. It is bad that a public treasure should be in the possession of a private man in America, but we took the first step in lightly letting it disappear into the private collection of a man in England. I know all about the genuine national tradition which treated the aristocracy as constituting the state; but these very foreign purchases go to prove that we ought to have had a state independent of the aristocracy. It is true that rich Americans do sometimes covet the monuments of our culture in a fashion that rightly revolts us as vulgar and irrational. They are said sometimes to want to take whole buildings away with them; and too many of such buildings are private and for sale. There were wilder stories of a millionaire wishing to transplant Glastonbury Abbey and similar buildings as if they were portable shrubs in pots. It is obvious that it is nonsense as well as vandalism to separate Glastonbury Abbey from Glastonbury. I can understand a man venerating it as a ruin; and I can understand a man despising it as a rubbish-heap. But it is senseless to insult a thing in order to idolatrise it; it is meaningless to desecrate the shrine in order to worship the stones. That sort of thing is the bad side of American appetite and ambition; and we are perfectly right to see it not only as a deliberate blasphemy but as an unconscious buffoonery. But there is another side to the American tradition, which is really too much lacking in our own tradition. And it is illustrated in this idea of preserving Washington as a sort of paradise of impersonal politics without personal commerce. Nobody could buy the White House or the Washington Monument; it may be hinted (as by an inhabitant of Glastonbury) that nobody wants to; but nobody could if he did want to. There is really a certain air of serenity and security about the place, lacking in every other American town. It is increased, of course, by the clear blue skies of that half-southern province, from which smoke has been banished. The effect is not so much in the mere buildings, though they are classical and often beautiful. But whatever else they have built, they have built a great blue dome, the largest dome in the world. And the place does express something in the inconsistent idealism of this strange people;

and here at least they have lifted it higher than all the sky-scrapers, and set it in a stainless sky.

IN THE AMERICAN COUNTRY

The sharpest pleasure of a traveller is in finding the things which he did not expect, but which he might have expected to expect. I mean the things that are at once so strange and so obvious that they must have been noticed, yet somehow they have not been noted. Thus I had heard a thousand things about Jerusalem before I ever saw it; I had heard rhapsodies and disparagements of every description. Modern rationalistic critics, with characteristic consistency, had blamed it for its accumulated rubbish and its modern restoration, for its antiquated superstition and its up-to-date vulgarity. But somehow the one impression that had never pierced through their description was the simple and single impression of a city on a hill, with walls coming to the very edge of slopes that were almost as steep as walls; the turreted city which crowns a cone-shaped hill in so many mediaeval landscapes. One would suppose that this was at once the plainest and most picturesque of all the facts; yet somehow, in my reading, I had always lost it amid a mass of minor facts that were merely details. We know that a city that is set upon a hill cannot be hid; and yet it would seem that it is exactly the hill that is hid; though perhaps it is only hid from the wise and the understanding. I had a similar and simple impression when I discovered America. I cannot avoid the phrase; for it would really seem that each man discovers it for himself.

Thus I had heard a great deal, before I saw them, about the tall and dominant buildings of New York. I agree that they have an instant effect on the imagination; which I think is increased by the situation in which they stand, and out of which they arose. They are all the more impressive because the building, while it is vertically so vast, is horizontally almost narrow. New York is an island, and has all the intensive romance of an island. It is a thing of almost infinite height upon very finite foundations. It is almost like a lofty lighthouse upon a lonely rock. But this story of the sky-scrapers, which I had often heard, would by itself give a curiously false impression of the freshest and most curious characteristic of American architecture. Told only in terms of these great towers of stone and brick in the big industrial cities, the story would tend too much to an impression of something cold and colossal like the monuments of Asia. It would suggest a modern Babylon altogether too Babylonian. It would imply that a man of the new world was a sort of new Pharaoh, who built not so much a pyramid as a pagoda of pyramids. It would suggest houses built by mammoths out of mountains; the cities reared by elephants in their own elephantine school of architecture. And New York does recall the most famous of all sky-scrapers—the tower of Babel. She recalls it none the less because there is no doubt about the confusion of tongues. But in truth the very reverse is true of most of the buildings in America. I had no sooner passed out into the suburbs of New York on the way to Boston than I began to see something else quite contrary and far more curious. I saw forests upon forests of small houses stretching away to the horizon as literal forests do; villages and towns and cities. And they were, in another sense, literally like forests. They were all made of wood. It was almost as fantastic to an English eye as if they had been all made of cardboard. I had long outlived the silly old joke that referred to Americans as if they all lived in the backwoods. But, in a sense, if they do not live in the woods, they are not yet out of the wood.

I do not say this in any sense as a criticism. As it happens, I am particularly fond of wood. Of all the superstitions which our fathers took lightly enough to love, the most natural seems to me the notion it is lucky to touch wood. Some of them affect me the less as superstitions, because I feel them as symbols. If humanity had really thought Friday unlucky it would have talked about bad Friday instead of good Friday. And while I feel the thrill of thirteen at a table, I am not so sure that it is the most miserable of all human fates to fill the places of the Twelve Apostles. But the idea that there was something cleansing or wholesome about the touching of wood seems to me one of those ideas which are truly popular, because they are truly poetic. It is probable enough that the conception came originally from the healing of the wood of the Cross; but that only clinches the divine coincidence. It is like that other divine coincidence that the Victim was a carpenter, who might almost have made His own cross. Whether we take the mystical or the mythical explanation, there is obviously a very deep connection between the human working in wood and such plain and pathetic mysticism. It gives something like a touch of the holy childishness to the tale, as if that terrible engine could be a toy. In the same fashion a child fancies that mysterious and sinister horse, which was the downfall of Troy, as something plain and staring, and perhaps spotted, like his own rocking-horse in the nursery.

It might be said symbolically that Americans have a taste for rocking-horses, as they certainly have a taste for rocking-chairs. A flippant critic might suggest that they select rocking-chairs so that, even when they are sitting down, they need not be sitting still. Something of this restlessness in the race may really be involved in the matter; but I think the deeper significance of the rocking-chair may still be found in the deeper symbolism of the rocking-horse. I think there is behind all this fresh and facile use of wood a certain spirit that is childish in the good sense of the word; something that is innocent, and easily pleased. It is not altogether untrue, still less is it unfriendly, to say that the landscape seems to be dotted with dolls' houses. It is the true tragedy of every fallen son of Adam that he has grown too big to live in a doll's house. These things seem somehow to escape the irony of time by not even challenging it; they are too temporary even to be merely temporal. These people are not building tombs; they are not, as in the fine image of Mrs. Meynell's poem, merely building ruins. It is not easy to imagine the ruins of a doll's house; and that is why a doll's house is an everlasting habitation. How far it promises a political permanence is a matter for further discussion; I am only describing the mood of discovery; in which all these cottages built of lath, like the palaces of a pantomime, really seemed coloured like the clouds of morning; which are both fugitive and eternal.

There is also in all this an atmosphere that comes in another sense from the nursery. We hear much of Americans being educated on English literature; but I think few Americans realise how much English children have been educated on American literature. It is true, and it is inevitable, that they can only be educated on rather old-fashioned American literature. Mr. Bernard Shaw, in one of his plays, noted truly the limitations of the young American millionaire, and especially the staleness of his English culture; but there is necessarily another side to it. If the American talked more of Macaulay than of Nietzsche, we should probably talk more of Emerson than of Ezra Pound. Whether this staleness is necessarily a disadvantage is, of course, a different question. But, in any case, it is true that the old American books were often the books of our childhood, even in the literal sense of the books of our nursery. I know few men in England who have not left their boyhood to some extent lost and entangled in the forests of *Huckleberry Finn*. I know few women in England, from the most revolutionary Suffragette to the most carefully preserved Early Victorian, who will not confess to having passed a happy childhood with the Little Women of Miss Alcott. *Helen's Babies* was the first and by far the best book in the modern scriptures of baby-worship. And about all this old-fashioned American literature there was an undefinable savour that satisfied, and even fed, our growing minds. Perhaps it was the smell of growing things; but I am far from certain that it was not simply the smell of wood. Now that all the memory comes back to me, it seems to come back heavy in a hundred forms with the fragrance and the touch of timber. There was the perpetual reference to the wood-pile, the perpetual background of the woods. There was something crude and clean about everything; something fresh and strange about those far-off houses, to which I could not then have put a name. Indeed, many things become clear in this wilderness of wood, which could only be expressed in symbol and even in fantasy. I will not go so far as to say that it shortened the transition from Log Cabin to White House; as if the White House were itself made of white wood (as Oliver Wendell Holmes said), 'that cuts like cheese, but lasts like iron for things like these.' But I will say that the experience illuminates some other lines by Holmes himself:—

Little I ask, my wants are few,
I only ask a hut of stone.

I should not have known, in England, that he was already asking for a good deal even in asking for that. In the presence of this wooden world the very combination of words seems almost a contradiction, like a hut of marble, or a hovel of gold.

It was therefore with an almost infantile pleasure that I looked at all this promising expansion of fresh-cut timber and thought of the housing shortage at home. I know not by what incongruous movement of the mind there swept across me, at the same moment, the thought of things ancestral and hoary with the light of ancient dawns. The last war brought back body-armour; the next war may bring back bows and arrows. And I suddenly had a memory of old wooden houses in London; and a model of Shakespeare's town.

It is possible indeed that such Elizabethan memories may receive a check or a chill when the traveller comes, as he sometimes does, to the outskirts of one of these strange hamlets of new frame-houses, and is confronted with a placard inscribed in enormous letters, 'Watch Us Grow.' He can always imagine that he sees the timbers swelling before his eyes like pumpkins in some super-tropical summer. But he may have formed the conviction that no such proclamation could be found outside Shakespeare's town. And indeed there is a serious criticism here, to any one who knows history; since the things that grow are not always the things that remain; and pumpkins of that expansiveness have a tendency to burst. I was always told that Americans were harsh, hustling, rather rude and perhaps vulgar; but they were very practical and the future belonged to them. I confess I felt a fine shade of difference; I liked the Americans; I thought they were sympathetic, imaginative, and full of fine enthusiasms; the one thing I could not always feel clear about was their future. I believe they were happier in their frame-houses than most people in most houses; having democracy, good education, and a hobby of work; the one doubt that did float across me was something like, 'Will all this be here at all in two hundred years?' That was the first impression produced by the wooden houses that seemed like the waggons of gipsies; it is a serious impression, but there is an answer to it. It is an answer that opens on the traveller more and more as he goes westward, and finds the little towns dotted about the vast central prairies. And the answer is agriculture. Wooden houses may or may not last; but farms will last; and farming will always last.

The houses may look like gipsy caravans on a heath or common; but they are not on a heath or common. They are on the most productive and prosperous land, perhaps, in the modern world. The houses might fall down like shanties, but the fields would remain; and whoever tills those fields will count for a great deal in the affairs of humanity. They are already counting for a great deal, and possibly for too much, in the affairs of America. The real criticism of the Middle West is concerned with two facts, neither of which has been yet adequately appreciated by the educated class in England. The first is that the turn of the world has come, and the turn of the agricultural countries with it. That is the meaning of the resurrection of Ireland; that is the meaning of the practical surrender of the Bolshevist Jews to the Russian peasants. The other is that in most places these peasant societies carry on what may be called the Catholic tradition. The Middle West is perhaps the one considerable place where they still carry on the Puritan tradition. But the Puritan tradition was originally a tradition of the town; and the second truth about the Middle West turns largely on its moral relation to the town. As I shall suggest presently, there is much in common between this agricultural society of America and the great agricultural societies of Europe. It tends, as the agricultural society nearly always does, to some decent degree of democracy. The agricultural society tends to the agrarian law. But in Puritan America there is an additional problem, which I can hardly explain without a periphrasis.

There was a time when the progress of the cities seemed to mock the decay of the country. It is more and more true, I think, to-day that it is rather the decay of the cities that seems to poison the progress and promise of the countryside. The cinema boasts of being a substitute for the tavern, but I think it a very bad substitute. I think so quite apart from the question about fermented liquor. Nobody enjoys cinemas more than I, but to enjoy them a man has only to look and not even to listen, and in a tavern he has to talk. Occasionally, I admit, he has to fight; but he need never move at the movies. Thus in the real village inn are the real village politics, while in the other are only the remote and unreal metropolitan politics. And those central city politics are not only cosmopolitan politics but corrupt politics. They corrupt everything that they reach, and this is the real point about many perplexing questions.

For instance, so far as I am concerned, it is the whole point about feminism and the factory. It is very largely the point about feminism and many other callings, apparently more cultured than the factory, such as the law court and the political platform. When I see women so wildly anxious to tie themselves to all this machinery of the modern city my first feeling is not indignation, but that dark and ominous sort of pity with which we should see a crowd rushing to embark in a leaking ship under a lowering storm. When I see wives and mothers going in for business government I not only regard it as a bad business but as a bankrupt business. It seems to me very much as if the peasant women, just before the French Revolution, had insisted on being made duchesses or (as is quite as logical and likely) on being made dukes.

It is as if those ragged women, instead of crying out for bread, had cried out for powder and patches. By the time they were wearing them they would be the only people wearing them. For powder and patches soon went out of fashion, but bread does not go out of fashion. In the same way, if women desert the family for the factory, they may find they have only done it for a deserted factory. It would have been very unwise of the lower orders to claim all the privileges of the higher orders in the last days of the French monarchy. It would have been very laborious to learn the science of heraldry or the tables of precedence when all such things were at once most complicated and most moribund. It would be tiresome to be taught all those tricks just when the whole bag of tricks was coming to an end. A French satirist might have written a fine apologue about Jacques Bonhomme coming up to Paris in his wooden shoes and demanding to be made Gold Stick in Waiting in the name of Liberty, Equality, and Fraternity; but I fear the stick in waiting would be waiting still.

One of the first topics on which I heard conversation turning in America was that of a very interesting book called *Main Street*, which involves many of these questions of the modern industrial and the eternal feminine. It is simply the story, or perhaps rather the study than the story, of a young married woman in one of the multitudinous little towns on the great central plains of America; and of a sort of struggle between her own more restless culture and the provincial prosperity of her neighbours. There are a number of true and telling suggestions in the book, but the one touch which I found tingling in the memory of many readers was the last sentence, in which the master of the house, with unshaken simplicity, merely asks for the whereabouts of some domestic implement; I think it was a screw-driver. It seems to me a harmless request, but from the way people talked about it one might suppose he had asked for a screw-driver to screw down the wife in her coffin. And a great many advanced persons would tell us that wooden house in which she lived really was like a wooden coffin. But this appears to me to be taking a somewhat funereal view of the life of humanity.

For, after all, on the face of it at any rate, this is merely the life of humanity, and even the life which all humanitarians have striven to give to humanity. Revolutionists have treated it not only as the normal but even as the ideal. Revolutionary wars have been waged to establish this; revolutionary heroes have fought, and revolutionary martyrs have died, only to build such a wooden house for such a worthy family. Men have taken the sword and perished by the sword in order that the poor gentleman might have liberty to look for his screw-driver. For there is here a fact about America that is almost entirely unknown in England. The English have not in the least realised the real strength of America. We in England hear a great deal, we hear far too much, about the economic energy of industrial America, about the money of Mr. Morgan, or the machinery of Mr. Edison. We never realise that while we in England suffer from the same sort of successes in capitalism and clockwork, we have not got what the Americans have got; something at least to balance it in the way of a free agriculture, a vast field of free farms dotted with small freeholders. For the reason I shall mention in a moment, they are not perhaps in the fullest and finest sense a peasantry. But they are in the practical and political sense a pure peasantry, in that their comparative equality is a true counterweight to the toppling injustice of the towns.

And, even in places like that described as Main Street, that comparative equality can immediately be felt. The men may be provincials, but they are certainly citizens; they consult on a common basis. And I repeat that in this, after all, they do achieve what many prophets and righteous men have died to achieve. This plain village, fairly prosperous, fairly equal, untaxed by tyrants and untroubled by wars, is after all the place which reformers have regarded as their aim; whenever reformers have used their wits sufficiently to have any aim. The march to Utopia, the march to the Earthly Paradise, the march to the New Jerusalem, has been very largely the march to Main Street. And the latest modern sensation is a book written to show how wretched it is to live there.

All this is true, and I think the lady might be more contented in her coffin, which is more comfortably furnished than most of the coffins where her fellow creatures live. Nevertheless, there is an answer to this, or at least a modification of it. There is a case for the lady and a case against the gentleman and the screw-driver. And when we have noted what it really is, we have noted the real disadvantage in a situation like that of modern America, and especially the Middle West. And with that we come back to the truth with which I started this speculation; the truth that few have yet realised, but of which I, for one, am more and more convinced—that industrialism is spreading because it is decaying; that only the dust and ashes of its dissolution are choking up the growth of natural things everywhere and turning the green world grey.

In this relative agricultural equality the Americans of the Middle West are far in advance of the English of the twentieth century. It is not their fault if they are still some centuries behind the English of the twelfth century. But the defect by which they fall short of being a true peasantry is that they do not produce their own spiritual food, in the same sense as their own material food. They do not, like some peasantries, create other kinds of culture besides the kind called agriculture. Their culture comes from the great cities; and that is where all the evil comes from.

If a man had gone across England in the Middle Ages, or even across Europe in more recent times, he would have found a culture which showed its vitality by its variety. We know the adventures of the three brothers in the old fairy tales who passed across the endless plain from city to city, and found one kingdom ruled by a wizard and another wasted by a dragon, one people living in castles of crystal and another sitting by fountains of wine. These are but legendary enlargements of the real adventures of a traveller passing from one patch of peasantry to another, and finding women wearing strange head-dresses and men singing new songs.

A traveller in America would be somewhat surprised if he found the people in the city of St. Louis all wearing crowns and crusading armour in honour of their patron saint. He might even feel some faint surprise if he found all the citizens of Philadelphia clad in a composite costume, combining that of a Quaker with that of a Red Indian, in honour of the noble treaty of William Penn. Yet these are the sort of local and traditional things that would really be found giving variety to the valleys of mediaeval Europe. I myself felt a perfectly genuine and generous exhilaration of freedom and fresh enterprise in new places like Oklahoma. But you would hardly find in Oklahoma what was found in Oberammergau. What goes to Oklahoma is not the peasant play, but the cinema. And the objection to the cinema is not so much that it goes to Oklahoma as that it does not come from Oklahoma. In other words, these people have on the economic side a much closer approach than we have to economic freedom. It is not for us, who have allowed our land to be stolen by squires and then vulgarised by sham squires, to sneer at such colonists as merely crude and prosaic. They at least have really kept something of the simplicity and, therefore, the dignity of democracy; and that democracy may yet save their country even from the calamities of wealth and science.

But, while these farmers do not need to become industrial in order to become industrious, they do tend to become industrial in so far as they become intellectual. Their culture, and to some great extent their creed, do come along the railroads from the great modern urban centres, and bring with them a blast of death and a reek of rotting things. It is that influence that alone prevents the Middle West from progressing towards the Middle Ages.

For, after all, linked up in a hundred legends of the Middle Ages, may be found a symbolic pattern of hammers and nails and saws; and there is no reason why they should not have also sanctified screw-drivers. There is no reason why the screw-driver that seemed such a trifle to the author should not have been borne in triumph down Main Street like a sword of state, in some pageant of the Guild of St. Joseph of the Carpenters or St. Dunstan of the Smiths. It was the Catholic poetry and piety that filled common life with something that is lacking in the worthy and virile democracy of the West. Nor are Americans of intelligence so ignorant of this as some may suppose. There is an admirable society called the Mediaevalists in Chicago; whose name and address will strike many as suggesting a certain struggle of the soul against the environment. With the national heartiness they blazon their note-paper with heraldry and the hues of Gothic windows; with the national high spirits they assume the fancy dress of friars; but any one who should essay to laugh at them instead of with them would find out his mistake. For many of them do really know a great deal about mediaevalism; much more than I do, or most other men brought up on an island that is crowded with its cathedrals. Something of the same spirit may be seen in the beautiful new plans and buildings of Yale, deliberately modelled not on classical harmony but on Gothic irregularity and surprise. The grace and energy of the mediaeval architecture resurrected by a man like Mr. R. A. Cram of Boston has behind it not merely artistic but historical and ethical enthusiasm; an enthusiasm for the Catholic creed which made mediaeval civilisation. Even on the huge Puritan plains of the Middle West the influence strays in the strangest fashion. And it is notable that among the pessimistic epitaphs of the Spoon River Anthology, in that churchyard compared with which most churchyards are cheery, among the suicides and secret drinkers and monomaniacs and hideous hypocrites of that happy village, almost the only record of respect and a recognition of wider hopes is dedicated to the Catholic priest.

But Main Street is Main Street in the main. Main Street is Modern Street in its multiplicity of mildly half-educated people; and all these historic things are a thousand miles from them. They have not heard the ancient noise either of arts or arms; the building of the cathedral or the marching of the crusade. But at least they have not deliberately slandered the crusade and defaced the cathedral. And if they have not produced the peasant arts, they can still produce the peasant crafts. They can sow and plough and reap and live by these everlasting things; nor shall the foundations of their state be moved. And the memory of those colossal fields, of those fruitful deserts, came back the more readily into my mind because I finished these reflections in the very heart of a modern industrial city, if it can be said to have a heart. It was in fact an English industrial city, but it struck me that it might very well be an American one. And it also struck me that we yield rather too easily to America the dusty palm of industrial enterprise, and feel far too little apprehension about greener and fresher vegetables. There is a story of an American who carefully studied all the sights of London or Rome or Paris, and came to the conclusion that 'it had nothing on Minneapolis.' It seems to me that Minneapolis has nothing on Manchester. There were the same grey vistas of shops full of rubber tyres and metallic appliances; a man felt that he might walk a day without seeing a blade of grass; the whole horizon was so infinite with efficiency. The factory chimneys might have been Pittsburg; the sky-signs might have been New York. One looked up in a sort of despair at the sky, not for a sky-sign but in a sense for a sign, for some sentence of significance and judgment; by the instinct that makes any man in such a scene seek for the only thing that has not been made by men. But even that was illogical, for it was night, and I could only expect to see the stars, which might have reminded me of Old Glory; but that was not the sign that oppressed me. All the ground was a wilderness of stone and all the buildings a forest of brick; I was far in the interior of a labyrinth of lifeless things. Only, looking up, between two black chimneys and a telegraph pole, I saw vast and far and faint, as the first men saw it, the silver pattern of the Plough.

THE AMERICAN BUSINESS MAN

It is a commonplace that men are all agreed in using symbols, and all differ about the meaning of the symbols. It is obvious that a Russian republican might come to identify the eagle as a bird of empire and therefore a bird of prey. But when he ultimately escaped to the land of the free, he might find the same bird on the American coinage figuring as a bird of freedom. Doubtless, he might find many other things to surprise him in the land of the free, and many calculated to make him think that the bird, if not imperial, was at least rather imperious. But I am not discussing those exceptional details here. It is equally obvious that a Russian reactionary might cross the world with a vow of vengeance against the red flag. But that authoritarian might have some difficulties with the authorities, if he shot a man for using the red flag on the railway between Willesden and Clapham Junction.

But, of course, the difficulty about symbols is generally much more subtle than in these simple cases. I have remarked elsewhere that the first thing which a traveller should write about is the thing which he has not read about. It may be a small or secondary thing, but it is a thing that he has seen and not merely expected to see.

I gave the example of the great multitude of wooden houses in America; we might say of wooden towns and wooden cities. But after he has seen such things, his next duty is to see the meaning of them; and here a great deal of complication and controversy is possible. The thing probably does not mean what he first supposes it to mean on the face of it; but even on the face of it, it might mean many different and even opposite things.

For instance, a wooden house might suggest an almost savage solitude; a rude shanty put together by a pioneer in a forest; or it might mean a very recent and rapid solution of the housing problem, conducted cheaply and therefore on a very large scale. A wooden house might suggest the very newest thing in America or one of the very oldest things in England. It might mean a grey ruin at Stratford or a white exhibition at Earl's Court.

It is when we come to this interpretation of international symbols that we make most of the international mistakes. Without the smallest error of detail, I will promise to prove that Oriental women are independent because they wear trousers, or Oriental men subject because they wear skirts. Merely to apply it to this case, I will take the example of two very commonplace and trivial objects of modern life—a walking stick and a fur coat.

As it happened, I travelled about America with two sticks, like a Japanese nobleman with his two swords. I fear the simile is too stately. I bore more resemblance to a cripple with two crutches or a highly ineffectual version of the devil on two sticks. I carried them both because I valued them both, and did not wish to risk losing either of them in my erratic travels. One is a very plain grey stick from the woods of Buckinghamshire, but as I took it with me to Palestine it partakes of the character of a pilgrim's staff. When I can say that I have taken the same stick to Jerusalem and to Chicago, I think the stick and I may both have a rest. The other, which I value even more, was given me by the Knights of Columbus at Yale, and I wish I could think that their chivalric title allowed me to regard it as a sword.

Now, I do not know whether the Americans I met, struck by the fastidious foppery of my dress and appearance, concluded that it is the custom of elegant English dandies to carry two walking sticks. But I do know that it is much less common among Americans than among Englishmen to carry even one. The point, however, is not merely that more sticks are carried by Englishmen than by Americans; it is that the sticks which are carried by Americans stand for something entirely different.

In America a stick is commonly called a cane, and it has about it something of the atmosphere which the poet described as the nice conduct of the clouded cane. It would be an exaggeration to say that when the citizens of the United States see a man carrying a light stick, they deduce that if he does that he does nothing else. But there is about it a faint flavour of luxury and lounging, and most of the energetic citizens of this energetic society avoid it by instinct.

Now, in an Englishman like myself, carrying a stick may imply lounging, but it does not imply luxury, and I can say with some firmness that it does not imply dandyism. In a great many Englishmen it means the very opposite even of lounging. By one of those fantastic paradoxes which are the mystery of nationality, a walking stick often actually means walking. It frequently suggests the very reverse of the beau with his clouded cane; it does not suggest a town type, but rather specially a country type. It rather implies the kind of Englishman who tramps about in lanes and meadows and knocks the tops off thistles. It suggests the sort of man who has carried the stick through his native woods, and perhaps even cut it in his native woods.

There are plenty of these vigorous loungers, no doubt, in the rural parts of America, but the idea of a walking stick would not especially suggest them to Americans; it would not call up such figures like a fairy wand. It would be easy to trace back the difference to many English origins, possibly to aristocratic origins, to the idea of the old squire, a man vigorous and even rustic, but trained to hold a useless staff rather than a useful tool. It might be suggested that American citizens do at least so far love freedom as to like to have their hands free. It might be suggested, on the other hand, that they keep their hands for the handles of many machines. And that the hand on a handle is less free than the hand on a stick or even a tool. But these again are controversial questions and I am only noting a fact.

If an Englishman wished to imagine more or less exactly what the impression is, and how misleading it is, he could find something like a parallel in what he himself feels about a fur coat. When I first found myself among the crowds on the main floor of a New York hotel, my rather exaggerated impression of the luxury of the place was largely produced by the number of men in fur coats, and what we should consider rather ostentatious fur coats, with all the fur outside.

Now an Englishman has a number of atmospheric but largely accidental associations in connection with a fur coat. I will not say that he thinks a man in a fur coat must be a wealthy and wicked man; but I do say that in his own ideal and perfect vision a wealthy and wicked man would wear a fur coat. Thus I had the sensation of standing in a surging mob of American millionaires, or even African millionaires; for the millionaires of Chicago must be like the Knights of the Round Table compared with the millionaires of Johannesburg.

But, as a matter of fact, the man in the fur coat was not even an American millionaire, but simply an American. It did not signify luxury, but rather necessity, and even a harsh and almost heroic necessity. Orson probably wore a fur coat; and he was brought up by bears, but not the bears of Wall Street. Eskimos are generally represented as a furry folk; but they are not necessarily engaged in delicate financial operations, even in the typical and appropriate occupation called freezing out. And if the American is not exactly an arctic traveller rushing from pole to pole, at least he is often literally fleeing from ice to ice. He has to make a very extreme distinction between outdoor and indoor clothing. He has to live in an icehouse outside and a hothouse inside; so hot that he may be said to construct an icehouse inside that. He turns himself into an icehouse and warms himself against the cold until he is warm enough to eat ices. But the point is that the same coat of fur which in England would indicate the sybarite life may here very well indicate the strenuous life; just as the same walking stick which would here suggest a lounger would in England suggest a plodder and almost a pilgrim.

And these two trifles are types which I should like to put, by way of proviso and apology, at the very beginning of any attempt at a record of any impressions of a foreign society. They serve merely to illustrate the most important impression of all, the impression of how false all impressions may be. I suspect that most of the very false impressions have come from the careful record of very true facts. They have come from the fatal power of observing the facts without being able to observe the truth. They came from seeing the symbol with the most vivid clarity and being blind to all that it symbolises. It is as if a man who knew no Greek should imagine that he could read a Greek inscription because he took the Greek R for an English P or the Greek long E for an English H. I do not mention this merely as a criticism on other people's impressions of America, but as a criticism on my own. I wish it to be understood that I am well aware that all my views are subject to this sort of potential criticism, and that even when I am certain of the facts I do not profess to be certain of the deductions.

In this chapter I hope to point out how a misunderstanding of this kind affects the common impression, not altogether unfounded, that the Americans talk about dollars. But for the moment I am merely anxious to avoid a similar misunderstanding when I talk about Americans. About the dogmas of democracy, about the right of a people to its own symbols, whether they be coins or customs, I am convinced, and no longer to be shaken. But about the meaning of those symbols, in silver or other substances, I am always open to correction. That error is the price we pay for the great glory of nationality. And in this sense I am quite ready, at the start, to warn my own readers against my own opinions.

The fact without the truth is futile; indeed the fact without the truth is false. I have already noted that this is especially true touching our observations of a strange country; and it is certainly true touching one small fact which has swelled into a large fable. I mean the fable about America commonly summed up in the phrase about the Almighty Dollar. I do not think the dollar is almighty in America; I fancy many things are mightier, including many ideals and some rather insane ideals. But I think it might be maintained that the dollar has another of the attributes of deity. If it is not omnipotent it is in a sense omnipresent. Whatever Americans think about dollars, it is, I think, relatively true that they talk about dollars. If a mere mechanical record could be taken by the modern machinery of dictaphones and stenography, I do not think it probable that the mere word 'dollars' would occur more often in any given number of American conversations than the mere word 'pounds' or 'shillings' in a similar number of English conversations. And these statistics, like nearly all statistics, would be utterly useless and even fundamentally false. It is as if we should calculate that the word 'elephant' had been mentioned a certain number of times in a particular London street, or so many times more often than the word 'thunderbolt' had been used in Stoke Poges. Doubtless there are statisticians capable of carefully collecting those statistics also; and doubtless there are scientific social reformers capable of legislating on the basis of them. They would probably argue from the elephantine imagery of the London street that such and such a percentage of the householders were megalomaniacs and required medical care and police coercion. And doubtless their calculations, like nearly all such calculations, would leave out the only important point; as that the street was in the immediate neighbourhood of the Zoo, or was yet more happily situated under the benignant shadow of the Elephant and Castle. And in the same way the mechanical calculation about the mention of dollars is entirely useless unless we have some moral understanding of why they are mentioned. It certainly does not mean merely a love of money; and if it did, a love of money may mean a great many very different and even contrary things. The love of money is very different in a peasant or in a pirate, in a miser or in a gambler, in a great financier or in a man doing some practical and productive work. Now this difference in the conversation of American and English business men arises, I think, from certain much deeper things in the American which are generally not understood by the Englishman. It also arises from much deeper things in the Englishman, of which the Englishman is even more ignorant.

To begin with, I fancy that the American, quite apart from any love of money, has a great love of measurement. He will mention the exact size or weight of things, in a way which appears to us as irrelevant. It is as if we were to say that a man came to see us carrying three feet of walking stick and four inches of cigar. It is so in cases that have no possible connection with any avarice or greed for gain. An American will praise the prodigal generosity of some other man in giving up his own estate for the good of the poor. But he will generally say that the philanthropist gave them a 200-acre park, where an Englishman would think it quite sufficient to say that he gave them a park. There is something about this precision which seems suitable to the American atmosphere; to the hard sunlight, and the cloudless skies, and the glittering detail of the architecture and the landscape; just as the vaguer English version is consonant to our mistier and more impressionist scenery. It is also connected perhaps with something more boyish about the younger civilisation; and corresponds to the passionate particularity with which a boy will distinguish the uniforms of regiments, the rigs of ships, or even the colours of tram tickets. It is a certain godlike appetite for things, as distinct from thoughts.

But there is also, of course, a much deeper cause of the difference; and it can easily be deduced by noting the real nature of the difference itself. When two business men in a train are talking about dollars I am not so foolish as to expect them to be talking about the philosophy of St. Thomas Aquinas. But if they were two English business men I should not expect them to be talking about business. Probably it would be about some sport; and most probably some sport in which they themselves never dreamed of indulging. The approximate difference is that the American talks about his work and the Englishman about his holidays. His ideal is not labour but leisure. Like every other national characteristic, this is not primarily a point for praise or blame; in essence it involves neither and in effect it involves both. It is certainly connected with that snobbishness which is the great sin of English society. The Englishman does love to conceive himself as a sort of country gentleman; and his castles in the air are all castles in Scotland rather than in Spain. For, as an ideal, a Scotch castle is as English as a Welsh rarebit or an Irish stew. And if he talks less about money I fear it is sometimes because in one sense he thinks more of it. Money is a mystery in the old and literal sense of something too sacred for speech. Gold is a god; and like the god of some agnostics has no name and is worshipped only in his works. It is true in a sense that the English gentleman wishes to have enough money to be able to forget it. But it may be questioned whether he does entirely forget it. As against this weakness the American has succeeded, at the price of a great deal of crudity and clatter, in making general a very real respect for work. He has partly disenchanted the dangerous glamour of the gentleman, and in that sense has achieved some degree of democracy; which is the most difficult achievement in the world.

On the other hand, there is a good side to the Englishman's day-dream of leisure, and one which the American spirit tends to miss. It may be expressed in the word 'holiday' or still better in the word 'hobby.' The Englishman, in his character of Robin Hood, really has got two strings to his bow. Indeed the Englishman really is well represented by Robin Hood; for there is always something about him that may literally be called outlawed, in the sense of being extra-legal or outside the rules. A Frenchman said of Browning that his centre was not in the middle; and it may be said of many an Englishman that his heart is not where his treasure is. Browning expressed a very English sentiment when he said:—

I like to know a butcher paints,
A baker rhymes for his pursuit,
Candlestick-maker much acquaints
His soul with song, or haply mute
Blows out his brains upon the flute.

Stevenson touched on the same insular sentiment when he said that many men he knew, who were meat-salesmen to the outward eye, might in the life of contemplation sit with the saints. Now the extraordinary achievement of the American meat-salesman is that his poetic enthusiasm can really be for meat sales; not for money but for meat. An American commercial traveller asked me, with a religious fire in his eyes, whether I did not think that salesmanship could be an art. In England there are many salesmen who are sincerely fond of art; but seldom of the art of salesmanship. Art is with them a hobby; a thing of leisure and liberty. That is why the English traveller talks, if not of art, then of sport. That is why the two city men in the London train, if they are not talking about golf, may be talking about gardening. If they are not talking about dollars, or the equivalent of dollars, the reason lies much deeper than any superficial praise or blame touching the desire for wealth. In the English case, at least, it lies very deep in the English spirit. Many of the greatest English things have had this lighter and looser character of a hobby or a holiday experiment. Even a masterpiece has often been a by-product. The works of Shakespeare come out so casually that they can be attributed to the most improbable people; even to Bacon. The sonnets of Shakespeare are picked up afterwards as if out of a wastepaper basket. The immortality of Dr. Johnson does not rest on the written leaves he collected, but entirely on the words he wasted, the words he scattered to the winds. So great a thing as Pickwick is almost a kind of accident; it began as something secondary and grew into something primary and pre-eminent. It began with mere words written to illustrate somebody else's pictures; and swelled like an epic expanded from an epigram. It might almost be said that in the case of Pickwick the author began as the servant of the artist. But, as in the same story of Pickwick, the servant became greater than the master. This incalculable and accidental quality, like all national qualities, has its strength and weakness; but it does represent a certain reserve fund of interests in the Englishman's life; and distinguishes him from the other extreme type, of the millionaire who works till he drops, or who drops because he stops working. It is the great achievement of American civilisation that in that country it really is not cant to talk about the dignity of labour. There is something that might almost be called the sanctity of labour; but it is subject to the profound law that when anything less than the highest becomes a sanctity, it tends also to become a superstition. When the candlestick-maker does not blow out his brains upon the flute there is always a danger that he may blow them out somewhere else, owing to depressed conditions in the candlestick market.

Now certainly one of the first impressions of America, or at any rate of New York, which is by no means the same thing as America, is that of a sort of mob of business men, behaving in many ways in a fashion very different from that of the swarms of London city men who go up every day to the city. They sit about in groups with Red-Indian gravity, as if passing the pipe of peace; though, in fact, most of them are smoking cigars and some of them are eating cigars. The latter strikes me as one of the most peculiar of transatlantic tastes, more peculiar than that of chewing gum. A man will sit for hours consuming a cigar as if it were a sugar-stick; but I should imagine it to be a very disagreeable sugar-stick. Why he attempts to enjoy a cigar without lighting it I do not know; whether it is a more economical way of carrying a mere symbol of commercial conversation; or whether something of the same queer outlandish morality that draws such a distinction between beer and ginger beer draws an equally ethical distinction between touching tobacco and lighting it. For the rest, it would be easy to make a merely external sketch full of things equally strange; for this can always be done in a strange country. I allow for the fact of all foreigners looking alike; but I fancy that all those hard-featured faces, with spectacles and shaven jaws, do look rather alike, because they all like to make their faces hard. And with the mention of their mental attitude we realise the futility of any such external sketch. Unless we can see that these are something more than men smoking cigars and talking about dollars we had much better not see them at all.

It is customary to condemn the American as a materialist because of his worship of success. But indeed this very worship, like any worship, even devil-worship, proves him rather a mystic than a materialist. The Frenchman who retires from business when he has money enough to drink his wine and eat his omelette in peace might much more plausibly be called a materialist by those who do not prefer to call him a man of sense. But Americans do worship success in the abstract, as a sort of ideal vision. They follow success rather than money; they follow money rather than meat and drink. If their national life in one sense is a perpetual game of poker, they are playing excitedly for chips or counters as well as for coins. And by the ultimate test of material enjoyment, like the enjoyment of an omelette, even a coin is itself a counter. The Yankee cannot eat chips as the Frenchman can eat chipped potatoes; but neither can he swallow red cents as the Frenchman swallows red wine. Thus when people say of a Yankee that he worships the dollar, they pay a compliment to his fine spirituality more true and delicate than they imagine. The dollar is an idol because it is an image; but it is an image of success and not of enjoyment.

That this romance is also a religion is shown in the fact that there is a queer sort of morality attached to it. The nearest parallel to it is something like the sense of honour in the old duelling days. There is not a material but a distinctly moral savour about the implied obligation to collect dollars or to collect chips. We hear too much in England of the phrase about 'making good'; for no sensible Englishman favours the needless interlarding of English with scraps of foreign languages. But though it means nothing in English, it means something very particular in American. There is a fine shade of distinction between succeeding and making good, precisely because there must always be a sort of ethical echo in the word good. America does vaguely feel a man making good as something analogous to a man being good or a man doing good. It is connected with his serious self-respect and his sense of being worthy of those he loves. Nor is this curious crude idealism wholly insincere even when it drives him to what some of us would call stealing; any more than the duellist's honour was insincere when it drove him to what some would call murder. A very clever American play which I once saw acted contained a complete working model of this morality. A girl was loyal to, but distressed by, her engagement to a young man on whom there was a sort of cloud of humiliation. The atmosphere was exactly what it would have been in England if he had been accused of cowardice or card-sharping. And there was nothing whatever the matter with the poor young man except that some rotten mine or other in Arizona had not 'made good.' Now in England we should either be below or above that ideal of good. If we were snobs, we should be content to know that he was a gentleman of good connections, perhaps too much accustomed to private means to be expected to be businesslike. If we were somewhat larger-minded people, we should know that he might be as wise as Socrates and as splendid as Bayard and yet be unfitted, perhaps one should say therefore be unfitted, for the dismal and dirty gambling of modern commerce. But whether we were snobbish enough to admire him for being an idler, or chivalrous enough to admire him for being an outlaw, in neither case should we ever really and in our hearts despise him for being a failure. For it is this inner verdict of instinctive idealism that is the point at issue. Of course there is nothing new, or peculiar to the new world, about a man's engagement practically failing through his financial failure. An English girl might easily drop a man because he was poor, or she might stick to him faithfully and defiantly although he was poor. The point is that this girl was faithful but she was not defiant; that is, she was not proud. The whole psychology of the situation was that she shared the weird worldly idealism of her family, and it was wounded as her patriotism would have been wounded if he had betrayed his country. To do them justice, there was nothing to show that they would have had any real respect for a royal duke who had inherited millions; what the simple barbarians wanted was a man who could 'make good.' That the process of making good would probably drag him through the mire of everything bad, that he would make good by bluffing, lying, swindling, and grinding the faces of the poor, did not seem to trouble them in the least. Against this fanaticism there is this shadow of truth even in the fiction of aristocracy; that a gentleman may at least be allowed to be good without being bothered to make it.

Another objection to the phrase about the almighty dollar is that it is an almighty phrase, and therefore an almighty nuisance. I mean that it is made to explain everything, and to explain everything much too well; that is, much too easily. It does not really help people to understand a foreign country; but it gives them the fatal illusion that they do understand it. Dollars stood for America as frogs stood for France; because it was necessary to connect particular foreigners with something, or it would be so easy to confuse a Moor with a Montenegrin or a Russian with a Red Indian. The only cure for this sort of satisfied familiarity is the shock of something really unfamiliar. When people can see nothing at all in American democracy except a Yankee running after a dollar, then the only thing to do is to trip them up as they run after the Yankee, or run away with their notion of the Yankee, by the obstacle of certain odd and obstinate facts that have no relation to that notion. And, as a matter of fact, there are a number of such obstacles to any such generalisation; a number of notable facts that have to be reconciled somehow to our previous notions. It does not matter for this purpose whether the facts are favourable or unfavourable, or whether the qualities are merits or defects; especially as we do not even understand them sufficiently to say which they are. The point is that we are brought to a pause, and compelled to attempt to understand them rather better than we do. We have found the one thing that we did not expect; and therefore the one thing that we cannot explain. And we are moved to an effort, probably an unsuccessful effort, to explain it.

For instance, Americans are very unpunctual. That is the last thing that a critic expects who comes to condemn them for hustling and haggling and vulgar ambition. But it is almost the first fact that strikes the spectator on the spot. The chief difference between the humdrum English business man and the hustling American business man is that the hustling American business man is always late. Of course there is a great deal of difference between coming late and coming too late. But I noticed the fashion first in connection with my own lectures; touching which I could heartily recommend the habit of coming too late. I could easily understand a crowd of commercial Americans not coming to my lectures at all; but there was something odd about their coming in a crowd, and the crowd being expected to turn up some time after the appointed hour. The managers of these lectures (I continue to call them lectures out of courtesy to myself) often explained to me that it was quite useless to begin properly until about half an hour after time. Often people were still coming in three-quarters of an hour or even an hour after time. Not that I objected to that, as some lecturers are said to do; it seemed to me an agreeable break in the monotony; but as a characteristic of a people mostly engaged in practical business, it struck me as curious and interesting. I have grown accustomed to being the most unbusinesslike person in any given company; and it gave me a sort of dizzy exaltation to find I was not the most unpunctual person in that company. I was afterwards told by many Americans that my impression was quite correct; that American unpunctuality was really very prevalent, and extended to much more important things. But at least I was not content to lump this along with all sorts of contrary things that I did not happen to like, and call it America. I am not sure of what it really means, but I rather fancy that though it may seem the very reverse of the hustling, it has the same origin as the hustling. The American is not punctual because he is not punctilious. He is impulsive, and has an impulse to stay as well as an impulse to go. For, after all, punctuality belongs to the same order of ideas as punctuation; and there is no punctuation in telegrams. The order of clocks and set hours which English business has always observed is a good thing in its own way; indeed I think that in a larger sense it is better than the other way. But it is better because it is a protection against hustling, not a promotion of it. In other words, it is better because it is more civilised; as a great Venetian merchant prince clad in cloth of gold was more civilised; or an old English merchant drinking port in an oak-panelled room was more civilised; or a little French shopkeeper shutting up his shop to play dominoes is more civilised. And the reason is that the American has the romance of business and is monomaniac, while the Frenchman has the romance of life and is sane. But the romance of business really is a romance, and the Americans are really romantic about it. And that romance, though it revolves round pork or petrol, is really like a love-affair in this; that it involves not only rushing but also lingering.

The American is too busy to have business habits. He is also too much in earnest to have business rules. If we wish to understand him, we must compare him not with the French shopkeeper when he plays dominoes, but with the same French shopkeeper when he works the guns or mans the trenches as a conscript soldier. Everybody used to the punctilious Prussian standard of uniform and parade has noticed the roughness and apparent laxity of the French soldier, the looseness of his clothes, the unsightliness of his heavy knapsack, in short his inferiority in every detail of the business of war except fighting. There he is much too swift to be smart. He is much too practical to be precise. By a strange illusion which can lift pork-packing almost to the level of patriotism, the American has the same free rhythm in his romance of business. He varies his conduct not to suit the clock but to suit the case. He gives more time to more important and less time to less important things; and he makes up his time-table as he goes along. Suppose he has three appointments; the first, let us say, is some mere trifle of erecting a tower twenty storeys high and exhibiting a sky-sign on the top of it; the second is a business discussion about the possibility of printing advertisements of soft drinks on the table-napkins at a restaurant; the third is attending a conference to decide how the populace can be prevented from using chewing-gum and the manufacturers can still manage to sell it. He will be content merely to glance at the sky-sign as he goes by in a trolley-car or an automobile; he will then settle down to the discussion with his partner about the table-napkins, each speaker indulging in long monologues in turn; a peculiarity of much American conversation. Now if in the middle of one of these monologues, he suddenly thinks that the vacant space of the waiter's shirt-front might also be utilised to advertise the Gee Whiz Ginger Champagne, he will instantly follow up the new idea in all its aspects and possibilities, in an even longer monologue; and will never think of looking at his watch while he is rapturously looking at his waiter. The consequence is that he will come late into the great social movement against chewing-gum, where an Englishman would probably have arrived at the proper hour. But though the Englishman's conduct is more proper, it need not be in all respects more practical. The Englishman's rules are better for the business of life, but not necessarily for the life of business. And it is true that for many of these Americans business is the business of life. It is really also, as I have said, the romance of life. We shall admire or deplore this spirit, accordingly as we are glad to see trade irradiated with so much poetry, or sorry to see so much poetry wasted on trade. But it does make many people happy, like any other hobby; and one is disposed to add that it does fill their imaginations like any other delusion. For the true criticism of all this commercial romance would involve a criticism of this historic phase of commerce. These people are building on the sand, though it shines like gold, and for them like fairy gold; but the world will remember the legend about fairy gold. Half the financial operations they follow deal with things that do not even exist; for in that sense all finance is a fairy tale. Many of them are buying and selling things that do nothing but harm; but it does them good to buy and sell them. The claim of the romantic salesman is better justified than he realises. Business really is romance; for it is not reality.

There is one real advantage that America has over England, largely due to its livelier and more impressionable ideal. America does not think that stupidity is practical. It does not think that ideas are merely destructive things. It does not think that a genius is only a person to be told to go away and blow his brains out; rather it would open all its machinery to the genius and beg him to blow his brains in. It might attempt to use a natural force like Blake or Shelley for very ignoble purposes; it would be quite capable of asking Blake to take his tiger and his golden lions round as a sort of Barnum's Show, or Shelley to hang his stars and haloed clouds among the lights of Broadway. But it would not assume that a natural force is useless, any more than that Niagara is useless. And there is a very definite distinction here touching the intelligence of the trader, whatever we may think of either course touching the intelligence of the artist. It is one thing that Apollo should be employed by Admetus, although he is a god. It is quite another thing that Apollo should always be sacked by Admetus, because he is a god. Now in England, largely owing to the accident of a rivalry and therefore a comparison with France, there arose about the end of the eighteenth century an extraordinary notion that there was some sort of connection between dullness and success. What the Americans call a bonehead became what the English call a hard-headed man. The merchants of London evinced their contempt for the fantastic logicians of Paris by living in a permanent state of terror lest somebody should set the Thames on fire. In this as in much else it is much easier to understand the Americans if we connect them with the French who were their allies than with the English who were their enemies. There are a great many Franco-American resemblances which the practical Anglo-Saxons are of course too hard-headed (or boneheaded) to see. American history is haunted with the shadow of the Plebiscitary President; they have a tradition of classical architecture for public buildings. Their cities are planned upon the squares of Paris and not upon the labyrinth of London. They call their cities Corinth and Syracuse, as the French called their citizens Epaminondas and Timoleon. Their soldiers wore the French kepi; and they make coffee admirably, and do not make tea at all. But of all the French elements in America the most French is this real practicality. They know that at certain times the most businesslike of all qualities is 'l'audace, et encore de l'audace, et toujours de l'audace.' The publisher may induce the poet to do a pot-boiler; but the publisher would cheerfully allow the poet to set the Mississippi on fire, if it would boil his particular pot. It is not so much that Englishmen are stupid as that they are afraid of being clever; and it is not so much that Americans are clever as that they do not try to be any stupider than they are. The fire of French logic has burnt that out of America as it has burnt it out of Europe, and of almost every place except England. This is one of the few points on which English insularity really is a disadvantage. It is the fatal notion that the only sort of commonsense is to be found in compromise, and that the only sort of compromise is to be found in confusion. This must be clearly distinguished from the commonplace about the utilitarian world not rising to the invisible values of genius.

Under this philosophy the utilitarian does not see the utility of genius, even when it is quite visible. He does not see it, not because he is a utilitarian, but because he is an idealist whose ideal is dullness. For some time the English aspired to be stupid, prayed and hoped with soaring spiritual ambition to be stupid. But with all their worship of success, they did not succeed in being stupid. The natural talents of a great and traditional nation were always breaking out in spite of them. In spite of the merchants of London, Turner did set the Thames on fire. In spite of our repeatedly explained preference for realism to romance, Europe persisted in resounding with the name of Byron. And just when we had made it perfectly clear to the French that we despised all their flamboyant tricks, that we were a plain prosaic people and there was no fantastic glory or chivalry about us, the very shaft we sent against them shone with the name of Nelson, a shooting and a falling star.

PRESIDENTS AND PROBLEMS

All good Americans wish to fight the representatives they have chosen. All good Englishmen wish to forget the representatives they have chosen. This difference, deep and perhaps ineradicable in the temperaments of the two peoples, explains a thousand things in their literature and their laws. The American national poet praised his people for their readiness 'to *rise* against the never-ending audacity of elected persons.' The English national anthem is content to say heartily, but almost hastily, 'Confound their politics,' and then more cheerfully, as if changing the subject, 'God Save the King.' For this is especially the secret of the monarch or chief magistrate in the two countries. They arm the President with the powers of a King, that he may be a nuisance in politics. We deprive the King even of the powers of a President, lest he should remind us of a politician. We desire to forget the never-ending audacity of elected persons; and with us therefore it really never does end. That is the practical objection to our own habit of changing the subject, instead of changing the ministry. The King, as the Irish wit observed, is not a subject; but in that sense the English crowned head is not a King. He is a popular figure intended to remind us of the England that politicians do not remember; the England of horses and ships and gardens and good fellowship. The Americans have no such purely social symbol; and it is rather the root than the result of this that their social luxury, and especially their sport, are a little lacking in humanity and humour. It is the American, much more than the Englishman, who takes his pleasures sadly, not to say savagely.

The genuine popularity of constitutional monarchs, in parliamentary countries, can be explained by any practical example. Let us suppose that great social reform, The Compulsory Haircutting Act, has just begun to be enforced. The Compulsory Haircutting Act, as every good citizen knows, is a statute which permits any person to grow his hair to any length, in any wild or wonderful shape, so long as he is registered with a hairdresser who charges a shilling. But it imposes a universal close-shave (like that which is found so hygienic during a curative detention at Dartmoor) on all who are registered only with a barber who charges threepence. Thus, while the ornamental classes can continue to ornament the street with Piccadilly weepers or chin-beards if they choose, the working classes demonstrate the care with which the State protects them by going about in a fresher, cooler, and cleaner condition; a condition which has the further advantage of revealing at a glance that outline of the criminal skull, which is so common among them. The Compulsory Haircutting Act is thus in every way a compact and convenient example of all our current laws about education, sport, liquor and liberty in general. Well, the law has passed and the masses, insensible to its scientific value, are still murmuring against it. The ignorant peasant maiden is averse to so extreme a fashion of bobbing her hair; and does not see how she can even be a flapper with nothing to flap. Her father, his mind already poisoned by Bolshevists, begins to wonder who the devil does these things, and why. In proportion as he knows the world of to-day, he guesses that the real origin may be quite obscure, or the real motive quite corrupt. The pressure may have come from anybody who has gained power or money anyhow. It may come from the foreign millionaire who owns all the expensive hairdressing saloons; it may come from some swindler in the cutlery trade who has contracted to sell a million bad razors. Hence the poor man looks about him with suspicion in the street; knowing that the lowest sneak or the loudest snob he sees may be directing the government of his country. Anybody may have to do with politics; and this sort of thing is politics. Suddenly he catches sight of a crowd, stops, and begins wildly to cheer a carriage that is passing. The carriage contains the one person who has certainly not originated any great scientific reform. He is the only person in the commonwealth who is not allowed to cut off other people's hair, or to take away other people's liberties. He at least is kept out of politics; and men hold him up as they did an unspotted victim to appease the wrath of the gods. He is their King, and the only man they know is not their ruler. We need not be surprised that he is popular, knowing how they are ruled.

The popularity of a President in America is exactly the opposite. The American Republic is the last mediaeval monarchy. It is intended that the President shall rule, and take all the risks of ruling. If the hair is cut he is the haircutter, the magistrate that bears not the razor in vain. All the popular Presidents, Jackson and Lincoln and Roosevelt, have acted as democratic despots, but emphatically not as constitutional monarchs. In short, the names have become curiously interchanged; and as a historical reality it is the President who ought to be called a King.

But it is not only true that the President could correctly be called a King. It is also true that the King might correctly be called a President. We could hardly find a more exact description of him than to call him a President. What is expected in modern times of a modern constitutional monarch is emphatically that he should preside. We expect him to take the throne exactly as if he were taking the chair. The chairman does not move the motion or resolution, far less vote it; he is not supposed even to favour it. He is expected to please everybody by favouring nobody. The primary essentials of a President or Chairman are that he should be treated with ceremonial respect, that he should be popular in his personality and yet impersonal in his opinions, and that he should actually be a link between all the other persons by being different from all of them. This is exactly what is demanded of the constitutional monarch in modern times. It is exactly the opposite to the American position; in which the President does not preside at all. He moves; and the thing he moves may truly be called a motion; for the national idea is perpetual motion. Technically it is called a message; and might often actually be called a menace. Thus we may truly say that the King presides and the President reigns. Some would prefer to say that the President rules; and some Senators and members of Congress would prefer to say that he rebels. But there is no doubt that he moves; he does not take the chair or even the stool, but rather the stump.

Some people seem to suppose that the fall of President Wilson was a denial of this almost despotic ideal in America. As a matter of fact it was the strongest possible assertion of it. The idea is that the President shall take responsibility and risk; and responsibility means being blamed, and risk means the risk of being blamed. The theory is that things are done by the President; and if things go wrong, or are alleged to go wrong, it is the fault of the President. This does not invalidate, but rather ratifies the comparison with true monarchs such as the mediaeval monarchs. Constitutional princes are seldom deposed; but despots were often deposed. In the simpler races of sunnier lands, such as Turkey, they were commonly assassinated. Even in our own history a King often received the same respectful tribute to the responsibility and reality of his office. But King John was attacked because he was strong, not because he was weak. Richard the Second lost the crown because the crown was a trophy, not because it was a trifle. And President Wilson was deposed because he had used a power which is such, in its nature, that a man must use it at the risk of deposition. As a matter of fact, of course, it is easy to exaggerate Mr. Wilson's real unpopularity, and still more easy to exaggerate Mr. Wilson's real failure. There are a great many people in America who justify and applaud him; and what is yet more interesting, who justify him not on pacifist and idealistic, but on patriotic and even military grounds. It is especially insisted by some that his demonstration, which seemed futile as a threat against Mexico, was a very far-sighted preparation for the threat against Prussia. But in so far as the democracy did disagree with him, it was but the occasional and inevitable result of the theory by which the despot has to anticipate the democracy.

Thus the American King and the English President are the very opposite of each other; yet they are both the varied and very national indications of the same contemporary truth. It is the great weariness and contempt that have fallen upon common politics in both countries. It may be answered, with some show of truth, that the new American President represents a return to common politics; and that in that sense he marks a real rebuke to the last President and his more uncommon politics. And it is true that many who put Mr. Harding in power regard him as the symbol of something which they call normalcy; which may roughly be translated into English by the word normality. And by this they do mean, more or less, the return to the vague capitalist conservatism of the nineteenth century. They might call Mr. Harding a Victorian if they had ever lived under Victoria. Perhaps these people do entertain the extraordinary notion that the nineteenth century was normal. But there are very few who think so, and even they will not think so long. The blunder is the beginning of nearly all our present troubles. The nineteenth century was the very reverse of normal. It suffered a most unnatural strain in the combination of political equality in theory with extreme economic inequality in practice. Capitalism was not a normalcy but an abnormalcy. Property is normal, and is more normal in proportion as it is universal. Slavery may be normal and even natural, in the sense that a bad habit may be second nature. But Capitalism was never anything so human as a habit; we may say it was never anything so good as a bad habit. It was never a custom; for men never grew accustomed to it. It was never even conservative; for before it was even created wise men had realised that it could not be conserved. It was from the first a problem; and those who will not even admit the Capitalist problem deserve to get the Bolshevist solution. All things considered, I cannot say anything worse of them than that.

The recent Presidential election preserved some trace of the old Party System of America; but its tradition has very nearly faded like that of the Party System of England. It is easy for an Englishman to confess that he never quite understood the American Party System. It would perhaps be more courageous in him, and more informing, to confess that he never really understood the British Party System. The planks in the two American platforms may easily be exhibited as very disconnected and ramshackle; but our own party was as much of a patchwork, and indeed I think even more so. Everybody knows that the two American factions were called 'Democrat' and 'Republican.' It does not at all cover the case to identify the former with Liberals and the latter with Conservatives. The Democrats are the party of the South and have some true tradition from the Southern aristocracy and the defence of Secession and State Rights. The Republicans rose in the North as the party of Lincoln, largely condemning slavery. But the Republicans are also the party of Tariffs, and are at least accused of being the party of Trusts. The Democrats are the party of Free Trade; and in the great movement of twenty years ago the party of Free Silver. The Democrats are also the party of the Irish; and the stones they throw at Trusts are retorted by stones thrown at Tammany. It is easy to see all these things as curiously sporadic and bewildering; but I am inclined to think that they are as a whole more coherent and rational than our own old division of Liberals and Conservatives. There is even more doubt nowadays about what is the connecting link between the different items in the old British party programmes. I have never been able to understand why being in favour of Protection should have anything to do with being opposed to Home Rule; especially as most of the people who were to receive Home Rule were themselves in favour of Protection. I could never see what giving people cheap bread had to do with forbidding them cheap beer; or why the party which sympathises with Ireland cannot sympathise with Poland. I cannot see why Liberals did not liberate public-houses or Conservatives conserve crofters. I do not understand the principle upon which the causes were selected on both sides; and I incline to think that it was with the impartial object of distributing nonsense equally on both sides. Heaven knows there is enough nonsense in American politics too; towering and tropical nonsense like a cyclone or an earthquake. But when all is said, I incline to think that there was more spiritual and atmospheric cohesion in the different parts of the American party than in those of the English party; and I think this unity was all the more real because it was more difficult to define. The Republican party originally stood for the triumph of the North, and the North stood for the nineteenth century; that is for the characteristic commercial expansion of the nineteenth century; for a firm faith in the profit and progress of its great and growing cities, its division of labour, its industrial science, and its evolutionary reform. The Democratic party stood more loosely for all the elements that doubted whether this development was democratic or was desirable; all that looked back to Jeffersonian idealism and the serene abstractions of the eighteenth century, or forward to Bryanite idealism and some simplified Utopia founded on grain rather than gold. Along with this went, not at all unnaturally, the last and lingering sentiment of the Southern squires, who remembered a more rural civilisation that seemed by comparison romantic. Along with this went, quite logically, the passions and the pathos of the Irish, themselves a rural civilisation, whose basis is a religion or what the nineteenth century tended to call a superstition. Above all, it was perfectly natural that this tone of thought should favour local liberties, and even a revolt on behalf of local liberties, and should distrust the huge machine of centralised power called the Union. In short, something very near the truth was said by a suicidally silly Republican orator, who was running Blaine for the Presidency, when he denounced the Democratic party as supported by 'Rome, rum, and rebellion.' They seem to me to be three excellent things in their place; and that is why I suspect that I should have belonged to the Democratic party, if I had been born in America when there was a Democratic party. But I fancy that by this time even this general distinction has become very dim. If I had been an American twenty years ago, in the time of the great Free Silver campaign, I should certainly never have hesitated for an instant about my sympathies or my side. My feelings would have been exactly those that are nobly expressed by Mr. Vachell Lindsay, in a poem bearing the characteristic title of 'Bryan, Bryan, Bryan, Bryan.' And, by the way, nobody can begin to sympathise with America whose soul does not to some extent begin to swing and dance to the drums and gongs of Mr. Vachell Lindsay's great orchestra; which has the note of his whole nation in this: that a refined person can revile it a hundred times over as violent and brazen and barbarous and absurd, but not as insincere; there is something in it, and that something is the soul of many million men. But the poet himself, in the political poem referred to, speaks of Bryan's fall over Free Silver as 'defeat of my boyhood, defeat of my dream'; and it is only too probable that the cause has fallen as well as the candidate. The William Jennings Bryan of later years is not the man whom I should have seen in my youth, with the visionary eyes of Mr. Vachell Lindsay. He has become a commonplace Pacifist, which is in its nature the very opposite of a revolutionist; for if men will fight rather than sacrifice humanity on a golden cross, it cannot be wrong for them to resist its being sacrificed to an iron cross. I came into very indirect contact with Mr. Bryan when I was in America, in a fashion that made me realise how hard it has become to recover the illusions of a Bryanite. I believe that my lecture agent was anxious to arrange a debate, and I threw out a sort of loose challenge to the effect that woman's suffrage had weakened the position of woman; and while I was away in the wilds of Oklahoma my lecture agent (a man of blood-curdling courage and enterprise) asked Mr. Bryan to debate with me. Now Mr. Bryan is one of the greatest orators of modern history, and there is no conceivable reason why he should trouble to debate with a wandering lecturer. But as a matter of fact he expressed himself in the most magnanimous and courteous terms about my personal position, but said (as I understood) that it would be improper to debate on female suffrage as it was already a part of the political system. And when I heard that, I could not help a sigh; for I recognised something that I knew only too well on the front benches of my own beloved land. The great and glorious demagogue had degenerated into a statesman. I had never expected for a moment that the great orator could be bothered to debate with me at all; but it had never occurred to me, as a general moral principle, that two educated men were for ever forbidden to talk sense about a particular topic, because a lot of other people had already voted on it. What is the matter with that attitude is the loss of the freedom of the mind. There can be no liberty of thought unless it is ready to unsettle what has recently been settled, as well as what has long been settled. We are perpetually being told in the papers that what is wanted is a strong man who will do things. What is wanted is a strong man who will undo things; and that will be a real test of strength.

Anyhow, we could have believed, in the time of the Free Silver fight, that the Democratic party was democratic with a small d. In Mr. Wilson it was transfigured, his friends would say into a higher and his foes into a hazier thing. And the Republican reaction against him, even where it has been healthy, has also been hazy. In fact, it has been not so much the victory of a political party as a relapse into repose after certain political passions; and in that sense there is a truth in the strange phrase about normalcy; in the sense that there is nothing more normal than going to sleep. But an even larger truth is this; it is most likely that America is no longer concentrated on these faction fights at all, but is considering certain large problems upon which those factions hardly troubled to take sides. They are too large even to be classified as foreign policy distinct from domestic policy. They are so large as to be inside as well as outside the state. From an English standpoint the most obvious example is the Irish; for the Irish problem is not a British problem, but also an American problem. And this is true even of the great external enigma of Japan. The Japanese question may be a part of foreign policy for America, but it is a part of domestic policy for California. And the same is true of that other intense and intelligent Eastern people, the genius and limitations of which have troubled the world so much longer. What the Japs are in California, the Jews are in America. That is, they are a piece of foreign policy that has become imbedded in domestic policy; something which is found inside but still has to be regarded from the outside. On these great international matters I doubt if Americans got much guidance from their party system; especially as most of these questions have grown very recently and rapidly to enormous size. Men are left free to judge of them with fresh minds. And that is the truth in the statement that the Washington Conference has opened the gates of a new world.

On the relations to England and Ireland I will not attempt to dwell adequately here. I have already noted that my first interview was with an Irishman, and my first impression from that interview a vivid sense of the importance of Ireland in Anglo-American relations; and I have said something of the Irish problem, prematurely and out of its proper order, under the stress of that sense of urgency. Here I will only add two remarks about the two countries respectively. A great many British journalists have recently imagined that they were pouring oil upon the troubled waters, when they were rather pouring out oil to smooth the downward path; and to turn the broad road to destruction into a butter-slide. They seem to have no notion of what to do, except to say what they imagine the very stupidest of their readers would be pleased to hear, and conceal whatever the most intelligent of their readers would probably like to know. They therefore informed the public that 'the majority of Americans' had abandoned all sympathy with Ireland, because of its alleged sympathy with Germany; and that this majority of Americans was now ardently in sympathy with its English brothers across the sea. Now to begin with, such critics have no notion of what they are saying when they talk about the majority of Americans. To anybody who has happened to look in, let us say, on the city of Omaha, Nebraska, the remark will have something enormous and overwhelming about it. It is like saying that the majority of the inhabitants of China would agree with the Chinese Ambassador in a preference for dining at the Savoy rather than the Ritz. There are millions and millions of people living in those great central plains of the North American Continent of whom it would be nearer the truth to say that they have never heard of England, or of Ireland either, than to say that their first emotional movement is a desire to come to the rescue of either of them. It is perfectly true that the more monomaniac sort of Sinn Feiner might sometimes irritate this innocent and isolated American spirit by being pro-Irish. It is equally true that a traditional Bostonian or Virginian might irritate it by being pro-English. The only difference is that large numbers of pure Irishmen are scattered in those far places, and large numbers of pure Englishmen are not. But it is truest of all to say that neither England nor Ireland so much as crosses the mind of most of them once in six months. Painting up large notices of 'Watch Us Grow,' making money by farming with machinery, together with an occasional hold-up with six-shooters and photographs of a beautiful murderess or divorcée, fill up the round of their good and happy lives, and fleet the time carelessly as in the golden age.

But putting aside all this vast and distant democracy, which is the real 'majority of Americans,' and confining ourselves to that older culture on the eastern coast which the critics probably had in mind, we shall find the case more comforting but not to be covered with cheap and false comfort. Now it is perfectly true that any Englishman coming to this eastern coast, as I did, finds himself not only most warmly welcomed as a guest, but most cordially complimented as an Englishman. Men recall with pride the branches of their family that belong to England or the English counties where they were rooted; and there are enthusiasms for English literature and history which are as spontaneous as patriotism itself. Something of this may be put down to a certain promptitude and flexibility in all American kindness, which is never sufficiently stodgy to be called good nature. The Englishman does sometimes wonder whether if he had been a

Russian, his hosts would not have remembered remote Russian aunts and uncles and disinterred a Muscovite great-grandmother; or whether if he had come from Iceland, they would not have known as much about Icelandic sagas and been as sympathetic about the absence of Icelandic snakes. But with a fair review of the proportions of the case he will dismiss this conjecture, and come to the conclusion that a number of educated Americans are very warmly and sincerely sympathetic with England.

What I began to feel, with a certain creeping chill, was that they were only too sympathetic with England. The word sympathetic has sometimes rather a double sense. The impression I received was that all these chivalrous Southerners and men mellow with Bostonian memories were *rallying* to England. They were on the defensive; and it was poor old England that they were defending. Their attitude implied that somebody or something was leaving her undefended, or finding her indefensible. The burden of that hearty chorus was that England was not so black as she was painted; it seemed clear that somewhere or other she was being painted pretty black. But there was something else that made me uncomfortable; it was not only the sense of being somewhat boisterously forgiven; it was also something involving questions of power as well as morality. Then it seemed to me that a new sensation turned me hot and cold; and I felt something I have never before felt in a foreign land. Never had my father or my grandfather known that sensation; never during the great and complex and perhaps perilous expansion of our power and commerce in the last hundred years had an Englishman heard exactly that note in a human voice. England was being *pitied*. I, as an Englishman, was not only being pardoned but pitied. My country was beginning to be an object of compassion, like Poland or Spain. My first emotion, full of the mood and movement of a hundred years, was one of furious anger. But the anger has given place to anxiety; and the anxiety is not yet at an end.

It is not my business here to expound my view of English politics, still less of European politics or the politics of the world; but to put down a few impressions of American travel. On many points of European politics the impression will be purely negative; I am sure that most Americans have no notion of the position of France or the position of Poland. But if English readers want the truth, I am sure this is the truth about their notion of the position of England. They are wondering, or those who are watching are wondering, whether the term of her success is come and she is going down the dark road after Prussia. Many are sorry if this is so; some are glad if it is so; but all are seriously considering the probability of its being so. And herein lay especially the horrible folly of our Black-and-Tan terrorism over the Irish people. I have noted that the newspapers told us that America had been chilled in its Irish sympathies by Irish detachment during the war. It is the painful truth that any advantage we might have had from this we ourselves immediately proceeded to destroy. Ireland *might* have put herself wrong with America by her attitude about Belgium, if England had not instantly proceeded to put herself more wrong by her attitude towards Ireland. It is quite true that two blacks do not make a white; but you cannot send a black to reproach people with tolerating blackness; and this is quite as true when one is a Black Brunswicker and the other a Black-and-Tan. It is true that since then England has made surprisingly sweeping concessions; concessions so large as to increase the amazement that the refusal should have been so long. But unfortunately the combination of the two rather clinches the conception of our decline. If the concession had come before the terror, it would have looked like an attempt to emancipate, and would probably have succeeded. Coming so abruptly after the terror, it looked only like an attempt to tyrannise, and an attempt that failed. It was partly an inheritance from a stupid tradition, which tried to combine what it called firmness with what it called conciliation; as if when we made up our minds to soothe a man with a five-pound note, we always took care to undo our own action by giving him a kick as well. The English politician has often done that; though there is nothing to be said of such a fool, except that he has wasted a fiver. But in this case he gave the kick first, received a kicking in return, and *then* gave up the money; and it was hard for the bystanders to say anything except that he had been badly beaten. The combination and sequence of events seems almost as if it were arranged to suggest the dark and ominous parallel. The first action looked only too like the invasion of Belgium, and the second like the evacuation of Belgium. So that vast and silent crowd in the West looked at the British Empire, as men look at a great tower that has begun to lean. Thus it was that while I found real pleasure, I could not find unrelieved consolation in the sincere compliments paid to my country by so many cultivated Americans; their memories of homely corners of historic counties from which their fathers came, of the cathedral that dwarfs the town, or the inn at the turning of the road. There was something in their voices and the look in their eyes which from the first disturbed me. So I have heard good Englishmen, who died afterwards the death of soldiers, cry aloud in 1914, 'It seems impossible, of those jolly Bavarians!' or, 'I will never believe it, when I think of the time I had at Heidelberg!'

But there are other things besides the parallel of Prussia or the problem of Ireland. The American press is much freer than our own; the American public is much more familiar with the discussion of corruption than our own; and it is much more conscious of the corruption of our politics than we are. Almost any man in America may speak of the Marconi Case; many a man in England does not even know what it means. Many imagine that it had something to do with the propriety of politicians speculating on the Stock Exchange. So that it means a great deal to Americans to say that one figure in that drama is ruling India and another is ruling Palestine. And this brings me to another problem, which is also dealt with much more openly in America than in England. I mention it here only because it is a perfect model of the misunderstandings in the modern world. If any one asks for an example of exactly how the important part of every story is left out, and even the part that is reported is not understood, he could hardly have a stronger case than the story of Henry Ford of Detroit.

When I was in Detroit I had the pleasure of meeting Mr. Ford, and it really was a pleasure. He is a man quite capable of views which I think silly to the point of insanity; but he is not the vulgar benevolent boss. It must be admitted that he is a millionaire; but he cannot really be convicted of being a philanthropist. He is not a man who merely wants to run people; it is rather his views that run him, and perhaps run away with him. He has a distinguished and sensitive face; he really invented things himself, unlike most men who profit by inventions; he is something of an artist and not a little of a fighter. A man of that type is always capable of being wildly wrong, especially in the sectarian atmosphere of America; and Mr. Ford has been wrong before and may be wrong now. He is chiefly known in England for a project which I think very preposterous; that of the Peace Ship, which came to Europe during the war. But he is not known in England at all in connection with a much more important campaign, which he has conducted much more recently and with much more success; a campaign against the Jews like one of the Anti-Semitic campaigns of the Continent. Now any one who knows anything of America knows exactly what the Peace Ship would be like. It was a national combination of imagination and ignorance, which has at least some of the beauty of innocence. Men living in those huge, hedgeless inland plains know nothing about frontiers or the tragedy of a fight for freedom; they know nothing of alarum and armaments or the peril of a high civilisation poised like a precious statue within reach of a mailed fist. They are accustomed to a cosmopolitan citizenship, in which men of all bloods mingle and in which men of all creeds are counted equal. Their highest moral boast is humanitarianism; their highest mental boast is enlightenment. In a word, they are the very last men in the world who would seem likely to pride themselves on a prejudice against the Jews. They have no religion in particular, except a sincere sentiment which they would call 'true Christianity,' and which specially forbids an attack on the Jews. They have a patriotism which prides itself on assimilating all types, including the Jews. Mr. Ford is a pure product of this pacific world, as was sufficiently proved by his pacifism. If a man of that sort has discovered that there is a Jewish problem, it is because there is a Jewish problem. It is certainly not because there is an Anti-Jewish prejudice. For if there had been any amount of such racial and religious prejudice, he would have been about the very last sort of man to have it. His particular part of the world would have been the very last place to produce it. We may well laugh at the Peace Ship, and its wild course and inevitable shipwreck; but remember that its very wildness was an attempt to sail as far as possible from the castle of Front-de-Bœuf. Everything that made him Anti-War should have prevented him from being Anti-Semite. We may mock him for being mad on peace; but we cannot say that he was so mad on peace that he made war on Israel.

It happened that, when I was in America, I had just published some studies on Palestine; and I was besieged by Rabbis lamenting my 'prejudice.' I pointed out that they would have got hold of the wrong word, even if they had not got hold of the wrong man. As a point of personal autobiography, I do not happen to be a man who dislikes Jews; though I believe that some men do. I have had Jews among my most intimate and faithful friends since my boyhood, and I hope to have them till I die. But even if I did have a dislike of Jews, it would be illogical to call that dislike a prejudice. Prejudice is a very lucid Latin word meaning the bias which a man has before he considers a case. I might be said to be prejudiced against a Hairy Ainu because of his name, for I have never been on terms of such intimacy with him as to correct my preconceptions. But if after moving about in the modern world and meeting Jews, knowing Jews, doing business with Jews, and reading and hearing about Jews, I came to the conclusion that I did not like Jews, my conclusion certainly would not be a prejudice. It would simply be an opinion; and one I should be perfectly entitled to hold; though as a matter of fact I do not hold it. No extravagance of hatred merely following on *experience* of Jews can properly be called a prejudice.

Now the point is that this new American Anti-Semitism springs from experience and nothing but experience. There is no prejudice for it to spring from. Or rather the prejudice is all the other way. All the traditions of that democracy, and very creditable traditions too, are in favour of toleration and a sort of idealistic indifference. The sympathies in which these nineteenth-century people were reared were all against Front-de-Bœuf and in favour of Rebecca. They inherited a prejudice against Anti-Semitism; a prejudice of Anti-Anti-Semitism. These people of the plains have found the Jewish problem exactly as they might have struck oil; because it is *there*, and not even because they were looking for it. Their view of the problem, like their use of the oil, is not always satisfactory; and with parts of it I entirely disagree. But the point is that the thing which I call a problem, and others call a prejudice, has now appeared in broad daylight in a new country where there is no priestcraft, no feudalism, no ancient superstition to explain it. It has appeared because it *is* a problem; and those are the best friends of the Jews, including many of the Jews themselves, who are trying to find a solution. That is the meaning of the incident of Mr. Henry Ford of Detroit; and you will hardly hear an intelligible word about it in England.

The talk of prejudice against the Japs is not unlike the talk of prejudice against the Jews. Only in this case our indifference has really the excuse of ignorance. We used to lecture the Russians for oppressing the Jews, before we heard the word Bolshevist and began to lecture them for being oppressed by the Jews. In the same way we have long lectured the Californians for oppressing the Japs, without allowing for the possibility of their foreseeing that the oppression may soon be the other way. As in the other case, it may be a persecution but it is not a prejudice. The Californians know more about the Japanese than we do; and our own colonists when they are placed in the same position generally say the same thing. I will not attempt to deal adequately here with the vast international and diplomatic problems which arise with the name of the new power in the Far East. It is possible that Japan, having imitated European militarism, may imitate European pacifism. I cannot honestly pretend to know what the Japanese mean by the one any more than by the other. But when Englishmen, especially English Liberals like myself, take a superior and censorious attitude towards Americans and especially Californians, I am moved to make a final remark. When a considerable number of Englishmen talk of the grave contending claims of our friendship with Japan and our friendship with America, when they finally tend in a sort of summing up to dwell on the superior virtues of Japan, I may be permitted to make a single comment.

We are perpetually boring the world and each other with talk about the bonds that bind us to America. We are perpetually crying aloud that England and America are very much alike, especially England. We are always insisting that the two are identical in all the things in which they most obviously differ. We are always saying that both stand for democracy, when we should not consent to stand their democracy for half a day. We are always saying that at least we are all Anglo-Saxons, when we are descended from Romans and Normans and Britons and Danes, and they are descended from Irishmen and Italians and Slavs and Germans. We tell a people whose very existence is a revolt against the British Crown that they are passionately devoted to the British Constitution. We tell a nation whose whole policy has been isolation and independence that with us she can bear safely the White Man's Burden of universal empire. We tell a continent crowded with Irishmen to thank God that the Saxon can always rule the Celt. We tell a populace whose very virtues are lawless that together we uphold the Reign of Law. We recognise our own law-abiding character in people who make laws that neither they nor anybody else can abide. We congratulate them on clinging to all they have cast away, and on imitating everything which they came into existence to insult. And when we have established all these nonsensical analogies with a nonexistent nation, we wait until there is a crisis in which we really are at one with America, and then we falter and threaten to fail her. In a battle where we really are of one blood, the blood of the great white race throughout the world, when we really have one language, the fundamental alphabet of Cadmus and the script of Rome, when we really do represent the same reign of law, the common conscience of Christendom and the morals of men baptized, when we really have an implicit faith and honour and type of freedom to summon up our souls as with trumpets—*then* many of us begin to weaken and waver and wonder whether there is not something very nice about little yellow men, whose heroic stories revolve round polygamy and suicide, and whose heroes wore two swords and worshipped the ancestors of the Mikado.

PROHIBITION IN FACT AND FANCY

I went to America with some notion of not discussing Prohibition. But I soon found that well-to-do Americans were only too delighted to discuss it over the nuts and wine. They were even willing, if necessary, to dispense with the nuts. I am far from sneering at this; having a general philosophy which need not here be expounded, but which may be symbolised by saying that monkeys can enjoy nuts but only men can enjoy wine. But if I am to deal with Prohibition, there is no doubt of the first thing to be said about it. The first thing to be said about it is that it does not exist. It is to some extent enforced among the poor; at any rate it was intended to be enforced among the poor; though even among them I fancy it is much evaded. It is certainly not enforced among the rich; and I doubt whether it was intended to be. I suspect that this has always happened whenever this negative notion has taken hold of some particular province or tribe. Prohibition never prohibits. It never has in history; not even in Moslem history; and it never will. Mahomet at least had the argument of a climate and not the interest of a class. But if a test is needed, consider what part of Moslem culture has passed permanently into our own modern culture. You will find the one Moslem poem that has really pierced is a Moslem poem in praise of wine. The crown of all the victories of the Crescent is that nobody reads the Koran and everybody reads the Rubaiyat.

Most of us remember with satisfaction an old picture in *Punch*, representing a festive old gentleman in a state of collapse on the pavement, and a philanthropic old lady anxiously calling the attention of a cabman to the calamity. The old lady says, 'I'm sure this poor gentleman is ill,' and the cabman replies with fervour, 'Ill! I wish I 'ad 'alf 'is complaint.'

We talk about unconscious humour; but there is such a thing as unconscious seriousness. Flippancy is a flower whose roots are often underground in the subconsciousness. Many a man talks sense when he thinks he is talking nonsense; touches on a conflict of ideas as if it were only a contradiction of language, or really makes a parallel when he means only to make a pun. Some of the *Punch* jokes of the best period are examples of this; and that quoted above is a very strong example of it. The cabman meant what he said; but he said a great deal more than he meant. His utterance contained fine philosophical doctrines and distinctions of which he was not perhaps entirely conscious. The spirit of the English language, the tragedy and comedy of the condition of the English people, spoke through him as the god spoke through a teraph-head or brazen mask of oracle. And the oracle is an omen; and in some sense an omen of doom.

Observe, to begin with, the sobriety of the cabman. Note his measure, his moderation; or to use the yet truer term, his temperance. He only wishes to have half the old gentleman's complaint. The old gentleman is welcome to the other half, along with all the other pomps and luxuries of his superior social station. There is nothing Bolshevist or even Communist about the temperance cabman. He might almost be called Distributist, in the sense that he wishes to distribute the old gentleman's complaint more equally between the old gentleman and himself. And, of course, the social relations there represented are very much truer to life than it is fashionable to suggest. By the realism of this picture Mr. Punch made amends for some more snobbish pictures, with the opposite social moral. It will remain eternally among his real glories that he exhibited a picture in which the cabman was sober and the gentleman was drunk. Despite many ideas to the contrary, it was emphatically a picture of real life. The truth is subject to the simplest of all possible tests. If the cabman were really and truly drunk he would not be a cabman, for he could not drive a cab. If he had the whole of the old gentleman's complaint, he would be sitting happily on the pavement beside the old gentleman; a symbol of social equality found at last, and the levelling of all classes of mankind. I do not say that there has never been such a monster known as a drunken cabman; I do not say that the driver may not sometimes have approximated imprudently to three-quarters of the complaint, instead of adhering to his severe but wise conception of half of it. But I do say that most men of the world, if they spoke sincerely, could testify to more examples of helplessly drunken gentlemen put inside cabs than of helplessly drunken drivers on top of them. Philanthropists and officials, who never look at people but only at papers, probably have a mass of social statistics to the contrary; founded on the simple fact that cabmen can be cross-examined about their habits and gentlemen cannot. Social workers probably have the whole thing worked out in sections and compartments, showing how the extreme intoxication of cabmen compares with the parallel intoxication of costermongers; or measuring the drunkenness of a dustman against the drunkenness of a crossing-sweeper. But there is more practical experience embodied in the practical speech of the English; and in the proverb that says 'as drunk as a lord.'

Now Prohibition, whether as a proposal in England or a pretence in America, simply means that the man who has drunk less shall have no drink, and the man who has drunk more shall have all the drink. It means that the old gentleman shall be carried home in the cab drunker than ever; but that, in order to make it quite safe for him to drink to excess, the man who drives him shall be forbidden to drink even in moderation. That is what it means; that is all it means; that is all it ever will mean. It tends to that in Moslem countries; where the luxurious and advanced drink champagne, while the poor and fanatical drink water. It means that in modern America; where the wealthy are all at this moment sipping their cocktails, and discussing how much harder labourers can be made to work if only they can be kept from festivity. This is what it means and all it means; and men are divided about it according to whether they believe in a certain transcendental concept called 'justice,' expressed in a more mystical paradox as the equality of men. So long as you do not believe in justice, and so long as you are rich and really confident of remaining so, you can have Prohibition and be as drunk as you choose.

I see that some remarks by the Rev. R. J. Campbell, dealing with social conditions in America, are reported in the press. They include some observations about Sinn Fein in which, as in most of Mr. Campbell's allusions to Ireland, it is not difficult to detect his dismal origin, or the acrid smell of the smoke of Belfast. But the remarks about America are valuable in the objective sense, over and above their philosophy. He believes that Prohibition will survive and be a success, nor does he seem himself to regard the prospect with any special disfavour. But he frankly and freely testifies to the truth I have asserted; that Prohibition does not prohibit, so far as the wealthy are concerned. He testifies to constantly seeing wine on the table, as will any other grateful guest of the generous hospitality of America; and he implies humorously that he asked no questions about the story told him of the old stocks in the cellars. So there is no dispute about the facts; and we come back as before to the principles. Is Mr. Campbell content with a Prohibition which is another name for Privilege? If so, he has simply absorbed along with his new theology a new morality which is different from mine. But he does state both sides of the inequality with equal logic and clearness; and in these days of intellectual fog that alone is like a ray of sunshine.

Now my primary objection to Prohibition is not based on any arguments against it, but on the one argument for it. I need nothing more for its condemnation than the only thing that is said in its defence. It is said by capitalists all over America; and it is very clearly and correctly reported by Mr. Campbell himself. The argument is that employees work harder, and therefore employers get richer. That this idea should be taken calmly, by itself, as the test of a problem of liberty, is in itself a final testimony to the presence of slavery. It shows that people have completely forgotten that there is any other test except the servile test. Employers are willing that workmen should have exercise, as it may help them to do more work. They are even willing that workmen should have leisure; for the more intelligent capitalists can see that this also really means that they can do more work. But they are not in any way willing that workmen should have fun; for fun only increases the happiness and not the utility of the worker. Fun is freedom; and in that sense is an end in itself. It concerns the man not as a worker but as a citizen, or even as a soul; and the soul in that sense is an end in itself. That a man shall have a reasonable amount of comedy and poetry and even fantasy in his life is part of his spiritual health, which is for the service of God; and not merely for his mechanical health, which is now bound to the service of man. The very test adopted has all the servile implication; the test of what we can get out of him, instead of the test of what he can get out of life.

Mr. Campbell is reported to have suggested, doubtless rather as a conjecture than a prophecy, that England may find it necessary to become teetotal in order to compete commercially with the efficiency and economy of teetotal America. Well, in the eighteenth and early nineteenth centuries there was in America one of the most economical and efficient of all forms of labour. It did not happen to be feasible for the English to compete with it by copying it. There were so many humanitarian prejudices about in those days. But economically there seems to be no reason why a man should not have prophesied that England would be forced to adopt American Slavery then, as she is urged to adopt American Prohibition now. Perhaps such a prophet would have prophesied rightly. Certainly it is not impossible that universal Slavery might have been the vision of Calhoun as universal Prohibition seems to be the vision of Campbell. The old England of 1830 would have said that such a plea for slavery was monstrous; but what would it have said of a plea for enforced water-drinking? Nevertheless, the nobler Servile State of Calhoun collapsed before it could spread to Europe. And there is always the hope that the same may happen to the far more materialistic Utopia of Mr. Campbell and Soft Drinks.

Abstract morality is very important; and it may well clear the mind to consider what would be the effect of Prohibition in America, if it were introduced there. It would, of course, be a decisive departure from the tradition of the Declaration of Independence. Those who deny that are hardly serious enough to demand attention. It is enough to say that they are reduced to minimising that document in defence of Prohibition, exactly as the slave-owners were reduced to minimising it in defence of Slavery. They are reduced to saying that the Fathers of the Republic meant no more than that they would not be ruled by a king. And they are obviously open to the reply which Lincoln gave to Douglas on the slavery question; that if that great charter was limited to certain events in the eighteenth century, it was hardly worth making such a fuss about in the nineteenth—or in the twentieth. But they are also open to another reply which is even more to the point, when they pretend that Jefferson's famous preamble only means to say that monarchy is wrong. They are maintaining that Jefferson only meant to say something that he does not say at all. The great preamble does not say that all monarchical government must be wrong; on the contrary, it rather implies that most government is right. It speaks of human governments in general as justified by the necessity of defending certain personal rights. I see no reason whatever to suppose that it would not include any royal government that does defend those rights. Still less do I doubt what it would say of a republican government that does destroy those rights.

But what are those rights? Sophists can always debate about their degree; but even sophists cannot debate about their direction. Nobody in his five wits will deny that Jeffersonian democracy wished to give the law a general control in more public things, but the citizens a more general liberty in private things. Wherever we draw the line, liberty can only be personal liberty; and the most personal liberties must at least be the last liberties we lose. But to-day they are the first liberties we lose. It is not a question of drawing the line in the right place, but of beginning at the wrong end. What are the rights of man, if they do not include the normal right to regulate his own health, in relation to the normal risks of diet and daily life? Nobody can pretend that beer is a poison as prussic acid is a poison; that all the millions of civilised men who drank it all fell down dead when they had touched it. Its use and abuse is obviously a matter of judgment; and there can be no personal liberty, if it is not a matter of private judgment. It is not in the least a question of drawing the line between liberty and licence. If this is licence, there is no such thing as liberty. It is plainly impossible to find any right more individual or intimate. To say that a man has a right to a vote, but not a right to a voice about the choice of his dinner, is like saying that he has a right to his hat but not a right to his head.

Prohibition, therefore, plainly violates the rights of man, if there are any rights of man. What its supporters really mean is that there are none. And in suggesting this, they have all the advantages that every sceptic has when he supports a negation. That sort of ultimate scepticism can only be retorted upon itself, and we can point out to them that they can no more prove the right of the city to be oppressive than we can prove the right of the citizen to be free. In the primary metaphysics of such a claim, it would surely be easier to make it out for a single conscious soul than for an artificial social combination. If there are no rights of men, what are the rights of nations? Perhaps a nation has no claim to self-government. Perhaps it has no claim to good government. Perhaps it has no claim to any sort of government or any sort of independence. Perhaps they will say *that* is not implied in the Declaration of Independence. But without going deep into my reasons for believing in natural rights, or rather in supernatural rights (and Jefferson certainly states them as supernatural), I am content here to note that a man's treatment of his own body, in relation to traditional and ordinary opportunities for bodily excess, is as near to his self-respect as social coercion can possibly go; and that when that is gone there is nothing left. If coercion applies to that, it applies to everything; and in the future of this controversy it obviously will apply to everything. When I was in America, people were already applying it to tobacco. I never can see why they should not apply it to talking. Talking often goes with tobacco as it goes with beer; and what is more relevant, talking may often lead both to beer and tobacco. Talking often drives a man to drink, both negatively in the form of nagging and positively in the form of bad company. If the American Puritan is so anxious to be a *censor morum*, he should obviously put a stop to the evil communications that really corrupt good manners. He should reintroduce the Scold's Bridle among the other Blue Laws for a land of blue devils. He should gag all gay deceivers and plausible cynics; he should cut off all flattering lips and the tongue that speaketh proud things. Nobody can doubt that nine-tenths of the harm in the world is done simply by talking. Jefferson and the old democrats allowed people to talk, not because they were unaware of this fact, but because they were fettered by this old fancy of theirs about freedom and the rights of man. But since we have already abandoned that doctrine in a final fashion, I cannot see why the new principle should not be applied intelligently; and in that case it would be applied to the control of conversation. The State would provide us with forms already filled up with the subjects suitable for us to discuss at breakfast; perhaps allowing us a limited number of epigrams each. Perhaps we should have to make a formal application in writing, to be allowed to make a joke that had just occurred to us in conversation. And the committee would consider it in due course. Perhaps it would be effected in a more practical fashion, and the private citizens would be shut up as the public-houses were shut up. Perhaps they would all wear gags, which the policeman would remove at stated hours; and their mouths would be opened from one to three, as now in England even the public-houses are from time to time accessible to the public. To some this will sound fantastic; but not so fantastic as Jefferson would have thought Prohibition. But there is one sense in which it is indeed fantastic, for by hypothesis it leaves out the favouritism that is the fundamental of the whole matter. The only sense in which we can say that logic will never go so far as this is that logic will never go the length of equality. It is perfectly possible that the same forces that have forbidden beer may go on to forbid tobacco. But they will in a special and limited sense forbid tobacco—but not cigars. Or at any rate not expensive cigars. In America, where large numbers of ordinary men smoke rather ordinary cigars, there would be doubtless a good opportunity of penalising a very ordinary pleasure. But the Havanas of the millionaire will be all right. So it will be if ever the Puritans bring back the Scold's Bridle and the statutory silence of the populace. It will only be the populace that is silent. The politicians will go on talking.

These I believe to be the broad facts of the problem of Prohibition; but it would not be fair to leave it without mentioning two other causes which, if not defences, are at least excuses. The first is that Prohibition was largely passed in a sort of fervour or fever of self-sacrifice, which was a part of the passionate patriotism of America in the war. As I have remarked elsewhere, those who have any notion of what that national unanimity was like will smile when they see America made a model of mere international idealism. Prohibition was partly a sort of patriotic renunciation; for the popular instinct, like every poetic instinct, always tends at great crises to great gestures of renunciation. But this very fact, while it makes the inhumanity far more human, makes it far less final and convincing. Men cannot remain standing stiffly in such symbolical attitudes; nor can a permanent policy be founded on something analogous to flinging a gauntlet or uttering a battle-cry. We might as well expect all the Yale students to remain through life with their mouths open, exactly as they were when they uttered the college yell. It would be as reasonable as to expect them to remain through life with their mouths shut, while the wine-cup which has been the sacrament of all poets and lovers passed round among all the youth of the world. This point appeared very plainly in a discussion I had with a very thoughtful and sympathetic American critic, a clergyman writing in an Anglo-Catholic magazine. He put the sentiment of these healthier Prohibitionists, which had so much to do with the passing of Prohibition, by asking, 'May not a man who is asked to give up his blood for his country be asked to give up his beer for his country?' And this phrase clearly illuminates all the limitations of the case. I have never denied, in principle, that it might in some abnormal crisis be lawful for a government to lock up the beer, or to lock up the bread. In that sense I am quite prepared to treat the sacrifice of beer in the same way as the sacrifice of blood. But is my American critic really ready to treat the sacrifice of blood in the same way as the sacrifice of beer? Is bloodshed to be as prolonged and protracted as Prohibition? Is the normal noncombatant to shed his gore as often as he misses his drink? I can imagine people submitting to a special regulation, as I can imagine them serving in a particular war. I do indeed despise the political knavery that deliberately passes drink regulations as war measures and then preserves them as peace measures. But that is not a question of whether drink and drunkenness are wrong, but of whether lying and swindling are wrong. But I never denied that there might need to be exceptional sacrifices for exceptional occasions; and war is in its nature an exception. Only, if war is the exception, why should Prohibition be the rule? If the surrender of beer is worthy to be compared to the shedding of blood, why then blood ought to be flowing for ever like a fountain in the public squares of Philadelphia and New York. If my critic wants to complete his parallel, he must draw up rather a remarkable programme for the daily life of the ordinary citizens. He must suppose that, through all their lives, they are paraded every day at lunch time and prodded with bayonets to show that they will shed their blood for their country. He must suppose that every evening, after a light repast of poison gas and shrapnel, they are made to go to sleep in a trench under a permanent drizzle of shell-fire. It is surely obvious that if this were the normal life of the citizen, the citizen would have no normal life. The common sense of the thing is that sacrifices of this sort are admirable but abnormal. It is not normal for the State to be perpetually regulating our days with the discipline of a fighting regiment; and it is not normal for the State to be perpetually regulating our diet with the discipline of a famine. To say that every citizen must be subject to control in such bodily things is like saying that every Christian ought to tear himself with red-hot pincers because the Christian martyrs did their duty in time of persecution. A man has a right to control his body, though in a time of martyrdom he may give his body to be burned; and a man has a right to control his bodily health, though in a state of siege he may give his body to be starved. Thus, though the patriotic defence was a sincere defence, it is a defence that comes back on the defenders like a boomerang. For it proves only that Prohibition ought to be ephemeral, unless war ought to be eternal.

The other excuse is much less romantic and much more realistic. I have already said enough of the cause which is really realistic. The real power behind Prohibition is simply the plutocratic power of the pushing employers who wish to get the last inch of work out of their workmen. But before the progress of modern plutocracy had reached this stage, there was a predetermining cause for which there was a much better case. The whole business began with the problem of black labour. I have not attempted in this book to deal adequately with the question of the negro. I have refrained for a reason that may seem somewhat sensational; that I do not think I have anything particularly valuable to say or suggest. I do not profess to understand this singularly dark and intricate matter; and I see no use in men who have no solution filling up the gap with sentimentalism. The chief thing that struck me about the coloured people I saw was their charming and astonishing cheerfulness. My sense of pathos was appealed to much more by the Red Indians; and indeed I wish I had more space here to do justice to the Red Indians. They did heroic service in the war; and more than justified their glorious place in the day-dreams and nightmares of our boyhood. But the negro problem certainly demands more study than a sight-seer could give it; and this book is controversial enough about things that I have really considered, without permitting it to exhibit me as a sight-seer who shoots at sight. But I believe that it was always common ground to people of common sense that the enslavement and importation of negroes had been the crime and catastrophe of American history. The only difference was originally that one side thought that, the crime once committed, the only reparation was their freedom; while the other thought that, the crime once committed, the only safety was their slavery. It was only comparatively lately, by a process I shall have to indicate elsewhere, that anything like a positive case for slavery became possible. Now among the many problems of the presence of an alien and at least recently barbaric figure among the citizens, there was a very real problem of drink. Drink certainly has a very exceptionally destructive effect upon negroes in their native countries; and it was alleged to have a peculiarly demoralising effect upon negroes in the United States; to call up the passions that are the particular temptation of the race and to lead to appalling outrages that are followed by appalling popular vengeance. However this may be, many of the states of the American Union, which first forbade liquor to citizens, meant simply to forbid it to negroes. But they had not the moral courage to deny that negroes are citizens. About all their political expedients necessarily hung the load that hangs so heavy on modern politics; hypocrisy. The superior race had to rule by a sort of secret society organised against the inferior. The American politicians dared not disfranchise the negroes; so they coerced everybody in theory and only the negroes in practice. The drinking of the white men became as much a conspiracy as the shooting by the white horsemen of the Ku-Klux Klan. And in that connection, it may be remarked in passing that the comparison illustrates the idiocy of supposing that the moral sense of mankind will ever support the prohibition of drinking as if it were something like the prohibition of shooting. Shooting in America is liable to take a free form, and sometimes a very horrible form; as when private bravos were hired to kill workmen in the capitalistic interests of that pure patron of disarmament, Carnegie. But when some of the rich Americans gravely tell us that their drinking cannot be interfered with, because they are only using up their existing stocks of wine, we may well be disposed to smile. When I was there, at any rate, they were using them up very fast; and with no apparent fears about the supply. But if the Ku-Klux Klan had started suddenly shooting everybody they didn't like in broad daylight, and had blandly explained that they were only using up the stocks of their ammunition, left over from the Civil War, it seems probable that there would at least have been a little curiosity about how much they had left. There might at least have been occasional inquiries about how long it was likely to go on. It is even conceivable that some steps might have been taken to stop it.

No steps are taken to stop the drinking of the rich, chiefly because the rich now make all the rules and therefore all the exceptions, but partly because nobody ever could feel the full moral seriousness of this particular rule. And the truth is, as I have indicated, that it was originally established as an exception and not as a rule. The emancipated negro was an exception in the community, and a certain plan was, rightly or wrongly, adopted to meet his case. A law was made professedly for everybody and practically only for him. Prohibition is only important as marking the transition by which the trick, tried successfully on black labour, could be extended to all labour. We in England have no right to be Pharisaic at the expense of the Americans in this matter; for we have tried the same trick in a hundred forms. The true philosophical defence of the modern oppression of the poor would be to say frankly that we have ruled them so badly that they are unfit to rule themselves. But no modern oligarch is enough of a man to say this. For like all virile cynicism it would have an element of humility; which would not mix with the necessary element of hypocrisy. So we proceed, just as the Americans do, to make a law for everybody and then evade it for ourselves. We have not the honesty to say that the rich may bet because they can afford it; so we forbid any man to bet in any place; and then say that a place is not a place. It is exactly as if there were an American law allowing a negro to be murdered because he is not a man within the meaning of the Act. We have not the honesty to drive the poor to school because they are ignorant; so we pretend to drive everybody; and then send inspectors to the slums but not to the smart streets. We apply the same ingenuous principle; and are quite as undemocratic as Western democracy. Nevertheless there is an element in the American case which cannot be present in ours; and this chapter may well conclude upon so important a change.

America can now say with pride that she has abolished the colour bar. In this matter the white labourer and the black labourer have at last been put upon an equal social footing. White labour is every bit as much enslaved as black labour; and is actually enslaved by a method and a model only intended for black labour. We might think it rather odd if the exact regulations about flogging negroes were reproduced as a plan for punishing strikers; or if industrial arbitration issued its reports in the precise terminology of the Fugitive Slave Law. But this is in essentials what has happened; and one could almost fancy some negro orgy of triumph, with the beating of gongs and all the secret violence of Voodoo, crying aloud to some ancestral Mumbo Jumbo that the Poor White Trash was being treated according to its name.

FADS AND PUBLIC OPINION

A foreigner is a man who laughs at everything except jokes. He is perfectly entitled to laugh at anything, so long as he realises, in a reverent and religious spirit, that he himself is laughable. I was a foreigner in America; and I can truly claim that the sense of my own laughable position never left me. But when the native and the foreigner have finished with seeing the fun of each other in things that are meant to be serious, they both approach the far more delicate and dangerous ground of things that are meant to be funny. The sense of humour is generally very national; perhaps that is why the internationalists are so careful to purge themselves of it. I had occasion during the war to consider the rights and wrongs of certain differences alleged to have arisen between the English and American soldiers at the front. And, rightly or wrongly, I came to the conclusion that they arose from the failure to understand when a foreigner is serious and when he is humorous. And it is in the very nature of the best sort of joke to be the worst sort of insult if it is not taken as a joke.

The English and the American types of humour are in one way directly contrary. The most American sort of fun involves a soaring imagination, piling one house on another in a tower like that of a sky-scraper. The most English humour consists of a sort of bathos, of a man returning to the earth his mother in a homely fashion; as when he sits down suddenly on a butter-slide. English farce describes a man as being in a hole. American fantasy, in its more aspiring spirit, describes a man as being up a tree. The former is to be found in the cockney comic songs that concern themselves with hanging out the washing or coming home with the milk. The latter is to be found in those fantastic yarns about machines that turn live pigs into pig-skin purses or burning cities that serve to hatch an egg. But it will be inevitable, when the two come first into contact, that the bathos will sound like vulgarity and the extravagance will sound like boasting.

Suppose an American soldier said to an English soldier in the trenches, 'The Kaiser may want a place in the sun; I reckon he won't have a place in the solar system when we begin to hustle.' The English soldier will very probably form the impression that this is arrogance; an impression based on the extraordinary assumption that the American means what he says. The American has merely indulged in a little art for art's sake, and abstract adventure of the imagination; he has told an American short story. But the Englishman, not understanding this, will think the other man is boasting, and reflecting on the insufficiency of the English effort. The English soldier is very likely to say something like, 'Oh, you'll be wanting to get home to your old woman before that, and asking for a kipper with your tea.' And it is quite likely that the American will be offended in his turn at having his arabesque of abstract beauty answered in so personal a fashion. Being an American, he will probably have a fine and chivalrous respect for his wife; and may object to her being called an old woman. Possibly he in turn may be under the extraordinary delusion that talking of the old woman really means that the woman is old. Possibly he thinks the mysterious demand for a kipper carries with it some charge of ill-treating his wife; which his national sense of honour swiftly resents. But the real cross-purposes come from the contrary direction of the two exaggerations, the American making life more wild and impossible than it is, and the Englishman making it more flat and farcical than it is; the one escaping from the house of life by a skylight and the other by a trap-door.

This difficulty of different humours is a very practical one for practical people. Most of those who profess to remove all international differences are not practical people. Most of the phrases offered for the reconciliation of severally patriotic peoples are entirely serious and even solemn phrases. But human conversation is not conducted in those phrases. The normal man on nine occasions out of ten is rather a flippant man. And the normal man is almost always the national man. Patriotism is the most popular of all the virtues. The drier sort of democrats who despise it have the democracy against them in every country in the world. Hence their international efforts seldom go any farther than to effect an international reconciliation of all internationalists. But we have not solved the normal and popular problem until we have an international reconciliation of all nationalists.

It is very difficult to see how humour can be translated at all. When Sam Weller is in the Fleet Prison and Mrs. Weller and Mr. Stiggins sit on each side of the fireplace and weep and groan with sympathy, old Mr. Weller observes, 'Vell, Sammy, I hope you find your spirits rose by this 'ere lively visit.' I have never looked up this passage in the popular and successful French version of *Pickwick*; but I confess I am curious as to what French past-participle conveys the precise effect of the word 'rose.' A translator has not only to give the right translation of the right word but the right translation of the wrong word. And in the same way I am quite prepared to suspect that there are English jokes which an Englishman must enjoy in his own rich and romantic solitude, without asking for the sympathy of an American. But Englishmen are generally only too prone to claim this fine perception, without seeing that the fine edge of it cuts both ways. I have begun this chapter on the note of national humour because I wish to make it quite clear that I realise how easily a foreigner may take something seriously that is not serious. When I think something in America is really foolish, it may be I that am made a fool of. It is the first duty of a traveller to allow for this; but it seems to be the very last thing that occurs to some travellers. But when I seek to say something of what may be called the fantastic side of America, I allow beforehand that some of it may be meant to be fantastic. And indeed it is very difficult to believe that some of it is meant to be serious. But whether or no there is a joke, there is certainly an inconsistency; and it is an inconsistency in the moral make-up of America which both puzzles and amuses me.

The danger of democracy is not anarchy but convention. There is even a sort of double meaning in the word 'convention'; for it is also used for the most informal and popular sort of parliament; a parliament not summoned by any king. The Americans come together very easily without any king; but their coming together is in every sense a convention, and even a very conventional convention. In a democracy riot is rather the exception and respectability certainly the rule. And though a superficial sight-seer should hesitate about all such generalisations, and certainly should allow for enormous exceptions to them, he does receive a general impression of unity verging on uniformity. Thus Americans all dress well; one might almost say that American women all look well; but they do not, as compared with Europeans, look very different. They are in the fashion; too much in the fashion even to be conspicuously fashionable. Of course there are patches, both Bohemian and Babylonian, of which this is not true, but I am talking of the general tone of a whole democracy. I have said there is more respectability than riot; but indeed in a deeper sense the same spirit is behind both riot and respectability. It is the same social force that makes it possible for the respectable to boycott a man and for the riotous to lynch him. I do not object to it being called 'the herd instinct,' so long as we realise that it is a metaphor and not an explanation.

Public opinion can be a prairie fire. It eats up everything that opposes it; and there is the grandeur as well as the grave disadvantages of a natural catastrophe in that national unity. Pacifists who complained in England of the intolerance of patriotism have no notion of what patriotism can be like. If they had been in America, after America had entered the war, they would have seen something which they have always perhaps subconsciously dreaded, and would then have beyond all their worst dreams detested; and the name of it is democracy. They would have found that there are disadvantages in birds of a feather flocking together; and that one of them follows on a too complacent display of the white feather. The truth is that a certain flexible sympathy with eccentrics of this kind is rather one of the advantages of an aristocratic tradition. The imprisonment of Mr. Debs, the American Pacifist, which really was prolonged and oppressive, would probably have been shortened in England where his opinions were shared by aristocrats like Mr. Bertrand Russell and Mr. Ponsonby. A man like Lord Hugh Cecil could be moved to the defence of conscientious objectors, partly by a true instinct of chivalry; but partly also by the general feeling that a gentleman may very probably have aunts and uncles who are quite as mad. He takes the matter personally, in the sense of being able to imagine the psychology of the persons. But democracy is no respecter of persons. It is no respecter of them, either in the bad and servile or in the good and sympathetic sense. And Debs was nothing to democracy. He was but one of the millions. This is a real problem, or question in the balance, touching different forms of government; which is, of course, quite neglected by the idealists who merely repeat long words. There was during the war a society called the Union of Democratic Control, which would have been instantly destroyed anywhere where democracy had any control, or where there was any union. And in this sense the United States have most emphatically got a union. Nevertheless I think there is something rather more subtle than this simple popular solidity behind the assimilation of American citizens to each other. There is something even in the individual ideals that drives towards this social sympathy. And it is here that we have to remember that biological fancies like the herd instinct are only figures of speech, and cannot really cover anything human. For the Americans are in some ways a very self-conscious people. To compare their social enthusiasm to a stampede of cattle is to ask us to believe in a bull writing a diary or a cow looking in a looking-glass. Intensely sensitive by their very vitality, they are certainly conscious of criticism and not merely of a blind and brutal appetite. But the peculiar point about them is that it is this very vividness in the self that often produces the similarity. It may be that when they are unconscious they are like bulls and cows. But it is when they are self-conscious that they are like each other.

Individualism is the death of individuality. It is so, if only because it is an 'ism.' Many Americans become almost impersonal in their worship of personality. Where their natural selves might differ, their ideal selves tend to be the same. Anybody can see what I mean in those strong self-conscious photographs of American business men that can be seen in any American magazine. Each may conceive himself to be a solitary Napoleon brooding at St. Helena; but the result is a multitude of Napoleons brooding all over the place. Each of them must have the eyes of a mesmerist; but the most weak-minded person cannot be mesmerised by more than one millionaire at a time. Each of the millionaires must thrust forward his jaw, offering (if I may say so) to fight the world with the same weapon as Samson. Each of them must accentuate the length of his chin, especially, of course, by always being completely clean-shaven. It would be obviously inconsistent with Personality to prefer to wear a beard. These are of course fantastic examples on the fringe of American life; but they do stand for a certain assimilation, not through brute gregariousness, but rather through isolated dreaming. And though it is not always carried so far as this, I do think it is carried too far. There is not quite enough unconsciousness to produce real individuality. There is a sort of worship of will-power in the abstract, so that people are actually thinking about how they can will, more than about what they want. To this I do think a certain corrective could be found in the nature of English eccentricity. Every man in his humour is most interesting when he is unconscious of his humour; or at least when he is in an intermediate stage between humour in the old sense of oddity and in the new sense of irony. Much is said in these days against negative morality; and certainly most Americans would show a positive preference for positive morality. The virtues they venerate collectively are very active virtues; cheerfulness and courage and vim, otherwise zip, also pep and similar things. But it is sometimes forgotten that negative morality is freer than positive morality. Negative morality is a net of a larger and more open pattern, of which the lines or cords constrict at longer intervals. A man like Dr. Johnson could grow in his own way to his own stature in the net of the Ten Commandments; precisely because he was convinced there were only ten of them. He was not compressed into the mould of positive beauty, like that of the Apollo Belvedere or the American citizen.

This criticism is sometimes true even of the American woman, who is certainly a much more delightful person than the mesmeric millionaire with his shaven jaw. Interviewers in the United States perpetually asked me what I thought of American women, and I confessed a distaste for such generalisations which I have not managed to lose. The Americans, who are the most chivalrous people in the world, may perhaps understand me; but I can never help feeling that there is something polygamous about talking of women in the plural at all; something unworthy of any American except a Mormon. Nevertheless, I think the exaggeration I suggest does extend in a less degree to American women, fascinating as they are. I think they too tend too much to this cult of impersonal personality. It is a description easy to exaggerate even by the faintest emphasis; for all these things are subtle and subject to striking individual exceptions. To complain of people for being brave and bright and kind and intelligent may not unreasonably appear unreasonable. And yet there is something in the background that can only be expressed by a symbol, something that is not shallowness but a neglect of the subconsciousness and the vaguer and slower impulses; something that can be missed amid all that laughter and light, under those starry candelabra of the ideals of the happy virtues. Sometimes it came over me, in a wordless wave, that I should like to see a sulky woman. How she would walk in beauty like the night, and reveal more silent spaces full of older stars! These things cannot be conveyed in their delicate proportion even in the most detached description. But the same thing was in the mind of a white-bearded old man I met in New York, an Irish exile and a wonderful talker, who stared up at the tower of gilded galleries of the great hotel, and said with that spontaneous movement of style which is hardly heard except from Irish talkers: 'And I have been in a village in the mountains where the people could hardly read or write; but all the men were like soldiers, and all the women had pride.'

It sounds like a poem about an Earthly Paradise to say that in this land the old women can be more beautiful than the young. Indeed, I think Walt Whitman, the national poet, has a line somewhere almost precisely to that effect. It sounds like a parody upon Utopia, and the image of the lion lying down with the lamb, to say it is a place where a man might almost fall in love with his mother-in-law. But there is nothing in which the finer side of American gravity and good feeling does more honourably exhibit itself than in a certain atmosphere around the older women. It is not a cant phrase to say that they grow old gracefully; for they do really grow old. In this the national optimism really has in it the national courage. The old women do not dress like young women; they only dress better. There is another side to this feminine dignity in the old, sometimes a little lost in the young, with which I shall deal presently. The point for the moment is that even Whitman's truly poetic vision of the beautiful old women suffers a little from that bewildering multiplicity and recurrence that is indeed the whole theme of Whitman. It is like the green eternity of Leaves of Grass. When I think of the eccentric spinsters and incorrigible grandmothers of my own country, I cannot imagine that any one of them could possibly be mistaken for another, even at a glance. And in comparison I feel as if I had been travelling in an Earthly Paradise of more decorative harmonies; and I remember only a vast cloud of grey and pink as of the plumage of cherubim in an old picture. But on second thoughts, I think this may be only the inevitable effect of visiting any country in a swift and superficial fashion; and that the grey and pink cloud is probably an illusion, like the spinning prairies scattered by the wheel of the train.

Anyhow there is enough of this equality, and of a certain social unity favourable to sanity, to make the next point about America very much of a puzzle. It seems to me a very real problem, to which I have never seen an answer even such as I shall attempt here, why a democracy should produce fads; and why, where there is so genuine a sense of human dignity, there should be so much of an impossible petty tyranny. I am not referring solely or even specially to Prohibition, which I discuss elsewhere. Prohibition is at least a superstition, and therefore next door to a religion; it has some imaginable connection with moral questions, as have slavery or human sacrifice. But those who ask us to model ourselves on the States which punish the sin of drink forget that there are States which punish the equally shameless sin of smoking a cigarette in the open air. The same American atmosphere that permits Prohibition permits of people being punished for kissing each other. In other words, there are States psychologically capable of making a man a convict for wearing a blue neck-tie or having a green front-door, or anything else that anybody chooses to fancy. There is an American atmosphere in which people may some day be shot for shaking hands, or hanged for writing a post-card.

As for the sort of thing to which I refer, the American newspapers are full of it and there is no name for it but mere madness. Indeed it is not only mad, but it calls itself mad. To mention but one example out of many, it was actually boasted that some lunatics were teaching children to take care of their health. And it was proudly added that the children were 'health-mad.' That it is not exactly the object of all mental hygiene to make people mad did not occur to them; and they may still be engaged in their earnest labours to teach babies to be valetudinarians and hypochondriacs in order to make them healthy. In such cases, we may say that the modern world is too ridiculous to be ridiculed. You cannot caricature a caricature. Imagine what a satirist of saner days would have made of the daily life of a child of six, who was actually admitted to be mad on the subject of his own health. These are not days in which that great extravaganza could be written; but I dimly see some of its episodes like uncompleted dreams. I see the child pausing in the middle of a cart-wheel, or when he has performed three-quarters of a cart-wheel, and consulting a little note-book about the amount of exercise per diem. I see him pausing half-way up a tree, or when he has climbed exactly one-third of a tree; and then producing a clinical thermometer to take his own temperature. But what would be the good of imaginative logic to prove the madness of such people, when they themselves praise it for being mad?

There is also the cult of the Infant Phenomenon, of which Dickens made fun and of which educationalists make fusses. When I was in America another newspaper produced a marvellous child of six who had the intellect of a child of twelve. The only test given, and apparently one on which the experiment turned, was that she could be made to understand and even to employ the word 'annihilate.' When asked to say something proving this, the happy infant offered the polished aphorism, 'When common sense comes in, superstition is annihilated.' In reply to which, by way of showing that I also am as intelligent as a child of twelve, and there is no arrested development about me, I will say in the same elegant diction, 'When psychological education comes in, common sense is annihilated.' Everybody seems to be sitting round this child in an adoring fashion. It did not seem to occur to anybody that we do not particularly want even a child of twelve to talk about annihilating superstition; that we do not want a child of six to talk like a child of twelve, or a child of twelve to talk like a man of fifty, or even a man of fifty to talk like a fool. And on the principle of hoping that a little girl of six will have a massive and mature brain, there is every reason for hoping that a little boy of six will grow a magnificent and bushy beard.

Now there is any amount of this nonsense cropping up among American cranks. Anybody may propose to establish coercive Eugenics; or enforce psychoanalysis—that is, enforce confession without absolution. And I confess I cannot connect this feature with the genuine democratic spirit of the mass. I can only suggest, in concluding this chapter, two possible causes rather peculiar to America, which may have made this great democracy so unlike all other democracies, and in this so manifestly hostile to the whole democratic idea.

The first historical cause is Puritanism; but not Puritanism merely in the sense of Prohibitionism. The truth is that prohibitions might have done far less harm as prohibitions, if a vague association had not arisen, on some dark day of human unreason, between prohibition and progress. And it was the progress that did the harm, not the prohibition. Men can enjoy life under considerable limitations, if they can be sure of their limited enjoyments; but under Progressive Puritanism we can never be sure of anything. The curse of it is not limitation; it is unlimited limitation. The evil is not in the restriction; but in the fact that nothing can ever restrict the restriction. The prohibitions are bound to progress point by point; more and more human rights and pleasures must of necessity be taken away; for it is of the nature of this futurism that the latest fad is the faith of the future, and the most fantastic fad inevitably makes the pace. Thus the worst thing in the seventeenth-century aberration was not so much Puritanism as sectarianism. It searched for truth not by synthesis but by subdivision. It not only broke religion into small pieces, but it was bound to choose the smallest piece. There is in America, I believe, a large religious body that has felt it right to separate itself from Christendom because it cannot believe in the morality of wearing buttons. I do not know how the schism arose; but it is easy to suppose, for the sake of argument, that there had originally existed some Puritan body which condemned the frivolity of ribbons though not of buttons. I was going to say of badges but not buttons; but on reflection I cannot bring myself to believe that any American, however insane, would object to wearing badges. But the point is that as the holy spirit of progressive prophesy rested on the first sect because it had invented a new objection to ribbons, so that holy spirit would then pass from it to the new sect who invented a further objection to buttons. And from them it must inevitably pass to any rebel among them who shall choose to rise and say that he disapproves of trousers because of the existence of trouser-buttons. Each secession in turn must be right because it is recent, and progress must progress by growing smaller and smaller. That is the progressive theory, the legacy of seventeenth-century sectarianism, the dogma implied in much modern politics, and the evident enemy of democracy. Democracy is reproached with saying that the majority is always right. But progress says that the minority is always right. Progressives are prophets; and fortunately not all the people are prophets. Thus in the atmosphere of this slowly dying sectarianism anybody who chooses to prophesy and prohibit can tyrannise over the people. If he chooses to say that drinking is always wrong, or that kissing is always wrong, or that wearing buttons is always wrong, people are afraid to contradict him for fear they should be contradicting their own great-grandchild. For their superstition is an inversion of the ancestor-worship of China; and instead of vainly appealing to something that is dead, they appeal to something that may never be born.

There is another cause of this strange servile disease in American democracy. It is to be found in American feminism, and feminist America is an entirely different thing from feminine America. I should say that the overwhelming majority of American girls laugh at their female politicians at least as much as the majority of American men despise their male politicians. But though the aggressive feminists are a minority, they are in this atmosphere which I have tried to analyse; the atmosphere in which there is a sort of sanctity about the minority. And it is this superstition of seriousness that constitutes the most solid obstacle and exception to the general and almost conventional pressure of public opinion. When a fad is frankly felt to be anti-national, as was Abolitionism before the Civil War, or Pro-Germanism in the Great War, or the suggestion of racial admixture in the South at all times, then the fad meets far less mercy than anywhere else in the world; it is snowed under and swept away. But when it does not thus directly challenge patriotism or popular ideas, a curious halo of hopeful solemnity surrounds it, merely because it is a fad, but above all if it is a feminine fad. The earnest lady-reformer who really utters a warning against the social evil of beer or buttons is seen to be walking clothed in light, like a prophetess. Perhaps it is something of the holy aureole which the East sees shining around an idiot.

But I think there is another explanation, feminine rather than feminist, and proceeding from normal women and not from abnormal idiots. It is something that involves an old controversy, but one upon which I have not, like so many politicians, changed my opinion. It concerns the particular fashion in which women tend to regard, or rather to disregard, the formal and legal rights of the citizen. In so far as this is a bias, it is a bias in the directly opposite direction from that now lightly alleged. There is a sort of underbred history going about, according to which women in the past have always been in the position of slaves. It is much more to the point to note that women have always been in the position of despots. They have been despotic because they ruled in an area where they had too much common sense to attempt to be constitutional. You cannot grant a constitution to a nursery; nor can babies assemble like barons and extort a Great Charter. Tommy cannot plead a Habeas Corpus against going to bed; and an infant cannot be tried by twelve other infants before he is put in the corner. And as there can be no laws or liberties in a nursery, the extension of feminism means that there shall be no more laws or liberties in a state than there are in a nursery. The woman does not really regard men as citizens but as children. She may, if she is a humanitarian, love all mankind; but she does not respect it. Still less does she respect its votes. Now a man must be very blind nowadays not to see that there is a danger of a sort of amateur science or pseudo-science being made the excuse for every trick of tyranny and interference. Anybody who is not an anarchist agrees with having a policeman at the corner of the street; but the danger at present is that of finding the policeman half-way down the chimney or even under the bed. In other words, it is a danger of turning the policeman into a sort of benevolent burglar. Against this protests are already being made, and will increasingly be made, if men retain any instinct of independence or dignity at all. But to complain of the woman interfering in the home will always sound like complaining of the oyster intruding into the oyster-shell. To object that she has too much power over education will seem like objecting to a hen having too much to do with eggs. She has already been given an almost irresponsible power over a limited region in these things; and if that power is made infinite it will be even more irresponsible. If she adds to her own power in the family all these alien fads external to the family, her power will not only be irresponsible but insane. She will be something which may well be called a nightmare of the nursery; a mad mother. But the point is that she will be mad about other nurseries as well as her own, or possibly instead of her own. The results will be interesting; but at least it is certain that under this softening influence government of the people, by the people, for the people, will most assuredly perish from the earth.

But there is always another possibility. Hints of it may be noted here and there like muffled gongs of doom. The other day some people preaching some low trick or other, for running away from the glory of motherhood, were suddenly silenced in New York; by a voice of deep and democratic volume. The prigs who potter about the great plains are pygmies dancing round a sleeping giant. That which sleeps, so far as they are concerned, is the huge power of human unanimity and intolerance in the soul of America. At present the masses in the Middle West are indifferent to such fancies or faintly attracted by them, as fashions of culture from the great cities. But any day it may not be so; some lunatic may cut across their economic rights or their strange and buried religion; and then he will see something. He will find himself running like a nigger who has wronged a white woman or a man who has set the prairie on fire. He will see something which the politicians fan in its sleep and flatter with the name of the people, which many reactionaries have cursed with the name of the mob, but which in any case has had under its feet the crowns of many kings. It was said that the voice of the people is the voice of God; and this at least is certain, that it can be the voice of God to the wicked. And the last antics of their arrogance shall stiffen before something enormous, such as towers in the last words that Job heard out of the whirlwind; and a voice they never knew shall tell them that his name is Leviathan, and he is lord over all the children of pride.

THE EXTRAORDINARY AMERICAN

When I was in America I had the feeling that it was far more foreign than France or even than Ireland. And by foreign I mean fascinating rather than repulsive. I mean that element of strangeness which marks the frontier of any fairyland, or gives to the traveller himself the almost eerie title of the stranger. And I saw there more clearly than in countries counted as more remote from us, in race or religion, a paradox that is one of the great truths of travel.

We have never even begun to understand a people until we have found something that we do not understand. So long as we find the character easy to read, we are reading into it our own character. If when we see an event we can promptly provide an explanation, we may be pretty certain that we had ourselves prepared the explanation before we saw the event. It follows from this that the best picture of a foreign people can probably be found in a puzzle picture. If we can find an event of which the meaning is really dark to us, it will probably throw some light on the truth. I will therefore take from my American experiences one isolated incident, which certainly could not have happened in any other country I have ever clapped eyes on. I have really no notion of what it meant. I have heard even from Americans about five different conjectures about its meaning. But though I do not understand it, I do sincerely believe that if I did understand it, I should understand America.

It happened in the city of Oklahoma, which would require a book to itself, even considered as a background. The State of Oklahoma is a district in the south-west recently reclaimed from the Red Indian territory. What many, quite incorrectly, imagine about all America is really true of Oklahoma. It is proud of having no history. It is glowing with the sense of having a great future—and nothing else. People are just as likely to boast of an old building in Nashville as in Norwich; people are just as proud of old families in Boston as in Bath. But in Oklahoma the citizens do point out a colossal structure, arrogantly affirming that it wasn't there last week. It was against the colours of this crude stage scenery, as of a pantomime city of pasteboard, that the fantastic figure appeared which still haunts me like a walking note of interrogation. I was strolling down the main street of the city, and looking in at a paper-stall vivid with the news of crime, when a stranger addressed me; and asked me, quite politely but with a curious air of having authority to put the question, what I was doing in that city.

He was a lean brown man, having rather the look of a shabby tropical traveller, with a grey moustache and a lively and alert eye. But the most singular thing about him was that the front of his coat was covered with a multitude of shining metallic emblems made in the shape of stars and crescents. I was well accustomed by this time to Americans adorning the lapels of their coats with little symbols of various societies; it is a part of the American passion for the ritual of comradeship. There is nothing that an American likes so much as to have a secret society and to make no secret of it. But in this case, if I may put it so, the rash of symbolism seemed to have broken out all over the man, in a fashion that indicated that the fever was far advanced. Of this minor mystery, however, his first few sentences offered a provisional explanation. In answer to his question, touching my business in Oklahoma, I replied with restraint that I was lecturing. To which he replied without restraint, but rather with an expansive and radiant pride, 'I also am lecturing. I am lecturing on astronomy.'

So far a certain wild rationality seemed to light up the affair. I knew it was unusual, in my own country, for the Astronomer Royal to walk down the Strand with his coat plastered all over with the Solar System. Indeed, it was unusual for any English astronomical lecturer to advertise the subject of his lectures in this fashion. But though it would be unusual, it would not necessarily be unreasonable. In fact, I think it might add to the colour and variety of life, if specialists did adopt this sort of scientific heraldry. I should like to be able to recognise an entomologist at sight by the decorative spiders and cockroaches crawling all over his coat and waistcoat. I should like to see a conchologist in a simple costume of shells. An osteopath, I suppose, would be agreeably painted so as to resemble a skeleton, while a botanist would enliven the street with the appearance of a Jack-in-the-Green. So while I regarded the astronomical lecturer in the astronomical coat as a figure distinguishable, by a high degree of differentiation, from the artless astronomers of my island home (enough their simple loveliness for me) I saw in him nothing illogical, but rather an imaginative extreme of logic. And then came another turn of the wheel of topsy-turvydom, and all the logic was scattered to the wind.

Expanding his starry bosom and standing astraddle, with the air of one who owned the street, the strange being continued, 'Yes, I am lecturing on astronomy, anthropology, archaeology, palaeontology, embryology, eschatology,' and so on in a thunderous roll of theoretical sciences apparently beyond the scope of any single university, let alone any single professor. Having thus introduced himself, however, he got to business. He apologised with true American courtesy for having questioned me at all, and excused it on the ground of his own exacting responsibilities. I imagined him to mean the responsibility of simultaneously occupying the chairs of all the faculties already mentioned. But these apparently were trifles to him, and something far more serious was clouding his brow.

'I feel it to be my duty,' he said, 'to acquaint myself with any stranger visiting this city; and it is an additional pleasure to welcome here a member of the Upper Ten.' I assured him earnestly that I knew nothing about the Upper Ten, except that I did not belong to them; I felt, not without alarm, that the Upper Ten might be another secret society. He waved my abnegation aside and continued, 'I have a great responsibility in watching over this city. My friend the mayor and I have a great responsibility.' And then an extraordinary thing happened. Suddenly diving his hand into his breast-pocket, he flashed something before my eyes like a hand-mirror; something which disappeared again almost as soon as it appeared. In that flash I could only see that it was some sort of polished metal plate, with some letters engraved on it like a monogram. But the reward of a studious and virtuous life, which has been spent chiefly in the reading of American detective stories, shone forth for me in that hour of trial; I received at last the prize of a profound scholarship in the matter of imaginary murders in tenth-rate magazines. I remembered who it was who in the Yankee detective yarn flashes before the eyes of Slim Jim or the Lone Hand Crook a badge of metal sometimes called a shield. Assuming all the desperate composure of Slim Jim himself, I replied, 'You mean you are connected with the police authorities here, don't you? Well, if I commit a murder here, I'll let you know.' Whereupon that astonishing man waved a hand in deprecation, bowed in farewell with the grace of a dancing master; and said, 'Oh, those are not things we expect from members of the Upper Ten.'

Then that moving constellation moved away, disappearing in the dark tides of humanity, as the vision passed away down the dark tides from Sir Galahad and, starlike, mingled with the stars.

That is the problem I would put to all Americans, and to all who claim to understand America. Who and what was that man? Was he an astronomer? Was he a detective? Was he a wandering lunatic? If he was a lunatic who thought he was an astronomer, why did he have a badge to prove he was a detective? If he was a detective pretending to be an astronomer, why did he tell a total stranger that he was a detective two minutes after saying he was an astronomer? If he wished to watch over the city in a quiet and unobtrusive fashion, why did he blazon himself all over with all the stars of the sky, and profess to give public lectures on all the subjects of the world? Every wise and well-conducted student of murder stories is acquainted with the notion of a policeman in plain clothes. But nobody could possibly say that this gentleman was in plain clothes. Why not wear his uniform, if he was resolved to show every stranger in the street his badge? Perhaps after all he had no uniform; for these lands were but recently a wild frontier rudely ruled by vigilance committees. Some Americans suggested to me that he was the Sheriff; the regular hard-riding, free-shooting Sheriff of Bret Harte and my boyhood's dreams. Others suggested that he was an agent of the Ku-Klux Klan, that great nameless revolution of the revival of which there were rumours at the time; and that the symbol he exhibited was theirs. But whether he was a sheriff acting for the law, or a conspirator against the law, or a lunatic entirely outside the law, I agree with the former conjectures upon one point. I am perfectly certain he had something else in his pocket besides a badge. And I am perfectly certain that under certain circumstances he would have handled it instantly, and shot me dead between the gay bookstall and the crowded trams. And that is the last touch to the complexity; for though in that country it often seems that the law is made by a lunatic, you never know when the lunatic may not shoot you for keeping it. Only in the presence of that citizen of Oklahoma I feel I am confronted with the fullness and depth of the mystery of America. Because I understand nothing, I recognise the thing that we call a nation; and I salute the flag.

But even in connection with this mysterious figure there is a moral which affords another reason for mentioning him. Whether he was a sheriff or an outlaw, there was certainly something about him that suggested the adventurous violence of the old border life of America; and whether he was connected with the police or no, there was certainly violence enough in his environment to satisfy the most ardent policeman. The posters in the paper-shop were placarded with the verdict in the Hamon trial; a *cause célèbre* which reached its crisis in Oklahoma while I was there. Senator Hamon had been shot by a girl whom he had wronged, and his widow demanded justice, or what might fairly be called vengeance. There was very great excitement culminating in the girl's acquittal. Nor did the Hamon case appear to be entirely exceptional in that breezy borderland. The moment the town had received the news that Clara Smith was free, newsboys rushed down the street shouting, 'Double stabbing outrage near Oklahoma,' or 'Banker's throat cut on Main Street,' or otherwise resuming their regular mode of life. It seemed as much as to say, 'Do not imagine that our local energies are exhausted in shooting a Senator,' or 'Come, now, the world is young, even if Clara Smith is acquitted, and the enthusiasm of Oklahoma is not yet cold.'

But my particular reason for mentioning the matter is this. Despite my friend's mystical remarks about the Upper Ten, he lived in an atmosphere of something that was at least the very reverse of a respect for persons. Indeed, there was something in the very crudity of his social compliment that smacked, strangely enough, of that egalitarian soil. In a vaguely aristocratic country like England, people would never dream of telling a total stranger that he was a member of the Upper Ten. For one thing, they would be afraid that he might be. Real snobbishness is never vulgar; for it is intended to please the refined. Nobody licks the boots of a duke, if only because the duke does not like his boots cleaned in that way. Nobody embraces the knees of a marquis, because it would embarrass that nobleman. And nobody tells him he is a member of the Upper Ten, because everybody is expected to know it. But there is a much more subtle kind of snobbishness pervading the atmosphere of any society trial in England. And the first thing that struck me was the total absence of that atmosphere in the trial at Oklahoma. Mr. Hamon was presumably a member of the Upper Ten, if there is such a thing. He was a member of the Senate or Upper House in the American Parliament; he was a millionaire and a pillar of the Republican party, which might be called the respectable party; he is said to have been mentioned as a possible President. And the speeches of Clara Smith's counsel, who was known by the delightfully Oklahomite title of Wild Bill McLean, were wild enough in all conscience; but they left very little of my friend's illusion that members of the Upper Ten could not be accused of crimes. Nero and Borgia were quite presentable people compared with Senator Hamon when Wild Bill McLean had done with him. But the difference was deeper, and even in a sense more delicate than this. There is a certain tone about English trials, which does at least begin with a certain scepticism about people prominent in public life being abominable in private life. People do vaguely doubt the criminality of 'a man in that position'; that is, the position of the Marquise de Brinvilliers or the Marquis de Sade. *Prima facie*, it would be an advantage to the Marquis de Sade that he was a marquis. But it was certainly against Hamon that he was a millionaire. Wild Bill did not minimise him as a bankrupt or an adventurer; he insisted on the solidity and size of his fortune, he made mountains out of the 'Hamon millions,' as if they made the matter much worse; as indeed I think they do. But that is because I happen to share a certain political philosophy with Wild Bill and other wild buffaloes of the prairies. In other words, there is really present here a democratic instinct against the domination of wealth. It does not prevent wealth from dominating; but it does prevent the domination from being regarded with any affection or loyalty. Despite the man in the starry coat, the Americans have not really any illusions about the Upper Ten. McLean was appealing to an implicit public opinion when he pelted the Senator with his gold.

But something more is involved. I became conscious, as I have been conscious in reading the crime novels of America, that the millionaire was taken as a type and not an individual. This is the great difference; that America recognises rich crooks as a *class*. Any Englishman might recognise them as individuals. Any English romance may turn on a crime in high life; in which the baronet is found to have poisoned his wife, or the elusive burglar turns out to be the bishop. But the English are not always saying, either in romance or reality, 'What's to be done, if our food is being poisoned by all these baronets?' They do not murmur in indignation, 'If bishops will go on burgling like this, something must be done.' The whole point of the English romance is the exceptional character of a crime in high life. That is not the tone of American novels or American newspapers or American trials like the trial in Oklahoma. Americans may be excited when a millionaire crook is caught, as when any other crook is caught; but it is at his being caught, not at his being discovered. To put the matter shortly, England recognises a criminal class at the bottom of the social scale. America also recognises a criminal class at the top of the social scale. In both, for various reasons, it may be difficult for the criminals to be convicted; but in America the upper class of criminals is recognised. In both America and England, of course, it exists.

This is an assumption at the back of the American mind which makes a great difference in many ways; and in my opinion a difference for the better. I wrote merely fancifully just now about bishops being burglars; but there is a story in New York, illustrating this, which really does in a sense attribute a burglary to a bishop. The story was that an Anglican Lord Spiritual, of the pompous and now rather antiquated school, was pushing open the door of a poor American tenement with all the placid patronage of the squire and rector visiting the cottagers, when a gigantic Irish policeman came round the corner and hit him a crack over the head with a truncheon on the assumption that he was a house-breaker. I hope that those who laugh at the story see that the laugh is not altogether against the policeman; and that it is not only the policeman, but rather the bishop, who had failed to recognise some fine logical distinctions. The bishop, being a learned man, might well be called upon (when he had sufficiently recovered from the knock on the head) to define what is the exact difference between a house-breaker and a home-visitor; and why the home-visitor should not be regarded as a house-breaker when he will not behave as a guest. An impartial intelligence will be much less shocked at the policeman's disrespect for the home-visitor than by the home-visitor's disrespect for the home.

But that story smacks of the western soil, precisely because of the element of brutality there is in it. In England snobbishness and social oppression are much subtler and softer; the manifestations of them at least are more mellow and humane. In comparison there is indeed something which people call ruthless about the air of America, especially the American cities. The bishop may push open the door without an apology, but he would not break open the door with a truncheon; but the Irish policeman's truncheon hits both ways. It may be brutal to the tenement dweller as well as to the bishop; but the difference and distinction is that it might really be brutal to the bishop. It is because there is after all, at the back of all that barbarism, a sort of negative belief in the brotherhood of men, a dark democratic sense that men are really men and nothing more, that the coarse and even corrupt bureaucracy is not resented exactly as oligarchic bureaucracies are resented. There is a sense in which corruption is not so narrow as nepotism. It is upon this queer cynical charity, and even humility, that it has been possible to rear so high and uphold so long that tower of brass, Tammany Hall. The modern police system is in spirit the most inhuman in history, and its evil belongs to an age and not to a nation. But some American police methods are evil past all parallel; and the detective can be more crooked than a hundred crooks. But in the States it is not only possible that the policeman is worse than the convict, it is by no means certain that he thinks that he is any better. In the popular stories of O. Henry there are light allusions to tramps being kicked out of hotels which will make any Christian seek relief in strong language and a trust in heaven—not to say in hell. And yet books even more popular than O. Henry's are those of the 'sob-sisterhood' who swim in lachrymose lakes after love-lorn spinsters, who pass their lives in reclaiming and consoling such tramps. There are in this people two strains of brutality and sentimentalism which I do not understand, especially where they mingle; but I am fairly sure they both work back to the dim democratic origin. The Irish policeman does not confine himself fastidiously to bludgeoning bishops; his truncheon finds plenty of poor people's heads to hit; and yet I believe on my soul he has a sort of sympathy with poor people not to be found in the police of more aristocratic states. I believe he also reads and weeps over the stories of the spinsters and the reclaimed tramps; in fact, there is much of such pathos in an American magazine (my sole companion on many happy railway journeys) which is not only devoted to detective stories, but apparently edited by detectives. In these stories also there is the honest, popular astonishment at the Upper Ten expressed by the astronomical detective, if indeed he was a detective and not a demon from the dark Red-Indian forests that faded to the horizon behind him. But I have set him as the head and text of this chapter because with these elements of the Third Degree of devilry and the Seventh Heaven of sentimentalism I touch on elements that I do not understand; and when I do not understand, I say so.

THE REPUBLICAN IN THE RUINS

The heathen in his blindness bows down to wood and stone; especially to a wood-cut or a lithographic stone. Modern people put their trust in pictures, especially scientific pictures, as much as the most superstitious ever put it in religious pictures. They publish a portrait of the Missing Link as if he were the Missing Man, for whom the police are always advertising; for all the world as if the anthropoid had been photographed before he absconded. The scientific diagram may be a hypothesis; it may be a fancy; it may be a forgery. But it is always an idol in the true sense of an image; and an image in the true sense of a thing mastering the imagination and not the reason. The power of these talismanic pictures is almost hypnotic to modern humanity. We can never forget that we have seen a portrait of the Missing Link; though we should instantly detect the lapse of logic into superstition, if we were told that the old Greek agnostics had made a statue of the Unknown God. But there is a still stranger fashion in which we fall victims to the same trick of fancy. We accept in a blind and literal spirit, not only images of speculation, but even figures of speech. The nineteenth century prided itself on having lost its faith in myths, and proceeded to put all its faith in metaphors. It dismissed the old doctrines about the way of life and the light of the world; and then it proceeded to talk as if the light of truth were really and literally a light, that could be absorbed by merely opening our eyes; or as if the path of progress were really and truly a path, to be found by merely following our noses. Thus the purpose of God is an idea, true or false; but the purpose of Nature is merely a metaphor; for obviously if there is no God there is no purpose. Yet while men, by an imaginative instinct, spoke of the purpose of God with a grand agnosticism, as something too large to be seen, something reaching out to worlds and to eternities, they speak of the purpose of Nature in particular and practical problems of curing babies or cutting up rabbits. This power of the modern metaphor must be understood, by way of an introduction, if we are to understand one of the chief errors, at once evasive and pervasive, which perplex the problem of America.

America is always spoken of as a young nation; and whether or no this be a valuable and suggestive metaphor, very few people notice that it is a metaphor at all. If somebody said that a certain deserving charity had just gone into trousers, we should recognise that it was a figure of speech, and perhaps a rather surprising figure of speech. If somebody said that a daily paper had recently put its hair up, we should know it could only be a metaphor, and possibly a rather strained metaphor. Yet these phrases would mean the only thing that can possibly be meant by calling a corporate association of all sorts of people 'young'; that is, that a certain institution has only existed for a certain time. I am not now denying that such a corporate nationality may happen to have a psychology comparatively analogous to the psychology of youth. I am not even denying that America has it. I am only pointing out, to begin with, that we must free ourselves from the talismanic tyranny of a metaphor which we do not recognise as a metaphor. Men realised that the old mystical doctrines were mystical; they do not realise that the new metaphors are metaphorical. They have some sort of hazy notion that American society must be growing, must be promising, must have the virtues of hope or the faults of ignorance, merely *because* it has only had a separate existence since the eighteenth century. And that is exactly like saying that a new chapel must be growing taller, or that a limited liability company will soon have its second teeth.

Now in truth this particular conception of American hopefulness would be anything but hopeful for America. If the argument really were, as it is still vaguely supposed to be, that America must have a long life before it, because it only started in the eighteenth century, we should find a very fatal answer by looking at the other political systems that did start in the eighteenth century. The eighteenth century was called the Age of Reason; and there is a very real sense in which the other systems were indeed started in a spirit of reason. But starting from reason has not saved them from ruin. If we survey the Europe of to-day with real clarity and historic comprehension, we shall see that it is precisely the most recent and the most rationalistic creations that have been ruined. The two great States which did most definitely and emphatically deserve to be called modern states were Prussia and Russia. There was no real Prussia before Frederick the Great; no real Russian Empire before Peter the Great. Both those innovators recognised themselves as rationalists bringing a new reason and order into an indeterminate barbarism; and doing for the barbarians what the barbarians could not do for themselves. They did not, like the kings of England or France or Spain or Scotland, inherit a sceptre that was the symbol of a historic and patriotic people. In this sense there was no Russia but only an Emperor of Russia. In this sense Prussia was a kingdom before it was a nation; if it ever was a nation. But anyhow both men were particularly modern in their whole mood and mind. They were modern to the extent of being not only anti-traditional, but almost anti-patriotic. Peter forced the science of the West on Russia to the regret of many Russians. Frederick talked the French of Voltaire and not the German of Luther. The two experiments were entirely in the spirit of Voltairean rationalism; they were built in broad daylight by men who believed in nothing but the light of common day; and already their day is done.

If then the promise of America were in the fact that she is one of the latest births of progress, we should point out that it is exactly the latest born that were the first to die. If in this sense she is praised as young, it may be answered that the young have died young, and have not lived to be old. And if this be confused with the argument that she came in an age of clarity and scepticism, uncontaminated by old superstitions, it could still be retorted that the works of superstition have survived the works of scepticism. But the truth is, of course, that the real quality of America is much more subtle and complex than this; and is mixed not only of good and bad, and rational and mystical, but also of old and new. That is what makes the task of tracing the true proportions of American life so interesting and so impossible.

To begin with, such a metaphor is always as distracting as a mixed metaphor. It is a double-edged tool that cuts both ways; and consequently opposite ways. We use the same word 'young' to mean two opposite extremes. We mean something at an early stage of growth, and also something having the latest fruits of growth. We might call a commonwealth young if it conducted all its daily conversation by wireless telegraphy; meaning that it was progressive. But we might also call it young if it conducted all its industry with chipped flints; meaning that it was primitive. These two meanings of youth are hopelessly mixed up when the word is applied to America. But what is more curious, the two elements really are wildly entangled in America. America is in some ways what is called in advance of the times, and in some ways what is called behind the times; but it seems a little confusing to convey both notions by the same word.

On the one hand, Americans often are successful in the last inventions. And for that very reason they are often neglectful of the last but one. It is true of men in general, dealing with things in general, that while they are progressing in one thing, such as science, they are going back in another thing, such as art. What is less fully realised is that this is true even as between different methods of science. The perfection of wireless telegraphy might well be followed by the gross imperfection of wires. The very enthusiasm of American science brings this out very vividly. The telephone in New York works miracles all day long. Replies from remote places come as promptly as in a private talk; nobody cuts anybody off; nobody says, 'Sorry you've been troubled.' But then the postal service of New York does not work at all. At least I could never discover it working. Letters lingered in it for days and days, as in some wild village of the Pyrenees. When I asked a taxi-driver to drive me to a post-office, a look of far-off vision and adventure came into his eyes, and he said he had once heard of a post-office somewhere near West Ninety-Seventh Street. Men are not efficient in everything, but only in the fashionable thing. This may be a mark of the march of science; it does certainly in one sense deserve the description of youth. We can imagine a very young person forgetting the old toy in the excitement of a new one.

But on the other hand, American manners contain much that is called young in the contrary sense; in the sense of an earlier stage of history. There are whole patches and particular aspects that seem to me quite Early Victorian. I cannot help having this sensation, for instance, about the arrangement for smoking in the railway carriages. There are no smoking carriages, as a rule; but a corner of each of the great cars is curtained off mysteriously, that a man may go behind the curtain and smoke. Nobody thinks of a woman doing so. It is regarded as a dark, bohemian, and almost brutally masculine indulgence; exactly as it was regarded by the dowagers in Thackeray's novels. Indeed, this is one of the many such cases in which extremes meet; the extremes of stuffy antiquity and cranky modernity. The American dowager is sorry that tobacco was ever introduced; and the American suffragette and social reformer is considering whether tobacco ought not to be abolished. The tone of American society suggests some sort of compromise, by which women will be allowed to smoke, but men forbidden to do so.

In one respect, however, America is very old indeed. In one respect America is more historic than England; I might almost say more archaeological than England. The record of one period of the past, morally remote and probably irrevocable, is there preserved in a more perfect form as a pagan city is preserved at Pompeii. In a more general sense, of course, it is easy to exaggerate the contrast as a mere contrast between the old world and the new. There is a superficial satire about the millionaire's daughter who has recently become the wife of an aristocrat; but there is a rather more subtle satire in the question of how long the aristocrat has been aristocratic. There is often much misplaced mockery of a marriage between an upstart's daughter and a decayed relic of feudalism; when it is really a marriage between an upstart's daughter and an upstart's grandson. The sentimental socialist often seems to admit the blue blood of the nobleman, even when he wants to shed it; just as he seems to admit the marvellous brains of the millionaire, even when he wants to blow them out. Unfortunately (in the interests of social science, of course) the sentimental socialist never does go so far as bloodshed or blowing out brains; otherwise the colour and quality of both blood and brains would probably be a disappointment to him. There are certainly more American families that really came over in the *Mayflower* than English families that really came over with the Conqueror; and an English county family clearly dating from the time of the *Mayflower* would be considered a very traditional and historic house. Nevertheless, there are ancient things in England, though the aristocracy is hardly one of them. There are buildings, there are institutions, there are even ideas in England which do preserve, as in a perfect pattern, some particular epoch of the past, and even of the remote past. A man could study the Middle Ages in Lincoln as well as in Rouen; in Canterbury as well as in Cologne. Even of the Renaissance the same is true, at least on the literary side; if Shakespeare was later he was also greater than Ronsard. But the point is that the spirit and philosophy of the periods were present in fullness and in freedom. The guildsmen were as Christian in England as they were anywhere; the poets were as pagan in England as they were anywhere. Personally I do not admit that the men who served patrons were freer than those who served patron saints. But each fashion had its own kind of freedom; and the point is that the English, in each case, had the fullness of that kind of freedom. But there was another ideal of freedom which the English never had at all; or, anyhow, never expressed at all. There was another ideal, the soul of another epoch, round which we built no monuments and wrote no masterpieces. You will find no traces of it in England; but you will find them in America.

The thing I mean was the real religion of the eighteenth century. Its religion, in the more defined sense, was generally Deism, as in Robespierre or Jefferson. In the more general way of morals and atmosphere it was rather Stoicism, as in the suicide of Wolfe Tone. It had certain very noble and, as some would say, impossible ideals; as that a politician should be poor, and should be proud of being poor. It knew Latin; and therefore insisted on the strange fancy that the Republic should be a public thing. Its Republican simplicity was anything but a silly pose; unless all martyrdom is a silly pose. Even of the prigs and fanatics of the American and French Revolutions we can often say, as Stevenson said of an American, that 'thrift and courage glowed in him.' And its virtue and value for us is that it did remember the things we now most tend to forget; from the dignity of liberty to the danger of luxury. It did really believe in self-determination, in the self-determination of the self, as well as of the state. And its determination was really determined. In short, it believed in self-respect; and it is strictly true even of its rebels and regicides that they desired chiefly to be respectable. But there were in it the marks of religion as well as respectability; it had a creed; it had a crusade. Men died singing its songs; men starved rather than write against its principles. And its principles were liberty, equality, and fraternity, or the dogmas of the Declaration of Independence. This was the idea that redeemed the dreary negations of the eighteenth century; and there are still corners of Philadelphia or Boston or Baltimore where we can feel so suddenly in the silence its plain garb and formal manners, that the walking ghost of Jefferson would hardly surprise us.

There is not the ghost of such a thing in England. In England the real religion of the eighteenth century never found freedom or scope. It never cleared a space in which to build that cold and classic building called the Capitol. It never made elbow-room for that free if sometimes frigid figure called the Citizen.

In eighteenth-century England he was crowded out, partly perhaps by the relics of better things of the past, but largely at least by the presence of much worse things in the present. The worst things kept out the best things of the eighteenth century. The ground was occupied by legal fictions; by a godless Erastian church and a powerless Hanoverian king. Its realities were an aristocracy of Regency dandies, in costumes made to match Brighton Pavilion; a paganism not frigid but florid. It was a touch of this aristocratic waste in Fox that prevented that great man from being a glorious exception. It is therefore well for us to realise that there is something in history which we did not experience; and therefore probably something in Americans that we do not understand. There was this idealism at the very beginning of their individualism. There was a note of heroic publicity and honourable poverty which lingers in the very name of Cincinnati.

But I have another and special reason for noting this historical fact; the fact that we English never made anything upon the model of a capitol, while we can match anybody with the model of a cathedral. It is far from improbable that the latter model may again be a working model. For I have myself felt, naturally and for a long time, a warm sympathy with both those past ideals, which seem to some so incompatible. I have felt the attraction of the red cap as well as the red cross, of the Marseillaise as well as the Magnificat. And even when they were in furious conflict I have never altogether lost my sympathy for either. But in the conflict between the Republic and the Church, the point often made against the Church seems to me much more of a point against the Republic. It is emphatically the Republic and not the Church that I venerate as something beautiful but belonging to the past. In fact I feel exactly the same sort of sad respect for the republican ideal that many mid-Victorian free-thinkers felt for the religious ideal. The most sincere poets of that period were largely divided between those who insisted, like Arnold and Clough, that Christianity might be a ruin, but after all it must be treated as a picturesque ruin; and those, like Swinburne, who insisted that it might be a picturesque ruin, but after all it must be treated as a ruin. But surely their own pagan temple of political liberty is now much more of a ruin than the other; and I fancy I am one of the few who still take off their hats in that ruined temple. That is why I went about looking for the fading traces of that lost cause, in the old-world atmosphere of the new world.

But I do not, as a fact, feel that the cathedral is a ruin; I doubt if I should feel it even if I wished to lay it in ruins. I doubt if Mr. M'Cabe really thinks that Catholicism is dying, though he might deceive himself into saying so. Nobody could be naturally moved to say that the crowded cathedral of St. Patrick in New York was a ruin, or even that the unfinished Anglo-Catholic cathedral at Washington was a ruin, though it is not yet a church; or that there is anything lost or lingering about the splendid and spirited Gothic churches springing up under the inspiration of Mr. Cram of Boston. As a matter of feeling, as a matter of fact, as a matter quite apart from theory or opinion, it is not in the religious centres that we now have the feeling of something beautiful but receding, of something loved but lost. It is exactly in the spaces cleared and levelled by America for the large and sober religion of the eighteenth century; it is where an old house in Philadelphia contains an old picture of Franklin, or where the men of Maryland raised above their city the first monument of Washington. It is there that I feel like one who treads alone some banquet hall deserted, whose lights are fled, whose garlands dead, and all save he departed. It is then that I feel as if I were the last Republican.

But when I say that the Republic of the Age of Reason is now a ruin, I should rather say that at its best it is a ruin. At its worst it has collapsed into a death-trap or is rotting like a dunghill. What is the real Republic of our day as distinct from the ideal Republic of our fathers, but a heap of corrupt capitalism crawling with worms; with those parasites, the professional politicians? I was re-reading Swinburne's bitter but not ignoble poem, 'Before a Crucifix,' in which he bids Christ, or the ecclesiastical image of Christ, stand out of the way of the onward march of a political idealism represented by United Italy or the French Republic. I was struck by the strange and ironic exactitude with which every taunt he flings at the degradation of the old divine ideal would now fit the degradation of his own human ideal. The time has already come when we can ask his Goddess of Liberty, as represented by the actual Liberals, 'Have *you* filled full men's starved-out souls; have *you* brought freedom on the earth?' For every engine in which these old free-thinkers firmly and confidently trusted has itself become an engine of oppression and even of class oppression. Its free parliament has become an oligarchy. Its free press has become a monopoly. If the pure Church has been corrupted in the course of two thousand years, what about the pure Republic that has rotted into a filthy plutocracy in less than a hundred?

O, hidden face of man, wheresoever
The years have woven a viewless veil,
If thou wert verily man's lover
What did thy love or blood avail?
Thy blood the priests make poison of;
And in gold shekels coin thy love.

Which has most to do with shekels to-day, the priests or the politicians? Can we say in any special sense nowadays that clergymen, as such, make a poison out of the blood of the martyrs? Can we say it in anything like the real sense, in which we do say that yellow journalists make a poison out of the blood of the soldiers?

But I understand how Swinburne felt when confronted by the image of the carven Christ, and, perplexed by the contrast between its claims and its consequences, he said his strange farewell to it, hastily indeed, but not without regret, not even really without respect. I felt the same myself when I looked for the last time on the Statue of Liberty.

FOOTNOTE:
_ In the conclusion of this chapter I mean by the Republic not merely the American Republic, but the whole modern representative system, as in France or even in England.

IS THE ATLANTIC NARROWING?

A certain kind of question is asked very earnestly in our time. Because of a certain logical quality in it, connected with premises and data, it is very difficult to answer. Thus people will ask what is the hidden weakness in the Celtic race that makes them everywhere fail or fade away; or how the Germans contrived to bring all their organisation into a state of such perfect efficiency; and what was the significance of the recent victory of Prussia. Or they will ask by what stages the modern world has abandoned all belief in miracles; and the modern newspapers ceased to print any news of murders. They will ask why English politics are free from corruption; or by what mental and moral training certain millionaires were enabled to succeed by sheer force of character; in short, they will ask why plutocrats govern well and how it is that pigs fly, spreading their pink pinions to the breeze or delighting us as they twitter and flutter from tree to tree. The logical difficulty of answering these questions is connected with an old story about Charles the Second and a bowl of goldfish, and with another anecdote about a gentleman who was asked, 'When did you leave off beating your wife?' But there is something analogous to it in the present discussions about the forces drawing England and America together. It seems as if the reasoners hardly went far enough back in their argument, or took trouble enough to disentangle their assumptions. They are still moving with the momentum of the peculiar nineteenth-century notion of progress; of certain very simple tendencies perpetually increasing and needing no special analysis. It is so with the international *rapprochement* I have to consider here.

In other places I have ventured to express a doubt about whether nations can be drawn together by an ancient rumour about races; by a sort of prehistoric chit-chat or the gossip of the Stone Age. I have ventured farther; and even expressed a doubt about whether they ought to be drawn together, or rather dragged together, by the brute violence of the engines of science and speed. But there is yet another horrible doubt haunting my morbid mind, which it will be better for my constitution to confess frankly. And that is the doubt about whether they are being drawn together at all.

It has long been a conversational commonplace among the enlightened that all countries are coming closer and closer to each other. It was a conversational commonplace among the enlightened, somewhere about the year 1913, that all wars were receding farther and farther into a barbaric past. There is something about these sayings that seems simple and familiar and entirely satisfactory when we say them; they are of that consoling sort which we can say without any of the mental pain of thinking what we are saying. But if we turn our attention from the phrases we use to the facts that we talk about, we shall realise at least that there are a good many facts on the other side and examples pointing the other way. For instance, it does happen occasionally, from time to time, that people talk about Ireland. He would be a very hilarious humanitarian who should maintain that Ireland and England have been more and more assimilated during the last hundred years. The very name of Sinn Fein is an answer to it, and the very language in which that phrase is spoken. Curran and Sheil would no more have dreamed of uttering the watchword of 'Repeal' in Gaelic than of uttering it in Zulu. Grattan could hardly have brought himself to believe that the real repeal of the Union would actually be signed in London in the strange script as remote as the snaky ornament of the Celtic crosses. It would have seemed like Washington signing the Declaration of Independence in the picture-writing of the Red Indians. Ireland has clearly grown away from England; and her language, literature, and type of patriotism are far less English than they were. On the other hand, no one will pretend that the mass of modern Englishmen are much nearer to talking Gaelic or decorating Celtic crosses. A hundred years ago it was perfectly natural that Byron and Moore should walk down the street arm in arm. Even the sight of Mr. Rudyard Kipling and Mr. W. B. Yeats walking down the street arm in arm would now arouse some remark.

I could give any number of other examples of the same new estrangement of nations. I could cite the obvious facts that Norway and Sweden parted company not very long ago, that

Austria and Hungary have again become separate states. I could point to the mob of new nations that have started up after the war; to the fact that the great empires are now nearly all broken up; that the Russian Empire no longer directs Poland, that the Austrian Empire no longer directs Bohemia, that the Turkish Empire no longer directs Palestine. Sinn Fein is the separatism of the Irish. Zionism is the separatism of the Jews. But there is one simple and sufficing example, which is here more to my purpose, and is at least equally sufficient for it. And that is the deepening national difference between the Americans and the English.

Let me test it first by my individual experience in the matter of literature. When I was a boy I read a book like *The Autocrat of the Breakfast-Table* exactly as I read another book like *The Book of Snobs*. I did not think of it as an American book, but simply as a book. Its wit and idiom were like those of the English literary tradition; and its few touches of local colour seemed merely accidental, like those of an Englishman who happened to be living in Switzerland or Sweden. My father and my father's friends were rightly enthusiastic for the book; so that it seemed to come to me by inheritance like *Gulliver's Travels* or *Tristram Shandy*. Its language was as English as Ruskin, and a great deal more English than Carlyle. Well, I have seen in later years an almost equally wide and well-merited popularity of the stories of O. Henry. But never for one moment could I or any one else reading them forget that they were stories by an American about America. The very first fact about them is that they are told with an American accent, that is, in the unmistakable tones of a brilliant and fascinating foreigner. And the same is true of every other recent work of which the fame has managed to cross the Atlantic. We did not say that *The Spoon River Anthology* was a new book, but that it was a new book from America. It was exactly as if a remarkable realistic novel was reported from Russia or Italy. We were in no danger of confusing it with the 'Elegy in a Country Churchyard.' People in England who heard of Main Street were not likely to identify it with a High Street; with the principal thoroughfare in any little town in Berkshire or Buckinghamshire. But when I was a boy I practically identified the boarding-house of the Autocrat with any boarding-house I happened to know in Brompton or Brighton. No doubt there were differences; but the point is that the differences did not pierce the consciousness or prick the illusion. I said to myself, 'People are like this in boarding-houses,' not 'People are like this in Boston.'

This can be seen even in the simple matter of language, especially in the sense of slang. Take, for instance, the delightful sketch in the causerie of Oliver Wendell Holmes; the character of the young man called John. He is the very modern type in every modern country who does specialise in slang. He is the young fellow who is something in the City; the everyday young man of the Gilbertian song, with a stick and a pipe and a half-bred black-and-tan. In every country he is at once witty and commonplace. In every country, therefore, he tends both to the vivacity and the vulgarity of slang. But when he appeared in Holmes's book, his language was not very different from what it would have been in a Brighton instead of a Boston boarding-house; or, in short, if the young man called John had more commonly been called 'Arry. If he had appeared in a modern American book, his language would have been almost literally unintelligible. At the least an Englishman would have had to read some of the best sentences twice, as he sometimes has to read the dizzy and involved metaphors of O. Henry. Nor is it an answer that this depended on the personalities of the particular writers. A comparison between the real journalism of the time of Holmes and the real journalism of the time of Henry reveals the same thing. It is the expansion of a slight difference of style into a luxuriant difference of idiom; and the process continued indefinitely would certainly produce a totally different language.

After a few centuries the signatures of American ambassadors would look as fantastic as Gaelic, and the very name of the Republic be as strange as Sinn Fein.

It is true that there has been on the surface a certain amount of give and take; or at least, as far as the English are concerned, of take rather than give. But it is true that it was once all the other way; and indeed the one thing is something like a just nemesis of the other. Indeed, the story of the reversal is somewhat singular, when we come to think of it. It began in a certain atmosphere and spirit of certain well-meaning people who talked about the English-speaking race; and were apparently indifferent to how the English was spoken, whether in the accent of a Jamaican negro or a convict from Botany Bay. It was their logical tendency to say that Dante was a Dago. It was their logical punishment to say that Disraeli was an Englishman. Now there may have been a period when this Anglo-American amalgamation included more or less equal elements from England and America. It never included the larger elements, or the more valuable elements of either. But, on the whole, I think it true to say that it was not an allotment but an interchange of parts; and that things first went all one way and then all the other. People began by telling the Americans that they owed all their past triumphs to England; which was false. They ended up by telling the English that they would owe all their future triumphs to America; which is if possible still more false. Because we chose to forget that New York had been New Amsterdam, we are now in danger of forgetting that London is not New York. Because we insisted that Chicago was only a pious imitation of Chiswick, we may yet see Chiswick an inferior imitation of Chicago. Our Anglo-Saxon historians attempted that conquest in which Howe and Burgoyne had failed, and with infinitely less justification on their side. They attempted the great crime of the Anglicisation of America. They have called down the punishment of the Americanisation of England. We must not murmur; but it is a heavy punishment.

It may lift a little of its load, however, if we look at it more closely; we shall then find that though it is very much on top of us, it is only on top. In that sense such Americanisation as there is is very superficial. For instance, there is a certain amount of American slang picked up at random; it appears in certain pushing types of journalism and drama. But we may easily dwell too much on this tragedy; of people who have never spoken English beginning to speak American. I am far from suggesting that American, like any other foreign language, may not frequently contribute to the common culture of the world phrases for which there is no substitute; there are French phrases so used in England and English phrases in France. The word 'high-brow,' for instance, is a real discovery and revelation, a new and necessary name for something that walked nameless but enormous in the modern world, a shaft of light and a stroke of lightning. That comes from America and belongs to the world, as much as 'The Raven' or *The Scarlet Letter* or the novels of Henry James belong to the world. In fact, I can imagine Henry James originating it in the throes of self-expression, and bringing out a word like 'high-browed,' with a sort of gentle jerk, at the end of searching sentences which groped sensitively until they found the phrase. But most of the American slang that is borrowed seems to be borrowed for no particular reason. It either has no point or the point is lost by translation into another context and culture. It is either something which does not need any grotesque and exaggerative description, or of which there already exists a grotesque and exaggerative description more native to our tongue and soil. For instance, I cannot see that the strong and simple expression 'Now it is for you to pull the police magistrate's nose' is in any way strengthened by saying, 'Now it is up to you to pull the police magistrate's nose.' When Tennyson says of the men of the Light Brigade 'Theirs but to do and die,' the expression seems to me perfectly lucid. 'Up to them to do and die' would alter the metre without especially clarifying the meaning. This is an example of ordinary language being quite adequate; but there is a further difficulty that even wild slang comes to sound like ordinary language. Very often the English have already as humorous and fanciful idiom of their own, only that through habit it has lost its humour. When Keats wrote the line, 'What pipes and timbrels, what wild ecstasy!' I am willing to believe that the American humorist would have expressed the same sentiment by beginning the sentence with 'Some pipe!' When that was first said, somewhere in the wilds of Colorado, it was really funny; involving a powerful understatement and the suggestion of a mere sample. If a spinster has informed us that she keeps a bird, and we find it is an ostrich, there will be considerable point in the Colorado satirist saying inquiringly, 'Some bird?' as if he were offering us a small slice of a small plover. But if we go back to this root and rationale of a joke, the English language already contains quite as good a joke. It is not necessary to say, 'Some bird'; there is a far finer irony in the old expression, 'Something like a bird.' It suggests that the speaker sees something faintly and strangely birdlike about a bird; that it remotely and almost irrationally reminds him of a bird; and that there is about ostrich plumes a yard long something like the faint and delicate traces of a feather. It has every quality of imaginative irony, except that nobody even imagines it to be ironical. All that happens is that people get tired of that turn of phrase, take up a foreign phrase and get tired of that, without realising the point of either. All that happens is that a number of weary people who used to say, 'Something like a bird,' now say, 'Some bird,' with undiminished weariness. But they might just as well use dull and decent English; for in both cases they are only using jocular language without seeing the joke.

There is indeed a considerable trade in the transplantation of these American jokes to England just now. They generally pine and die in our climate, or they are dead before their arrival; but we cannot be certain that they were never alive. There is a sort of unending frieze or scroll of decorative designs unrolled ceaselessly before the British public, about a hen-pecked husband, which is indistinguishable to the eye from an actual self-repeating pattern like that of the Greek Key, but which is imported as if it were as precious and irreplaceable as the Elgin Marbles. Advertisement and syndication make mountains out of the most funny little mole-hills; but no doubt the mole-hills are picturesque enough in their own landscape. In any case there is nothing so national as humour; and many things, like many people, can be humorous enough when they are at home. But these American jokes are boomed as solemnly as American religions; and their supporters gravely testify that they are funny, without seeing the fun of it for a moment. This is partly perhaps the spirit of spontaneous institutionalism in American democracy, breaking out in the wrong place. They make humour an institution; and a man will be set to tell an anecdote as if to play the violin. But when the story is told in America it really is amusing; and when these jokes are reprinted in England they are often not even intelligible. With all the stupidity of the millionaire and the monopolist, the enterprising proprietor prints jokes in England which are necessarily unintelligible to nearly every English person; jokes referring to domestic and local conditions quite peculiar to America. I saw one of these narrative caricatures the other day in which the whole of the joke (what there was of it) turned on the astonishment of a housewife at the absurd notion of not having an ice-box. It is perfectly true that nearly every ordinary American housewife possesses an ice-box. An ordinary English housewife would no more expect to possess an ice-box than to possess an iceberg. And it would be about as sensible to tow an iceberg to an English port all the way from the North Pole, as to trail that one pale and frigid joke to Fleet Street all the way from the New York papers. It is the same with a hundred other advertisements and adaptations. I have already confessed that I took a considerable delight in the dancing illuminations of Broadway—in Broadway. Everything there is suitable to them, the vast interminable thoroughfare, the toppling houses, the dizzy and restless spirit of the whole city. It is a city of dissolving views, and one may almost say a city in everlasting dissolution. But I do not especially admire a burning fragment of Broadway stuck up opposite the old Georgian curve of Regent Street. I would as soon express sympathy with the Republic of Switzerland by erecting a small Alp, with imitation snow, in the middle of St. James's Park.

But all this commercial copying is very superficial; and above all, it never copies anything that is really worth copying. Nations never *learn* anything from each other in this way. We have many things to learn from America; but we only listen to those Americans who have still to learn them. Thus, for instance, we do not import the small farm but only the big shop. In other words, we hear nothing of the democracy of the Middle West, but everything of the plutocracy of the middleman, who is probably as unpopular in the Middle West as the miller in the Middle Ages. If Mr. Elihu K. Pike could be transplanted bodily from the neighbourhood of his home town of Marathon, Neb., with his farm and his frame-house and all its fittings, and they could be set down exactly in the spot now occupied by Selfridge's (which could be easily cleared away for the purpose), I think we could really get a great deal of good by watching him, even if the watching were inevitably a little too like watching a wild beast in a cage or an insect under a glass case. Urban crowds could collect every day behind a barrier or railing, and gaze at Mr. Pike pottering about all day in his ancient and autochthonous occupations. We could see him growing Indian corn with all the gravity of an Indian; though it is impossible to imagine Mrs. Pike blessing the cornfield in the manner of Minnehaha. As I have said, there is a certain lack of humane myth and mysticism about this Puritan peasantry. But we could see him transforming the maize into pop-corn, which is a very pleasant domestic ritual and pastime, and is the American equivalent of the glory of roasting chestnuts. Above all, many of us would learn for the first time that a man can really live and walk about upon something more productive than a pavement; and that when he does so he can really be a free man, and have no lord but the law. Instead of that, America can give nothing to London but those multiple modern shops, of which it has too many already. I know that many people entertain the innocent illusion that big shops are more efficient than small ones; but that is only because the big combinations have the monopoly of advertisement as well as trade. The big shop is not in the least remarkable for efficiency; it is only too big to be blamed for its inefficiency. It is secure in its reputation for always sacking the wrong man. A big shop, considered as a place to shop in, is simply a village of small shops roofed in to keep out the light and air; and one in which none of the shopkeepers is really responsible for his shop. If any one has any doubts on this matter, since I have mentioned it, let him consider this fact: that in practice we never do apply this method of commercial combination to anything that matters very much. We do not go to the surgical department of the Stores to have a portion of our brain removed by a delicate operation; and then pass on to the advocacy department to employ one or any of its barristers, when we are in temporary danger of being hanged. We go to men who own their own tools and are responsible for the use of their own talents. And the same truth applies to that other modern method of advertisement, which has also so largely fallen across us like the gigantic shadow of America. Nations do not arm themselves for a mortal struggle by remembering which sort of submarine they have seen most often on the hoardings. They can do it about something like soap, precisely because a nation will not perish by having a second-rate sort of soap, as it might by having a second-rate sort of submarine. A nation may indeed perish slowly by having a second-rate sort of food or drink or medicine; but that is another and much longer story, and the story is not ended yet. But nobody wins a great battle at a great crisis because somebody has told him that Cadgerboy's Cavalry Is the Best. It may be that commercial enterprise will eventually cover these fields also, and advertisement-agents will provide the instruments of the surgeon and the weapons of the soldier. When that happens, the armies will be defeated and the patients will die. But though we modern people are indeed patients, in the sense of being merely receptive and accepting things with astonishing patience, we are not dead yet; and we have lingering gleams of sanity.

For the best things do not travel. As I appear here as a traveller, I may say with all modesty that the best people do not travel either. Both in England and America the normal people are the national people; and I repeat that I think they are growing more and more national. I do not think the abyss is being bridged by cosmopolitan theories; and I am sure I do not want it bridged by all this slang journalism and blatant advertisement. I have called all that commercial publicity the gigantic shadow of America. It may be the shadow of America, but it is not the light of America. The light lies far beyond, a level light upon the lands of sunset, where it shines upon wide places full of a very simple and a very happy people; and those who would see it must seek for it.

LINCOLN AND LOST CAUSES

It has already been remarked here that the English know a great deal about past American literature, but nothing about past American history. They do not know either, of course, as well as they know the present American advertising, which is the least important of the three. But it is worth noting once more how little they know of the history, and how illogically that little is chosen. They have heard, no doubt, of the fame and the greatness of Henry Clay. He is a cigar. But it would be unwise to cross-examine any Englishman, who may be consuming that luxury at the moment, about the Missouri Compromise or the controversies with Andrew Jackson. And just as the statesman of Kentucky is a cigar, so the state of Virginia is a cigarette. But there is perhaps one exception, or half-exception, to this simple plan. It would perhaps be an exaggeration to say that Plymouth Rock is a chicken. Any English person keeping chickens, and chiefly interested in Plymouth Rocks considered as chickens, would nevertheless have a hazy sensation of having seen the word somewhere before. He would feel subconsciously that the Plymouth Rock had not always been a chicken. Indeed, the name connotes something not only solid but antiquated; and is not therefore a very tactful name for a chicken. There would rise up before him something memorable in the haze that he calls his history; and he would see the history books of his boyhood and old engravings of men in steeple-crowned hats struggling with sea-waves or Red Indians. The whole thing would suddenly become clear to him if (by a simple reform) the chickens were called Pilgrim Fathers.

Then he would remember all about it. The Pilgrim Fathers were champions of religious liberty; and they discovered America. It is true that he has also heard of a man called Christopher Columbus; but that was in connection with an egg. He has also heard of somebody known as Sir Walter Raleigh; and though his principal possession was a cloak, it is also true that he had a potato, not to mention a pipe of tobacco. Can it be possible that he brought it from Virginia, where the cigarettes come from? Gradually the memories will come back and fit themselves together for the average hen-wife who learnt history at the English elementary schools, and who has now something better to do. Even when the narrative becomes consecutive, it will not necessarily become correct. It is not strictly true to say that the Pilgrim Fathers discovered America. But it is quite as true as saying that they were champions of religious liberty. If we said that they were martyrs who would have died heroically in torments rather than tolerate any religious liberty, we should be talking something like sense about them, and telling the real truth that is their due. The whole Puritan movement, from the Solemn League and Covenant to the last stand of the last Stuarts, was a struggle *against* religious toleration, or what they would have called religious indifference. The first religious equality on earth was established by a Catholic cavalier in Maryland. Now there is nothing in this to diminish any dignity that belongs to any real virtues and virilities in the Pilgrim Fathers; on the contrary, it is rather to the credit of their consistency and conviction. But there is no doubt that the note of their whole experiment in New England was intolerance, and even inquisition. And there is no doubt that New England was then only the newest and not the oldest of these colonial experiments. At least two Cavaliers had been in the field before any Puritans. And they had carried with them much more of the atmosphere and nature of the normal Englishman than any Puritan could possibly carry. They had established it especially in Virginia, which had been founded by a great Elizabethan and named after the great Elizabeth. Before there was any New England in the North, there was something very like Old England in the South. Relatively speaking, there is still.

Whenever the anniversary of the *Mayflower* comes round, there is a chorus of Anglo-American congratulation and comradeship, as if this at least were a matter on which all can agree. But I knew enough about America, even before I went there, to know that there are a good many people there at any rate who do not agree with it. Long ago I wrote a protest in which I asked why Englishmen had forgotten the great state of Virginia, the first in foundation and long the first in leadership; and why a few crabbed Nonconformists should have the right to erase a record that begins with Raleigh and ends with Lee, and incidentally includes Washington. The great state of Virginia was the backbone of America until it was broken in the Civil War. From Virginia came the first great Presidents and most of the Fathers of the Republic. Its adherence to the Southern side in the war made it a great war, and for a long time a doubtful war. And in the leader of the Southern armies it produced what is perhaps the one modern figure that may come to shine like St. Louis in the lost battle, or Hector dying before holy Troy.

Again, it is characteristic that while the modern English know nothing about Lee they do know something about Lincoln; and nearly all that they know is wrong. They know nothing of his Southern connections, nothing of his considerable Southern sympathy, nothing of the meaning of his moderation in face of the problem of slavery, now lightly treated as self-evident. Above all, they know nothing about the respect in which Lincoln was quite un-English, was indeed the very reverse of English; and can be understood better if we think of him as a Frenchman, since it seems so hard for some of us to believe that he was an American. I mean his lust for logic for its own sake, and the way he kept mathematical truths in his mind like the fixed stars. He was so far from being a merely practical man, impatient of academic abstractions, that he reviewed and revelled in academic abstractions, even while he could not apply them to practical life. He loved to repeat that slavery was intolerable while he tolerated it, and to prove that something ought to be done while it was impossible to do it. This was probably very bewildering to his brother-politicians; for politicians always whitewash what they do not destroy. But for all that this inconsistent consistency beat the politicians at their own game, and this abstracted logic proved the most practical of all. For when the chance did come to do something, there was no doubt about the thing to be done. The thunderbolt fell from the clear heights of heaven; it had not been tossed about and lost like a common missile in the market-place. The matter is worth mentioning, because it has a moral for a much larger modern question. A wise man's attitude towards industrial capitalism will be very like Lincoln's attitude towards slavery. That is, he will manage to endure capitalism; but he will not endure a defence of capitalism. He will recognise the value, not only of knowing what he is doing, but of knowing what he would like to do. He will recognise the importance of having a thing clearly labelled in his own mind as bad, long before the opportunity comes to abolish it. He may recognise the risk of even worse things in immediate abolition, as Lincoln did in abolitionism. He will not call all business men brutes, any more than Lincoln would call all planters demons; because he knows they are not. He will regard many alternatives to capitalism as crude and inhuman, as Lincoln regarded John Brown's raid; because they are. But he will clear his *mind* from cant about capitalism; he will have no doubt of what is the truth about Trusts and Trade Combines and the concentration of capital; and it is the truth that they endure under one of the ironic silences of heaven, over the pageants and the passing triumphs of hell.

But the name of Lincoln has a more immediate reference to the international matters I am considering here. His name has been much invoked by English politicians and journalists in connection with the quarrel with Ireland. And if we study the matter, we shall hardly admire the tact and sagacity of those journalists and politicians.

History is an eternal tangle of cross-purposes; and we could not take a clearer case, or rather a more complicated case, of such a tangle, than the facts lying behind a political parallel recently mentioned by many politicians. I mean the parallel between the movement for Irish independence and the attempted secession of the Southern Confederacy in America. Superficially any one might say that the comparison is natural enough; and that there is much in common between the quarrel of the North and South in Ireland and the quarrel of the North and South in America. In both cases the South was on the whole agricultural, the North on the whole industrial. True, the parallel exaggerates the position of Belfast; to complete it we must suppose the whole Federal system to have consisted of Pittsburg. In both the side that was more successful was felt by many to be less attractive. In both the same political terms were used, such as the term 'Union' and 'Unionism.' An ordinary Englishman comes to America, knowing these main lines of American history, and knowing that the American knows the similar main lines of Irish history. He knows that there are strong champions of Ireland in America; possibly he also knows that there are very genuine champions of England in America. By every possible historical analogy, he would naturally expect to find the pro-Irish in the South and the pro-English in the North. As a matter of fact, he finds almost exactly the opposite. He finds Boston governed by Irishmen, and Nashville containing people more pro-English than Englishmen. He finds Virginians not only of British blood, like George Washington, but of British opinions almost worthy of George the Third.

But I do not say this, as will be seen in a moment, as a criticism of the comparative Toryism of the South. I say it as a criticism of the superlative stupidity of English propaganda. On another page I remark on the need for a new sort of English propaganda; a propaganda that should be really English and have some remote reference to England. Now if it were a matter of making foreigners feel the real humours and humanities of England, there are no Americans so able or willing to do it as the Americans of the Southern States. As I have already hinted, some of them are so loyal to the English humanities, that they think it their duty to defend even the English inhumanities. New England is turning into New Ireland. But Old England can still be faintly traced in Old Dixie. It contains some of the best things that England herself has had, and therefore (of course) the things that England herself has lost, or is trying to lose. But above all, as I have said, there are people in these places whose historic memories and family traditions really hold them to us, not by alliance but by affection. Indeed, they have the affection in spite of the alliance. They love us in spite of our compliments and courtesies and hands across the sea; all our ambassadorial salutations and speeches cannot kill their love. They manage even to respect us in spite of the shady Jew stockbrokers we send them as English envoys, or the 'efficient' men, who are sent out to be tactful with foreigners because they have been too tactless with trades unionists. This type of traditional American, North or South, really has some traditions connecting him with England; and though he is now in a very small minority, I cannot imagine why England should wish to make it smaller. England once sympathised with the South. The South still sympathises with England. It would seem that the South, or some elements in the South, had rather the advantage of us in political firmness and fidelity; but it does not follow that that fidelity will stand every shock. And at this moment, and in this matter, of all things in the world, our political propagandists must try to bolster British Imperialism up, by kicking Southern Secession when it is down. The English politicians eagerly point out that we shall be justified in crushing Ireland exactly as Sumner and Stevens crushed the most English part of America. It does not seem to occur to them that this comparison between the Unionist triumph in America and a Unionist triumph in Britain is rather hard upon our particular sympathisers, who did not triumph. When England exults in Lincoln's victory over his foes, she is exulting in his victory over her own friends. If her diplomacy continues as delicate and chivalrous as it is at present, they may soon be her only friends. England will be defending herself at the expense of her only defenders. But however this may be, it is as well to bear witness to some of the elements of my own experience; and I can answer for it, at least, that there are some people in the South who will not be pleased at being swept into the rubbish heap of history as rebels and ruffians; and who will not, I regret to say, by any means enjoy even being classed with Fenians and Sinn Feiners.

Now touching the actual comparison between the conquest of the Confederacy and the conquest of Ireland, there are, of course, a good many things to be said which politicians cannot be expected to understand. Strange to say, it is not certain that a lost cause was never worth winning; and it would be easy to argue that the world lost very much indeed when that particular cause was lost. These are not days in which it is exactly obvious that an agricultural society was more dangerous than an industrial one. And even Southern slavery had this one moral merit, that it was decadent; it has this one historic advantage, that it is dead. The Northern slavery, industrial slavery, or what is called wage slavery, is not decaying but increasing; and the end of it is not yet. But in any case, it would be well for us to realise that the reproach of resembling the Confederacy does not ring in all ears as an unanswerable condemnation. It is scarcely a self-evident or sufficient argument, to some hearers, even to prove that the English are as delicate and philanthropic as Sherman, still less that the Irish are as criminal and lawless as Lee. Nor will it soothe every single soul on the American continent to say that the English victory in Ireland will be followed by a reconstruction, like the reconstruction exhibited in the film called 'The Birth of a Nation.' And, indeed, there is a further inference from that fine panorama of the exploits of the Ku-Klux Klan. It would be easy, as I say, to turn the argument entirely in favour of the Confederacy. It would be easy to draw the moral, not that the Southern Irish are as wrong as the Southern States, but that the Southern States were as right as the Southern Irish. But upon the whole, I do not incline to accept the parallel in that sense any more than in the opposite sense. For reasons I have already given elsewhere, I do believe that in the main Abraham Lincoln was right. But right in what?

If Lincoln was right, he was right in guessing that there was not really a Northern nation and a Southern nation, but only one American nation. And if he has been proved right, he has been proved right by the fact that men in the South, as well as the North, do now feel a patriotism for that American nation. His wisdom, if it really was wisdom, was justified not by his opponents being conquered, but by their being converted. Now, if the English politicians must insist on this parallel, they ought to see that the parallel is fatal to themselves. The very test which proved Lincoln right has proved them wrong. The very judgment which may have justified him quite unquestionably condemns them. We have again and again conquered Ireland, and have never come an inch nearer to converting Ireland. We have had not one Gettysburg, but twenty Gettysburgs; but we have had no Union. And that is where, as I have remarked, it is relevant to remember that flying fantastic vision on the films that told so many people what no histories have told them. I heard when I was in America rumours of the local reappearance of the Ku-Klux Klan; but the smallness and mildness of the manifestation, as compared with the old Southern or the new Irish case, is alone a sufficient example of the exception that proves the rule. To approximate to any resemblance to recent Irish events, we must imagine the Ku-Klux Klan riding again in more than the terrors of that vision, wild as the wind, white as the moon, terrible as an army with banners. If there were really such a revival of the Southern action, there would equally be a revival of the Southern argument. It would be clear that Lee was right and Lincoln was wrong; that the Southern States were national and were as indestructible as nations. If the South were as rebellious as Ireland, the North would be as wrong as England.

But I desire a new English diplomacy that will exhibit, not the things in which England is wrong but the things in which England is right. And England is right in England, just as she is wrong in Ireland; and it is exactly that rightness of a real nation in itself that is at once most difficult and most desirable to explain to foreigners. Now the Irishman, and to some extent the American, has remained alien to England, largely because he does not truly realise that the Englishman loves England, still less can he really imagine why the Englishman loves England. That is why I insist on the stupidity of ignoring and insulting the opinions of those few Virginians and other Southerners who really have some inherited notion of why Englishmen love England; and even love it in something of the same fashion themselves. Politicians who do not know the English spirit when they see it at home, cannot of course be expected to recognise it abroad. Publicists are eloquently praising Abraham Lincoln, for all the wrong reasons; but fundamentally for that worst and vilest of all reasons—that he succeeded. None of them seems to have the least notion of how to look for England in England; and they would see something fantastic in the figure of a traveller who found it elsewhere, or anywhere but in New England. And it is well, perhaps, that they have not yet found England where it is hidden in England; for if they found it, they would kill it.

All I am concerned to consider here is the inevitable failure of this sort of Anglo-American propaganda to create a friendship. To praise Lincoln as an Englishman is about as appropriate as if we were praising Lincoln as an English town. We are talking about something totally different. And indeed the whole conversation is rather like some such cross-purposes about some such word as 'Lincoln'; in which one party should be talking about the President and the other about the cathedral. It is like some wild bewilderment in a farce, with one man wondering how a President could have a church-spire, and the other wondering how a church could have a chin-beard. And the moral is the moral on which I would insist everywhere in this book; that the remedy is to be found in disentangling the two and not in entangling them further. You could not produce a democrat of the logical type of Lincoln merely out of the moral materials that now make up an English cathedral town, like that on which Old Tom of Lincoln looks down. But on the other hand, it is quite certain that a hundred Abraham Lincolns, working for a hundred years, could not build Lincoln Cathedral. And the farcical allegory of an attempt to make Old Tom and Old Abe embrace to the glory of the illogical Anglo-Saxon language is but a symbol of something that is always being attempted, and always attempted in vain. It is not by mutual imitation that the understanding can come. It is not by erecting New York sky-scrapers in London that New York can learn the sacred significance of the towers of Lincoln. It is not by English dukes importing the daughters of American millionaires that England can get any glimpse of the democratic dignity of American men. I have the best of all reasons for knowing that a stranger can be welcomed in America; and just as he is courteously treated in the country as a stranger, so he should always be careful to treat it as a strange land. That sort of imaginative respect, as for something different and even distant, is the only beginning of any attachment between patriotic peoples. The English traveller may carry with him at least one word of his own great language and literature; and whenever he is inclined to say of anything 'This is passing strange,' he may remember that it was no inconsiderable Englishman who appended to it the answer, 'And therefore as a stranger give it welcome.'

WELLS AND THE WORLD STATE

There was recently a highly distinguished gathering to celebrate the past, present, and especially future triumphs of aviation. Some of the most brilliant men of the age, such as Mr. H. G. Wells and Mr. J. L. Garvin, made interesting and important speeches, and many scientific aviators luminously discussed the new science. Among their graceful felicitations and grave and quiet analyses a word was said, or a note was struck, which I myself can never hear, even in the most harmless after-dinner speech, without an impulse to leap up and yell, and smash the decanters and wreck the dinner-table.

Long ago, when I was a boy, I heard it with fury; and never since have I been able to understand any free man hearing it without fury. I heard it when Bloch, and the old prophets of pacifism by panic, preached that war would become too horrible for patriots to endure. It sounded to me like saying that an instrument of torture was being prepared by my dentist, that would finally cure me of loving my dog. And I felt it again when all these wise and well-meaning persons began to talk about the inevitable effect of aviation in bridging the Atlantic, and establishing alliance and affection between England and America.

I resent the suggestion that a machine can make me bad. But I resent quite equally the suggestion that a machine can make me good. It might be the unfortunate fact that a coolness had arisen between myself and Mr. Fitzarlington Blenkinsop, inhabiting the suburban villa and garden next to mine; and I might even be largely to blame for it. But if somebody told me that a new kind of lawn-mower had just been invented, of so cunning a structure that I should be forced to become a bosom-friend of Mr. Blenkinsop whether I liked it or not, I should be very much annoyed. I should be moved to say that if that was the only way of cutting my grass I would not cut my grass, but continue to cut my neighbour. Or suppose the difference were even less defensible; suppose a man had suffered from a trifling shindy with his wife. And suppose somebody told him that the introduction of an entirely new vacuum-cleaner would compel him to a reluctant reconciliation with his wife. It would be found, I fancy, that human nature abhors that vacuum. Reasonably spirited human beings will not be ordered about by bicycles and sewing-machines; and a sane man will not be made good, let alone bad, by the things he has himself made. I have occasionally dictated to a typewriter, but I will not be dictated to by a typewriter, even of the newest and most complicated mechanism; nor have I ever met a typewriter, however complex, that attempted such a tyranny.

Yet this and nothing else is what is implied in all such talk of the aeroplane annihilating distinctions as well as distances; and an international aviation abolishing nationalities. This and nothing else was really implied in one speaker's prediction that such aviation will almost necessitate an Anglo-American friendship. Incidentally, I may remark, it is not a true suggestion even in the practical and materialistic sense; and the speaker's phrase refuted the speaker's argument. He said that international relations must be more friendly when men can get from England to America in a day. Well, men can already get from England to Germany in a day; and the result was a mutual invitation of which the formalities lasted for five years. Men could get from the coast of England to the coast of France very quickly, through nearly all the ages during which those two coasts were bristling with arms against each other. They could get there very quickly when Nelson went down by that Burford Inn to embark for Trafalgar; they could get there very quickly when Napoleon sat in his tent in that camp at Boulogne that filled England with alarums of invasion. Are these the amiable and pacific relations which will unite England and America, when Englishmen can get to America in a day? The shortening of the distance seems quite as likely, so far as that argument goes, to facilitate that endless guerila warfare which raged across the narrow seas in the Middle Ages; when French invaders carried away the bells of Rye, and the men of those flats of East Sussex gloriously pursued and recovered them. I do not know whether American privateers, landing at Liverpool, would carry away a few of the more elegant factory chimneys as a substitute for the superstitious symbols of the past. I know not if the English, on ripe reflection, would essay with any enthusiasm to get them back. But anyhow it is anything but self-evident that people cannot fight each other because they are near to each other; and if it were true, there would never have been any such thing as border warfare in the world. As a fact, border warfare has often been the one sort of warfare which it was most difficult to bring under control. And our own traditional position in face of this new logic is somewhat disconcerting. We have always supposed ourselves safer because we were insular and therefore isolated. We have been congratulating ourselves for centuries on having enjoyed peace because we were cut off from our neighbours. And now they are telling us that we shall only enjoy peace when we are joined up with our neighbours. We have pitied the poor nations with frontiers, because a frontier only produces fighting; and now we are trusting to a frontier as the only thing that will produce friendship. But, as a matter of fact, and for a far deeper and more spiritual reason, a frontier will not produce friendship. Only friendliness produces friendship. And we must look far deeper into the soul of man for the thing that produces friendliness.

But apart from this fallacy about the facts, I feel, as I say, a strong abstract anger against the idea, or what some would call the ideal. If it were true that men could be taught and tamed by machines, even if they were taught wisdom or tamed to amiability, I should think it the most tragic truth in the world. A man so improved would be, in an exceedingly ugly sense, losing his soul to save it. But in truth he cannot be so completely coerced into good; and in so far as he is incompletely coerced, he is quite as likely to be coerced into evil. Of the financial characters who figure as philanthropists and philosophers in such cases, it is strictly true to say that their good is evil. The light in their bodies is darkness, and the highest objects of such men are the lowest objects of ordinary men. Their peace is mere safety, their friendship is mere trade; their international friendship is mere international trade. The best we can say of that school of capitalism is that it will be unsuccessful. It has every other vice, but it is not practical. It has at least the impossibility of idealism; and so far as remoteness can carry it, that Inferno is indeed a Utopia. All the visible manifestations of these men are materialistic; but at least their visions will not materialise. The worst we suffer; but the best we shall at any rate escape. We may continue to endure the realities of cosmopolitan capitalism; but we shall be spared its ideals.

But I am not primarily interested in the plutocrats whose vision takes so vulgar a form. I am interested in the same thing when it takes a far more subtle form, in men of genius and genuine social enthusiasm like Mr. H. G. Wells. It would be very unfair to a man like Mr. Wells to suggest that in his vision the Englishman and the American are to embrace only in the sense of clinging to each other in terror. He is a man who understands what friendship is, and who knows how to enjoy the motley humours of humanity. But the political reconstruction which he proposes is too much determined by this old nightmare of necessitarianism. He tells us that our national dignities and differences must be melted into the huge mould of a World State, or else (and I think these are almost his own words) we shall be destroyed by the instruments and machinery we have ourselves made. In effect, men must abandon patriotism or they will be murdered by science. After this, surely no one can accuse Mr. Wells of an undue tenderness for scientific over other types of training. Greek may be a good thing or no; but nobody says that if Greek scholarship is carried past a certain point, everybody will be torn in pieces like Orpheus, or burned up like Semele, or poisoned like Socrates. Philosophy, theology and logic may or may not be idle academic studies; but nobody supposes that the study of philosophy, or even of theology, ultimately forces its students to manufacture racks and thumb-screws against their will; or that even logicians need be so alarmingly logical as all that. Science seems to be the only branch of study in which people have to be waved back from perfection as from a pestilence. But my business is not with the scientific dangers which alarm Mr. Wells, but with the remedy he proposes for them; or rather with the relation of that remedy to the foundation and the future of America. Now it is not too much to say that Mr. Wells finds his model in America. The World State is to be the United States of the World. He answers almost all objections to the practicability of such a peace among states, by pointing out that the American States have such a peace, and by adding, truly enough, that another turn of history might easily have seen them broken up by war. The pattern of the World State is to be found in the New World.

Oddly enough, as it seems to me, he proposes almost cosmic conquests for the American Constitution, while leaving out the most successful thing in that Constitution. The point appeared in answer to a question which many, like myself, must have put in this matter; the question of despotism and democracy. I cannot understand any democrat not seeing the danger of so distant and indirect a system of government. It is hard enough anywhere to get representatives to represent. It is hard enough to get a little town council to fulfil the wishes of a little town, even when the townsmen meet the town councillors every day in the street, and could kick them down the street if they liked. What the same town councillors would be like if they were ruling all their fellow-creatures from the North Pole or the New Jerusalem, is a vision of Oriental despotism beyond the towering fancies of Tamberlane. This difficulty in all representative government is felt everywhere, and not least in America. But I think that if there is one truth apparent in such a choice of evils, it is that monarchy is at least better than oligarchy; and that where we have to act on a large scale, the most genuine popularity can gather round a particular person like a Pope or a President of the United States, or even a dictator like Caesar or Napoleon, rather than round a more or less corrupt committee which can only be defined as an obscure oligarchy. And in that sense any oligarchy is obscure. For people to continue to trust twenty-seven men it is necessary, as a preliminary formality, that people should have heard of them. And there are no twenty-seven men of whom everybody has heard as everybody in France had heard of Napoleon, as all Catholics have heard of the Pope or all Americans have heard of the President. I think the mass of ordinary Americans do really elect their President; and even where they cannot control him at least they watch him, and in the long run they judge him. I think, therefore, that the American Constitution has a real popular institution in the Presidency. But Mr. Wells would appear to want the American Constitution without the Presidency. If I understand his words rightly, he seems to want the great democracy without its popular institution. Alluding to this danger, that the World State might be a world tyranny, he seems to take tyranny entirely in the sense of autocracy. He asks whether the President of the World State would not be rather too tremendous a person, and seems to suggest in answer that there need not even be any such person. He seems to imply that the committee controlling the planet could meet almost without any one in the chair, certainly without any one on the throne. I cannot imagine anything more manifestly made to be a tyranny than such an acephalous aristocracy. But while Mr. Wells's decision seems to me strange, his reason for it seems to me still more extraordinary.

He suggests that no such dictator will be needed in his World State because 'there will be no wars and no diplomacy.' A World State ought doubtless to go round the world; and going round the world seems to be a good training for arguing in a circle. Obviously there will be no wars and no war-diplomacy if something has the power to prevent them; and we cannot deduce that the something will not want any power. It is rather as if somebody, urging that the Germans could only be defeated by uniting the Allied commands under Marshal Foch, had said that after all it need not offend the British Generals because the French supremacy need only be a fiction, the Germans being defeated. We should naturally say that the German defeat would only be a reality because the Allied command was not a fiction. So the universal peace would only be a reality if the World State were not a fiction. And it could not be even a state if it were not a government. This argument amounts to saying, first that the World State will be needed because it is strong, and then that it may safely be weak because it will not be needed.

Internationalism is in any case hostile to democracy. I do not say it is incompatible with it; but any combination of the two will be a compromise between the two. The only purely popular government is local, and founded on local knowledge. The citizens can rule the city because they know the city; but it will always be an exceptional sort of citizen who has or claims the right to rule over ten cities, and these remote and altogether alien cities. All Irishmen may know roughly the same sort of things about Ireland; but it is absurd to say they all know the same things about Iceland, when they may include a scholar steeped in Icelandic sagas or a sailor who has been to Iceland. To make all politics cosmopolitan is to create an aristocracy of globe-trotters. If your political outlook really takes in the Cannibal Islands, you depend of necessity upon a superior and picked minority of the people who have been to the Cannibal Islands; or rather of the still smaller and more select minority who have come back.

Given this difficulty about quite direct democracy over large areas, I think the nearest thing to democracy is despotism. At any rate I think it is some sort of more or less independent monarchy, such as Andrew Jackson created in America. And I believe it is true to say that the two men whom the modern world really and almost reluctantly regards with impersonal respect, as clothed by their office with something historic and honourable, are the Pope and the President of the United States.

But to admire the United States as the United States is one thing. To admire them as the World State is quite another. The attempt of Mr. Wells to make America a sort of model for the federation of all the free nations of the earth, though it is international in intention, is really as narrowly national, in the bad sense, as the desire of Mr. Kipling to cover the world with British Imperialism, or of Professor Treitschke to cover it with Prussian Pan-Germanism. Not being schoolboys, we no longer believe that everything can be settled by painting the map red. Nor do I believe it can be done by painting it blue with white spots, even if they are called stars. The insufficiency of British Imperialism does not lie in the fact that it has always been applied by force of arms. As a matter of fact, it has not. It has been effected largely by commerce, by colonisation of comparatively empty places, by geographical discovery and diplomatic bargain. Whether it be regarded as praise or blame, it is certainly the truth that among all the things that have called themselves empires, the British has been perhaps the least purely military, and has least both of the special guilt and the special glory that goes with militarism. The insufficiency of British Imperialism is not that it is imperial, let alone military. The insufficiency of British Imperialism is that it is British; when it is not merely Jewish. It is that just as a man is no more than a man, so a nation is no more than a nation; and any nation is inadequate as an international model. Any state looks small when it occupies the whole earth. Any polity is narrow as soon as it is as wide as the world. It would be just the same if Ireland began to paint the map green or Montenegro were to paint it black. The objection to spreading anything all over the world is that, among other things, you have to spread it very thin.

But America, which Mr. Wells takes as a model, is in another sense rather a warning. Mr. Wells says very truly that there was a moment in history when America might well have broken up into independent states like those of Europe. He seems to take it for granted that it was in all respects an advantage that this was avoided. Yet there is surely a case, however mildly we put it, for a certain importance in the world still attaching to Europe. There are some who find France as interesting as Florida; and who think they can learn as much about history and humanity in the marble cities of the Mediterranean as in the wooden towns of the Middle West. Europe may have been divided, but it was certainly not destroyed; nor has its peculiar position in the culture of the world been destroyed. Nothing has yet appeared capable of completely eclipsing it, either in its extension in America or its imitation in Japan. But the immediate point here is perhaps a more important one. There is now no creed accepted as embodying the common sense of all Europe, as the Catholic creed was accepted as embodying it in mediaeval times. There is no culture broadly superior to all others, as the Mediterranean culture was superior to that of the barbarians in Roman times. If Europe were united in modern times, it would probably be by the victory of one of its types over others, possibly over all the others. And when America was united finally in the nineteenth century, it *was* by the victory of one of its types over others. It is not yet certain that this victory was a good thing. It is not yet certain that the world will be better for the triumph of the North over the Southern traditions of America. It may yet turn out to be as unfortunate as a triumph of the North Germans over the Southern traditions of Germany and of Europe.

The men who will not face this fact are men whose minds are not free. They are more crushed by Progress than any pietists by Providence. They are not allowed to question that whatever has recently happened was all for the best. Now Progress is

Providence without God. That is, it is a theory that everything has always perpetually gone right by accident. It is a sort of atheistic optimism, based on an everlasting coincidence far more miraculous than a miracle. If there be no purpose, or if the purpose permits of human free will, then in either case it is almost insanely unlikely that there should be in history a period of steady and uninterrupted progress; or in other words a period in which poor bewildered humanity moves amid a chaos of complications, without making a single mistake. What has to be hammered into the heads of most normal newspaper-readers today is that Man has made a great many mistakes. Modern Man has made a great many mistakes. Indeed, in the case of that progressive and pioneering character, one is sometimes tempted to say that he has made nothing but mistakes. Calvinism was a mistake, and Capitalism was a mistake, and Teutonism and the flattery of the Northern tribes were mistakes. In the French the persecution of Catholicism by the politicians was a mistake, as they found out in the Great War; when the memory gave Irish or Italian Catholics an excuse for hanging back. In England the loss of agriculture and therefore of food-supply in war, and the power to stand a siege, was a mistake. And in America the introduction of the negroes was a mistake; but it may yet be found that the sacrifice of the Southern white man to them was even more of a mistake.

The reason of this doubt is in one word. We have not yet seen the end of the whole industrial experiment; and there are already signs of it coming to a bad end. It may end in Bolshevism. It is more likely to end in the Servile State. Indeed, the two things are not so different as some suppose, and they grow less different every day. The Bolshevists have already called in Capitalists to help them to crush the free peasants. The Capitalists are quite likely to call in Labour Leaders to whitewash their compromise as social reform or even Socialism. The cosmopolitan Jews who are the Communists in the East will not find it so very hard to make a bargain with the cosmopolitan Jews who are Capitalists in the West. The Western Jews would be willing to admit a nominal Socialism. The Eastern Jews have already admitted that their Socialism is nominal. It was the Bolshevist leader himself who said, 'Russia is again a Capitalist country.' But whoever makes the bargain, and whatever is its precise character, the substance of it will be servile. It will be servile in the only rational and reliable sense; that is, an arrangement by which a mass of men are ensured shelter and livelihood, in return for being subjected to a law which obliges them to continue to labour. Of course it will not be called the Servile State; it is very probable that it will be called the Socialist State. But nobody seems to realise how very near all the industrial countries are to it. At any moment it may appear in the simple form of compulsory arbitration; for compulsory arbitration dealing with private employers is by definition slavery. When workmen receive unemployment pay, and at the same time arouse more and more irritation by going on strike, it may seem very natural to give them the unemployment pay for good and forbid them the strike for good; and the combination of those two things is by definition slavery. And Trotsky can beat any Trust magnate as a strike-breaker; for he does not even pretend that his compulsory labour is a free bargain. If Trotsky and the Trust magnate come to a working compromise, that compromise will be a Servile State. But it will also be the supreme and by far the most constructive and conclusive result of the industrial movement in history; of the power of machinery or money; of the huge populations of the modern cities; of scientific inventions and resources; of all the things before which the agricultural society of the Southern Confederacy went down. But even those who cannot see that commercialism may end in the triumph of slavery can see that the Northern victory has to a great extent ended in the triumph of commercialism. And the point at the moment is that this did definitely mean, even at the time, the triumph of one American type over another American type; just as much as any European war might mean the triumph of one European type over another. A victory of England over France would be a victory of merchants over peasants; and the victory of Northerners over Southerners was a victory of merchants over squires. So that that very unity, which Mr. Wells contrasts so favourably with war, was not only itself due to a war, but to a war which had one of the most questionable and even perilous of the results of war. That result was a change in the balance of power, the predominance of a particular partner, the exaltation of a particular example, the eclipse of excellent traditions when the defeated lost their international influence. In short, it made exactly the same sort of difference of which we speak when we say that 1870 was a disaster to Europe, or that it was necessary to fight Prussia lest she should Prussianise the whole world. America would have been very different if the leadership had remained with Virginia. The world would have been very different if America had been very different. It is quite reasonable to rejoice that the issue went as it did; indeed, as I have explained elsewhere, for other reasons I do on the whole rejoice in it. But it is certainly not self-evident that it is a matter for rejoicing. One type of American state conquered and subjugated another type of American state; and the virtues and value of the latter were very largely lost to the world. So if Mr. Wells insists on the parallel of a United States of Europe, he must accept the parallel of a Civil War of Europe. He must suppose that the peasant countries crush the industrial countries or vice versa; and that one or other of them becomes the European tradition to the neglect of the other. The situation which seems to satisfy him so completely in America is, after all, the situation which would result in Europe if the Germanic Empires, let us say, had entirely arrested the special development of the Slavs; or if the influence of France had really broken off short under a blow from Britain. The Old South had qualities of humane civilisation which have not sufficiently survived; or at any rate have not sufficiently spread. It is true that the decline of the agricultural South has been considerably balanced by the growth of the agricultural West. It is true, as I have occasion to emphasise in another place, that the West does give the New America something that is nearly a normal peasantry, as a pendant to the industrial towns. But this is not an answer; it is rather an augmentation of the argument. In so far as America is saved it is saved by being patchy; and would be ruined if the Western patch had the same fate as the Southern patch. When all is said, therefore, the advantages of American unification are not so certain that we can apply them to a world unification. The doubt could be expressed in a great many ways and by a great many examples. For that matter, it is already being felt that the supremacy of the Middle West in politics is inflicting upon other localities exactly the sort of local injustice that turns provinces into nations struggling to be free. It has already inflicted what amounts to religious persecution, or the imposition of an alien morality, on the wine-growing civilisation of California. In a word, the American system is a good one as governments go; but it is too large, and the world will not be improved by making it larger. And for this reason alone I should reject this second method of uniting England and America; which is not only Americanising England, but Americanising everything else.

But the essential reason is that a type of culture came out on top in America and England in the nineteenth century, which cannot and would not be tolerated on top of the world. To unite all the systems at the top, without improving and simplifying their social organisation below, would be to tie all the tops of the trees together where they rise above a dense and poisonous jungle, and make the jungle darker than before. To create such a cosmopolitan political platform would be to build a roof above our own heads to shut out the sunlight, on which only usurers and conspirators clad in gold could walk about in the sun. This is no moment when industrial intellectualism can inflict such an artificial oppression upon the world. Industrialism itself is coming to see dark days, and its future is very doubtful. It is split from end to end with strikes and struggles for economic life, in which the poor not only plead that they are starving, but even the rich can only plead that they are bankrupt. The peasantries are growing not only more prosperous but more politically effective; the Russian moujik has held up the Bolshevist Government of Moscow and Petersburg; a huge concession has been made by England to Ireland; the League of Nations has decided for Poland against Prussia. It is not certain that industrialism will not wither even in its own field; it is certain that its intellectual ideas will not be allowed to cover every field; and this sort of cosmopolitan culture is one of its ideas. Industrialism itself may perish; or on the other hand industrialism itself may survive, by some searching and scientific reform that will really guarantee economic security to all. It may really purge itself of the accidental maladies of anarchy and famine; and continue as a machine, but at least as a comparatively clean and humanely shielded machine; at any rate no longer as a man-eating machine. Capitalism may clear itself of its worst corruptions by such reform as is open to it; by creating humane and healthy conditions for labour, and setting the labouring classes to work under a lucid and recognised law. It may make Pittsburg one vast model factory for all who will model themselves upon factories; and may give to all men and women in its employment a clear social status in which they can be contented and secure. And on the day when that social security is established for the masses, when industrial capitalism has achieved this larger and more logical organisation and found peace at last, a strange and shadowy and ironic triumph, like an abstract apology, will surely hover over all those graves in the Wilderness where lay the bones of so many gallant gentlemen; men who had also from their youth known and upheld such a social stratification, who had the courage to call a spade a spade and a slave a slave.

A NEW MARTIN CHUZZLEWIT

The aim of this book, if it has one, is to suggest this thesis; that the very worst way of helping Anglo-American friendship is to be an Anglo-American. There is only one thing lower, of course, which is being an Anglo-Saxon. It is lower, because at least Englishmen do exist and Americans do exist; and it may be possible, though repulsive, to imagine an American and an Englishman in some way blended together. But if Angles and Saxons ever did exist, they are all fortunately dead now; and the wildest imagination cannot form the weakest idea of what sort of monster would be made by mixing one with the other. But my thesis is that the whole hope, and the only hope, lies not in mixing two things together, but rather in cutting them very sharply asunder. That is the only way in which two things can succeed sufficiently in getting outside each other to appreciate and admire each other. So long as they are different and yet supposed to be the same, there can be nothing but a divided mind and a staggering balance. It may be that in the first twilight of time man and woman walked about as one quadruped. But if they did, I am sure it was a quadruped that reared and bucked and kicked up its heels. Then the flaming sword of some angel divided them, and they fell in love with each other.

Should the reader require an example a little more within historical range, or a little more subject to critical tests, than the above prehistoric anecdote (which I need not say was revealed to me in a vision) it would be easy enough to supply them both in a hypothetical and a historical form. It is obvious enough in a general way that if we begin to subject diverse countries to an identical test, there will not only be rivalry, but what is far more deadly and disastrous, superiority. If we institute a competition between Holland and Switzerland as to the relative grace and agility of their mountain guides, it will be clear that the decision is disproportionately easy; it will also be clear that certain facts about the configuration of Holland have escaped our international eye. If we establish a comparison between them in skill and industry in the art of building dykes against the sea, it will be equally clear that the injustice falls the other way; it will also be clear that the situation of Switzerland on the map has received insufficient study. In both cases there will not only be rivalry but very unbalanced and unjust rivalry; in both cases, therefore, there will not only be enmity but very bitter or insolent enmity. But so long as the two are sharply divided there can be no enmity because there can be no rivalry. Nobody can argue about whether the Swiss climb mountains better than the Dutch build dykes; just as nobody can argue about whether a triangle is more triangular than a circle is round.

This fancy example is alphabetically and indeed artificially simple; but, having used it for convenience, I could easily give similar examples not of fancy but of fact. I had occasion recently to attend the Christmas festivity of a club in London for the exiles of one of the Scandinavian nations. When I entered the room the first thing that struck my eye, and greatly raised my spirits, was that the room was dotted with the colours of peasant costumes and the specimens of peasant craftsmanship. There were, of course, other costumes and other crafts in evidence; there were men dressed like myself (only better) in the garb of the modern middle classes; there was furniture like the furniture of any other room in London. Now, according to the ideal formula of the ordinary internationalist, these things that we had in common ought to have moved me to a sense of the kinship of all civilisation. I ought to have felt that as the Scandinavian gentleman wore a collar and tie, and I also wore a collar and tie, we were brothers and nothing could come between us. I ought to have felt that we were standing for the same principles of truth because we were wearing the same pair of trousers; or rather, to speak with more precision, similar pairs of trousers. Anyhow, the pair of trousers, that cloven pennon, ought to have floated in fancy over my head as the banner of Europe or the League of Nations. I am constrained to confess that no such rush of emotions overcame me; and the topic of trousers did not float across my mind at all. So far as those things were concerned, I might have remained in a mood of mortal enmity, and cheerfully shot or stabbed the best dressed gentleman in the room. Precisely what did warm my heart with an abrupt affection for that northern nation was the very thing that is utterly and indeed lamentably lacking in my own nation. It was something corresponding to the one great gap in English history, corresponding to the one great blot on English civilisation. It was the spiritual presence of a peasantry, dressed according to its own dignity, and expressing itself by its own creations.

The sketch of America left by Charles Dickens is generally regarded as something which is either to be used as a taunt or covered with an apology. Doubtless it was unduly critical, even of the America of that day; yet curiously enough it may well be the text for a true reconciliation at the present day. It is true that in this, as in other things, the Dickensian exaggeration is itself exaggerated. It is also true that, while it is over-emphasised, it is not allowed for. Dickens tended too much to describe the United States as a vast lunatic asylum; but partly because he had a natural inspiration and imagination suited to the description of lunatic asylums. As it was his finest poetic fancy that created a lunatic over the garden wall, so it was his fancy that created a lunatic over the western sea. To read some of the complaints, one would fancy that Dickens had deliberately invented a low and farcical America to be a contrast to his high and exalted England. It is suggested that he showed America as full of rowdy bullies like Hannibal Chollop, or ridiculous wind-bags like Elijah Pogram, while England was full of refined and sincere spirits like Jonas Chuzzlewit, Chevy Slime, Montague Tigg, and Mr. Pecksniff. If *Martin Chuzzlewit* makes America a lunatic asylum, what in the world does it make England? We can only say a criminal lunatic asylum. The truth is, of course, that Dickens so described them because he had a genius for that sort of description; for the making of almost maniacal grotesques of the same type as Quilp or Fagin. He made these Americans absurd because he was an artist in absurdity; and no artist can help finding hints everywhere for his own peculiar art. In a word, he created a laughable Pogram for the same reason that he created a laughable Pecksniff; and that was only because no other creature could have created them.

It is often said that we learn to love the characters in romances as if they were characters in real life. I wish we could sometimes love the characters in real life as we love the characters in romances. There are a great many human souls whom we should accept more kindly, and even appreciate more clearly, if we simply thought of them as people in a story. *Martin Chuzzlewit* is itself indeed an unsatisfactory and even unfortunate example; for it is, among its author's other works, a rather unusually harsh and hostile story. I do not suggest that we should feel towards an American friend that exact shade or tint of tenderness that we feel towards Mr. Hannibal Chollop. Our enjoyment of the foreigner should rather resemble our enjoyment of Pickwick than our enjoyment of Pecksniff. But there is this amount of appropriateness even in the particular example; that Dickens did show in both countries how men can be made amusing to each other. So far the point is not that he made fun of America, but that he got fun out of America. And, as I have already pointed out, he applied exactly the same method of selection and exaggeration to England. In the other English stories, written in a more amiable mood, he applied it in a more amiable manner; but he could apply it to an American too, when he was writing in that mood and manner. We can see it in the witty and withering criticism delivered by the Yankee traveller in the musty refreshment room of Mugby Junction; a genuine example of a genuinely American fun and freedom satirising a genuinely British stuffiness and snobbery. Nobody expects the American traveller to admire the refreshments at Mugby Junction; but he might admire the refreshment at one of the Pickwickian inns, especially if it contained Pickwick. Nobody expects Pickwick to like Pogram; but he might like the American who made fun of Mugby Junction. But the point is that, while he supported him in making fun, he would also think him funny. The two comic characters could admire each other, but they would also be amused at each other. And the American would think the Englishman funny because he was English; and a very good reason too. The Englishman would think the American amusing because he was American; nor can I imagine a better ground for his amusement.

Now many will debate on the psychological possibility of such a friendship founded on reciprocal ridicule, or rather on a comedy of comparisons. But I will say of this harmony of humours what Mr. H. G. Wells says of his harmony of states in the unity of his World State. If it be truly impossible to have such a peace, then there is nothing possible except war. If we cannot have friends in this fashion, then we shall sooner or later have enemies in some other fashion. There is no hope in the pompous impersonalities of internationalism.

And this brings us to the real and relevant mistake of Dickens. It was not in thinking his Americans funny, but in thinking them foolish because they were funny. In this sense it will be noticed that Dickens's American sketches are almost avowedly superficial; they are descriptions of public life and not private life. Mr. Jefferson Brick had no private life. But Mr. Jonas Chuzzlewit undoubtedly had a private life; and even kept some parts of it exceeding private. Mr. Pecksniff was also a domestic character; so was Mr. Quilp. Mr. Pecksniff and Mr. Quilp had slightly different ways of surprising their families; Mr. Pecksniff by playfully observing 'Boh!' when he came home; Mr. Quilp by coming home at all. But we can form no picture of how Mr. Hannibal Chollop playfully surprised his family; possibly by shooting at them; possibly by not shooting at them. We can only say that he would rather surprise us by having a family at all. We do not know how the Mother of the Modern Gracchi managed the Modern Gracchi; for her maternity was rather a public than a private office. We have no romantic moonlit scenes of the love-making of Elijah Pogram, to balance against the love story of Seth Pecksniff. These figures are all in a special sense theatrical; all facing one way and lit up by a public limelight. Their ridiculous characters are detachable from their real characters, if they have any real characters. And the author might perfectly well be right about what is ridiculous, and wrong about what is real. He might be as right in smiling at the Pograms and the Bricks as in smiling at the Pickwicks and the Boffins. And he might still be as wrong in seeing Mr. Pogram as a hypocrite as the great Buzfuz was wrong in seeing Mr. Pickwick as a monster of revolting heartlessness and systematic villainy. He might still be as wrong in thinking Jefferson Brick a charlatan and a cheat as was that great disciple of Lavater, Mrs. Wilfer, in tracing every wrinkle of evil cunning in the face of Mrs. Boffin. For Mr. Pickwick's spectacles and gaiters and Mrs. Boffin's bonnets and boudoir are after all superficial jokes; and might be equally well seen whatever we saw beneath them. A man may smile and smile and be a villain; but a man may also make us smile and not be a villain. He may make us smile and not even be a fool. He may make us roar with laughter and be an exceedingly wise man.

Now that is the paradox of America which Dickens never discovered. Elijah Pogram was far more fantastic than his satirist thought; and the most grotesque feature of Brick and Chollop was hidden from him. The really strange thing was that Pogram probably did say, 'Rough he may be. So air our bars. Wild he may be. So air our buffalers,' and yet was a perfectly intelligent and public-spirited citizen while he said it. The extraordinary thing is that Jefferson Brick may really have said, 'The libation of freedom must sometimes be quaffed in blood,' and yet Jefferson Brick may have served freedom, resisting unto blood. There really has been a florid school of rhetoric in the United States which has made it quite possible for serious and sensible men to say such things. It is amusing simply as a difference of idiom or costume is always amusing; just as English idiom and English costume are amusing to Americans. But about this kind of difference there can be no kind of doubt. So sturdy not to say stuffy a materialist as Ingersoll could say of so shoddy not to say shady a financial politician as Blaine, 'Like an arméd warrior, like a pluméd knight, James G. Blaine strode down the hall of Congress, and flung his spear full and true at the shield of every enemy of his country and every traducer of his fair name.' Compared with that, the passage about bears and buffaloes, which Mr. Pogram delivered in defence of the defaulting post-master, is really a very reasonable and appropriate statement. For bears and buffaloes are wild and rough and in that sense free; while pluméd knights do not throw their lances about like the assegais of Zulus. And the defaulting post-master was at least as good a person to praise in such a fashion as James G. Blaine of the Little Rock Railway. But anybody who had treated Ingersoll or Blaine merely as a fool and a figure of fun would have very rapidly found out his mistake. But Dickens did not know Brick or Chollop long enough to find out his mistake. It need not be denied that, even after a full understanding, he might still have found things to smile at or to criticise. I do not insist on his admitting that Hannibal Chollop was as great a hero as Hannibal, or that Elijah Pogram was as true a prophet as Elijah. But I do say very seriously that they had something about their atmosphere and situation that made possible a sort of heroism and even a sort of prophecy that were really less natural at that period in that Merry England whose comedy and common sense we sum up under the name of Dickens. When we joke about the name of Hannibal Chollop, we might remember of what nation was the general who dismissed his defeated soldiers at Appomatox with words which the historian has justly declared to be worthy of Hannibal: 'We have fought through this war together. I have done my best for you.' It is not fair to forget Jefferson, or even Jefferson Davis, entirely in favour of Jefferson Brick.

For all these three things, good, bad, and indifferent, go together to form something that Dickens missed, merely because the England of his time most disastrously missed it. In this case, as in every case, the only way to measure justly the excess of a foreign country is to measure the defect of our own country. For in this matter the human mind is the victim of a curious little unconscious trick, the cause of nearly all international dislikes. A man treats his own faults as original sin and supposes them scattered everywhere with the seed of Adam. He supposes that men have then added their own foreign vices to the solid and simple foundation of his own private vices. It would astound him to realise that they have actually, by their strange erratic path, avoided his vices as well as his virtues. His own faults are things with which he is so much at home that he at once forgets and assumes them abroad. He is so faintly conscious of them in himself that he is not even conscious of the absence of them in other people. He assumes that they are there so that he does not see that they are not there. The Englishman takes it for granted that a Frenchman will have all the English faults. Then he goes on to be seriously angry with the Frenchman for having dared to complicate them by the French faults. The notion that the Frenchman has the French faults and *not* the English faults is a paradox too wild to cross his mind.

He is like an old Chinaman who should laugh at Europeans for wearing ludicrous top-hats and curling up their pig-tails inside them; because obviously all men have pig-tails, as all monkeys have tails. Or he is like an old Chinese lady who should justly deride the high-heeled shoes of the West, considering them a needless addition to the sufficiently tight and secure bandaging of the foot; for, of course, all women bind up their feet, as all women bind up their hair. What these Celestial thinkers would not think of, or allow for, is the wild possibility that we do not have pig-tails although we do have top-hats, or that our ladies are not silly enough to have Chinese feet, though they are silly enough to have high-heeled shoes. Nor should we necessarily have come an inch nearer to the Chinese extravagances even if the chimney-pot hat rose higher than a factory chimney or the high heels had evolved into a sort of stilts. By the same fallacy the Englishman will not only curse the French peasant as a miser, but will also try to tip him as a beggar. That is, he will first complain of the man having the surliness of an independent man, and then accuse him of having the servility of a dependent one. Just as the hypothetical Chinaman cannot believe that we have top-hats but not pig-tails, so the Englishman cannot believe that peasants are not snobs even when they are savages. Or he sees that a Paris paper is violent and sensational; and then supposes that some millionaire owns twenty such papers and runs them as a newspaper trust. Surely the Yellow Press is present everywhere to paint the map yellow, as the British Empire to paint it red. It never occurs to such a critic that the French paper is violent because it is personal, and personal because it belongs to a real and responsible person, and not to a ring of nameless millionaires. It is a pamphlet, and not an anonymous pamphlet. In a hundred other cases the same truth could be illustrated; the situation in which the black man first assumes that all mankind is black, and then accuses the rest of the artificial vice of painting their faces red and yellow, or the hypocrisy of white-washing themselves after the fashion of whited sepulchres. The particular case of it now before us is that of the English misunderstanding of America; and it is based, as in all these cases, on the English misunderstanding of England.

For the truth is that England has suffered of late from not having enough of the free shooting of Hannibal Chollop; from not understanding enough that the libation of freedom must sometimes be quaffed in blood. The prosperous Englishman will not admit this; but then the prosperous Englishman will not admit that he has suffered from anything. That is what he is suffering from. Until lately at least he refused to realise that many of his modern habits had been bad habits, the worst of them being contentment. For all the real virtue in contentment evaporates, when the contentment is only satisfaction and the satisfaction is only self-satisfaction. Now it is perfectly true that America and not England has seen the most obvious and outrageous official denials of liberty. But it is equally true that it has seen the most obvious flouting of such official nonsense, far more obvious than any similar evasions in England. And nobody who knows the subconscious violence of the American character would ever be surprised if the weapons of Chollop began to be used in that most lawful lawlessness. It is perfectly true that the libation of freedom must sometimes be drunk in blood, and never more (one would think) than when mad millionaires forbid it to be drunk in beer. But America, as compared with England, is the country where one can still fancy men obtaining the libation of beer by the libation of blood. Vulgar plutocracy is almost omnipotent in both countries; but I think there is now more kick of reaction against it in America than in England. The Americans may go mad when they make laws; but they recover their reason when they disobey them. I wish I could believe that there was as much of that destructive repentance in England; as indeed there certainly was when Cobbett wrote. It faded gradually like a dying fire through the Victorian era; and it was one of the very few realities that Dickens did not understand. But any one who does understand it will know that the days of Cobbett saw the last lost fight for English democracy; and that if he had stood at that turning of the historic road, he would have wished a better fate to the frame-breakers and the fury against the first machinery, and luck to the Luddite fires.

Anyhow, what is wanted is a new Martin Chuzzlewit, told by a wiser Mark Tapley. It is typical of something sombre and occasionally stale in the mood of Dickens when he wrote that book, that the comic servant is not really very comic. Mark Tapley is a very thin shadow of Sam Weller. But if Dickens had written it in a happier mood, there might have been a truer meaning in Mark Tapley's happiness. For it is true that this illogical good humour amid unreason and disorder is one of the real virtues of the English people. It is the real advantage they have in that adventure all over the world, which they were recently and reluctantly induced to call an Empire. That receptive ridicule remains with them as a secret pleasure when they are colonists—or convicts. Dickens might have written another version of the great romance, and one in which America was really seen gaily by Mark instead of gloomily by Martin. Mark Tapley might really have made the best of America. Then America would have lived and danced before us like Pickwick's England, a fairyland of happy lunatics and lovable monsters, and we might still have sympathised as much with the rhetoric of Lafayette Kettle as with the rhetoric of Wilkins Micawber, or with the violence of Chollop as with the violence of Boythorn. That new Martin Chuzzlewit will never be written; and the loss of it is more tragic than the loss of *Edwin Drood*. But every man who has travelled in America has seen glimpses and episodes in that untold tale; and far away on the Red-Indian frontiers or in the hamlets in the hills of Pennsylvania, there are people whom I met for a few hours or for a few moments, whom I none the less sincerely like and respect because I cannot but smile as I think of them. But the converse is also true; they have probably forgotten me; but if they remember they laugh.

THE SPIRIT OF AMERICA

I suggest that diplomatists of the internationalist school should spend some of their money on staging farces and comedies of cross-purposes, founded on the curious and prevalent idea that England and America have the same language. I know, of course, that we both inherit the glorious tongue of Shakespeare, not to mention the tune of the musical glasses; but there have been moments when I thought that if we spoke Greek and they spoke Latin we might understand each other better. For Greek and Latin are at least fixed, while American at least is still very fluid. I do not know the American language, and therefore I do not claim to distinguish between the American language and the American slang. But I know that highly theatrical developments might follow on taking the words as part of the English slang or the English language. I have already given the example of calling a person 'a regular guy,' which in the States is a graceful expression of respect and esteem, but which on the stage, properly handled, might surely lead the way towards a divorce or duel or something lively. Sometimes coincidence merely clinches a mistake, as it so often clinches a misprint. Every proof-reader knows that the worst misprint is not that which makes nonsense but that which makes sense; not that which is obviously wrong but that which is hideously right. He who has essayed to write 'he got the book,' and has found it rendered mysteriously as 'he got the boob' is pensively resigned. It is when it is rendered quite lucidly as 'he got the boot' that he is moved to a more passionate mood of regret. I have had conversations in which this sort of accident would have wholly misled me, if another accident had not come to the rescue. An American friend of mine was telling me of his adventures as a cinema-producer down in the south-west where real Red Indians were procurable. He said that certain Indians were 'very bad actors.' It passed for me as a very ordinary remark on a very ordinary or natural deficiency. It would hardly seem a crushing criticism to say that some wild Arab chieftain was not very good at imitating a farmyard; or that the Grand Llama of Thibet was rather clumsy at making paper boats. But the remark might be natural in a man travelling in paper boats, or touring with an invisible farmyard for his menagerie. As my friend was a cinema-producer, I supposed he meant that the Indians were bad cinema actors. But the phrase has really a high and austere moral meaning, which my levity had wholly missed. A bad actor means a man whose actions are bad or morally reprehensible. So that I might have embraced a Red Indian who was dripping with gore, or covered with atrocious crimes, imagining there was nothing the matter with him beyond a mistaken choice of the theatrical profession. Surely there are here the elements of a play, not to mention a cinema play. Surely a New England village maiden might find herself among the wigwams in the power of the formidable and fiendish 'Little Blue Bison,' merely through her mistaken sympathy with his financial failure as a Film Star. The notion gives me glimpses of all sorts of dissolving views of primeval forests and flamboyant theatres; but this impulse of irrelevant theatrical production must be curbed. There is one example, however, of this complication of language actually used in contrary senses, about which the same figure can be used to illustrate a more serious fact.

Suppose that, in such an international interlude, an English girl and an American girl are talking about the fiancé of the former, who is coming to call. The English girl will be haughty and aristocratic (on the stage), the American girl will of course have short hair and skirts and will be cynical; Americans being more completely free from cynicism than any people in the world. It is the great glory of Americans that they are not cynical; for that matter, English aristocrats are hardly ever haughty; they understand the game much better than that. But on the stage, anyhow, the American girl may say, referring to her friend's fiancé, with a cynical wave of the cigarette, 'I suppose he's bound to come and see you.' And at this the blue blood of the Vere de Veres will boil over; the English lady will be deeply wounded and insulted at the suggestion that her lover only comes to see her because he is forced to do so. A staggering stage quarrel will then ensue, and things will go from bad to worse; until the arrival of an Interpreter who can talk both English and American. He stands between the two ladies waving two pocket dictionaries, and explains the error on which the quarrel turns. It is very simple; like the seed of all tragedies. In English 'he is bound to come and see you' means that he is obliged or constrained to come and see you. In American it does not. In American it means that he is bent on coming to see you, that he is irrevocably resolved to do so, and will surmount any obstacle to do it. The two young ladies will then embrace as the curtain falls.

Now when I was lecturing in America I was often told, in a radiant and congratulatory manner, that such and such a person was bound to come and hear me lecture. It seemed a very cruel form of conscription, and I could not understand what authority could have made it compulsory. In the course of discovering my error, however, I thought I began to understand certain American ideas and instincts that lie behind this American idiom. For as I have urged before, and shall often urge again, the road to international friendship is through really understanding jokes. It is in a sense through taking jokes seriously. It is quite legitimate to laugh at a man who walks down the street in three white hats and a green dressing gown, because it is unfamiliar; but after all the man has *some* reason for what he does; and until we know the reason we do not understand the story, or even understand the joke. So the outlander will always seem outlandish in custom or costume; but serious relations depend on our getting beyond the fact of difference to the things wherein it differs. A good symbolical figure for all this may be found among the people who say, perhaps with a self-revealing simplicity, that they are bound to go to a lecture.

If I were asked for a single symbolic figure summing up the whole of what seems eccentric and interesting about America to an Englishman, I should be satisfied to select that one lady who complained of Mrs. Asquith's lecture and wanted her money back. I do not mean that she was typically American in complaining; far from it. I, for one, have a great and guilty knowledge of all that amiable American audiences will endure without complaint. I do not mean that she was typically American in wanting her money; quite the contrary. That sort of American spends money rather than hoards it; and when we convict them of vulgarity we acquit them of avarice. Where she was typically American, summing up a truth individual and indescribable in any other way, is that she used these words: 'I've risen from a sick-bed to come and hear her, and I want my money back.'

The element in that which really amuses an Englishman is precisely the element which, properly analysed, ought to make him admire an American. But my point is that only by going through the amusement can he reach the admiration. The amusement is in the vision of a tragic sacrifice for what is avowedly a rather trivial object. Mrs. Asquith is a candid lady of considerable humour; and I feel sure she does not regard the experience of hearing her read her diary as an ecstasy for which the sick should thus suffer martyrdom. She also is English; and had no other claim but to amuse Americans and possibly to be amused by them. This being so, it is rather as if somebody said, 'I have risked my life in fire and pestilence to find my way to the music hall,' or, 'I have fasted forty days in the wilderness sustained by the hope of seeing Totty Toddles do her new dance.'

And there is something rather more subtle involved here. There is something in an Englishman which would make him feel faintly ashamed of saying that he had fasted to hear Totty Toddles, or risen from a sick-bed to hear Mrs. Asquith. He would feel that it was undignified to confess that he had wanted mere amusement so much; and perhaps that he had wanted anything so much. He would not like, so to speak, to be seen rushing down the street after Totty Toddles, or after Mrs. Asquith, or perhaps after anybody. But there is something in it distinct from a mere embarrassment at admitting enthusiasm. He might admit the enthusiasm if the object seemed to justify it; he might perfectly well be serious about a serious thing. But he cannot understand a person being proud of serious sacrifices for what is not a serious thing. He does not like to admit that a little thing can excite him; that he can lose his breath in running, or lose his balance in reaching, after something that might be called silly.

Now that is where the American is fundamentally different. To him the enthusiasm itself is meritorious. To him the excitement itself is dignified. He counts it a part of his manhood to fast or fight or rise from a bed of sickness for something, or possibly for anything. His ideal is not to be a lock that only a worthy key can open, but a 'live wire' that anything can touch or anybody can use. In a word, there is a difference in the very definition of virility and therefore of virtue. A live wire is not only active, it is also sensitive. Thus sensibility becomes actually a part of virility. Something more is involved than the vulgar simplification of the American as the irresistible force and the Englishman as the immovable post. As a fact, those who speak of such things nowadays generally mean by something irresistible something simply immovable, or at least something unalterable, motionless even in motion, like a cannon ball; for a cannon ball is as dead as a cannon. Prussian militarism was praised in that way—until it met a French force of about half its size on the banks of the Marne. But that is not what an American means by energy; that sort of Prussian energy is only monotony without repose. American energy is not a soulless machine; for it is the whole point that he puts his soul into it. It is a very small box for so big a thing; but it is not an empty box. But the point is that he is not only proud of his energy, he is proud of his excitement. He is not ashamed of his emotion, of the fire or even the tear in his manly eye, when he tells you that the great wheel of his machine breaks four billion butterflies an hour.

That is the point about American sport; that it is not in the least sportive. It is because it is not very sportive that we sometimes say it is not very sporting. It has the vices of a religion. It has all the paradox of original sin in the service of aboriginal faith. It is sometimes untruthful because it is sincere. It is sometimes treacherous because it is loyal. Men lie and cheat for it as they lied for their lords in a feudal conspiracy, or cheated for their chieftains in a Highland feud. We may say that the vassal readily committed treason; but it is equally true that he readily endured torture. So does the American athlete endure torture. Not only the self-sacrifice but the solemnity of the American athlete is like that of the American Indian. The athletes in the States have the attitude of the athletes among the Spartans, the great historical nation without a sense of humour. They suffer an ascetic régime not to be matched in any monasticism and hardly in any militarism. If any tradition of these things remains in a saner age, they will probably be remembered as a mysterious religious order of fakirs or dancing dervishes, who shaved their heads and fasted in honour of Hercules or Castor and Pollux. And that is really the spiritual atmosphere though the gods have vanished; and the religion is subconscious and therefore irrational. For the problem of the modern world is that it has continued to be religious when it has ceased to be rational. Americans really would starve to win a cocoa-nut shy. They would fast or bleed to win a race of paper boats on a pond. They would rise from a sick-bed to listen to Mrs. Asquith.

But it is the real reason that interests me here. It is certainly not that Americans are so stupid as not to know that cocoa-nuts are only cocoa-nuts and paper boats only made of paper. Americans are, on an average, rather more intelligent than Englishmen; and they are well aware that Hercules is a myth and that Mrs. Asquith is something of a mythologist. It is not that they do not know that the object is small in itself; it is that they do really believe that the enthusiasm is great in itself. They admire people for being impressionable. They admire people for being excited. An American so struggling for some disproportionate trifle (like one of my lectures) really feels in a mystical way that he is right, because it is his whole morality to be keen. So long as he wants something very much, whatever it is, he feels he has his conscience behind him, and the common sentiment of society behind him, and God and the whole universe behind him. Wedged on one leg in a hot crowd at a trivial lecture, he has self-respect; his dignity is at rest. That is what he means when he says he is bound to come to the lecture.

Now the Englishman is fond of occasional larks. But these things are not larks; nor are they occasional. It is the essential of the Englishman's lark that he should think it a lark; that he should laugh at it even when he does it. Being English myself, I like it; but being English myself, I know it is connected with weaknesses as well as merits. In its irony there is condescension and therefore embarrassment. This patronage is allied to the patron, and the patron is allied to the aristocratic tradition of society. The larks are a variant of laziness because of leisure; and the leisure is a variant of the security and even supremacy of the gentleman. When an undergraduate at Oxford smashes half a hundred windows he is well aware that the incident is merely a trifle. He can be trusted to explain to his parents and guardians that it was merely a trifle. He does not say, even in the American sense, that he was bound to smash the windows. He does not say that he had risen from a sick-bed to smash the windows. He does not especially think he has risen at all; he knows he has descended (though with delight, like one diving or sliding down the banisters) to something flat and farcical and full of the English taste for the bathos. He has collapsed into something entirely commonplace; though the owners of the windows may possibly not think so. This rather indescribable element runs through a hundred English things, as in the love of bathos shown even in the sound of proper names; so that even the yearning lover in a lyric yearns for somebody named Sally rather than Salome, and for a place called Wapping rather than a place called Westermain. Even in the relapse into rowdiness there is a sort of relapse into comfort. There is also what is so large a part of comfort; carelessness. The undergraduate breaks windows because he does not care about windows, not because he does care about more fresh air like a hygienist, or about more light like a German poet. Still less does he heroically smash a hundred windows because they come between him and the voice of Mrs. Asquith. But least of all does he do it because he seriously prides himself on the energy apart from its aim, and on the will-power that carries it through. He is not 'bound' to smash the windows, even in the sense of being bent upon it. He is not bound at all but rather relaxed; and his violence is not only a relaxation but a laxity. Finally, this is shown in the fact that he only smashes windows when he is in the mood to smash windows; when some fortunate conjunction of stars and all the tints and nuances of nature whisper to him that it would be well to smash windows. But the American is always ready, at any moment, to waste his energies on the wilder and more suicidal course of going to lectures. And this is because to him such excitement is not a mood but a moral ideal. As I note in another connection, much of the English mystery would be clear to Americans if they understood the word 'mood.' Englishmen are very moody, especially when they smash windows. But I doubt if many Americans understand exactly what we mean by the mood; especially the passive mood.

It is only by trying to get some notion of all this that an Englishman can enjoy the final crown and fruit of all international friendship; which is really liking an American to be American. If we only think that parts of him are excellent because parts of him are English, it would be far more sensible to stop at home and possibly enjoy the society of a whole complete Englishman. But anybody who does understand this can take the same pleasure in an American being American that he does in a thunderbolt being swift and a barometer being sensitive. He can see that a vivid sensibility and vigilance really radiate outwards through all the ramifications of machinery and even of materialism. He can see that the American uses his great practical powers upon very small provocation; but he can also see that there is a kind of sense of honour, like that of a duellist, in his readiness to be provoked. Indeed, there is some parallel between the American man of action, however vulgar his aims, and the old feudal idea of the gentleman with a sword at his side. The gentleman may have been proud of being strong or sturdy; he may too often have been proud of being thick-headed; but he was not proud of being thick-skinned. On the contrary, he was proud of being thin-skinned. He also seriously thought that sensitiveness was a part of masculinity. It may be very absurd to read of two Irish gentlemen trying to kill each other for trifles, or of two Irish-American millionaires trying to ruin each other for trash. But the very pettiness of the pretext and even the purpose illustrates the same conception; which may be called the virtue of excitability. And it is really this, and not any rubbish about iron will-power and masterful mentality, that redeems with romance their clockwork cosmos and its industrial ideals. Being a live wire does not mean that the nerves should be like wires; but rather that the very wires should be like nerves.

Another approximation to the truth would be to say that an American is really not ashamed of curiosity. It is not so simple as it looks. Men will carry off curiosity with various kinds of laughter and bravado, just as they will carry off drunkenness or bankruptcy. But very few people are really proud of lying on a door-step, and very few people are really proud of longing to look through a key-hole. I do not speak of looking through it, which involves questions of honour and self-control; but few people feel that even the desire is dignified. Now I fancy the American, at least by comparison with the Englishman, does feel that his curiosity is consistent with his dignity, because dignity is consistent with vivacity. He feels it is not merely the curiosity of Paul Pry, but the curiosity of Christopher Columbus. He is not a spy but an explorer; and he feels his greatness rather grow with his refusal to turn back, as a traveller might feel taller and taller as he neared the source of the Nile or the North-West Passage. Many an Englishman has had that feeling about discoveries in dark continents; but he does not often have it about discoveries in daily life. The one type does believe in the indignity and the other in the dignity of the detective. It has nothing to do with ethics in the merely external sense. It involves no particular comparison in practical morals and manners. It is something in the whole poise and posture of the self; of the way a man carries himself. For men are not only affected by what they are; but still more, when they are fools, by what they think they are; and when they are wise, by what they wish to be.

There are truths that have almost become untrue by becoming untruthful. There are statements so often stale and insincere that one hesitates to use them, even when they stand for something more subtle. This point about curiosity is not the conventional complaint against the American interviewer. It is not the ordinary joke against the American child. And in the same way I feel the danger of it being identified with the cant about 'a young nation' if I say that it has some of the attractions, not of American childhood, but of real childhood. There is some truth in the tradition that the children of wealthy Americans tend to be too precocious and luxurious. But there is a sense in which we can really say that if the children are like adults, the adults are like children. And that sense is in the very best sense of childhood. It is something which the modern world does not understand. It is something that modern Americans do not understand, even when they possess it; but I think they do possess it.

The devil can quote Scripture for his purpose; and the text of Scripture which he now most commonly quotes is, 'The kingdom of heaven is within you.' That text has been the stay and support of more Pharisees and prigs and self-righteous spiritual bullies than all the dogmas in creation; it has served to identify self-satisfaction with the peace that passes all understanding. And the text to be quoted in answer to it is that which declares that no man can receive the kingdom except as a little child. What we are to have inside is the childlike spirit; but the childlike spirit is not entirely concerned about what is inside. It is the first mark of possessing it that one is interested in what is outside. The most childlike thing about a child is his curiosity and his appetite and his power of wonder at the world. We might almost say that the whole advantage of having the kingdom within is that we look for it somewhere else.

THE SPIRIT OF ENGLAND

Nine times out of ten a man's broad-mindedness is necessarily the narrowest thing about him. This is not particularly paradoxical; it is, when we come to think of it, quite inevitable. His vision of his own village may really be full of varieties; and even his vision of his own nation may have a rough resemblance to the reality. But his vision of the world is probably smaller than the world. His vision of the universe is certainly much smaller than the universe. Hence he is never so inadequate as when he is universal; he is never so limited as when he generalises. This is the fallacy in the many modern attempts at a creedless creed, at something variously described as essential Christianity or undenominational religion or a world faith to embrace all the faiths in the world. It is that every sectarian is more sectarian in his unsectarianism than he is in his sect. The emancipation of a Baptist is a very Baptist emancipation. The charity of a Buddhist is a very Buddhist charity, and very different from Christian charity. When a philosophy embraces everything it generally squeezes everything, and squeezes it out of shape; when it digests it necessarily assimilates. When a theosophist absorbs Christianity it is rather as a cannibal absorbs Christian missionaries. In this sense it is even possible for the larger thing to be swallowed by the smaller; and for men to move about not only in a Clapham sect but in a Clapham cosmos under Clapham moon and stars.

But if this danger exists for all men, it exists especially for the Englishman. The Englishman is never so insular as when he is imperial; except indeed when he is international. In private life he is a good friend and in practical politics generally a good ally. But theoretical politics are more practical than practical politics. And in theoretical politics the Englishman is the worst ally the world ever saw. This is all the more curious because he has passed so much of his historical life in the character of an ally. He has been in twenty great alliances and never understood one of them. He has never been farther away from European politics than when he was fighting heroically in the thick of them. I myself think that this splendid isolation is sometimes really splendid; so long as it is isolation and does not imagine itself to be imperialism or internationalism. With the idea of being international, with the idea of being imperial, comes the frantic and farcical idea of being impartial. Generally speaking, men are never so mean and false and hypocritical as when they are occupied in being impartial. They are performing the first and most typical of all the actions of the devil; they are claiming the throne of God. Even when it is not hypocrisy but only mental confusion, it is always a confusion worse and worse confounded. We see it in the impartial historians of the Victorian Age, who now seem far more Victorian than the partial historians. Hallam wrote about the Middle Ages; but Hallam was far less mediaeval than Macaulay; for Macaulay was at least a fighter. Huxley had more mediaeval sympathies than Herbert Spencer for the same reason; that Huxley was a fighter. They both fought in many ways for the limitations of their own rationalistic epoch; but they were nearer the truth than the men who simply assumed those limitations as rational. The war of the controversionalists was a wider thing than the peace of the arbiters. And in the same way the Englishman never cuts a less convincing figure before other nations than when he tries to arbitrate between them.

I have by this time heard a great deal about the necessity of saving Anglo-American friendship, a necessity which I myself feel rather too strongly to be satisfied with the ambassadorial and editorial style of achieving it. I have already said that the worst style of all is to be Anglo-American; or, as the more illiterate would express, to be Anglo-Saxon. I am more and more convinced that the way for the Englishman to do it is to be English; but to know that he is English and not everything else as well. Thus the only sincere answer to Irish nationalism is English nationalism, which is a reality; and not English imperialism, which is a reactionary fiction, or English internationalism, which is a revolutionary one.

For the English are reviled for their imperialism because they are not imperialistic. They dislike it, which is the real reason why they do it badly; and they do it badly, which is the real reason why they are disliked when they do it. Nobody calls France imperialistic because she has absorbed Brittany. But everybody calls England imperialistic because she has not absorbed Ireland. The Englishman is fixed and frozen for ever in the attitude of a ruthless conqueror; not because he has conquered such people, but because he has not conquered them; but he is always trying to conquer them with a heroism worthy of a better cause. For the really native and vigorous part of what is unfortunately called the British Empire is not an empire at all, and does not consist of these conquered provinces at all. It is not an empire but an adventure; which is probably a much finer thing. It was not the power of making strange countries similar to our own, but simply the pleasure of seeing strange countries because they were different from our own. The adventurer did indeed, like the third son, set out to seek his fortune, but not primarily to alter other people's fortunes; he wished to trade with people rather than to rule them. But as the other people remained different from him, so did he remain different from them. The adventurer saw a thousand strange things and remained a stranger. He was the Robinson Crusoe on a hundred desert islands; and on each he remained as insular as on his own island.

What is wanted for the cause of England to-day is an Englishman with enough imagination to love his country from the outside as well as the inside. That is, we need somebody who will do for the English what has never been done for them, but what is done for any outlandish peasantry or even any savage tribe. We want people who can make England attractive; quite apart from disputes about whether England is strong or weak. We want somebody to explain, not that England is everywhere, but what England is anywhere; not that England is or is not really dying, but why we do not want her to die. For this purpose the official and conventional compliments or claims can never get any farther than pompous abstractions about Law and Justice and Truth; the ideals which England accepts as every civilised state accepts them, and violates as every civilised state violates them. That is not the way in which the picture of any people has ever been painted on the sympathetic imagination of the world. Enthusiasts for old Japan did not tell us that the Japs recognised the existence of abstract morality; but that they lived in paper houses or wrote letters with paint-brushes. Men who wished to interest us in Arabs did not confine themselves to saying that they are monotheists or moralists; they filled our romances with the rush of Arab steeds or the colours of strange tents or carpets. What we want is somebody who will do for the Englishman with his front garden what was done for the Jap and his paper house; who shall understand the Englishman with his dog as well as the Arab with his horse. In a word, what nobody has really tried to do is the one thing that really wants doing. It is to make England attractive as a nationality, and even as a small nationality.

For it is a wild folly to suppose that nations will love each other because they are alike. They will never really do that unless they are really alike; and then they will not be nations. Nations can love each other as men and women love each other, not because they are alike but because they are different. It can easily be shown, I fancy, that in every case where a real public sympathy was aroused for some unfortunate foreign people, it has always been accompanied with a particular and positive interest in their most foreign customs and their most foreign externals. The man who made a romance of the Scotch Highlander made a romance of his kilt and even of his dirk; the friend of the Red Indians was interested in picture writing and had some tendency to be interested in scalping. To take a more serious example, such nations as Serbia had been largely commended to international consideration by the study of Serbian epics, or Serbian songs. The epoch of negro emancipation was also the epoch of negro melodies. Those who wept over Uncle Tom also laughed over Uncle Remus. And just as the admiration for the Redskin almost became an apology for scalping, the mysterious fascination of the African has sometimes almost led us into the fringes of the black forest of Voodoo. But the sort of interest that is felt even in the scalp-hunter and the cannibal, the torturer and the devil-worshipper, that sort of interest has never been felt in the Englishman.

And this is the more extraordinary because the Englishman is really very interesting. He is interesting in a special degree in this special manner; he is interesting because he is individual. No man in the world is more misrepresented by everything official or even in the ordinary sense national. A description of English life must be a description of private life. In that sense there is no public life. In that sense there is no public opinion. There have never been those prairie fires of public opinion in England which often sweep over America. At any rate, there have never been any such popular revolutions since the popular revolutions of the Middle Ages. The English are a nation of amateurs; they are even a nation of eccentrics. An Englishman is never more English than when he is considered a lunatic by the other Englishmen. This can be clearly seen in a figure like Dr. Johnson, who has become national not by being normal but by being extraordinary. To express this mysterious people, to explain or suggest why they like tall hedges and heavy breakfasts and crooked roads and small gardens with large fences, and why they alone among Christians have kept quite consistently the great Christian glory of the open fireplace, here would be a strange and stimulating opportunity for any of the artists in words, who study the souls of strange peoples. That would be the true way to create a friendship between England and America, or between England and anything else; yes, even between England and Ireland. For this justice at least has already been done to Ireland; and as an indignant patriot I demand a more equal treatment for the two nations.

I have already noted the commonplace that in order to teach internationalism we must talk nationalism. We must make the nations as nations less odious or mysterious to each other. We do not make men love each other by describing a monster with a million arms and legs, but by describing the men as men, with their separate and even solitary emotions. As this has a particular application to the emotions of the Englishman, I will return to the topic once more. Now Americans have a power that is the soul and success of democracy, the power of spontaneous social organisation. Their high spirits, their humane ideals are really creative, they abound in unofficial institutions; we might almost say in unofficial officialism. Nobody who has felt the presence of all the leagues and guilds and college clubs will deny that Whitman was national when he said he would build states and cities out of the love of comrades. When all this communal enthusiasm collides with the Englishman, it too often seems literally to leave him cold. They say he is reserved; they possibly think he is rude. And the Englishman, having been taught his own history all wrong, is only too likely to take the criticism as a compliment. He admits that he is reserved because he is stern and strong; or even that he is rude because he is shrewd and candid. But as a fact he is not rude and not especially reserved; at least reserve is not the meaning of his reluctance. The real difference lies, I think, in the fact that American high spirits are not only high but level; that the hilarious American spirit is like a plateau, and the humorous English spirit like a ragged mountain range.

The Englishman is moody; which does not in the least mean that the Englishman is morose. Dickens, as we all feel in reading his books, was boisterously English. Dickens was moody when he wrote *Oliver Twist*; but he was also moody when he wrote *Pickwick*. That is, he was in another and much healthier mood. The mood was normal to him in the sense that nine times out of ten he felt and wrote in that humorous and hilarious mood. But he was, if ever there was one, a man of moods; and all the more of a typical Englishman for being a man of moods. But it was because of this, almost entirely, that he had a misunderstanding with America.

In America there are no moods, or there is only one mood. It is the same whether it is called hustle or uplift; whether we regard it as the heroic love of comrades or the last hysteria of the herd instinct. It has been said of the typical English aristocrats of the Government offices that they resemble certain ornamental fountains and play from ten till four; and it is true that an Englishman, even an English aristocrat, is not always inclined to play any more than to work. But American sociability is not like the Trafalgar fountains. It is like Niagara. It never stops, under the silent stars or the rolling storms. There seems always to be the same human heat and pressure behind it; it is like the central heating of hotels as explained in the advertisements and announcements. The temperature can be regulated; but it is not. And it is always rather overpowering for an Englishman, whose mood changes like his own mutable and shifting sky. The English mood is very like the English weather; it is a nuisance and a national necessity.

If any one wishes to understand the quarrel between Dickens and the Americans, let him turn to that chapter in *Martin Chuzzlewit*, in which young Martin has to receive endless defiles and deputations of total strangers each announced by name and demanding formal salutation. There are several things to be noticed about this incident. To begin with, it did not happen to Martin Chuzzlewit; but it did happen to Charles Dickens. Dickens is incorporating almost without alteration a passage from a diary in the middle of a story; as he did when he included the admirable account of the prison petition of John Dickens as the prison petition of Wilkins Micawber. There is no particular reason why even the gregarious Americans should so throng the portals of a perfectly obscure steerage passenger like young Chuzzlewit. There was every reason why they should throng the portals of the author of *Pickwick* and *Oliver Twist*. And no doubt they did. If I may be permitted the aleatory image, you bet they did. Similar troops of sociable human beings have visited much more insignificant English travellers in America, with some of whom I am myself acquainted. I myself have the luck to be a little more stodgy and less sensitive than many of my countrymen; and certainly less sensitive than Dickens. But I know what it was that annoyed him about that unending and unchanging stream of American visitors; it was the unending and unchanging stream of American sociability and high spirits. A people living on such a lofty but level tableland do not understand the ups and downs of the English temperament; the temper of a nation of eccentrics or (as they used to be called) of humorists. There is something very national in the very name of the old play of *Every Man in His Humour*. But the play more often acted in real life is 'Every Man Out of His Humour.' It is true, as Matthew Arnold said, that an Englishman wants to do as he likes; but it is not always true even that he likes what he likes. An Englishman can be friendly and yet not feel friendly. Or he can be friendly and yet not feel hospitable. Or he can feel hospitable and yet not welcome those whom he really loves. He can think, almost with tears of tenderness, about people at a distance who would be bores if they came in at the door.

American sociability sweeps away any such subtlety. It cannot be expected to understand the paradox or perversity of the Englishman, who thus can feel friendly and avoid friends. That is the truth in the suggestion that Dickens was sentimental. It means that he probably felt most sociable when he was solitary. In all these attempts to describe the indescribable, to indicate the real but unconscious differences between the two peoples, I have tried to balance my words without the irrelevant bias of praise and blame. Both characteristics always cut both ways. On one side this comradeship makes possible a certain communal courage, a democratic derision of rich men in high places, that is not easy in our smaller and more stratified society. On the other hand the Englishman has certainly more liberty, if less equality and fraternity. But the richest compensation of the Englishman is not even in the word 'liberty,' but rather in the word 'poetry.' That humour of escape or seclusion, that genial isolation, that healing of wounded friendship by what Christian Science would call absent treatment, that is the best atmosphere of all for the creation of great poetry; and out of that came 'bare ruined choirs where late the sweet birds sang' and 'Thou wast not made for death, immortal bird.' In this sense it is indeed true that poetry is emotion remembered in tranquillity; which may be extended to mean affection remembered in loneliness. There is in it a spirit not only of detachment but even of distance; a spirit which does desire, as in the old English rhyme, to be not only over the hills but also far away. In other words, in so far as it is true that the Englishman is an exception to the great truth of Aristotle, it is because he is not so near to Aristotle as he is to Homer. In so far as he is not by nature a political animal, it is because he is a poetical animal. We see it in his relations to the other animals; his quaint and almost illogical love of dogs and horses and dependants whose political rights cannot possibly be defined in logic. Many forms of hunting or fishing are but an excuse for the same thing which the shameless literary man does without any excuse. Sport is speechless poetry. It would be easy for a foreigner, by taking a few liberties with the facts, to make a satire about the sort of silent Shelley who decides ultimately to shoot the skylark. It would be easy to answer these poetic suggestions by saying that he himself might be responsible for ruining the choirs where late the sweet birds sang, or that the immortal bird was likely to be mortal when he was out with his gun. But these international satires are never just; and the real relations of an Englishman and an English bird are far more delicate. It would be equally easy and equally unjust to suggest a similar satire against American democracy; and represent Americans merely as birds of a feather who can do nothing but flock together. But this would leave out the fact that at least it is not the white feather; that democracy is capable of defiance and of death for an idea. Touching the souls of great nations, these criticisms are generally false because they are critical.

But when we are quite sure that we rejoice in a nation's strength, then and not before we are justified in judging its weakness. I am quite sure that I rejoice in any democratic success without *arrière pensée*; and nobody who knows me will credit me with a covert sneer at civic equality. And this being granted, I do think there is a danger in the gregariousness of American society. The danger of democracy is not anarchy; on the contrary, it is monotony. And it is touching this that all my experience has increased my conviction that a great deal that is called female emancipation has merely been the increase of female convention. Now the males of every community are far too conventional; it was the females who were individual and criticised the conventions of the tribe. If the females become conventional also, there is a danger of individuality being lost. This indeed is not peculiar to America; it is common to the whole modern industrial world, and to everything which substitutes the impersonal atmosphere of the State for the personal atmosphere of the home. But it is emphasised in America by the curious contradiction that Americans do in theory value and even venerate the individual. But individualism is still the foe of individuality. Where men are trying to compete with each other they are trying to copy each other. They become featureless by 'featuring' the same part. Personality, in becoming a conscious ideal, becomes a common ideal. In this respect perhaps there is really something to be learnt from the Englishman with his turn or twist in the direction of private life. Those who have travelled in such a fashion as to see all the American hotels and none of the American houses are sometimes driven to the excess of saying that the Americans have no private life. But even if the exaggeration has a hint of truth, we must balance it with the corresponding truth; that the English have no public life. They on their side have still to learn the meaning of the public thing, the republic; and how great are the dangers of cowardice and corruption when the very State itself has become a State secret.

The English are patriotic; but patriotism is the unconscious form of nationalism. It is being national without understanding the meaning of a nation. The Americans are on the whole too self-conscious, kept moving too much in the pace of public life, with all its temptations to superficiality and fashion; too much aware of outside opinion and with too much appetite for outside criticism. But the English are much too unconscious; and would be the better for an increase in many forms of consciousness, including consciousness of sin. But even their sin is ignorance of their real virtue. The most admirable English things are not the things that are most admired by the English, or for which the English admire themselves. They are things now blindly neglected and in daily danger of being destroyed. It is all the worse that they should be destroyed, because there is really nothing like them in the world. That is why I have suggested a note of nationalism rather than patriotism for the English; the power of seeing their nation as a nation and not as the nature of things. We say of some ballad from the Balkans or some peasant costume in the Netherlands that it is unique; but the good things of England really are unique. Our very isolation from continental wars and revolutionary reconstructions have kept them unique. The particular kind of beauty there is in an English village, the particular kind of humour there is in an English public-house, are things that cannot be found in lands where the village is far more simply and equally governed, or where the vine is far more honourably served and praised. Yet we shall not save them by merely sinking into them with the conservative sort of contentment, even if the commercial rapacity of our plutocratic reforms would allow us to do so. We must in a sense get far away from England in order to behold her; we must rise above patriotism in order to be practically patriotic; we must have some sense of more varied and remote things before these vanishing virtues can be seen suddenly for what they are; almost as one might fancy that a man would have to rise to the dizziest heights of the divine understanding before he saw, as from a peak far above a whirlpool, how precious is his perishing soul.

THE FUTURE OF DEMOCRACY

The title of this final chapter requires an apology. I do not need to be reminded, alas, that the whole book requires an apology. It is written in accordance with a ritual or custom in which I could see no particular harm, and which gives me a very interesting subject, but a custom which it would be not altogether easy to justify in logic. Everybody who goes to America for a short time is expected to write a book; and nearly everybody does. A man who takes a holiday at Trouville or Dieppe is not confronted on his return with the question, 'When is your book on France going to appear?' A man who betakes himself to Switzerland for the winter sports is not instantly pinned by the statement, 'I suppose your History of the Helvetian Republic is coming out this spring?' Lecturing, at least my kind of lecturing, is not much more serious or meritorious than ski-ing or sea-bathing; and it happens to afford the holiday-maker far less opportunity of seeing the daily life of the people. Of all this I am only too well aware; and my only defence is that I am at least sincere in my enjoyment and appreciation of America, and equally sincere in my interest in its most serious problem, which I think a very serious problem indeed; the problem of democracy in the modern world. Democracy may be a very obvious and facile affair for plutocrats and politicians who only have to use it as a rhetorical term. But democracy is a very serious problem for democrats. I certainly do not apologise for the word democracy; but I do apologise for the word future. I am no Futurist; and any conjectures I make must be taken with the grain of salt which is indeed the salt of the earth; the decent and moderate humility which comes from a belief in free will. That faith is in itself a divine doubt. I do not believe in any of the scientific predictions about mankind; I notice that they always fail to predict any of the purely human developments of men; I also notice that even their successes prove the same truth as their failures; for their successful predictions are not about men but about machines. But there are two things which a man may reasonably do, in stating the probabilities of a problem, which do not involve any claim to be a prophet. The first is to tell the truth, and especially the neglected truth, about the tendencies that have already accumulated in human history; any miscalculation about which must at least mislead us in any case. We cannot be certain of being right about the future; but we can be almost certain of being wrong about the future, if we are wrong about the past. The other thing that he can do is to note what ideas necessarily go together by their own nature; what ideas will triumph together or fall together. Hence it follows that this final chapter must consist of two things. The first is a summary of what has really happened to the idea of democracy in recent times; the second a suggestion of the fundamental doctrine which is necessary for its triumph at any time.

The last hundred years has seen a general decline in the democratic idea. If there be anybody left to whom this historical truth appears a paradox, it is only because during that period nobody has been taught history, least of all the history of ideas. If a sort of intellectual inquisition had been established, for the definition and differentiation of heresies, it would have been found that the original republican orthodoxy had suffered more and more from secessions, schisms, and backslidings. The highest point of democratic idealism and conviction was towards the end of the eighteenth century, when the American Republic was 'dedicated to the proposition that all men are equal.' It was then that the largest number of men had the most serious sort of conviction that the political problem could be solved by the vote of peoples instead of the arbitrary power of princes and privileged orders. These men encountered various difficulties and made various compromises in relation to the practical politics of their time; in England they preserved aristocracy; in America they preserved slavery. But though they had more difficulties, they had less doubts. Since their time democracy has been steadily disintegrated by doubts; and these political doubts have been contemporary with and often identical with religious doubts. This fact could be followed over almost the whole field of the modern world; in this place it will be more appropriate to take the great American example of slavery. I have found traces in all sorts of intelligent quarters of an extraordinary idea that all the Fathers of the Republic owned black men like beasts of burden because they knew no better, until the light of liberty was revealed to them by John Brown and Mrs. Beecher Stowe. One of the best weekly papers in England said recently that even those who drew up the Declaration of Independence did not include negroes in its generalisation about humanity. This is quite consistent with the current convention, in which we were all brought up; the theory that the heart of humanity broadens in ever larger circles of brotherhood, till we pass from embracing a black man to adoring a black beetle. Unfortunately it is quite inconsistent with the facts of American history. The facts show that, in this problem of the Old South, the eighteenth century was *more* liberal than the nineteenth century. There was *more* sympathy for the negro in the school of Jefferson than in the school of Jefferson Davis. Jefferson, in the dark estate of his simple Deism, said the sight of slavery in his country made him tremble, remembering that God is just. His fellow Southerners, after a century of the world's advance, said that slavery in itself was good, when they did not go farther and say that negroes in themselves were bad. And they were supported in this by the great and growing modern suspicion that nature is unjust. Difficulties seemed inevitably to delay justice, to the mind of Jefferson; but so they did to the mind of Lincoln. But that the slave was human and the servitude inhuman—that was, if anything, clearer to Jefferson than to Lincoln. The fact is that the utter separation and subordination of the black like a beast was a *progress*; it was a growth of nineteenth-century enlightenment and experiment; a triumph of science over superstition. It was 'the way the world was going,' as Matthew Arnold reverentially remarked in some connection; perhaps as part of a definition of God. Anyhow, it was not Jefferson's definition of God. He fancied, in his far-off patriarchal way, a Father who had made all men brothers; and brutally unbrotherly as was the practice, such democratical Deists never dreamed of denying the theory. It was not until the scientific sophistries began that brotherhood was really disputed. Gobineau, who began most of the modern talk about the superiority and inferiority of racial stocks, was seized upon eagerly by the less generous of the slave-owners and trumpeted as a new truth of science and a new defence of slavery. It was not really until the dawn of Darwinism, when all our social relations began to smell of the monkey-house, that men thought of the barbarian as only a first and the baboon as a second cousin. The full servile philosophy has been a modern and even a recent thing; made in an age whose invisible deity was the Missing Link. The Missing Link was a true metaphor in more ways than one; and most of all in its suggestion of a chain.

By a symbolic coincidence, indeed, slavery grew more brazen and brutal under the encouragement of more than one movement of the progressive sort. Its youth was renewed for it by the industrial prosperity of Lancashire; and under that influence it became a commercial and competitive instead of a patriarchal and customary thing. We may say with no exaggerative irony that the unconscious patrons of slavery were Huxley and Cobden. The machines of Manchester were manufacturing a great many more things than the manufacturers knew or wanted to know; but they were certainly manufacturing the fetters of the slave, doubtless out of the best quality of steel and iron. But this is a minor illustration of the modern tendency, as compared with the main stream of scepticism which was destroying democracy. Evolution became more and more a vision of the break-up of our brotherhood, till by the end of the nineteenth century the genius of its greatest scientific romancer saw it end in the anthropophagous antics of the Time Machine. So far from evolution lifting us above the idea of enslaving men, it was providing us at least with a logical and potential argument for eating them. In the case of the American negroes, it may be remarked, it does at any rate permit the preliminary course of roasting them. All this materialistic hardening, which replaced the remorse of Jefferson, was part of the growing evolutionary suspicion that savages were not a part of the human race, or rather that there was really no such thing as the human race. The South had begun by agreeing reluctantly to the enslavement of men. The South ended by agreeing equally reluctantly to the emancipation of monkeys.

That is what had happened to the democratic ideal in a hundred years. Anybody can test it by comparing the final phase, I will not say with the ideal of Jefferson, but with the ideal of Johnson. There was far more horror of slavery in an eighteenth-century Tory like Dr. Johnson than in a nineteenth-century Democrat like Stephen Douglas. Stephen Douglas may be mentioned because he is a very representative type of the age of evolution and expansion; a man thinking in continents, like Cecil Rhodes, human and hopeful in a truly American fashion, and as a consequence cold and careless rather than hostile in the matter of the old mystical doctrines of equality. He 'did not care whether slavery was voted up or voted down.' His great opponent Lincoln did indeed care very much. But it was an intense individual conviction with Lincoln exactly as it was with Johnson. I doubt if the spirit of the age was not much more behind Douglas and his westward expansion of the white race. I am sure that more and more men were coming to be in the particular mental condition of Douglas; men in whom the old moral and mystical ideals had been undermined by doubt but only with a negative effect of indifference. Their positive convictions were all concerned with what some called progress and some imperialism. It is true that there was a sincere sectional enthusiasm against slavery in the North; and that the slaves were actually emancipated in the nineteenth century. But I doubt whether the Abolitionists would ever have secured Abolition. Abolition was a by-product of the Civil War; which was fought for quite other reasons. Anyhow, if slavery had somehow survived to the age of Rhodes and Roosevelt and evolutionary imperialism, I doubt if the slaves would ever have been emancipated at all. Certainly if it had survived till the modern movement for the Servile State, they would never have been emancipated at all. Why should the world take the chains off the black man when it was just putting them on the white? And in so far as we owe the change to Lincoln, we owe it to Jefferson. Exactly what gives its real dignity to the figure of Lincoln is that he stands invoking a primitive first principle of the age of innocence, and holding up the tables of an ancient law, *against* the trend of the nineteenth century; repeating, 'We hold these truths to be self-evident; that all men are created equal, that they are endowed by their Creator, etc.,' to a generation that was more and more disposed to say something like this: 'We hold these truths to be probable enough for pragmatists; that all things looking like men were evolved somehow, being endowed by heredity and environment with no equal rights, but very unequal wrongs,' and so on. I do not believe that creed, left to itself, would ever have founded a state; and I am pretty certain that, left to itself, it would never have overthrown a slave state. What it did do, as I have said, was to produce some very wonderful literary and artistic flights of sceptical imagination. The world did have new visions, if they were visions of monsters in the moon and Martians striding about like spiders as tall as the sky, and the workmen and capitalists becoming two separate species, so that one could devour the other as gaily and greedily as a cat devours a bird. No one has done justice to the meaning of Mr. Wells and his original departure in fantastic fiction; to these nightmares that were the last apocalypse of the nineteenth century. They meant that the bottom had fallen out of the mind at last, that the bridge of brotherhood had broken down in the modern brain, letting up from the chasms this infernal light like a dawn. All had grown dizzy with degree and relativity; so that there would not be so very much difference between eating dog and eating darkie, or between eating darkie and eating dago. There were different sorts of apes; but there was no doubt that we were the superior sort.

Against all this irresistible force stood one immovable post. Against all this dance of doubt and degree stood something that can best be symbolised by a simple example. An ape cannot be a priest, but a negro can be a priest. The dogmatic type of Christianity, especially the Catholic type of Christianity, had riveted itself irrevocably to the manhood of all men. Where its faith was fixed by creeds and councils it could not save itself even by surrender. It could not gradually dilute democracy, as could a merely sceptical or secular democrat. There stood, in fact or in possibility, the solid and smiling figure of a black bishop. And he was either a man claiming the most towering spiritual privileges of a man, or he was the mere buffoonery and blasphemy of a monkey in a mitre. That is the point about Christian and Catholic democracy; it is not that it is necessarily at any moment more democratic, it is that its indestructible minimum of democracy really is indestructible. And by the nature of things that mystical democracy was destined to survive, when every other sort of democracy was free to destroy itself. And whenever democracy destroying itself is suddenly moved to save itself, it always grasps at rag or tag of that old tradition that alone is sure of itself. Hundreds have heard the story about the mediaeval demagogue who went about repeating the rhyme

When Adam delved and Eve span,
Who was then the gentleman?

Many have doubtless offered the obvious answer to the question, 'The Serpent.' But few seem to have noticed what would be the more modern answer to the question, if that innocent agitator went about propounding it. 'Adam never delved and Eve never span, for the simple reason that they never existed. They are fragments of a Chaldeo-Babylonian mythos, and Adam is only a slight variation of Tag-Tug, pronounced Uttu. For the real beginning of humanity we refer you to Darwin's *Origin of Species*.' And then the modern man would go on to justify plutocracy to the mediaeval man by talking about the Struggle for Life and the Survival of the Fittest; and how the strongest man seized authority by means of anarchy, and proved himself a gentleman by behaving like a cad. Now I do not base my beliefs on the theology of John Ball, or on the literal and materialistic reading of the text of Genesis; though I think the story of Adam and Eve infinitely less absurd and unlikely than that of the prehistoric 'strongest man' who could fight a hundred men. But I do note the fact that the idealism of the leveller could be put in the form of an appeal to Scripture, and could not be put in the form of an appeal to Science. And I do note also that democrats were still driven to make the same appeal even in the very century of Science. Tennyson was, if ever there was one, an evolutionist in his vision and an aristocrat in his sympathies. He was always boasting that John Bull was evolutionary and not revolutionary, even as these Frenchmen. He did not pretend to have any creed beyond faintly trusting the larger hope. But when human dignity is really in danger, John Bull has to use the same old argument as John Ball. He tells Lady Clara Vere de Vere that 'the gardener Adam and his wife smile at the claim of long descent'; their own descent being by no means long. Lady Clara might surely have scored off him pretty smartly by quoting from 'Maud' and 'In Memoriam' about evolution and the eft that was lord of valley and hill. But Tennyson has evidently forgotten all about Darwin and the long descent of man. If this was true of an evolutionist like Tennyson, it was naturally ten times truer of a revolutionist like Jefferson. The Declaration of Independence dogmatically bases all rights on the fact that God created all men equal; and it is right; for if they were not created equal, they were certainly evolved unequal.

There is no basis for democracy except in a dogma about the divine origin of man. That is a perfectly simple fact which the modern world will find out more and more to be a fact. Every other basis is a sort of sentimental confusion, full of merely verbal echoes of the older creeds. Those verbal associations are always vain for the vital purpose of constraining the tyrant. An idealist may say to a capitalist, 'Don't you sometimes feel in the rich twilight, when the lights twinkle from the distant hamlet in the hills, that all humanity is a holy family?' But it is equally possible for the capitalist to reply with brevity and decision, 'No, I don't,' and there is no more disputing about it further than about the beauty of a fading cloud. And the modern world of moods is a world of clouds, even if some of them are thunderclouds.

For I have only taken here, as a convenient working model, the case of negro slavery; because it was long peculiar to America and is popularly associated with it. It is more and more obvious that the line is no longer running between black and white but between rich and poor. As I have already noted in the case of Prohibition, the very same arguments of the inevitable suicide of the ignorant, of the impossibility of freedom for the unfit, which were once applied to barbarians brought from Africa are now applied to citizens born in America. It is argued even by industrialists that industrialism has produced a class submerged below the status of emancipated mankind. They imply that the Missing Link is no longer missing, even from England or the Northern States, and that the factories have manufactured their own monkeys. Scientific hypotheses about the feeble-minded and the criminal type will supply the masters of the modern world with more and more excuses for denying the dogma of equality in the case of white labour as well as black. And any man who knows the world knows perfectly well that to tell the millionaires, or their servants, that they are disappointing the sentiments of Thomas Jefferson, or disregarding a creed composed in the eighteenth century, will be about as effective as telling them that they are not observing the creed of St. Athanasius or keeping the rule of St. Benedict.

The world cannot keep its own ideals. The secular order cannot make secure any one of its own noble and natural conceptions of secular perfection. That will be found, as time goes on, the ultimate argument for a Church independent of the world and the secular order. What has become of all those ideal figures from the Wise Man of the Stoics to the democratic Deist of the eighteenth century? What has become of all that purely human hierarchy of chivalry, with its punctilious pattern of the good knight, its ardent ambition in the young squire? The very name of knight has come to represent the petty triumph of a profiteer, and the very word squire the petty tyranny of a landlord. What has become of all that golden liberality of the Humanists, who found on the high tablelands of the culture of Hellas the very balance of repose in beauty that is most lacking in the modern world? The very Greek language that they loved has become a mere label for snuffy and snobbish dons, and a mere cock-shy for cheap and half-educated utilitarians, who make it a symbol of superstition and reaction. We have lived to see a time when the heroic legend of the Republic and the Citizen, which seemed to Jefferson the eternal youth of the world, has begun to grow old in its turn. We cannot recover the earthly estate of knighthood, to which all the colours and complications of heraldry seemed as fresh and natural as flowers. We cannot re-enact the intellectual experiences of the Humanists, for whom the Greek grammar was like the song of a bird in spring. The more the matter is considered the clearer it will seem that these old experiences are now only alive, where they have found a lodgment in the Catholic tradition of Christendom, and made themselves friends for ever. St. Francis is the only surviving troubadour. St. Thomas More is the only surviving Humanist. St. Louis is the only surviving knight.

It would be the worst sort of insincerity, therefore, to conclude even so hazy an outline of so great and majestic a matter as the American democratic experiment, without testifying my belief that to this also the same ultimate test will come. So far as that democracy becomes or remains Catholic and Christian, that democracy will remain democratic. In so far as it does not, it will become wildly and wickedly undemocratic. Its rich will riot with a brutal indifference far beyond the feeble feudalism which retains some shadow of responsibility or at least of patronage. Its wage-slaves will either sink into heathen slavery, or seek relief in theories that are destructive not merely in method but in aim; since they are but the negations of the human appetites of property and personality. Eighteenth-century ideals, formulated in eighteenth-century language, have no longer in themselves the power to hold all those pagan passions back. Even those documents depended upon Deism; their real strength will survive in men who are still Deists; and the men who are still Deists are more than Deists. Men will more and more realise that there is no meaning in democracy if there is no meaning in anything; and that there is no meaning in anything if the universe has not a centre of significance and an authority that is the author of our rights. There is truth in every ancient fable, and there is here even something of it in the fancy that finds the symbol of the Republic in the bird that bore the bolts of Jove. Owls and bats may wander where they will in darkness, and for them as for the sceptics the universe may have no centre; kites and vultures may linger as they like over carrion, and for them as for the plutocrats existence may have no origin and no end; but it was far back in the land of legends, where instincts find their true images, that the cry went forth that freedom is an eagle, whose glory is gazing at the sun.

Made in the USA
Monee, IL
03 October 2022

c023a4ef-76a0-4351-9857-056367cb30a2R01